CHEAT CODE CODE OVERLOAD WINTER

Look for faces like this throughout Cheat Code Overload to find the latest and greatest games and the cheats to make playing them even more fun!

P9-EKI-405

MICROSOFT XBOX 360®

GAMES

XBOX 360

2010 FIFA WORLD CUP SOUTH AFRICA

ADIDAS U11 TEAM
Go to EA Extras in My 2010
FIFA World Cup. Select
Unlockable Code Entry and enter
WSBJPJYODFYQIIGK.

FINAL MATCH BALL
Go to EA Extras in My 2010
FIFA World Cup. Select
Unlockable Code Entry and enter
FGWIXGFXTNSICLSS

ADIDAS ADIPURE III TRX (BLACK/SUN)
Go to EA Extras in My 2010
FIFA World Cup. Select
Unlockable Code Entry and enter
HHDOPWPMIXZQOJOZ

ADIDAS F50 ADIZERO (BLACK/SUN/SUN)
Go to EA Extras in My 2010
FIFA World Cup. Select
Unlockable Code Entry and enter
SGFSTZPPXCHHMJMH

ADIDAS F50 ADIZERO (CHAMELEON)
Go to EA Extras in My 2010
FIFA World Cup. Select
Unlockable Code Entry and enter
VOKMNEZTJOQPULUT

ADIDAS F50 ADIZERO (SUN/BLACK/GOLD)
Go to EA Extras in My 2010
FIFA World Cup. Select
Unlockable Code Entry and enter
YOZCCVIFJGKQJWTW

ADIDAS PREDATOR X (BLACK/SUN)
Go to EA Extras in My 2010
FIFA World Cup. Select
Unlockable Code Entry and enter
OCEGZCUHXOBSBNFU

COCA-COLA CELEBRATIONS
Go to EA Extras in My 2010 FIFA
World Cup. Select Unlockable
Code Entry and enter the
following:

CELEBRATION	CODE	HOW TO PERFORM
Baby Cradle	UGSIMLBHLFPUBFJY	Left Trigger + A
Dance	KBRRWKUIRSTWUJQW	Left Trigger + B
Dying Fly	DVMNJPBTLHJZGECP	Left Trigger + X
Flying Dive	DBQDUXQTRWTVXYDC	Left Trigger + Y
Prancing Bird	TWVBIXYACAOLGOWO	Right Bumper + B
River Dance	MIKAKPUMEEWNTQVE	Right Bumper + X
Side Slide	VNDWDUDLMGRNHDNV	Right Bumper + Y
Speed Skating	LHEHJZTPYYQDJQXB	Right Bumper + A

AMPED 3

ALL SLEDS
Select Cheat Codes from the
Options menu and press Right
Trigger, X, Left Trigger, Down,
Right, Left Bumper, Left Trigger,
Right Trigger, Y, X.

ALL GEAR
Select Cheat Codes from the
Options menu and press Y, Down,
Up, Left, Right, Left Bumper, Right,
Right Trigger, Right Trigger, Right
Bumper.

ALL TRICKS
Select Cheat Codes from the
Options menu and press Left
Bumper, Right Trigger, Y, Up,
Down, X, Left Trigger, Left, Right
Bumper, Right Trigger.

ALL LEVELS
Select Cheat Codes from the
Options menu and press X, Y, Up,
Left, Left Bumper, Left Bumper,
Right Trigger, X, Y, Left Trigger.

ALL CONFIGS

Select Cheat Codes from the Options menu and press Down, X, Right, Left Bumper, Right, Right Bumper, X, Right Trigger, Left Trigger, Y.

SUPER SPINS

Select Cheat Codes from the Options menu and press X (x4), Y (x3), X.

AWESOME METER ALWAYS FULL

Select Cheat Codes from the Options menu and press Up, Right Trigger, X, Y, Left Bumper, X, Down, Left Bumper, Right Trigger, Right Bumper.

ALL AWESOMENESS

Select Cheat Codes from the Options menu and press Right Bumper, Right Bumper, Down, Left, Up, Right Trigger, X, Right Bumper, X, X.

ALL BUILD LICENSES

Select Cheat Codes from the Options menu and press Left, Right Trigger, Left Bumper, Right Trigger, X, X, Y, Down, Up, X.

ALL BUILD OBJECTS

Select Cheat Codes from the Options menu and press Left Trigger, Right Trigger, Up, Up, Right Bumper, Left, Right, X, Y, Left Bumper.

ALL CHALLENGES

Select Cheat Codes from the Options menu and press Right, Left Bumper, Left Trigger, X, Left, Right Bumper, Right Trigger, Y, Left Trigger, X.

LOUD SPEAKERS

Select Cheat Codes from the Options menu and press Y, Right Trigger, Right Trigger, Left Bumper, Down, Down, Left, Left, Right, Left Bumper.

LOW GRAVITY BOARDERS

Select Cheat Codes from the Options menu and press Right Trigger, Down, Down, Up, X, Left Bumper, Y, Right Trigger, Y, Down.

NO AI

Select Cheat Codes from the Options menu and press X, X, Left Bumper, Down, Right, Right, Up, Y, Y, Left Trigger.

ALL MUSIC

Select Cheat Codes from the Options menu and press Up, Left, Right Trigger, Right Bumper, Right Trigger, Up, Down, Left, Y, Left Trigger.

AVATAR: THE LAST AIRBENDER — THE BURNING EARTH

UNLIMITED HEALTH

Select Code Entry from the Extras menu and enter 65049.

DOUBLE DAMAGE

Select Code Entry from the Extras menu and enter 90210.

MAXIMUM LEVEL

Select Code Entry from the Extras menu and enter 89121.

UNLIMITED SPECIALS

Select Code Entry from the Extras menu and enter 66206.

ONE-HIT DISHONOR

Select Code Entry from the Extras menu and enter 28260.

ALL BONUS GAMES

Select Code Entry from the Extras menu and enter 99801.

UNLOCKS GALLERY

Select Code Entry from the Extras menu and enter 85061.

BAJA: EDGE OF CONTROL

ALL VEHICLES AND TRACKS

Select Cheat Codes from the Options menu and enter SHOWTIME.

ALL PARTS

Select Cheat Codes from the Options menu and enter SUPERMAX.

BAKUGAN BATTLE BRAWLERS

1,000 BP
Enter 33204429 as your name.

5,000 BP
Enter 42348294 as your name.

10,000 BP
Enter 46836478 as your name.

100,000 BP
Enter 18499753 as your name.

500,000 BP
Enter 26037947 as your name.

BAND HERO

MOST CHARACTERS UNLOCKED
Select Input Cheats from the options and enter Blue, Yellow, Green, Yellow, Red, Green, Red, Yellow.

ELECTRIKA STEEL UNLOCKED
Select Input Cheats from the options and enter Blue, Blue, Red, Yellow, Red, Yellow, Blue, Blue.

ALL HOPO MODE
Select Input Cheats from the options and enter Red, Green, Blue, Green, Blue, Green, Red, Green.

ALWAYS SLIDE
Select Input Cheats from the options and enter Yellow, Green, Yellow, Yellow, Yellow, Red, Blue, Red.

AUTO KICK
Select Input Cheats from the options and enter Yellow, Green, Yellow, Blue, Blue, Red, Blue, Red.

FOCUS MODE
Select Input Cheats from the options and enter Yellow, Yellow, Green, Green, Red, Red, Blue, Blue.

HUD FREE MODE
Select Input Cheats from the options and enter Green, Red, Green, Red, Yellow, Blue, Green, Red.

PERFORMANCE MODE
Select Input Cheats from the options and enter Yellow, Yellow, Blue, Green, Blue, Red, Red, Red.

AIR INSTRUMENTS
Select Input Cheats from the options and enter Blue, Yellow, Blue, Red, Red, Yellow, Green, Yellow.

INVISIBLE ROCKER
Select Input Cheats from the options and enter Green, Red, Yellow, Green, Yellow, Blue, Yellow, Green.

In Treasure Trove Cove, enter the Sandcastle and spell CHEAT by using your Beak Buster on the desired letter. A sound will confirm the entry of the letter. The following cheats will now be available for you. Two things to keep in mind: First, no sound will confirm the correct letter. Secondly, ignore the spaces in the phrases—just spell the entire phrase out.

AREA OPENING CHEATS

ACCESS CLANKER'S CAVERN
THERES NOWHERE DANKER THAN IN WITH CLANKER

ACCESS MAD MONSTER MANSION
THE JIGGYS NOW MADE WHOLE INTO THE MANSION YOU CAN STROLL

ACCESS GOBI'S VALLEY
GOBIS JIGGY IS NOW DONE TREK ON IN AND GET SOME SUN

ACCESS RUSTY BUCKET BAY
WHY NOT TAKE A TRIP INSIDE GRUNTYS RUSTY SHIP

ACCESS CLICK CLOCK WOOD
THIS ONES GOOD AS YOU CAN ENTER THE WOOD

ACCESS FREEZEEZY PEAK
THE JIGGYS DONE SO OFF YOU GO INTO FREEZEEZY PEAK AND ITS SNOW

ACCESS BUBBLEGLOOP SWAMP
NOW INTO THE SWAMP YOU CAN STOMP

HIDDEN EGG CHEATS

The Hidden Egg cheats will only work if you have been to the level previously.

REVEAL THE BLUE EGG IN GOBI'S VALLEY BEHIND THE LOCKED GATE IN THE ROCK WALL
A DESERT DOOR OPENS WIDE ANCIENT SECRETS WAIT INSIDE

REVEAL THE PURPLE EGG IN TREASURE TROVE COVE IN SHARKFOOD ISLAND
OUT OF THE SEA IT RISES TO REVEAL MORE SECRET PRIZES

REVEAL THE ICE KEY IN FREEZEEZY PEAK IN THE ICE CAVE
NOW YOU CAN SEE A NICE ICE KEY WHICH YOU CAN HAVE FOR FREE

REVEAL THE LIGHT BLUE EGG IN GRUNTILDA'S LAIR—YOU'LL FIND IT IN THE CASK MARKED WITH AN X
DONT YOU GO AND TELL HER ABOUT THE SECRET IN HER CELLAR

REVEAL THE GREEN EGG IN MAD MONSTER MANSION IN THE SAME ROOM AS LOGGO THE TOILET
AMIDST THE HAUNTED GLOOM A SECRET IN THE BATHROOM

REVEAL THE YELLOW EGG IN CLICK CLOCK WOOD IN NABNUTS' TREE HOUSE
NOW BANJO WILL BE ABLE TO SEE IT ON NABNUTS TABLE

REVEAL THE RED EGG IN RUSTY BUCKET BAY IN THE CAPTAIN'S CABIN
THIS SECRET YOULL BE GRABBIN IN THE CAPTAINS CABIN

NOTE DOOR CHEATS

These codes will pop the note doors open without having to find the required notes.

DOOR 2
THESE GO RIGHT ON THROUGH NOTE DOOR TWO

DOOR 3
NOTE DOOR THREE GET IN FOR FREE

DOOR 4
TAKE A TOUR THROUGH NOTE DOOR FOUR

DOOR 5
USE THIS CHEAT NOTE DOOR FIVE IS BEAT

DOOR 6
THIS TRICKS USED TO OPEN NOTE DOOR SIX

DOOR 7
THE SEVENTH NOTE DOOR IS NOW NO MORE

SWITCH AND OBSTACLE CHEATS FOR GRUNTILDA'S LAIR

These will allow you to alter certain obstacles throughout Gruntilda's Lair. Sometimes, the cheat will even remove them completely.

RAISE THE PIPES NEAR CLANKER'S CAVERN
BOTH PIPES ARE THERE TO CLANKERS LAIR

RAISE THE LARGE PIPE NEAR CLANKER'S CAVERN
YOULL CEASE TO GRIPE WHEN UP GOES A PIPE

UNLOCK THE PATH NEAR CLANKER'S CAVERN THAT LEADS TO THE CLICK CLOCK WOOD PICTURE
ONCE IT SHONE BUT THE LONG TUNNEL GRILLE IS GONE

REVEAL THE PODIUM FOR THE CLICK CLOCK WOOD JIGGY
DONT DESPAIR THE TREE JIGGY PODIUM IS NOW THERE

UNLOCK THE PATH INSIDE THE GIANT WITCH STATUE, NEAR BUBBLEGLOOP SWAMP (OPEN THE GRILL)
SHES AN UGLY BAT SO LETS REMOVE HER GRILLE AND HAT

UNLOCK THE PATH TO THE FREEZEEZY PEAK PICTURE BEHIND THE ICE CUBE
ITS YOUR LUCKY DAY AS THE ICE BALL MELTS AWAY

UNLOCK PASSAGES BLOCKED BY COBWEBS
WEBS STOP YOUR PLAY SO TAKE THEM AWAY

REVEAL A JIGGY IN GRUNTILDA'S STATUE BY SMASHING THE EYE NEAR MAD MONSTER MANSION
GRUNTY WILL CRY NOW YOUVE SMASHED HER EYE

RAISE THE WATER LEVEL NEAR RUSTY BUCKET BAY
UP YOU GO WITHOUT A HITCH UP TO THE WATER LEVEL SWITCH

UNLOCK THE PATH TO THE CRYPT NEAR MAD MONSTER MANSION (REMOVE THE GATE)
YOU WONT HAVE TO WAIT NOW THERES NO CRYPT GATE

REMOVE THE COFFIN LID IN THE CRYPT
THIS SHOULD GET RID OF THE CRYPT COFFIN LID

CRUMBLE ALL BREAKABLE WALLS
THEY CAUSE TROUBLE BUT NOW THEYRE RUBBLE

ACTIVATE SPECIAL PADS

Skip the lesson from Bottles by entering these codes.

ACTIVATE THE FLY PAD
YOU WONT BE SAD NOW YOU CAN USE THE FLY PAD

ACTIVATE THE SHOCK JUMP PAD
YOULL BE GLAD TO SEE THE SHOCK JUMP PAD

EXTRA HEALTH CHEAT

Skip the note-hunt and get that extra health by entering this cheat.

AN ENERGY BAR TO GET YOU FAR
Remember, to enter a code you must first enter the word CHEAT in the Sandcastle.

BANJO-TOOIE

REGAIN ENERGY
Go to the Code Chamber in the Mayahem Temple and access the scroll on the wall. If you have been awarded this cheat by Cheato, enter HONEYBACK. If not, enter CHEATOKCABYENOH.

FALLS DON'T HURT
Go to the Code Chamber in the Mayahem Temple and access the scroll on the wall. If you have been awarded this cheat by Cheato, enter FALLPROOF. If not, enter CHEATOFOORPLLAF.

HOMING EGGS
Go to the Code Chamber in the Mayahem Temple and access the scroll on the wall. If you have been awarded this cheat, enter HOMING. If not, enter CHEATOGNIMOH.

DOUBLES MAXIMUM EGGS

Go to the Code Chamber in the Mayahem Temple and access the scroll on the wall. If you have been awarded this cheat by Cheato, enter EGGS. If not, enter CHEATOSGGE.

DOUBLES MAXIMUM FEATHERS

Go to the Code Chamber in the Mayahem Temple and access the scroll on the wall. If you have been awarded this cheat by Cheato, enter FEATHERS. If not, enter CHEATOSREHTAEF.

JOLLY ROGER LAGOON'S JUKEBOX

Go to the Code Chamber in the Mayahem Temple and access the scroll on the wall. If you have been awarded this cheat, enter JUKEBOX. If not, enter CHEATOXOBEKUJ.

SIGNS IN JIGGYWIGGY'S TEMPLE GIVE HINTS TO GET EACH JIGGY

Go to the Code Chamber in the Mayahem Temple and access the scroll on the wall. If you have been awarded this cheat, enter GETJIGGY. If not, enter CHEATOYGGIJTEG.

ALL LEVELS

Go to the Code Chamber in the Mayahem Temple and enter JIGGYWIGGYSPECIAL.

SPEED BANJO

Go to the Code Chamber in the Mayahem Temple and enter SUPERBANJO.

SPEED ENEMIES

Go to the Code Chamber in the Mayahem Temple and enter SUPERBADDY.

INFINITE EGGS & FEATHERS

Go to the Code Chamber in the Mayahem Temple and enter NESTKING.

INFINITE HONEY

Go to the Code Chamber in the Mayahem Temple and enter HONEYKING.

BATTLEFIELD: BAD COMPANY

M60

Select Unlocks from the Multiplayer menu, press Start, and enter try4ndrunf0rcov3r.

QBU88

Select Unlocks from the Multiplayer menu, press Start, and enter your3mynextt4rget.

UZI

Select Unlocks from the Multiplayer menu, press Start, and enter cov3r1ngthecorn3r.

FIND ALL FIVE WEAPONS

SNIPER RIFLE

You received a weapon unlock code for this gun if you pre-ordered the game.

MACHINE GUN

Receive a weapon unlock code for this gun after signing up for the newsletter at www.findallfive.com.

SUB-MACHINE GUN

Download the demo and reach rank 4 to receive an unlock code for this weapon.

ASSAULT RIFLE

Go to veteran.battlefield.com and register your previous Battlefield games to receive an unlock code for this weapon.

SEMI-AUTOMATIC SHOTGUN

Check your online stats at www.findallfive.com to get an unlock code for this weapon.

BATTLEFIELD 2: MODERN COMBAT

ALL WEAPONS

During a game, hold Right Bumper + Left Bumper and quickly press Right, Right, Down, Up, Left, Left.

BATTLESTATIONS: MIDWAY

ALL CAMPAIGN AND CHALLENGE MISSIONS

At the mission select, hold Right Bumper + Left Bumper + Right Trigger + Left Trigger and press X.

OVERLOAD

XBOX 360

BAYONETTA

In Chapter 2, after Verse 3, find the phones in the plaza area. Stand in front of the appropriate phone and enter the following codes. The left phone is used for Weapons, the right phone is for Accessories, and the far phone is for Characters.

These codes require a certain amount of halos to be used. You will lose these halos immediately after entering the code.

WEAPONS

BAZILLIONS
Required Halos: 1 Million
Up, Up, Up, Up, Down, Down, Down, Down, Left, Right, Left, Right, Y

PILLOW TALK
Required Halos: 1 Million
Up, Up, Up, Up, Down, Down, Down, Down, Left, Right, Left, Right, A

RODIN
Required Halos: 5 Million
Up, Up, Up, Up, Down, Down, Down, Down, Left, Right, Left, Right, Left Bumper

ACCESSORIES

BANGLE OF TIME
Required Halos: 3 Million
Up, Up, Up, Up, Down, Down, Down, Down, Left, Right, Left, Right, Left Trigger

CLIMAX BRACELET
Required Halos: 5 Million
Up, Up, Up, Up, Down, Down, Down, Down, Left, Right, Left, Right, Right Trigger

ETERNAL TESTIMONY
Required Halos: 2 Million
Up, Up, Up, Up, Down, Down, Down, Down, Left, Right, Left, Right, Right Bumper

CHARACTERS

JEANNE
Required Halos: 1 Million
Up, Up, Up, Up, Down, Down, Down, Down, Left, Right, Left, Right, B

LITTLE ZERO
Required Halos: 5 Million
Up, Up, Up, Up, Down, Down, Down, Down, Left, Right, Left, Right, X

BEAT'N GROOVY

ALTERNATE CONTROLS
At the Title screen, press Up, Up, Down, Down, Left, Right, Left, Right, B, A.

THE BEATLES: ROCK BAND

BONUS PHOTOS
At the title screen, press Blue, Yellow, Orange, Orange, Orange, Blue, Blue, Blue, Yellow, Orange.

BEN 10: ALIEN FORCE VILGAX ATTACKS

Level Skip Pause the game and enter Portal in the Cheats menu.

UNLOCK ALL SPECIAL ATTACKS FOR ALL FORMS
Pause the game and enter Everythingproof in the Cheats menu.

UNLOCK ALL ALIEN FORMS
Pause the game and enter Primus in the Cheats menu.

TOGGLE INVULNERABILITY ON AND OFF
Pause the game and enter Xlmrsmoothy in the Cheats menu.

GIVES PLAYER FULL HEALTH
Pause the game and enter Herotime in the Cheats menu.

QUICK ENERGY REGENERATION
Pause the game and enter Generator in the Cheats menu.

These cheats disable Achievements. To remove the cheats, you will need to start a new game.

1,000,000 DNA
Pause the game, select Cheats, and enter Cash.

REGENERATE HEALTH
Pause the game, select Cheats, and enter Health.

REGENERATE ENERGY
Pause the game, select Cheats, and enter Energy.

UPGRADE EVERYTHING
Pause the game, select Cheats, and enter Upgrade.

ALL LEVELS
Pause the game, select Cheats, and enter Levels.

ENEMIES DO DOUBLE DAMAGE/PLAYER DOES ½ DAMAGE
Pause the game, select Cheats, and enter Hard.

UNLOCKS RATH
Pause the game, select Cheats, and enter Primus.

BIOLOGY BATTLE

INCREASED CONFLICT LEVEL IN GLOBAL CHALLENGE MODE
At the Global Challenge Mode lobby, press A to access the game controls/ start screen. At this screen, hold Y and press A.

BIONIC COMMANDO REARMED

The following challenge rooms can be found in the Challenge Room list. Only one code can be active at a time.

AARON SEDILLO'S CHALLENGE ROOM (CONTEST WINNER)
At the Title screen, press Right, Down, Left, Up, Left Bumper, Right Bumper, Y, Y, X, X, Start.

EUROGAMER CHALLENGE ROOM:
At the Title screen, press Down, Up, Down, Up, Left, Left Bumper, X, Left Bumper, X, Y, Start.

GAMESRADAR CHALLENGE ROOM:
At the Title screen, press Right Bumper, Y, X, X, Up, Down, Left Bumper, Left Bumper, Up, Down, Start.

IGN CHALLENGE ROOM:
At the Title screen, press Up, Down, Y, X, X, Y, Down, Up, Left Bumper, Left Bumper, Start.

MAJOR NELSON CHALLENGE ROOM
At the Title screen, press Left Bumper, X, X, X, Right, Down, Left Bumper, Left, Y, Down, Start.

BLACKLIGHT: TANGO DOWN

UNLOCK CODES
Select Unlock Code from Help & Options and enter the following. These tags can be used on your customized weapons.

TAG	UNLOCK CODE
Alienware Black	Alienwarec8pestU
Alienware	Al13nwa4re5acasE
AMD VISION	4MDB4quprex
AMD VISION	AMD3afrUnap
ATi	AT1hAqup7Su
Australia Flag	AUS9eT5edru
Austria Flag	AUTF6crAS5u
Belgium Flag	BELS7utHAsP
Blacklight	R41nB0wu7p3
Blacklight	Ch1pBLuS9PR
Canada Flag	CANfeprUtr5
Denmark Flag	DENdathe8HU
E3 Dog Tags	E3F6crAS5u

TAG	UNLOCK CODE
Famitsu Magazine	Fam1tsuprusWe2e
Finland Flag	FINw3uthEfe
France Flag	FRApRUyUT4a
Germany Flag	GERtRE4a4eS
Holland Flag	HOLb8e6UWuh
Hong Kong Flag	HOKYeQuKuw3
India Flag	INDs4u8RApr
Ireland Flag	IRE8ruGejec
Italy Flag	ITAQ7Swu9re
Jace Hall Show	J4ceH4llstuFaCh4
Japan Flag	JPNj7fazebR

XBOX 360

TAG	UNLOCK CODE
Korea Flag	KORpaphA9uK
Mexico Flag	MEX5Usw2YAd
New Zealand Flag	NZLxut32eSA
Norway Flag	NOR3Waga8wa
Orange Scorpion	Ch1pMMRSc0rp
Order Logo Chip	Ch1p0RD3Ru02
Pink Brass Knuckles	H4rtBr34kerio4u
Portugal Flag	PORQ54aFrEY
Razer	R4z3erzu8habuC
Russia Flag	RUS7rusteXe
Singapore Flag	SINvuS8E2aC
Spain Flag	ESPChE4At5p
Storm Lion Comics	StormLion9rAVaZ2

TAG	UNLOCK CODE
Storm Lion Comics	St0rmLi0nB4qupre
Sweden Flag	SWEt2aPHutr
Switzerland Flag	SWIsTE8tafU
Taiwan Flag	TAW8udukUP2
United Kingdom Flag	UKv4D3phed
United States Flag	USAM3spudre
Upper Playground	UPGr0undv2FUDame
Upper Playground	UPGr0undWupraf4u
UTV Lightning Logo chip	Ch1p1GN1u0S
Yellow Teddy Bear	Denek1Ju3aceH7
Zombie Studios Logo Chip	Ch1pZ0MB1Et7

BLAZING ANGELS: SQUADRONS OF WWII

ALL MISSIONS, MEDALS, & PLANES
At the Main menu hold Left Trigger + Right Trigger and press X, Left Bumper, Right Bumper, Y, Y, Right Bumper, Left Bumper, X.

GOD MODE
Pause the game, hold Left Trigger and press X, Y, Y, X. Release Left Trigger, hold Right Trigger and press Y, X, X, Y. Re-enter the code to disable it.

INCREASED DAMAGE
Pause the game, hold Left Trigger and press Left Bumper, Left Bumper, Right Bumper. Release Left Trigger, hold Right Trigger and press Right Bumper, Right Bumper, Left Bumper. Re-enter the code to disable it.

BLAZING ANGELS 2: SECRET MISSIONS OF WWII

Achievements are disabled when using these codes.

ALL MISSIONS AND PLANES UNLOCKED
At the Main menu, hold Left Trigger + Right Trigger, and press X, Left Bumper, Right Bumper, Y, Y, Right Bumper, Left Bumper, X.

GOD MODE
Pause the game, and press X, Y, Y, X. Release Left Trigger, hold Right Trigger and press Y, X, X, Y. Re-enter the code to disable it.

INCREASED DAMAGE WITH ALL WEAPONS
Pause the game, and press Left Bumper, Left Bumper, Right Bumper. Release Left Trigger, hold Right Trigger, and press Right Bumper, Right Bumper, Left Bumper. Re-enter the code to disable it.

BLITZ: THE LEAGUE

The following codes work for Quick Play mode:

UNLIMITED UNLEASH
Select Codes from Extras and enter BIGDOGS.

DOUBLE UNLEASH ICONS
Select Codes from Extras and enter PIPPED.

STAMINA OFF
Select Codes from Extras and enter NOTTIRED.

UNLIMITED CLASH ICONS
Select Codes from Extras and enter CLASHY.

TWO PLAYER CO-OP
Select Codes from Extras and enter CHUWAY.

BALL TRAIL ALWAYS ON
Select Codes from Extras and enter ONFIRE.

BEACH BALL
Select Codes from Extras and enter BOUNCY.

BLITZ: THE LEAGUE II

TOUCHDOWN CELEBRATIONS
Press these button combinations when given the chance after scoring a touchdown

CELEBRATION	CODE	CELEBRATION	CODE
Ball Spike	A, A, A, B	Knockout	X, X, Y, Y
Beer Chug	A, A, B, B	Man Crush	X, X, X, Y
Dance Fever	Y, Y, Y, A	Nut Shot	Y, Y, B, A
Get Down	B, A, B, Y	Pylon Darts	A, B, A, B
Golf Putt	A, X, Y, B	The Pooper	Y, X, A, B
Helmet Fling	A, X, A, X		

BLUR

BMW CONCEPT 1 SERIES TII CHROME
In the Multiplayer Showroom, highlight the BMW Concept 1 Series tii and press Left Trigger, Right Trigger, Left Trigger, Right Trigger.

FULLY UPGRADE FORD BRONCO
In the Multiplayer Showroom, highlight the Ford Bronco and press Left Trigger, Right Trigger, Left Trigger, Right Trigger.

AVATAR AWARDS

AWARD	EARNED BY
Wreck Tee	Earn the Been there, got the T-shirt Achievement
Friend Rechallenge Tee	Defeat a friends rechallenge.
Legend Tee	Unlock first Legend Rank in multiplayer.
Showdown Tee	Complete Showdown
Sticker Tee	Complete the Sticker Book.

BROTHERS IN ARMS: HELL'S HIGHWAY

ALL CHAPTERS
Select Enter Codes from the Options and enter GIMMECHAPTERS.

ALL RECON POINTS
Select Enter Codes from the Options and enter 0ZNDRBICRA.

KILROY DETECTOR
Select Enter Codes from the Options and enter SH2VYIVNZF.

TWO MULTIPLAYER SKINS
Select Enter Codes from the Options and enter HI9WTPXSUK.

BULLY: SCHOLARSHIP EDITION

FULL HEALTH
During a game and with a second controller, hold Left Bumper and press Right Trigger, Right Trigger, Right Trigger.

MONEY
During a game and with a second controller, hold Left Bumper and press Y, X, B, A.

INFINITE AMMO
During a game and with a second controller, hold Left Bumper and press Up, Down, Up, Down. Re-enter code to disable it.

ALL WEAPONS
During a game and with a second controller, hold Left Bumper and press Up, Up, Up, Up.

ALL GYM GRAPPLE MOVES
During a game and with a second controller, hold Left Bumper and press Up, Left, Down, Down, Y, X, A, A.

ALL HOBO MOVES
During a game and with a second controller, hold Left Bumper and press Up, Left, Down, Right, Y, X, A, B

BURNOUT PARADISE

BEST BUY CAR
Pause the game and select Sponsor Product Code from the Under the Hood menu. Enter Bestbuy. Need the A License to use this car offline.

CIRCUIT CITY CAR
Pause the game and select Sponsor Product Code from the Under the Hood menu. Enter Circuitcity. Need Burnout Paradise License to use this car offline.

GAMESTOP CAR
Pause the game and select Sponsor Product Code from the Under the Hood menu. Enter Gamestop. Need the A License to use this car offline.

WALMART CAR
Pause the game and select Sponsor Product Code from the Under the Hood menu. Enter Walmart. Need the Burnout Paradise License to use this car offline.

"STEEL WHEELS" GT
Pause the game and select Sponsor Product Code from the Under the Hood menu. Enter G23X 5K8Q GX2V 04B1 or E60J 8Z7T MS8L 51U6.

LICENSES

LICENSE	NUMBER OF WINS NEEDED
D	2
C	7
B	16
A	26
Burnout Paradise	45
Elite License	All events

CABELA'S DANGEROUS HUNTS 2009

.470 NITRO EXPRESS HIGH CALIBER RIFLE
Select Enter Special Code from the Extras menu and enter 101987.

CALL OF DUTY 4: MODERN WARFARE

ARCADE MODE
After a complete playthrough of the game, Arcade Mode becomes available from the Main menu.

UNLOCKABLE CHEATS

After completing the game, cheats are unlocked based on how many intelligence pieces were gathered. These cheats cannot be used during Arcade Mode. They may also disable the ability to earn Achievements.

CHEAT	INTEL ITEMS	DESCRIPTION
CoD Noir	2	Black and white
Photo-Negative	4	Inverses colors
Super Contrast	6	Increases contrast
Ragtime Warfare	8	Black and white, scratches fill screen, double speed, piano music
Cluster Bombs	10	Four extra grenade explosions after frag grenade explodes
A Bad Year	15	Enemies explode into a bunch of old tires when killed
Slow-Mo Ability	20	Melee button enables/disables slow-motion mode
Infinite Ammo	30	Unlimited ammo and no need to reload. Doesn't work for single-shot weapons such as RPG.

CALL OF DUTY: WORLD AT WAR

ZOMBIE MODE
Complete Campaign mode.

CALL OF JUAREZ: BOUND IN BLOOD

EXCLUSIVE CONTENT
Select Enter Code from Exclusive Content and enter 735S653J. This code unlocks extra money for equipment in single-player mode, a silver weapon in multiplayer, and an exclusive weapon for the first two chapters.

CARS

UNLOCK EVERYTHING
Select Cheat Codes from the Options and enter IF900HP.

ALL CHARACTERS
Select Cheat Codes from the Options and enter YAYCARS.

ALL CHARACTER SKINS
Select Cheat Codes from the Options and enter R4MONE.

ALL MINI-GAMES AND COURSES
Select Cheat Codes from the Options and enter MATTL66.

FAST START
Select Cheat Codes from the Options and enter IMSPEED.

INFINITE BOOST
Select Cheat Codes from the Options and enter VROOOOM.

ART
Select Cheat Codes from the Options and enter CONC3PT.

VIDEOS
Select Cheat Codes from the Options and enter WATCHIT.

CARS MATER-NATIONAL

ALL ARCADE RACES, MINI-GAMES, AND WORLDS
Select Codes/Cheats from the options and enter PLAYALL.

ALL CARS
Select Codes/Cheats from the options and enter MATTEL07.

ALTERNATE LIGHTNING MCQUEEN COLORS
Select Codes/Cheats from the options and enter NCEDUDZ.

ALL COLORS FOR OTHERS
Select Codes/Cheats from the options and enter PAINTIT.

UNLIMITED TURBO
Select Codes/Cheats from the options and enter ZZOOOOM.

EXTREME ACCELERATION
Select Codes/Cheats from the options and enter 0TO200X.

EXPERT MODE
Select Codes/Cheats from the options and enter VRYFAST.

ALL BONUS ART
Select Codes/Cheats from the options and enter BUYTALL.

XBOX 360

CASTLEVANIA: HARMONY OF DESPAIR

HARD MODE
Complete Chapter 6 to unlock Hard Mode for Chapter 1.

ALUCARD GAMERPIC
Complete Chapter 6 in single player.

JAPANESE VOICES
At the character's color select, hold Right Trigger and press A.

CASTLEVANIA: LORDS OF SHADOW

CHEAT MENU
At the loading screen, press Up, Up, Down, Down, Left, Right, Left, Right, B, A. Using this cheat disables Achievements and saving.

SNAKE OUTFIT
Defeat the game. In the Extras menu, toggle Solid Eye and Bandanna on.

VAMPIRE WARGAME
During Chapter 6-3: Castle Hall, beat the Vampire Wargame to unlock it in the Extras menu.

CASTLEVANIA: SYMPHONY OF THE NIGHT

Before using the following codes, complete the game with 170%.

PLAY AS RICHTER BELMONT
Enter RICHTER as your name.

ALUCARD WITH AXELORD ARMOR
Enter AXEARMOR as your name.

ALUCARD WITH 99 LUCK AND OTHER STATS ARE LOW
Enter X-X!V"Q as your name.

COMIC JUMPER: THE ADVENTURES OF CAPTAIN SMILEY

AVATAR AWARDS

AWARD	EARNED BY
Captain Smiley Giant Head	Complete the whole game
Gerda T-Shirt (female only)	Complete the 1st Level
Star T-Shirt (male only)	Complete the 1st Level

COMMAND & CONQUER 3: TIBERIUM WARS

FREE NOD SHADOW SQUADS
During a NOD game, pause and press Left, Right, Up, Up, Up, Down, RB, LB, LB, B. This code does not work in Skirmish or Career.

CONDEMNED: CRIMINAL ORIGINS

ALL LEVELS
Enter ShovelFighter as a profile name.

CONDEMNED 2: BLOODSHOT

ALL BONUS ART
Create a profile with the name ShovelFighter. Use this profile to start a game and all of the bonus art is unlocked.

COSTUME QUEST

AVATAR AWARDS

AWARD	EARNED BY
Pumpkin Pail	Start a new game.
Pumpkin Mask	Complete the game.

CRACKDOWN 2

AVATAR AWARDS

AWARD	EARNED BY
Orb Shirt (Male and Female)	Have First Blood achievement from Crackdown
Freaky Slippers (Male and Female)	Earn First Hurdle achievement
Ruffian Hat	Earn Hope Springs Savior achievement
Level 1 Agent Suit (Male and Female)	Earn Light Bringer achievement
Official Agency Hoodie (Male and Female)	Earn Jack of all Trades achievement

DOWNLOADABLE CONTENT: TOY BOX

AVATAR AWARDS

AWARD	EARNED BY
Green Agent Helmet	Download Toy Box DLC
Green Agent Suit	Earn Rocketeer achievement

CRASH BANDICOOT: MIND OVER MUTANT

A cheat can be deactivated by re-entering the code.

FREEZE ENEMIES WITH TOUCH
Pause the game, hold Right Trigger and press Down, Down, Down, Up.

ENEMIES DROP X4 DAMAGE
Pause the game, hold Right Trigger and press Up, Up, Up, Left.

ENEMIES DROP PURPLE FRUIT
Pause the game, hold Right Trigger and press Up, Down, Down, Up.

ENEMIES DROP SUPER KICK
Pause the game, hold Right Trigger and press Up, Right, Down, Left.

ENEMIES DROP WUMPA FRUIT
Pause the game, hold Right Trigger and press Right, Right, Right, Up.

SHADOW CRASH
Pause the game, hold Right Trigger and press Left, Right, Left, Right.

DEFORMED CRASH
Pause the game, hold Right Trigger and press Left, Left, Left, Down.

CRASH OF THE TITANS

BIG HEAD CRASH
Pause the game, hold the Right Trigger, and press X, X, Y, A.

SHADOW CRASH
Pause the game, hold the Right Trigger, and press Y, X, Y, A.

DAMNATION

INSANE DIFFICULTY
Select Enter Code from Unlockables and enter Revenant.

VORPAL MECHANICAL REPEATER
Select Enter Code from Unlockables and enter BlowOffSomeSteam.

BIG HEAD MODE
Select Enter Code from Unlockables and enter LincolnsTopHat.

CUSTOM CHARACTERS
Select Enter Code from Unlockables and enter PeoplePerson.

CUSTOM LOADOUT
Select Enter Code from Unlockables and enter LockNLoad.

DARK MESSIAH OF MIGHT AND MAGIC: ELEMENTS

EXCLUSIVE MAP
Select Exclusive content from the Main menu. Select Exclusivity code and enter 5684219998871395. You can access it through Aranthir's office, in chapter 8.

XBOX 360

THE DARKNESS

DARKLING OUTFITS

Even Darklings can make a fashion statement. Support your mini minions with an ensemble fit for murderous monsters by collecting these fun and colorful outfits.

OUTFIT	MENTIONED IN	AREA	LOCATION
Potato Sack	Chapter 1	Chinatown	Sitting against alley wall near metro exit
Jungle	Chapter 1	Hunters Point Alley	Inside hidden room
Roadworker	Chapter 3	City Hall station	Inside train car
Lumberjack	Side Objectives	Cutrone objective	Inside Cutrone's apartment
Fireman	Side Objectives	Pajamas objective	Inside room 261
Construction	Side Objectives	Mortarello objective	Inside room of last mission
Baseball	N/A	Dial: 555-4263	N/A
Golfshirt	N/A	Dial: 555-5664	N/A

PHONE NUMBERS

Dialing 'D' for Darkness isn't the only number to punch on a telephone. Sure, you called every number you found on those hard-to-get Collectibles, but you certainly haven't found *all* of the phone numbers. Pay close to attention to the environment as you hunt down Uncle Paulie. Chances are, you overlooked a phone number or two without even knowing it as you ripped out a goon's heart. All 25 'secret' phone numbers are scattered throughout New York and can be seen on anywhere from flyers and storefronts to garbage cans and posters. Dial 18 of the 25 numbers on a phone—in no specific order—to unlock the final secret of the game.

555-6118	555-1847	555-6667	555-4569
555-9985	555-1037	555-1206	555-9528
555-3285	555-5723	555-8024	555-6322
555-9132	555-6893	555-2402	555-6557
555-2309	555-4372	555-9723	555-5289
555-6205	555-7658	555-1233	555-3947
555-9562	555-7934	555-7892	555-8930
555-3243	555-3840	555-2349	555-6325
555-4565	555-9898	555-7613	555-6969

DARKSIDERS

HARVESTER FOR 0 SOULS

Pause the game and select Enter Code from the Options. Enter The Hollow Lord.

DEAD RISING 2

KNIGHT ARMOR

Wearing this armor doubles Chuck's health. When his health falls below half, the armor is destroyed.

PIECE OF ARMOR	OBTAINED BY
Full Beard Moustache	In the back of Wave of Style located in Royal Flush Plaza.
Knight Armor	Finish the game with the S ending.
Knight Boots	$2,000,000 at Moe's Maginations pawnshop on the Platinum Strip.
Knight Helmet	Rescue Jack in Meet the Family and then win at poker in Ante Up.

UNLOCKABLE OUTFITS

The following items are unlocked by performing the corresponding task.

ITEM	OBTAINED BY
Bowling Shirt, Diner Waitress, Hunting Jacket, and Overalls	Import a save game from Case Zero.
Champion Jacket	Earn the Win Big! Achievement. Get this by finishing in first place in a TIR Episode.
Dealer Outfit	Earn Chuck Greene: Cross Dresser? Achievement. Get this by changing into all the clothes in the game.
Hockey Mask	Earn the Head Trauma Achievement. Get this by using every type of melee weapon on a zombie.
Orange Prison Outfit	Earn the Judge, Jury, and Executioner Achievement. Get this by killing 10 psychos.
Tattered Clothes	Earn the Zombie Fu Achievement. Get this by killing 1,000 zombies barehanded.
TIR Helmet	Earn $1,000,000 in Terror is Reality.
TIR Outfit	Earn $5,000,000 in Terror is Reality.
Willamette Mall Security Uniform	Earn Hero of Fortune City Achievement. Get this by rescuing 50 survivors.

DEAD SPACE

REFILL STASIS AND KINESIS ENERGY
Pause the game and press X, Y, Y, X, Y.

REFILL OXYGEN
Pause the game and press X, X, Y (x3).

ADD 2 POWER NODES
Pause the game and press Y, X (x3), Y. *This code can only be used once.*

ADD 5 POWER NODES
Pause the game and press Y, X, Y, X, X, Y, X, X, Y, X, X, Y. *This code can only be used once.*

1,000 CREDITS
Pause the game and press X (x3), Y, X. *This code can only be used once.*

2,000 CREDITS
Pause the game and press X (x3), Y, Y. *This code can only be used once.*

5,000 CREDITS
Pause the game and press X (x3), Y, X, Y. *This code can only be used once.*

10,000 CREDITS
Pause the game and press X, Y (x3), X, X, Y. *This code can only be used once.*

DEAD TO RIGHTS: RETRIBUTION

AVATAR AWARDS

AWARD	EARNED BY
GAC Armor	Earn the Best cop this city's ever had Achievement. Get this by completing the game on Officer difficulty.
GAC Helmet	Earn the Boom! Achievement. Get this by getting 30 headshots in any level, on Officer or greater difficulty.
GCPD Shirt	Earn the Brawler Achievement. Get this by completing any level (excluding the Prologue) without firing a shot.
Jack and Shadow Shirt	Earn the Finish him Shadow! Achievement. Get this by combining Jack and Shadow to kill 20 enemies in any level, on Officer or greater.
Logo Shirt	Earn the Protect the Innocent Achievement. Get this by saving the hostages.

XBOX 360

DEADLIEST WARRIOR: THE GAME

Enabling the cheats does not affect Achievements, but they are disabled when going online.

PLAYER 1 GOD MODE
At the main menu, press Up, A, X, B, Y, Down

PLAYER 2 GOD MODE
At the main menu, press Down, B, X, A, Y, Up

SLICE MODE
At the main menu, press Left Trigger, X, A, X, A, Right Trigger.

SUDDEN DEATH
At the main menu, press X, Right Bumper, Up, Down, Left Bumper, A.

ZOMBIE MODE
At the main menu, press Y, A, A, A, X, B.

AVATAR AWARDS

AWARD	EARNED BY
Samurai Kikou (Armor)	Complete Arcade mode with every character on Hard difficulty.
Samurai Kabuto with Somen (Helmet)	Complete Arcade mode with every character on Deadliest difficulty.

DEATHSPANK

AVATAR AWARDS

AWARD	EARNED BY
Dragon Hatchling	Complete Ms. Heybenstances quest to rescue the hatchlings.
Unicorn Poop T-shirt	Kill the twin dragons guarding the artifact.

DEFENSE GRID: THE AWAKENING

The following cheats will disable Achievements.

100,000 RESOURCES
Click and hold the Right Thumbstick and press Right, Right, Right, Right

CORES CANNOT BE TAKEN
Click and hold the Right Thumbstick and press Up, Left, Down, Right

FREE CAMERA MODE
Click and hold the Right Thumbstick and press Down, Up, Down, Down

INSTANT VICTORY
Click and hold the Right Thumbstick and press Up, Up, Up, Up

KILL ALL ALIENS
Click and hold the Right Thumbstick and press Left, Right, Left, Right

KILL ALL ALIENS CARRYING CORES
Click and hold the Right Thumbstick and press Up, Down, Down, Up

LEVEL SELECT
Click and hold the Right Thumbstick and press Up, Up, Down, Down, Left, Right, Left, Right

SELF-DESTRUCT (INSTANT DEFEAT)
Click and hold the Right Thumbstick and press Down, Down, Down, Down

TOGGLE TARGET RETICULE
Click and hold the Right Thumbstick and press Down, Up, Down, Up

UNLOCK ALL TOWER TYPES
Click and hold the Right Thumbstick and press Up, Down, Left, Right

DEF JAM: ICON

IT'S GOING DOWN BY YUNG JOC
At the Title Screen, after "Press Start Button" appears, press Down, B, A, Right.

MAKE IT RAIN BY FAT JOE AND FIGHT AS FAT JOE
At the Title Screen, after "Press Start Button" appears, press B, Up, Right, Left, Y.

DESTROY ALL HUMANS! PATH OF THE FURON

After entering the following codes, select Customize from the Options to activate them.

60S APPEARANCE
Select Unlock Content from Extras and enter M13Ni95L.

70S APPEARANCE
Select Unlock Content from Extras and enter S63bf2kd.

BIKER OUTFIT
Select Unlock Content from Extras and enter 1gb57M2x.

CHEF OUTFIT
Select Unlock Content from Extras and enter 51c24KiW.

GANGSTER OUTFIT
Select Unlock Content from Extras and enter J5d99bPz.

KUNG FU OUTFIT
Select Unlock Content from Extras and enter Ly11r98H.

MIME OUTFIT
Select Unlock Content from Extras and enter 7qd33J1n.

VELVET OUTFIT
Select Unlock Content from Extras and enter F9sT5v88.

SAUCER ATTACHMENTS
Select Unlock Content from Extras and enter V81fvUW3.

SAUCER SKINS
Select Unlock Content from Extras and enter X91mw7zp.

DIRT 2

Win the given events to earn the following cars:

CAR	EVENT
Ford RS200 Evolution	Rally Cross World Tour
Toyota Stadium Truck	Landrush World Tour
Mitsubishi Pajero Dakar 1993	Raid World Tour
Dallenbach Special	Trailblazer World Tour
1995 Subaru Impreza WRX STi	Colin McRae Challenge
Colin McRae R4 [X Games]	X Games Europe
Mitsubishi Lancer Evolution X [X Games]	X Games Asia
Subaru Impreza WRX STi [X Games]	X Games America
Ford Escort MKII and MG Metro 6R4	All X Games events

DJ HERO

Select Cheats from Options and enter the following. Some codes will disable high scores and progress. Cheats cannot be used in tutorials and online.

UNLOCK ALL CONTENT
Enter tol0.

ALL CHARACTER ITEMS
Enter uNA2.

ALL VENUES
Enter Wv1u.

ALL DECKS
Enter LAuP.

ALL HEADPHONES
Enter 62Db.

ALL MIXES
Enter 82xl.

AUTO SCRATCH
Enter it6j.

AUTO EFFECTS DIAL
Enter ab1l.

AUTO FADER
Enter sl5d.

AUTO TAPPER
Enter zith.

AUTO WIN EUPHORIA
Enter r3a9.

BLANK PLINTHS
Enter ipr0.

HAMSTER SWITCH
Enter 7geo.

HYPER DECK MODE
Enter 76st.

SHORT DECK
Enter 51uc.

BLACK AND WHITE
Enter b!99.

EDGE EFFECT
Enter 2u4u.

INVISIBLE DJ
Enter oh5t.

MIDAS
Enter 4pe5.

PITCH BLACK OUT
Enter d4kr.

PLAY IN THE BEDROOM
Enter g7nh.

XBOX 360

RAINBOW
Enter ?jy!.

ANY DJ, ANY SETLIST
Enter 0jj8.

DAFT PUNK'S CONTENT
Enter d1g?.

DJ AM'S CONTENT
Enter k07u.

DJ JAZZY JEFF'S CONTENT
Enter n1fz.

DJ SHADOW'S CONTENT
Enter omxv.

DJ Z-TRIP'S CONTENT
Enter 5rtg.

GRANDMASTER FLASH'S CONTENT
Enter ami8.

DJ HERO 2

ALL BONUS CONTENT
Select Cheats from the Options. Choose Retail Cheats and enter VIP Pass.

DAVID GUETTA
Select Cheats from the Options. Choose Retail Cheats and enter Guetta Blaster.

DEADMAU5
Select Cheats from the Options. Choose Retail Cheats and enter Open The Trap.

DON KING PRESENTS: PRIZEFIGHTER

Re-enter a code to disable the cheat.

INVULNERABILITY
Select Enter Unlock Code from the Extras menu and enter SHIELDOFSTEEL.

MAXIMUM STATS
Select Enter Unlock Code from the Extras menu and enter BROUSSARDMODE.

INFINITE ADRENALINE
Select Enter Unlock Code from the Extras menu and enter FISTOFTHENORTHSHIELDS.

INFINITE STAMINA
Select Enter Unlock Code from the Extras menu and enter FEELTHEBURN.

SKIP GETUP GAME
Select Enter Unlock Code from the Extras menu and enter NEVERQUIT.

PLAY AS RICARDO MAYORGA
Select Enter Unlock Code from the Extras menu and enter POTSEMAG.

GREAT MOMENTS IN BOXING VIDEO
Select Enter Unlock Code from the Extras menu and enter 1BESTBUYBEST.

EAT LEAD: THE RETURN OF MATT HAZARD

MAXIMUM HAZARD DIFFICULTY
At the difficulty select, press Up, Up, Down, Down, Left, Right, Left, Right.

ERAGON

FURY MODE
Pause the game, hold Left Bumper + Right Bumper + Left Trigger + Right Trigger and press X, X, B, B.

EVERY EXTEND EXTRA EXTREME

FINE ADJUSTMENT MENU
At the Start screen, press Left Bumper, Right Bumper, Left Bumper, Right Bumper, Left Bumper, Right Bumper, Left Bumper, Right Bumper.

FAR CRY INSTINCTS PREDATOR

EVOLUTION GAME
Select the Cheat menu option from the Main menu or the pause menu and enter GiveMeltAll.

HEAL
Select the Cheat menu option from the Main menu or the pause menu and enter ImJackCarver.

INFINITE ADRENALINE
Select the Cheat menu option from the Main menu or the pause menu and enter Bloodlust.

INFINITE AMMO
Select the Cheat menu option from the Main menu or the pause menu and enter UnleashHell.

ENABLE EVOLUTIONS
Select the Cheat menu option from the Main menu or the pause menu and enter FeralAttack.

ALL MAPS
Select the Cheat menu option from the Main menu or the pause menu and enter GiveMeTheMaps.

FAR CRY 2

BONUS MISSIONS
Select Promotional Content from the Additional Content menu and enter the following codes. Each code gives four or six extra missions.

6aPHuswe
Cr34ufrE
2Eprunef
JeM8SpaW
tr99pUkA

FATAL FURY SPECIAL

CHEAT MENU
During a game, hold Start and push A + X + Y.

F.E.A.R.

ALL MISSIONS
Sign in with F3ARDAY1 as your Profile Name. Using this cheat will disable Achievements.

FIGHT NIGHT ROUND 3

ALL VENUES
Create a champ with a first name of NEWVIEW.

FLATOUT: ULTIMATE CARNAGE

MOB CAR IN SINGLE EVENTS
Select Enter Code from Extras and enter BIGTRUCK.

PIMPSTER IN SINGLE EVENTS
Select Enter Code from Extras and enter RUTTO.

ROCKET IN SINGLE EVENTS
Select Enter Code from Extras and enter KALJAKOPPA.

FRACTURE

EXCLUSIVE PRE-ORDER SKIN
Pause the game and press Up, Right, Left, Down, Up, Left, Right, Down.

FROGGER

BIG FROGGER
At the One/Two-Player screen, press Up, Up, Down, Down, Left, Right, Left, Right, B, A.

XBOX 360

FUEL

CAMO ARMY HELMET
Select Bonus Codes from the Options menu and enter 48992519.

ROAD ADDICT JACKET
Select Bonus Codes from the Options menu and enter 20061977.

SPEED ANGEL SHORTS
Select Bonus Codes from the Options menu and enter 91031985.

BUTTERFLY LIVERY FOR SLUDGERAY VEHICLE
Select Bonus Codes from the Options menu and enter 18021974.

LIGHTNING BOLT LIVERY FOR MUDHOG VEHICLE
Select Bonus Codes from the Options menu and enter 17121973.

WARRIOR VEHICLE
Select Bonus Codes from the Options menu and enter 18041851.

GAMERBOTS: THIRD-ROBOT SHOOTING

300,000 GP
Enter 24162444 as a gift code.

DEMON SWORD
Enter 39121412 as a gift code.

DUAL FLAME
Enter 34094035 as a gift code.

SPIKED CLUB
Enter 56095802 as a gift code.

STAR SLICER
Enter 55122302 as a gift code.

GAROU: MARK OF THE WOLVES

PLAY AS GRANT
Highlight Dong Hwan, hold Start, and press Up, Up, Down, Down, Up, Down. Press any button while still holding Start.

PLAY AS KAIN
Highlight Jae Hoon, hold Start, and press Down, Down, Up, Up, Down, Up. Press any button while still holding Start.

RANDOM CHARACTER SELECT
At the character select, hold Start and press a button.

G.I. JOE: THE RISE OF COBRA

CLASSIC DUKE
At the Main menu, press Left, Up, X, Up, Right, Y.

CLASSIC SCARLETT
At the Main menu, press Right, Up, Down, Down, Y.

THE GODFATHER: THE GAME

FULL AMMO
Pause the game and press Y, Left, Y, Right, X, Right Thumbstick.

FULL HEALTH
Pause the game and press Left, X, Right, Y, Right, Left Thumbstick.

UNLOCK ENTIRE FILM ARCHIVE
After loading a game and before joining the family, press Y, X, Y, X, X, Left Thumbstick. Select Film Archive to view the films.

THE GODFATHER II

These codes can only be used once every few minutes.

$5,000
While in Don view, press X, Y, X, X, Y, click Left Analog Stick.

FULL HEALTH
While in Don view, press Left, X, Right, Y, Right, click Left Analog Stick.

FULL AMMO
While in Don view, press Y, Left, Y, Right, X, click Right Analog Stick.

GRAND THEFT AUTO IV

CHEATS
Call the following phone numbers with Niko's phone to activate the cheats. Some cheats may affect the missions and achievements.

VEHICLE	PHONE NUMBER
Change weather	468-555-0100
Get weapons	486-555-0100
Get different weapons	486-555-0150
Raise wanted level	267-555-0150
Remove wanted level	267-555-0100
Restore armor	362-555-0100
Restore health	482-555-0100
Restore armor, health, and ammo	482-555-0100

SPAWN VEHICLES
Call the following phone numbers with Niko's phone to spawn the corresponding vehicle.

VEHICLE	PHONE NUMBER
Annihilator	359-555-0100
Cognoscenti	227-555-0142
Comet	227-555-0175
FIB Buffalo	227-555-0100
Jetmax	938-555-0100
NRG-900	625-555-0100
Sanchez	625-555-0150
SuperGT	227-555-0168
Turismo	227-555-0147

MAP LOCATIONS
Access a computer in game and enter the following URL:
www.whattheydonotwantyoutoknow.com.

GRAND THEFT AUTO IV: THE BALLAD OF GAY TONY

CHEATS
Call the following phone numbers with your phone to activate the cheats. Some cheats may affect the missions and achievements.

CHEAT	PHONE NUMBER
Get weapons	486-555-0100
Get different weapons	486-555-0150
Raise wanted level	267-555-0150
Remove wanted level	267-555-0100
Restore armor	362-555-0100
Restore armor, health, and ammo	482-555-0100
Parachute	359-555-7272
Change Weather	468-555-0100

SPAWN VEHICLES

Call the following phone numbers with your phone to spawn the corresponding vehicle.

VEHICLE	PHONE NUMBER
Akuma	625-555-0200
Annihilator	359-555-0100
APC	272-555-8265
Bullet GT	227-555-9666
Buzzard	359-555-2899
Cognoscenti	227-555-0142
Comet	227-555-0175
FIB Buffalo	227-555-0100

VEHICLE	PHONE NUMBER
Floater	938-555-0150
Jetmax	938-555-0100
NRG-900	625-555-0100
Sanchez	625-555-0150
Super GT	227-555-0168
Turismo	227-555-0147
Vader	625-555-3273

GRAND THEFT AUTO IV: THE LOST AND DAMNED

CHEATS

Call the following phone numbers with your phone to activate the cheats. Some cheats may affect the missions and achievements.

BONUS	PHONE NUMBER
Get weapons	486-555-0100
Get different weapons	486-555-0150
Raise wanted level	267-555-0150
Remove wanted level	267-555-0100
Restore armor	362-555-0100
Restore armor, health, and ammo	482-555-0100

SPAWN VEHICLES

Call the following phone numbers with your phone to spawn the corresponding vehicle.

VEHICLE	PHONE NUMBER
Annihilator	359-555-0100
Burrito	826-555-0150
Double T	245-555-0125
FIB Buffalo	227-555-0100

VEHICLE	PHONE NUMBER
Hakuchou	245-555-0199
Hexer	245-555-0150
Innovation	245-555-0100
Slamvan	826-555-0100

GRID

ALL DRIFT CARS

Select Bonus Codes from the Options. Then choose Enter Code and enter TUN58396.

ALL MUSCLE CARS

Select Bonus Codes from the Options. Then choose Enter Code and enter MUS59279.

BUCHBINDER EMOTIONAL ENGINEERING BMW 320SI

Select Bonus Codes from the Options. Then choose Enter Code and enter F93857372. You can use this in Race Day or in GRID World once you've started your own team.

EBAY

Select Bonus Codes from the Options. Then choose Enter Code and enter DAFJ55E01473M0. You can use this in Race Day or in GRID World once you've started your own team.

GAMESTATION BMW 320SI

Select Bonus Codes from the Options. Then choose Enter Code and enter G29782655. You can use this in Race Day or in GRID World once you've started your own team.

MICROMANIA PAGANI ZONDA R

Select Bonus Codes from the Options. Then choose Enter Code and enter M38572343. You can use this in Race Day or in GRID World once you've started your own team.

PLAY.COM ASTON MARTIN DBR9

Select Bonus Codes from the Options. Then choose Enter Code and enter P47203845. You can use this in Race Day or in GRID World once you've started your own team.

To enter the following cheats, strum the guitar with the given buttons held. For example, if it says Yellow + Orange, hold Yellow and Orange as you strum. Air Guitar, Precision Mode, and Performance Mode can be toggled on and off from the Cheats menu. You can also change between five different levels of Hyperspeed at this menu.

UNLOCK EVERYTHING

Select Cheats from the Options. Choose Enter Cheat and enter Green + Red + Blue + Orange, Green + Red + Yellow + Blue, Green + Red + Yellow + Orange, Green + Yellow + Blue + Orange, Green + Red + Yellow + Blue, Red + Yellow + Blue + Orange, Green + Red + Yellow + Blue, Green + Yellow + Blue + Orange, Green + Red + Yellow + Blue, Green + Red + Yellow + Orange, Green + Red + Yellow + Orange, Green + Red + Yellow + Blue, Green + Red + Yellow + Orange. No sounds play while this code is entered.

An easier way to show this code is by representing Green as 1 down to Orange as 5. For example, if you have 1345, you would hold down Green + Yellow + Blue + Orange while strumming. 1245 + 1234 + 1235 + 1345 + 1234 + 2345 + 1234 + 1345 + 1234 + 1235 + 1235 + 1234 + 1235.

ALL SONGS

Select Cheats from the Options. Choose Enter Cheat and enter Yellow + Orange, Red + Blue, Red + Orange, Green + Blue, Red + Yellow, Yellow + Orange, Red + Yellow, Red + Blue, Green + Yellow, Green + Yellow, Yellow + Blue, Yellow + Blue, Yellow + Orange, Yellow + Orange, Yellow + Blue, Yellow, Red, Red + Yellow, Red, Yellow, Orange.

NO FAIL

Select Cheats from the Options. Choose Enter Cheat and enter Green + Red, Blue, Green + Red, Green + Yellow, Blue, Green + Yellow, Red + Yellow, Orange, Red + Yellow, Green + Yellow, Yellow, Green + Yellow, Green + Red.

AIR GUITAR

Select Cheats from the Options. Choose Enter Cheat and enter Blue + Yellow, Green + Yellow, Green + Yellow, Red + Blue, Red + Blue, Red + Yellow, Red + Yellow, Blue + Yellow, Green + Yellow, Green + Yellow, Red + Blue, Red + Blue, Red + Yellow, Red + Yellow, Green + Yellow, Green + Yellow, Red + Yellow, Red + Yellow.

HYPERSPEED

Select Cheats from the Options. Choose Enter Cheat and enter Orange, Blue, Orange, Yellow, Orange, Blue, Orange, Yellow, Red, Green + Red, Green + Red, Red + Yellow, Red + Yellow, Red + Blue, Red + Blue, Yellow + Blue, Yellow + Orange, Yellow + Orange.

PERFORMANCE MODE

Select Cheats from the Options. Choose Enter Cheat and enter Red + Yellow, Red + Blue, Red + Orange, Red + Blue, Red + Yellow, Green + Blue, Red + Yellow, Red + Blue.

EASY EXPERT

Select Cheats from the Options. Choose Enter Cheat and enter Green + Red, Green + Yellow, Yellow + Blue, Red + Blue, Blue + Orange, Yellow + Orange, Red + Yellow, Red + Blue.

PRECISION MODE

Select Cheats from the Options. Choose Enter Cheat and enter Green + Red, Green + Red, Green + Red, Red + Yellow, Red + Yellow, Red + Blue, Red + Blue, Yellow + Blue, Yellow + Orange, Yellow + Orange, Green + Red, Green + Red, Green + Red, Red + Yellow, Red + Yellow, Red + Blue, Red + Blue, Yellow + Blue, Yellow + Orange, Yellow + Orange.

BRET MICHAELS SINGER

Select Cheats from the Options. Choose Enter Cheat and enter Green + Red, Green + Red, Green + Red, Green + Blue, Green + Blue, Green + Blue, Red + Blue, Red, Red, Red, Red + Blue, Red, Red, Red, Red + Blue, Red, Red, Red.

GUITAR HERO 5

ALL HOPOS
Select Input Cheats from the Options menu and enter Green, Green, Blue, Green, Green, Green, Yellow, Green.

ALWAYS SLIDE
Select Input Cheats from the Options menu and enter Green, Green, Red, Red, Yellow, Blue, Yellow, Blue.

AUTO KICK
Select Input Cheats from the Options menu and enter Yellow, Green, Red, Blue, Blue, Blue, Blue, Red.

FOCUS MODE
Select Input Cheats from the Options menu and enter Yellow, Green, Red, Green, Yellow, Blue, Green, Green.

HUD FREE MODE
Select Input Cheats from the Options menu and enter Green, Red, Green, Green, Yellow, Green, Green, Green.

PERFORMANCE MODE
Select Input Cheats from the Options menu and enter Yellow, Yellow, Blue, Red, Blue, Green, Red, Red.

AIR INSTRUMENTS
Select Input Cheats from the Options menu and enter Red, Red, Blue, Yellow, Green, Green, Green, Yellow.

INVISIBLE ROCKER
Select Input Cheats from the Options menu and enter Green, Red, Yellow, Yellow, Yellow, Blue, Blue, Green.

ALL CHARACTERS
Select Input Cheats from the Options menu and enter Blue, Blue, Green, Green, Red, Green, Red, Yellow.

CONTEST WINNER 1
Select Input Cheats from the Options menu and enter Green, Green, Red, Red, Yellow, Red, Yellow, Blue.

GUITAR HERO: AEROSMITH

To enter the following cheats, strum the guitar with the given buttons held. For example, if it says Yellow + Orange, hold Yellow and Orange as you strum. Air Guitar, Precision Mode, and Performance Mode can be toggled on and off from the Cheats menu. You can also change between five different levels of Hyperspeed at this menu.

ALL SONGS
Red + Yellow, Green + Red, Green + Red, Red + Yellow, Red + Yellow, Green + Red, Red + Yellow, Red + Yellow, Green + Red, Green + Red, Red + Yellow, Red + Yellow, Green + Red, Red + Yellow, Red + Blue.

AIR GUITAR
Red + Yellow, Green + Red, Red + Yellow, Red + Yellow, Red + Blue, Red + Blue, Red + Blue, Red + Blue, Red + Blue, Yellow + Blue, Yellow + Blue, Yellow + Orange

HYPERSPEED

Yellow + Orange, Yellow + Orange, Yellow + Orange, Yellow + Orange, Yellow + Orange, Red + Yellow, Red + Yellow, Red + Yellow, Red + Yellow, Red + Blue, Red + Blue, Red + Blue, Red + Blue, Red + Blue, Yellow + Blue, Yellow + Orange, Yellow + Orange.

NO FAIL

Select Cheats from the Options. Choose Enter Cheat and enter Green + Red, Blue, Green + Red, Green + Yellow, Blue, Green + Yellow, Red + Yellow, Orange, Red + Yellow, Green + Yellow, Yellow, Green + Yellow, Green + Red.

PERFORMANCE MODE

Green + Red, Green + Red, Red + Orange, Red + Blue, Green + Red, Green + Red, Red + Orange, Red + Blue

PRECISION MODE

Red + Yellow, Red + Blue, Red + Blue, Red + Yellow, Red + Yellow, Yellow + Blue, Yellow + Blue, Yellow + Blue, Red + Blue, Red + Yellow, Red + Blue, Red + Blue, Red + Yellow, Red + Yellow, Yellow + Blue, Yellow + Blue, Yellow + Blue, Red + Blue.

GUITAR HERO: METALLICA

Once entered, the cheats must be activated in the Cheats menu.

METALLICA COSTUMES

Select Cheats from Settings and enter Green, Red, Yellow, Blue, Blue, Yellow, Red, Green.

HYPERSPEED

Select Cheats from Settings and enter Green, Blue, Red, Yellow, Yellow, Red, Green, Green.

PERFORMANCE MODE

Select Cheats from Settings and enter Yellow, Yellow, Blue, Red, Blue, Green, Red, Red.

INVISIBLE ROCKER

Select Cheats from Settings and enter Green, Red, Yellow (x3), Blue, Blue, Green.

AIR INSTRUMENTS

Select Cheats from Settings and enter Red, Red, Blue, Yellow, Green (x3), Yellow.

ALWAYS DRUM FILL

Select Cheats from Settings and enter Red (x3), Blue, Blue, Green, Green, Yellow.

AUTO KICK

Select Cheats from Settings and enter Yellow, Green, Red, Blue (x4), Red. With this cheat activated, the bass pedal is automatically hit.

ALWAYS SLIDE

Select Cheats from Settings and enter Green, Green, Red, Red, Yellow, Red, Yellow, Blue. All Guitar Notes Become Touch Pad Sliding Notes.

BLACK HIGHWAY

Select Cheats from Settings and enter Yellow, Red, Green, Red, Green, Red, Red, Blue.

FLAME COLOR

Select Cheats from Settings and enter Green, Red, Green, Blue, Red, Red, Yellow, Blue.

GEM COLOR

Select Cheats from Settings and enter Blue, Red, Red, Green, Red, Green, Red, Yellow.

STAR COLOR

Select Cheats from Settings and enter Press Red, Red, Yellow, Red, Blue, Red, Red, Blue.

ADDITIONAL LINE 6 TONES

Select Cheats from Settings and enter Green, Red, Yellow, Blue, Red, Yellow, Blue, Green.

VOCAL FIREBALL

Select Cheats from Settings and enter Red, Green, Green, Yellow, Blue, Green, Yellow, Green.

GUITAR HERO: SMASH HITS

ALWAYS DRUM FILL
Select Cheats from the Options menu and enter Green, Green, Red, Red, Blue, Blue, Yellow, Yellow.

ALWAYS SLIDE
Select Cheats from the Options menu and enter Blue, Yellow, Red, Green, Blue, Green, Green, Yellow.

AIR INSTRUMENTS
Select Cheats from the Options menu and enter Yellow, Red, Blue, Green, Yellow, Red, Red, Red.

INVISIBLE ROCKER
Select Cheats from the Options menu and enter Blue, Red, Red, Red, Red, Yellow, Blue, Green.

PERFORMANCE MODE
Select Cheats from the Options menu and enter Blue, Red, Yellow, Yellow, Red, Red, Yellow, Yellow.

HYPERSPEED
Select Cheats from the Options menu and enter Red, Green, Blue, Yellow, Green, Yellow, Red, Red. This unlocks the HyperGuitar, HyperBass, and HyperDrums cheats.

AUTO KICK
Select Cheats from the Options menu and enter Blue, Green, Red, Yellow, Red, Yellow, Red, Yellow.

GEM COLOR
Select Cheats from the Options menu and enter Red, Red, Red, Blue, Blue, Blue, Yellow, Green.

FLAME COLOR
Select Cheats from the Options menu and enter Yellow, Blue, Red, Green, Yellow, Red, Green, Blue.

STAR COLOR
Select Cheats from the Options menu and enter Green, Red, Green, Yellow, Green, Blue, Yellow, Red.

VOCAL FIREBALL
Select Cheats from the Options menu and enter Green, Blue, Red, Red, Yellow, Yellow, Blue, Blue.

EXTRA LINE 6 TONES
Select Cheats from the Options menu and enter Green, Red, Yellow, Blue, Red, Yellow, Blue, Green.

GUITAR HERO: VAN HALEN

ALWAYS DRUM FILL
Select Input Cheats from the Options menu and enter Red, Red, Red, Blue, Blue, Green, Green, Yellow.

ALWAYS SLIDE
Select Input Cheats from the Options menu and enter Green, Green, Red, Red, Yellow, Red, Yellow, Blue.

AUTO KICK
Select Input Cheats from the Options menu and enter Yellow, Green, Red, Blue, Blue, Blue, Blue, Red.

HYPERSPEED
Select Input Cheats from the Options menu and enter Green, Blue, Red, Yellow, Yellow, Red, Green, Green. This allows you to enable Hyperguitar, Hyperbass, and Hyperdrums.

PERFORMANCE MODE
Select Input Cheats from the Options menu and enter Yellow, Blue, Red, Blue, Green, Red, Red.

AIR INSTRUMENTS
Select Input Cheats from the Options menu and enter Red, Red, Blue, Yellow, Green, Green, Green, Yellow.

INVISIBLE ROCKER
Select Input Cheats from the Options menu and enter Green, Red, Yellow, Yellow, Yellow, Blue, Blue, Green.

BLACK HIGHWAY
Select Input Cheats from the Options menu and enter Yellow, Red, Green, Red, Green, Red, Red, Blue.

FLAME COLOR
Select Input Cheats from the Options menu and enter Green, Red, Green, Blue, Red, Red, Yellow, Blue.

GEM COLOR
Select Input Cheats from the Options menu and enter Blue, Red, Red, Green, Red, Green, Red, Yellow.

STAR COLOR
Select Input Cheats from the Options menu and enter Red, Red, Yellow, Red, Blue, Red, Red, Blue.

VOCAL FIREBALL
Select Input Cheats from the Options menu and enter Red, Green, Green, Yellow, Blue, Green, Yellow, Green.

EXTRA LINE 6 TONES
Select Input Cheats from the Options menu and enter Green, Red, Yellow, Blue, Red, Yellow, Blue, Green.

GUITAR HERO: WARRIORS OF ROCK

Select Extras from Options to toggle the following on and off. Some cheats will disable Achievements.

ALL CHARACTERS
Select Cheats from the Options menu and enter Blue, Green, Green, Red, Green, Red, Yellow, Blue.

ALL VENUES
Select Cheats from the Options menu and enter Red, Blue, Blue, Red, Red, Blue, Blue, Red.

ALWAYS SLIDE
Select Cheats from the Options menu and enter Blue, Green, Green, Red, Red, Yellow, Blue, Yellow.

ALL HOPOS
Select Cheats from the Options menu and enter Green (x3), Blue, Green (x3), Yellow. Most notes become hammer-ons or pull-offs.

INVISIBLE ROCKER
Select Cheats from the Options menu and enter Green, Green, Red, Yellow (x3), Blue, Blue.

AIR INSTRUMENTS
Select Cheats from the Options menu and enter Yellow, Red, Red, Blue, Yellow, Green (x3).

FOCUS MODE
Select Cheats from the Options menu and enter Green, Yellow, Green, Red, Green, Yellow, Blue, Green. This removes the busy background.

HUD FREE MODE
Select Cheats from the Options menu and enter Green, Green, Red, Green, Green, Yellow, Green, Green.

PERFORMANCE MODE
Select Cheats from the Options menu and enter Red, Yellow, Yellow, Blue, Red, Blue, Green, Red.

COLOR SHUFFLE
Select Cheats from the Options menu and enter Blue, Green, Blue, Red, Yellow, Green, Red, Yellow.

MIRROR GEMS
Select Cheats from the Options menu and enter Blue, Blue, Red, Blue, Green, Green, Red, Green.

RANDOM GEMS
Select Cheats from the Options menu and enter Green, Green, Red, Red, Yellow, Red, Yellow, Blue.

GUITAR HERO WORLD TOUR

The following cheats can be toggled on and off at the Cheats menu.

QUICKPLAY SONGS

Select Cheats from the Options menu, choose Enter New Cheat and press Blue, Blue, Red, Green, Green, Blue, Blue, Yellow.

ALWAYS SLIDE

Select Cheats from the Options menu, choose Enter New Cheat and press Green, Green, Red, Red, Yellow, Red, Yellow, Blue.

AT&T BALLPARK

Select Cheats from the Options menu, choose Enter New Cheat and press Yellow, Green, Red, Red, Green, Blue, Red, Yellow.

AUTO KICK

Select Cheats from the Options menu, choose Enter New Cheat and press Yellow, Green, Red, Blue (x4), Red.

EXTRA LINE 6 TONES

Select Cheats from the Options menu, choose Enter New Cheat and press Green, Red, Yellow, Blue, Red, Yellow, Blue, Green.

FLAME COLOR

Select Cheats from the Options menu, choose Enter New Cheat and press Green, Red, Green, Blue, Red, Red, Yellow, Blue.

GEM COLOR

Select Cheats from the Options menu, choose Enter New Cheat and press Blue, Red, Red, Green, Red, Green, Red, Yellow.

STAR COLOR

Select Cheats from the Options menu, choose Enter New Cheat and press Red, Red, Yellow, Red, Blue, Red, Red, Blue.

AIR INSTRUMENTS

Select Cheats from the Options menu, choose Enter New Cheat and press

Red, Red, Blue, Yellow, Green (x3), Yellow.

HYPERSPEED

Select Cheats from the Options menu, choose Enter New Cheat and press Green, Blue, Red, Yellow, Yellow, Red, Green, Green. These show up in the menu as HyperGuitar, HyperBass, and HyperDrums.

PERFORMANCE MODE

Select Cheats from the Options menu, choose Enter New Cheat and press Yellow, Yellow, Blue, Red, Blue, Green, Red, Red.

INVISIBLE ROCKER

Select Cheats from the Options menu, choose Enter New Cheat and press Green, Red, Yellow (x3), Blue, Blue, Green.

VOCAL FIREBALL
Select Cheats from the Options menu, choose Enter New Cheat and press Red, Green, Green, Yellow, Blue, Green, Yellow, Green.

AARON STEELE!
Select Cheats from the Options menu, choose Enter New Cheat and press Blue, Red, Yellow (x5), Green.

JONNY VIPER
Select Cheats from the Options menu, choose Enter New Cheat and press Blue, Red, Blue, Blue, Yellow (x3), Green.

NICK
Select Cheats from the Options menu, choose Enter New Cheat and press Green, Red, Blue, Green, Red, Blue, Blue, Green.

RINA
Select Cheats from the Options menu, choose Enter New Cheat and press Blue, Red, Green, Green, Yellow (x3), Green.

HALO 3

TOGGLE HIDE WEAPON
During a local game, hold Left Bumper + Right Bumper + Left Stick + A + Down.

TOGGLE SHOW COORDINATES
During a local game, hold Left Bumper + Right Bumper + Left Stick + A + Up.

TOGGLE BETWEEN PAN-CAM AND NORMAL
During a local game, hold Left Stick + Right Stick and press Left when Show Coordinates is active.

HALO REACH

AVATAR AWARDS

AWARD	EARNED BY
Carter's Helmet	Clear a Campaign mission on Legendary without dying—Save and quit toward the end of a mission. Resume the game and finish mission without dying to earn this award easily.
Emile's Helmet	Earn a Bulltrue medal in either multiplayer or Firefight Matchmaking
Jorge's Helmet	Earn a Killtacular in multiplayer Matchmaking
Jun's Helmet	Kill 100 enemies in a row without dying in either the Campaign or Firefight
Kat's Helmet	Avenge teammate's death in multiplayer Matchmaking

HARRY POTTER AND THE HALF-BLOOD PRINCE

BONUS TWO-PLAYER DUELING ARENA CASTLE GATES
At the Rewards menu, press Right, Right, Down, Down, Left, Right, Left, Right, Left, Right, Start.

HYDRO THUNDER HURRICANE

AVATAR AWARDS

AWARD	EARNED BY
Hydro Thunder Hurricane T-Shirt	Get 500 points.
Razorback Toy Boat	Earn 18,500 points.

IDOLMASTER: LIVE FOR YOU!

MAMI

At the character select, press R3 while on Ami.

SHORT-HAIRED MIKI

At the character select, press R3 while on Miki.

IRON MAN

CLASSIC ARMOR

Clear One Man Army vs. Mercs.

EXTREMIS ARMOR

Clear One Man Army vs. Maggia.

MARK II ARMOR

Clear One Man Army vs. Ten Rings.

HULKBUSTER ARMOR

Clear One Man Army vs. AIM-X. Can also be unlocked when clear game save data from Incredible Hulk is stored on the same console.

SILVER CENTURION ARMOR

Clear Mission 13: Showdown.

CLASSIC MARK I ARMOR

Clear One Man Army vs. AIM.

JUICED 2: HOT IMPORT NIGHTS

HIDDEN CHALLENGE AND A MITSUBISHI PROTOTYPE X

Select Cheats and Codes from the DNA Lab menu and enter DOPX. Defeat the challenge to earn the Mitsubishi Prototype X.

HIDDEN CHALLENGE AND A NISSAN 350Z

Select Cheats and Codes from the DNA Lab menu and enter PRGN. Defeat the challenge to earn the Nissan 350Z.

HIDDEN CHALLENGE AND A NISSAN SKYLINE R34 GT-R

Select Cheats and Codes from the DNA Lab menu and enter JWRS. Defeat the challenge to earn the Nissan Skyline R34 GT-R.

HIDDEN CHALLENGE AND A SALEEN S7

Select Cheats and Codes from the DNA Lab menu and enter WIKF. Defeat the challenge to earn the Saleen S7.

HIDDEN CHALLENGE AND A SEAT LEON CUPRA R

Select Cheats and Codes from the DNA Lab menu and enter FAMQ. Defeat the challenge to earn the Seat Leon Cupra R.

HIDDEN CHALLENGE AND AN AUDI TT 1.8 QUATTRO

Select Cheats and Codes from the DNA Lab menu and enter YTHZ. Defeat the challenge to earn the Audi TT 1.8 Quattro.

HIDDEN CHALLENGE AND A BMW Z4

Select Cheats and Codes from the DNA Lab menu and enter GVDL. Defeat the challenge to earn the BMW Z4.

HIDDEN CHALLENGE AND A HOLDEN MONARO

Select Cheats and Codes from the DNA Lab menu and enter RBSG. Defeat the challenge to earn the Holden Monaro.

HIDDEN CHALLENGE AND A HYUNDAI COUPE 2.7 V6

Select Cheats and Codes from the DNA Lab menu and enter BSLU. Defeat the challenge to earn the Hyundai Coupe 2.7 V6.

HIDDEN CHALLENGE AND AN INFINITY G35

Select Cheats and Codes from the DNA Lab menu and enter MRHC. Defeat the challenge to earn the Infinity G35.

HIDDEN CHALLENGE AND A KOENIGSEGG CCX

Select Cheats and Codes from the DNA Lab menu and enter KDTR. Defeat the challenge to earn the Koenigsegg CCX.

ISLAND FROM LOST

Grab a plane and fly to the small island in the northwest corner of the map. The plane explodes and falls to the ground as you fly over. There are several references to the show, including a hatch in the southwest corner of the island.

KUNG FU PANDA

INFINITE CHI
Select Cheats from the Extra menu and press Down, Right, Left, Up, Down.

INVINCIBILITY
Select Cheats from the Extra menu and press Down, Down, Right, Up, Left.

FULL UPGRADES
Select Cheats from the Extra menu and press Left, Right, Down, Left, Up.

4X DAMAGE MULTIPLAYER
Select Cheats from the Extra menu and press Up, Down, Up, Right, Left.

ALL MULTIPLAYER CHARACTERS
Select Cheats from the Extra menu and press Left, Down, Left, Right, Down.

DRAGON WARRIOR OUTFIT IN MULTIPLAYER
Select Cheats from the Extra menu and press Left, Down, Right, Left, Up.

ALL OUTFITS
Select Cheats from the Extra menu and press Right, Left, Down, Up, Right.

LARA CROFT AND THE GUARDIAN OF LIGHT

LARA CROFT HEAVY JUNGLE OUTFIT
Complete the game.

LARA CROFT JUNGLE OUTFIT
Score 1,410,000 points.

LARA CROFT BIKER OUTFIT
Score 1,900,000 points.

LARA CROFT LEGEND OUTFIT
Defeat Xolotl.

DOPPELGANGER OUTFIT
Score 2,400,000 points.

LEFT 4 DEAD 2

AVATAR AWARDS

AWARD	EARNED BY
Med Kit	Defeat all campaigns
Left 4 Dead 2 Hat	Play any map in The Passing
Gnome	Play any 6 Mutations
Left 4 Dead 2 Shirt	Win 10 games in Scavenge
Bull Shifters (Ellis) Shirt	Win 10 games in Versus
Depeche Mode (Rochelle) Shirt	Rescue Gnome Chompski from Dark Carnival
Zombie Hand Shirt	Kill 10,000 infected

OVERLOAD

THE LEGEND OF SPYRO: DAWN OF THE DRAGON

UNLIMITED LIFE
Pause the game, hold Left Bumper and press Right, Right, Down, Down, Left with the Left Control Stick.

UNLIMITED MANA
Pause the game, hold Right Bumper and press Up, Right, Up, Left, Down with the Left Control Stick.

MAXIMUM XP
Pause the game, hold Right Bumper and press Up, Left, Left, Down, Up with the Left Control Stick.

ALL ELEMENTAL UPGRADES
Pause the game, hold Left Bumper and press Left, Up, Down, Up, Right with the Left Control Stick.

LEGENDS OF WRESTLEMANIA

ANIMAL'S SECOND COSTUME
Select Cheat Codes from the Options menu and enter TheRoadWarriorAnimal.

BRUTUS BEEFCAKE'S SECOND COSTUME
Select Cheat Codes from the Options menu and enter BrutusTheBarberShop!.

IRON SHIEK'S SECOND COSTUME
Select Cheat Codes from the Options menu and enter IronSheikCamelClutch.

JIMMY HART'S SECOND COSTUME
Select Cheat Codes from the Options menu and enter WithManagerJimmyHart.

KOKO B WARE'S SECOND COSTUME
Select Cheat Codes from the Options menu and enter TheBirdmanKokoBWare!.

THE ROCK'S SECOND COSTUME
Select Cheat Codes from the Options menu and enter UnlockTheRockBottom!.

SGT. SLAUGHTER'S SECOND COSTUME
Select Cheat Codes from the Options menu and enter CobraClutchSlaughter.

SHAWN MICHAELS'S SECOND COSTUME
Select Cheat Codes from the Options menu and enter ShawnsSweetChinMusic.

UNDERTAKER'S SECOND COSTUME
Select Cheat Codes from the Options menu and enter UndertakersTombstone.

LEGO BATMAN

BATCAVE CODES
Using the computer in the Batcave, select Enter Code and enter the following codes.

CHARACTERS

CHARACTER	CODE
Alfred	ZAQ637
Batgirl	JKR331
Bruce Wayne	BDJ327
Catwoman (Classic)	M1AAWW
Clown Goon	HJK327
Commissioner Gordon	DDP967
Fishmonger	HGY748

CHARACTER	CODE
Freeze Girl	XVK541
Joker Goon	UTF782
Joker Henchman	YUN924
Mad Hatter	JCA283
Man-Bat	NYU942
Military Policeman	MKL382
Nightwing	MVY759
Penguin Goon	NKA238

CHARACTER	CODE
Penguin Henchman	BJH782
Penguin Minion	KJP748
Poison Ivy Goon	GTB899
Police Marksman	HKG984
Police Officer	JRY983
Riddler Goon	CRY928
Riddler Henchman	XEU824

CHARACTER	CODE
S.W.A.T.	HTF114
Sailor	NAV592
Scientist	JFL786
Security Guard	PLB946
The Joker (Tropical)	CCB199
Yeti	NJL412
Zoo Sweeper	DWR243

VEHICLES

VEHICLE	CODE
Bat-Tank	KNTT4B
Bruce Wayne's Private Jet	LEA664
Catwoman's Motorcycle	HPL826
Garbage Truck	DUS483
Goon Helicopter	GCH328
Harbor Helicopter	CHP735
Harley Quinn's Hammer Truck	RDT637
Mad Hatter's Glider	HS000W
Mad Hatter's Steamboat	M4DM4N
Mr. Freeze's Iceberg	ICYICE

VEHICLE	CODE
The Joker's Van	JUK657
Mr. Freeze's Kart	BCT229
Penguin Goon Submarine	BTN248
Police Bike	LJP234
Police Boat	PLC999
Police Car	KJL832
Police Helicopter	CWR732
Police Van	MAC788
Police Watercraft	VJD328
Riddler's Jet	HAHAHA
Robin's Submarine	TTF453
Two-Face's Armored Truck	EFE933

CHEATS

CHEAT	CODE
Always Score Multiply	9LRGNB
Fast Batarangs	JRBDCB
Fast Walk	ZOLM6N
Flame Batarang	D8NYWH
Freeze Batarang	XPN4NG
Extra Hearts	ML3KHP
Fast Build	EVG26J
Immune to Freeze	JXUDY6
Invincibility	WYD5CP
Minikit Detector	ZXGH9J

CHEAT	CODE
More Batarang Targets	XWP645
Piece Detector	KHJ554
Power Brick Detector	MMN786
Regenerate Hearts	HJH7HJ
Score x2	N4NR3E
Score x4	CX9MAT
Score x6	MLVNF2
Score x8	WCCDB9
Score x10	18HW07

LEGO HARRY POTTER: YEARS 1-4

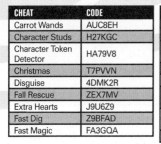

RED BRICK EXTRAS

Once you have access to The Leaky Cauldron, enter Wiseacre's Wizarding Supplies from Diagon Alley. Go upstairs to enter the following. Pause the game and select Extras to toggle the cheats on/off.

CHEAT	CODE
Carrot Wands	AUC8EH
Character Studs	H27KGC
Character Token Detector	HA79V8
Christmas	T7PVVN
Disguise	4DMK2R
Fall Rescue	ZEX7MV
Extra Hearts	J9U6Z9
Fast Dig	Z9BFAD
Fast Magic	FA3GQA

CHEAT	CODE
Gold Brick Detector	84QNQN
Hogwarts Crest Detector	TTMC6D
Ice Rink	F88VUW
Invincibility	QQWC6B
Red Brick Detector	7AD7HE
Regenerate Hearts	89ML2W
Score x2	74YKR7

XBOX 360

CHEAT	CODE
Score x4	J3WHNK
Score x6	XK9ANE
Score x8	HUFV2H
Score x10	H8X69Y

CHEAT	CODE
Silhouettes	HZBVX7
Singing Mandrake	BMEU6X
Stud Magnet	67FKWZ

WISEACRE SPELLS

Once you have access to The Leaky Cauldron, enter Wiseacre's Wizarding Supplies from Diagon Alley. Go upstairs to enter the following. You need to learn Wingardium Leviosa before you can use these cheats.

SPELL	CODE
Accio	VE9VV7
Anteoculatia	QFB6NR
Calvorio	6DNR6L
Colovaria	9GJ442
Engorgio Skullus	CD4JLX
Entomorphis	MYN3NB
Flipendo	ND2L7W
Glacius	ERA9DR
Herbifors	H8FTHL
Incarcerous	YEB9Q9

SPELL	CODE
Locomotor Mortis	2M2XJ6
Multicorfors	JK6QRM
Redactum Skullus	UW8LRH
Rictusempra	2UCA3M
Slugulus Eructo	U6EE8X
Stupefy	UWDJ4Y
Tarantallegra	KWWQ44
Trip Jinx	YZNRF6

EEYLOPS GOLD BRICKS

Once you have access to The Leaky Cauldron, enter Wiseacre's Wizarding Supplies from Diagon Alley. Go upstairs to enter the following. To access the LEGO Builder, visit Gringott's Bank at the end of Diagon Alley.

GOLD BRICK	CODE
1	QE4VC7
2	FY8H97
3	3MQT4P
4	PQPM7Z
5	ZY2CPA
6	3GMTP6

GOLD BRICK	CODE
7	XY6VYZ
8	TUNC4W
9	EJ42Q6
10	GFJCV9
11	DZCY6G

LEGO INDIANA JONES: THE ORIGINAL ADVENTURES

CHARACTERS

Approach the blackboard in the Classroom and enter the following codes.

CHARACTER	CODE
Bandit	12N68W
Bandit Swordsman	1MK4RT
Barranca	04EM94
Bazooka Trooper (Crusade)	MK83R7
Bazooka Trooper (Raiders)	S93Y5R
Belloq	CHN3YU
Belloq (Jungle)	TDR197
Belloq (Robes)	VEO29L
British Commander	B73EUA
British Officer	VJ5TI9
British Soldier	DJ5I2W
Captain Katanga	VJ3TT3
Chatter Lal	ENW936
Chatter Lal (Thuggee)	CNH4RY
Chen	3NK48T
Colonel Dietrich	2K9RKS
Colonel Vogel	8EAL4H
Dancing Girl	C7EJ21
Donovan	3NFTU8

CHARACTER	CODE
Elsa (Desert)	JSNRT9
Elsa (Officer)	VMJ5US
Enemy Boxer	8246RB
Enemy Butler	VJ48W3
Enemy Guard	VJ7R51
Enemy Guard (Mountains)	YR47WM
Enemy Officer	572E61
Enemy Officer (Desert)	2MK45O
Enemy Pilot	B84ELP
Enemy Radio Operator	1MF94R
Enemy Soldier (Desert)	4NSU7Q
Fedora	V75YSP
First Mate	0GIN24
Grail Knight	NE6THI
Hovitos Tribesman	H0V1SS
Indiana Jones (Desert Disguise)	4J8S4M
Indiana Jones (Officer)	VJ85OS

CHARACTER	CODE
Jungle Guide	24PF34
Kao Kan	WMO46L
Kazim	NRH23J
Kazim (Desert)	3M29TJ
Lao Che	2NK479
Maharajah	NFK5N2
Major Toht	13NS01
Masked Bandit	N48SF0
Mola Ram	FJUR31
Monkey Man	3RF6YJ
Pankot Assassin	2NKT72
Pankot Guard	VN28RH
Sherpa Brawler	VJ37WJ

CHARACTER	CODE
Sherpa Gunner	ND762W
Slave Child	0E3ENW
Thuggee	VM683E
Thuggee Acolyte	T2R3F9
Thuggee Slave Driver	VBS7GW
Village Dignitary	KD48TN
Village Elder	4682E1
Willie (Dinner Suit)	VK93R7
Willie (Pajamas)	MEN4IP
Wu Han	3NSLT8

EXTRAS

Approach the blackboard in the Classroom and enter the following codes. Some cheats need to be enabled by selecting Extras from the pause menu.

CHEAT	CODE
Artifact Detector	VIKED7
Beep Beep	VNF59Q
Character Treasure	VIES2R
Disarm Enemies	VKRNS9
Disguises	4ID1N6
Fast Build	V83SLO
Fast Dig	378RS6
Fast Fix	FJ59WS
Fertilizer	B1GW1F
Ice Rink	33GM7J
Parcel Detector	VUT673
Poo Treasure	WWQ1SA

CHEAT	CODE
Regenerate Hearts	MDLP69
Secret Characters	3X44AA
Silhouettes	3HE85H
Super Scream	VN3R7S
Super Slap	0P1TA5
Treasure Magnet	H86LA2
Treasure x10	VI3PS8
Treasure x2	VM4TS9
Treasure x4	VLWEN3
Treasure x6	V84RYS
Treasure x8	A72E1M

LEGO INDIANA JONES 2: THE ADVENTURE CONTINUES

Pause the game, select Enter Secret Code from the Extras menu, and enter the following.

CHARACTERS

CHARACTER	CODE
Belloq (Priest)	FTL48S
Dovchenko	WL4T6N
Enemy Boxer	7EQF47
Henry Jones	4CSAKH
Indiana Jones	PGWSEA
Indiana Jones: 2	FGLKYS
Indiana Jones (Collect)	DZFY9S
Indiana Jones (Desert)	M4C34K
Indiana Jones (Desert Disguise)	2W8QR3
Indiana Jones (Dinner Suit)	QUNZUT
Indiana Jones (Kali)	J2XS97

CHARACTER	CODE
Indiana Jones (Officer)	3FQFKS
Interdimensional Being	PXT4UP
Lao Che	7AWX3J
Mannequin (Boy)	2UJQWC
Mannequin (Girl)	3PGSEL
Mannequin (Man)	QPWDMM
Mannequin (Woman)	U7SMVK
Mola Ram	82RMC2
Mutt	2GKS62
Salah	E88YRP
Willie	94RUAJ

EXTRAS

EFFECT	CODE
Beep Beep	UU3VSC
Disguise	Y9TE98
Fast Build	SNXC2F
Fast Dig	XYAN83
Fast Fix	3Z7PJX

EFFECT	CODE
Fearless	TUXNZF
Ice Rink	TY9P4U
Invincibility	6JBB65
Poo Money	SZFAAE
Score x3	PEHHPZ

XBOX 360

EFFECT	CODE		EFFECT	CODE
Score x4	UXGTB3		Silhouettes	FQGPYH
Score X6	XWLJEY		Snake Whip	2U7YCV
Score x8	S5UZCP		Stud Magnet	EGSM5B
Score x10	V7JYBU			

LEGO STAR WARS: THE COMPLETE SAGA

The following still need to be purchased after entering the codes.

CHARACTERS

ADMIRAL ACKBAR
At the bar in Mos Eisley Cantina, select Enter Code and enter ACK646.

BATTLE DROID (COMMANDER)
At the bar in Mos Eisley Cantina, select Enter Code and enter KPF958.

BOBA FETT (BOY)
At the bar in Mos Eisley Cantina, select Enter Code and enter GGF539.

BOSS NASS
At the bar in Mos Eisley Cantina, select Enter Code and enter HHY697.

CAPTAIN TARPALS
At the bar in Mos Eisley Cantina, select Enter Code and enter QRN714.

COUNT DOOKU
At the bar in Mos Eisley Cantina, select Enter Code and enter DDD748.

DARTH MAUL
At the bar in Mos Eisley Cantina, select Enter Code and enter EUK421.

EWOK
At the bar in Mos Eisley Cantina, select Enter Code and enter EWK785.

GENERAL GRIEVOUS
At the bar in Mos Eisley Cantina, select Enter Code and enter PMN576.

GREEDO
At the bar in Mos Eisley Cantina, select Enter Code and enter ZZR636.

IG-88
At the bar in Mos Eisley Cantina, select Enter Code and enter GIJ989.

IMPERIAL GUARD
At the bar in Mos Eisley Cantina, select Enter Code and enter GUA850.

JANGO FETT
At the bar in Mos Eisley Cantina, select Enter Code and enter KLJ897.

KI-ADI MUNDI
At the bar in Mos Eisley Cantina, select Enter Code and enter MUN486.

LUMINARA
At the bar in Mos Eisley Cantina, select Enter Code and enter LUM521.

PADMÉ
At the bar in Mos Eisley Cantina, select Enter Code and enter VBJ322.

R2-Q5
At the bar in Mos Eisley Cantina, select Enter Code and enter EVILR2.

STORMTROOPER
At the bar in Mos Eisley Cantina, select Enter Code and enter NBN431.

TAUN WE
At the bar in Mos Eisley Cantina, select Enter Code and enter PRX482.

VULTURE DROID
At the bar in Mos Eisley Cantina, select Enter Code and enter BDC866.

WATTO
At the bar in Mos Eisley Cantina, select Enter Code and enter PLL967.

ZAM WESELL
At the bar in Mos Eisley Cantina, select Enter Code and enter 584HJF.

SKILLS

DISGUISE
At the bar in Mos Eisley Cantina, select Enter Code and enter BRJ437.

FORCE GRAPPLE LEAP
At the bar in Mos Eisley Cantina, select Enter Code and enter CLZ738.

VEHICLES

DROID TRIFIGHTER
At the bar in Mos Eisley Cantina, select Enter Code and enter AAB123.

IMPERIAL SHUTTLE
At the bar in Mos Eisley Cantina, select Enter Code and enter HUT845.

TIE INTERCEPTOR
At the bar in Mos Eisley Cantina, select Enter Code and enter INT729.

TIE FIGHTER
At the bar in Mos Eisley Cantina, select Enter Code and enter DBH897.

ZAM'S AIRSPEEDER
At the bar in Mos Eisley Cantina, select Enter Code and enter UUU875.

BEACH TROOPER

At Mos Eisley Canteena, select Enter Code and enter UCK868. You must still select Characters and purchase this character for 20,000 studs.

BEN KENOBI (GHOST)

At Mos Eisley Canteena, select Enter Code and enter BEN917. You must still select Characters and purchase this character for 1,100,000 studs.

BESPIN GUARD

At Mos Eisley Canteena, select Enter Code and enter VHY832. You must still select Characters and purchase this character for 15,000 studs.

BIB FORTUNA

At Mos Eisley Canteena, select Enter Code and enter WTY721. You must still select Characters and purchase this character for 16,000 studs.

BOBA FETT

At Mos Eisley Canteena, select Enter Code and enter HLP221. You must still select Characters and purchase this character for 175,000 studs.

DEATH STAR TROOPER

At Mos Eisley Canteena, select Enter Code and enter BNC332. You must still select Characters and purchase this character for 19,000 studs.

EWOK

At Mos Eisley Canteena, select Enter Code and enter TTT289. You must still select Characters and purchase this character for 34,000 studs.

GAMORREAN GUARD

At Mos Eisley Canteena, select Enter Code and enter YZF999. You must still select Characters and purchase this character for 40,000 studs.

GONK DROID

At Mos Eisley Canteena, select Enter Code and enter NFX582. You must still select Characters and purchase this character for 1,550 studs.

GRAND MOFF TARKIN

At Mos Eisley Canteena, select Enter Code and enter SMG219. You must still select Characters and purchase this character for 38,000 studs.

GREEDO

At Mos Eisley Canteena, select Enter Code and enter NAH118. You must still select Characters and purchase this character for 60,000 studs.

HAN SOLO (HOOD)

At Mos Eisley Canteena, select Enter Code and enter YWM840. You must still select Characters and purchase this character for 20,000 studs.

IG-88

At Mos Eisley Canteena, select Enter Code and enter NXL973. You must still select Characters and purchase this character for 30,000 studs.

IMPERIAL GUARD

At Mos Eisley Canteena, select Enter Code and enter MMM111. You must still select Characters and purchase this character for 45,000 studs.

IMPERIAL OFFICER

At Mos Eisley Canteena, select Enter Code and enter BBV889. You must still select Characters and purchase this character for 28,000 studs.

IMPERIAL SHUTTLE PILOT

At Mos Eisley Canteena, select Enter Code and enter VAP664. You must still select Characters and purchase this character for 29,000 studs.

IMPERIAL SPY

At Mos Eisley Canteena, select Enter Code and enter CVT125. You must still select Characters and purchase this character for 13,500 studs.

JAWA

At Mos Eisley Canteena, select Enter Code and enter JAW499. You must still select Characters and purchase this character for 24,000 studs.

LOBOT

At Mos Eisley Canteena, select Enter Code and enter UUB319. You must still select Characters and purchase this character for 11,000 studs.

PALACE GUARD

At Mos Eisley Canteena, select Enter Code and enter SGE549. You must still select Characters and purchase this character for 14,000 studs.

REBEL PILOT

At Mos Eisley Canteena, select Enter Code and enter CYG336. You must still select Characters and purchase this character for 15,000 studs.

OVERLOAD

XBOX 360

REBEL TROOPER (HOTH)
At Mos Eisley Canteena, select Enter Code and enter EKU849. You must still select Characters and purchase this character for 16,000 studs.

SANDTROOPER
At Mos Eisley Canteena, select Enter Code and enter YDV451. You must still select Characters and purchase this character for 14,000 studs.

SKIFF GUARD
At Mos Eisley Canteena, select Enter Code and enter GBU888. You must still select Characters and purchase this character for 12,000 studs.

SNOWTROOPER
At Mos Eisley Canteena, select Enter Code and enter NYU989. You must still select Characters and purchase this character for 16,000 studs.

STORMTROOPER
At Mos Eisley Canteena, select Enter Code and enter PTR345. You must still select Characters and purchase this character for 10,000 studs.

THE EMPEROR
At Mos Eisley Canteena, select Enter Code and enter HHY382. You must still select Characters and purchase this character for 275,000 studs.

TIE FIGHTER
At Mos Eisley Canteena, select Enter Code and enter HDY739. You must still select Characters and purchase this item for 60,000 studs.

TIE FIGHTER PILOT
At Mos Eisley Canteena, select Enter Code and enter NNZ316. You must still select Characters and purchase this character for 21,000 studs.

TIE INTERCEPTOR
At Mos Eisley Canteena, select Enter Code and enter QYA828. You must still select Characters and purchase this item for 40,000 studs.

TUSKEN RAIDER
At Mos Eisley Canteena, select Enter Code and enter PEJ821. You must still select Characters and purchase this character for 23,000 studs.

UGNAUGHT
At Mos Eisley Canteena, select Enter Code and enter UGN694. You must still select Characters and purchase this character for 36,000 studs.

LOONEY TUNES: ACME ARSENAL

UNLIMITED AMMO
At the Cheat menu, press Down, Left, Up, Right, Down, Left, Up, Right, Down.

LOST PLANET: EXTREME CONDITION

The following codes are for Single Player Mode on Easy Difficulty only.

500 THERMAL ENERGY
Pause the game and press Up, Up, Down, Down, Left, Right, Left, Right, X, Y, Right Bumper + Left Bumper.

INFINITE AMMUNITION
Pause the game and press Right Trigger, Right Bumper, Y, X, Right, Down, Left, Left Bumper, Left Trigger, Right Trigger, Right Bumper, Y, X, Right, Down, Left, Left Bumper, Left Trigger, Right Trigger, Left Trigger, Left Bumper, Right Bumper, Y, Left, Down, X, Right Bumper + Left Bumper.

INFINITE HEALTH
Pause the game and press Down (x3), Up, Y, Up, Y, Up, Y, Up(x3), Down, X, Down, X, Down, X, Left, Y, Right, X, Left, Y, Right, X, Right Bumper + Left Bumper.

CHANGE CAMERA ANGLE IN CUT SCENES
During a cut scene, press B, A, X, Y, B, A, X, Y, B, A, X, Y.

LOST PLANET: EXTREME CONDITION COLONIES EDITION

The following cheats only work for Easy Campaign, Score Attack, and Trial Battle. Each code must be reentered for every level.

+500 THERMAL ENERGY

Pause the game and enter: Up, Up, Down, Down, Left, Right, Left, Right, X, Y, Right Bumper + Left Bumper. This code can be used more than once.

INFINITE AMMUNITION

Pause the game and enter: Right Trigger, Right Bumper, Y, X, Right, Down, Left, Left Bumper, Left Trigger, Right Trigger, Right Bumper, Y, X, Right, Down, Left, Left Bumper, Left Trigger, Right Trigger, Left Trigger, Left Bumper, Right Bumper, Y, Left, Down, X, Right Bumper + Left Bumper.

INFINITE HEALTH

Pause the game and enter: Down (x3), Up, Y, Up, Y, Up, Y, Up (x3), Down, X, Down, X, Down, X, Left, Y, Right, X, Left, Y, Right, X, Right Bumper + Left Bumper.

USE WAYNE'S FINAL VS DURING END CREDITS

During the ending credits, before the words TEST PLAYER comes on screen, press and hold the following buttons to control Wayne's LP-9999 VS during credits.
Left Trigger, Left Bumper, Right Trigger, Right Bumper, X, Y, B.

LOST PLANET 2

Go to the Customization screen from My Page and select Character Parts. Press Y to access the LP2 Slot Machine and then press X to enter the following passwords:

T-SHIRT 1
Enter 73154986.

T-SHIRT 11
Enter 25060016.

T-SHIRT 4
Enter 40358056.

T-SHIRT 12
Enter 65162980.

T-SHIRT 5
Enter 96725729.

T-SHIRT 13
Enter 56428338.

T-SHIRT 6
Enter 21899787.

T-SHIRT 14
Enter 18213092.

T-SHIRT 7
Enter 52352345.

T-SHIRT 15
Enter 26797358.

T-SHIRT 8
Enter 63152256.

T-SHIRT 16
Enter 71556463.

T-SHIRT 9
Enter 34297758.

T-SHIRT 17
Enter 31354816.

T-SHIRT 10
Enter 88020223.

T-SHIRT 18
Enter 12887439.

ALBERT WESKER

Have a save game from Resident Evil 5. Albert Wesker can also be unlocked from the LP2 Slot Machine by entering 72962792. This character model can be found in Customization under Preset Models.

FRANK WEST

Have a save game from Lost Planet. Frank West can also be unlocked from the LP2 Slot Machine by entering 83561942. This character model can be found in Customization under Preset Models.

LUCHA LIBRE AAA HEROES DEL RING

LITTLE ONES

At the character select, press Up, Up, Down, Down, Left, Right, Left, Right. Play with them to unlock the Little Ones Can Too Achievement.

MARVEL ULTIMATE ALLIANCE

UNLOCK ALL SKINS
At the Team menu, press Up, Down, Left, Right, Left, Right, Start.

UNLOCKS ALL HERO POWERS
At the Team menu, press Left, Right, Up, Down, Up, Down, Start.

ALL HEROES TO LEVEL 99
At the Team menu, press Up, Left, Up, Left, Down, Right, Down, Right, Start.

UNLOCK ALL HEROES
At the Team menu, press Up, Up, Down, Down, Left, Left, Left, Start.

UNLOCK DAREDEVIL
At the Team menu, press Left, Left, Right, Right, Up, Down, Up, Down, Start.

UNLOCK SILVER SURFER
At the Team menu, press Down, Left, Left, Up, Right, Up, Down, Left, Start.

GOD MODE
During gameplay, press Up, Down, Up, Down, Up, Left, Down, Right, Start.

TOUCH OF DEATH
During gameplay, press Left, Right, Down, Down, Right, Left, Start.

SUPER SPEED
During gameplay, press Up, Left, Up, Right, Down, Right, Start.

FILL MOMENTUM
During gameplay, press Left, Right, Right, Left, Up, Down, Down, Up, Start.

UNLOCK ALL COMICS
At the Review menu, press Left, Right, Right, Left, Up, Up, Right, Start.

UNLOCK ALL CONCEPT ART
At the Review menu, press Down, Down, Down, Right, Right, Left, Down, Start.

UNLOCK ALL CINEMATICS
At the Review menu, press Up, Left, Left, Up, Right, Right, Up, Start.

UNLOCK ALL LOAD SCREENS
At the Review menu, press Up, Down, Right, Left, Up, Up Down, Start.

UNLOCK ALL COURSES
At the Comic Missions menu, press Up, Right, Left, Down, Up, Right, Left, Down, Start.

MARVEL: ULTIMATE ALLIANCE 2

These codes will disable the ability to save.

GOD MODE
During a game, press Up, Down, Up, Down, Up, Left, Down, Right, Start.

UNLIMITED FUSION
During a game, press Right, Right, Up, Down, Up, Up, Left, Start.

UNLOCK ALL POWERS
During a game, press Left, Right, Up, Down, Up, Down, Start.

UNLOCK ALL HEROES
During a game, press Up, Up, Down, Down, Left, Left, Left, Start.

UNLOCK ALL SKINS
During a game, press Up, Down, Left, Right, Left, Right, Start.

UNLOCK JEAN GREY
During a game, press Left, Left, Right, Right, Up, Down, Up, Down, Start.

UNLOCK HULK
During a game, press Down, Left, Left, Up, Right, Up, Down, Left, Start.

UNLOCK THOR
During a game, press Up, Right, Right, Down, Right, Down, Left, Right, Start.

UNLOCK ALL AUDIO LOGS
At the main menu, press Left, Right, Right, Left, Up, Up, Right, Start.

UNLOCK ALL DOSSIERS
At the main menu, press Down, Down, Down, Right, Right, Left, Down, Start.

UNLOCK ALL MOVIES
At the main menu, press Up, Left, Left, Up, Right, Right, Up, Start.

MEDAL OF HONOR: AIRBORNE

Using the following cheats disables saves and achievements. During a game, hold Left Bumper + Right Bumper, and press X, B, Y, A, A. This brings up an Enter Cheat screen. Now you can enter the following:

FULL AMMO
Hold Left Bumper + Right Bumper and press B, B, Y, X, A, Y.

FULL HEALTH
Hold Left Bumper + Right Bumper and press Y, X, X, Y, A, B.

MERCENARIES 2: WORLD IN FLAMES

These codes work with the updated version of Mercenaries 2 only. The cheats will keep you from earning achievements, but anything earned up to that point remains. You can still save with the cheats, but be careful if you want to earn trophies. Quit the game without saving to return to normal.

CHEAT MODE

Access your PDA by pressing Back. Press Left Bumper, Right Bumper, Right Bumper, Left Bumper, Right Bumper, Left Bumper, Left Bumper, Right Bumper, Right Bumper, Right Bumper, Left Bumper and close the PDA. You then need to accept the agreement that says achievements are disabled. Now you can enter the following cheats.

INVINCIBILITY

Access your PDA and press Up, Down, Left, Down, Right, Right. This activates invincibility for you and anyone who joins your game.

INFINITE AMMO

Access your PDA and press Up, Down, Left, Right, Left, Left.

GIVE ALL VEHICLES

Access your PDA and press Up, Down, Left, Right, Right, Left.

GIVE ALL SUPPLIES

Access your PDA and press Left, Right, Right, Left, Up, Up, Left, Up.

GIVE ALL AIRSTRIKES (EXCEPT NUKE)

Access your PDA and press Right, Left, Down, Up, Right, Left, Down, Up.

GIVE NUKE

Access your PDA and press Up, Up, Down, Down, Left, Right, Left, Right.

FILL FUEL

Access your PDA and press Up, Up, Up, Down, Down, Down.

ALL COSTUMES

Access your PDA and press Up, Right, Down, Left, Up.

GRAPPLING HOOK

Access your PDA and press Up, Left, Down, Right, Up.

MONDAY NIGHT COMBAT

AVATAR AWARDS

AWARD	EARNED BY
Mascot Mask	Meet the Mascot in Monday Night Combat Tutorial-kill the mascot in the tutorial.
Monday Night Combat T-Shirt	Earn the Exhibitor Achievement Get this by completing "Exhibition" Blitz mode.

MONSTER MADNESS: BATTLE FOR SUBURBIA

Pause the game and press Up, Up, Down, Down, Left, Right, Left, Right, B, A. This brings up a screen where you can enter the following cheats. With the use of some cheats profile saving, level progression, and Xbox Live Achievements are disabled until you return to the Main menu.

EFFECT	CHEAT
Animal Sounds	patrickdugan
Disable Tracking Cameras	ihatefunkycameras
Faster Music	upthejoltcola
First Person	morgythemole
Infinite Secondary Items	stevebrooks
Objects Move Away from Player	southpeak
Remove Film Grain	reverb

MOTOGP 07

ALL CHALLENGES

At the Main menu, press Right, Up, B, A, B, A, Left, Down, Y.

ALL CHAMPIONSHIPS

At the Main menu, press Right, Up, B, Y, Right, Up, B, Y, Right, Up, B, Y.

ALL LIVERIES
At the Main menu, press Right, A, Left, Left, Y, Left, A, Down, Y.

ALL TRACKS
At the Main menu, press Left, A, Right, Down, Y, B, A, B, Y.

ALL RIDERS
At the Main menu, press Right, Up, B, B, A, Down, Up, B, Down, Up, B.

MX VS. ATV REFLEX

MX VEHICLES FOR PURCHASE
Select Enter Cheat Code from the Options and enter brapbrap.

ATV VEHICLES FOR PURCHASE
Select Enter Cheat Code from the Options and enter couches.

JUSTIN BRAYTON, KTM MX BIKES AND ATVS IN ARCADE MODE
Select Enter Cheat Code from the Options and enter readytorace.

ALL AVAILABLE RIDER GEAR
Select Enter Cheat Code from the Options and enter gearedup.

ALL EVENT LOCATIONS IN ARCADE MODE
Select Enter Cheat Code from the Options and enter whereto.

ALL AVAILABLE HELMETS
Select Enter Cheat Code from the Options and enter skullcap.

ALL AI OPPONENTS
Select Enter Cheat Code from the Options and enter allai.

ALL AVAILABLE BOOTS
Select Enter Cheat Code from the Options and enter kicks.

ALL AVAILABLE GOGGLES
Select Enter Cheat Code from the Options and enter windows.

MX VS. ATV UNTAMED

ALL RIDING GEAR
Select Cheat Codes from the Options and enter crazylikea.

27 GRAPHICS
Select Cheat Codes from the Options and enter STICKERS.

ALL HANDLEBARS
Select Cheat Codes from the Options and enter nohands.

NARUTO: THE BROKEN BOND

NEW SASUKE
At The Character Select press Up, Down, X, X, Y, X, Y, B.

UCHIHA MADARA
At the Character Select press X, X, X, Y, X, B, B, A, A, Y.

NINE TAILS NARUTO
At the Character Select press X, X, Y, Y, X, Y, X, Y, X, X.

NASCAR 08

ALL CHASE MODE CARS
Select cheat codes from the options menu and enter checkered flag.

FANTASY DRIVERS
Select cheat codes from the options menu and enter race the pack.

EA SPORTS CAR
Select cheat codes from the options menu and enter ea sports car.

WALMART CAR AND TRACK
Select cheat codes from the options menu and enter walmart everyday.

NASCAR 09

ALL FANTASY DRIVERS
Select EA Extras from My NASCAR, choose Cheat Codes and enter CHECKERED FLAG.

WAL-MART CAR & CHICAGO PIER RACETRACK
Select EA Extras from My Nascar, choose Cheat Codes and enter WALMART EVERYDAY.

NBA 2K9

2K SPORTS TEAM
Select Codes from the Features menu and enter 2ksports.

NBA 2K TEAM
Select Codes from the Features menu and enter nba2k.

2K CHINA TEAM
Select Codes from the Features menu and enter 2kchina.

SUPERSTARS
Select Codes from the Features menu and enter llmohffae.

VC TEAM
Select Codes from the Features menu and enter vcteam.

ABA BALL
Select Codes from the Features menu and enter payrespect.

2009 ALL-STAR UNIFORMS
Select Codes from the Features menu and enter llaveyfonus.

NBA 2K10

ABA BALL
Select Codes from Options and enter payrespect.

2K CHINA TEAM
Select Codes from Options and enter 2kchina.

NBA 2K TEAM
Select Codes from Options and enter nba2k.

2K SPORTS TEAM
Select Codes from Options and enter 2ksports.

VISUAL CONCEPTS TEAM
Select Codes from Options and enter vcteam.

CAVFANATICS JERSEY FOR THE CAVALIERS
Select Codes from the Options menu and enter aifnaatccv.

HARDWOOD CLASSIC JERSEYS
Select Codes from the Options menu and enter wasshcicsl. This code gives Hardwood Classic Jerseys for the Cavaliers, Jazz, Magic, Raptors, timberwolves, Trail Blazers, and Warriors.

LATIN NIGHTS JERSEYS
Select Codes from the Options menu and enter aihinntslgt. This code gives Latin Nights jerseys for Bulls, Heat, Knicks, Lakers, Mavericks, Rockets, Spurs, and Suns.

NBA ALL-STAR JERSEYS
Select Codes from the Options menu and enter otnresla.

XBOX 360

NBA GREEN JERSEYS

Select Codes from the Options menu and enter nreogge. This code gives green uniforms for the Bobcats, Bulls, and Nuggets.

MARDI GRAS JERSEY FOR THE HORNETS

Select Codes from the Options menu and enter asrdirmga.

RACING JERSEY FOR THE BOBCATS

Select Codes from the Options menu and enter agsntrccai.

RIP CITY JERSEY FOR THE BLAZERS

Select Codes from the Options menu and enter ycprtii.

SECOND ROAD JERSEYS

Select Codes from the Options menu and enter eydonscar. This code gives Second Road Jerseys for the Grizzlies, Hawks, Mavericks, and Rockets.

ST. PATRICK'S DAY JERSEYS

Select Codes from the Options menu and enter riiasgerh. This code gives St. Patrick's Day jerseys for the Bulls, Celtics, Knicks, and Raptors.

NBA 2K11

MJ: CREATING A LEGEND

In Features, select Codes from the Extras menu. Choose Enter Code and enter icanbe23.

2K CHINA TEAM

In Features, select Codes from the Extras menu. Choose Enter Code and enter 2kchina.

2K SPORTS TEAM

In Features, select Codes from the Extras menu. Choose Enter Code and enter 2Ksports.

NBA 2K TEAM

In Features, select Codes from the Extras menu. Choose Enter Code and enter nba2k.

VC TEAM

In Features, select Codes from the Extras menu. Choose Enter Code and enter vcteam.

ABA BALL

In Features, select Codes from the Extras menu. Choose Enter Code and enter payrespect.

NBA LIVE 09

SUPER DUNKS MODE

Use the Sprite vending machine in the practice area and enter spriteslam.

NBA LIVE 10

CHARLOTTE BOBCATS' 2009/2010 RACE DAY ALTERNATE JERSEYS

Select Options from My NBA Live and go to Select Codes. Enter ceobdabacarstcy.

NEW ORLEANS HORNETS' 2009/2010 MARDI GRAS ALTERNATE JERSEYS

Select Options from My NBA Live and go to Select Codes. Enter nishrag1rosmad0.

ALTERNATE JERSEYS

Select Options from My NBA Live and go to Select Codes. Enter ndnba1rooaesdc0. This unlocks alternate jerseys for Atlanta Hawks, Dallas Mavericks, Houston Rockets, and Memphis Grizzlies.

MORE HARDWOOD CLASSICS NIGHTS JERSEYS

Select Options from My NBA Live and go to Select Codes. Enter hdogdrawhoticns. This unlocks Hardwood Classics Nights jerseys for Cleveland Cavaliers, Golden State Warriors, Minnesota Timberwolves, Orlando Magic, Philadelphia 76ers.

ADIDAS EQUATIONS

Select Options from My NBA Live and go to Select Codes. Enter adaodqauieints1.

ADIDAS TS CREATORS WITH ANKLE BRACES

Select Options from My NBA Live and go to Select Codes. Enter atciadsstsdhecf.

ADIDAS TS SUPERNATURAL COMMANDERS

Select Options from My NBA Live and go to Select Codes. Enter andsicdsmatdnsr.

ADIDAS TS SUPERNATURAL CREATORS

Select Options from My NBA Live and go to Select Codes. Enter ard8siscdnatstr.

AIR MAX LEBRON VII

Select Options from My NBA Live and go to Select Codes. Enter ere1nbvlaoeknii, 2ovnaebnkrielei, 3rioabeneikenvl, ri4boenanekilve, ivl5brieekaeonn, or n6ieirvalkeeobn.

KOBE V

Select Options from My NBA Live and go to Select Codes. Enter ovze1bimenkoko0, m0kveokoiebozn2, eev0nbimokk3ozo, or bmo4inozeeo0kvk.

JORDAN CP3 IIIS

Select Options from My NBA Live and go to Select Codes. Enter iaporcdian3ejis.

JORDAN MELO M6S

Select Options from My NBA Live and go to Select Codes. Enter emlarmeoo6ajdsn.

JORDAN SIXTY PLUSES

Select Options from My NBA Live and go to Select Codes. Enter aondsuilyjrspxt.

NIKE HUARACHE LEGIONS

Select Options from My NBA Live and go to Select Codes. Enter aoieuchrahelgn.

NIKE KD 2S

Select Options from My NBA Live and go to Select Codes. Enter kk2tesaosepinrd.

NIKE ZOOM FLIP'NS

Select Options from My NBA Live and go to Select Codes. Enter epfnozaeminolki.

NBA STREET HOMECOURT

ALL TEAMS

At the Main menu, hold Right Bumper + Left Bumper and press Left, Right, Left, Right.

ALL COURTS

At the Main menu, hold Right Bumper + Left Bumper and press Up, Right, Down, Left.

BLACK/RED BALL

At the Main menu, hold Right Bumper + Left Bumper and press Up, Down, Left, Right.

NEED FOR SPEED CARBON

CASTROL CASH

At the main menu, press Down, Up, Left, Down, Right, Up, X, B. This will give you 10,000 extra cash.

INFINITE CREW CHARGE

At the main menu, press Down, Up, Up, Right, Left, Left, Right, X.

INFINITE NITROUS

At the main menu, press Left, Up, Left, Down, Left, Down, Right, X.

INFINITE SPEEDBREAKER

At the main menu, press Down, Right, Right, Left, Right, Up, Down, X.

NEED FOR SPEED CARBON LOGO VINYLS

At the main menu, press Right, Up, Down, Up, Down, Left, Right, X.

NEED FOR SPEED CARBON SPECIAL LOGO VINYLS

At the main menu, press Up, Up, Down, Down, Down, Down, Up, X.

NEED FOR SPEED MOST WANTED

BURGER KING CHALLENGE

At the Title screen, press Up, Down, Up, Down, Left, Right, Left, Right.

CASTROL SYNTEC VERSION OF THE FORD GT

At the Title screen, press Left, Right, Left, Right, Up, Down, Up, Down.

MARKER FOR BACKROOM OF THE ONE-STOP SHOP

At the Title screen, press Up, Up, Down, Down, Left, Right, Up, Down.

JUNKMAN ENGINE

At the Title screen, press Up, Up, Down, Down, Left, Right, Up, Down.

PORSCHE CAYMAN

At the Title screen, press Left, Right, Right, Right, Right, Left, Right, Down.

XBOX 360

NEED FOR SPEED PROSTREET

$2,000
Select Career and then choose Code Entry. Enter 1MA9X99.

$4,000
Select Career and then choose Code Entry. Enter W2IOLL01.

$8,000
Select Career and then choose Code Entry. Enter L1IS97A1.

$10,000
Select Career and then choose Code Entry. Enter 1MI9K7E1.

$10,000
Select Career and then choose Code Entry. Enter CASHMONEY.

$10,000
Select Career and then choose Code Entry. Enter REGGAME.

AUDI TT
Select Career and then choose Code Entry. Enter ITSABOUTYOU.

CHEVELLE SS
Select Career and then choose Code Entry. Enter HORSEPOWER.

COKE ZERO GOLF GTI
Select Career and then choose Code Entry. Enter COKEZERO.

DODGE VIPER
Select Career and then choose Code Entry. Enter WORLDSLONGESTLASTING.

MITSUBISHI LANCER EVOLUTION
Select Career and then choose Code Entry. Enter MITSUBISHIGOFAR.

UNLOCK ALL BONUSES
Select Career and then choose Code Entry. Enter UNLOCKALLTHINGS.

5 REPAIR MARKERS
Select Career and then choose Code Entry. Enter SAFETYNET.

ENERGIZER VINYL
Select Career and then choose Code Entry. Enter ENERGIZERLITHIUM.

CASTROL SYNTEC VINYL
Select Career and then choose Code Entry. Enter CASTROLSYNTEC. This also gives you $10,000.

NEED FOR SPEED UNDERCOVER

$10,000
Select Secret Codes from the Options menu and enter $EDSOC.

DIE-CAST BMW M3 E92
Select Secret Codes from the Options menu and enter)B7@B=.

DIE-CAST LEXUS IS F
Select Secret Codes from the Options menu and enter 0;5M2;.

NEEDFORSPEED.COM LOTUS ELISE
Select Secret Codes from the Options menu and enter -KJ3=E.

DIE-CAST NISSAN 240SX (S13)
Select Secret Codes from the Options menu and enter ?P:COL.

DIE-CAST PORSCHE 911 TURBO
Select Secret Codes from the Options menu and enter >8P:I;.

SHELBY TERLINGUA
Select Secret Codes from the Options menu and enter NeedForSpeedShelbyTerlingua.

DIE-CAST VOLKSWAGEN R32
Select Secret Codes from the Options menu and enter!2ODBJ:.

NHL 2K9

3RD JERSEYS
From the Features menu, enter R6y34bsH52 as a code.

NHL 2K10

THIRD JERSEYS
Select Cheats from the Extras menu and enter G8r23Bty56.

VISUAL CONCEPTS TEAM
Select Cheats from the Extras menu and enter vcteam.

NHL 10

THIRD JERSEYS
At the EA Extras screen, enter rwyhafwh6ekyjcmr

TIPPMANN X-7 AK-47 SCENARIO PAINTBALL MARKER
Select Field Gear and press Up, Up, Right, Right, Down, Down, Left, Left.

OPERATION FLASHPOINT: DRAGON RISING

AMBUSH BONUS MISSION
Select Cheats from the Options menu and enter AmbushU454.

CLOSE QUARTERS BONUS MISSION
Select Cheats from the Options menu and enter CloseQ8M3

COASTAL STRONGHOLD BONUS MISSION
Select Cheats from the Options menu and enter StrongM577

DEBRIS FIELD BONUS MISSION
Select Cheats from the Options menu and enter OFPWEB2

ENCAMPMENT BONUS MISSION
Select Cheats from the Options menu and enter OFPWEB1

NIGHT RAID BONUS MISSION
Select Cheats from the Options menu and enter RaidT18Z

THE ORANGE BOX

HALF-LIFE 2
The following codes work for Half-Life 2, Half-Life 2: Episode One, and Half-Life 2: Episode Two.

CHAPTER SELECT
While playing, press Left, Left, Left, Left, Left Bumper, Right, Right, Right, Right, Right Bumper. Pause the game and select New Game to skip to another chapter.

RESTORE HEALTH (25 POINTS)
While playing, press Up, Up, Down, Down, Left, Right, Left, Right, B, A.

RESTORE AMMO FOR CURRENT WEAPON
While playing, press Y, B, A, X, Right Bumper, Y, X, A, B, Right Bumper.

INVINCIBILITY
While playing, press Left Shoulder, Up, Right Shoulder, Up, Left Shoulder, Left Shoulder, Up, Right Shoulder, Right Shoulder, Up.

PORTAL

CHAPTER SELECT
While playing, press Left, Left, Left, Left, Left Bumper, Right, Right, Right, Right, Right Bumper. Pause the game and select New Game to skip to another chapter.

GET A BOX
While playing, press Down, B, A, B, Y, Down, B, A, B, Y.

ENERGY BALL
While playing, press Up, Y, Y, X, X, A, A, B, B, Up.

PORTAL PLACEMENT ANYWHERE
While playing, press Y, A, B, A, B, Y, Y, A, Left, Right.

PORTALGUN ID 0
While playing, press Up, Left, Down, Right, Up, Left, Down, Right, Y, Y.

PORTALGUN ID 1
While playing, press Up, Left, Down, Right, Up, Left, Down, Right, X, X.

PORTALGUN ID 2
While playing, press Up, Left, Down, Right, Up, Left, Down, Right, A, A.

PORTALGUN ID 3
While playing, press Up, Left, Down, Right, Up, Left, Down, Right, B, B.

UPGRADE PORTALGUN
While playing, press X, B, Left Bumper, Right Bumper, Left, Right, Left Bumper, Right Bumper, Left Trigger, Right Trigger.

PERFECT DARK

PERFECT DARK ZERO SAVE CHEATS
If you have a save from Perfect Dark Zero on your hard drive, you get the following: All Guns (Solo), Cloaking Device, Hurricane Fists, and Weapon Stash Radar.

PRINCE OF PERSIA

SANDS OF TIME PRINCE/FARAH SKINS

Select Skin Manager from the Extras menu. Press Y and enter 52585854. This gives you the Sands of Time skin for the Prince and Farah from Sands of Time for the Princess. Access them from the Skin Manager

PRINCE ALTAIR IBN LA-AHAD SKIN

At the Main menu, press Y for Exclusive Content. Create an Ubisoft account. Then select "Altair Skin for Prince" to unlock.

PROTOTYPE

BODY SURFING ABILITY

Select Cheats from the Extras menu and enter Right, Right, Left, Down, Up, Up, Up, Down.

QUAKE 4

ALL WEAPONS, FULL ARMOR, HEALTH & AMMO

Press the Back button to access the Objectives, then press Up, Up, Down, Down, Left, Right, Left, Right, B, A.

FULL AMMO

Press the Back button to access the Objectives, then press B, A, X, Y, Left, Right, Left.

FULL HEALTH

Press the Back button to access the Objectives, then press B, A, B, A, Up, Up, Down, X.

RATATOUILLE

UNLIMITED RUNNING

At the cheat code screen, enter SPEEDY.

ALL MULTIPLAYER AND SINGLE PLAYER MINI-GAMES

At the cheat code screen, enter MATTELME.

RED FACTION: GUERRILLA

WRECKING CREW MAPS

Select Extras from the Options menu, choose Enter Code, and then enter MAPMAYHEM.

GOLDEN SLEDGEHAMMER, SINGLE PLAYER

Select Extras from the Options menu, choose Enter Code, and then enter HARDHITTER.

RED DEAD REDEMPTION

CHEATS

Select Cheats from Options and enter the following codes. Cheats disable Trophies and saving.

CHEAT	CODE
Invincibility	HE GIVES STRENGTH TO THE WEAK

CHEAT	CODE
Infinite Dead Eye	I DON'T UNDERSTAND IMNFINITY
Infinite Horse Stamina	MAKE HAY WHILE THE SUN SHINES
Infinite Ammo	ABUNDANCE IS EVERYWHERE
Money ($500)	THE ROOT OF ALL EVIL, WE THANK YOU!
Coach	NOW WHO PUT THAT THERE?
Horse	BEASTS AND MAN TOGETHER
Good Guy	IT AINT PRIDE. IT'S HONOR
Famous	I AM ONE OF THEM FAMOUS FELLAS
Diplomatic Immunity	I WISH I WORKED FOR UNCLE SAM
Decrease Bounty	THEY SELL SOULS CHEAP HERE
Gun Set 1	IT'S MY CONSTITUTIONAL RIGHT
Gun Set 2	I'M AN AMERICAN. I NEED GUNS
Who?	HUMILITY BEFORE THE LORD
Old School (Sepia)	THE OLD WAYS IS THE BEST WAYS
Man in Uniform (Bureau, US Army, and US Marshal uniforms)	I LOVE A MAN IN UNIFORM
Sharp Dressed Man (Gentleman's Suit)	DON'T YOU LOOK FINE AND DANDY
Lewis and Clark (All areas)	YOU GOT YOURSELF A FINE PAIR OF EYES
Gang Chic (Treasure Hunter outfit)	YOU THINK YOU TOUGH, MISTER?
Jack Attack (Play as Jack)	OH MY SON, MY BLESSED SON

CHEAT	CODE
Hic (Drunk)	I'M DRUNK AS A SKUNK AND TWICE AS SMELLY

AVATAR AWARDS

AWARD	EARNED BY
Sombrero	Shoot the hat off of an enemy.
Black on Red RDR Logo T-Shirt (Male and Female)	Open chest in burnt down house in Riley's Charge.
Yellow Rockstar Logo T-Shirt (Male and Female)	Open the chest in the attic of John Marston's Beechers Hope house.
Gentleman's Attire/Lady's Finest	Complete Skin It To Win It Social Club Challenge
Posse T-Shirt (Male and Female)	High score in Strike It Rich Social Club Challenge

RESONANCE OF FATE

Once you have reached Chapter 7, search Leanne's closet. As she speaks her first line, enter the following codes to unlock more outfits.

8-BIT GIRL SHIRT
Up, Up, Down, Down, Left, Right, Left, Right, Y, X

CLUB FAMITSU SHIRT
Y, Y, Up, Up, X, X, Left, Left, Left Bumper, Right Bumper

GEMAGA SHIRT
Right Trigger, Left Trigger, Left Bumper, Right Bumper, Y, Y, Y, X, X, Up

HIRAKOU SHIRT
X, Y, Left Bumper, Left Bumper, Right Bumper, Right Bumper, Click Left Thumbstick, Click Left Thumbstick, Up, Down

XBOX 360

OVERLOAD

PLATFORM LOGO SHIRT
Left, Up, Right, Down, Right Bumper, Right Bumper, Left Bumper, Left Bumper, Y, Click Left Thumbstick

POLITAN SUIT
Click Right Thumbstick (x3), Right, Left, Y, X, Left Trigger, Right Trigger, Left Bumper. This requires you to have the Reindeer Suit first.

ROBERT LUDLUM'S THE BOURNE CONSPIRACY

LIGHT MACHINE GUNS HAVE SILENCERS
Select Enter Code from the Cheats screen and enter whattheymakeyougive.

EXTRAS UNLOCKED — CONCEPT ART
Select Enter Code from the Cheats screen and enter lastchancemarie. Select Concept Art from the Extras menu.

EXTRAS UNLOCKED — MUSIC TRACKS
Select Enter Code from the Cheats screen and enter jasonbourneisdead. This unlocks Treadstone Appointment and Manheim Suite in the Music Selector found in the Extras menu.

ROCK BAND

ALL SONGS
At the title screen, press Red, Yellow, Blue, Red, Red, Blue, Blue, Red, Yellow, Blue. Saving and all network features are disabled with this code.

TRANSPARENT INSTRUMENTS
Complete the Hall of Fame concert with that instrument.

GOLD INSTRUMENT
Complete the Solo Tour with that instrument.

SILVER INSTRUMENT
Complete the Bonus Tour with that instrument.

ROCK BAND 2

Most of these codes disable saving, achievements, and Xbox LIVE play.

UNLOCK ALL SONGS
Select Modify Game from the Extras menu, choose Enter Unlock Code and press Red, Yellow, Blue, Red, Red, Blue, Blue, Red, Yellow, Blue or Y, B, X, Y, Y, X, X, Y, B, X. Toggle this cheat on or off from the Modify Game menu.

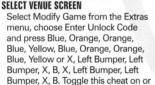

SELECT VENUE SCREEN
Select Modify Game from the Extras menu, choose Enter Unlock Code and press Blue, Orange, Orange, Blue, Yellow, Blue, Orange, Orange, Blue, Yellow or X, Left Bumper, Left Bumper, X, B, X, Left Bumper, Left Bumper, X, B. Toggle this cheat on or off from the Modify Game menu.

NEW VENUES ONLY
Select Modify Game from the Extras menu, choose Enter Unlock Code and press Red, Red, Red, Red, Yellow, Yellow, Yellow, Yellow or Y (x4), B (x4). Toggle this cheat on or off from the Modify Game menu.

PLAY THE GAME WITHOUT A TRACK
Select Modify Game from the Extras menu, choose Enter Unlock Code and press Blue, Blue, Red, Red, Yellow, Yellow, Blue, Blue or X, X, Y, Y, B, B, X, X. Toggle this cheat on or off from the Modify Game menu.

AWESOMENESS DETECTION

Select Modify Game from the Extras menu, choose Enter Unlock Code and press Yellow, Blue, Orange, Yellow, Blue, Orange, Yellow, Blue, Orange or B, X, Left Bumper, B, X, Left Bumper, B, X, Left Bumper. Toggle this cheat on or off from the Modify Game menu.

STAGE MODE

Select Modify Game from the Extras menu, choose Enter Unlock Code and press Blue, Yellow, Red, Blue, Yellow, Red, Blue, Yellow, Red or X, B, Y, X, B, Y, X, B, Y. Toggle this cheat on or off from the Modify Game menu.

ROCK BAND 3

GUILD X-79 GUITAR

At the main menu, press Blue, Orange, Orange, Blue, Orange, Orange, Blue, Blue.

OVATION D-2010 GUITAR

At the main menu, press Orange, Blue, Orange, Orange, Blue, Blue, Orange, Blue.

ROCKET KNIGHT

ALL CHARACTER SKINS

At the title screen, press Up, Up, Down, Down, Left, Right, Left, Right, B, A, Start.

ROCKSTAR GAMES PRESENTS TABLE TENNIS

Use of the following codes will disable achievements.

SWEATY CHARACTER VIEWER

After loading the map and before accepting the match, press Right Trigger, Up, Down, Left Trigger, Left, Right, Y, X, X, Y.

SMALL CROWD AUDIO

After loading the map and before accepting the match, press Down, Down, Down, Left Bumper, Left Trigger, Left Bumper, Left Trigger.

BIG BALL

After loading the map and before accepting the match, press Left, Right, Left, Right, Up, Up, Up, X.

COLORBLIND SPINDICATOR (ONLY IN NEWER PATCH)

After loading the map and before accepting the match, press Up, Down, X, X, Y, Y.

SILHOUETTE MODE

After loading the map and before accepting the match, press Up, Down, Y, Y, Left Bumper, Left Trigger, Right Trigger, Right Bumper.

BIG PADDLES CHEAT (ONLY IN NEWER PATCH)

After loading the map and before accepting the match, press Up, Left, Up, Right, Up, Down, Up, Up, X, X.

UNLOCK ALL

After loading the map and before accepting the match, press Up, Right, Down, Left, Left Bumper, Right, Up, Left, Down, Right Bumper.

VINTAGE AUDIO

After loading the map and before accepting the match, press Up, Up, Down, Down, Left, Right, Left, Right, Left Bumper, Right Bumper.

BIG CROWD AUDIO

After loading the map and before accepting the match, press Up, Up, Up, Right Bumper, Right Trigger, Right Bumper, Right Trigger.

OFFLINE GAMERTAGS

After loading the map and before accepting the match, press X, Y, X, Y, X, Y, Left Trigger, Right Trigger, Down, Down, Down.

SAINTS ROW

Pause the game and select Dial from your phone. Enter the following codes and then press Call. Select Cheats to enable the first set of codes, the ones that start with "#." You cannot earn achievements if using these cheats. Note that vehicles are delivered to your garage.

XBOX 360

CODE NAME	DIAL
Give Cash	#MONEY
Full Health	#FULLHEALTH
Repair Car	#778
Infinite Ammo	#AMMO
Infinite Sprint	#SPRINT
No Cop Notoriety	#NOCOPS
No Gang Notoriety	#NOGANGS
Evil Cars	#EVILCARS
Clear Skies	#SUNNY
Wrath of God	#10
44	#SHEPHERD
12 Gauge	#12GAUGE
Ambulance	#AMBULANCE
Anchor	#ANCHOR
Ant	#ANT
Aqua	#A7UA
Hannibal	#42664225
Hollywood	#HOLLYWOOD
Jackrabbit	#JACKRABBIT
The Job	#THEJOB
K6	#K6KRUKOV
Keystone	#KEYSTONE
Knife	#KNIFE
Komodo	#KOMODO
La Fuerza	#LAFUER9A
Mag	#MAG
McManus	#MACMANUS
Mockingbird	#MOCKINGBIRD
Molotov	#MOLOTOV
Nelson	#635766
Newman	#NEWMAN
Nightstick	#NIGHTSTICK
AR40	#AR40XTND
AS12	#AS12RIOT
Baron	#BARON
Baseball Bat	#BASEBALL
Betsy	#BETSY
Bulldog	#BULLDOG

CODE NAME	DIAL
Cavallaro	#CAVALLARO
Compton	#COMPTON
Cosmos	#COSMOS
Destiny	#DESTINY
Justice	#JUSTICE
FBI	#FBI
Ferdelance	#FERDELANCE
Gdhc	#GDHC50
Grenade	#GRENADE
Gunslinger	#GUNSLINGER
Halberd	#HALBERD
Hammerhead	#HAMMERHEAD
Hannibal	#42664225
Zenith	#9ENITH
Zimos	#9IMOS
Zircon	#9IRCON
Nordberg	#NORDBERG
NR4	#NR4
Pimp Cane	#PIMPCANE
Pipebomb	#PIPEBOMB
Quasar	#7UASAR
Quota	#7UOTA
Rattler	#RATTLER
Reaper	#REAPER
RPG	#ROCKET
Shogun	#SHOGUN
SKR7	#SKRSPREE
T3K	#T3KURBAN
Taxi	#TAXI
Titan	#TITAN
Tombstone	#TOMBSTONE
Traxxmaster	#TRAXXMASTER
VICE9	#Vice9
Vortex	#VORTEX
Voxel	#VOXEL
GameStop	#42637867
Chicken Ned	5552445 (select Homies from your Phone to access Chicken Ned)

For the following codes, select the Phone Book to call.

CODE NAME	DIAL
EagleLine Yellow	5550180174
Big Willy's Cab	5558198415
Brown Baggers	5553765
Crash Landing	5556278
The Dead Cow	5556238
Emergency	911
Eye for an Eye	5555966
Freckle Bitch's	5556328
Grounds for Divorce	5559473

CODE NAME	DIAL
Impression	5553248
Legal Lee's	5559467
Lik-a-Chick	5553863
On the Fence	5557296
On the Rag	5555926
On Thin Ice	5552564
Rim Jobs	5553493
$tock$	5552626
Suicide Hotline	5554876837
TNA Taxis	5554558008

CHEAT CODES

Select Dial from the Phone menu and enter these numbers followed by the Call button. Activate the cheats by selecting Cheats from the Phone menu. Enabling a cheat prevents the acquisition of Achievements

PLAYER ABILITY

CHEAT	NUMBER	CHEAT	NUMBER
Give Cash	#2274666399	Car Mass Hole	#2
No Cop Notoriety	#50	Infinite Ammo	#11
No Gang Notoriety	#51	Heaven Bound	#12
Infinite Sprint	#6	Add Police Notoriety	#4
Full Health	#1	Add Gang Notoriety	#35
Player Pratfalls	#5	Never Die	#36
Milk Bones	#3	Unlimited Clip	#9

VEHICLES

CHEAT	NUMBER	CHEAT	NUMBER
Repair Car	#1056	Anchor	#1041
Venom Classic	#1079	Blaze	#1044
Five-0	#1055	Sabretooth	#804
Stilwater Municipal	#1072	Sandstorm	#805
Baron	#1047	Kaneda	#801
Attrazione	#1043	Widowmaker	#806
Zenith	#1081	Kenshin	#802
Vortex	#1080	Melbourne	#803
Phoenix	#1064	Miami	#826
Bootlegger	#1049	Python	#827
Raycaster	#1068	Hurricane	#825
Hollywood	#1057	Shark	#828
Justice	#1058	Skipper	#829
Compton	#1052	Mongoose	#1062
Eiswolf	#1053	Superiore	#1073
Taxi	#1074	Tornado	#713
Ambulance	#1040	Horizon	#711
Backhoe	#1045	Wolverine	#714
Bagboy	#1046	Snipes 57	#712
Rampage	#1067	Bear	#1048
Reaper	#1069	Toad	#1077
The Job	#1075	Kent	#1059
Quota	#1066	Oring	#1063
FBI	#1054	Longhauler	#1061
Mag	#1060	Atlasbreaker	#1042
Bulldog	#1050	Septic Avenger	#1070
Quasar	#1065	Shaft	#1071
Titan	#1076	Bulldozer	#1051
Varsity	#1078		

WEAPONS

CHEAT	NUMBER	CHEAT	NUMBER
AR-50	#923	Baseball Bat	#926
K6	#935	Knife	#936
GDHC	#932	Molotov	#940
NR4	#942	Grenade	#933
44	#921	Nightstick	#941
Tombstone	#956	Pipebomb	#945
T3K	#954	RPG	#946
VICE9	#957	Crowbar	#955
AS14 Hammer	#925	Pimp Cane	#944
12 Gauge	#920	AR200	#922
SKR-9	#951	AR-50/Grenade Launcher	#924
McManus 2010	#938	Chainsaw	#927

CHEAT	NUMBER
Fire Extinguisher	#928
Flamethrower	#929
Flashbang	#930
GAL43	#931
Kobra	#934
Machete	#937
Mini-gun	#939
Pepperspray	#943

CHEAT	NUMBER
Annihilator RPG	#947
Samurai Sword	#948
Satchel Charge	#949
Shock Paddles	#950
Sledgehammer	#952
Stungun	#953
XS-2 Ultimax	#958
Pimp Slap	#969

WEATHER

CHEAT	NUMBER
Clear Skies	#78669
Heavy Rain	#78666
Light Rain	#78668
Overcast	#78665

CHEAT	NUMBER
Time Set Midnight	#2400
Time Set Noon	#1200
Wrath Of God	#666

WORLD

CHEAT	NUMBER
Super Saints	#8
Super Explosions	#7
Evil Cars	#16
Pedestrian War	#19

CHEAT	NUMBER
Drunk Pedestrians	#15
Raining Pedestrians	#20
Low Gravity	#18

SAMURAI SHODOWN 2

PLAY AS KUROKO IN 2-PLAYER
At the character select, press Up, Down, Left, Up, Down, Right + X.

SCOTT PILGRIM VS. THE WORLD: THE GAME

PLAY AS SAME CHARACTER
At the title screen, press Down, Right Bumper, Up, Left Bumper, Y, B.

HEART SWORD
At the title screen, press X, X, X, A, B, A, Y, Y.

BLOOD MODE
At the title screen, press A, B, A, X, A, B, B.

BOSS RUSH MODE
Pause the game on the overworld and press **Right, Right, B, Right Bumper, Right, Right, B, Right Bumper.**

ZOMBIE MODE
At the title screen, press Down, Up, Right, Down, Up, Right, Down, Up, Right, Right, Right.

SOUND CHECK BONUS LEVEL
Pause the game on the overworld and press Left Bumper, Left Bumper, Left Bumper, Right Bumper, Right Bumper, Right Bumper, Left Bumper, Right Bumper.

CHANGE MONEY TO ANIMALS
At the title screen, press Up, Up, Down, Down, Up, Up, Up, Up.

SEGA SUPERSTARS TENNIS

UNLOCK CHARACTERS
Complete the following missions to unlock the corresponding character.

CHARACTER	COMPLETE THIS MISSION
Alex Kidd	Mission 1 of Alex Kidd's World
Amy Rose	Mission 2 of Sonic the Hedgehog's World
Gilius	Mission 1 of Golden Axe's World
Gum	Mission 12 of Jet Grind Radio's World
Meemee	Mission 8 of Super Monkey Ball's World
Pudding	Mission 1 of Space Channel 5's World
Reala	Mission 2 of NiGHTs' World
Shadow The Hedgehog	Mission 14 of Sonic the Hedgehog's World

SHANK

KUNG FU SHANK
Reach 1000 kills. Press Start for a tally.

SHANK THE GIMP
Kill 500 creatures.

HORROR SHANK
Get 100 kills with the Chainsaw.

WHITE PAJAMAS SHANK
Perform a 100-hit combo.

RED PAJAMAS SHANK
Perform a 150-hit combo.

DANCE SHANK
Complete single player campaign on Normal.

WILDMAN SHANK
Complete single player campaign on Hard.

SHANK THE SPARTAN
Complete Backstory Co-op mode.

ANY-S
Defeat the single player campaign, then pause a game and press Up, Up, Down, Down, Left, Right, Left, Right, B, A.

DEATHSPANK
Defeat the single player campaign, then pause a game and press Up + X + Down + B + Left + Y + Right + A.

SHREK THE THIRD

10,000 GOLD COINS
At the gift shop, press Up, Up, Down, Up, Right, Left.

SILENT HILL: HOMECOMING

YOUNG ALEX COSTUME
At the Title screen, press Up, Up, Down, Down, Left, Right, Left, Right, B.

THE SIMPSONS GAME

After unlocking the following, the outfits can be changed at the downstairs closet in the Simpson's house. The Trophies can be viewed at different locations in the house: Bart's room, Lisa's room, Marge's room, and the garage.

BART'S OUTFITS AND TROPHIES (POSTER COLLECTION)
At the Main menu, press Right, Left, X, X, Y, Right Thumbstick.

HOMER'S OUTFITS AND TROPHIES (BEER BOTTLE COLLECTION)
At the Main menu, press Left, Right, Y, Y, X, Left Thumbstick.

LISA'S OUTFITS AND TROPHIES (DOLLS)
At the Main menu, press X, Y, X, X, Y, Left Thumbstick.

MARGE'S OUTFITS AND TROPHIES (HAIR PRODUCTS)
At the Main menu, press Y, X, Y, Y, X, Right Thumbstick.

THE SIMS 3

CHEATS
Load your family, press Start, and hold Left Bumper + Left Trigger + Right Bumper + Right Trigger. The game prompts you to save another file before activating the cheats. Spoot the Llama is now available in Misc Décor. Place it in your lot and click it to access the cheats. This disables Achievements and challenges.

SKATE

EXCLUSIVE BEST BUY CLOTHES
At the Main menu, press Up, Down, Left, Right, X, Right Bumper, Y, Left Bumper. You can get the clothes at Reg's or Slappy's Skate Shop. Find it under Skate.

DEM BONES CHARACTER
Break each bone in your body at least three times.

SKATE 2

BIG BLACK
Select Enter Cheat from the Extras menu and enter letsdowork.

3D MODE
Select Enter Cheat from the Extras menu and enter strangeloops. Use glasses to view in 3D.

SKATE 3

HOVERBOARD MODE
In Free Play, select Extras from the Options. Choose Enter Cheat Code and enter mcfly.

MINI SKATER MODE
In Free Play, select Extras from the Options. Choose Enter Cheat Code and enter miniskaters.

ZOMBIE MODE
In Free Play, select Extras from the Options. Choose Enter Cheat Code and enter zombie.

ISAAC CLARK FROM DEADSPACE
In Free Play, select Extras from the Options. Choose Enter Cheat Code and enter deadspacetoo.

DEM BONES
Beat most of the Hall of Meat Challenges.

MEAT MAN
Beat all Hall of Meat Challenges.

RESETS OBJECTS TO ORIGINAL POSITIONS
In Free Play, select Extras from the Options. Choose Enter Cheat Code and enter streetsweeper.

SOLDIER OF FORTUNE: PAYBACK

ACR-2 SNIPER RIFLE
At the difficulty select, press Up, Up, Down, Left, Right, Right, Down.

SONIC THE HEDGEHOG 4: EPISODE I

AVATAR AWARDS

AWARD	EARNED BY
Sonic Costume (Body)	After collecting the 7 Chaos Emeralds, defeat the final boss 1 more time
Sonic Costume (Head)	Collect all rings during ending after the final stage.

SOULCASTER

PASSWORD
Select Continue and enter JUSTIN BAILEY ------ ------ as a password. This starts you midway through the game, on hard difficulty, with plenty of money. This password is a reference to a password from Metroid.

SPIDER-MAN: FRIEND OR FOE

NEW GREEN GOBLIN AS A SIDEKICK
While standing in the Helicarrier between levels, press Left, Down, Right, Right, Down, Left.

SANDMAN AS A SIDEKICK
While standing in the Helicarrier between levels, press Right, Right, Right, Up, Down, Left.

VENOM AS A SIDEKICK
While standing in the Helicarrier between levels, press Left, Left, Right, Up, Down, Down.

5000 TECH TOKENS
While standing in the Helicarrier between levels, press Up, Up, Down, Down, Left, Right.

SPIDER-MAN: SHATTERED DIMENSIONS

The following can be entered after completing the tutorial.

IRON SPIDER SUIT
At the main menu, press Up, Right, Right, Right, Left, Left, Left, Down, Up.

NEGATIVE ZONE SUIT
At the main menu, press Left, Right, Right, Down, Right, Down, Up, Left.

SCARLET SPIDER SUIT
At the main menu, press Right, Up, Left, Right, Up, Left, Right, Up, Left, Right.

SPLIT/ SECOND

HANZO FX350 CX (COMPUTER SPIELE) IN QUICK PLAY
At the Options menu, press X, Up, X, Up, X, Up.

RYBACK COYOTE AMX IN QUICK PLAY
At the Options menu, press Left, X, Left, X, Left, X, Left, X, Left, X, Left, X, Right.

RYBACK MOHAWK XDX (DISNEY XD) IN QUICK PLAY
At the Options menu, press X, Down, X, Down, X, Down.

STAR TREK: D-A-C

KOBAYASHI MARU CHEAT & ACHIEVEMENT
Once a match begins, pause the game and press Left Trigger, Y, X, X, Y, Right Trigger. This increases your rate of fire and regeneration. This also unlocks the Kobayashi Maru achievement.

STAR WARS THE CLONE WARS: REPUBLIC HEROES

BIG HEAD MODE
Pause the game, select Shop, and enter Up, Down, Left, Right, Left, Right, Down, Up in Cheats.

MINI-GUN
Pause the game, select Shop, and enter Down, Left, Right, Up, Right, Up, Left, Down in Cheats.

ULTIMATE LIGHTSABER
Pause the game, select Shop, and enter Right, Down, Down, Up, Left, Up, Up, Down in Cheats.

LIGHTSABER THROW UPGRADE
Pause the game, select Shop, and enter Left, Left, Right, Right, Up, Down, Down, Up in Combat Upgrades.

SPIDER DROID UPGRADE
Pause the game, select Shop, and enter Up, Left, Down, Left, Right, Left, Left, Left in Droid-Jak Upgrades.

STAR WARS: THE FORCE UNLEASHED

CHEAT CODES

Pause the game and select Input Code. Here you can enter the following codes. Activating any of the following cheat codes will disable some unlockables, and you will be unable to save your progress.

CHEAT	CODE
All Force Powers at Max Power	KATARN
All Force Push Ranks	EXARKUN
All Saber Throw Ranks	ADEGAN
All Repulse Ranks	DATHOMIR
All Saber Crystals	HURRIKANE
All Talents	JOCASTA
Deadly Saber	LIGHTSABER

COMBOS

Pause the game and select Input Code. Here you can enter the following codes. Activating any of the following cheat codes will disable some unlockables, and you will be unable to save your progress.

COMBO	CODE
All Combos	MOLDYCROW
Aerial Ambush	VENTRESS
Aerial Assault	EETHKOTH
Aerial Blast	YADDLE
Impale	BRUTALSTAB
Lightning Bomb	MASSASSI
Lightning Grenade	RAGNOS
Saber Slam	PLOKOON
Saber Sling	KITFISTO
Sith Saber Flurry	LUMIYA
Sith Slash	DARAGON
Sith Throw	SAZEN
New Combo	FREEDON
New Combo	MARAJADE

ALL DATABANK ENTRIES

Pause the game and select Input Code. Enter OSSUS.

MIRRORED LEVEL

Pause the game and select Input Code. Enter MINDTRICK. Re-enter the code to return level to normal.

SITH MASTER DIFFICULTY

Pause the game and select Input Code. Enter SITHSPAWN.

COSTUMES

Pause the game and select Input Code. Here you can enter the following codes.

COSTUME	CODE
All Costumes	SOHNDANN
Bail Organa	VICEROY
Ceremonial Jedi Robes	DANTOOINE
Drunken Kota	HARDBOILED
Emperor	MASTERMIND
Incinerator Trooper	PHOENIX
Jedi Adventure Robe	HOLOCRON
Kashyyyk Trooper	TK421GREEN
Kota	MANDALORE
Master Kento	WOOKIEE
Proxy	PROTOTYPE
Scout Trooper	FERRAL
Shadow Trooper	BLACKHOLE
Sith Stalker Armor	KORRIBAN
Snowtrooper	SNOWMAN
Stormtrooper	TK421WHITE
Stormtrooper Commander	TK421BLUE

STAR WARS: THE FORCE UNLEASHED II

BOBA FETT COSTUME
Pause the game, select Cheat Codes from the Options, and enter MANDALORE.

DARK APPRENTICE COSTUME
Pause the game, select Cheat Codes from the Options, and enter VENTRESS.

GENERAL KOTA COSTUME
Pause the game, select Cheat Codes from the Options, and enter RAHM.

NEIMOIDIAN COSTUME
Pause the game, select Cheat Codes from the Options, and enter GUNRAY.

REBEL COMMANDO COSTUME
Pause the game, select Cheat Codes from the Options, and enter SPECFORCE.

REBEL SOLDIER COSTUME
Pause the game, select Cheat Codes from the Options, and enter REBELSCUM.

SABER GUARD COSTUME
Pause the game, select Cheat Codes from the Options, and enter MORGUKAI.

SITH ACOLYTE COSTUME
Pause the game, select Cheat Codes from the Options, and enter HAAZEN.

STORMTROOPER COSTUME
Pause the game, select Cheat Codes from the Options, and enter TK421.

TERROR TROOPER COSTUME
Pause the game, select Cheat Codes from the Options, and enter SHADOW.

TRAINING DROID COSTUME
Pause the game, select Cheat Codes from the Options, and enter HOLODROID.

REPULSE FORCE POWER
Pause the game, select Cheat Codes from the Options, and enter MAREK.

SABRE THROW
Pause the game, select Cheat Codes from the Options, and enter TRAYA.

WISDOM LIGHTSABER CRYSTALS
Pause the game, select Cheat Codes from the Options, and enter SOLARI.

TRAINING GEAR
Have a save game from Star Wars: The Force Unleashed.

CEREMONIAL ROBES
Have a save game from Star Wars: The Force Unleashed with the Light Side ending.

SITH STALKER ARMOR
Have a save game from Star Wars: The Force Unleashed with the Dark Side ending.

STREET FIGHTER IV

ALTERNATE STAGES
At the stage select, hold Left Bumper or Right Bumper and select a stage.

STUNTMAN IGNITION

3 PROPS IN STUNT CREATOR MODE
Select Cheats from Extras and enter COOLPROP.

ALL ITEMS UNLOCKED FOR CONSTRUCTION MODE
Select Cheats from Extras and enter NOBLEMAN.

MVX SPARTAN
Select Cheats from Extras and enter fastride.

ALL CHEATS
Select Cheats from Extras and enter Wearefrozen. This unlocks the following cheats: Slo-mo Cool, Thrill Cam, Vision Switcher, Nitro Addiction, Freaky Fast, and Ice Wheels.

ALL CHEATS
Select Cheats from Extras and enter Kungfoopete.

ICE WHEELS CHEAT
Select Cheats from Extras and enter IceAge.

NITRO ADDICTION CHEAT
Select Cheats from Extras and enter TheDuke.

VISION SWITCHER CHEAT
Select Cheats from Extras and enter GFXMODES.

SUPER MEAT BOY

AVATAR AWARDS

AWARD	EARNED BY
Super Meat Boy	Beat the Light World.
Super Meat Boy T-Shirt	Play the first few levels.

SUPER PUZZLE FIGHTER II TURBO HD REMIX

PLAY AS AKUMA
At the character select, highlight Hsien-Ko and press Down.

PLAY AS DAN
At the character select, highlight Donovan and press Down.

PLAY AS DEVILOT
At the character select, highlight Morrigan and press Down.

PLAY AS ANITA
At the character select, hold Left Bumper + Right Bumper and choose Donovan.

PLAY AS HSIEN-KO'S TALISMAN
At the character select, hold Left Bumper + Right Bumper and choose Hsien-Ko.

PLAY AS MORRIGAN AS A BAT
At the character select, hold Left Bumper + Right Bumper and choose Morrigan.

PLAY AS ANITA
At the character select, hold Left Bumper + Right Bumper and choose Donovan.

PLAY AS HSIEN-KO'S TALISMAN
At the character select, hold Left Bumper + Right Bumper and choose Hsien-Ko.

PLAY AS MORRIGAN AS A BAT
At the character select, hold Left Bumper + Right Bumper and choose Morrigan.

SUPER STREET FIGHTER II TURBO HD REMIX

The following codes give you the classic fighters in Classic Arcade Mode. Select the character, quickly enter the given code, and select him/her again.

CLASSIC BALROG
Right, Left, Left, Right

CLASSIC BLANKA
Left, Right (x3)

CLASSIC CAMMY
Up, Up, Down, Down

CLASSIC CHUN-LI
Down (x3), Up

CLASSIC DEE JAY
Down, Down, Up, Up

CLASSIC DHALSIM
Down, Up (x3)

CLASSIC E. HONDA
Up (x3), Down

CLASSIC FEI LONG
Left, Left, Right, Right

CLASSIC GUILE
Up, Down (x3)

CLASSIC KEN
Left (x3), Right

CLASSIC M. BISON
Down, Up, Up, Down

CLASSIC RYU
Right (x3), Left

CLASSIC SAGAT
Up, Down (x3), Up

CLASSIC T. HAWK
Right, Right, Left, Left

CLASSIC VEGA
Left, Right, Right, Left

CLASSIC ZANGIEF
Left, Right (x3)

SUPER STREET FIGHTER IV

BARREL BUSTER AND CAR CRUSHER BONUS STAGES
Beat Arcade Mode in any difficulty

COLORS AND TAUNTS
Colors 1 and 2 plus the first taunt for each fighter are available from the start. For colors 11 & 12, start a game with a Street Fighter IV save game on your system. To earn the rest of the colors and taunts, you need to fight a certain number of matches with that character.

COLOR	# OF MATCHES
3	2
4	4
5	6
6	8
7	10
8	12
9	14
10	16

TAUNT	# OF MATCHES
2	1
3	3
4	5
5	7
6	9
7	11
8	13
9	15
10	16

SUPERMAN RETURNS: THE VIDEOGAME

GOD MODE
Pause the game, select Options and press Up, Up, Down, Down, Left, Right, Left, Right, Y, X.

INFINITE CITY HEALTH
Pause the game, select Options and press Y, Right, Y, Right, Up, Left, Right, Y.

ALL POWER-UPS
Pause the game, select Options and press Left, Y, Right, X, Down, Y, Up, Down, X, Y, X.

ALL UNLOCKABLES
Pause the game, select Options and press Left, Up, Right, Down, Y, X, Y, Up, Right, X.

FREE ROAM AS BIZARRO
Pause the game, select Options and press Up, Right, Down, Right, Up, Left, Down, Right, Up.

SURF'S UP

ALL CHAMPIONSHIP LOCATIONS
Select Cheat Codes from the Extras menu and enter FREEVISIT.

ALL LEAF SLIDE STAGES
Select Cheat Codes from the Extras menu and enter GOINGDOWN.

ALL MULTIPLAYER LEVELS
Select Cheat Codes from the Extras menu and enter MULTIPASS.

ALL BOARDS
Select Cheat Codes from the Extras menu and enter MYPRECIOUS.

XBOX 360

ASTRAL BOARD
Select Cheat Codes from the Extras menu and enter ASTRAL.

MONSOON BOARD
Select Cheat Codes from the Extras menu and enter MONSOON.

TINE SHOCKWAVE BOARD
Select Cheat Codes from the Extras menu and enter TINYSHOCKWAVE.

ALL CHARACTER CUSTOMIZATIONS
Select Cheat Codes from the Extras menu and enter TOPFASHION.

PLAY AS ARNOLD
Select Cheat Codes from the Extras menu and enter TINYBUTSTRONG.

PLAY AS ELLIOT
Select Cheat Codes from the Extras menu and enter SURPRISEGUEST.

PLAY AS GEEK
Select Cheat Codes from the Extras menu and enter SLOWANDSTEADY.

PLAY AS TANK EVANS
Select Cheat Codes from the Extras menu and enter IMTHEBEST.

PLAY AS TATSUHI KOBAYASHI
Select Cheat Codes from the Extras menu and enter KOBAYASHI.

PLAY AS ZEKE TOPANGA
Select Cheat Codes from the Extras menu and enter THELEGEND.

ALL VIDEOS AND SPEN GALLERY
Select Cheat Codes from the Extras menu and enter WATCHAMOVIE.

ART GALLERY
Select Cheat Codes from the Extras menu and enter NICEPLACE.

THRILLVILLE: OFF THE RAILS

$50,000
While in a park, press X, B, Y, X, B, Y, A.

500 THRILL POINTS
While in a park, press B, X, Y, B, X, Y, X.

ALL PARKS
While in a park, press X, B, Y, X, B, Y, X.

ALL RIDES IN CURRENT PARK
While in a park, press X, B, Y, X, B, Y, Y.

MISSION UNLOCK
While in a park, press X, B, Y, X, B, Y, B.

ALL MINI-GAMES IN PARTY PLAY
While in a park, press X, B, Y, X, B, Y, Right.

TIGER WOODS PGA TOUR 08

ALL COURSES
Select Password from EA Sports Extras and enter greensfees.

ALL GOLFERS
Select Password from EA Sports Extras and enter allstars.

TIGER WOODS PGA TOUR 09

SPECTATORS BIG HEAD MODE
Select EA SPORTS Extras from My Tiger '09, choose Password and enter cephalus.

TIMESHIFT

KRONE IN MULTIPLAYER
Select Multiplayer from the Options menu. Highlight Model and press Left to get to Krone. Press Y and enter RXYMCPENCJ.

TMNT

CHALLENGE MAP 2
At the Main menu, hold the Left Bumper and press A, A, B, A.

DON'S BIG HEAD GOODIE
At the Main menu, hold the Left Bumper and press B, Y, A, X.

TOM CLANCY'S ENDWAR

EUROPEAN ENFORCER CORPS
Go to Community and Extras, highlight Downloadable Content and press Y. Enter EUCA20.

RUSSIAN SPETZNAZ BATTALION
Go to Community and Extras, highlight Downloadable Content and press Y. Enter SPZT17.

RUSSIAN SPETZNAZ GUARD BRIGADE
Go to Community and Extras, highlight Downloadable Content and press Y. Enter SPZA39.

US JOINT STRIKE FORCE BATTALION
Go to Community and Extras, highlight Downloadable Content and press Y. Enter JSFA35.

TOM CLANCY'S GHOST RECON ADVANCED WARFIGHTER

ALL MISSIONS
At the Mission Select screen, hold Back + Left Trigger + Right Trigger and press Y, Right Bumper, Y, Right Bumper, X.

FULL HEALTH
Pause the game, hold Back + Left Trigger + Right Trigger and press Left Bumper, Left Bumper, Right Bumper, X, Right Bumper, Y.

INVINCIBLE
Pause the game, hold Back + Left Trigger + Right Trigger and press Y, Y, X, Right Bumper, X, Left Bumper.

TEAM INVINCIBLE
Pause the game, hold Back + Left Trigger + Right Trigger and press X, X, Y, Right Bumper, Y, Left Bumper.

UNLIMITED AMMO
Pause the game, hold Back + Left Trigger + Right Trigger and press Right Bumper, Right Bumper, Left Bumper, X, Left Bumper, Y.

TOM CLANCY'S GHOST RECON ADVANCED WARFIGHTER 2

FAMAS IN QUICK MISSION MODE
Create a new campaign with the name: GRAW2QUICKFAMAS.

TOM CLANCY'S HAWX

A-12 AVENGER II
At the hangar, hold Left Trigger and press X, Left Bumper, X, Right Bumper, Y, X.

F-18 HARV
At the hangar, hold Left Trigger and press Left Bumper, Y, Left Bumper, Y, Left Bumper, X.

FB-22 STRIKE RAPTOR
At the hangar, hold Left Trigger and press Right Bumper, X, Right Bumper, X, Right Bumper, Y.

TOM CLANCY'S RAINBOW SIX VEGAS

The following codes work in single player only.

BIG HEADS
Pause the game, hold Left Trigger and press B, X, A, Y, Left Thumbstick, Y, A, X, B, Right Thumbstick.

CHANGE BULLET TRACER COLOR
Pause the game, hold Left Trigger and press Left Thumbstick, Left Thumbstick, A, Right Thumbstick, Right Thumbstick, B, Left Thumbstick, Left Thumbstick, X, Right Thumbstick, Right Thumbstick, Y.

ONE-SHOT KILLS
Pause the game, hold the Left Bumper and press Left Thumbstick, Right Thumbstick, Left Thumbstick, Right Thumbstick, A, B, Left Thumbstick, Right Thumbstick, Left Thumbstick, Right Thumbstick, X, Y.

THIRD PERSON VIEW
Pause the game, hold Left Trigger and press X, B, X, B, Left Thumbstick, Left Thumbstick, Y, A, Y, A, Right Thumbstick, Right Thumbstick.

OVERLOAD

XBOX 360

TOM CLANCY'S RAINBOW SIX VEGAS 2

GI JOHN DOE MODE
Pause the game, hold the Right Bumper and press Left Thumbstick, Left Thumbstick, A, Right Thumbstick, Right Thumbstick, B, Left Thumbstick, Left Thumbstick, X, Right Thumbstick, Right Thumbstick, Y.

SUPER RAGDOLL
Pause the game, hold the Right Bumper and press A, A, B, B, X, X, Y, Y, A, B, X, Y.

THIRD-PERSON MODE
Pause the game, hold the Right Bumper and press X, B, X, B, Left Thumbstick, Left Thumbstick, Y, A, Y, A, Right Thumbstick, Right Thumbstick.

TAR-21 ASSAULT RIFLE
At the Character Customization screen, hold Right Bumper and press Down, Down, Up, Up, X, B, X, B, Y, Up, Up, Y.

MULTIPLAYER MAP: COMCAST EVENT
Select Extras from the Main menu. Choose Comcast Gift and enter Comcast Faster.

M468 ASSAULT RIFLE
While customizing your character, hold down RB and press Up, Y, Down, A, Left, X, Right, B, Left, Left, Right, X

TOMB RAIDER: LEGEND

You must unlock the following codes in the game before using them.

BULLETPROOF
During a game, hold Left Trigger and press A, Right Trigger, Y, Right Trigger, X, Left Bumper.

DRAIN ENEMY HEALTH
During a game, hold Left Trigger and press X, B, A, Left Bumper, Right Trigger, Y.

INFINITE ASSAULT RIFLE AMMO
During a game, hold Left Bumper and press A, B, A, Left Trigger, X, Y.

INFINITE GRENADE LAUNCHER AMMO
During a game, hold Left Bumper and press Left Trigger, Y, Right Trigger, B, Left Trigger, X.

INFINITE SHOTGUN AMMO
During a game, hold Left Bumper and press Right Trigger, B, X, Left Trigger, X, A.

INFINITE SMG AMMO
During a game, hold Left Bumper and press B, Y, Left Trigger, Right Trigger, A, B.

EXCALIBUR
During a game, hold Left Bumper and press Y, A, B, Right Trigger, Y, Left Trigger.

SOUL REAVER
During a game, hold Left Bumper and press A, Right Trigger, B, Right Trigger, Left Trigger, X.

1-SHOT KILL
During a game, hold Left Trigger and press Y, A, Y, X, Left Bumper, B.

TEXTURELESS MODE
During a game, hold Left Trigger and press Left Bumper, A, B, A, Y, Right Trigger.

TOMB RAIDER: UNDERWORLD

BULLETPROOF LARA
During a game, hold Left Trigger and press A, Right Trigger, Y, Right Trigger, X, LB.

ONE-SHOT KILL
During a game, hold Left Trigger and press Y, A, Y, X, Left Bumper, B.

SHOW ENEMY HEALTH
During a game, hold Left Trigger and press X, B, A, Left Bumper, Right Trigger, Y.

TONY HAWK RIDE

RYAN SHECKLER
Select Cheats from the Options menu and enter SHECKLERSIG.

QUICKSILVER 80'S LEVEL
Select Cheats from the Options menu and enter FEELINGEIGHTIES.

SPONSOR ITEMS

As you progress through Career mode and move up the rankings, you gain sponsors. Each sponsor comes with its own Create-a-Skater item.

RANK	CAS ITEM UNLOCKED
Rank 040	Adio Kenny V2 Shoes
Rank 050	Quiksilver_Hoody_3
Rank 060	Birdhouse Tony Hawk Deck
Rank 080	Vans No Skool Gothic Shoes
Rank 100	Volcom Scallero Jacket
Rank 110	eS Square One Shoes

RANK	CAS ITEM UNLOCKED
Rank 120	Almost Watch What You Say Deck
Rank 140	DVS Adage Shoe
Rank 150	Element Illuminate Deck
Rank 160	Etnies Sheckler White Lavender Shoes
Complete Skateshop Goal	Stereo Soundwave Deck

SKATERS

You must unlock all of the skaters, except for Tony Hawk, by completing challenges in the Career Mode. They are playable in Free Skate and 2-Player modes.

SKATER	HOW TO UNLOCK
Tony Hawk	Always unlocked
Lyn-z Adams Hawkins	Complete Pro Challenge
Bob Burquist	Complete Pro Challenge
Dustin Dollin	Complete Pro Challenge
Nyjah Huston	Complete Pro Challenge
Bam Margera	Complete Pro Challenge
Rodney Mullen	Complete Pro Challenge
Paul Rodriguez	Complete Pro Challenge
Ryan Sheckler	Complete Pro Challenge
Daewon Song	Complete Pro Challenge
Mike Vallely	Complete Pro Challenge
Stevie Willams	Complete Pro Challenge

SKATER	HOW TO UNLOCK
Travis Barker	Complete Pro Challenge
Kevin Staab	Complete Pro Challenge
Zombie	Complete Pro Challenge
Christaian Hosoi	Rank #1
Jason Lee	Complete Final Tony Hawk Goal
Photographer	Unlock Shops
Security Guard	Unlock School
Bum	Unlock Car Factory
Beaver Mascot	Unlock High School
Real Estate Agent	Unlock Downtown
Filmer	Unlock High School
Skate Jam Kid	Rank #4
Dad	Rank #1
Colonel	All Gaps
Nerd	Complete School Spirit Goal

CHEAT CODES

Select Cheat Codes from the Options menu to enter the following codes. You can access some of these codes from the Options menu.

CODE	WHAT IT UNLOCKS
plus44	Travis Barker
hohohosoi	Christian Hosoi
notmono	Jason Lee
mixitup	Kevin Staab
strangefellows	Dad & Skater Jam Kid
themedia	Photog Girl & Filmer
militarymen	Colonel & Security Guard
jammypack	Always Special
balancegalore	Perfect Rail
frontandback	Perect Manual
shellshock	Unlimited Focus
shescaresme	Big Realtor
birdhouse	Inkblot Deck

CODE	WHAT IT UNLOCKS
allthebest	Full Stats
needaride	All Decks unlocked and free, except for Inkblot Deck and Gamestop Deck
yougotitall	All specials unlocked and in player's special list and set as owned in Skate Shop
wearelosers	Nerd and a Bum
manineedadate	Beaver Mascot
suckstobedead	Officer Dick
HATEDANDPROUD	The Vans unlockable item

TONY HAWK'S PROVING GROUND

Select Cheat Codes from the Options and enter the following cheats. Some codes need to be enabled by selecting Cheats from the Options during a game.

UNLOCK	CHEAT	UNLOCK	CHEAT
Unlocks Boneman	CRAZYBONEMAN	Unlocks all CAS items	GIVEMESTUFF
Unlocks Bosco	MOREMILK	Unlocks all Decks	LETSGOSKATE
Unlocks Cam	NOTACAMERA	Unlock all Game Movies	WATCHTHIS
Unlocks Cooper	THECOOP		
Unlocks Eddie X	SKETCHY		
Unlocks El Patinador	PILEDRIVER	Unlock all Lounge Bling Items	SWEETSTUFF
Unlocks Eric	FLYAWAY		
Unlocks Mad Dog	RABBIES	Unlock all Lounge Themes	LAIDBACKLOUNGE
Unlocks MCA	INTERGALACTIC	Unlock all Rigger Pieces	IMGONNABUILD
Unlocks Mel	NOTADUDE		
Unlocks Rube	LOOKSSMELLY	Unlock all Video Editor Effects	TRIPPY
Unlocks Spence	DAPPER		
Unlocks Shayne	MOVERS	Unlock all Video Editor Overlays	PUTEMONTOP
Unlocks TV Producer	SHAKER	All specials unlocked and in player's special list	LOTSOFTRICKS
Unlock FDR	THEPREZPARK		
Unlock Lansdowne	THELOCALPARK		
Unlock Air & Space Museum	THEINDOORPARK	Full Stats	BEEFEDUP
Unlocks all Fun Items	OVERTHETOP	Give player +50 skill points	NEEDSHELP

The following cheats lock you out of the Leaderboards:

UNLOCK	CHEAT	UNLOCK	CHEAT
Unlocks Perfect Manual	STILLAINTFALLIN	Unlocks 100% branch completion in NTT	FOREVERNAILED
Unlocks Perfect Rail	AINTFALLIN		
Unlock Super Check	BOOYAH	No Bails	ANDAINTFALLIN
Unlocks Unlimited Focus	MYOPIC	You can not use the Video Editor with the following cheats:	
Unlock Unlimited Slash Grind	SUPERSLASHIN	Invisible Man	THEMISSING
		Mini Skater	TINYTATER
		No Board	MAGICMAN

TRANSFORMERS REVENGE OF THE FALLEN

LOW GRAVITY MODE
Select Cheat Code and enter A, X, Y, Left Thumbstick, Y, Left Thumbstick.

NO WEAPON OVERHEAT
Select Cheat Code and enter Left Thumbstick, X, A, Left Thumbstick, Y, Left Bumper.

ALWAYS IN OVERDRIVE MODE
Select Cheat Code and enter Left Bumper, B, Left Bumper, A, X, Right Thumbstick.

UNLIMITED TURBO
Select Cheat Code and enter B, Left Thumbstick, X, Right Thumbstick, A, Y.

NO SPECIAL COOLDOWN TIME
Select Cheat Code and enter Right Thumbstick, X, Right Thumbstick, Right Thumbstick, X, A.

INVINCIBILITY
Select Cheat Code and enter Right Thumbstick, A, X, Left Thumbstick, X, X.

4X ENERGON FROM DEFEATED ENEMIES
Select Cheat Code and enter Y, X, B, Right Thumbstick, A, Y.

INCREASED WEAPON DAMAGE, ROBOT FORM
Select Cheat Code and enter Y, Y, Right Thumbstick, A, Left Bumper, Y.

INCREASED WEAPON DAMAGE, VEHICLE FORM
Select Cheat Code and enter Y, B, Right Bumper, X, Right Thumbstick, Left Thumbstick.

MELEE INSTANT KILLS
Select Cheat Code and enter Right Thumbstick, A, Left Bumper, B, Right Thumbstick, Left Bumper.

LOWER ENEMY ACCURACY
Select Cheat Code and enter X, Left Thumbstick, Right Thumbstick, Left Thumbstick, Right Thumbstick, Right Bumper.

INCREASED ENEMY HEALTH
Select Cheat Code and enter B, X, Left Bumper, B, Right Thumbstick, Y.

INCREASED ENEMY DAMAGE
Select Cheat Code and enter Left Bumper, Y, A, Y, Right Thumbstick, Right Thumbstick.

INCREASED ENEMY ACCURACY
Select Cheat Code and enter Y, Y, B, A, X, Left Bumper.

SPECIAL KILLS ONLY MODE
Select Cheat Code and enter B, B, Right Bumper, B, A, Left Thumbstick.

UNLOCK ALL SHANGHAI MISSIONS & ZONES
Select Cheat Code and enter Y, Left Thumbstick, Right Thumbstick, Left Bumper, Y, A.

UNLOCK ALL WEST COAST MISSIONS & ZONES
Select Cheat Code and enter Left Bumper, Right Bumper, Right Thumbstick, Y, Right Thumbstick, B.

UNLOCK ALL DEEP SIX MISSIONS & ZONES
Select Cheat Code and enter X, Right Bumper, Y, B, A, Left Bumper.

UNLOCK ALL EAST COAST MISSIONS & ZONES
Select Cheat Code and enter Right Thumbstick, Left Thumbstick, Right Bumper, A, B, X.

UNLOCK ALL CAIRO MISSIONS & ZONES
Select Cheat Code and enter Right Thumbstick, Y, A, Y, Left Thumbstick, Left Bumper.

UNLOCK AND ACTIVATE ALL UPGRADES
Select Cheat Code and enter Left Bumper, Y, Left Bumper, B, X, X.

TRANSFORMERS: THE GAME

The following cheats disable saving and achievements:

INFINITE HEALTH
At the Main menu, press Left, Left, Up, Left, Right, Down, Right.

INFINITE AMMO
At the Main menu, press Up, Down, Left, Right, Up, Up, Down.

NO MILITARY OR POLICE
At the Main menu, press Right, Left, Right, Left, Right, Left, Right.

ALL MISSIONS
At the Main menu, press Down, Up, Left, Right, Right, Right, Up, Down.

BONUS CYBERTRON MISSIONS
At the Main menu, press Right, Up, Up, Down, Right, Left, Left.

GENERATION 1 SKIN: JAZZ
At the Main menu, press Left, Up, Down, Down, Left, Up, Right.

GENERATION 1 SKIN: MEGATRON
At the Main menu, press Down, Left, Left, Down, Right, Right, Up.

GENERATION 1 SKIN: OPTIMUS PRIME
At the Main menu, press Down, Right, Left, Up, Down, Down, Left.

GENERATION 1 SKIN: ROBOVISION OPTIMUS PRIME
At the Main menu, press Down, Down, Up, Up, Right, Right, Right.

GENERATION 1 SKIN: STARSCREAM
At the Main menu, press Right, Down, Left, Left, Down, Up, Up.

TROPICO 3

CHEAT MENU
During a game, click the Left Thumbstick and Right Thumbstick and hold them down. Add Back + Start to open the cheat menu. Activating any cheats disables achievements.

UFC 2009 UNDISPUTED

MASK
Win three consecutive fights by submission in Career Mode.

PUNKASS
Earn the TapouT sponsorship in Career Mode.

SKYSKRAPE
At the Title screen, press Up, Up, Up, Down, Left, Right, Up, Start.

UFC 2010 UNDISPUTED

BJ PENN (BLACK SHORTS)
At the main menu, press Left Bumper, Right Bumper, Left Trigger, Right Trigger, Right Trigger, Left Trigger, Right Bumper, Left Bumper, Y, X, X, Y, start.

SHAQUILLE O'NEAL
At the main menu, press Right, Up, Left, Right, Down, Left, Up, Right, Down, Left, X, Y, Y, X, Start.

TAPOUT CREW - MASK, PUNKASS, SKYSCRAPE
At the main menu, press Down, Down, Up, Right, Left, Down, Back, Start.

UNDERTOW

GAMER PIC 1 — SCUBA DIVER
Total 100 kills.

GAMER PIC 2 — ATLANTIS MAN
Total 10,000 kills.

VIRTUA TENNIS 3

KING & DUKE
At the Main menu, press Up, Up, Down, Down, Left, Right, Left Bumper, Right Bumper.

ALL COURTS
At the Main menu, press Up, Up, Down, Down, Left, Right, Left, Right.

ALL GEAR
At the Main menu, press Left, Right, B, Left, Right, B, Up, Down.

WIN ONE MATCH TO WIN TOURNAMENT
At the Main menu, press B, Left, B, Right, B, Up, B, Down.

VIRTUAL ON: ORATORIO TANGRAM VER5.66

PLAY AS ALPHA RAIDEN
After defeating Arcade Mode with Raiden, do the following at the Character Select screen: highlight Apharmd B, press X, highlight Apharmd S, press X, highlight Dordray, press X, X, highlight Specineff, press X, X, highlight Fei-Yen, press X, X, highlight Cypher, press X (x3).

PLAY AS ALPHA TEMJIN
After defeating Arcade Mode with Temjin, do the following at the Character Select screen: highlight Temjin, press X, highlight Random, press X, highlight Raiden, press X, X, highlight Bal-Bados, press X, X, highlight Angelan, press X, X, highlight Grys-Vok, press X (x3).

VIVA PIÑATA

NEW ITEMS IN PET STORE
Select New Garden and enter chewnicorn as the name.

NEW ITEMS IN PET STORE
Select New Garden and enter goobaa as the name.

NEW ITEMS IN PET STORE
Select New Garden and enter bullseye as the name.

NEW ITEMS IN PET STORE
Select New Garden and enter kittyfloss as the name.

VIVA PIÑATA: PARTY ANIMALS

CLASSIC GAMER AWARD ACHIEVEMENT
At the START screen, press Up, Up, Down, Down, Left, Right, Left, Right, B, A. This earns you 10 points toward your Gamerscore.

VIVA PIÑATA: TROUBLE IN PARADISE

CREDITS
Select Play Garden and name your garden Piñata People. This unlocks the ability to view the credits on the Main menu.

The following cheats will disable saving. The five possible characters starting with Wall-E and going down are: Wall-E, Auto, EVE, M-O, GEL-A Steward.

ALL BONUS FEATURES UNLOCKED
Select Cheats from the Bonus Features menu and enter Wall-E, Auto, EVE, GEL-A Steward.

ALL GAME CONTENT UNLOCKED
Select Cheats from the Bonus Features menu and enter M-O, Auto, GEL-A Steward, EVE.

ALL SINGLE PLAYER LEVELS UNLOCKED
Select Cheats from the Bonus Features menu and enter Auto, GEL-A Steward, M-O, Wall-E.

ALL MULTIPLAYER MAPS UNLOCKED
Select Cheats from the Bonus Features menu and enter EVE, M-O, GEL-A Steward, Auto.

ALL HOLIDAY COSTUMES UNLOCKED
Select Cheats from the Bonus Features menu and enter Auto, Auto, GEL-A Steward, GEL-A Steward.

ALL MULTIPLAYER COSTUMES UNLOCKED
Select Cheats from the Bonus Features menu and enter GEL-A Steward, Wall-E, M-O, Auto.

UNLIMITED HEALTH UNLOCKED
Select Cheats from the Bonus Features menu and enter Wall-E, M-O, Auto, M-O.

WALL-E: MAKE ANY CUBE AT ANY TIME
Select Cheats from the Bonus Features menu and enter Auto, M-O, Auto, M-O.

WALL-EVE: MAKE ANY CUBE AT ANY TIME
Select Cheats from the Bonus Features menu and enter M-O, GEL-A Steward, EVE, EVE.

WALL-E WITH A LASER GUN AT ANY TIME
Select Cheats from the Bonus Features menu and enter Wall-E, EVE, EVE, Wall-E.

WALL-EVE WITH A LASER GUN AT ANY TIME
Select Cheats from the Bonus Features menu and enter GEL-A Steward, EVE, M-O, Wall-E.

WALL-E: PERMANENT SUPER LASER UPGRADE
Select Cheats from the Bonus Features menu and enter Wall-E, Auto, EVE, M-O.

EVE: PERMANENT SUPER LASER UPGRADE
Select Cheats from the Bonus Features menu and enter EVE, Wall-E, Wall-E, Auto.

CREDITS
Select Cheats from the Bonus Features menu and enter Auto, Wall-E, GEL-A Steward, M-O.

WANTED: WEAPONS OF FATE

HEALTH IMPROVEMENT
Select Secret Codes and enter 0100 1100.

ONE SHOT ONE KILL
Select Secret Codes and enter 0111 0010.

PLAY WITH SPECIAL SUIT
Select Secret Codes and enter 0110 0001.

SUPER WEAPONS
Select Secret Codes and enter 0100 1111.

UNLIMITED ADRENALINE
Select Secret Codes and enter 0110 1101.

UNLIMITED AMMO
Select Secret Codes and enter 0110 1111.

PLAY AS AIRPLANE BODYGUARD
Select Secret Codes and enter 0101 0111.

PLAY AS CROSS
Select Secret Codes and enter 0101 0100.

PLAY AS JANICE
Select Secret Codes and enter 0100 0100.

PLAY AS WESLY
Select Secret Codes and enter 0100 0011.

CINEMATIC MODE
Select Secret Codes and enter 0111 0100.

CLOSE COMBAT MODE
Select Secret Codes and enter 0110 0101.

HEADSHOT MODE
Select Secret Codes and enter 0110 0111.

WWE SMACKDOWN! VS. RAW 2008

HBK AND HHH'S DX OUTFIT
Select Cheat Codes from the Options and enter DXCostume69K2.

KELLY KELLY'S ALTERNATE OUTFIT
Select Cheat Codes from the Options and enter KellyKG12R.

BRET HART
Complete the March 31, 1996 Hall of Fame challenge by defeating Bret Hart with Shawn Michaels in a One-On-One 30-Minute Iron Man Match on Legend difficulty. Purchase from WWE Shop for $210,000.

MICK FOLEY
Complete the June 28, 1998 Hall of Fame challenge by defeating Mick Foley with The Undertaker in a Hell In a Cell Match on Legend difficulty. Purchase from WWE Shop for $210,000.

MR. MCMAHON
Win or successfully defend a championship (WWE or World Heavyweight) at WrestleMania in WWE 24/7 GM Mode. Purchase from WWE Shop for $110,000.

THE ROCK
Complete the April 1, 2001 Hall of Fame challenge by defeating The Rock with Steve Austin in a Single Match on Legend Difficulty. Purchase from WWE Shop for $210,000.

STEVE AUSTIN
Complete the March 23, 1997 Hall of Fame challenge by defeating Steve Austin with Bret Hart in a Submission Match on Legend Difficulty. Purchase from WWE Shop for $210,000.

TERRY FUNK
Complete the April 13, 1997 Hall of Fame challenge by defeating Tommy Dreamer, Sabu and Sandman with any Superstar in an ECW Extreme Rules 4-Way Match on Legend difficulty. Purchase from WWE Shop for $210,000.

MR. MCMAHON BALD
Must unlock Mr. McMahon as a playable character first. Purchase from WWE Shop for $60,000.

WWE SMACKDOWN VS. RAW 2009

BOOGEYMAN
Select Cheat Codes from My WWE and enter BoogeymanEatsWorms!!.

GENE SNITSKY
Select Cheat Codes from My WWE and enter UnlockSnitskySvR2009.

HAWKINS & RYDER
Select Cheat Codes from My WWE and enter Ryder&HawkinsTagTeam.

JILLIAN HALL
Select Cheat Codes from My WWE and enter PlayAsJillianHallSvR.

LAYLA
Select Cheat Codes from My WWE and enter UnlockECWDivaLayla09.

RIC FLAIR
Select Cheat Codes from My WWE and enter FlairWooooooooooooooo.

TAZZ
Select Cheat Codes from My WWE and enter UnlockECWTazzSvR2009.

VINCENT MCMAHON
Select Cheat Codes from My WWE and enter VinceMcMahonNoChance.

HORNSWOGGLE AS MANAGER
Select Cheat Codes from My WWE and enter HornswoggleAsManager.

CHRIS JERICHO COSTUME B
Select Cheat Codes from My WWE and enter AltJerichoModelSvR09.

CM PUNK COSTUME B
Select Cheat Codes from My WWE and enter CMPunkAltCostumeSvR!.

REY MYSTERIO COSTUME B
Select Cheat Codes from My WWE and enter BooyakaBooyaka619SvR.

SATURDAY NIGHT'S MAIN EVENT ARENA
Select Cheat Codes from My WWE and enter SatNightMainEventSvR.

WWE SMACKDOWN VS. RAW 2010

THE ROCK
Select Cheat Codes from the Options menu and enter The Great One.

DIRT SHEET BRAWL AND OFFICE STAGE BRAWL
Select Cheat Codes from the Options menu and enter BonusBrawl.

JOHN CENA'S NEW COSTUME
Select Cheat Codes from the Options menu and enter CENATION.

RANDY ORTON'S NEW COSTUME
Select Cheat Codes from the Options menu and enter ViperRKO.

SANTINO MARELLA'S NEW COSTUME
Select Cheat Codes from the Options menu and enter Milan Miracle.

SHAWN MICHAELS' NEW COSTUME
Select Cheat Codes from the Options menu and enter Bow Down.

TRIPLE H'S NEW COSTUME
Select Cheat Codes from the Options menu and enter Suck IT!.

WWE SMACKDOWN VS. RAW 2011

JOHN CENA (ENTRANCE/CIVILIAN)
In My WWE, select Cheat Codes from the Options and enter SLURPEE.

TRIBUTE TO THE TROOPS ARENA
In My WWE, select Cheat Codes from the Options and enter 8thannualtribute.

ALL OF RANDY ORTON'S COSTUMES
In My WWE, select Cheat Codes from the Options and enter apexpredator.

WORLD OF OUTLAWS: SPRINT CARS

$5,000,000
Enter your name as CHICMCHIM.

ALL TRACKS
Enter your name as JOEYJOEJOE.

ALL DRIVERS
Enter your name as MITYMASTA.

X-MEN ORIGINS: WOLVERINE

CLASSIC WOLVERINE OUTFIT
During a game, press A, X, B, X, A, Y, A, Y, A, X, B, B, X, R3. This code disables achievements.

DOUBLE ENEMY REFLEX POINTS
During a game, press A, A, X, X, Y, Y, B, B, Y, Y, X, X, A, A, R3. This code disables achievements.

INFINITE RAGE
During a game, press Y, X, X, Y, B, B, Y, A, A, Y, R3. This code disables achievements.

INVINCIBLE
During a game, press X, A, A, X, Y, Y, X, B, B, X, R3. This code disables achievements.

CLASSIC WOLVERINE CHALLENGE/OUTFIT
Find any two Classic Wolverine action figures to unlock this challenge. Defeat Classic Wolverine in combat to unlock the Classic Wolverine outfit.

ORIGINAL WOLVERINE CHALLENGE/OUTFIT
Find any two Original Wolverine action figures to unlock this challenge. Defeat Original Wolverine in combat to unlock the Original Wolverine outfit.

X-FORCE WOLVERINE CHALLENGE/OUTFIT
Find any two X-Force Wolverine action figures to unlock this challenge. Defeat X-Force Wolverine in combat to unlock the X-Force Wolverine outfit.

YOU'RE IN THE MOVIES

ALL TRAILERS AND DIRECTOR'S MODE
At the options screen, press Left Bumper, Right Bumper, Left Bumper, Right Bumper, Y.

ZOMBIE APOCALYPSE

7 DAYS OF HELL MODE
Complete Day 55.

HARDCORE MODE
Survive for seven straight days.

CHAINSAW ONLY MODE
Complete a day only using the chainsaw.

TURBO MODE
Get a 100 multiplier.

ZOOMAROOM

ALL COSTUMES, TIERS, & DOUBLE JUMP
At the Title screen, press Left Trigger, Right Trigger, Left Trigger, Right Trigger, X, X, Left Bumper, Right Bumper.

OVERLOAD

XBOX 360

MICROSOFT XBOX 360®
ACHIEVEMENTS

GAMES

2010 FIFA WORLD CUP

ACHIEVEMENTS

NAME	GOAL/REQUIREMENT	POINT VALUE
Single Star Group Stage	Finish the Group Stage in the Online 2010 FIFA World Cup™ with a 1/2 - 1 star team.	30
Two Star Group Stage	Finish the Group Stage in the Online FIFA World Cup™ with a 1.5 - 2 star team.	20
Three Star Group Stage	Finish the Group Stage in the Online FIFA World Cup™ with a 2.5 - 3 star team.	5
Against all odds	Win the Online 2010 FIFA World Cup™ with a 1/2 - 1 star team.	75
Ultimate Underdogs	Win the Online 2010 FIFA World Cup™ with a 1.5 - 2 star team.	50
Played well as a team	Win the Online FIFA World Cup™ with a 2.5 - 3 star team.	15
Dream Come True	Advance past the group stage in the Online FIFA World Cup™ with a team rated 3 stars or lower.	5

NAME	GOAL/REQUIREMENT	POINT VALUE
Undefeated Group Stage	Win all three group games and advance to the knockout stage in the Online FIFA World Cup™.	15
Hospitality and Victories	As the lead profile advance through the group stage as South Africa in 2010 FIFA World Cup™	10
We'll just score more	As the lead profile Concede 14+ In the Finals & Win the World Cup™. Semi-Pro or higher difficulty.	10
Concede No Goals	As the lead profile Advance to the round of 16 without conceding a goal: Semi-pro+ difficulty	10
Defend, Defend, Defend	Lift the World Cup™ Trophy in the 2010 FIFA World Cup™ scoring 11 or fewer total goals :Lead Profile	10
Second Trip, First Goal	Qualify & Score in the finals using any team that's been to the finals & not scored :Lead profile	10
First Team Selection	Get promoted to the First team and play a match in Captain your Country.	15
Managers First Choice	With a Virtual Pro play a game as the #1 ranked squad member in Captain your Country.	15
Co-op Success	All four co-op players get a match rating of 7 or above in a captain your country match.	5
Practice Penalty Kicks	Score at least 5 penalty Kicks in Penalty Shootout Practice	10
Masterful Performance	Finish a captain your country where one of the players wins an end of tournament award.	20
The Captain	In a Captain your Country campaign play a game as the captain for your country's first team.	10
Solid Performer	Achieve an average match rating of 8 at the end of a single Captain your Country campaign.	10
Fair Play	In a single Captain your country campaign Receive no match bans.	5
Hold the Line	Earn a match rating of 8 or above as a Defender in Captain your Country.	5
Most Hat-tricks	In Captain your Country score 2 or more hat-tricks in the Finals to beat the standing record.	20
2010 FIFA World Cup™ Mastery	Defeat all 32 teams that qualified for the 2010 FIFA World Cup™.	125
2006 FIFA World Cup™ Final	Beat France using Italy on Semi-Pro or Higher Difficulty.	10
2002 FIFA World Cup™ Final	Beat Germany using Brazil on Semi-Pro or Higher Difficulty.	10
1998 FIFA World Cup™ Final	Defeat Brazil using France on Semi-Pro or Higher Difficulty.	10
Lightning Quick Strike	Score in under 90 seconds to beat the standing record for fastest goal in a World Cup™ finals match.	20
Europe Qualifier	As the lead profile qualify as a team from Europe in 2010 FIFA World Cup™.	20
Asia Qualifier	As the lead profile qualify as a team from Asia in 2010 FIFA World Cup™.	20
Oceania Qualifier	As the lead profile qualify as a team from Oceania in 2010 FIFA World Cup™.	20
CONCACAF Qualifier	As the lead profile qualify as a team from CONCACAF in 2010 FIFA World Cup™.	20
South America Qualifier	As the lead profile qualify as a team from South America in 2010 FIFA World Cup™.	20
Africa Qualifier	As the lead profile qualify as a team from Africa in 2010 FIFA World Cup™.	20
World Cup™ Winner	As the lead profile win the FIFA World Cup™ Final in 2010 FIFA World Cup™.	125
Victorious!	Win the FIFA World Cup™ in a Captain your Country campaign.	100
Shameful	I've quit out of at least 5 ranked matches while losing.	0

SECRET ACHIEVEMENTS

NAME	GOAL/REQUIREMENT	POINT VALUE
First time on the world stage	Play with a team in the Online FIFA World Cup™ that's never qualified for the real World Cup Finals.	15
adidas Golden Shoe	Beat the standing record by scoring 10 goals in an Online FIFA World Cup™ with a single player.	25
Better luck needed next time	Finish the group stage without advancing to the Knockout stage of the Online 2010 FIFA World Cup™	20

XBOX 360 ACHIEVEMENTS

NAME	GOAL/REQUIREMENT	POINT VALUE
Practice Makes Perfect	Enter the training grounds to practice after a loss.	5
Pressure Cooker	Score in a penalty shootout using your Virtual Pro and win the game.	15
2 Button Mentor	Play and win a co-op game where at least one user is on 2 Button Controls.	10
2010 FIFA World Cup™ Fever	Challenge and defeat someone with this achievement in the Online FIFA World Cup™.	10

ALIENS VS. PREDATOR

ACHIEVEMENTS

NAME	GOAL/REQUIREMENT	POINT VALUE
Not Bad for A Human	Get all the Aliens vs Predator achievements	50
Game Over, Man!	Complete all three Campaigns	30
Club hopper	Survive The 'Party' at The Club	15
Exit Strategy	Escape from C-Block	15
You Have My Sympathies	Help Van Zandt	15
Regicide	Defeat the Matriarch	15
I Will Never Leave You...	Locate Tequila	15
...That's A Promise	Get Tequila to surgery	15
One Big Bug	Defeat the Praetorian	15
Get to The Chopper!	Recover Weyland's datapad	30
Come to Mama	Liberate the Matriarch	15
Breaking Quarantine	Escape from the Research Lab	15
Grunt Hunt	Wipe out all of the Marines in the Colony	15
Under Pressure	Solve the riddle of the Ruins	15
Grim Reaper	Harvest all available civilians in the Alien Campaign	15
Alien vs Predator	Create a new species	30
It Uses The Jungle	Find a way through Gateway	15
Fallen Comrade	Find the Youngbloods in the Jungle	15
Matter of Honor	Discover the Elite Predator's fate	15
Eyes of The Demon	Retrieve the ancient mask	15
World of Hurt	Survive trial by combat	15
Breaking and Entering	Find a way into the Research Lab	15
Reclaimer	Retrieve the second artifact	15
Extinction Agenda	Destroy the Abomination	30
Stay Frosty	Complete Marine Campaign on Hard difficulty setting	15
I Admire its Purity	Complete Alien Campaign on Hard difficulty setting	15
It Ain't No Man	Complete Predator Campaign on Hard difficulty setting	15
I LOVE the Corps!	Complete Marine Campaign on Nightmare difficulty setting	30
Magnificent, Isn't It?	Complete Alien Campaign on Nightmare difficulty setting	30
One Ugly Mother	Complete Predator Campaign on Nightmare difficulty setting	30
Harsh Language	Discover all 67 Audio Diaries	15
Quite A Specimen	Destroy all 50 Royal Jelly Containers	15
Fortune and Glory	Find all 45 Predator trophy belts	15
Scatter Shot	As a team, kill 20 enemies in under 60 seconds in a Survivor match.	15
I Like to Keep This Handy	Kill 2 enemies with one shot with the shotgun	15
Spin Doctor	Kill two enemies with one throw of the Battle Disc	15
Let's Rock!	Kill 5 enemies with one burst from the smartgun	15
Elite Sniper	Kill 10 enemies with head shots from the scoped rifle	15
Stick Around	Kill 20 enemies with the Combi Stick	15
Gunslinger	Kill 30 enemies with the pistol	30
Welcome to The War	Play and complete your first Ranked Match in standard Deathmatch mode	15
Killer Instinct	Win your first Ranked Match in standard Deathmatch mode	15

NAME	GOAL/REQUIREMENT	POINT VALUE
Serial Killer	Win 10 Ranked Matches in any Deathmatch mode	30
Very Tough Hombre	Kill 10 enemies in a row without dying in a Ranked Match	15
Persecution Complex	Achieve Persecutor status more than once in any Ranked Match	15
The Six Pack	Play with six friends in a Ranked Match	30
Ain't Got Time to Bleed	Heal or regenerate 30 blocks of health in Survivor	15
The Uninfected	Finish a Ranked Infestation match as the only remaining prey	30
Welcome to The Party	Get 6000 XP in Ranked Matches	30
Real Nasty Habit	Get 18060 XP in Ranked Matches	50

ALPHA PROTOCOL

ACHIEVEMENTS

NAME	GOAL/REQUIREMENT	POINT VALUE
Operation True Heirs	Complete Operation True Heirs.	75
Basic Training	Complete the Training Mission.	50
Alpha Protocol	Complete Operation Desert Spear.	75
Operation Blood Feud	Complete Operation Blood Feud.	75
Operation Deus Vult	Complete Operation Deus Vult.	75
Full Circle	Complete Alpha Protocol.	125
Hardcore	Complete Alpha Protocol on Hard difficulty setting.	25
Evolution of an Action Hero	Complete the Alpha Protocol using the Recruit background.	10
Desert Spear	Assassinate Sheikh Shaheed.	25
Ask Questions First, Shoot Later	Refrain from killing in cold blood.	15
Judge, Jury, and Executioner	Let your gun do the talking.	15
Thorton, Inc.	Turn all your enemies into allies in one single career.	10
Ladies' Man	Romance all the ladies in Alpha Protocol in a single career.	10
No Time For Love	Complete the game without being seduced.	20
Hard to Read	Use each stance at least 25% across 90 dialogue stance choices.	10
Social Butterfly	Gain Liked reputation status of 3 people (who must all Like you at the same time).	10
Antisocial	Get 3 people to hate you (who must all hate you at the same time).	10
Ready For Anything	Acquire the vast majority of Intel available in the game.	5
Pistol Mastery	Score 100 Critical Hits with the Pistol.	5
SMG Havoc	Achieve the maximum SMG Critical Hit Multiplier 7 times in your career.	5
Shotgun Crowd Control	Score 100 Critical Hits with the Shotgun.	5
Assault Rifle Marksmanship	Score 100 head shots with the Assault Rifle.	5
Black Belt	Defeat 50 enemies with CQC.	5
Lurker	Evade or Takedown 75 enemies across your career.	5
One With The Shadows	Complete 3 missions with less than 5 kills and with no enemies alerted to your presence.	5
Technophile	Complete 5 missions wherein 6 different gadgets are used.	5
Building a Deadlier Mousetrap	Have 100 placed devices detonate.	5
Breaking and Entering	Pick 10 locks.	5
Circuit Breaker	Bypass 20 electronic devices.	5
Data Theft	Hack 10 computers.	5

SECRET ACHIEVEMENTS

NAME	GOAL REQUIREMENTS	POINT VALUE
Friends Before Strangers	You saved Madison Saint James from certain death.	25

XBOX 360 ACHIEVEMENTS

NAME	GOAL REQUIREMENTS	POINT VALUE
Hard Choices	The Roman History Museum is safe, thanks to your efforts.	25
Keeping the Peace	You prevented a riot from killing hundreds in Taipei.	25
Secret Service	You prevented the assassination of President Ronald Sung.	25
Stay of Execution	You allowed Sheikh Shaheed to live.	25
No Compromise, No Mercy	Choosing your own path, you put an end to Halbech and Alpha Protocol.	25
Savage Love	You gained the affection of SIE and allowed her to consummate her lust.	5
Exclusive Interview	You and Scarlet Lake had a romantic trist.	5
Crime Buster	You reconciled with Alpha Protocol and put Halbech out of business.	25
Rising Star	You joined Halbech and put an end to Alpha Protocol.	25
Price For Lying	You killed Surkov for lying to you.	5
Russian Alliance	You forged a partnership with Sergei Surkov.	5
A Price On Mercy	You spared Konstantin Brayko.	25
One Less Gangster	Konstantin Brayko is dead by your hand.	25
Youth Trumps Experience	By carefully pushing his buttons, you provoked Marburg into fighting to the death.	5
Respected Enemies	You gained Marburg's respect and bested him in battle.	5
Never Trust A Sociopath	You successfully alienated "secret agent" Steven Heck.	5
A Plot Uncovered	You discovered the identity of Sung's assassin.	5
Office Romance	Your working relationship with Mina Tang turned into something more.	5
Rome-ance	You became more than friends with Madison Saint James.	5

BATMAN ARKHAM ASYLUM

ACHIEVEMENTS

NAME	GOAL/REQUIREMENT	POINT VALUE
Big Bang	Complete story mode on Easy difficulty	50
Bigger Bang	Complete story mode on Normal difficulty	50
Biggest Bang	Complete story mode on Hard difficulty	50
Party Pooper	Time to break up this party	10
Freeflow Combo 20	Complete a combo of 20 moves (any play mode)	10
Freeflow Combo 40	Complete a combo of 40 moves (any play mode)	10
Night Glider	Glide continuously for over 100m	5
Rope-A-Dope-A-Dope	String up one henchman and drop him to surprise a second (any play mode)	10
Mano-A-Mano	Take on a beast in hand to hand combat	10
Catch!	Catch a Batarang (any play mode)	5
Freeflow Combo 5	Complete a combo of 5 moves (any play mode)	5
Freeflow Combo 10	Complete a combo of 10 moves (any play mode)	5
Freeflow Perfection	Perform a perfect combo including all of Batman's combat moves (any play mode)	10
Freakshow Rodeo	Ride a beast and unleash its power	10
Freeflow Bronze	Achieve 8 medals on combat challenges	10
Freeflow Silver	Achieve 16 medals on combat challenges	25
Freeflow Gold	Achieve 24 medals on combat challenges	50
Predator Bronze	Achieve 8 medals on predator challenges	10
Predator Silver	Achieve 16 medals on predator challenges	25
Predator Gold	Achieve 24 medals on predator challenges	50
Invisible Predator	Complete one predator challenge by using only Silent Takedowns and without being detected	10
Flawless Freeflow Fighter	Complete one combat challenge without taking damage	10
Crack The E Nigma	Solve every riddle on the island	20
Arkham Analyst	Solve 5% of Riddler challenges	20
Cryptic Investigator	Solve 10% of Riddler challenges	20
Lateral Thinker	Solve 25% of Riddler challenges	20
Mystery Solver	Solve 40% of Riddler challenges	20

NAME	GOAL/REQUIREMENT	POINT VALUE
Conundrum Cracker	Solve 55% of Riddler challenges	20
Mental Athlete	Solve 70% of Riddler challenges	20
Riddle Resolver	Solve 85% of Riddler challenges	20
World's Greatest Detective	Solve Arkham's biggest mystery	20
Perfect Knight	100% Complete	75

SECRET ACHIEVEMENTS

NAME	GOAL/REQUIREMENT	POINT VALUE
Shocking Rescue	Take down Zsasz in the Patient Pacification Chamber	10
Leave No Man Behind	Rescue the guards and henchman from the Joker toxin in Decontamination	10
Malpractice Needs More Practice	Survive the onslaught from the deformed Joker henchman	10
Born Free	Escape from Intensive Treatment to the island surface	10
Just What The Doctors Ordered	Save all the doctors in Medical	10
Daydreamer	Survive the nightmare of the Scarecrow's fear gas	10
Baneful Payback	Defeat Bane	25
Breaking And Entering	Gain access to Arkham Mansion after it is locked down by the Joker	10
Recurring Nightmare	Face your biggest fears and keep your sanity	10
Zsasz Cut Down To Size	Save Dr. Young from being killed by Victor Zsasz	10
Solitary Confinement	Capture and lock up Harley Quinn	25
Double Trouble	Defeat two Titan Henchmen at once	25
Resist The Fear	Conquer the effects of the Scarecrow's fear gas	50
Crocodile Tears	Venture into Killer Croc's lair and come out alive	50
Poisoned Ivy	Defeat the giant Titan Ivy plant	50

BATTLEFIELD BAD COMPANY 2

ACHIEVEMENTS

NAME	GOAL/REQUIREMENT	POINT VALUE
I knew we'd make it	Campaign: finish Operation Aurora	15
Retirement just got postponed.	Campaign: finish Cold War	15
It's bad for my karma man!	Campaign: finish Heart of Darkness	15
They got all your intel?	Campaign: finish Upriver	15
Salvage a vehicle.	Campaign: finish Crack the Sky	15
Alright, here it is.	Campaign: finish Snowblind	15
Nobody ever drowned in sweat	Campaign: finish Heavy Metal	15
Ghost rider's here!	Campaign: finish High Value Target	15
Sierra Foxtrot 1079	Campaign: finish Sangre del Toro	15
Thanks for the smokes, brother!	Campaign: finish No One Gets Left Behind	15
Save me some cheerleaders.	Campaign: finish Zero Dark Thirty	15
Turn on a light.	Campaign: finish Force Multiplier	15
P.S. Invasion cancelled, sir.	Campaign: finish Airborne	30
It sucks to be right.	Campaign: finish Airborne on Hard	50
New Shiny Gun	Campaign: find 5 collectable weapons	15
Guns Guns Guns	Campaign: find 15 collectable weapons	50
Link to the Past	Campaign: destroy 1 satellite uplink	15
Communication Issues	Campaign: destroy 15 satellite uplinks	15
Complete Blackout	Campaign: destroy all satellite uplinks	50
Ten Blades	Campaign: 10 melee kills	15
Taxi!	Campaign: drive 5 km in any land vehicle	15

NAME	GOAL/REQUIREMENT	POINT VALUE
Destruction	Campaign: destroy 100 objects	15
Destruction Part 2	Campaign: destroy 1000 objects	30
Demolish	Campaign: demolish 1 house	15
Demolish Part 2	Campaign: demolish 50 houses	30
Assault Rifle Aggression	Campaign: 50 kills with assault rifles	15
Sub Machine Gun Storm	Campaign: 50 kills with sub machine guns	15
Light Machine Gun Lash Out	Campaign: 50 kills with light machine guns	15
Sniper Rifle Strike	Campaign: 50 kills with sniper rifles	15
Wall of Shotgun	Campaign: 50 kills with shotguns	15
Multiplayer Knowledge	Online: reach Rank 10 (Sergeant I)	15
Multiplayer Elite	Online: reach Rank 22 (Warrant Officer I)	50
Assault Expert	Online: unlock 3 weapons in the Assault kit	15
Engineer Expert	Online: unlock 3 weapons in the Engineer kit	15
Medic Expert	Online: unlock 3 weapons in the Medic kit	15
Recon Expert	Online: unlock 3 weapons in the Recon kit	15
Battlefield Expert	Online: obtain all unlocks in any kit or all Vehicle unlocks	50
15 Minutes of Fame	Online: play for 15 minutes	15
Mission... Accomplished.	Online: in a round do one kill with the knife, the M60 and the RPG-7	15
Pistol Man	Online: get 5 kills with every handgun in the game	15
Airkill	Online: roadkill an enemy with any helicopter	15
Et Tu, Brute?	Online: knife 5 friends	15
Demolition Man	Online: get 20 demolish kills	15
Careful Guidance	Online: destroy an enemy helicopter with a stationary RPG	15
The Dentist	Online: do a headshot kill with the repair tool	15
Won Them All	Online: win a round in all online game modes	15
Squad Player	Online: obtain the Gold Squad Pin 5 times	30
Combat Service Support	Online: do 10 resupplies, repairs, heals, revives and motion mine spot assists	15
Award Aware	Online: obtain 10 unique awards	15
Award Addicted	Online: obtain 50 unique awards	30

DOWNLOADABLE CONTENT: WEAPONS PACK 1

NAME	GOAL/REQUIREMENT	POINT VALUE
SPECACT Assault Elite	Get all SPECACT Assault awards	15
SPECACT Engineer Elite	Get all SPECACT Engineer awards	15
SPECACT Medic Elite	Get all SPECACT Medic awards	15
SPECACT Recon Elite	Get all SPECACT Recon awards	15

DOWNLOADABLE CONTENT: ONSLAUGHT

NAME	GOAL/REQUIREMENT	POINT VALUE
Valpariso Conquered	Successfully complete Valpariso in Onslaught mode on any difficulty	10
Valpariso Veteran	Successfully complete Valpariso in Onslaught mode on Hardcore difficulty	20
Isla Inocentes Conquered	Successfully complete Isla Inocentes in Onslaught mode on any difficulty	10
Isla Inocentes Veteran	Successfully complete Isla Inocentes in Onslaught mode on Hardcore difficulty	20
Atacama Desert Conquered	Successfully complete Atacama Desert in Onslaught mode on any difficulty	10
Atacama Desert Veteran	Successfully complete Atacama Desert in Onslaught mode on Hardcore difficulty	20
Nelson Bay Conquered	Successfully complete Nelson Bay in Onslaught mode on any difficulty	10
Nelson Bay Veteran	Successfully complete Nelson Bay in Onslaught mode on Hardcore difficulty	20

ACHIEVEMENTS

NAME	GOAL/REQUIREMENT	POINT VALUE
Bought a Slot	Buy one Plasmid or Tonic Slot at a Gatherer's Garden.	5
Max Plasmid Slots	Fully upgrade to the maximum number of Plasmid Slots.	10
Upgraded a Weapon	Upgrade any weapon at a Power to the People Station.	10
Fully Upgraded a Weapon	Install the third and final upgrade to any of your weapons.	10
All Weapon Upgrades	Find all 14 Power to the People weapon upgrades in the game.	20
Prolific Hacker	Successfully hack at least one of every type of machine.	20
Master Hacker	Hack 30 machines at a distance with the Hack Tool.	20
First Research	Research a Splicer with the Research Camera.	5
One Research Track	Max out one Research Track.	20
Research Master	Max out research on all 9 research subjects.	20
Grand Daddy	Defeat 3 Big Daddies without dying during the fight.	25
Master Gatherer	Gather 600 ADAM with Little Sisters.	30
Fully Upgraded a Plasmid	Fully upgrade one of your Plasmids to the level 3 version at a Gatherer's Garden.	10
All Plasmids	Find or purchase all 11 basic Plasmid types.	20
Trap Master	Kill 30 enemies using only Traps.	15
Master Protector	Get through a Gather with no damage and no one getting to the Little Sister.	15
Big Spender	Spend 2000 dollars at Vending Machines.	15
Dealt with Every Little Sister	Either Harvest or Save every Little Sister in the game.	50
Against All Odds	Finish the game on the hardest difficulty level.	30
Big Brass Balls	Finish the game without using Vita-Chambers.	25
Rapture Historian	Find 100 audio diaries.	40
Unnatural Selection	Score your first kill in a non-private match.	10
Welcome to Rapture	Complete your first non-private match.	10
Disgusting Frankenstein	Become a Big Daddy for the first time in a non-private match.	10
"Mr. Bubbles-- No!"	Take down your first Big Daddy in a non-private match.	20
Mother Goose	Save your first Little Sister in a non-private match.	20
Two-Bit Heroics	Complete your first trial in a non-private match.	10
Parasite	Achieve Rank 10.	10
Little Moth	Achieve Rank 20.	20
Skin Job	Achieve Rank 30.	20
Choose the Impossible	Achieve Rank 40.	50
Proving Grounds	Win your first non-private match.	20
Man About Town	Play at least one non-private match on each multiplayer map.	10

SECRET ACHIEVEMENTS

NAME	GOAL/REQUIREMENT	POINT VALUE
Daddy's Home	Found your way back into the ruins of Rapture.	10
Protector	Defended yourself against Lamb's assault in the train station.	20
Sinclair's Solution	Joined forces with Sinclair in Ryan Amusements.	20
Confronted Grace	Confronted Lamb's lieutenant in Pauper's Drop.	10
Defeated the Preacher	Defeated the Preacher.	20
Nose for News	Uncovered the secret of Dionysus Park.	20
Found Lamb's Hideout	Gained access to Lamb's stronghold.	20
Reunion	Reunited with your original Little Sister.	50
Heading to the Surface	Headed to the surface on the side of Sinclair's escape pod.	25
Escape	Escaped Rapture.	100
9-Irony	Paid your respects to the founder of Rapture.	5

OVERLOAD

XBOX 360 ACHIEVEMENTS

NAME	GOAL/REQUIREMENT	POINT VALUE
Distance Hacker	Used the Hack Tool to hack an object at a distance.	5
Unbreakable	Defended yourself against the Big Sister without dying.	20
Look at You, Hacker	Killed 50 enemies using only hacked Security.	15
Adopted a Little Sister	Adopted a new Little Sister for the first time.	5
Savior	Saved every Little Sister and spared Grace, Stanley and Gil.	25
Counterattack	Killed an enemy with its own projectile.	5

DOWNLOADABLE CONTENT: RAPTURE METRO PACK

NAME	GOAL/REQUIREMENT	POINT VALUE
Aqua Incognita	Play at least one non-private match on each downloadable content map.	25
Territorial	Win a non-private match in each of the 6 new maps.	25
Reincarnation	Use Rebirth to start again!	100

DOWNLOADABLE CONTENT: THE PROTECTOR TRIALS

NAME	GOAL/REQUIREMENT	POINT VALUE
Litmus Test	Earn 6 stars in the Protector Trials	5
Acid Test	Earn 18 stars in the Protector Trial	10
Trial By Fire	Earn 36 stars in the Protector Trials	15
Enemy of the Family	Earn an A rank in all Protector Trials	15
Perfect Protector	Collect 100% of the ADAM in a single Protector Trial	20
Get a Bigger Bucket	Collect 50% of the ADAM available in all Protector Trials	25

SECRET ACHIEVEMENTS

NAME	GOAL/REQUIREMENT	POINT VALUE
Guardian Angel	Completed all bonus Protector Trials.	10

DOWNLOADABLE CONTENT: MINERVA'S DEN

NAME	GOAL/REQUIREMENT	POINT VALUE
Garbage Collection	Destroy all 10 Vacuum Bots in Minerva's Den	10
Lancer Killer	Kill a Lancer Big Daddy	10
ADAM Addict	Resolve all the Little Sisters in Minerva's Den	10

SECRET ACHIEVEMENTS

NAME	GOAL/REQUIREMENT	POINT VALUE
Login	Reached Rapture Central Computing Operations	20
Root Access Granted	Reached Computer Core Access	20
Logout	Escaped Minerva's Den	50
SUDO	Wrested control of the Thinker from Reed Wahl	20
High Score	Get 9999 points in a single game of spitfire	10

BORDERLANDS

ACHIEVEMENTS

NAME	GOAL/REQUIREMENT	POINT VALUE
Paid in Fyrestone	Complete 5 missions in the Arid Badlands	5
Made in Fyrestone	Complete all missions in the Arid Badlands	15
Paid in New Haven	Complete 5 missions in the Rust Commons	10
Made in New Haven	Complete all missions in the Rust Commons	20
My Brother is an Italian Plumber	Kill an enemy by stomping on its head	15
Speedy McSpeederton	Race around the Ludicrous Speedway in under 31 seconds	10
You call this archaeology?	Apply an elemental artifact	20
Ding! Newbie	Earn level 5	5
Ding! Novice	Earn level 10	10

NAME	GOAL/REQUIREMENT	POINT VALUE
Ding! Expert	Earn level 20	20
Ding! Hardcore	Earn level 30	30
Ding! Sleepless	Earn level 40	40
Discovered Skag Gully	Discover Skag Gully	5
Discovered Sledge's Safe House	Discover Sledge's Safe House	5
Discovered Headstone Mine	Discover Headstone Mine	5
Discovered Trash Coast	Discover Trash Coast	5
Discovered The Scrapyard	Discover The Scrapyard	10
Discovered Krom's Canyon	Discover Krom's Canyon	10
Discovered Crimson Lance Enclave	Discover Crimson Lance Enclave	15
Discovered Eridian Promontory	Discover Eridian Promontory	15
Ding! Champion	Earn level 50	50
Get A Little Blood on the Tires	Kill 25 enemies by ramming them with any vehicle	20
Rootinest, Tootinest, Shootinest	Kill 5 Rakk in under 10 seconds	10
Pandora-dog Millionaire	Earn $1,000,000	50
Fence	Sell 50 guns to a shop	25
Can't We Get BEYOND Thunderdome?	Win an arena match	25
Duel-icious	Win a duel against another player	15
Group LF Healer	Rescue a groupmate from death in a co-op game	25
There's No "I" In "Team"	Complete 15 missions in co-op	30
And They'll Tell Two Friends	Play in a co-op game with either an employee of Gearbox or someone who has this achievement	10
Weapon Aficionado	Reach proficiency level 10 with any weapon type	20
Duelinator	Win a duel without taking damage	35
Facemelter	Kill 25 enemies with corrosive weapons	25
1.21 Gigawatts	Kill 25 enemies with shock weapons	25
Pyro	Kill 25 enemies with incendiary weapons	25
Master Exploder	Kill 25 enemies with explosive weapons	15
There are some who call me...Tim	Equip a class mod for your character	25
Fully Loaded	Rescue enough Claptraps to earn 42 inventory slots	10
Truly Outrageous	Kill an enemy with the Siren's action skill	15
Careful, He Bites	Kill 15 enemies with the Hunter's action skill	15
Reckless Abandon	Kill 15 enemies with the Berserker's action skill	15
Down in Front!	Kill 15 enemies with the Soldier's action skill	15

SECRET ACHIEVEMENTS

NAME	GOAL/REQUIREMENT	POINT VALUE
12 Days of Pandora	Mastered the technology of Pandora	30
Wanted: Sledge	Killed Sledge	10
Wanted: Krom	Killed Krom	20
Wanted: Flynt	Killed Flynt	30
Destroyed the Hive	Killed the Rakk Hive	40
Destroyed The Destroyer	Killed the Vault Boss	50
United We Stand	Defeated the Rakk Hive, the Vault Boss, Sledge, Krom, or Flynt in a co-op game	35
You're on a boat!	I bet you never thought you'd be here.	15

XBOX 360 ACHIEVEMENTS

ACHIEVEMENTS

NAME	GOAL/REQUIREMENT	POINT VALUE
Got a Car and a Date	Completed "Welcome to the Age of Metal"	15
Start a Revolution	Completed "Exploited in the Bowels of Hell"	15
Thick as a Baby's Arm	Completed "Lair of the Metal Queen"	15
Hair Remover	Completed "Battle for Bladehenge"	15
French Kiss Instructor	Completed "Pilgrimage of Screams"	15
Chicks n' Booze n' Stuff	Completed "Sanctuary of Sin"	15
Ran to the Hills	Completed "It's Raining Death"	15
Fistfull of Fog	Completed "Dry Ice, Wet Graves"	15
No More Tears	Completed "Sea of Black Tears"	15
Groupie	Completed Campaign mode on Easy	25
Roadie	Completed Campaign mode on Normal	25
Legend	Completed Campaign mode on Brutal	25
Overkill	Completed all hunting secondary missions	20
Squeal Like a Chicken	Completed all racing secondary missions	20
Protector	Completed 20 ambush, outpost defense, or mortar secondary missions	20
Metal God	Achieved 100% completion on the stats screen	50
Serpent Samaritan	Freed 40 Bound Serpents	10
Serpent Spanker	Freed 80 Bound Serpents	15
Serpent Savior	Freed all 120 Bound Serpents	25
One Hit Wonder	Purchased 1 upgrade in the Motor Forge	5
Loyal Customer	Purchased all upgrades in the Motor Forge	25
Virtuoso	Learned all guitar solos	20
Tourist	Viewed all vistas	20
Now You Must Tell the Tale	View all Legends	20
Voices From Beyond	Unlocked all songs in the Mouth of Metal	20
Flowerslave	Summoned all Motor Forges	20
Practice Bloody Practice	Won an AI Stage Battle - any difficulty	10
Iron Fist	Won an AI Stage Battle - Brutal difficulty	20
Victör	Won a ranked multiplayer match	10
Subjügator	Won 10 ranked multiplayer matches	20
Cönquerer	Won 50 ranked multiplayer matches	50
Master of the Flame	Double Teamed with every Ironheade unit	20
Master of the Tear	Double Teamed with every Drowning Doom unit	20
Master of the Blood	Double Teamed with every Tainted Coil unit	20
Armchair General	Won a Stage Battle by yourself against the AI without attacking	20
Favored	Acquired 3,000 Fire Tributes	30
Sellout	Spent 250,000 fans - any mode	30
Some Demon Flesh on your Bumper	Slayed 150 enemies with the Deuce - any mode	20
I've never touched an axe before	Personally smote 300 enemies - any mode	30
Silence, groundwalker!	Gained 5 or more seconds of hang time in a single jump - any mode	10
Six Degrees of Schafer	Played with or against another player who has this Achievement	15
Ringleader	Trapped 15 enemies in one ring of fire with the Fire Baron's Double Team	15
Painkiller	Killed 25 enemies with the grinder of one Rock Crusher	15
Dollpocalypse	Hit 6 enemies with the explosion from a Brood's Double Team	15
Euthanasia	Hit 15 enemies with one Agony Ball using the Pain Lifter's Double Team	15
Death From Above	Killed 20 enemies with one Bleeding Death	15
Coolest Thing Ever	Jumped over a Hextadon in the Deuce	15
Beast Master	Rode every animal in the world	15
Boar Bather	Rode a Razorfire Boar into the Sea of Black Tears and live to tell the tale.	50
Quill Tosser	Killed a Tollusk using only Ground Urchins	20

ACHIEVEMENTS

NAME	GOAL/REQUIREMENT	POINT VALUE
Death to Dictators	Take down Castro with a headshot.	15
Sacrifice	Ensure your squad escapes safely from Cuba.	10
Vehicular Slaughter	Destroy all enemies on vehicles during the prison break.	25
Slingshot Kid	Destroy all slingshot targets in 3 attempts.	15
Give me liberty	Escape Vorkuta.	10
VIP	Receive orders from Lancer.	10
A safer place	Sabotage the Soviet space program.	10
Tough Economy	Use no more than 6 TOW guided missiles to destroy the tanks in the defense of Khe Sanh.	15
Looks don't count	Break the siege in the battle of Khe Sanh.	10
Raining Pain	Rack up a body count of 20 NVA using air support in Hue City.	15
The Dragon Within	Kill 10 NVA with Dragon's Breath rounds.	15
SOG Rules	Retrieve the dossier and the defector from Hue City.	10
Heavy Hand	Use the Grim Reaper to destroy the MG emplacement.	15
Up close and personal	Silently take out 3 VC.	15
Double Trouble	Use only dual wield weapons to escape Kowloon.	10
Broken English	Escape Kowloon.	10
Lord Nelson	Destroy all targets and structures while making your way up the river.	25
Never get off the boat	Find the Soviet connection in Laos.	10
Pathfinder	Guide the squad through the Soviet outpost without them getting killed.	50
Mr. Black OP	Enter the Soviet relay station undetected.	50
With extreme prejudice	Get to the POW compound in the Hind using only rockets.	25
Russian bar-b-q	Incinerate 10 enemies with the flamethrower attachment in the POW compound.	15
Light Foot	Escape the ship with 2:15 left on the timer in Veteran.	30
Some wounds never heal	Escape the Past.	10
I hate monkeys	Kill 7 monkeys in under 10 seconds in the Rebirth labs.	15
No Leaks	Make it through the NOVA 6 gas without dying on Rebirth Island.	50
Clarity	Crack the code.	10
Double Whammy	Destroy both helicopters with one Valkyrie rocket from the deck of the ship.	15
Stand Down	Complete the campaign on any difficulty.	35
BLACK OP MASTER	Complete the campaign on Hardened or Veteran difficulty.	100
Frag Master	Kill 5 enemies with a single frag grenade in the campaign.	15
Sally Likes Blood	Demonstrate killer economic sensibilities by taking down 3 enemies with a single bullet.	15
Unconventional Warfare	Use the explosive bolts to kill 30 enemies in the campaign.	15
Cold Warrior	Complete "Operation 40," "Vorkuta," and "Executive Order" on Veteran difficulty.	25
Down and Dirty	Complete "SOG" and "The Defector" on Veteran difficulty.	25
It's your funeral	Complete "Numbers," "Project Nova," and "Victor Charlie" on Veteran difficulty.	25
Not Today	Complete "Crash Site," "WMD," and "Payback" on Veteran difficulty.	25
Burn Notice	Complete "Rebirth" and "Redemption" on Veteran difficulty.	25
Closer Analysis	Find all the hidden intel.	15
Date Night	Watch a film or clip with a friend.	15
In The Money	Finish 5 Wager Matches "in the money."	20
Ready For Deployment	Reach rank 10 in Combat Training.	15

XBOX 360 ACHIEVEMENTS

NAME	GOAL/REQUIREMENT	POINT VALUE
The Collector	Buy every weapon off the walls in a single Zombies game.	20
Hands Off the Merchandise	Kill the Pentagon thief before it can steal your load-out.	20
Sacrificial Lamb	Shoot at or be shot by an ally with a Pack-a-Punch crossbow and kill six zombies with the explosion.	15
"Insert Coin"	Access the terminal and battle the forces of the Cosmic Silverback in Dead Ops Arcade.	5
Easy Rhino	In Dead Ops Arcade, use a Speed Boost to blast through 20 or more enemies at one time.	10

SECRET ACHIEVEMENTS

NAME	GOAL/REQUIREMENT	POINT VALUE
See Me, Stab Me, Heal Me	Fire a Pack-a-Punched Ballistic Knife at a downed ally to revive them from a distance.	15
Just ask me nicely	Break free from the torture chair.	15
Eaten by a Grue	Play Zork on the terminal.	15

CALL OF DUTY: MODERN WARFARE 2

ACHIEVEMENTS

NAME	GOAL/REQUIREMENT	POINT VALUE
Back in the Saddle	Help train the local militia.	15
Danger Close	Get hand picked for Shepherd's elite squad.	15
Cold Shoulder	Infiltrate the snowy mountain side base.	15
Tag 'em and bag 'em	Find Rojas in the Favelas.	15
Royale with Cheese	Defend Burger Town.	15
Soap on a Rope	Storm the gulag.	15
Desperate Times	Execute the plan to help the Americans.	15
Whiskey Hotel	Take back Whiskey Hotel.	15
The Pawn	Assault Makarov's safe house.	15
Out of the Frying Pan…	Complete the mission in the airplane graveyard.	15
For the Record	Complete the Single Player campaign on any difficulty.	35
The Price of War	Complete the single player campaign on Hardened or Veteran Difficulty.	90
First Day of School	Complete 'S.S.D.D' and 'Team Player' on Veteran Difficulty.	25
Black Diamond	Complete 'Cliffhanger' on Veteran Difficulty.	25
Turistas	Complete 'Takedown' and 'The Hornet's Nest' on Veteran Difficulty.	25
Red Dawn	Complete 'Wolverines!' and 'Exodus' on Veteran Difficulty.	25
Prisoner #627	Complete 'The Only Easy Day... Was Yesterday' and 'The Gulag' on Veteran Difficulty.	25
Ends Justify the Means	Complete 'Contingency' on Veteran Difficulty	25
Homecoming	Complete 'Of Their Own Accord', 'Second Sun', and 'Whiskey Hotel' on Veteran Difficulty.	25
Queen takes Rook	Complete 'Loose Ends' and 'The Enemy of My Enemy' on Veteran Difficulty.	25
Off the Grid	Complete 'Just Like Old Times' and 'Endgame' on Veteran Difficulty.	25
Pit Boss	Run The Pit in 'S.S.D.D' and finish with a final time under 30 seconds.	10
Ghost	Plant the C4 in 'Cliffhanger' without alerting or injuring anyone in the blizzard.	10
Colonel Sanderson	Kill 7 chickens in under 10 seconds in 'The Hornet's Nest'.	10
Gold Star	Earn 1 star in Special Ops.	20
Hotel Bravo	Earn 4 stars in Special Ops.	20
Charlie On Our Six	Earn 8 stars in Special Ops.	20
It Goes to Eleven	Earn at least 1 star in 11 different Special Op missions.	20

NAME	GOAL/REQUIREMENT	POINT VALUE
Operational Asset	Earn all 3 stars in at least 5 different Special Op missions.	20
Blackjack	Earn 21 stars in Special Ops.	20
Honor Roll	Earn at least 1 star in each Special Op mission.	20
Operative	Earn all 3 stars in at least 10 different Special Op missions.	30
Specialist	Earn 30 stars in Special Ops.	30
Professional	Earn all 3 stars in at least 15 different Special Op missions.	30
Star 69	Earn 69 stars in Special Ops.	90
Downed but Not Out	Kill 4 enemies in a row while downed in Special Ops.	10
I'm the Juggernaut…	Kill a Juggernaut in Special Ops.	10
Ten plus foot-mobiles	Kill at least 10 enemies with one Predator missile in Single Player or Special Ops.	10
Unnecessary Roughness	Use a riot shield to beat down an enemy in Single Player or Special Ops.	10
Knock-knock	Kill 4 enemies with 4 shots during a slow-mo breach in Single Player or Special Ops.	10
Some Like it Hot	Kill 6 enemies in a row using a thermal weapon in Single Player or Special Ops.	10
Two Birds with One Stone	Kill 2 enemies with a single bullet in Single Player or Special Ops.	10
The Road Less Traveled	Collect 22 enemy intel items.	10
Leave No Stone Unturned	Collect 45 enemy intel items.	10
Drive By	Kill 20 enemies in a row while driving a vehicle in Single Player or Special Ops.	10
The Harder They Fall	Kill 2 rappelling enemies in a row before they land on their feet in Single Player or Special Ops.	10
Desperado	Kill 5 enemies in a row using 5 different weapons or attachments in Single Player or Special Ops.	10
Look Ma Two Hands	Kill 10 enemies in a row using akimbo weapons in Single Player or Special Ops.	10
No Rest For the Wary	Knife an enemy without him ever knowing you were there in Single Player or Special Ops.	10
Three-some	Kill at least 3 enemies with a single shot from a grenade launcher in Single Player or Special Ops.	10

DANTE'S INFERNO

ACHIEVEMENTS

NAME	GOAL/REQUIREMENT	POINT VALUE
Slaughter at Acre	Fight against the prisoner at Acre	5
Abandon All Hope	Break through the Gates of Hell	15
Sentence the Judge	Defeat King Minos	25
Lovers Torn Asunder	Defeat Marc Antony	25
The Great Worm	Defeat Cerberus	25
Like Father Like Son	Defeat Alighiero	25
Gates of Dis	Enter the lower circles of The Inferno	35
The Harrowing	Escape Heresy	35
Brotherhood	Defeat Francesco	40
Bitter Sweet	Save Beatrice	50
Lucifer's Match	Defeat the Emperor of the Woeful Realm	100
Precious	Find a Beatrice stone	10
Power of the Cross	Find all 3 Beatrice stones	20
Footsteps of a Traitor	Find 10 pieces of silver	10
Betrayed with a Kiss	Find 20 pieces of silver	10
Well Done, Judas	Find All 30 pieces of silver	20
Relic Hunter	Find a relic	10
Light Relics	Find all Holy relics	20
Dark Relics	Find all Unholy relics	20
Forbidden Love	Find and absolve both Francesca da Polenta and Paolo Malatesta	20
Old Friend	Find and absolve Brunetto Latini	20

NAME	GOAL/REQUIREMENT	POINT VALUE
The Damned	Punish or absolve all 27 shades of The Inferno	50
The Guide	Collect all Virgil commentaries	40
Soul Reaper	Collect 60,000 Souls	50
Burning Eyes	Send Charon back into the abyss	10
Warming Up	Perform a 50 hit combo	10
Masterpiece	Perform a 200 hit combo	10
Poetry in Motion	Perform a 666 hit combo	20
Holy Warrior	Kill 30 Minions	10
Demon Slayer	Kill 30 Demons	10
Bad Nanny	Kill 20 Unbaptized Babies	10
Indigestion	Kill 5 Gluttons	10
Confessional	Kill 5 Heretics	10
Countermeasures	Kill 20 enemies using a counter move	10
Superstition	Kill 20 enemies using magic	10
Give Me Strength	Open 20 Health fountains	10
Sorcerer's Apprentice	Open 20 Mana fountains	10
Light in the Dark	Reach Holy Level 7	30
Death's Apprentice	Reach Unholy Level 7	30
Holy Man	Max out the Holy path	30
Man of Evil	Max out the Unholy path	30
Gates of Hell	Defeat all enemy waves in the Gates of Hell Arena	60
Dark Forest	Complete the Dark Forest on any difficulty	20
Clear Path Not Lost	Complete the Dark Forest without getting lost once	20

DJ HERO

ACHIEVEMENTS

NAME	GOAL/REQUIREMENT	POINT VALUE
My First Set	Complete a setlist on any difficulty setting.	5
The Full Set	Complete all mixes at any difficulty setting.	30
Super Scratchin'	Successfully perform 10,000 scratches.	20
Harsh Fader	Successfully perform 5,000 crossfader moves.	20
Freestyle DJ	Trigger every Effects Zone and every Freestyle Sample Zone in any mix on hard difficulty or above.	10
Special Effects!	Turn the effects dial during every Effects Zone in any mix at any difficulty (not in the tutorial).	5
No Mistakes Allowed	Successfully perform all scratches in any mix on hard difficulty or above.	20
Tap King	Successfully press the platter button(s) for all tap icons in any mix on hard difficulty or above.	20
Fantastic Fader	Successfully perform all crossfades and crossfade spikes in any mix on hard difficulty or above.	20
Superstar DJ	Get a 100% Hits in any mix on hard difficulty or above.	30
Good Times	Earn 10 stars by playing any of the mixes in the Grandmaster Flash Presents setlist.	15
Multiplier Madness	Achieve an 8X multiplier during any mix (not in the tutorial).	5
REEEWIINNNNDD!!!	Perform 4 rewinds without missing any icons in any mix on any difficulty.	15
Graduation	Complete the tutorial Learn to DJ - Advanced Techniques.	10
Double Trouble	Complete a 2 player one on one local game (DJ v DJ only).	10
Supporting Act	Join and complete 3 online games.	5
Headliner	Host and complete an online game.	5
Win Online	Win 10 online games.	25
New Jack	Complete your first mix (not in the tutorial).	1
Four Star	Earn 4 stars in any mix on hard difficulty.	4
Five Star	Earn 5 stars in any mix on expert difficulty.	5
The Gift of Music	Unlock a bonus mix on any set list (where available).	10
Hello World	Have your score posted to the online leaderboard.	5
My 50 Pence	Attain a 50 streak in any mix on hard difficulty or above using a DJ Hero™ Turntable Controller.	5

NAME	GOAL/REQUIREMENT	POINT VALUE
Tonight We DJ in Hell!	Attain a 300 streak in any mix on expert difficulty using a DJ Hero™ Turntable Controller.	30
200 Deep	Attain a 200 streak in any mix on hard difficulty or above using a DJ Hero™ Turntable Controller.	15
All Over the World	Complete a mix in every venue.	15
Five in Ten	Earn 5 stars in any 10 mixes on medium difficulty or above.	20
Four in Twenty	Earn 4 Stars in any 20 mixes on medium difficulty or above.	25
Five in Twenty	Earn 5 Stars in any 20 mixes on medium difficulty or above.	35
Props!	Watch the entire credits.	5
Legendary Status	Earn 5 stars in every mix on hard difficulty or above.	80
The Grandmaster!	Earn 5 stars in every mix on medium difficulty or above.	35
360 Degrees	Perform a 360 degree rewind in any mix without missing any icons on hard or expert difficulty.	20
720 Degrees	Perform a 720 degree rewind in any mix without missing any icons on hard or expert difficulty.	35
The New Style	Construct and play all the mixes of a quicklist online with another player.	10
Guitar and DJ	Play the Guitar DJ mode with one player as the DJ and the other as the Guitarist.	15
Spin Back King	Perform 20 rewinds.	20
Walk-in Wardrobe	Complete any 10 mixes in 10 different outfits.	10
The Vinyl Cut	Earn 20 stars by playing any of the mixes in The Vinyl Cut setlist.	50
DJ Shadow Presents...	Earn 15 stars by playing any of the mixes in the DJ Shadow Presents setlist.	30
Bonus Bangers	Unlock all available bonus mixes from all setlists.	35
Turntable Perfection	Earn 5 stars in every mix on expert difficulty.	100
Here Comes the Hot Starter!	Earn 50 Hot Starts in any complete mixes.	25
Shout Out	Complete any mix using a microphone in a single player game.	5
Euphoria DJ	Complete all the Perfect Regions and activate Euphoria in any mix on hard difficulty or above.	15
Euphoric Hoarder	Complete all the Perfect Regions in any mix on hard difficulty or above, without using Euphoria.	20
The Power of Two	Both players activate Euphoria and Star Power simultaneously in Guitar DJ Mode.	15
The Choice Is Yours	Play an 8 mix custom setlist on medium difficulty or above and get at least 3 stars on all mixes.	15
Master Blaster	Complete a setlist using the Ghetto Blaster deck.	20

FABLE 2

ACHIEVEMENTS

NAME	GOAL/REQUIREMENT	POINT VALUE
The Pooch Pamperer	Play fetch with your dog, or see another Hero's dog play.	5
The Archaeologist	Dig up something the dog has discovered, or see another Hero do so.	5
The Dog Trainer	Teach your dog a trick, or see another Hero's dog learn one.	5
The Persuader	Convince a villager to give you a present, or see another Hero do so.	5
The Show-off	Impress a villager with a perfect expression, or see another Hero do so.	5
The Romantic	Take a villager on a perfect date, or tag along to one. Location and expressions are all-important.	10
The Spouse	Marry a villager, or attend the wedding of another Hero.	10
The Parent	Have a child, or be there for the birth of another Hero's child.	10
The Hunter	Kill a sweet, innocent, fluffy bunny rabbit (remember, safety's off!)	5
The Gargoyle	Find the gargoyles' legendary treasure.	25

NAME	GOAL/REQUIREMENT	POINT VALUE
The Chicken Kicker	Kick a chicken a good distance, or see one getting kicked.	5
The Cliff Diver	Cliff dive 500 feet, or see another Hero do so.	5
The Workhorse	A Hero must achieve a high-enough chain while performing a job.	10
The Hero of Many Names	Change your Hero's title, or see another Hero change theirs.	5
The Teaser	Make bandits respond to expressions with fear, anger, mirth, and confusion... during combat!	5
The Property Magnate	A property must be sold for twice the price it was bought for.	10
The Rogue	Steal something undetected from a building while there are people nearby, or see another Hero do so.	5
The Illustrated Hero	Tattoo every part of your Hero's body, or see another Hero do so.	5
The Executioner	Sacrifice ten people in the Temple of Shadows, or see another Hero do so.	10
The Gambler	A Hero must win 500 gold at a pub game in one sitting, having tried each game type at least once.	10
The Bigamist	Get married a second time, whilst already married, or attend the second wedding of another Hero.	10
The Swinger	Take part in a debauched bedroom party with several participants.	5
The Pied Piper	Start a party where at least five villagers are dancing, or see another Hero do so.	10
The Party Animal	Get five villagers drunk in under three minutes, or see another Hero do so.	10
The Menace To Society	Commit an act of public indecency, or see another Hero commit one.	5
The Black Knight	Shoot the weapons from a hollow man's hands, blow off his head and then kill him for good!	10
The Duellist	String together a full-speed chain attack, or see another Hero do so.	10
The Sharpshooter	Hit three enemies with one shot, or see another Hero do so.	10
The Archmage	A Hero must kill five human enemies with one spell.	10
The Ruler of Albion	Amass a 2.5 million gold real estate empire, or be there when another Hero does.	100
The Hoarder	Collect every silver key, or see another Hero do so.	25
The Goth	A Hero must dye their hair black, and wear a black outfit and black makeup.	5
The Completionist	Get all expressions, pet tricks and abilities, or see another Hero do so.	50
The Paragon	Reach 100% good or evil, or see another Hero do so.	15
The Extremist	Reach 100% purity or corruption, or see another Hero do so.	15
The Celebrity	Reach 50,000 renown, or see another Hero do so.	50
The Artisan	Succeed at one job to Level 5, or see another Hero do so.	10
The Dollcatcher	Collect all the Hero dolls, or see another Hero collect them.	10
The Muse	Inspire the Bard to compose songs celebrating your great deeds.	5
The Companions	Perform a perfect co-op expression.	10
The Double Threat	Get a co-op combat bonus.	10
The Philanthropist	Send a gift to an Xbox LIVE friend, or watch another Hero send one.	10
The Whippersnapper	A child Hero must collect five gold pieces.	25
The New Hero	The terror of Bower Lake must be defeated.	50
The Hero of Strength	Complete The Hero of Strength.	100
The Hero of Will	Complete The Hero of Will.	100
The Hero of Skill	Complete The Hero of Skill.	100
The Sacrifice	A Hero must choose 'The Needs of the Many'.	25
The Family	A Hero must choose 'The Needs of The Few'.	25
The Egomaniac	A Hero must choose 'The Needs of the One'.	25
The Collector	Acquire all the mystery items in The Box of Secrets shop, or see another Hero do so.	25
The Meteorologist	Bring all of Knothole Island's weather problems under control, or help another Hero to do so.	50

NAME	GOAL/REQUIREMENT	POINT VALUE
The Bibliophile	Find all the books detailing the history of Knothole Island, or help another Hero to do so.	25
The Nutcracker	Score 25 groin shots, or see another Hero do so.	10
The Paramour	Make love 25 times, or see another Hero do so.	10
The Concierge	Open all the Demon Doors in Albion, or see another Hero do so.	30
The Visionary	Take a look into the future, or see another Hero do so.	50
The Con Artist	Find all 10 of Murgo's statuettes, or see another Hero do so.	25
The Howler	Scare five people while dressed as a balverine, or see another Hero do so.	10
The Ghastly Jester	Make five people laugh while dressed as a hobbe, or see another Hero do so.	10
The Repugnant	Disgust five people while dressed as a hollow man, or see another Hero do so.	10
The Gladiator	Score a total high score of 20,000 points or more in the Colosseum, or see another Hero do so.	30
The Multiplicator	Achieve a multiplier of 10 or more in the Colosseum, or see another Hero do so.	20
The Combatant	Defeat the necromancer in the Colosseum, or see another Hero do so.	20
The Fowl Player	Dress as a chicken and kick five chickens during the Colosseum battles, or see another Hero do so.	10
The Colourist	Collect the dyes hidden in Murgo's magical items, or see another Hero do so.	15

FABLE 3

ACHIEVEMENTS

NAME	GOAL/REQUIREMENT	POINT VALUE
The Guild Seal	Unleash your heroic potential.	10
And So It Begins	Win the support of the Dwellers.	20
Swift Justice	Win the support of the Swift Brigade.	20
The Resistance	Win the support of Bowerstone.	50
Distant Friends	Win the support of Aurora.	20
The Ruler of Albion	Become the ruler of Albion.	80
For Albion!	This is where you *spoiler* the great, big *spoiler* and then it all *spoiler*.	80
Save The Princess!	Rescue the princess from the evil Baron.	10
Ghost Brothers	Make sure Max and Sam get home in time for tea.	10
Tragical-Comical-Historical	Help the celebrated thespians Lambert and Pinch put on the world's greatest play.	10
The Dark Sanctum	Reinstate an ancient, evil temple.	10
Island Paradise	Establish the island of Driftwood.	10
Knight Jumps Chesty	Defeat Chesty at his own game.	10
Coronation Chicken	Perform a royal judgment while dressed as a chicken.	10
Spellweaver	Combine two gauntlets to cast a "woven" spell.	5
Archmage	Cast all 15 possible spell combinations.	20
Total Warrior	Kill enemies with melee, ranged and spell attacks.	10
Pull!	Send an enemy flying into the air and kill him while he's airborne.	10
Gunning For Glory	Kill 500 enemies using firearms.	20
If It Bleeds, We Can Kill It	Kill 500 enemies using melee weapons.	20
Wizard's Revenge	Kill 500 enemies using magic.	20
Super Hero	Fully upgrade your Melee, Ranged, and Magic abilities on the Road to Rule.	50
You Can't Bring Me Down	Complete Fable III without being knocked out in combat.	50
My Weapon's Better Than Yours	Complete 3 unique upgrades on one of the legendary weapons found around Albion.	25
I Am The Keymaster	Collect all 50 Silver Keys and 4 Gold Keys.	30
Flower Power	Collect all 30 Auroran flowers.	30
Gnome Invasion	Destroy all 50 gnomes.	30

NAME	GOAL/REQUIREMENT	POINT VALUE
Brightwall Book Club	Collect all 30 rare books for the Brightwall Academy.	30
Digger	Dig up 50 items.	15
We Need Guns, Lots Of Guns	Collect all 50 legendary weapons. They won't all appear in your world, so trade with other Heroes!	20
Fashion Victim	Collect every item of clothing.	20
He's a Woman. She's a Man	Wear a full set of clothing intended for the opposite sex.	5
Dye Hippie, Dye	Dye each part of an outfit you're wearing a different color and have long hair.	5
Hand in Hand	Hold hands with someone.	5
Long Distance Relationship	Get married to another Xbox LIVE player.	10
Cross-Dimensional Conception	Have a child with another Xbox LIVE player.	10
Online Merger	Enter into a business partnership with another Xbox LIVE player.	10
Barrel of Laughs	Kill 30 enemies with explosive barrels.	10
We Can Be Heroes	Earn 1,000 gold in henchman wages in another Hero's world.	10
Kaboom!	Score 2000 on the Mourningwood Fort mortar game.	10
Lute Hero Tour	Play in each town as a 5 star lute player.	10
Touched By A Hero	Use touch expressions to interact with 20 different people.	10
Popularity Contest	Make 20 Friends.	15
Remodelling	Remodel 5 different houses by changing the furniture.	10
Magnate Personality	Build a property empire worth 2,000,000 gold.	50
Crime Spree	Get a 15,000 gold bounty placed on your head.	10
Henry VIII	As ruler of Albion, get married 6 times and kill 2 of your spouses.	10
Chest Grandmaster	Unlock all of the chests on the Road To Rule.	40
Tough Love	Save the maximum amount of Albion citizens.	10
Adopt Or Die	Adopt a child.	5

FALLOUT: NEW VEGAS

ACHIEVEMENTS

NAME	GOAL/REQUIREMENT	POINT VALUE
New Kid	Reach 10th level.	10
Up and Comer	Reach 20th level.	20
The Boss	Reach 30th level.	30
Ol' Buddy Ol' Pal	Recruit any companion.	10
The Whole Gang's Here	Recruit all companions.	25
Crafty	Craft 20 items.	15
Mod Machine	Install 20 weapon mods.	15
Walker of the Mojave	Discover 50 locations.	10
Master of the Mojave	Discover 125 locations.	25
Globe Trotter	Discover all snow globes.	25
You Run Barter Town	Sell 10,000 caps worth of goods.	15
Blast Mastery	Cause 10,000 damage with Energy Weapons.	15
Love the Bomb	Cause 10,000 damage with Explosives.	15
Lead Dealer	Cause 10,000 damage with Guns.	15
No Tumbler Fumbler	Pick 25 locks.	15
Stim-ply Amazing	Heal 10,000 points of damage with Stimpaks.	15
New Vegas Samurai	Cause 10,000 damage with Melee Weapons.	15
Jury Rigger	Repair 30 items.	15
Hack the Mojave	Hack 25 terminals.	15
Artful Pocketer	Pick 50 pockets.	15
Outstanding Orator	Make 50 Speech challenges.	15
Desert Survivalist	Heal 10,000 points of damage with food.	15
Old-Tyme Brawler	Cause 10,000 damage with Unarmed weapons.	15
Know When to Fold Them	Win 3 games of Caravan.	10

NAME	GOAL/REQUIREMENT	POINT VALUE
One Armed Bandit	Play 10 spins of Slots.	10
Little Wheel	Play 10 spins of Roulette.	10
Double Down	Play 10 hands of Blackjack.	10
Caravan Master	Win 30 games of Caravan.	30
The Courier Who Broke the Bank	Get banned from all the Strip's casinos.	30
Hardcore	Play the game from start to finish in Hardcore Mode.	100
Ain't That a Kick in the Head	Complete Ain't That a Kick in the Head.	10
They Went That-a-Way	Complete They Went That-a-Way.	25
Ring-a-Ding-Ding	Complete Ring-a-Ding-Ding.	25
The House Always Wins	Complete The House Always Wins.	30
For the Republic	Complete For the Republic.	30
Render Unto Caesar	Complete Render Unto Caesar.	30
Wild Card	Complete Wild Card.	30
All or Nothing	Complete All or Nothing.	15
Veni, Vidi, Vici	Complete Veni, Vidi, Vici.	15
Eureka!	Complete Eureka!	15
No Gods, No Masters	Complete No Gods, No Masters.	15
Come Fly With Me	Complete Come Fly With Me.	20
Talent Pool	Complete Talent Pool.	20
Return to Sender	Complete Return to Sender.	20
Arizona Killer	Complete Arizona Killer.	20
You'll Know It When It Happens	Complete You'll Know It When It Happens.	20
G.I. Blues	Complete G.I. Blues.	20
That Lucky Old Sun	Complete That Lucky Old Sun.	20
Volare!	Complete Volare!	20
The Legend of the Star	Complete The Legend of the Star.	20

FIFA 11

ACHIEVEMENTS

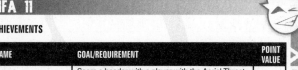

XBOX 360 ACHIEVEMENTS

NAME	GOAL/REQUIREMENT	POINT VALUE
Aerial Threat	Score a header with a player with the Aerial Threat Specialty	10
Against the Odds	Win a Head to Head Ranked Match using a weaker team	10
All My Own Work	Win a Match with Manual Controls (auto-switching must be set to 'Manual')	10
Always Friendly	Cross for a Friend to score	10
Anything in Particular?	Visit the FIFA 11 Store	5
Around the World	Play a match with a team from every league	25
Back of the Net	Score 5 goals in one Arena kick-about	5
Club Glory	Win the Cup as part of an online Pro Club	25
Crosser	Create a goal with a cross with a player with the Crossing Specialty	10
Distance Shooter	Score from outside the box with a player with the Distance Shooter Specialty	10
Eat My Goal	Upload a Video to EA SPORTS™ Football World	5
Established Keeper	Play a season as a Goalkeeper in Career Mode	50
Experimental	Play 5 consecutive Head to Head Ranked Matches with different teams	15
First Time Out	Win an online Friends League match	10
Folklore	Become a Legend as a player in Career Mode	25
Founding Member	Include a Creation Centre Team in a Kick-Off match	25
Good Form	Play 5 consecutive Head to Head Ranked Matches without losing	20
Home & Away	Play & win in every Stadium	50
Home Maker	Change the Home Stadium of any team	5
Hundred & Counting	Play 100 Head to Head Ranked Matches	100

NAME	GOAL/REQUIREMENT	POINT VALUE
In for the Win	Take a Head to Head Ranked Match to extra time with a weaker team	10
In the Game	Create a Virtual Pro	5
It's in the Blood!	Go from being a Player to the Manager (or Player Manager) in Career Mode	25
Look at me!	Download your Game Face from EA SPORTS™ Football World	25
Mastermind	Have a substitute score a goal in Career Mode	10
New Choons	Import your own sounds into the game using the Custom Music & Chants feature	10
Once in a lifetime	Score as the Goalkeeper in any match	10
One Club Man	Play 50 matches for the same online Pro Club	50
One to Remember	Save a highlight to the Replay Theatre	5
Perfect Keeping	Play as the Goalkeeper in a Kick-Off match & finish with 100% Saving Accuracy	15
Picture Perfect	Upload a Screenshot to EA SPORTS™ Football World	5
Playmaker	Create a goal with a player with the Playmaker Specialty	10
Poacher	Score from inside the box with a player with the Poacher Specialty	10
Record Holder	Get your name on any Career Mode Leaderboard	25
Rising Talent	Complete 100 Accomplishments with your Virtual Pro	25
Safe Hands	Play any match as the Goalkeeper with no Assistance	10
Team Training	Play a Practice Match with your online Pro Club	10
Training Time	Work on your skills in any Arena Practice Mode	5
Virtual Debut	Play an online Pro Club or Pro Ranked match with your Virtual Pro	25
Virtual Football	Play a Pro Clubs match as a team of 10 or more	25
Virtual Legend	Play 500 matches with your Virtual Pro	100
Warming the Gloves	Make 10 saves in 1 Arena kick-about	10
Woodwork & In!	Score off the post or cross bar in a match	10
Good Week!	Get yourself selected in the Team of the Week in Career Mode	15
Great Month!	Win the Manager of the Month award in Career Mode	25

SECRET ACHIEVEMENTS

NAME	GOAL/REQUIREMENT	POINT VALUE
FIFA for Life	Spend 50 hours on the pitch	100

FINAL FANTASY ✕III

ACHIEVEMENTS

NAME	GOAL/REQUIREMENT	POINT VALUE
Commando's Seal	Mastered the Commando role.	15
Ravager's Seal	Mastered the Ravager role.	15
Sentinel's Seal	Mastered the Sentinel role.	15
Saboteur's Seal	Mastered the Saboteur role.	15
Synergist's Seal	Mastered the Synergist role.	15
Medic's Seal	Mastered the Medic role.	15
Limit Breaker	Dealt 100,000+ damage with a single attack.	30
Adamant Will	Felled a heavyweight of the lowerworld wilds.	30
Master's Seal	Fully developed all characters.	30
Treasure Hunter	Held every weapon and accessory.	80
Loremaster	Discerned the full attributes of 100 enemies.	80

SECRET ACHIEVEMENTS

NAME	GOAL/REQUIREMENT	POINT VALUE
Instrument of Fate	Took the first steps toward challenging an unjust fate.	15
Instrument of Dissent	Survived the Purge to confront a greater peril.	15

NAME	GOAL/REQUIREMENT	POINT VALUE
Instrument of Tragedy	Strode into danger's den and paid the consequences.	15
Instrument of Flight	Slipped through the net and lived to fight the day.	15
Instrument of Vengeance	Resolved to be more than a victim of circumstance,	15
Instrument of Survival	Evaded pursuers, though memories of the past still gave chase.	15
Instrument of Rebellion	Made plans to infiltrate enemy-occupied territory.	15
Instrument of Shame	Carried the burden of guilt to the end of the line.	15
Instrument of Wrath	Took the fight to the enemy's door.	15
Instrument of Truth	Recognized the true threat to the world's future.	15
Instrument of Hope	Traveled to the world below, seeking a way to alternate fate.	15
Instrument of Faith	Defied destiny's charge and embarked on a different path.	30
Instrument of Change	Witnessed the dawn of a new crystal legend.	95
Pulsian Pioneer	Took over 10,000 steps on the lowerworld surface	15
Gysahl Wreath	Discovered buried treasure with a little help from a chocobo.	15
Kelger's Cup	Completed all low-level Cie'th Stone missions.	15
Xezat's Chalice	Completed all mid-level Cie'th Stone missions.	15
Dorgann's Trophy	Completed all high-level Cie'th Stone missions.	30
Galuf's Grail	Completed all Cie'th Stone missions.	30
L'Cie Paragon	Earned a 5-star ranking for all Cie'th Stone missions.	80
Exorcist	Triumphed over undying lowerworld souls in seven fierce battles.	30
Floraphobe	Toppled a green terror and cut an oversized succulent down to size.	30
Natural Selector	Passed Titan's trials.	30
Superstar	Earned a 5-star ranking in the battle to determine the world's fate.	80

GEARS OF WAR 2

ACHIEVEMENTS

NAME	GOAL/REQUIREMENT	POINT VALUE
Green as Grass	Train the rook (any difficulty)	10
It's a Trap!	Story progression in Act 1, Chapter 2	10
Escort Service	Story progression in Act 1, Chapter 4	10
Girl About Town	Story progression in Act 1, Chapter 6	10
That Sinking Feeling	Story progression in Act 2, Chapter 4	10
Freebaird!	Story progression in Act 2, Chapter 5	10
Heartbroken	Story progression in Act 2, Chapter 6	10
Longitude and Attitude	Story progression in Act 3, Chapter 3	10
Tanks for the Memories	Story progression in Act 3, Chapter 4	10
Water Sports	Story progression in Act 3, Chapter 6	10
There's a Time for Us	Story progression in Act 4, Chapter 2	10
Better Wrapped in Beacon	Story progression in Act 4, Chapter 3	10
Have Fun Storming the Castle	Story progression in Act 4, Chapter 6	10
And the Horse You Rode in On	Story progression in Act 5, Chapter 1	10
You Are the Support, Son	Story progression in Act 5, Chapter 2	10
Brumak Rodeo	Story progression in Act 5, Chapter 4	10
Does This Look Infected to You?	Story progression in Act 5, Chapter 5	10
Tourist of Duty	Complete all campaign acts on Casual Difficulty	25
Guerilla Tactician	Complete all campaign acts on Normal Difficulty	50
Artist of War	Complete all campaign acts on Hardcore Difficulty	75
Suicide Missionary	Complete all campaign acts on Insane Difficulty	150
Collector	Recover 5 collectibles (any difficulty)	5
Name	Goal/Requirement	Point Value

NAME	GOAL/REQUIREMENT	POINT VALUE
Pack Rat	Recover 20 collectibles (any difficulty)	15
Completionist	Recover all 41 collectibles (any difficulty)	30
One-Night Stand	Complete 1 chapter in co-op on any difficulty (Marcus or Dom)	10
Open Relationship	Complete 10 chapters in co-op on any difficulty (Marcus or Dom)	30
Friends with Benefits	Complete all acts in co-op on any difficulty (Marcus or Dom)	50
Once More, With Feeling	Perform 30 perfect active reloads (any mode)	10
Takes a Licking	Melee 30 Tickers (any mode)	30
Organ Grinder	Kill 30 enemies with a cover mounted Mulcher (any mode)	10
Shock and Awe	Kill 30 enemies with the heavy Mortar (any mode)	10
Said the Spider to the Fly	Kill 10 enemies with a planted grenade (any mode)	10
Crowd Control	Melee 10 enemies down with the Boomshield equipped (any mode)	10
Smells Like Victory	Kill 30 enemies with the Scorcher Flamethrower (any mode)	10
Variety is the Spice of Death	Kill an enemy with every weapon in the game (any mode)	30
Seriously 2.0	Kill 100,000 enemies (any mode)	50
Standing Here, Beside Myself	Win 3 matches of Wingman (public)	10
Beat the Meatflag	Capture 10 meatflags in Submission (public)	10
It's Good to be the King	Win 10 rounds of Guardian as the leader (public)	10
You Go Ahead, I'll Be Fine	Win three matches of King of the Hill (public)	10
Back to Basic	Successfully complete the 5 lessons of multiplayer Training Grounds	10
Party Like It's 1999	Play 1999 rounds of multiplayer (any mode)	30
Around the World, Again	Win a multiplayer match on each map (any mode)	30
Dirty, Dirty Horde	Survive the first 10 waves of Horde (any difficulty, any map)	20
Hoard the Horde	Survive all 50 waves of Horde (any difficulty, any map)	30
Crossed Swords	Win 10 chainsaw duels (any mode)	10
A Parting Gift	Kill 10 enemies with a grenade while down but not out (any mode)	20
Pound of Flesh	Use a meatshield to save your life 10 times (any mode)	10
Photojournalist	Submit a spectator photo	10
Kick 'Em When They're Down	Perform all 11 unique executions on a downed enemy	10

GRAND THEFT AUTO IV: THE BALLAD OF GAY TONY

ACHIEVEMENTS

NAME	GOAL/REQUIREMENT	POINT VALUE
TBoGT: Gone Down	Complete all base jumps.	5
TBoGT: Diamonds Forever	Complete the Trinity.	5
TBoGT: Four Play	Hit a flag with a golf ball four times.	10
TBoGT: Bear Fight	Win the L.C. Cage Fighters championship.	15
TBoGT: Catch the Bus	Dance perfectly in both Tony's nightclubs.	15
TBoGT: Snow Queen	Complete 25 drug wars.	20
TBoGT: Adrenaline Junkie	Freefall for the longest possible time.	25
TBoGT: Maestro	Finish the Ballad.	30
TBoGT: Past the Velvet Rope	Score 80% or above in all missions.	45
TBoGT: Gold Star	Score 100% in all missions.	80

GAME COMPLETION ON HARDCORE

CAMPAIGN ACH	TYPE	DIFFICULTY	PTS	DESCRIPTION
Completed Act 1 on Hardcore	Campaign	Medium	20	Complete Act 1 on Hardcore Difficulty.
Completed Act 2 on Hardcore	Campaign	Medium	20	Complete Act 2 on Hardcore Difficulty.
Completed Act 3 on Hardcore	Campaign	Medium	20	Complete Act 3 on Hardcore Difficulty.
Completed Act 4 on Hardcore	Campaign	Medium	20	Complete Act 4 on Hardcore Difficulty.
Completed Act 5 on Hardcore	Campaign	Medium	20	Complete Act 5 on Hardcore Difficulty.
Soldier (unlocks Gamer Pic)	Campaign	Medium	20	Complete all Acts on Hardcore Difficulty.

GAME COMPLETION ON INSANE

CAMPAIGN ACH	TYPE	DIFFICULTY	PTS	DESCRIPTION
Completed Act 1 on Insane	Campaign	Hard	30	Complete Act 1 on Insane Difficulty.
Completed Act 2 on Insane	Campaign	Hard	30	Complete Act 2 on Insane Difficulty.
Completed Act 3 on Insane	Campaign	Hard	30	Complete Act 3 on Insane Difficulty.
Completed Act 4 on Insane	Campaign	Hard	30	Complete Act 4 on Insane Difficulty.
Completed Act 5 on Insane	Campaign	Hard	30	Complete Act 5 on Insane Difficulty.
Commando (unlocks Gamer Pic)	Campaign	Hard	30	Complete all Acts on Insane Difficulty.

COG TAGS

CAMPAIGN ACH	TYPE	DIFFICULTY	PTS	DESCRIPTION
Time to Remember	Campaign	Easy	10	Recover 10 COG Tags (on any difficulty).
Honor Bound	Campaign	Medium	20	Recover 20 COG Tags (on any difficulty).
For the Fallen	Campaign	Hard	30	Recover 30 COG Tags (on any difficulty).

KILLING BOSSES

CAMPAIGN ACH	TYPE	DIFFICULTY	PTS	DESCRIPTION
My Love for You is Like a Truck	Campaign	Hard	30	Defeat a Berserker on Hardcore Difficulty.
Broken Fingers	Campaign	Hard	30	Defeat a Corpser on Hardcore Difficulty.
A Dish Best Served Cold	Campaign	Hard	30	Defeat General RAAM on Hardcore Difficulty.

GAME SKILLS

CAMPAIGN ACH	TYPE	DIFFICULTY	PTS	DESCRIPTION
Zen and the Art of Reloading	Campaign	Easy	10	Perform 25 Perfect Active Reloads (on any difficulty).
Zen and the Art Part 2	Campaign	Medium	20	Perform 5 Perfect Active Reloads in a row (on any difficulty).
Clusterluck	Campaign	Medium	20	Kill 3 enemies at once 10 different times (on any difficulty).

CO-OP ACHIEVEMENTS

CO-OP SPECIFIC ACH	TYPE	DIFFICULTY	PTS	DESCRIPTION
Dom-curious	Co-op	Easy	10	Complete 1 chapter as Dominic Santiago on any difficulty.
Domination	Co-op	Medium	20	Complete 10 chapters as Dominic Santiago on any difficulty.
I Can't Quit You Dom	Co-op	Hard	30	Complete all Acts in Co-Op on any difficulty.

VERSUS ACHIEVEMENTS

VERSUS ACH	TYPE	DIFFICULTY	PTS	DESCRIPTION
Don't You Die on Me	Versus	Easy	10	Revive 100 teammates in Ranked Matches.
A Series of Tubes	Versus	Medium	20	Host 50 complete Ranked Matches.

XBOX 360 ACHIEVEMENTS

WEAPON MASTERY

CAMPAIGN ACH	TYPE	DIFFICULTY	PTS	DESCRIPTION
Fall Down Go Boom	Versus	Easy	10	Kill 100 enemies in Ranked Matches with the Boomshot.
Pistolero	Versus	Medium	20	Kill 100 enemies in Ranked Matches with a Pistol.
The Nuge	Versus	Medium	20	Kill 100 enemies in Ranked Matches with the Torquebow.
I Spy With My Little Eye	Versus	Medium	20	Kill 100 enemies in Ranked Matches with the Longshot.
Don't Hurt 'Em	Versus	Medium	20	Kill 100 enemies in Ranked Matches with the Hammer of Dawn.

HUMILIATION MASTERY

CAMPAIGN ACH	TYPE	DIFFICULTY	PTS	DESCRIPTION
It's a Massacre	Versus	Easy	10	Kill 100 enemies in Ranked Matches with the Chainsaw.
Curb Appeal	Versus	Medium	20	Kill 100 enemies in Ranked Matches with the Curb Stomp.
Capital Punishment	Versus	Medium	20	Kill 100 enemies in Ranked Matches with an Execution.
Crackdown	Versus	Medium	20	Kill 100 enemies in Ranked Matches with Melee.
Is it a Spider?	Versus	Medium	20	Kill 100 enemies in Ranked Matches with Grenade Tag.
The Money Shot	Versus	Medium	20	Kill 100 enemies in Ranked Matches with a Head Shot.

VERSUS SUCCESS

CAMPAIGN ACH	TYPE	DIFFICULTY	PTS	DESCRIPTION
Always Remember Your First	Versus	Easy	10	Finish playing a Versus Ranked Match.
Don't Hate the Player	Versus	Easy	10	Finish with the highest points in a Ranked Match.
Mix it Up	Versus	Medium	20	Win a Ranked Match in every Versus game type.
Can't Touch Us	Versus	Medium	20	Win 10 Ranked Matches without losing a Round.
Around the World	Versus	Hard	30	Win a Ranked Match on every Versus map.
Seriously… (unlocks Gamer Pic)	Versus	Hard	50	Kill 10,000 people in Versus Ranked Match total.

GRAND THEFT AUTO IV: THE LOST AND DAMNED

ACHIEVEMENTS

NAME	GOAL/REQUIREMENT	POINT VALUE
TLAD: One Percenter	Help Billy get his bike back.	5
TLAD: The Lost Boy	Become leader of The Lost.	25
TLAD: Easy Rider	Finish the story.	100
TLAD: Get Good Wood	In the bike races, whack off 69 bikers with a bat.	50
TLAD: Full Chat	Build Terry and Clay's toughness to 100%.	70

GUITAR HERO 5

ACHIEVEMENTS

NAME	GOAL/REQUIREMENT	POINT VALUE
Fest Quartet Quest	Play 10 4-Player RockFest Mode games of any type	20
The Grand Tour	Unlock every venue in the world, and then some	30
Going Gold	Complete 50 of the challenges at Gold or better	20
Going Platinum	Complete 50 of the challenges at Platinum or better	30
Going Diamond	Complete 50 of the challenges at Diamond	50
Iron Lungs	Complete a 25-phrase streak as a Vocalist	20

NAME	GOAL/REQUIREMENT	POINT VALUE
Sampler Plate	Play at least one song in Quickplay, Career and each Competitive game type	30
Producer	Create a music studio song	10
The Fabricated Four	Create a band of 4 created rockers and play a song with them	10
Quadruple Threat	Complete at least one challenge for every instrument at Gold level or better	30
Rocktopus	Make a standard 8 player Band v Band match online, win or lose	20
Ménage à Huit	Play an online match with 8 players, all on the same instrument	20
Outgoing	Complete 25 Pro Face Off matches online (Win or Lose)	10
Barbershop	Play a song with 4 Vocalists	10
Drumline	Play a song with 4 Drummers	10
String Quartet	Play a song with 4 Lead Guitarists	10
All Four Bass Are Belong to Us	Play a song with 4 Bass Guitarists	10
Explore the Studio Space	Read 5 Tooltips in GHMix	10
Play It To The Bone	Make and complete a setlist which is at least 1 hour long	20
Challenge of the Supergroup	Complete 5 band challenges at Gold or better	20
Crowd Pleaser	Fill your Rock Meter all the way	5
What's an LP?	Complete 14 songs in Quickplay	20
Young Star	Collect 25 Stars in Career	10
Rising Star	Collect 101 Stars in Career	20
Shooting Star	Collect 303 Stars in Career	30
Senior Commander	Earn 5 or more Stars on a song in Career or Quickplay	10
Super Star	Collect 505 Stars in Career	50
You Want More?	Play 5 encore gigs	10
Synchronized	Complete 20 Band Moments	10
The Streak	Complete a 1001 note streak	30
Crank It Up To 11	Achieve a maxed out band multiplier as a standard band	20
What's New?	Complete any tutorial's lesson on a new feature	5
No Mistakes Allowed	Streak through the entirety of a song in Quickplay or Career	20
Above And Beyond	Complete a song with an average individual multiplier above 4x	10
Score Big	Earn 500,000 points in a single song as a solo act	5
Score Bigger	Earn 1,000,000 points in a single song as a solo act or band	10
Score Biggest	Earn 3,000,000 points in a single song as a band	30
Our Powers Combined	As a 4 player standard band, all 4 players activate Star Power simultaneously	10
Box Set	Complete 100 songs in Quickplay	20
Juke Box	Complete 300 songs in Quickplay	30
Chanteuse	5 Star 'Ex-Girlfriend', 'Send A Little Love Token' and 'Only Happy When It Rains' as a Vocalist	10
Star Cluster	Collect 808 Stars in Career	100
Special Guest	Complete a song with your Xbox 360 Avatar	10
Representative	Complete a sponsor gig challenge at Diamond level	5

SECRET ACHIEVEMENTS

NAME	GOAL/REQUIREMENT	POINT VALUE
Over 9000!	Went super	5
Open Minded	Gave every one a chance	50
Starstruck	Had a brush with celebrity	20
Did You Finish Like We Did?	Came alive	5
The Traditional	Beat the game	50

GUITAR HERO: VAN HALEN

ACHIEVEMENTS

NAME	GOAL/REQUIREMENT	POINT VALUE
Have You Seen His Grades?	Complete a tutorial level.	5
It's Alive	Unlock Eddie's Frankenstein guitar.	5
Ouch!	Create a custom tattoo.	5
Intruder	Complete the career intro.	10
Van Halen	Complete a career on Beginner. (Band or Solo)	10
Every Band Wants Some!!	Complete a song with the full band. (4 player band)	10
They Ran With the Devil	All band members get a 50 note streak at the same time. (4 player band)	10
Somebody Get Them a Doctor	Hit 100% of the notes in a song as a band. (4 player band)	10
Atomic Power Punk	All band members activate Star Power at the same time. (4 player band)	10
Hung High	All band members earn an 8x multiplier at the same time. (4 player band)	10
EVH	Unlock all of the Van Halen instruments.	10
The Broken Combs	Complete a gig in West Hollywood.	15
Ain't Talkin' 'Bout Dallas	Complete a gig in Dallas.	15
Far Away Lands	Complete gigs in London and The Netherlands.	15
The Space Brothers	Complete gigs in Los Angeles and Rome.	15
Van Halen II	Complete a career on Easy. (Band or Solo)	15
Jump	Complete all Van Halen songs. (Band or Solo Career)	15
Rock Out Big Cities	Complete gigs in Berlin and New York City.	20
Unchained	Unlock all Van Halen characters.	20
Women and Children First	Complete a career on Medium. (Band or Solo)	25
Fair Warning	Complete a career on Hard. (Band or Solo)	35
The Tour is Ending	Complete a majority of the gigs. (Band or Solo)	35
Diver Down	Complete a career on Expert. (Band or Solo)	45
1984	Complete a career on Expert+. (Solo Drum)	55
The Woodshed	5 star guitar for 'Little Guitars', 'Cathedral', 'Spanish Fly', and 'Eruption'. (expert)	60
316	5 star all Van Halen songs on Bass Career. (expert)	65
Diamond in the Rough	5 star all Van Halen songs on Vocal Career. (expert)	70
Double Bass Master	5 star all Van Halen songs on Drum Career. (expert)	75
Guitar God	5 star all Van Halen songs on Guitar Career. (expert)	100
5150	Complete all Van Halen songs on every instrument. (Guitar, Bass, Drums, and Vocals)	100

SECRET ACHIEVEMENTS

NAME	GOAL/REQUIREMENT	POINT VALUE
Can I Borrow A Quarter?	You created a custom guitar.	5
Bang your Gong	Created a custom drum set.	5
Brown Sound	You rocked out as classic Eddie.	5
Break that String	You completed the song 'I Want It All' as Eddie playing guitar.	5
Beaten	You won a guest artist song playing with Eddie.	5
Born to Rock	You rocked out as classic Wolfgang.	5
The Ice Cream Man	You won a guest artist song playing with Dave.	5
Diamond Dave	You rocked out as classic Dave.	5
King Arthur	You rocked out as classic Alex.	5
I Have a Sound System	You created a band named 'Van Halen.'	5
Respect the Wind	You won a guest artist song playing with Alex.	5
Good Times	You performed on every instrument with a member of Van Halen.	10
I'm the One	You scored 225,000 playing 'I'm the One' on expert guitar.	10
You Really Got Me	You won a song as a band with Eddie, Alex, and Wolfgang.	10

NAME	GOAL/REQUIREMENT	POINT VALUE
Hot For High Scores	You scored 800,000 playing 'Hot for Teacher' with your band.	10
No Brown M&M's!!	You are now like a Van Halen encyclopedia!	15

GUITAR HERO: WARRIORS OF ROCK

ACHIEVEMENTS

NAME	GOAL/REQUIREMENT	POINT VALUE
Tracker of Deeds	Follow any five Hero Feed items (Xbox LIVE only)	10
Anthemic Archivist	Expand your song library to at least 115 songs of any type. Be creative!	10
Stellar Centurion	Deploy Star Power a total of 100 times (Quest)	20
Gem Collector	Hit a cumulative total of 75,000 notes (Quest)	20
Gem Hoarder	Hit a cumulative total of 150,000 notes (Quest)	30
Champion of Challenges	Target another person's score on any Challenge and earn a higher grade than they did (Local QP+)	20
Self Improver	Target your own score on a Challenge and earn a higher grade than you did previously (Local QP+)	10
Ultimate Answerer	Earn all Stars from any one song (excluding the Power Challenge) (QP+)	30
Scions of Excess	Earn an 11x Band multiplier with any 4-player Band configuration (QP+)	20
Player of the Ear Worm	Play any one non-GH(tm)Tracks song 10 or more times (QP+, Quest, Competitive)	10
Patron of the Arts	5-Star any GH(tm)Tracks song containing at least 200 notes (QP+)	10
Apostates of Orthodoxy	5-Star any song as a 4-player Non-Standard Band, with all players on Medium or higher (QP+)	10
Bearers of the Standard	5-Star any song as a 4-player Standard Band, with all players on Medium or higher (QP+)	10
Mythical Millionaire	Earn 1,000,000 points or more in a single play of a song in a Power Challenge (QP+)	20
Manager of Fate	Create and play a custom playlist of at least 5 songs, and earn 5 Stars on 5 of the songs (QP+)	10
Mocker of Fate	Create and play a 5-song random playlist, earning 5 Stars on each song (QP+)	10
Nauseous Numerologist	Beat any song with a final score of 133,337 (QP+, Competitive)	10
Mathematic Sharpshooters	Beat any song with a final score ending in 000 as a Band (QP+)	10
Gold Master	As a single player, earn Gold or higher on three or more Challenges on a single play of a song (QP+)	20
Diamond Master	As a single player, earn Diamond on two or more Challenges on a single play of a song (QP+)	20
Quick Learner	Full-Combo any tutorial exercise (no missed notes or overstrums)	10
The Siren	Recruit Warrior Judy (Quest)	20
The Trickster	Unleash Warrior Johnny (Quest)	20
The Vigil	Charm Warrior Casey (Quest)	20
The Brute	Release Warrior Lars (Quest)	20
The Eternal	Awaken Warrior Axel (Quest)	20
The Dynamo	Liberate Warrior Echo (Quest)	20
Divine Liberator	Free the Demigod of Rock (Quest)	30
Axe Claimer	Regain the Legendary Guitar (Quest)	30
Savior of Rock	Defeat the scourge of Rock (Quest)	50
Amateur Astrologer	Earn a total of 100 Stars (QP+)	10
Accomplished Astrologer	Earn a total of 500 Stars (QP+)	10
Adept Astrologer	Earn a total of 1000 Stars (QP+)	40
Pseudo Perfectionist	Dominate any 2 chapters of Quest (Earn all the Power Stars from any 2 chapters of Quest)	20
Ace Astrologer	Earn a total of 2000 Stars (QP+)	60
Partial Perfectionist	Dominate any 4 chapters of Quest (Earn all the Power Stars from any 4 chapters of Quest)	20
Perfect Perfectionist	Earn all the Power Stars from all character chapters (Quest)	60

OVERLOAD

XBOX 360 ACHIEVEMENTS

NAME	GOAL/REQUIREMENT	POINT VALUE
Motivated Improviser	Play 100 notes in a single GH(tm)Jam session	10
String Twins	Complete a song with only a Guitarist and Bassist, both earning the same score (QP+)	30
Altered Virtuoso	Earn 40 Power Stars on a single song (Quest)	20
Poor Boys	Beat Bohemian Rhapsody as a band with all on Medium or higher, and at least 2 vocalists (QP+)	10
The Meek	Beat 2112 Part 4 as a Standard band with 3 or more members, all on Medium or higher difficulty (QP+)	10
Giant Slayer	Beat Holy Wars... The Punishment Due as a solo Bassist on Hard or higher difficulty (QP+)	10
Chosen One	Beat Fury of the Storm as a solo Drummer on Hard or higher difficulty (QP+)	20
Hand Mutilator	Beat Black Widow of La Porte as a solo Expert Guitarist (QP+, no Powers)	30
The Recluse	Invoke Warrior Austin (Quest)	20
The Exalted	Summon Warrior Pandora (Quest)	20
Lucifer's Accountant	Beat any song with a final score which is evenly divisible by 6 (QP+)	10
Gold Standard	As a Standard Band, earn Gold or higher on 2 Band Challenges in a single play of a song (QP+)	20
Seasoned Competitor	Play Pro Faceoff, Momentum, Momentum+, Streakers, Do or Die, and Perfectionist at least once each	20

HALO 3: ODST

ACHIEVEMENTS

NAME	GOAL/REQUIREMENT	POINT VALUE
Listener	Find the first Audio Log.	5
Naughty Naughty	Killing things that are new and different is good, alone or with another ODST.	5
Tuned In	Find 3 Audio Logs, alone or with another ODST.	15
Audiophile	Find all Audio Logs, alone or with another ODST.	75
All Ears	Find 15 Audio Logs, alone or with another ODST.	30
Good Samaritan	Killing things that are new and different is bad, alone or with another ODST.	20
Both Tubes	Get 10 Rocket kills on Kizingo Boulevard.	5
Wraith Killer	Kill all Wraiths in Uplift Reserve.	5
Laser Blaster	Get 10 Spartan Laser kills on ONI Alpha Site.	5
I Like Fire	Kill 10 enemies with the Flamethrower on Data Hive.	5
Dome Inspector	Get 15 headshot kills on NMPD HQ.	5
Be Like Marty	In Firefight, finish a full round without killing a single enemy.	10
Firefight: Last Exit	Score over 200,000 points in Firefight on Last Exit.	10
Firefight: Chasm Ten	Score over 200,000 points in Firefight on Chasm Ten.	10
Vidmaster Challenge: Classic	Finish any level solo on Legendary, on LIVE, with no shots fired or grenades thrown.	25
Vidmaster Challenge: Déjà Vu	Complete Highway on 4-player Legendary LIVE co-op, with Iron, and no 'Hog or Scorpion.	25
Vidmaster Challenge: Endure	In Firefight, on any mission, pass the 4th Set on 4-player Heroic LIVE co-op.	25
Firefight: Windward	Score over 200,000 points in Firefight on Windward.	10
Firefight: Lost Platoon	Score over 200,000 points in Firefight on Lost Platoon.	10
Firefight: Crater	Score over 200,000 points in Firefight on Crater.	10
Firefight: Rally Point	Score over 200,000 points in Firefight on Rally Point.	10
Firefight: Alpha Site	Score over 200,000 points in Firefight on Alpha Site.	10
Firefight: Security Zone	Score over 200,000 points in Firefight on Security Zone.	10
Super Sleuth	Find the final clue unraveling the mystery, alone or with another ODST.	10
Pink and Deadly	Get 10 Needler supercombine kills on any covenant.	5
My Clothes!	Plasma Pistol Overcharge and quickly kill 10 Brutes.	5
Trading Down	Trade weapons with a fellow character.	5
Tayari Plaza	Complete Tayari Plaza on Normal, Heroic, or Legendary to unlock a new Firefight character.	30

NAME	GOAL/REQUIREMENT	POINT VALUE
Headcase	Finish any level with at least one Skull activated.	5
Ewww, Sticky	Get 5 sticky grenade kills in any level.	5
Tourist	Access and download the city map to your VISR.	5
Heal Up	Find the first Medical Kiosk and heal yourself.	5
Dark Times	Kill 5 enemies while using VISR mode.	5
Stunning!	Stun a vehicle with an overcharged plasma pistol and quickly kill the driver.	5
Boom, Headshot	Get 10 automag headshot kills in any level.	5
Uplift Reserve	Complete Uplift Reserve on Normal, Heroic, or Legendary to unlock a new Firefight character.	30
Campaign Complete: Heroic	Complete the Campaign on Heroic difficulty.	100
Campaign Complete: Normal	Complete the Campaign on Normal difficulty.	100
Campaign Complete: Legendary	Complete the Campaign on Legendary to unlock a new Firefight character.	100
Gumshoe	Find the 3rd clue unraveling the mystery, alone or with another ODST.	10
Junior Detective	Find the first clue unraveling the mystery.	10
Coastal Highway	Complete Coastal Highway on Normal, Heroic, or Legendary to unlock a new Firefight mission.	50
ONI Alpha Site	Complete ONI Alpha Site on Normal, Heroic, or Legendary to unlock a new Firefight mission.	30
Kizingo Boulevard	Complete Kizingo Blvd. on Normal, Heroic, or Legendary to unlock a new Firefight character.	30
NMPD HQ	Complete NMPD HQ on Normal, Heroic, or Legendary to unlock a new Firefight character.	30
Data Hive	Complete Data Hive on Normal, Heroic, or Legendary to unlock a new Firefight mission.	50
Kikowani Station	Complete Kikowani Station on Normal, Heroic, or Legendary.	30

HALO REACH

ACHIEVEMENTS

NAME	GOAL/REQUIREMENT	POINT VALUE
The Soldier We Need You To Be	Completed the Campaign on Normal difficulty.	25
Folks Need Heroes...	Completed the Campaign on Heroic difficulty.	50
Gods Must Be Strong	Completed the Campaign on Legendary difficulty.	125
A Monument To All Your Sins	Completed every mission in Halo: Reach alone, on Legendary.	150
We're Just Getting Started	Completed the 2nd mission on Normal or harder.	10
Protocol Dictates Action	Completed the 3rd mission on Normal or harder.	10
I Need A Weapon	Completed the 4th mission on Normal or harder.	10
To War	Completed the 5th mission on Normal or harder.	10
You Flew Pretty Good	Completed the 6th mission on Normal or harder.	10
Into The Howling Dark	Completed the 7th mission on Normal or harder.	10
Dust And Echoes	Completed the 8th mission on Normal or harder.	10
This Is Not Your Grave	Completed the 9th mission on Normal or harder.	10
Send Me Out...With A Bang	Completed the 10th mission on Normal or harder.	10
They've Always Been Faster	Cleared the 2nd mission without setting foot in a drivable vehicle.	25
Two Corpses In One Grave	Killed 2 vehicles at once with the Target Locator in the 3rd mission.	25
Banshees, Fast And Low	Hijacked a Banshee during the Reach Campaign.	25
Your Heresy Will Stay Your Feet	Killed the Elite Zealot before he escaped during the 5th mission.	25
If They Came To Hear Me Beg	Performed an Assassination against an Elite to survive a fall that would've been fatal.	25
Wake Up Buttercup	Destroyed the Corvette's engines & escort in under 3 minutes in the 6th mission on Heroic or harder.	25
Tank Beats Everything	Finished the 9th mission on Legendary with the Scorpion intact.	25

XBOX 360 ACHIEVEMENTS

NAME	GOAL/REQUIREMENT	POINT VALUE
Lucky Me	Earned a Triple Kill while Jetpacking in Campaign, Firefight or Matchmaking.	25
KEEP IT CLEAN	Killed 7 Moa during the 2nd mission of the Campaign.	5
I Didn't Train To Be A Pilot	Killed 3 of the anti-aircraft batteries during the 8th mission.	10
Doctor, Doctor	Used a Health Pack to replenish life after taking body damage.	5
That's A Knife	Performed an Assassination on an enemy.	10
I See You Favor A .45	Killed 10 enemies in a Firefight or Campaign session with the M6G pistol.	10
An Elegant Weapon	Killed 10 enemies in a Firefight or Campaign session with the DMR.	10
Swap Meet	Traded weapons with an AI ally in Campaign.	10
A Spoonful Of Blamite	Killed 10 enemies in Firefight or Campaign with a supercombine explosion.	10
Be My Wingman Anytime	Let a teammate spawn on you 5 times in an Invasion Matchmaking game.	5
Yes, Sensei	Earned a First Strike Medal in a Matchmaking game.	10
Skunked	Won a game of Invasion in the 1st phase.	10
What's A Killing Spree?	Earned a Killing Spree in multiplayer Matchmaking.	5
Crowd Control	Earned a Killionaire medal in Firefight.	10
Knife To A Gun Fight	As an Elite, killed 5 Spartan players in Matchmaking.	5
Score Attack	Scored 15,000 points in Score Attack Firefight Matchmaking.	10
Firestarter	Scored 50,000 points in a Firefight game.	10
Blaze Of Glory	Scored 200,000 points in a Firefight game.	25
Heat In The Pipe	Scored 1,000,000 points in a Firefight game.	75
Game, Set, Match	Completed a Firefight set on Legendary without dying.	25
Make It Rain	Purchased an item from the Armory that required the rank of Lt. Colonel.	10
The Start Of Something	Reached the rank of Corporal in the UNSC.	15
An Honor Serving	Reached the rank of Captain in the UNSC.	25
A Storage Solution	Used the File Browser to upload a file to your File Share.	5
A New Challenger	Completed all of the Daily Challenges in a given day.	10
Make It Drizzle	Purchased an item from the Armory.	10
Cool File, Bro	Recommended a file to someone.	5
Lemme Upgrade Ya	Advanced a Commendation to a Silver state.	10
One Down, 51 To Go	Completed a Weekly Challenge.	10

HOW TO TRAIN YOUR DRAGON

ACHIEVEMENTS

NAME	GOAL/REQUIREMENT	POINT VALUE
First Step	Win a fight in either Story mode or 1 Player Arcade mode.	5
Glory to Hiccup	Finish the Story mode with Hiccup.	15
Glory to Astrid	Finish the Story mode with Astrid.	15
Great Speaker	Talk to every person on the island in Story mode.	15
In Feathers	Catch 200 chickens.	15
More Wild Meat	Catch 200 sheep or boars.	15
New Champion	Win against the leader of the first Tournament.	10
Courageous	Win against the leader of the second Tournament.	10
Daring	Win against the leader of the third Tournament.	10
Fearless	Win against the leader of the fourth Tournament.	10
Unstoppable	Win the first Tournament without being defeated.	15
In Great Shape	Win the second Tournament without taking care of your dragons during it.	15
Valiant	Win the third Tournament always fighting the lowest rated opponent.	15
Brave	Win the fourth Tournament always fighting the highest rated opponent.	15

NAME	GOAL/REQUIREMENT	POINT VALUE
Invulnerable	Win the final Championship with none of your dragons being KO.	90
Weapon Master	Make a dragon finish all trainings.	15
Duelist	Win a wild fight.	15
Legendary Fighter	Win all wild fights.	30
Shopping Master	Spend 10,000 gold at the shop.	30
Cooking Master	Buy all recipes from the shop.	15
Rich Harvest	Gather 1,000 common ingredients.	15
Enlightened	Gather 100 rare ingredients.	15
Dragon Doctor	Have 4 dragons in a great shape in Story mode.	15
Final Evolution	Have a level 25 dragon.	30
All Stars	Have 4 level 25 dragons.	90
Belong to the Legend	Unlock all legendary dragons.	30
Perfectionist	Have a dragon with 20 points in a characteristic in Story mode.	15
Ultimate Customization	Unlock all customizations of a dragon family.	15
Perfect	Win 50 fights without being injured in 1 Player Arcade mode.	15
Conqueror	Win 100 fights in either 1 Player or 2 Players Arcade mode.	15
Commander	Win 10 fights in a row in 1 Player Arcade mode on Hard difficulty.	30
All for One	Win a fight with each default and Legendary dragons in 1 Player Arcade mode.	15
They Are Alive!	Win 20 fights in 1 Player Arcade mode with a team of dragons created with the Dragon Editor.	15
Exceptional Tamer	Win 20 fights in 1 Player Arcade mode with a team of custom dragons from the Story mode.	15
Game Over!	Win all the medals for all difficulty levels in each challenge.	30
Young Competitor	Earn a gold medal in any challenge on Novice difficulty.	5
Outstanding Competitor	Earn a gold medal in any challenge on Normal difficulty.	10
Extreme Competitor	Earn a gold medal in any challenge on Expert difficulty.	15
To Hit the Bull's Eyes	Clear 5 checkpoint rings in a row in the Looping Race challenge on Expert difficulty.	30
What an Artist!	Sculpt 10 ice blocks in a row in the Ice Sculpting challenge on Expert difficulty.	30
Shepherd Dragon	Bring back 5 brown sheep in a row in the Flying Shepherd challenge on Expert difficulty.	30
Brainy	Perform 6 sequences in a row in the Memory Torch challenge on Expert difficulty.	30
Precise	Recreate 3 dragons in a row without mistakes in the Puzzle Dragon challenge on Expert difficulty.	30
Success	Earn a gold medal in each challenge.	15
Viking Gold	Have 10,000 gold in Story mode.	30
Viking Inhabitant	Play more than 20 hours in Story or Arcade mode (primary profile only).	30
Ally or Enemy?	Import at least one dragon in Arcade mode.	10

IRON MAN 2

ACHIEVEMENTS

NAME	GOAL/REQUIREMENT	POINT VALUE
Access Denied	Prevent Roxxon from stealing the Stark Archives.	10
Deportation	Prevent the Russian separatists from deploying Roxxon Armigers.	15
Power Outage	Defeat the Crimson Dynamo.	15
Anti-PROTEAN	Destroy Project PROTEAN.	20
Improvisation Under Fire	Save Rhodey and the Stark mobile armory from the A.I.M. attack.	20
Operation Daybreak	Defeat A.I.M. and save the S.H.I.E.L.D. Helicarrier.	20
Stormbreaker	Shut down the GREENGRID power transmitter.	20
The Bigger They Are	Defeat ULTIMO.	30
Shake It Off	Recover from the Roxxon EMP attack.	3

OVERLORD

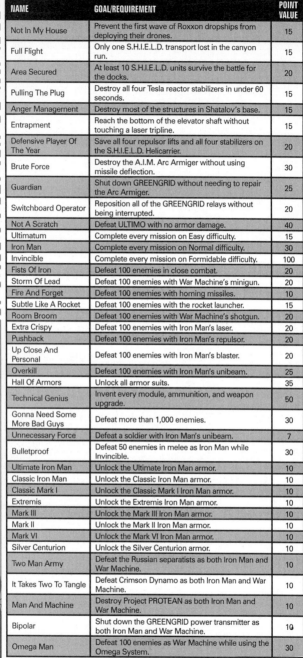

NAME	GOAL/REQUIREMENT	POINT VALUE
Not In My House	Prevent the first wave of Roxxon dropships from deploying their drones.	15
Full Flight	Only one S.H.I.E.L.D. transport lost in the canyon run.	15
Area Secured	At least 10 S.H.I.E.L.D. units survive the battle for the docks.	20
Pulling The Plug	Destroy all four Tesla reactor stabilizers in under 60 seconds.	15
Anger Management	Destroy most of the structures in Shatalov's base.	15
Entrapment	Reach the bottom of the elevator shaft without touching a laser tripline.	15
Defensive Player Of The Year	Save all four repulsor lifts and all four stabilizers on the S.H.I.E.L.D. Helicarrier.	20
Brute Force	Destroy the A.I.M. Arc Armiger without using missile deflection.	30
Guardian	Shut down GREENGRID without needing to repair the Arc Armiger.	25
Switchboard Operator	Reposition all of the GREENGRID relays without being interrupted.	20
Not A Scratch	Defeat ULTIMO with no armor damage.	40
Ultimatum	Complete every mission on Easy difficulty.	15
Iron Man	Complete every mission on Normal difficulty.	30
Invincible	Complete every mission on Formidable difficulty.	100
Fists Of Iron	Defeat 100 enemies in close combat.	20
Storm Of Lead	Defeat 100 enemies with War Machine's minigun.	20
Fire And Forget	Defeat 100 enemies with homing missiles.	10
Subtle Like A Rocket	Defeat 100 enemies with the rocket launcher.	15
Room Broom	Defeat 100 enemies with War Machine's shotgun.	20
Extra Crispy	Defeat 100 enemies with Iron Man's laser.	20
Pushback	Defeat 100 enemies with Iron Man's repulsor.	20
Up Close And Personal	Defeat 100 enemies with Iron Man's blaster.	20
Overkill	Defeat 100 enemies with Iron Man's unibeam.	25
Hall Of Armors	Unlock all armor suits.	35
Technical Genius	Invent every module, ammunition, and weapon upgrade.	50
Gonna Need Some More Bad Guys	Defeat more than 1,000 enemies.	30
Unnecessary Force	Defeat a soldier with Iron Man's unibeam.	7
Bulletproof	Defeat 50 enemies in melee as Iron Man while Invincible.	30
Ultimate Iron Man	Unlock the Ultimate Iron Man armor.	10
Classic Iron Man	Unlock the Classic Iron Man armor.	10
Classic Mark I	Unlock the Classic Mark I Iron Man armor.	10
Extremis	Unlock the Extremis Iron Man armor.	10
Mark III	Unlock the Mark III Iron Man armor.	10
Mark II	Unlock the Mark II Iron Man armor.	10
Mark VI	Unlock the Mark VI Iron Man armor.	10
Silver Centurion	Unlock the Silver Centurion armor.	10
Two Man Army	Defeat the Russian separatists as both Iron Man and War Machine.	10
It Takes Two To Tangle	Defeat Crimson Dynamo as both Iron Man and War Machine.	10
Man And Machine	Destroy Project PROTEAN as both Iron Man and War Machine.	10
Bipolar	Shut down the GREENGRID power transmitter as both Iron Man and War Machine.	10
Omega Man	Defeat 100 enemies as War Machine while using the Omega System.	30

JUST CAUSE 2

ACHIEVEMENTS

NAME	GOAL/REQUIREMENT	POINT VALUE
Top Agent	Bonus for completing the game on Normal difficulty.	20
Heroic Agent	Bonus for completing the game on Experienced difficulty.	30

NAME	GOAL/REQUIREMENT	POINT VALUE
Legendary Agent	Bonus for completing the game on Hardcore difficulty.	40
Gaining a Foothold	Complete 3 stronghold takeovers	10
Conqueror of Panau	Complete 9 stronghold takeovers.	20
A Trusted Ally	Complete 49 faction missions.	20
First Taste of Chaos	Cause chaos for the first time.	10
Saboteur	Complete 150 sabotages.	10
Destroyer	Complete 1000 sabotages.	20
Professional Hitman	Assassinate 25 colonels.	20
Up to the Challenge 1	Complete 10 challenges.	10
Up to the Challenge 2	Complete 50 challenges.	20
Leaving No Rock Unturned	Collect 1000 resource items.	25
Finders Keepers	Collect 100 resource items.	15
Faction Benefactor	Collect 150 faction items.	20
Globetrotter	Discover 100 locations.	20
Freeroamer 1	Reach 100% complete in 15 locations.	10
Freeroamer 2	Reach 100% complete in 100 locations.	20
Body Count	Kill 750 enemies.	15
Unarmed and Dangerous	Kill 50 enemies using melee attacks.	15
Gravity is a Bitch!	Kill 30 enemies by using the grappling hook and making them fall to their death.	15
Follow Me!	Kill 5 enemies by dragging them behind a vehicle with the grappling hook.	15
Hang 'em High!	Kill 30 enemies while they're suspended in the air with the grappling hook.	15
Wrecking Ball	Kill 5 enemies by smashing them with an object tethered to your vehicle with the grappling hook.	15
Piñata Party	Kill 5 enemies with the melee attack while they're suspended with the grappling hook.	15
Juggler	Kill 30 enemies while they're in mid air.	15
Road Rage	Kill 30 enemies by mowing them down with vehicles.	10
Marksman	Kill 50 enemies with head shots.	15
Killing Frenzy	Kill 20 enemies in 60 seconds.	20
Invincible Warrior	Kill 50 enemies in a row with inventory weapons without losing health.	20
Destruction Frenzy	Destroy 30 objects in 60 seconds.	10
Test Driver	Drive 30 different vehicles.	10
Trying Everything Once	Drive all 104 vehicles.	25
Road Trip	Travel 75 kilometers by land vehicle.	20
Please Step Out of the Vehicle	Hijack 50 enemy vehicles.	10
Stunt Driver	Get 100 stunt driver points.	10
Halfway there	Reach 50% completion in the normal mode or mercenary mode.	25
Parachute Climber	Open the parachute and then land on foot 300 meters above the starting height.	10
I Believe I Can Fly	Base jump 1000 meters.	10
Bridge Limbo	Fly an airplane under 30 unique bridges in Panau.	20
Stunt Flyer	Fly an airplane close to the ground for 30 seconds.	10
Perfectionist	Reach 75% completion in the normal mode or mercenary mode.	25
Top of the World	Stand on foot on the highest point of Panau	10

SECRET ACHIEVEMENTS

NAME	GOAL/REQUIREMENT	POINT VALUE
Welcome to Panau	Complete Story Mission 1.	10
Casino Bust	Complete Story Mission 2.	20
The White Tiger	Complete Story Mission 3.	30
Mountain Rescue	Complete Story Mission 4.	40
Three Kings	Complete Story Mission 5.	50
Into the Den	Complete Story Mission 6.	60
A Just Cause	Complete Story Mission 7.	70

XBOX 360 ACHIEVEMENTS

ACHIEVEMENTS

XBOX 360 ACHIEVEMENTS

NAME	GOAL/REQUIREMENT	POINT VALUE
Welcome to Shanghai	Complete 'Welcome to Shanghai' on any difficulty.	20
Street War	Complete 'The Details' on any difficulty.	20
Death Sentence	Complete 'Blood, Sweat and Tears' on any difficulty.	20
Nowhere to Hide	Complete 'Laying Low' on any difficulty.	25
Baby be Safe	Complete 'Coming Home' on any difficulty.	25
Lost Love	Complete 'A Thousand Cuts' on any difficulty.	25
Double Cross	Complete 'The Deal' on any difficulty.	25
Slow Train to Hell	Complete 'Out of Shanghai' on any difficulty.	30
Bring It Down	Complete 'Air Strike' on any difficulty.	30
Kill or Be Killed	Complete 'Resurrection' on any difficulty.	30
Dog Days	Complete Story Mode on any difficulty level.	60
Dead Men Rising	Complete Story Mode on Extreme.	60
Catch!	Push your human shield into an opponent in Story Mode.	10
Can It!	Kill 10 enemies with exploding canisters.	10
Mexican Showoff	Kill 5 enemies while downed before successfully recovering.	10
Sichuan Specialist	Escape the restaurant in 'Laying Low' without being downed on any difficulty.	10
Hand of God	Complete a Story Mode mission without dying once on any difficulty.	15
Chinese Waltz	Kill 5 enemies without losing your human shield.	10
Dance Off!	Execute 30 enemies while holding them as human shield.	10
Trigger Happy	Kill 5 enemies in 15 seconds with any pistol whilst not dropping your health below 90%.	15
Double Happiness	Kill 6 enemies in a row with a shotgun - all of them as one shot kills.	15
Steady Hand	Get 5 headshots in a row using the same clip.	15
You Want Blood?	1000 kills.	30
A Little Help From a Friend	Complete 1 mission in Co-op.	10
No Going Back	Complete 5 missions in Co-op.	20
End of the Road	Complete Story Mode in Co-op.	40
Giving a Hand	Finish 30 enemies your Co-op partner shot 'Down Not Dead'.	15
Got Your Back	Revive your Co-op partner 10 times.	10
Welcome	Successfully escape once in Arcade Mode or in any Multiplayer Ranked Match.	10
Doing Good	Successfully reach round 5 in Arcade Mode.	10
Love of Money	Successfully reach round 10 in Arcade Mode.	20
Greedy Bastard	Earn at least $5,000,000 in every level in Arcade Mode.	10
Lightning Looter	Reach $8,000,000 in under 6 minutes of actual playtime in Arcade Mode.	10
Safe Crime	Finish 5 rounds in a row without getting any penalties in Arcade Mode.	10
Battle Hardened	Complete one session in each Multiplayer Mode (Ranked Match).	15
Addict	Win 20 sessions of Cops & Robbers (Ranked Match).	20
The Cleaner	Escape as a traitor with 50% of any level's total loot in Arcade Mode or Multiplayer Ranked Match.	20
Escape from ...Anywhere	Successfully escape 25 times in Arcade Mode or in any Multiplayer Ranked Match.	25
D.I.Y.	Escape with more than $2,500,000 in a round of either Arcade Mode or Multiplayer Ranked Match.	20
Putting on the Ritz	End a round as Criminal Expert in a Fragile Alliance Ranked Match.	20
Blackjack and Hookers!	Accumulate $25,000,000 in your career (Arcade Mode and Multiplayer Ranked Match).	10
Most Wanted	Accumulate $50,000,000 in your career (Arcade Mode and Multiplayer Ranked Match).	25
Mastermind	Become criminal Mastermind (Highest Rank) in Multiplayer Ranked Match.	50

NAME	GOAL/REQUIREMENT	POINT VALUE
Rat Killer	Kill the Undercover Cop as the last surviving criminal and escape (Ranked Match).	20
Law Enforcer	Win as the Undercover Cop by killing all criminals yourself (Ranked Match).	20
Harry Houdini	Escape from being held as human shield in any Multiplayer mode (Ranked Match).	10
Unfinished Business	Kill a yellow carded criminal whilst Down Not Dead (Arcade Mode and Multiplayer Ranked Match).	10
Alpha Male	Have the most kills in a Cops & Robbers Ranked Match.	20
No I in TEAM	Earn the highest Criminal Loyalty level in Multiplayer Ranked Match.	15
There's an I in TRAITOR	Become Scum in a Multiplayer Mode (Ranked Match).	15

DOWNLOADABLE CONTENT: THE DOGGIE BAG

NAME	GOAL/REQUIREMENT	POINT VALUE
K9-Firepower	[Doggie Bag] Get 5 kills using canisters in a round of Multiplayer Ranked Match or Arcade Mode.	20
Escape From The Pound	[Doggie Bag] Escape on all levels at least once in Multiplayer Ranked Match or Arcade Mode.	20
Last in Show	[Doggie Bag] Escape as the last player on your own in a Multiplayer Ranked Match.	25
Rabid	[Doggie Bag] 1000 kills.	50
Under Dog	[Doggie Bag] In the last round of a 'Fragile Alliance' Ranked Match, climb from last to 1st place.	25
Good Doggie	[Doggie Bag] Escape with $100,000 or more in every round of a Multiplayer Ranked Match session.	20
The Dog Track	[Doggie Bag] Escape in less than 1½ minutes in Arcade Mode or Multiplayer Ranked Match.	20
Rex	[Doggie Bag] Get 150 criminal kills as a cop in 'Cops & Robbers' Ranked Matches.	20
Poodle	[Doggie Bag] Accumulate $25,000,000 during your career in Multiplayer Ranked Matches.	50

LEFT 4 DEAD 2

ACHIEVEMENTS

NAME	GOAL/REQUIREMENT	POINT VALUE
PRICE CHOPPER	Survive the Dead Center campaign.	20
MIDNIGHT RIDER	Survive the Dark Carnival campaign.	20
RAGIN' CAJUN	Survive the Swamp Fever campaign.	20
WEATHERMAN	Survive the Hard Rain campaign.	20
BRIDGE BURNER	Survive the Parish campaign.	20
STILL SOMETHING TO PROVE	Survive all campaigns on Expert.	35
THE REAL DEAL	Survive a campaign on Expert skill with Realism mode enabled.	35
CONFEDERACY OF CRUNCHES	Finish a campaign using only melee weapons.	30
HEAD HONCHO	Decapitate 200 Infected with a melee weapon.	15
CLUB DEAD	Use every melee weapon to kill Common Infected.	15
CHAIN OF COMMAND	Kill 100 Common Infected with the chainsaw.	15
TANK BURGER	Kill a Tank with melee weapons.	30
SHOCK JOCK	Revive 10 dead Survivors with the defibrillator.	30
THE QUICK AND THE DEAD	Revive 10 incapacitated Survivors while under the speed-boosting effects of adrenaline.	30
ARMORY OF ONE	Deploy an ammo upgrade and have your team use it.	15
BURNING SENSATION	Ignite 50 Common Infected with incendiary ammo.	15
DISMEMBERMENT PLAN	Kill 15 Infected with a single grenade launcher blast.	20
SEPTIC TANK	Use a bile bomb on a Tank.	15
CRASS MENAGERIE	Kill one of each Uncommon Infected.	20
DEAD IN THE WATER	Kill 10 swampy Mudmen while they are in the water.	20

OVERLORD

XBOX 360 ACHIEVEMENTS

NAME	GOAL/REQUIREMENT	POINT VALUE
ROBBED ZOMBIE	Collect 10 vials of Boomer vomit from infected CEDA agents you have killed.	15
CL0WND	Honk the noses of 10 Clowns.	15
FRIED PIPER	Using a Molotov, burn a Clown leading at least 10 Common Infected.	15
LEVEL A CHARGE	Kill a Charger with a melee weapon while they are charging.	15
ACID REFLEX	Kill a Spitter before she is able to spit.	15
A RIDE DENIED	Kill a Jockey within 2 seconds of it jumping on a Survivor.	15
STACHE WHACKER	Prove you are faster than Moustachio.	15
GONG SHOW	Prove you are stronger than Moustachio.	15
GUARDIN' GNOME	Rescue Gnome Chompski from the Carnival.	30
WING AND A PRAYER	Defend yourself at the crashed airliner without taking damage.	30
SOB STORY	Navigate the sugar mill and reach the safe room without killing any Witches.	30
VIOLENCE IN SILENCE	Navigate the impound lot and reach the cemetery safe room without tripping any alarms.	30
BRIDGE OVER TREBLED SLAUGHTER	Cross the bridge finale in less than three minutes.	30
HEARTWARMER	In a Versus round, leave the saferoom to defibrillate a dead teammate.	20
STRENGTH IN NUMBERS	Form a team and beat an enemy team in 4v4 Versus or Scavenge.	15
QUALIFIED RIDE	As the Jockey, ride a Survivor for more than 12 seconds.	15
BACK IN THE SADDLE	As the Jockey, ride the Survivors twice in a single life.	15
RODE HARD, PUT AWAY WET	As the Jockey, ride a Survivor and steer them into a Spitter's acid patch.	20
GREAT EXPECTORATIONS	As the Spitter, hit every Survivor with a single acid patch.	15
A SPITTLE HELP FROM MY FRIENDS	As the Spitter, spit on a Survivor being choked by a Smoker.	15
SCATTERING RAM	As the Charger, bowl through the entire enemy team in a single charge.	20
MEAT TENDERIZER	As the Charger, grab a Survivor and smash them into the ground for a solid 15 seconds.	20
LONG DISTANCE CARRIER	As the Charger, grab a Survivor and carry them over 80 feet.	15
BEAT THE RUSH	In a Survival round, get a medal only using melee weapons.	15
HUNTING PARTY	Win a game of Scavenge.	15
GAS GUZZLER	Collect 100 gas cans in Scavenge.	20
CACHE AND CARRY	Collect 15 gas cans in a single Scavenge round.	20
SCAVENGE HUNT	Stop the enemy team from collecting any gas cans during a Scavenge round.	15
FUEL CRISIS	Make a Survivor drop a gas can during overtime.	15
GAS SHORTAGE	Cause 25 gas can drops as a Special Infected.	20

DOWNLOADABLE CONTENT: THE PASSING

ACHIEVEMENTS

NAME	GOAL/REQUIREMENT	POINT VALUE
TORCH BEARER	Survive The Passing Campaign.	20
WEDDING CRASHER	As the Charger, grab a Survivor and crash them through 8 chairs at the wedding.	30
TIL IT GOES CLICK	Using the M60, kill 25 infected without letting go of the trigger.	20
GRAVE ROBBER	Collect 10 items dropped by a Fallen Survivor.	25
MUTANT OVERLORD	Play 6 Mutations.	30
FORE!	Knock off the heads of 18 infected with the golf club.	25
KILLING 'EM SWIFTLY TO THIS SONG	Play the new Midnight Riders song on a jukebox.	20
KITE LIKE A MAN	Kill a Tank only with damage from the original Survivors.	30
CACHE GRAB	Open 5 foot lockers.	20
PORT OF SCAVENGE	Play 5 full games of Scavenge on The Port.	30

ACHIEVEMENTS

NAME	GOAL/REQUIREMENT	POINT VALUE
Hero	Complete the first episode - Hero.	25
Super Hero	Complete the second episode - Hero.	25
Crusader	Complete the third episode - Hero.	25
Villain	Complete the first episode - Villain.	25
Super-villain	Complete the second episode - Villain.	25
Crime Lord.	Complete the third episode - Villain.	25
Sidekick	Complete a level in co-op.	15
Memorabilia	Collect all Memorabilia.	35
League of Assassins	Unlock all the Villain characters.	30
Justice League	Unlock all the Hero characters.	30
It's the car, right?	Unlock all Vehicles (Hero/Villain).	30
1007 Mountain Drive	Complete Wayne Manor bonus level.	30
Unbreakable	Finish a level without dying (Character) with no extras.	30
0000001 00000011	Build the giant LEGO Robot.	20
The city is safe... for now	100% game completion.	50
Cobblepot School of Driving	Smash all the cars in the robot level.	20
Vigilante	Rescue 25 civilians.	25
Be a Hero	Super Hero on every level.	40
Super Builder	Build 50 LEGO build-its.	20
Nice Outfit!	Collect all suits.	20
Dressed to Impress	Get all suit upgrades.	20
The Richest Man in Gotham	Max out the stud counter.	40
The Most Dangerous Man on Earth	Defeat Joker, Two-Face, Riddler and Catwoman as Batman.	20
Heads I win, tails you lose	Defeat 10 goons and 10 police officers with Two-Face in a level.	20
Who needs curiosity?	Defeat Catwoman 9 times.	20
Shot to the goon	Defeat 8 goons in 8 seconds.	20
Throwing up	Throw 50 policemen with superstrength.	20
Atomic Backbreaker	As Bane do the Backbreaker on Batman.	20
Oh, I got a live one here!	Shock 30 people with Joker's hand buzzer.	10
Kill-a-moth	Defeat Killer Moth.	20
Smash Gordon	Defeat Commissioner Gordon with Harley Quinn's Hammer.	20
Start of something wonderful	Shock the Joker with the Joker.	15
Boy Wonder	Perform 20 backflips in a row with Robin.	10
Thanks a million	Complete Arkham Bonus level.	30
Is it a bird? Is it a plane?	Glide for 9 seconds.	10
Gentlemen, start your screaming	Knock 5 people into the ground with a vehicle at once.	15
Natural Habitat	Smash all street lights in Episode 1 Chapter 1.	10
Make it snappy	Build the Croc ride on.	20
The Destroyer of Worlds	Destroy 12 objects at once with Bat Bombs.	15
There and back	Destroy 10 objects in one Batarang throw.	10
Kiss from a Rose	Eat 15 enemies with the Venus ride on .	15
Ice to see you.	Freeze 50 enemies as Mr. Freeze.	15
Say hello to my little friends	Destroy 20 policemen with penguin bombers.	15
Scare Tactics	Scare 5 enemies with Scarecrow.	10
Down the rabbit hole	Use Mad Hatter's mind control to walk 5 enemies to their deaths.	20
Eat floor... High fiber	Slam 20 goons into the floor with Batman.	15

LEGO ROCK BAND

ACHIEVEMENTS

NAME	GOAL/REQUIREMENT	POINT VALUE
New to the Scene	Complete your first gig on the World Tour	10
Tour de Force	Play at every venue on the World Tour	20
Veteran Performer	Complete all gigs on the World Tour (except for the Rock Marathon Setlist and Endless Setlist)	50
Long-Distance Rocker	Complete the Rock Marathon Setlist on the World Tour	30
Endless Shameless	Complete the Endless Setlist on the World Tour	50
Got Wheels	Purchase the 2nd vehicle on the World Tour	10
Sea Legs	Purchase the 3rd vehicle on the World Tour	10
Rotary Club	Purchase the 4th vehicle on the World Tour	10
Open Road	Purchase the 5th vehicle on the World Tour	10
Walking on Air	Purchase the 6th vehicle on the World Tour	10
Into the Deep	Purchase the 7th vehicle on the World Tour	10
Jet Setter	Purchase the 8th vehicle on the World Tour	10
Teleportation Nation	Unlock the Teleporter on the World Tour	10
Rock the House Down	Complete the Wreck 'n' Roll Rock Power Challenge	10
Pencil Pusher	Hire a Band Manager	10
You're Hired!	Hire an Entourage member	10
#1 Boss	Hire all Entourage members	40
Hovel, Sweet Hovel	Purchase one item of rock den furniture	10
House Proud	Spend 100,000 studs on rock den furniture	20
Luxury Living	Spend 1,000,000 studs on rock den furniture	40
Bare Essentials	Purchase an item of clothing	10
Appetite For Apparel	Spend 100,000 studs or more on items of clothing	20
Fashion Victim	Spend 1,000,000 studs or more on items of clothing	40
Gear Head	Purchase an instrument	10
Instrumental	Spend 1,000,000 studs or more on instruments	40
Local Legend	Get 100 fans	10
Fan-TASTIC	Get 1,000,000 fans	30
Twinkle, Twinkle	Get 100 Stars	10
Super Stars	Get 1000 Stars	30
Universal Acclaim	Complete the Story	50
Flawless Fretwork	Score 100% notes hit as a Guitarist	20
Flawless Drumming	Score 100% notes hit as a Drummer	20
Flawless Singing	Score a 100% rating as a Vocalist	20
Flawless Groove	Score 100% notes hit as a Bassist	20
Stud Farm	Achieve a 100% Stud Recovery during a performance	20
Brian MAY Be Jealous	100% a guitar solo on Expert	20
The Final Countdown	Score 100% on the Guitar Solo in "The Final Countdown" on Expert	40
All Four One!	Complete a song with four band members	20
Practice Makes Perfect	All four band members score 100% notes hit	50
Solid Gold, Easy Action!	Gold Star any song	50

SECRET ACHIEVEMENTS

NAME	GOAL/REQUIREMENT	POINT VALUE
Royal Command Performance	Kings of Rock 'n' Troll completed	10
No More Mr Ice Guy	Rock the Boat completed	10
Dooyafinkhesaurus	Securi-T-Rex completed	10
Rain King	Rock the Crop completed	10
Kickin' the Tentacles	Rocktopus completed	10
The School of Shock	Shock Band completed	10
Roadie Revolution	Road Crew hired	10
Armageddon Outta Here	Stop the Rock completed	10
Start Me Up	Rock-It Fuel completed	10

ACHIEVEMENTS

NAME	GOAL/REQUIREMENT	POINT VALUE
Complete Prologue A	Complete Episode 1 Chapter 0-A.	10
Complete Prologue B	Complete Episode 1 Chapter 0-B.	10
Complete Episode 1	Complete all the chapters in Episode 1.	10
Rookie	Complete the game on Easy.	10
Soldier	Complete the game on Normal.	10
Super Soldier	Complete the game on Hard.	15
Snow Pirate	Achieve a Career Level of Lv. 10.	10
Welcome to the Battle!	Play one Online match.	10

SECRET ACHIEVEMENTS

NAME	GOAL/REQUIREMENT	POINT VALUE
Complete Episode 2	Complete all the chapters in Episode 2.	10
Complete Episode 3	Complete all the chapters in Episode 3.	10
Complete Episode 4	Complete all the chapters in Episode 4.	10
Complete Episode 5	Complete all the chapters in Episode 5.	10
Complete Episode 6	Complete all the chapters in Episode 6.	10
100-Chapter Playback	Play through 100 chapters.	10
Instrument of Destruction	Defeat 9999 enemies (Akrid, VS, or enemy soldiers).	20
300-Chapter Playback	Play through 300 chapters.	30
200-Chapter Playback	Play through 200 chapters.	20
Ultimate Warrior	Complete the game on Extreme.	20
Snow Pirate Warrior	Achieve a Career Level of Lv. 30.	15
Snow Pirate Leader	Achieve a Career Level of Lv. 50.	20
Snow Pirate Commander	Achieve a Career Level of Lv. 80.	25
Rounder Chief	Achieve a Career Level of Lv. 99 with the Rounders.	30
Fight Junkie Berserker	Achieve a Career Level of Lv. 99 with the Fight Junkies.	30
First Among Snow Pirate Elites	Achieve a Career Level of Lv. 99 with the Snow Pirate Elites.	30
NEVEC Black Ops Commander	Achieve a Career Level of Lv. 99 with the NEVEC Black Ops.	30
Femmes Fatales Faction Leader	Achieve a Career Level of Lv. 99 with the Femmes Fatales.	30
Quintuple Factionalism	Achieve a Career Level of Lv. 99 with all 5 factions.	50
A Thousand Unmarked Graves	Defeat 1000 enemy soldiers.	15
Endangered Species	Defeat 3000 S- and M-sized Akrid.	15
VS Graveyard	Destroy 100 enemy VSs.	15
It's So Easy	Play any combination of chapters 39 times on Easy.	20
Monster Hunter	Defeat 30 bosses.	20
Thermal Energy Reactor	Accumulate a combined total of more than 99999 units of thermal energy.	10
Me Against the World	Complete 93 areas while online without the help of other players.	10
Prove Your Mettle	Unlock all the Abilities.	25
Weapons Master	Unlock all regular weapons and grenades.	25
Honeymoon Period	Celebrate your six-month anniversary with LOST PLANET 2.	20
A Collector's Collector	Unlock all items (weapons, Abilities, Noms de Guerre).	50
All in a Day's Work	Achieve 100 different Good Job awards.	20
Warrior of Many Names	Unlock 100 Noms de Guerre.	20
Centurion	Win 100 Online Ranked matches.	15
Slayer of a Thousand Men	Achieve 1000 kills in Online matches.	15
Hot Shot	Gain promotion to the rank of Gunner.	15
Two is Better Than One	Complete 386 areas with one or more other players.	10

XBOX 360 ACHIEVEMENTS

OVERLOAD

NAME	GOAL/REQUIREMENT	POINT VALUE
Let's Go VS Force!	Merge two VS units.	10
Professional Turncoat	Fight for a number of different factions in Faction Match.	10
War Vet	Play 500 Online matches.	15
Death Wish	Die more than 444 times.	10
Good Job, Soldier	Earn all the Good Job awards.	40
Committed 'til the End	Earn all the Good Job awards, items, and Career Levels available in the game.	100

MADDEN NFL 11

ACHIEVEMENTS

NAME	GOAL/REQUIREMENT	POINT VALUE
Very Special Teams	Return 2 kicks for touchdowns in one game with one player (no OTP)	100
Butterfingers	Force 3 fumbles in a game (no OTP)	50
Man Dozer	Rush for 50 yards after the first hit in one game (no OTP)	25
He's Got All Day	Stay in the pocket for 10 seconds (no OTP)	20
Did I Break It?	Win a game by at least 59 points (max qtr. length 7 min, no OTP)	40
Winning Isn't Everything	Catch 21 passes in a game with one player (no OTP)	75
Old Spice Swagger Return	Return a punt for a touchdown (no OTP)	45
Comeback Kids	Win after being behind in the last 2 min of a game (no OTP, min qtr. length 3 min)	40
No Offense	Intercept 5 passes in a game (no OTP)	50
Fantasy Freak	Rush for over 200 yards in a game with one player (no OTP)	25
The Elusive Man	Break 5 tackles in a game with one player (no OTP)	25
Perfect Game	Have a perfect passer rating in a game (no OTP)	50
Home Run	Break an 80+ yard touchdown run (no OTP)	25
Old Spice Swagger Pick 6	Intercept a pass and return it for a touchdown (no OTP)	25
YACtastic	Have over 100 YAC in one game (no OTP)	35
Pick Up 6	Win a Fight for the Fumble in the end zone for a TD (no OTP)	75
Deadly Accurate	Have a 92% or higher completion percentage in a game (min 20 att., no OTP)	30
Laces Out	Kick a 60+ yard Field Goal (no OTP)	40
Madden Moments	Complete the "Super Bowl Sunday" Madden Moment	100
Defensive Dominance	Hold your opponent to under 100 yards of offense (min qtr. len. 5 min, no OTP)	75
Sack Master	Record 5 sacks in a game with one player (no OTP)	25
Verizon Master Strategist	Create a custom Gameplan	5

SECRET ACHIEVEMENTS

NAME	GOAL/REQUIREMENT	POINT VALUE
Thanks For Coming	Play the Pro Bowl (Franchise Mode)	10
Nano	Tackle the QB before he can hand the ball off (no OTP)	10

MAFIA II

ACHIEVEMENTS

NAME	GOAL/REQUIREMENT	POINT VALUE
Viva la Resistenza!	Complete Chapter 1.	20
Home Sweet Home	Complete Chapter 2.	20
Back in Business	Do your first job for Mike Bruski.	10
Big Brother	Protect Francesca.	10
A Real Gentleman	Help the woman fix her car in Home Sweet Home.	10
The Price of Oil	Complete Chapter 3.	20
The Professional	Obtain the ration stamps without raising the alarm.	10
Mail Man	Sell all the gas stamps before the time runs out.	10
Night Shift	Complete Chapter 4.	20
Good Spirit	Complete Chapter 5.	20
Time Well Spent	Complete Chapter 6.	20
Last Respects	Complete Chapter 7.	30
The Wild Ones	Complete Chapter 8.	30
Man of Honor	Complete Chapter 9.	30
Checking Out	Complete Chapter 10.	40
Our Good Friend	Complete Chapter 11.	20
Wake Up Call	Help Leo out of a tricky situation without getting caught.	10
Chasing the Dragon	Complete Chapter 12.	40
Chop Chop!	Complete Chapter 13.	40
Men at Work	Complete Chapter 14.	50
Finish Him	Finish what you started.	50
Made Man	Finish the story on Medium difficulty level.	50
Tough Nut	Finish the story on Hard difficulty level.	100
Get Rich or Die Flyin'	Get all wheels of your car into the air for at least 20 meters and then touch the ground again.	10
Pedal to the Metal	Travel at 125 mph.	10
One Careful Owner	Travel a total of 50 miles in one vehicle.	10
Proper Scrapper	Sell 5 vehicles to Mike Bruski at the scrapyard.	10
Exporter	Sell 5 vehicles to Derek at the dock.	10
Cruise Control	Keep any vehicle at 30 mph or over for 5 or more minutes.	10
Hairdresser	Kill 5 enemies in rapid succession with a headshot.	10
Knucklehead	Kill a total of 30 enemies using melee attacks.	10
Stuck Up	Rob 5 stores in under 5 minutes.	10
The Enforcer	Kill 50 enemies.	10
Sharp Suiter	Buy your first luxury suit.	10
Tuned Ride	Upgrade one of your cars one level.	10
Dream Handling	Upgrade one of your cars to the maximum level.	10
Hard to Kill	The police want you dead. Survive for 10 minutes!	10
Collector's Item	Find at least one collectible in the game.	10
Petrol Head	Drive at least 30 different vehicles.	30
Ladies' Man	Find all of the Playboy magazines.	40
Card Sharp	Find all of the Wanted posters.	40
He Who Pays the Barber	Improve the dockworkers' haircuts.	10
A Lesson in Manners	Show that you know how to treat a lady.	10
Hey Joe	Clean up after Joe.	10
End of the Rainbow	Settle the score with the Irish once and for all.	10
The Mafia Never Forgets	Pay a visit to an old friend.	10
Out for Justice	Learn what it means to be a Scaletta.	30

DOWNLOADABLE CONTENT: JIMMY'S VENDETTA

NAME	GOAL/REQUIREMENT	POINT VALUE
First Step	Complete your first mission in "Jimmy's Vendetta."	10
Faster than Light	Achieve a 10x point multiplier in "Jimmy's Vendetta."	10
Explorer	Drive a total of 1,000 miles in vehicles in "Jimmy's Vendetta."	10
Armament King	Kill your enemies in "Jimmy's Vendetta" with every weapon available in the game.	10

OVERLORD

XBOX 360 ACHIEVEMENTS

NAME	GOAL/REQUIREMENT	POINT VALUE
Firebug	Destroy 100 vehicles in "Jimmy's Vendetta."	10
Sharpshooter	Kill 100 enemies by headshots in "Jimmy's Vendetta."	10
Carnapper	Finish all Car Dealer missions in "Jimmy's Vendetta."	50
Revenged	Finish "Jimmy's Vendetta" on any difficulty level.	100
Millionaire	Earn 1,000,000 points in "Jimmy's Vendetta."	20
Massacre	Kill 1,000 enemies in "Jimmy's Vendetta."	20

DOWNLOADABLE CONTENT: JOE'S ADVENTURES

NAME	GOAL/REQUIREMENT	POINT VALUE
What Witness?	Finish the Witness level in "Joe's Adventures."	10
Arctic Grave	Push the chief witness into the ice lake in "Joe's Adventures."	20
Dockyard Discord	Finish the Connection level in "Joe's Adventures."	20
Five Finger Discount	Finish the Supermarket level in "Joe's Adventures."	30
Mind the Goods	Finish the Cathouse level in "Joe's Adventures."	40
Same Shirt Different Day	Finish Joe's Adventures on any difficulty.	50
Hypersonic	Reach 2000 points for one velocity run in "Joe's Adventures."	20
Jacked Jumper	Reach 200 points for one Jump in "Joe's Adventures."	20
Driftin' Daddy-O	Reach 200 points for one Drift in "Joe's Adventures."	20
Jack of all Trades	Reach 10 different score actions in one mission in "Joe's Adventures."	20

MAGNA CARTA 2

ACHIEVEMENTS

NAME	GOAL/REQUIREMENT	POINT VALUE
Battle of Highwind Island	Complete the battle of Highwind Island.	10
Battle of Oldfox Canyon	Complete the battle of Oldfox Canyon.	20
Battle of Cota Mare	Complete the battle of Cota Mare.	30
Battle of Dunan Hill	Complete the battle of Dunan Hill.	40
Battle of Ruhalt Basin	Complete the battle of Ruhalt Basin.	50
First Quest Cleared	Clear the first quest.	5
10 Quests Cleared	Clear 10 quests.	5
50 Quests Cleared	Clear 50 quests.	10
80 Quests Cleared	Clear 80 quests.	20
All Quests Cleared	Clear all quests.	30
Co-op Technique: Juto & Zephie	Learn Co-op Technique for Juto & Zephie.	10
Style Master: 1 Handed Sword	Master Juto's 1 Handed Sword skill tree.	30
Style Master: 2 Handed Sword	Master Juto's 2 Handed Sword skill tree.	30
Style Master: Hammer	Master Argo's Hammer skill tree.	30
Style Master: Axe	Master Argo's Axe skill tree.	30
Style Master: Rod	Master Zephie's Rod skill tree.	30
Style Master: Fan	Master Zephie's Fan skill tree.	30
Style Master: Fireball	Master Crocell's Fireball skill tree.	30
Style Master: Knuckles	Master Crocell's Knuckle skill tree.	30
Style Master: Aroma	Master Celestine's Aroma skill tree.	30
Style Master: Bow	Master Celestine's Bow skill tree.	30
Style Master: Katana	Master Rue's Katana skill tree.	30
Style Master: Shuriken	Master Rue's Shuriken skill tree.	30
Weapon Enhanced	Use Enhancements on a weapon.	5
Obtained Item Recipe	Obtain an item recipe.	5
Obtained 6 Item Recipes	Obtain 6 item recipes.	10

NAME	GOAL/REQUIREMENT	POINT VALUE
Obtained All Item Recipes	Obtain all item recipes.	30
100 Chain Breaks	Complete 100 chain breaks.	10
300 Chain Breaks	Complete 300 chain breaks.	30
500 Chain Breaks	Complete 500 chain breaks.	50
Viewed Live Drama 1	View Live Drama 1	20
Viewed Live Drama 2	View Live Drama 2	20
Viewed Live Drama 3	View Live Drama 3	20
Weapon Collector: Juto	Collect all of Juto's weapons, including downloadable content.	30
Weapon Collector: Zephie	Collect all of Zephie's weapons, including downloadable content.	30
Weapon Collector: Argo	Collect all of Argo's weapons, including downloadable content.	30
Weapon Collector: Crocell	Collect all of Crocell's weapons, including downloadable content.	30
Weapon Collector: Celestine	Collect all of Celestine's weapons, including downloadable content.	30
Weapon Collector: Rue	Collect all of Rue's weapons, including downloadable content.	30

SECRET ACHIEVEMENTS

NAME	GOAL/REQUIREMENT	POINT VALUE
Escape from Belfort	Successfully escaped from Belfort.	60
Assault on Ruhalt Plateau	Completed the assault on Ruhalt Plateau.	70
Game Completed	Completed the game's main story.	80
Co-op Technique: Argo&Celestine	Learned Co-op Technique for Argo & Celestine.	10
Co-op Technique: Zephie & Rue	Learned Co-op Technique for Zephie & Rue.	10
Co-op Technique: Juto & Crocell	Learned Co-op Technique for Juto & Crocell.	20
Co-op Technique: Celestine & Rue	Learned Co-op Technique for Celestine & Rue.	20

MAJOR LEAGUE BASEBALL 2K10

ACHIEVEMENTS

NAME	GOAL/REQUIREMENT	POINT VALUE
Down But Not Out	Get a hit with 2 strikes on Pro or higher, in a non-simulated game.	5
Grab Some Pine	Get a strikeout to end the inning on Pro or higher, in a non-simulated game.	5
Run the Risk	Steal a base after the 6th inning tied or down by 1 run on Pro or higher, in a non-simulated game.	10
A Pitcher's Best Friend	Turn a double play on Pro or higher, in a non-simulated game.	10
To the Rescue	Bring in a pitcher, get a save with the tying run on base on Pro or higher, in a non-simulated game.	10
A Virtue	Face 10 pitches as the batter on Pro or higher, in a non-simulated game.	20
Don't Call it a Comeback	Win after being down by 4 after the 6th inning on Pro or higher, in a non-simulated game.	20
Keep on Truckin'	Truck the Catcher and score on Pro or higher, in a non-simulated game.	10
This is Why I'm Here	Be successful in a major league clutch moment in My Player Mode.	15
Trifectas Maximus	Throw a MAX pitch 3 consecutive times with Total Control on Pro or higher, in a non-simulated game.	10
One Man Show	Throw a Perfect Game or a No-Hitter on Pro or higher in a 9 inning game, in a non-simulated game.	80
Time to Run for Mayor	Hit 3 Home Runs in a single game with the same player on Pro or higher, in a non-simulated game.	30
I came, I saw...	Hit a Walk-off Home Run on Pro or higher, in a non-simulated game.	20

NAME	GOAL/REQUIREMENT	POINT VALUE
Stooges	Strikeout all three hitters in the inning on Pro or higher, in a non-simulated game.	10
High Crimes	Rob a Home Run on Pro or higher, in a non-simulated game.	20
Thou Shalt Not	Throw out a runner stealing a base on Pro or higher, in a non-simulated game.	10
State Farm™- The Road to Victory	Get 3 consecutive batters on base on Pro or higher, in a non-simulated game.	20
Still Kicking	Strike out a batter with a pitcher who has low composure on Pro or higher, in a non-simulated game.	10
It's Never Too Late	Get a 2-out RBI Hit on Pro or higher, in a non-simulated game.	10
The Call	Get called up to the Majors in My Player Mode.	20
The Goal	Accomplish a Team Season Goal in My Player Mode.	10
The Top	Become the #1 ranked player in your My Player organization.	30
The Star	Make the All-Star team in My Player Mode.	40
The Start	Get your player's overall rating to 65 in My Player Mode.	10
The Truth	Get your player's overall rating to 85 in My Player Mode.	20
The Hall	Make the Hall of Fame in My Player Mode.	80
One and O	Play and win opening day in Franchise Mode.	10
What's Your Ring Size?	Win a World Series® in Franchise Mode. (play at least 20 games)	80
Remember Me	Break a record in Franchise Mode. (play at least 20 games)	20
Booked a Ticket	Clinch a Postseason Berth in Franchise Mode. (play at least 20 games)	20
A Day in the Life	Play a game of MLB Today.	10
Mid-Summer Classic	Play the All-Star game in MLB Today.	40
King of the Hill	Get to the top of the Best of the Best ladder in Home Run Derby® Mode.	20
My Fellow Man	Complete and win an online league game.	10
The Team to Beat	Beat the New York Yankees in a completed online match.	10
Count it	Complete and win a ranked match.	10
The Road to Greatness	Complete and win 3 ranked matches in a row.	20
The spice of life	Complete 10 online matches using 10 different teams.	20
Domination	Strikeout 200 batters with your user profile.	20
Production	Drive in 250 RBI with your user profile.	20
A Whole New You	Choose a signature batting stance or pitching delivery in My Player or Create Player.	5
Learning the Ropes	Achieve gold in all the drills.	10
Hurlers	Unlock 20 pitcher cards.	10
Swingers	Unlock 25 hitter cards.	10

SECRET ACHIEVEMENTS

NAME	GOAL/REQUIREMENT	POINT VALUE
Round and Round We Go	Bat around (all 9 players bat in the same inning) on Pro or higher, in a non-simulated game.	30
EpidemiK	Complete an online game against a 2K developer or a player who already has this achievement.	20
Upset Alert	Use the Nationals in a completed ranked match.	10
Big Bang	Leadoff the game with a Home Run on Pro or higher, in a non-simulated game.	30
Back From the Brink	Get out of a bases loaded jam (0 outs, no runs scored) on Pro or higher, in a non-simulated game.	20
Hawkeye	Draw a walk on a full count on Pro or higher, in a non-simulated game.	10

ACHIEVEMENTS

NAME	GOAL/REQUIREMENT	POINT VALUE
Mission Accomplished	Topple a dictator.	5
Coalition of the Willing	Crash a castle.	20
Oceans No Longer Protect Us	Protect a city.	20
A House Divided	Defend your leaders.	20
If You're Not With Us	Choose a side.	10
Freedom Isn't Free	Raid a hideout.	20
Defending Our Way of Life	Rescue a hideout.	20
All Options on the Table	Defend a convoy.	20
Collateral Damage	Stop a convoy.	20
Fallen Star	Ambush your opponents.	20
Iron and Blood	Fight back an ambush.	20
Knowns and Unknowns	Repay a favor.	10
Alliance Reborn	Break and enter.	20
Grave and Growing	Free a country.	20
A More Perfect Union	Finish what you started.	10
I'm With Iron Man	Defeat all Act II and III missions as a Pro-Registration team.	30
I'm With Captain America	Defeat all Act II and III missions as an Anti-Registration team.	30
Legendary Schism	Defeat all Act I missions on Legendary Difficulty.	20
Legendary War	Defeat all Act II missions on Legendary Difficulty.	30
Legendary Alliance	Defeat all Act III missions on Legendary Difficulty.	30
Rookie Squad	Complete a map in Co-Op.	10
Experienced Allies	Complete 8 maps in Co-Op.	15
Decorated Veterans	Complete 24 maps in Co-Op.	30
Seek and Destroy	Complete all optional mission objectives.	15
Uncontained Aggression	You or other players on your team must destroy 250 health containers.	15
Undefeated Heroes	Defeat 12 mission bosses on Super Heroic or Legendary Difficulty without revival or map reload.	30
Immortal Heroics	Defeat 25 maps on Super Heroic or Legendary Difficulty without revival or map reload.	50
Back in Action	Perform 10 revivals.	10
Tactical Training	Perform all 5 recommended training Fusions in Latveria.	10
Heroes Unite	Perform 10 Fusions with another player-controlled hero in a Co-Op game.	10
United We Stand	Earn 20 high scores for each type of Fusion: Targeted, Guided, and Clearing.	30
Powers of Two	Perform all Fusions by combining every available pairing of 24 heroes.	50
Old Friends	Have 10 special conversations between characters with a history while in an HQ map.	10
Costume Collector	Unlock 23 alternate costumes.	10
Distinguished Service	Collect 50 Team Boosts.	10
Extraordinary Heroism	Collect 125 Team Boosts.	30
Above and Beyond	Collect 200 Team Boosts.	50
Listening In	Collect 30 Audio Logs.	20
Superior Intel	Collect 125 Dossiers.	20
Potential Evidence	Collect 10 Concept Art Bundles in HQ maps.	10
Trivia Buff	Correctly answer 15 Trivia questions.	10
Trivia Team-Up	Score 30 Trivia Fusions.	15
Trivia Genius	Earn all Trivia rewards.	30
Sim Team-Up	Earn Mission Succeeded on a Simulator Mission in Co-Op and return to the Simulator menu.	5
Sim Amateur	Earn 4 Bronze Medals from Simulator Missions.	10
Sim Expert	Earn 8 Silver Medals from Simulator Missions.	15
Sim Champion	Earn 12 Gold Medals from Simulator Missions.	30

NAME	GOAL/REQUIREMENT	POINT VALUE
Melee Training	Complete all melee training goals listed on the Stats page.	10
Power Training	Complete all Power training goals listed on the Stats page.	15
Every Trick in the Book	Complete all combat mastery goals listed on the Stats page.	30

MEDAL OF HONOR

ACHIEVEMENTS

NAME	GOAL/REQUIREMENT	POINT VALUE
Multiplayer: First rotation	Play online for 15 minutes	15
Multiplayer: Tour of Duty	Play online for 2 hours	15
Multiplayer: Heavy Fire Support	Fire 1000 bullets in a round (awarded at end of round)	15
Multiplayer: Boot camp	Play once as each class (min 2 min)	15
Multiplayer: Mission Training	Play Combat Mission	15
Multiplayer: Assault Training	Play Team Assault	15
Multiplayer: Secure Training	Play Sector Control	15
Multiplayer: Raid Training	Play Objective Raid	15
Multiplayer: Enlisted	Reach level 2 in any class	15
Multiplayer: Veteran	Reach level 4 in any class	15
Multiplayer: Triple Canopy	Reach level 8 in one class	15
Multiplayer: Mission Specialist	Play two hours of Combat Mission	20
Multiplayer: Assault Specialist	Play two hours of Team Assault	20
Multiplayer: Secure Specialist	Play two hours of Sector Control	20
Multiplayer: Raid Specialist	Play two hours of Objective Raid	20
Multiplayer: Forward Spotter	Deploy a missile strike support action (awarded at end of round)	20
Multiplayer: Fire Controller	Use each offensive support action once (awarded at end of round)	30
Multiplayer: Quartermaster	Get 1000 support points	30
Multiplayer: Tier 1	Reach top level in one class	35
Multiplayer: High Achiever	Be top 3 on the scoreboard ten times	40
First Incision	Single player: Complete First In	15
Welcome to the TOC	Single player: Complete Breaking Bagram	15
Develop the Situation	Single player: Complete Running with Wolves…	15
Unexpected Guests	Single player: Complete Dorothy's a Bitch	15
Full Battle Rattle	Single player: Complete Belly of the Beast	15
Bad Guy Jamboree	Single player: Complete Gunfighters	15
Friends From Afar	Single player: Complete Friends From Afar	15
Cliffhanger...	Single player: Complete Compromised	15
S.E.R.E.	Single player: Complete Neptune's Net	15
Eight Heroes Aboard	Single player: Complete Rescue the Rescuers	15
Smooth Operator	Single player: In First In, Kill the Hostage Taker with a Head Shot	10
The Sledgehammer	Single player: In Breaking Bagram, destroy 2 vehicles with a single 2000 lb Laser Guided Bomb	10
Dropping Deuce	Single player: Jump 7.5 meters high on the ATV	10
Fear the Reaper	Single player: In Dorothy's a Bitch, destroy the entire AQ Camp with the AC-130	10
Manic Suppression	Single player: In Belly of the Beast, defeat the DShK in under two minutes	20

NAME	GOAL/REQUIREMENT	POINT VALUE
It Takes A Village...Out	Single player: Destroy 30 buildings in Gunfighters Village	10
Like a Surgeon	Single player: While long range sniping, hit one of every body part	10
Feeding the Pig	Single player: In Compromised, get 15 kills with the M60	15
The Quiet Professional	Single player: In Neptune's Net, eliminate 13 enemies without alerting anyone	15
Timber!	Single player: In Rescue the Rescuers, chop down 5 trees with the Minigun	10
The Battle is Won...	Single player: Finish the game on Easy, Normal or Hard	50
...But the War Rages On.	Single player: Finish the game on Hard	75
Conspicuous Gallantry	Single player: Finish every level in the game on Tier 1 Mode under par time	100
The Scalpel	Single player: Achieve 20 total knife kills	15
Pistol Pete Showdown	Single player: Get a total of 30 pistol kills	15
Right in the Grape...	Single player: Get 7 headshots in a row with any weapon except the long range sniper rifle.	15
Crowd Control	Single player: Kill 5 enemies at once with a single hand grenade	15
Rangers Lead the Way	Single player: Finish all of Dante's missions	15
Never Quit	Single player: Finish all of Rabbit's missions	15
Have a Good One	Single player: Finish all of Deuce's missions	15

MX VS. ATV: REFLEX

ACHIEVEMENTS

NAME	GOAL/REQUIREMENT	POINT VALUE
Waypoint Series 1	Place 3rd or higher in the Waypoint Series 1 in the MotoCareer	15
Waypoint Series 2	Place 3rd or higher in the Waypoint Series 2 in the MotoCareer	15
Waypoint Series 3	Place 3rd or higher in the Waypoint Series 3 in the MotoCareer	15
National Series 1	Place 3rd or higher in the National Series 1 in the MotoCareer	15
National Series 2	Place 3rd or higher in the National Series 2 in the MotoCareer	15
National Series 3	Place 3rd or higher in the National Series 3 in the MotoCareer	30
Supercross Series 1	Place 3rd or higher in the Supercross Series 1 in the MotoCareer	15
Supercross Series 2	Place 3rd or higher in the Supercross Series 2 in the MotoCareer	15
Supercross Series 3	Place 3rd or higher in the Supercross Series 3 in the MotoCareer	30
Freestyle Series 1	Place 3rd or higher in the Freestyle Series 1 in the MotoCareer	15
Freestyle Series 2	Place 3rd or higher in the Freestyle Series 2 in the MotoCareer	15
Freestyle Series 3	Place 3rd or higher in the Freestyle Series 3 in the MotoCareer	15
Omnicross Series 1	Place 3rd or higher in the Omnicross Series 1 in the MotoCareer	15
Omnicross Series 2	Place 3rd or higher in the Omnicross Series 2 in the MotoCareer	15
Omnicross Series 3	Place 3rd or higher in the Omnicross Series 3 in the MotoCareer	15
Champion Sport Track Series 1	Place 3rd or higher in the Champion Sport Track Series 1 in the MotoCareer	15
Champion Sport Track Series 2	Place 3rd or higher in the Champion Sport Track Series 2 in the MotoCareer	15
Champion Sport Track Series 3	Place 3rd or higher in the Champion Sport Track Series 3 in the MotoCareer	15
Ironman of Offroad	Win all Series in the MotoCareer	75

NAME	GOAL/REQUIREMENT	POINT VALUE
Champion of Champions	Win all Face-Off Challenges in the MotoCareer	25
Greatest of All Time	Place 1st in all events in the MotoCareer	100
Gold Standard	Earn a Gold medal in any MotoCareer Free Ride Challenge	10
Precious Medals	Earn a Gold medal in all MotoCareer Free Ride Challenges	50
Step Into the Arena	Complete an Xbox LIVE Playlist Match	15
To the Victor…	Place 1st in an Xbox LIVE Playlist Match with 11 human opponents	15
Endurance	Complete 25 Xbox LIVE Playlist Matches	25
Long Live the King	Place 1st in 25 Xbox LIVE Playlist Matches	50
Leveler	Finish ahead of any opponent who has a higher Experience Level in a Xbox LIVE Playlist Match	15
You're It!	Win a Tag Mini-Game in an Xbox LIVE Playlist Match	15
Snake in the Grass	Win a Snake Mini-Game in an Xbox LIVE Playlist Match	15
Moto Skills	Complete MotoSkills 1, 2 and 3	15
Master Skills	Complete MotoSkills 4, 5 and 6	15
Trickster	Perform any airborne Trick and land successfully	15
Hat-Trick!	Perform three consecutive, unique airborne Tricks in one jump	15
Perfection	Earn a judge's score of 10.0 in a Freestyle Event	25
Freestylin'	Win a Freestyle Event in the MotoCareer without repeating a trick	25
Coming on Strong	Lap an Opponent in a Race	15
Ace in the Hole	Win 10 Holeshots	15
Showboat	Pull off three unique tricks in a Race Event	15
Tuning In	Adjust a Tuning Slider and save the new setting	5
Keeping it Clean	Complete a Race in a Machine with all body panels still attached to your vehicle	15
Skeletal Remains	Complete a Race in a Machine with no body panels remaining on your vehicle	15
Wreck-less	Avoid a Wreck in a Race	5
Close Calls!	Avoid 100 Wrecks	25
You are Legend	Place 1st in any Race on All-Time difficulty	25
Long Jumper	Land a jump distance of 300 feet or greater	15
Wheelie King	Hold a Wheelie trick for 150 feet or longer	15
Stoppie Master	Hold a Stoppie trick for 75 feet or longer	15

NBA 2K9

ACHIEVEMENTS

NAME	GOAL/REQUIREMENT	POINT VALUE
30 Assists	Record 30 assists or more with any team.	20
10 Blocks	Record 10 blocks or more with any team.	20
15 Steals	Record 15 steals or more with any team.	20
Rebound Margin +7	Win the rebound battle by a margin of +7 with any team.	20
15 Threes	Make 15 three pointers or more with any team.	15
Defensive FG%	Hold the opposing team's FG% below 40% with any team.	15
Lights Out	FG% over 55% for the game [minimum 40 FGAs] with any team.	15
Track Meet	Score at least 15 fastbreak points with any team.	15
Second Unit	Score at least 40 bench points with any team.	15
Inside Domination	Score at least 60 points in the paint with any team.	20
Good Hands	Record 20 assists with no more than 5 turnovers with any team.	20
All-Hustle	Record at least 10 offensive rebounds, 5 blocks and 5 steals with any team.	15
All-Heart	Start the 4th period losing by 10 or more points and win the game with any team.	15
3-For-All	Make at least 10 3pt FG's while shooting at least 45% from 3pt range with any team.	20

NAME	GOAL/REQUIREMENT	POINT VALUE
Ice Water	FT% over 85% with at least 15 FTA's with any team.	15
Lockdown	Record at least 10 blocks and 10 steals with any team.	20
Celtics vs Lakers	User controlled team must win this matchup on All-Star difficulty.	15
Spurs vs Suns	User controlled team must win this matchup on All-Star difficulty.	15
Cavaliers vs Wizards	User controlled team must win this matchup on All-Star difficulty.	15
Suns vs Mavericks	User controlled team must win this matchup on All-Star difficulty.	15
Lakers vs Clippers	User controlled team must win this matchup on All-Star difficulty.	15
East vs West	User controlled team must win this matchup on All-Star difficulty.	15
LeBron James	Record at least 35 points, 9 rebounds and 9 assists with LeBron James.	25
Dwyane Wade	Record at least 26 points, 5 rebounds and 7 assists with Dwyane Wade.	25
Kobe Bryant	Record at least 40 points, 5 rebounds and 5 assists with Kobe Bryant.	25
Allen Iverson	Record at least 30 points, 8 assists and 3 steals with Allen Iverson.	25
Steve Nash	Record at least 20 points and 15 assists with Steve Nash.	25
Dwight Howard	Record at least 20 points, 15 rebounds and 3 blocks with Dwight Howard.	25
Gilbert Arenas	Record at least 35 points, 3 steals and 5 threes with Gilbert Arenas.	25
Carmelo Anthony	Record at least 40 points and 8 rebounds with Carmelo Anthony.	25
Chris Paul	Record at least 20 points, 10 assists and 3 steals with Chris Paul.	25
Kevin Garnett	Record at least 20 points, 13 rebounds and 5 assists with Kevin Garnett.	25
Yao Ming	Record at least 30 points, 12 rebounds and 4 blocks with Yao Ming.	25
Chris Bosh	Record at least 30 points, 10 rebounds and 2 blocks with Chris Bosh.	25
Sprite Slam Dunk	Win the Sprite Slam Dunk Contest using LeBron James.	35
Dunk-Off	Defeat any challenger in a Dunk-Off.	35
Trivia	Answer 15 trivia questions correctly.	35
3pt Shootout	Win the 3pt Shootout.	15
Create Player	Use the Create Player feature.	10
2K Beats Playlist	Create a 2K Beats playlist.	10
Online Ranked Game	Win one online ranked game.	15
3 Online Ranked Streak	Win 3 online ranked games in a row.	15
5 Online Ranked Streak	Win 5 online ranked games in a row.	20
5 Online Ranked Wins	Win 5 online ranked games.	15
10 Online Ranked Wins	Win 10 online ranked games.	25
20 Online Ranked Wins	Win 20 online ranked games.	30
Team 2K	Beat a Team 2K member in an online game.	20
Good Teammate	Earn a positive "teammate rating" in the online Team-Up Mode.	20
Better to Give	Share any file type through 2K Share.	20
Reel Critic	Download a reel from ReelViewer and rate it.	10

NBA LIVE 09

ACHIEVEMENTS

NAME	GOAL/REQUIREMENT	POINT VALUE
Ice Water	Win a solo game in overtime vs. the CPU.	30
Well Rounded Player	Get a 'triple double' with your player in a solo Be a Pro game vs. the CPU.	50

NAME	GOAL/REQUIREMENT	POINT VALUE
Super GM	Fully upgrade your Dynasty Mode™ team staff.	100
Perimeter Man	Fully complete all of the 'Guard Station' challenges in the NBA LIVE Academy.	50
BMOC	Fully complete all of the 'Big Man Station' challenges in the NBA LIVE Academy.	50
Team Player	Fully complete all of the 'Team-Play Station' challenges in the NBA LIVE Academy.	50
Created a Monster	Score over 60 points with a created player in a solo game vs. the CPU.	25
The Past is Present	Play and win a solo NBA LIVE Rewind Game vs. the CPU.	25
Game of the Week	Play and win a 'Game of the Week' ranked match online.	30
BAP MVP	Win a Be a Pro game, receiving an 80 or higher Be a Pro rating with your player solo vs. the CPU.	30
David and Goliath	Defeat any team rated 10 points or higher in a solo match on Superstar difficulty vs. the CPU.	50
MVP	A player on your Dynasty Mode team wins the MVP of the regular season.	30
NBA Finals MVP	A player on your Dynasty Mode teams wins the NBA Finals MVP.	30
All-Star	A player on your Dynasty Mode team makes the NBA All-Star Game.	20
All-NBA	A player on your Dynasty Mode team makes the All-NBA team.	20
Clutch	On Superstar difficulty vs. the CPU, make two free throws in a row with under two minutes remaining.	20
G.O.A.T.	Win by at least 20 points in solo game on Superstar difficulty vs. the CPU.	60
The Comeback Kid	Win a solo game after being down by 20 points vs. the CPU.	40
Shock the World	Defeat Team USA in a solo match in the FIBA World Championship tournament vs. the CPU.	30
The Grinder	Play 20 ranked matches online.	100
Club Victory	Play and win a Team Play Club match.	50
Cool Off	Shut down a hot 'Shot Streak' by keeping his point total under 10 vs. the CPU (minimum 10 min. Q).	50
Old School	Win a game with no dunks or 3 point shots in a solo game vs. the CPU.	60

NHL 2K9

ACHIEVEMENTS

NAME	GOAL/REQUIREMENT	POINT VALUE
5 Goals	Achieve a total of 5 User Goals.	5
25 Goals	Achieve a total of 25 User Goals.	10
75 Goals	Achieve a total of 75 User Goals.	20
150 Goals	Achieve a total of 150 User Goals.	40
1000 Goals	Achieve a total of 1000 User Goals.	100
10 Assists	Achieve a total of 10 User Assists.	5
40 Assists	Achieve a total of 40 User Assists.	10
100 Assists	Achieve a total of 100 User Assists.	20
200 Assists	Achieve a total of 200 User Assists.	40
1500 Assists	Achieve a total of 1500 User Assists.	100
10 PIMs	Achieve a total of 10 User PIMs (Penalties in Minutes).	5
50 PIMs	Achieve a total of 50 User PIMs (Penalties in Minutes).	10
100 PIMs	Achieve a total of 100 User PIMs (Penalties in Minutes).	20
150 PIMs	Achieve a total of 150 User PIMs (Penalties in Minutes).	40
500 PIMs	Achieve a total of 500 User PIMs (Penalties in Minutes).	100
1 Win	Achieve a total of 1 User Wins.	5
15 Wins	Achieve a total of 15 User Wins.	10
50 Wins	Achieve a total of 50 User Wins.	20
100 Wins	Achieve a total of 100 User Wins.	40
150 Wins	Achieve a total of 150 User Wins.	100
Powerplay Specialist	Score three powerplay goals in one game.	20
Boom Goes the Dynamite	Score a goal from behind the blue line.	10

NAME	GOAL/REQUIREMENT	POINT VALUE
Kill It	Kill a full 2 minute 5 on 3 powerplays.	10
Skillful Skater	Score a goal after performing a 1-on-1 deke special move.	10
Masterful Scorer	Score a goal using a goalie deke special move.	10
Wraparound	Score on a wraparound goal.	5
Ride the Zamboni	Win the Zamboni mini-game.	40
Marty Turco	Get a shutout with Marty Turco in net while facing a minimum of 20 shots.	10
Jason Spezza	Get at least 6 points with Jason Spezza in a single game.	10
Joe Thornton	Get at least 2 goals, 3 assists and 4 PIMs with Joe Thornton in a single game.	10
Rick Nash	Get at least 3 points and a shootout goal in a win with Rick Nash.	10
Undisputed Champion	Win the Presidents' Trophy and Stanley Cup in a single season.	45
Reel Him In	Resign a Superstar (95+ overall) to your team.	15
Lumberjack	Get a hat trick with a player that's fully-bearded in the Stanley Cup playoffs.	15
Team 2K	Beat a Team 2K member or someone that has unlocked this achievement in an online game.	20
Good Teammate	Average an A teammate grade.	20
Alter Ego	Customize your Online Avatar.	20
Critic	Download and rate a reel from ReelViewer.	20

PES 2011

ACHIEVEMENTS

NAME	GOAL/REQUIREMENT	POINT VALUE
First Glory	Awarded for your first win.	10
Perfect 10	Awarded for winning 10 consecutive matches.	25
Come Back Win	Awarded for your first Come Back Win.	15
Last Gasp Winner	Awarded for scoring the Winner in Extra Time.	10
World Traveller	A Title awarded for playing at all featured Stadiums. (Excludes ones created in Edit Mode.)	20
The Gentleman	Awarded for committing less than 1 Foul per match on average in your last 10 Matches.	20
Possession Play	Awarded for having a Possession Rate of 60% or higher in your last 10 Matches.	25
Hat-trick Hero	Awarded for scoring 5 hat-tricks.	35
Predatory Striker	Awarded for playing over 20 Matches, averaging 2 plus goals per Match in your last 10.	40
Dead-ball Expert	Awarded for scoring 5 Direct Free-Kicks.	40
Long Ranger	Awarded for scoring from 35m out or more.	50
League Winner	Awarded for winning one of the top leagues in [Master League].	15
European Elite 16	Awarded for making the Knockout phase of the UEFA Champions League in [Master League].	20
Kings of Europe	Awarded for winning the Master League UEFA Champions League.	30
The Invincibles	Awarded for an undefeated season in Master League winning League, Cup and UEFA Champions League.	90
No.1 Club	Awarded for topping the Team Ranking in Master League.	50
World Footballer of the Year	Awarded if a member of your team wins World Footballer of the Year in Master League.	70
10 years of Service	An award to honor 10 years of service in Master League.	50
The Debutant	Awarded for your First Professional Appearance in Become a Legend.	10
International Cup Debut	Awarded for your First Appearance in the Become a Legend International Cup.	15
International Cup MVP	Awarded for being named International Cup Player of the Tournament in Become a Legend.	30
The Journeyman	A title awarded for playing at 10 different clubs across 6 countries in Become a Legend.	40

XBOX 360 ACHIEVEMENTS

NAME	GOAL/REQUIREMENT	POINT VALUE
The Super Hero	A title awarded for being named World Footballer of the Year in BECOME A LEGEND.	50
Mr. Consistency (Online)	Awarded for winning 75% of your Last 20 Ranked matches Online.	50
Made the Knockout phase	Awarded for making the Knockout phase of the UEFA Champions League.	40
European Champions	Awarded when you win the UEFA Champions League.	70
Kings of Latin America	A title awarded for winning the Copa Santander Libertadores.	80

PRINCE OF PERSIA

ACHIEVEMENTS

NAME	GOAL/REQUIREMENT	POINT VALUE
Wallrunner	Completing the Canyon.	10
Compass	Use the Compass.	10
Heal the Land	First Healing.	30
Saviour of the City of Light	Final Healing.	50
Explorer	Explore every part of every region.	20
Block Master	Block 50 attacks.	20
Deflect Master	Deflect 20 attacks.	20
Sword Master	Perform 14 hits in one combo.	20
Be gentle with her	Elika saves you fewer than 100 times in the whole game.	100
Improviser	Use the environment against an enemy.	10
Up against it	Win a wall mini-game in combat.	10
Ruined Citadel Runner	Run from the Sun Temple's Fertile Ground to the Fertile Ground in Windmills in 5 minutes.	10
Vale Runner	Run between the Fertile Grounds in the Construction Yards and Heaven's Stair in 6 minutes.	20
Royal Palace Runner	Run between the Fertile Grounds in the Royal Gardens and Coronation Halls in 4 minutes.	30
City of Light Runner	Run between the Fertile Grounds in the Tower of Ahriman and City of Light in 7 minutes.	40
Warrior Special	Dodge the Warrior's attacks 20 times in one battle.	20
Hunter Special	Deflect the Hunter's attacks 5 times in one battle.	20
Alchemist Special	Defeat the Alchemist without using the acrobatic button.	20
Concubine Special	Defeat the Concubine without using grab.	20
Light Seeds Finder	Collect 100 Light Seeds.	10
Light Seeds Collector	Collect 200 Light Seeds.	10
Light Seeds Provider	Collect 300 Light Seeds.	10
Light Seeds Locator	Collect 400 Light Seeds.	10
Light Seeds Harvester	Collect 500 Light Seeds.	10
Light Seeds Hoarder	Collect 600 Light Seeds.	10
Light Seeds Gatherer	Collect 700 Light Seeds.	10
Light Seeds Accumulator	Collect 800 Light Seeds.	10
Light Seeds Protector	Collect 900 Light Seeds.	10
Light Seeds master	Collect 1001 Light Seeds.	50
Speed Kill	Kill 10 generic enemies before they spawn.	10
Throw Master	Throw 10 Soldiers of Ahriman into pits.	10
Assassin View	Find the Assassin's view.	10
Titanic view	Find the Titanic View.	10
In Harmony	500 coop jumps.	10
Precious Time	Take one minute to think.	10
Where's that Temple?	Talk to Elika.	10
Getting to Know You	Get to know Elika by talking to her.	10
Good Company	Learn about the world, and Elika's history.	10
Climbing to New Heights!	Find the highest point in the world.	10
Sinking to New Depths!	Find the lowest point in the world.	10

NAME	GOAL/REQUIREMENT	POINT VALUE
Speed Demon	Finish the game in under 12 hours.	10
Combo Specialist	Find every combo in the game.	50
Leaving the Storm	Complete the Epilogue.	30
Bouncing From Here to There	Complete the puzzle with rebound in the Epilogue.	20
The Best Offence Is Good Defense	Defeat any enemy of the Epilogue by only starting a combo with a Deflect and Counter-Attack.	20
Change Once, Then Die	In the Epilogue, defeat the Shapeshifter with only one shape change.	20
A Fresco Of Light	Reach one Ormazd's fresco in the Epilogue.	10
All The Frescos	Reach all Ormazd's Frescos in the Epilogue.	20
Born Dead	Kill all the soldiers of the Epilogue before they spawn.	40

SECRET ACHIEVEMENTS

NAME	GOAL/REQUIREMENT	POINT VALUE
Into the Storm… Saved!	Congratulations, you have unlocked Elika's saving ability.	10
Death of a Concubine	Congratulations, you have killed the Concubine.	20
Now who's the Hunter?	Congratulations, you have killed the Hunter.	20
Death of a Warrior King	Congratulations, you have killed the Warrior.	20
Traitor's End	Congratulations, you have killed the Alchemist.	20
From Darkness...Light!	Congratulations, you have reimprisoned Ahriman.	30
To be continued...	Congratulations, the game is complete... the story has only just begun...	80
I Only Need a Hand or Twenty	Elika saves you fewer than 20 times in the whole Epilogue.	40
No Time to Waste	Complete the Epilogue in less than 2 hours.	40
What Once was There	First use of Energize in the Epilogue.	10

RED DEAD REDEMPTION

ACHIEVEMENTS

NAME	GOAL/REQUIREMENT	POINT VALUE
High Roller	Win over 2000 chips in a hand of Poker.	10
No Dice	Complete a game of Liar's Dice without losing a single die.	10
What About Hand Grenades?	Get a ringer in a game of Horseshoes.	10
Austin Overpowered	Complete Twin Rocks, Pike's Basin, and Gaptooth Breach Hideouts in Single Player.	25
Evil Spirits	Complete Tumbleweed and Tesoro Azul Hideouts in Single Player.	25
Instinto Asesino	Complete Fort Mercer and Nosalida Hideouts in Single Player.	25
Fightin' Around the World	Knock someone out in melee in every saloon in the game in Single Player.	5
Strange Things are Afoot	Complete a task for a Stranger.	10
People are Still Strange	Complete 15 tasks for Strangers.	25
Buckin' Awesome	Break the Kentucky Saddler, the American Standard-bred, and the Hungarian Half-bred.	10
Clemency Pays	Capture a bounty alive.	10
Exquisite Taste	Purchase a rare weapon from a gunsmith.	10
Bearly Legal	Kill and skin 18 grizzly bears.	5
He Cleans Up Well!	Obtain the Elegant Suit.	10
More than a Fistful	Earn $10,000 in Single Player.	10
Frontiersman	Obtain Legendary rank in any Single Player Ambient Challenge.	20
The Gunslinger	Score a headshot on any enemy using Expert targeting mode.	5

NAME	GOAL/REQUIREMENT	POINT VALUE
Man of Honor / Chivalry's Dead	Attain highest Fame rank and either highest Honor rank or lowest Honor rank.	25
Gold Medal	Earn a Gold Medal Rank for a combat mission in Single Player.	25
On the Trail of de Vaca	Uncover every location on the map in Single Player.	10
Friends in High Places	Use a pardon letter with more than $5000 bounty in Single Player.	10
Redeemed	Attain 100% in the Single Player Game Completion stat.	100
Mowing Them Down	Kill 500 enemies with a mounted weapon in any game mode.	20
In a Hail of Bullets	Kill 500 enemies with any pistol or revolver in any game mode.	20
Long Arm of Marston	Kill 500 enemies with any rifle, repeater, or shotgun in any game mode.	20
Bullseye	Get 250 headshots in any game mode.	20
Unnatural Selection	Kill one of every animal species in the game in any game mode.	20
Have Gun Will Travel	Complete all Hideouts in a single public Free Roam session.	20
Slow on the Draw	Get 10 assists in a single Hideout in a public Free Roam session.	10
Hit the Trail	Get from Blackwater to Escalera before sundown in a public Free Roam session.	10
Posse Up!	Create a posse and get the maximum number of members.	10
The Quick and Everyone Else...	Be the top scoring player in any three consecutive FFA games in public matches.	20
How the West Was Won	Reach the top rank for multiplayer experience.	20
Go Team!	Be on the winning team for four consecutive victories in any team based game in public matches.	20
Most Wanted	Become a Public Enemy for 10 minutes and escape alive in a public Free Roam session.	10
Red Dead Rockstar	Kill a Rockstar or someone with this achievement in a public multiplayer match.	10

SECRET ACHIEVEMENTS

NAME	GOAL/REQUIREMENT	POINT VALUE
That Government Boy	Complete "Exodus in America".	10
Land of Opportunity	Complete "The Assault on Fort Mercer".	30
Sons of Mexico	Complete "The Gates of El Presidio".	40
No More Fancy Words	Complete "An Appointed Time".	20
A Savage Soul	Complete "At Home with Dutch".	10
The Benefits of Civilization	Complete "And the Truth Will Set You Free".	90
Into the Sunset	Complete "The Last Enemy That Shall Be Destroyed".	100
Nurture or Nature?	Complete "Remember My Family".	50
Dastardly	Place a hogtied woman on the train tracks, and witness her death by train.	5
Spurred to Victory	Complete 20 story missions without switching to a new horse at a hitching post.	10
Heading South on a White Bronco	Evade the US Marshals while riding the Hungarian Half-Bred horse in Single Player.	5
Manifest Destiny	Kill the last buffalo in the Great Plains in Single Player.	5

DOWNLOADABLE CONTENT: OUTLAWS TO THE END

NAME	GOAL/REQUIREMENT	POINT VALUE
Well done	Complete a Co-Op mission.	5
Have posse, will travel	Complete all Co-Op missions.	15
2 guys, 1 Coop	Complete a Co-Op mission with just 2 people.	10
Stake a claim	Gold medal any Co-Op mission.	5
Struck gold	Gold medal all Co-Ops missions.	10
Friends indeed	Complete a Co-Op mission without anyone dying.	5
You rule!	Complete all Advanced Co-Op missions.	15

NAME	GOAL/REQUIREMENT	POINT VALUE
The mother lode	Gold medal all Advanced Co-Op missions.	20
Dodge this	Achieve a kill chain of 10 or more in any Advanced Co-Op mission.	10
Bulletproof	Complete a Co-Op mission without dying.	5

DOWNLOADABLE CONTENT: LEGENDS AND KILLERS

NAME	GOAL/REQUIREMENT	POINT VALUE
Call it a Comeback!	Come back from a 2-0 deficit and win a Hold Your Own game.	10
Who needs Deadeye?	Kill 3 or more players in a standoff or showdown.	10
Stick and Move	Get 3 kills with knives or throwing knives in a single competitive match.	10
Double bagger	Double capture 3 times in a single Gold Rush map.	10
Headhunter	Kill 5 players via headshot in a single Shootout or Gang Shootout.	10
Legendary	Reach level 50 and pass into Legend.	10
Hail Mary	Get a kill greater than 35 yards with a Tomahawk.	10
Axe Master	Complete all Tomahawk challenges in Single Player.	10
Original Gunslinger	Get 25 Deadeye kills with Red.	10
Reeeeal Good	Get 25 Dynamite kills with Pig Josh.	10

DOWNLOADABLE CONTENT: LIARS & CHEATS

NAME	GOAL/REQUIREMENT	POINT VALUE
Master Exploder	Complete the Explosive Rifle Single Player Challenge	10
Pa-Pa-Pa-Poker Ace	In a full Multiplayer Poker game, beat the table when blinds are at maximum	10
The Big Bluff	In a Multiplayer Poker game, win a hand by forcing someone with a better hand to fold	5
In A Van Down By The River	In a Multiplayer Poker game, win a hand on the last card when you were losing prior	5
Compulsive Liar	In a full Multiplayer Liar's Dice game, win without losing a single die	10
Good Call	In a single Multiplayer Liar's Dice game, successfully make a spot-on call	5
One Die to Rule Them All	In a Multiplayer Liar's Dice game, win with only one die left	5
Triple Crown	Get first place in all races in any Grand Prix	10
Peacewalker	Finish a single race without getting shot or killed, and without shooting a bullet	5
From Glue to Mon Dieu!	During a Grand Prix, finish a race in first after placing last in the previous race.	5
We Must Protect This House!	While on defense, do not allow the attacking team to capture any of their objectives	10
Avatar of Death	Successfully complete either round of a Stronghold map without dying	5
Legion of Boom	Get a triple kill while on the attacking team in Stronghold	5
Over 9001	Attain over 9,001 points in a single Free Roam session	5
Put the Posse on a Pedestal	Attain over 50,000 posse points in a single Free Roam session	5

RED FACTION GUERILLA

ACHIEVEMENTS

NAME	GOAL/REQUIREMENT	POINT VALUE
Welcoming Committee	Complete the Tutorial mission.	10
Martian Tea Party	Complete 2 missions for the Red Faction.	10
Spread the Word	Liberate Parker Sector.	10
Death From Above	Liberate Dust Sector.	20
Friendly Skies	Liberate Badlands Sector.	30
Don't Tread On Me	Liberate Oasis Sector.	40

NAME	GOAL/REQUIREMENT	POINT VALUE
Coup D'etat	Liberate Eos Sector.	50
Red Dawn	Liberate Mars.	100
Insurgent	Complete 5 Guerrilla Actions.	5
Guerrilla	Complete 25 Guerrilla Actions.	10
Freedom Fighter	Complete 50 Guerrilla Actions.	15
Revolutionary	Complete all Guerrilla Actions.	25
Clean and Righteous!	Destroy 5 High Importance targets.	15
Warp Speed	Beat all Transporter Pro times.	15
Got Any Fingers Left?	Beat all Pro times in Demolitions Master.	15
Lost Memories	Locate all missing radio tags.	25
Working the Land	Mine all ore locations.	25
Free Your Mind	Destroy all instances of propaganda.	25
One Man Army	Complete 25 killing sprees during the Campaign.	25
Disaster Area	Destroy 1 billion credits worth of EDF property.	50
Broken Supply Line	Destroy 250 EDF supply crates.	10
Power to the People	Raise the Morale of 3 sectors to 100%.	10
Tank Buster	Blow up 100 small hydrogen tanks.	10
Best Friends Forever	Kill 100 EDF with the sledgehammer during the Campaign.	10
Coming Down!	Destroy 50 EDF owned buildings.	10
Freed Space	Destroy 50 EDF flyers.	10
Just the Beginning	Win a Matchmaking match.	5
Start of Something Special	Play 5 Matchmaking matches.	5
Doing Your Part	Kill 10 enemies in a Matchmaking Match.	10
Juggernaut	Destroy a Siege target.	5
Doozer	Reconstruct a Damage Control target.	5
Grab Some Popcorn	Enter Spectator mode and enjoy the show!	5
Try Anything Once	Finish a match in every mode.	10
Check Your Map	Finish a match on every map in Multiplayer.	10
Tools of the Trade	Score a kill with every weapon in Multiplayer.	10
Field Tested	Earn 1,000 XP in Multiplayer.	10
Battle Scarred	Earn 10,000 XP in Multiplayer.	25
War Veteran	Earn 100,000 XP in Multiplayer.	50
A Winner is You!	Win 250 matchmaking games.	20
Topher Would Be Proud	Play 250 matchmaking games.	20
Courier of Pain	Score 5,000 kills in Multiplayer.	20
Experimenter	Complete 4 hidden challenges in Multiplayer.	10
Detective	Complete 8 hidden challenges in Multiplayer.	20
Mad Genius	Complete 16 hidden challenges in Multiplayer.	40
Jack of all Trades	Score 10 kills while wearing each backpack.	10
The High and Mighty	Kill a flying opponent using a remote charge stuck to them.	10
Party Time	Play all Wrecking Crew modes once.	10
Can't Get Enough	Play every mode on all maps in Wrecking Crew.	20
Wrecking Ball	Score 25 million points worth of destruction in Wrecking Crew.	40
Red Faction Member	Play online with another player who has completed the Campaign.	50
Bound By Blood	Complete Rescue.	30
Family Vengeance	Complete Retribution.	40
A Greater Purpose	Complete Redemption.	50
Deliverance Defender	Complete Marauder Actions.	20
Tumbling Down	Beat all Pro times in Mariner Valley Demo Masters and Transporters.	10
Mobile Bombs	Destroy 100 EDF vehicles.	10
Structural Integrity	Destroy all Medium and High Priority Targets in Mariner Valley.	20
Purge the Valley	Break the EDF Control of the Mariner Valley.	30
Ares' Bloodlust	Destroy the 4 Marauder War Totems.	20
The Power of One	Collect 75 Marauder Power Cells.	20

ACHIEVEMENTS

NAME	GOAL/REQUIREMENT	POINT VALUE
First Contact	This is just the beginning.	10
Maiden Mission	This is what pays the bills.	10
Bonus Hitter	You can land one more hit.	15
Tri-Attacker	You'll need to cooperate as a team of three.	15
Hundred Plus Club	This is the natural product of having weathered countless battles.	15
Bullet Barrage	It's all about positioning.	15
Resonance Miser	It'll take all three of you to tackle this challenge.	15
Hero Actor	Spend enough time in combat, and you'll cross this threshold.	15
Spite Monger	Perfect the timing for landing a bonus hit.	15
Extreme Spiker	There are more ways to deal extra damage than just a bonus hit.	15
Professional Hunter	Their lives have not been given up in vain.	15
Material Collector	They sometimes yield useful parts and materials.	15
Thousand Pitcher	Throw as hard as your little arms can stand.	15
The Iron Fist	A true warrior doesn't fear getting up close and personal.	15
Big Shot	You'll have to put mind, spirit, and body into it to hit this hard.	15
Material Creator	Become a regular down at the local shop.	15
Shopaholic	It's your money. Spend it how you like!	15
Customaestro	Laying out parts can become quite a puzzle.	15
Basel's Repairman	There's a lot of world left out there.	15
Four-Terminal Chain	Connect terminal effects to make them even more effective.	15

SECRET ACHIEVEMENTS

NAME	GOAL/REQUIREMENT	POINT VALUE
Prologue Complete	You've completed the prologue.	10
Chapter 1 Complete	You've completed the first chapter.	10
Chapter 2 Complete	You've completed the second chapter.	15
Chapter 3 Complete	You've completed the third chapter.	15
Chapter 4 Complete	You've completed the fourth chapter.	15
Chapter 5 Complete	You've completed the fifth chapter.	15
Chapter 6 Complete	You've completed the sixth chapter.	15
Chapter 7 Complete	You've completed the seventh chapter.	15
Chapter 8 Complete	You've completed the eighth chapter.	15
Chapter 9 Complete	You've completed the ninth chapter.	15
Chapter 10 Complete	You've completed the tenth chapter.	15
Chapter 11 Complete	You've completed the eleventh chapter.	15
Chapter 12 Complete	You've completed the twelfth chapter.	15
Chapter 13 Complete	You've completed the thirteenth chapter.	15
Chapter 14 Complete	You've completed the fourteenth chapter.	15
Chapter 15 Complete	You've completed the fifteenth chapter.	15
Game Complete	You've beat the game! Congratulations!	15
An Unfortunate Accident	A party member has been caught in an explosion and died.	15
Union Assault	You've defeated two or more enemies in a single attack.	15
A New Beginning	You've begun your second playthrough!	15
Tera-Driver	You've loaded over a terabit of data from the disc.	30
Disrespect Your Elders	You've defeated the Elderly Man. He's with the stars now!	30
Basel's Liberator	You've made all of Basel's hexes accessible again. Are you even human?!	30
Challenge Conqueror	You've defeated the top-ranked team, the Last Line! Amazing!	30
Kings of Neverland	You've cleared Neverland!	30
The Legendary Hunter	You've completed every mission in the game! The legend will never die!	90
Stardust Hunters	You've got a in every rank!	90
Lap Two Complete	You've finished your second playthrough! Congratulations, and thank you!	90

ROCK BAND 2

ACHIEVEMENTS

NAME	GOAL/REQUIREMENT	POINT VALUE
Solid Gold, Baby!	Gold Star a song	25
The Bachman-Turner Award	Maintain deployed Overdrive for 90 seconds	25
Flawless Fretwork	Score 100% notes hit as a guitarist on Expert	25
Flawless Guitar Solo	100% a guitar solo on Expert, using only the solo buttons	20
Flawless Drumming	Score 100% notes hit as a drummer on Expert	25
Flawless Singing	Score a 100% rating as a vocalist on Expert	25
Flawless Groove	Score 100% notes hit as bassist, up-strums only, on Expert	25
Comeback Kid	Defeat the last player that defeated you over Xbox LIVE in either Score Duel or Tug of War.	15
Victory!	Defeat a player in either Score Duel or Tug of War.	15
Band Savior	Be a savior three times during a single song	20
Overdrive Overdose	Achieve an 8x Band Multiplier	25
Hello Cleveland!	Deploy Vocal Overdrive 4 times in a single song	20
Million Point Club	Earn more than 1,000,000 points in a single song.	25
You're Hired!	Hire a staff member	10
Needs more Umlauts!	Make a band logo	10
The San Dimas 4th Annual Award	Compete in a Battle of the Bands event	15
You Killed the Radio Star	Make a music video in World Tour	15
Clothes to the Edge	Buy over $100,000 worth of items from the Rock Shop	20
Along for the Ride	Beat an instrument-specific challenge while playing another instrument	10
Challenge Novice	Complete either 25 challenges on Medium, 10 challenges on Hard, or 5 challenges on Expert	10
Challenge Master	Complete 25 Challenges on Hard Difficulty or 10 Challenges on Expert Difficulty	15
Challenge Savant	Complete 25 Challenges on Expert Difficulty	25
The Final Countdown	Unlock an Impossible Challenge	15
Groove Assassin	Beat the Impossible Bass Challenge	20
Lord of the Strings	Beat the Impossible Guitar Challenge	25
Stage Igniters	Beat the Impossible Band Challenge	25
AN-I-MAL!!!	Beat the Impossible Drum Challenge	25
Virtuoso	Beat the Impossible Vocal Challenge	25
West Coast Performer	Play a set on the West Coast of North America	10
Heartland Performer	Play a set in Middle America	10
East Coast Performer	Play a set on the East Coast of North America	10
God Save the Band	Play a set in the United Kingdom	10
Western Europe Performer	Play a set in Western Europe.	10
Eastern European Performer	Play a set in Eastern Europe	10
Worldwide Sensation	Gain access to every venue in the world	25
Road Dog	Play in every venue in the world	30
One Million Fans	Reach 1 million fans in World Tour	30
Open Road	Win a Bus in World Tour	20
Got Wheels	Win a Van in World Tour	20
Jet Setter	Win a Jet in World Tour	20
Beat It!	Complete all beats at 60 BPM or higher or half of the beats at 140 BPM or higher	10
The Beat Goes On	Complete all beats at 100 BPM or higher or half of the beats at 180 BPM or higher	20
Fill Me In	Complete all fills at 60 BPM or higher or half of the fills at 140 BPM or higher	10
Fill Legend	Complete all fills at 100 BPM or higher or half of the fills at 180 BPM or higher	20

SECRET ACHIEVEMENTS

NAME	GOAL/REQUIREMENT	POINT VALUE
Buy a Real Instrument Already!	Beat an "Impossible" Challenge with all players on Expert Difficulty	35
Rock Immortal Inductee	Joined the Rolling Stone Rock Immortals list	20
Vinyl Artist	Finished the Endless Setlist 2 in World Tour on Medium	20
Gold Artist	Finished the Endless Setlist 2 in World Tour on Hard	30
Platinum Artist	Finished the Endless Setlist 2 in World Tour on Expert	50
The Bladder of Steel Award	Completed the Endless Setlist 2 without pausing or failing.	25

ROCK BAND 3

ACHIEVEMENTS

NAME	GOAL/REQUIREMENT	POINT VALUE
Tune Up	Calibrate your audio/video setup for the optimal Rock Band 3 experience.	4
Self-Made Dude or Lady	Create a Character.	5
Best. Name. Ever.	Rename your band.	5
Well Connected	Connect your Rock Band 3 Band with rockband.com at http://www.rockband.com.	6
You Ain't Seen Nothing Yet	Maintain overdrive for 60 seconds.	20
Millionaire Club	Get 1,000,000 on one song.	25
Rock Band Master	5 Star on Medium (or 3 Star on a higher difficulty) any 50 Rock Band 3 songs.	25
Rock Band Legend	5 Star every song in Rock Band 3 on Hard.	30
Rock Band Immortal	5 Star every song in Rock Band 3 on Expert.	50
Alex's Luggage Combination	Beat a Rock Band 3 score of 12,345,678.	30
Hometown Threwdown	Complete the "Hometown Throwdown" Road Challenge.	20
Real Nor'easter	Complete "The Wicked Awesome Tour".	20
Hell Defrosted	Win all rewards on the "Hell Freezes Over" Road Challenge.	25
Wilderness Survival	Complete the "Through the Wilderness, Eh?" Road Challenge.	20
Major Mileage	Get 90 or more spades on "The Long Drive South" Road Challenge.	25
Party Animal	Completed the "Total Debauchery" Road Challenge.	20
The Connoisseur's Connoisseur	Get 90 or more spades on "The European Connoisseur" Road Challenge.	25
Mile High Club	Complete the "Really Frequent Flyers" Road Challenge.	25
Ultimate Road Warrior	Win all awards on the "Really Frequent Flyers" Road Challenge.	30
HOPO-cidal Maniac	Kill 53,596 Hammer-ons and Pull-offs.	25
Bleeding Fingers	Get 85% on all Guitar Solos in Rock Band 3 on Hard or Expert.	30
Guitar Perfectionist	Get 100% accuracy on Expert Guitar.	25
Guitar Apprentice	5 Star on Easy Guitar (or 3 Star on a higher difficulty) any 25 Rock Band 3 songs.	20
Bass Streaker	Get a streak of 500 notes on Bass.	10
Most Authentic Strummer	Hit 100% of the notes, only strumming up, on Hard Bass.	10
Bass Apprentice	5 Starred on Easy Bass (or 3 Starred on a higher difficulty) 25 Rock Band 3 songs.	20
Drum Roll, Please!	Nail a drum roll.	10
Fastest Feet	Hit 90% of the Kick notes in a song on Hard Drums.	15
Drums Apprentice	5 Star on Easy Drums (or 3 Star on a higher difficulty) any 25 Rock Band 3 songs.	20
Keys Streaker	Get a streak of 350 notes on Keys.	15

XBOX 360 ACHIEVEMENTS

NAME	GOAL/REQUIREMENT	POINT VALUE
Keys Apprentice	5 Star on Easy Keys (or 3 Star on a higher difficulty) any 25 Rock Band 3 songs.	20
Pro Bass Apprentice	5 Star on Easy Pro Bass (or 3 Star on a higher difficulty) any 25 Rock Band 3 songs.	20
Drum Trainer Initiate	Complete the introductory Pro Drum Trainer lessons.	15
Drum Trainer Graduate	Complete the final Pro Drum Trainer lessons.	30
Play a Real Guitar Already!	Play "The Hardest Button to Button" on Pro Guitar.	15
Pro Guitar to the Max	Max out your Score Multiplier meter on Pro Guitar.	15
Power Chords	Complete the "Power Chords" lessons in the Pro Guitar trainer.	15
Complex Chords	Complete the "More Chord Holding and Arpeggiation" Pro Guitar lessons.	25
Pro Guitar Apprentice	5 Star on Easy Pro Guitar (or 3 Star on a higher difficulty) any 25 Rock Band 3 songs.	20
Pro Keyboardist	Hit at least 90% of the notes in 3 songs on Expert Pro Keys.	15
Pro Keys Graduate	Complete the final Pro Keys trainers.	25
Pro Keys to the Max	Max out your Score Multiplier meter on Pro Keys.	15
Pro Keys Apprentice	5 Star on Easy Pro Keys (or 3 Star on a higher difficulty) any 25 Rock Band 3 songs.	20
Triple Awesome	Get a Triple Awesome while playing with Vocal Harmonies.	10
Is This Just Fantasy?	Hit all triple awesomes in "Bohemian Rhapsody" on Medium or a higher difficulty.	25
Vocals Showmanship	Deploy overdrive four times in a single song as a vocalist.	10
Tambourine Master	Hit 100% of the notes in a percussion section.	10
Vocal Virtuoso	Earn an Awesome rating on at least 90% of the phrases in 6 songs on Hard Vocals.	15
Vocal Apprentice	5 Star on Easy Vocals (or 3 Star on a higher difficulty) any 25 Rock Band 3 songs.	20
The Endless Setlist III	Successfully complete "The Endless Setlist III!"	50
Downloader	Play a downloaded song.	20
Mercurial Vocalist	Earn 5 stars on Vocals on a downloaded Queen song.	30
Live Free or Die	Beat all of the free downloadable songs for Rock Band.	25
Fistful of Awesome	Beat 5 downloaded songs.	15
Accountant's Dozen	Beat 12 downloaded songs.	15
Decent Collection	Beat 20 downloaded songs.	15
I Want It All	Play a downloaded Queen song.	15
Shameless Self-Promotion	Download and play three songs from a band that has Harmonix team members in it.	15
Just Another Band Out of Boston	5 Star any Boston song.	15
Face Melter	Melt faces by beating any three '80s Metal songs.	25
Dave Grohl Band	Beat 5 songs from any band that has had Dave Grohl as a member.	30
The Perfect Drug	Get a 200 note streak on "The Perfect Drug".	30

SAW

ACHIEVEMENTS

NAME	GOAL/REQUIREMENT	POINT VALUE
Treasure!	Unlock first container.	10
It Was An Accident	Kill first minion.	10
Self-Defense	Kill 10 minions.	15
Duress	Kill 20 minions.	20
Just Experimenting	Used Health Syringe for the first time	10
I Can Stop Anytime	Used 20 Health Syringes.	20
You've Wasted Your Life	Idle for five minutes.	5
Would You Like To Know More?	Find your first Asylum File.	20

NAME	GOAL/REQUIREMENT	POINT VALUE
Who Is The Jigsaw Killer?	Find your first Patient File.	15
Darwin Would Be Proud	Died once.	20
Kill Or Be Killed	Killed a Collared Minion with a collar detonation.	30
Give Me Five!	First kill with a Mannequin Arm.	10
Homerun	First kill with a Bat.	10
Sometimes It Sticks	First kill with a Nail Bat.	10
Cleaning Up	First kill with a Mop Handle.	10
Pipe Dream	First kill with a Pipe.	10
Surgeon	First kill with a Scalpel.	10
Penetrated	First kill with a Syringe.	10
You've Been Served	First kill with a Table Leg.	10
You'll Need This Afterwards	First kill with a Crutch.	10
Grave Digger	First kill with a Shovel.	10
Lights Off	First kill with a Table Lamp.	10
Hatchet Job	First kill with a Hatchet.	10
Fire Hazard	First kill with fire	10
Splitting Headache	First kill with Scissors.	10
Say Hello To My Little Friend	First kill with a Gun.	10
Wait For The Boom	First kill with an Explosive Mine.	10
Whoops!	First kill with a Stun Mine.	10
Choked Up	First kill with a Gas Mine.	10
I'm In Charge	Fought first NPC.	10
Curb Stomp	Stomped first Minion to death.	10
Merciless	Stomped five Minions to death.	20
Forced Entry	Unlocked first door.	10
Locksmith	Unlock 5 locked doors.	20
Professional	Unlock 20 locked doors.	50

SECRET ACHIEVEMENTS

NAME	GOAL/REQUIREMENT	POINT VALUE
It's A Trap!	Complete Reverse Bear Trap	40
What Was That?!?	First encounter with Pighead.	5
Hit And Run	Release Jennings from his Trap	40
Damaged Goods	Release Amanda from her trap	40
Absent Parent	Release Melissa from her Trap	40
Aphasia	Release Oswald from his Trap	40
Eager Student	Release Obi from his Trap	40
Born Victim	Release Jeff from his Trap	40
Violence Begets Violence	Kill the Pighead	40
Cost of the Truth	Complete Game using Truth Door	100
Never Truly Free	Complete game using Freedom Door.	100

SINGULARITY

ACHIEVEMENTS

NAME	GOAL/REQUIREMENT	POINT VALUE
Time Master	Completed Singularity on Hard Mode	60
Pistol Whipped	20 Centurion kills in single player campaign	10
A Salt and Battery	40 AR9 Valkyrie kills in single player campaign	10
Double Barrel	30 Volk S4 kills in single player campaign	10
The Slower the Better	25 Kasimov SNV-E99 slo-mo kills in single player campaign	15
No Time to Bleed	15 Autocannon kills without reloading in single player campaign	15
You're a Hit	20 Spikeshot kills in single player campaign	10
Roller Derby	20 Dethex Launcher kills in single player campaign	15
Drive By	15 Seeker kills in single player campaign	20

XBOX 360 ACHIEVEMENTS

NAME	GOAL/REQUIREMENT	POINT VALUE
Return to Sender	Kill 5 enemies by grabbing rockets and launching them back in single player campaign	20
Put the Dead in Deadlock	Kill 10 enemies inside a Deadlock in single player campaign	15
Up Close and Personal	Kill 20 enemies with Impulse in single player campaign	15
Fire and Ice	Kill 10 enemies with Propane Tanks or Cryo Tanks in single player campaign	20
Time Bandit	Grab 5 Shields from enemies in single player campaign	15
Ashes to Ashes	Age 15 soldiers to Dust in single player campaign	20
Night of the Living Revert	Turn 15 soldiers into Reverts in single player campaign	20
Fully Armed	Fully Upgraded 1 Weapon in single player campaign	20
E99 Tech Geek	Purchased 10 different Hero Upgrades in single player campaign	20
Time's on My Side	Purchased 5 different TMD Equipment items in single player campaign	20
Pen Pal	Used the TMD to find 15 Chrono-Notes in single player campaign	20
Stay After Class	Used the TMD to revert 10 Chalkboards in single player campaign	20
Revert Bomber	Killed 10 enemies by aging a Revert and having it explode near them in single player campaign	25
That Wheel?	Found the wheel. Will they ever explain this?	15
Mother My Brain Hurts	Discovered the strange E99 specimen and what it morphs people into	15
Extermination Expert	Play 5 public matches of Extermination	10
Extermination Addict	Play 100 public matches of Extermination	40
Extermination Master	Win 25 public matches of Extermination	25
CvS Master	Win 25 public matches of Creatures Vs. Soldiers	25
Creature Hater	Renew 25 beacons in Extermination (public match)	10
Creature Lover	Kill 15 soldiers with each creature (public match)	10
Fastball	Kill 15 soldiers with a Zek barrel (public match)	15
Zekky Style	Kill 15 soldiers from behind with the Zek (public match)	15
Hot Lunch Special	Kill 25 soldiers with the Revert puke (public match)	20
Bombs over Katorga	Kill 25 soldiers with the Radion's lob attack (public match)	20
In Yo Face	Possess 15 soldiers with tick leap attack (public match)	20
Talk to the Hand	Kill 25 creatures with the Bruiser's Impulse Power (public match)	20
Dr. Time	Use the Healer's power to restore 25 soldiers to full health (public match)	20
Don't Touch Me!	Kill 15 creatures with the Lurker's reflective shield damage from a melee hit (public match)	20
The VP Treatment	Possess a soldier, then shoot another soldier in the face (public match)	10
Blitzkrieg	Travel 585 meters using the Blitzer's Teleport power (public match)	20
Killer	Get highest number of kills in a public match	15
SECRET ACHIEVEMENTS		
Workers' District	Completed the Workers' District Mission	25
Research Facility	Completed the Research Facility Mission	25
Rail Line	Completed the Rail Line Mission	25
Central Docks	Completed the Central Docks Mission	25
E99 Processing Complex	Completed the E99 Processing Complex Mission	25
Singularity	Completed Singularity	25
The Good of the Many	You sacrificed yourself to stop Demichev	30
One TMD to Rule Them All	You chose to live and rule the world alone	30
The Needs of the Few	You chose to live and join Demichev	30

ACHIEVEMENTS

NAME	GOAL/REQUIREMENT	POINT VALUE
True Blue	Earn your BLUE SEGA License.	10
Amber De Amigo	Earn your AMBER SEGA License.	10
Red Out	Earn your RED SEGA License.	15
Virtual Bronze	Earn your BRONZE SEGA License.	20
Captain Silver	Earn your SILVER SEGA License.	30
Golden Acts	Earn your GOLD SEGA License.	80
Now There Are No Limits!	Win your first Grand Prix Cup.	10
Welcome to the Next Level!	Win every race within a Grand Prix Cup.	15
To be this good takes AGES!	Win every Grand Prix Cup.	30
Fighters Megamix	Take out an opponent with each character's All-Star Move.	30
Time Stalker	Set a Personal Best Time on any Time Trial course.	10
Clock Work	Set a Personal Best Time on every Time Trial course.	30
Shadow Dancing	Defeat a Staff Ghost on any Time Trial course.	10
Ghost Master	Defeat a Staff Ghost on every Time Trial course.	30
Mega Driver	Score AAA on any mission.	10
Crazy Box	Pass every mission.	15
Magical Sound Shower	Race to every piece of music.	30
Top of the Class	Score AAA on every mission.	30
Dreamarena	Play a friend over Xbox LIVE.	10
Racing Hero	Win any race over Xbox LIVE.	15
Outrunner	Lap a trailing player in a race over Xbox LIVE.	30
Death Adder	Take out opponents with items one hundred times over Xbox LIVE.	30
Lucky Dime	Purchase any item from the shopping menu.	10
High Roller	Purchase every item from the shopping menu.	15
Classic Collection	Win a race as each racer.	15
SEGA World	Complete a race on each course in Grand Prix, Single Race or Time Trial mode.	30
Power Drift	Perform a fifteen second Drift.	15
Turbo	Perform twenty Turbo-Boosts within a single lap of any event.	15
Triple Trouble	Perform three Tricks in one jump and make the landing.	15
Gaining Ground	Get a Turbo-Boost Start in any event.	10
Wheels of Fire	Perform a Turbo-Boost Start across 3 consecutive events.	15
Rolling Start	Complete Sonic's Test Drive.	15
Road Rampage	Take out three opponents with one All-Star Move.	15
After Burner	Take out three opponents with one triple-weapon.	15
Up 'N' Down	Take out a racer by manually directing an item.	10
Streets of Rage	Ram an opponent off the course without using a Weapon or Power-Up.	15
Wonder Boy	Win a race by crossing the finish line in reverse.	15
Altered Beast	Win a race while using an All-Star Move.	10
Last Survivor	Finish the first lap in last position and go on to win the race.	15
Super Hang-On	Win the race holding first place on each lap.	15
Project Rub	Complete any Race event without collisions.	15
Enduro Racer	Play one hundred events including any race, mission or time trial in any mode.	15
Ultimate Collection	Earn every achievement in the game.	100

SECRET ACHIEVEMENTS

NAME	GOAL/REQUIREMENT	POINT VALUE
Sonic Unleashed	Use Sonic's All-Star Move to take out Dr. Eggman and show him who's boss!	15
Feel the Magic	Use Amy's All-Star Move to send Sonic dizzy with love!	15

XBOX 360 ACHIEVEMENTS

NAME	GOAL/REQUIREMENT	POINT VALUE
Working Man	Use Ryo's All-Star Move to take out Jacky and Akira and show them who's the ultimate martial artist!	15
Giant Egg	Use Billy's All-Star Move to squash the Crows!	15
Top Skater	Perform three tricks in one jump with Beat on Tokyo-to - Shibuya Downtown.	15
The Chariot	Use Zobio and Zobiko to send one hundred Curien Mansion Creatures back to the grave.	15
Cat Mania	Summon the giant KapuKapu and gobble up Big the Cat for mouse revenge!	15

SPIDER-MAN: SHATTERED DIMENSIONS

ACHIEVEMENTS

NAME	GOAL/REQUIREMENT	POINT VALUE
Easy as pie!	Complete all levels on Easy	20
Is this normal?	Complete all levels on Normal	50
Hard pressed	Complete all levels on Hard	100
Lead on, M-Dubs!	Complete the Tutorial	5
End of Act 1	Complete Act 1 on any difficulty level	20
End of Act 2	Complete Act 2 on any difficulty level	20
End of Act 3	Complete Act 3 on any difficulty level	20
Getting warmed up	Defeat 100 enemies	10
In the zone	Defeat 500 enemies	20
Ain't no stoppin'!	Defeat 1000 enemies	50
Manifest Destiny	Complete the Web of Destiny	100
Bug collector	Collect all Hidden Spiders	50
The complete package	Unlock all Character upgrades	20
Smooth moves	Unlock all Combat upgrades	20
Uncle Benjamin	Execute a 100-hit combo (except the Tutorial)	10
Two hundo	Execute a 200-hit combo (except the Tutorial)	20
Missed me!	Defeat a boss on any difficulty level without taking damage	20
Close call!	Recover 10 times from a Critical Fall	10
Amazing!	Complete 4 levels with the highest rank in Hard mode	20
Sensational!!	Complete 8 levels with the highest rank in Hard mode	30
Spectacular!!!	Complete 12 levels with the highest rank in Hard mode	50
Hobbyist	Collect 125 Spider Emblems	10
Enthusiast	Collect 250 Spider Emblems	15
Fanatic	Collect 500 Spider Emblems	20
The Spider's shadow	Complete a Noir level without triggering an alarm	10
The Spider's bite	Keep Rage Mode active for one minute	10
The Spider's grace	Complete a 2099 freefall section without taking damage	10
The Spider's web	Defeat 50 enemies using the Amazing Charge Attack	10

SECRET ACHIEVEMENTS

NAME	GOAL/REQUIREMENT	POINT VALUE
Survival of the fittest	Defeat Kraven on any difficulty level	15
Something CAN stop Juggernaut!	Defeat Juggernaut on any difficulty level	15
Here's mud in your eye!	Defeat Sandman on any difficulty level	15
Now there's a shock	Defeat Electro on any difficulty level	15
Canceled!	Defeat Deadpool on any difficulty level	15
Minimized Carnage	Defeat Carnage on any difficulty level	15
Clipped wings	Defeat Hobgoblin on any difficulty level	15
Took the sting out of him	Defeat Scorpion on any difficulty level	15

NAME	GOAL/REQUIREMENT	POINT VALUE
Lay down your arms	Defeat Doc Ock on any difficulty level	15
The caged bird squawks	Defeat Vulture on any difficulty level	15
The hammer falls	Defeat Hammerhead on any difficulty level	15
Circus freak	Defeat Goblin on any difficulty level	15
Final curtain call	Defeat Mysterio on any difficulty level	50
No harm done	Complete any level without dying (except the Tutorial)	20

SUPER STREET FIGHTER IV

ACHIEVEMENTS

NAME	GOAL/REQUIREMENT	POINT VALUE
Overachiever	Attain all the Achievements! The path of the warrior demands this from those who walk on it!	0
Fashion Plate	Even a top rate fighter needs to coordinate properly! You gotta get all of the Colors first!	10
Dan the Man	Mastery of the Saikyo arts requires mastery of the Personal Action! Collect 'em all, punk!	10
Entitled	A Title does not tell all of a man, sir, but if I were to see one Title, I'd want them all...	50
Iconoclast	Oh my gosh, those Icons are so adorable! I gotta find Don-chan and catch 'em all!	50
Special Movement	Do a Special Move 100 times! If you're a true student of the Rindo-kan dojo, it's your duty!	10
EXtra! EXtra!	Battle requires courage! Train by using your EX Gauge to successfully land 100 EX Moves!	10
Super, Man!	To battle is to win a fight with overwhelming strength! Show me you can do 100 Super Combos!	10
Ultra, Man!	If yer gonna fight, give it your all, pal. Performing 100 Ultra Combos oughta do it, eh?	10
It Takes Focus	Your mission, should you wish to join Delta Red, is to connect with 100 Focus Attacks!	10
Superior Super	Trust your instincts and winning will come easy. Let's begin with 50 Super Combo finishes!	10
Ultimate Ultra	Candy always says you gotta win with style, so go out there and perform 50 Ultra Combo finishes!	10
Sunspotter	Amigo, perform 365 Super or Ultra Combo finishes against your opponents! The dawn is coming!	10
Absolute Perfection	Lauren's waiting, so how about you finish your fights quickly and get 30 Perfects. Sound good?	20
Clear Headed	Hey! Got time to kill? Try to clear Arcade Mode on Medium or higher! That's all you gotta do!	10
All Clear	To get strong takes lots of fighting! Clear Arcade Mode on Medium or higher with all characters!	10
Herculean Effort	Can you finish Arcade Mode on Medium or higher without using a continue? Show me you can!	10
Hard Times	To escape death is to beat the strongest of the strong. Finish Arcade Mode on Hardest, kid!	20
Long Time No See	Do you wish for defeat? If so, complete Arcade Mode on Hardest difficulty and beat Gouken!	50
Rival Schooled	See your future by clearing every Rival Battle on Medium or higher with every character.	20
Speed Freak	Finish each round in Arcade Mode on Medium or higher in 20 seconds or less. Too easy.	30
Good Start	All of nature must withstand a trial. You must clear 10 trials in Trial Mode to succeed.	10
Trail of Trials	There is no shortcut in the art of Yoga. Aim to clear any character's Trial Mode trials!	20
Trial Athlete	I shall assimilate all and be all-powerful! Clear all Trial Mode challenges, and so can you!	50
Oh! My Car!	Hee hee, destruction is so much fun! Score 80,000 points or more in the Car Crusher bonus stage!	10
Barrel of Laughs	No need for barrels without oil! Score 110,000 points or more in the Barrel Buster bonus stage!	10
It Begins	The fight starts here! Set your Title and Icon, and begin fighting on Xbox Live!	10

NAME	GOAL/REQUIREMENT	POINT VALUE
First Timer	I'll never forget my first time for Ryu's sake! Win one Ranked Match! Gotta aim for the top!	10
Threepeat	You think being this good is easy? Let's see you win 3 Ranked Matches in a row, champ!	20
Fivepeat	This is your real power, child? Show me it's not luck by winning 5 Ranked Matches in a row!	30
Tenpeat	Don't hold back your true potential! Win 10 Ranked Matches in a row!	50
Moving On Up	Ya need to do anything to reach the top of the food chain! Let's see a Rank Up via Ranked Match!	10
Now You C Me...	I wrestle only the strong! You shall rank up to C Rank if you wanna face me, comrade!	20
From C to Shining C	You think you're good, don't you? Prove it by ranking up all characters to C Rank!	50
Road to Victory	You wanna get that fight money? You're gonna have to win 10 Xbox LIVE matches first, sucka!	10
Battle Master	Only winners can attain such beauty. Win 30 Xbox LIVE matches and I may share my beauty secrets.	20
Legendary Fighter	I shall make you the right hand of Shadaloo if you can win 100 Xbox LIVE matches!	50
Worldly Warrior	Let's do this, amigo! Fight 50 Xbox LIVE matches, because that's the only way to become strong!	10
Bring it on!	No comrade, this will not do! We must become stronger, for our fans! Fight 100 Xbox LIVE matches!	20
This is Madness!	Fighting is fun, huh? Well then, let's aim for 300 Xbox LIVE matches fought, OK buddy?	50
Team Player	A 1-on-1 fight is fun, but it's more fun with friends! Try fighting in a Team Battle!	10
Team Mate	Win 1 Team Battle match, and you will learn that teamwork can help you become stronger!	10
Teamworker	A pro can win with any team. Win 10 Team Battles but don't forget, you have to win too!	30
Keep on Truckin'	If you want to focus on nothing but the fight, entering an Endless Battle is for you!	10
Three For The Road	In the pursuit of strength, one must have a goal! In Endless Battle win 3 matches in a row.	20
Endless Ten	Throw away your fears and focus on the fight! Win 10 fights in a row in Endless Battle!	50
Replayer	Watch 30 Replays via the Replay Channel! Isn't it fun watching people go at it tooth and nail!?	10
Endless Lobbyist	It's only natural for warriors to seek fights! Create 30 Endless Battle lobbies!	10
Team Lobbyist	Hey mon, battlin' is fun, no? Go out and create 30 Team Battle lobbies and enjoy the rhythm!	10
Quarter Up	Fight 30 opponents via Arcade Fight Request. It'd be easy with the right bait, he he.	10

SUPREME COMMANDER 2

ACHIEVEMENTS

NAME	GOAL/REQUIREMENT	POINT VALUE
Start Here	Complete both parts of the tutorial	10
Easy Going	Complete all three campaigns on 'Easy' difficulty	25
A Winner is You	Complete all three campaigns 'Normal' difficulty	75
Supremest Commander	Complete all three campaigns on 'Hard' difficulty	100
Knows it All	Complete all primary and secondary campaign objectives	25
Completist	Complete all hidden campaign objectives	25
Score Hoarder	Get a complete campaign score over 150,000	50
Replayer	Improve your score on any operation	5
Cakewalk	Win a skirmish or online match against any AI opponent	5
Good Game	Win a skirmish or online match against all AI opponents	20
Luddite	Win a skirmish or online match without building any Experimentals	10
To the Victor...	Win 25 skirmish or online matches	25

NAME	GOAL/REQUIREMENT	POINT VALUE
Rushin' Front	Win a skirmish or online match in less than five minutes	10
Sampling	Win a skirmish or online match with each faction	10
Dating	Play 10 skirmish or online matches with one faction	15
Committed Relationship	Play 25 skirmish or online matches with one faction	25
Sightseer	Win a skirmish or online match on every multiplayer map	20
Sharp Shooter	Destroy 10,000 units	25
Masster	Extract 1,000,000 mass	25
Master Builder	Build 10,000 units	25
Time Cruncher	Play the game for over 24 hours in total	50
Internet Commander	Win an online match	10
Friends	Win a co-op match vs AI	10
Ranker	Win a Ranked Match	10
Supreme Online Commander	Win 25 Ranked Matches	50
Good Friends	Win 10 co-op matches vs AI	20

SECRET ACHIEVEMENTS

NAME	GOAL/REQUIREMENT	POINT VALUE
Communication Breakdown	Complete the 'Prime Target' operation	10
Second Target	Complete the 'Off Base' operation	10
Deep Freeze	Complete the 'Strike While Cold' operation	10
Fatboy Parade	Complete the 'Titans of Industry' operation	15
Nuclear Strike	Complete the 'Factions or Family Plan' operation	15
Rodgers is Relievedis	Complete the 'End of an Alliance' operation	25
Barge Ahead	Complete the 'Delta Force' operationthe	10
Alarming	Complete the 'Lethal Weapons' operation	10
Prison Break	Complete the 'Back on the Chain Gang' operation	15
Hole in the Ground	Complete the 'Steamed' operation	15
Gorged	Complete the 'Cliff Diving' operation	20
Reunited	Complete the 'Prime Time' operation	25
Downloading	Complete the 'Fact Finder' operation	10
Bugs in the Systemthe	Complete the 'The Trouble With Technology' operation	20
Animal Magnetism	Complete the 'The Great Leap Forward' operation	10
Class Reunion	Complete the 'Gatekeeper' operation	20
Well Stocked	Complete the 'Surface Tension' operation	15
Terra Firma	Complete the 'The Final Countdown' operation	25
Survivor	Don't lose any units during the first attack in 'Prime Target'	10
Bot Lord	Complete 'Prime Time' with an army made up entirely of Assault Bots	15
Survivalist	Survive multiple waves after the download completes in 'Fact Finder'	15

TEKKEN 6

ACHIEVEMENTS

NAME	GOAL/REQUIREMENT	POINT VALUE
Give Your Fists a Rest	Defeat an enemy using a weapon in Scenario Campaign Mode.	15
Night at the Movies	Unlock a movie in Scenario Campaign Mode.	15
Item Connoisseur	Obtain a Rank S Item in Scenario Campaign Mode.	30
Treasure Amateur	Collect 50 treasures in Scenario Campaign Mode.	10
Treasure Enthusiast	Collect 100 treasures in Scenario Campaign Mode.	20
Treasure Master	Collect 200 treasures in Scenario Campaign Mode.	30
Enemy Hunting Amateur	Defeat 300 enemies in Scenario Campaign Mode.	10
Enemy Hunting Enthusiast	Defeat 1000 enemies in Scenario Campaign Mode.	20

NAME	GOAL/REQUIREMENT	POINT VALUE
Enemy Hunting Master	Defeat 2000 enemies in Scenario Campaign Mode.	30
Playing With Fire	Defeat 100 enemies with the Flamethrower in Scenario Campaign Mode.	15
Heavy Artillery	Defeat 100 enemies with the Gatling Gun in Scenario Campaign Mode.	15
Ready for Action	Pick up 300 health recovery items in Scenario Campaign Mode.	15
Brute Force	Defeat 100 enemies with the Lead Pipe in Scenario Campaign Mode.	15
Thirsty Fighter	Pick up 50 drink items in Scenario Campaign Mode.	15
Crate Breaker	Destroy 100 wooden crates in Scenario Campaign Mode.	15
Alien Hunter	Defeat 10 aliens in Scenario Campaign Mode.	20
Scenario Expert	Clear all of the stages in Scenario Campaign Mode.	30
King of the Hill	Knock 10 enemies in the water in Scenario Campaign Mode.	20
A Friend in Need	Rescue your downed partner 3 times in Scenario Campaign Mode (single player).	15
Combo Amateur	Perform a 10 chain combo in Scenario Campaign Mode.	10
Combo Enthusiast	Perform a 30 chain combo in Scenario Campaign Mode.	20
Combo Master	Perform a 50 chain combo in Scenario Campaign Mode.	30
Upgraded Assistant	Upgrade Alisa to the highest possible level.	15
What's So Special About It?	Obtain the Special Flag in Scenario Campaign Mode.	20
No Key For Me	Clear the Millennium Tower stage without the boot-up key in Scenario Campaign Mode.	45
Learning is Fun	Clear the tutorial stage in Scenario Campaign Mode.	15
Moving On Up	Win a Ranked Match in Online Mode.	20
No Pressure	Win a Player Match in Online Mode.	20
Fighting Amateur	Play 3 matches in Online Mode.	10
Fighting Enthusiast	Play 10 matches in Online Mode.	20
Fighting Master	Play 30 matches in Online Mode.	30
Arcade Addict	Clear the Arcade Battle in Offline Mode.	15
Team Toppler	Defeat 3 teams in Team Battle in Offline Mode.	15
Survival of the Fittest	Earn 10 consecutive wins in Survival in Offline Mode.	15
Practice Makes Perfect	Inflict a total of 1000 damage in Practice in Offline Mode.	15
Gallery Completionist	Complete the Gallery.	45
Ghost Vanquisher	Defeat 30 Ghosts.	20
Love That Money	Collect more than 5,000,000 G.	15
Machine Crusher	Defeat NANCY-MI847J.	30

SECRET ACHIEVEMENTS

NAME	GOAL/REQUIREMENT	POINT VALUE
Tekken Fanatic	Complete all other objectives.	10
Friend or Foe?	Reunite with your ally in Scenario Campaign Mode.	15
Locate the Target	Learn the whereabouts of Heihachi Mishima in Scenario Campaign Mode.	15
It's All Coming Back to Me	Recover your memory in Scenario Campaign Mode.	15
The Key to Victory	Obtain the boot-up key in Scenario Campaign Mode.	15
That's No Hero	Defeat the Hero in Scenario Campaign Mode.	15
The Destroyer Has Fallen	Defeat the Destroyer of Worlds in Scenario Campaign Mode.	15
Showdown	Win the final battle in Scenario Campaign Mode.	30
What a Nightmare	Clear the Nightmare Train stage in Scenario Campaign Mode.	30
Wooden Warrior	Clear the Subterranean Pavilion stage in Scenario Campaign Mode.	30
Eastern Explorer	Clear the Kigan Island stage in Scenario Campaign Mode.	30

TERMINATOR: SALVATION

ACHIEVEMENTS

NAME	GOAL/REQUIREMENT	POINT VALUE
L.A. 2016	Complete Chapter 1—L.A. 2016 on any difficulty	80
Thank Heaven	Complete Chapter 2—Thank Heaven on any difficulty	80
New Acquaintances	Complete Chapter 3—New Acquaintances on any difficulty	80
The Sights	Complete Chapter 4—The Sights on any difficulty	80
Underground	Complete Chapter 5—Underground on any difficulty	80
Into the Wild	Complete Chapter 6—Into the Wild on any difficulty	80
Angie	Complete Chapter 7—Angie on any difficulty	80
Every life is sacred	Complete Chapter 8—Every life is sacred on any difficulty	80
For the Resistance	Complete Chapter 9—For the Resistance on any difficulty	80
Seasoned Commander	Complete the Game—Become a commander on Medium difficulty	100
Veteran Commander	Complete the Game—Become a commander on Hard difficulty	180

TOM CLANCY'S SPLINTER CELL: CONVICTION

ACHIEVEMENTS

NAME	GOAL/REQUIREMENT	POINT VALUE
Realistic Difficulty	Complete single player story on "Realistic" difficulty	50
Co-op Realistic Difficulty	Complete the co-op story on "Realistic" difficulty	50
Quality Time	Invite a friend to join and participate in a co-op story or game mode session	20
Hunter	Complete any 1 map in "Hunter" game mode in co-op	10
Last Stand	Complete any 1 map in "Last Stand" game mode in co-op	10
Hunter Completionist	Complete all maps in "Hunter" game mode on rookie or normal difficulty	20
Hunter Master	Complete all maps in "Hunter" game mode on realistic difficulty	50
Last Stand Completionist	Complete all maps in "Last Stand" game mode on rookie or normal difficulty	20
Last Stand Master	Complete all maps in "Last Stand" game mode on realistic difficulty	50
Face-Off Completionist	Complete all maps in "Face-Off" game mode using any connection type	20
Face Off	Win one match in "Face-Off" game mode on any difficulty	10
Preparation Master	Complete all prepare & execute challenges	30
Stealth Master	Complete all vanish challenges	30
Best Of The Best	Complete all Splinter Cell challenges	30
Well-Rounded	Complete all challenges	50
Weapon Upgraded	Purchase all 3 upgrades for any 1 weapon	10
Gadget Upgraded	Purchase all 3 upgrades for any 1 gadget	10
Weapons Expert	Purchase all 3 upgrades for all weapons	20
Gadgets Expert	Purchase both upgrades for all gadgets	20
Weapons Collector	Unlock all weapons in the weapon vault	20
Variety	Purchase any 1 uniform	10
Accessorizing	Purchase any 1 accessory for any 1 uniform	10
Ready For Anything	Purchase all 9 accessories for all uniforms	20
Fashionable	Purchase all 6 texture variants for all uniforms	20
Perfect Hunter	Complete any map in Hunter without ever having been detected on realistic difficulty	20
Last Man Standing	In Last Stand, survive all enemy waves of any map in one session without failing on any difficulty	50
Revelations	Discover Anna Grimsdottir's dark secret	10

SECRET ACHIEVEMENTS

NAME	GOAL/REQUIREMENT	POINT VALUE
Merchant's Street Market	Complete Single Player Story "Merchant's Street Market" on any difficulty	20
Kobin's Mansion	Complete Single Player Story "Kobin's Mansion" on any difficulty	20
Price Airfield	Complete Single Player Story "Price Airfield" on any difficulty	20
Diwaniya, Iraq	Complete Single Player Story "Diwaniya, Iraq" on any difficulty	20
Washington Monument	Complete Single Player Story "Washington Monument" on any difficulty	20
White Box Laboratories	Complete Single Player Story "White Box Laboratories" on any difficulty	20
Lincoln Memorial	Complete Single Player Story "Lincoln Memorial" on any difficulty	20
Third Echelon HQ	Complete Single Player Story "Third Echelon HQ" on any difficulty	20
Michigan Ave. Reservoir	Complete Single Player Story "Michigan Ave. Reservoir" on any difficulty	20
Downtown District	Complete Single Player Story "Downtown District" on any difficulty	20
White House	Complete Single Player Story "White House" on any difficulty	20
St. Petersburg Banya	Complete CO-OP Story "St. Petersburg Banya" on any difficulty	20
Russian Embassy	Complete CO-OP Story "Russian Embassy" on any difficulty	20
Yastreb Complex	Complete CO-OP Story "Yastreb Complex" on any difficulty	20
Modzok Proving Grounds	Complete CO-OP Story "Modzok Proving Grounds" on any difficulty	20
Judge, Jury and Executioner	Take down Tom Reed	10
Man of Conviction	Allow Tom Reed to live	10
Survivor	Battle your CO-OP teammate and survive	10

TRANSFORMERS: REVENGE OF THE FALLEN

ACHIEVEMENTS

NAME	GOAL/REQUIREMENT	POINT VALUE
Down to Chinatown	Medal in all Autobot Shanghai Missions	20
West Side	Medal in all Autobot West Coast Missions	20
Aerialbot Assault	Medal in all Autobot Deep Six Missions	20
East Side	Medal in all Autobot East Coast Missions	20
The Dagger's Tip	Medal in all Autobot Cairo Missions	20
One Shall Stand	Defeat Megatron—Autobot Campaign	25
Now I've Seen It All	Unlock all Autobot Unlockables	50
Power to the People	Purchase All Autobot Upgrades	25
Awesome Achievement!	Eliminate 250 Decepticons—Autobot Campaign	25
Do the Math	Acquire 2,000,000 Energon in the Autobot Campaign	20
A True Autobot	Earn Platinum Medals on ALL Autobot Missions	75
Shanghai'd	Medal in all Decepticon Shanghai Missions	25
West Coast For The Win!	Medal in all Decepticon West Coast Missions	25
Rise of The Fallen	Medal in all Decepticon Deep Six Missions	25
Coast to Coast	Medal in all Decepticon East Coast Missions	25
Lies	Medal in all Decepticon Cairo Missions	25
One Shall Fall	Defeat Optimus Prime—Decepticon Campaign	25
Now I've Really Seen It All	Unlock all Decepticon Unlockables	50
Spoils of War	Purchase All Decepticon Upgrades	25
Bad Boys	Eliminate 350 Autobots—Decepticon Campaign	25
Break the Bank	Acquire 3,000,000 Energon in the Decepticon Campaign	25

NAME	GOAL/REQUIREMENT	POINT VALUE
A True Decepticon	Earn Platinum Medals on ALL Decepticon Missions	75
Platty For The Win!	Earn a Platinum Medal—Either Campaign	20
Golden Boy	Earn a Gold Medal—Either Campaign	15
Not Gold Enough	Earn a Silver Medal—Either Campaign	10
Cast in Bronze	Earn a Bronze Medal—Either Campaign	5
On the Board	Make it into the Top 100000 on SP Leaderboards—Either Campaign	15
Good Mojo	Make it into the Top 10000 on SP Leaderboards—Either Campaign	25
Bonecrusher	Make it into the Top 1000 on SP Leaderboards—Either Campaign	25
And So It Begins…	Unlock a Single Unlockable—Either Campaign	5
Grind On	Purchase an Upgrade—Either Campaign	5
Choices…	Unlock a New Zone—Either Campaign	5
You've Got The Touch	Fill OVERDRIVE Meter—Either Campaign	25
Choose a Side	Win one RANKED/PLAYER MATCH game as Autobots and one as Decepticons	15
Hold!	Win a Control Point round without losing a control point in a RANKED/PLAYER MATCH game	15
Follow the Leader	While playing One Shall Stand, as the leader, kill the opposing leader in a RANKED/PLAYER MATCH game	15
Life of the Party	Host one game of each game type in a PLAYER MATCH game	15
Smells Like Victory	Win a Match as Each of the 15 Default Characters	50

UFC 2010 UNDISPUTED

ACHIEVEMENTS

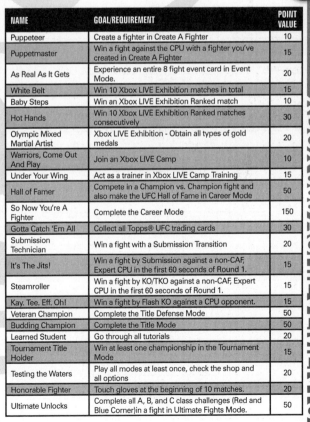

NAME	GOAL/REQUIREMENT	POINT VALUE
Puppeteer	Create a fighter in Create A Fighter	10
Puppetmaster	Win a fight against the CPU with a fighter you've created in Create A Fighter	15
As Real As It Gets	Experience an entire 8 fight event card in Event Mode.	20
White Belt	Win 10 Xbox LIVE Exhibition matches in total	15
Baby Steps	Win an Xbox LIVE Exhibition Ranked match	10
Hot Hands	Win 10 Xbox LIVE Exhibition Ranked matches consecutively	30
Olympic Mixed Martial Artist	Xbox LIVE Exhibition - Obtain all types of gold medals	20
Warriors, Come Out And Play	Join an Xbox LIVE Camp	10
Under Your Wing	Act as a trainer in Xbox LIVE Camp Training	15
Hall of Famer	Compete in a Champion vs. Champion fight and also make the UFC Hall of Fame in Career Mode	50
So Now You're A Fighter	Complete the Career Mode	150
Gotta Catch 'Em All	Collect all Topps® UFC trading cards	30
Submission Technician	Win a fight with a Submission Transition	20
It's The Jits!	Win a fight by Submission against a non-CAF, Expert CPU in the first 60 seconds of Round 1.	15
Steamroller	Win a fight by KO/TKO against a non-CAF, Expert CPU in the first 60 seconds of Round 1.	15
Kay. Tee. Eff. Oh!	Win a fight by Flash KO against a CPU opponent.	15
Veteran Champion	Complete the Title Defense Mode	50
Budding Champion	Complete the Title Mode	50
Learned Student	Go through all tutorials	20
Tournament Title Holder	Win at least one championship in the Tournament Mode	15
Testing the Waters	Play all modes at least once, check the shop and all options	20
Honorable Fighter	Touch gloves at the beginning of 10 matches.	20
Ultimate Unlocks	Complete all A, B, and C class challenges (Red and Blue Corner)in a fight in Ultimate Fights Mode.	50

NAME	GOAL/REQUIREMENT	POINT VALUE
Pound For Pound Champ	Win a Champion vs. Champion fight in Career Mode	50
Yellow Belt	Win 25 Xbox LIVE Ranked Matches	20
Purple Belt	Win 50 Xbox LIVE Ranked Matches	30
Brown Belt	Win 75 Xbox LIVE Ranked Matches	40
Black Belt	Win 100 Xbox LIVE Ranked Matches	50
Coming Up Next...	Download an Event for Event Mode	10
The Cessation Sensation!	Win by all methods of stoppage against the CPU. (KO, TKO, Submission, Doctor Stoppage)	25
Bobbin' And Weavin'	Dodge 3 consecutive strikes via sway (Outside of Tutorial Mode)	30
Blog Fodder	Complete a post-fight interview in Career Mode	15
Move Mastery	Reach "World Class" (Level 3) status with a technique or move.	25

SECRET ACHIEVEMENTS

NAME	GOAL/REQUIREMENT	POINT VALUE
Fighting with Pride	Now you're dirty boxing with Pride!	15
Cocky S.O.B.	No respect for your opponent.	10
It Slices, It Dices	Is there a doctor in the stadium!	15?

VANQUISH

ACHIEVEMENTS

NAME	GOAL/REQUIREMENT	POINT VALUE
One Day at DARPA	Complete all DARPA training exercises.	10
Space Normandy	Complete Act 1.	15
Storming Grand Hill	Complete Act 2.	15
I Don't Speak Kreon!	Complete Act 3.	15
My Way	Complete Act 4.	15
End to Major Combat Operations	Complete Act 5.	15
Survivor	Complete all Acts.	30
Operation Overlord II	Complete Act 1 on Hard difficulty or above.	25
Ain't Life Grand?	Complete Act 2 on Hard difficulty or above.	25
Cry on, Kreon!	Complete Act 3 on Hard difficulty or above.	25
The High Way	Complete Act 4 on Hard difficulty or above.	25
Mission Accomplished	Complete Act 5 on Hard difficulty or above.	25
ARS Operator	Complete all Acts on Hard difficulty or above.	50
Gun Runner	Scan and acquire all weapons.	10
King of the Hill	Level a weapon up to maximum operational capability.	20
Fight or Flight	Manually trigger AR Mode and destroy an enemy robot.	10
Adrenaline Rush	Manually trigger AR Mode and destroy three enemy robots in a row.	20
Going in for the Kill	Destroy ten enemy robots with melee attacks.	10
A Heartbreaker and Lifetaker	Destroy 100 enemy robots with melee attacks.	30
Helloooo, Nurse	Revive a friendly troop.	5
Knight in Shining White Armor	Revive 20 friendly troops.	15
Death Wish	Destroy three enemy robots while in damage-triggered AR Mode.	20
40 Yard Dash	Maintain a Boost dash to the limit of the ARS reactor without overheating.	30
Home Run	Destroy an incoming missile or grenade.	10
Home Run God	Destroy ten incoming missiles or grenades.	10
Brutality Bonus	Destroy a Romanov's arms and legs, then finish it with a melee attack.	10
Romanov This!	Destroy a Romanov with a melee attack.	20

NAME	GOAL/REQUIREMENT	POINT VALUE
The Hand of God	Destroy two Romanovs in a row using only melee attacks.	30
Robots Tend to Blow Up	Destroy three enemy robots at once with one hand grenade.	10
Hole-in-One	Destroy a Chicane with a hand grenade.	5
Short Circuit	Destroy ten enemy robots that have been disabled with an EMP emitter.	20
Two Birds with One Stone	Destroy two or more enemy robots at once with the LFE gun.	20
Trick Shot	Destroy three enemy robots at once with rocket launcher splash damage.	20
Flash! King of the Impossible	Destroy four enemies simultaneously with the Lock-on Laser.	30
Piece by Piece	Destroy the arms, head, and back of an KNRB-0 Argus robot.	20
That Ended Up Working Out Nicely	After taking control of the enemy transport in Act 2-2, do not let a single enemy escape.	10
Failure Breeds Success	Destroy two Argus robots in Act 2-3 while they are in bipedal mode.	15
Leibniz Defense Agency	Defend the Pangloss statue in Act 3-2.	10
Tightrope Walker	Destroy two cannons in Act 3-3 and complete the mission.	10
Fisher is the Other Sam	Proceed on the monorail in Act 3-4 without being spotted by the enemy troops or searchlights.	15
Flyswatter	Destroy all the floating turrets in Act 3-4.	20
Guardian	Do not allow any friendly armor to be destroyed during Act 3-5.	10
Hurry the #@$% Up!	Destroy five or more enemy transports from atop the Kreon in Act 3-7.	10
Civil Disobedience	Ignore the elevator start order in Act 4-1. Instead, hold position and destroy all reinforcements.	30
Buzzard Beater	Destroy the Buzzard without allowing it to reach ground level in Act 5-1.	30
Smoke 'em if ya got 'em!	Destroy 10 enemies distracted by cigarettes during one mission.	30
Auld Lang Syne	Destroy two enemy robots who have been distracted by a cigarette.	15
The Best of All Possible Worlds	Find and fire upon all of the Pangloss statues hidden on the colony.	30
Living Legend	Complete the game without dying, regardless of difficulty level.	50

SECRET ACHIEVEMENTS

NAME	GOAL/REQUIREMENT	POINT VALUE
Tactical Challenges	Complete all of the Tactical Challenges in VANQUIS	50H

WOLFENSTEIN

ACHIEVEMENTS

NAME	GOAL/REQUIREMENT	POINT VALUE
Safe Keeping	Finish a match on Bank, spending the majority of your time on the winning team. (1 min minimum)	10
Route Canal	Finish a match on Canals, spending the majority of your time on the winning team. (1 min minimum)	10
Chemical Burn	Finish a match on Chemical, spending the majority of your time on the winning team. (1 min minimum)	10
Facilitated	Finish a match on Facility, spending the majority of your time on the winning team. (1 min minimum)	10
Hospitalized	Finish a match on Hospital, spending the majority of your time on the winning team. (1 min minimum)	10
Mind your Manors	Finish a match on Manor, spending the majority of your time on the winning team. (1 min minimum)	10
Pirate Radio	Finish a match on Rooftops, spending the majority of your time on the winning team. (1 min minimum)	10
Shock and Awe	Finish a match on Tesla, spending the majority of your time on the winning team. (1 min minimum)	10

XBOX 360 ACHIEVEMENTS

NAME	GOAL/REQUIREMENT	POINT VALUE
Test Subject	Use every Veil ability once in multiplayer.	10
Veilophile	Spend 5 minutes in the Veil in multiplayer.	10
Ley Vacuum	Suck up 5 Veil Pools' worth of Veil energy in multiplayer.	10
Surgical Striker	Kill 200 enemy players using the Veil Strike in multiplayer.	30
Sneaky Pete	Kill 100 enemy players with the Satchel Charge in multiplayer.	30
Unholy Lifeline	Revive 250 teammates, including 10 revives in a single match in multiplayer.	30
Focal Point	Restore 5000 points of health to teammates using the Healing Aura in multiplayer.	30
Quartermaster	Give 100 Health Packs to teammates in multiplayer.	30
Run-gineer	Use Veil Speed for 30 minutes in multiplayer.	30
Engineering Corps	Complete 30 primary objectives and 50 secondary objectives in multiplayer.	30
Beatdown	Kill 50 enemies with melee attacks in a single player campaign.	30
Bubble Boy	Block 1000 shots with Shield power in a single player campaign.	20
Buster	Destroy 1000 breakable objects in a single player campaign.	20
Conservationist	Complete a story mission in the single player campaign without reloading a gun.	30
Endgame	Finish the single player campaign on any difficulty.	10
Gadget Freak	Purchase all the upgrades for one of your weapons in the single player campaign.	20
Game Hunter	Kill an enemy of every type in a single player campaign.	10
Gold Digger	Collect all the valuables in a single player campaign.	30
Gun Nut	Collect all the weapons in a single player campaign.	10
Honorary Geist	Spend two hours in the Veil in a single player campaign.	20
Nerd Rage	Complete the single player campaign on Hard or Über difficulty.	20
Librarian	Collect all the Tomes of Power in a single player campaign.	20
Man About Town	Complete all the Downtown missions in a single player campaign.	20
Blitzkrieg	Complete the single player campaign in under 12 hours.	30
Master Spy	Collect all the Intel in a single player campaign.	20
Monitor Tan	Collect every collectible in a single player campaign.	30
Newbie	Complete the Train Station mission in a single player campaign.	10
Rampage	Kill 200 enemies with Empower in a single player campaign.	20
Single Quarter	Complete the single player campaign with less than three deaths.	30
Slumming	Complete all the Midtown missions in a single player campaign.	10
Super Soldier	Complete the single player campaign on Über difficulty.	30
Time Out	Use the Mire power for more than an hour in a single player campaign.	20
Warchest	Collect more than $30,000 in a single player campaign.	20
Enemies in a Barrel	Kill 3 floating enemies.	20
Career Soldier	Reach Rank 25 in multiplayer.	15
Das Big Man	Reach Rank 50 in multiplayer.	15
Boot Camp	Get a kill with each Soldier weapon, the Satchel Charge and Veil Strike in multiplayer.	30
Heavy-Handed	Kill 200 enemy players with either the Panzerschreck or the Flammenwerfer in multiplayer.	30
Med School	Revive a player, supply a Health Pack, and heal someone using Healing Aura in multiplayer.	30
Basic Training	Complete a primary objective, supply an Ammo Pack, and use Veil Speed once in multiplayer.	30
Johnny-on-the-spot	Give 100 Ammo Packs to teammates in multiplayer.	30

WWE SMACKDOWN VS. RAW 2010

ACHIEVEMENTS

NAME	GOAL/REQUIREMENT	POINT VALUE
Story Designer	Create an original story using WWE STORY DESIGNER Mode.	20
2010 Hall of Fame Nominee	Induct a Superstar into the HALL OF FAME.	100
A Showman Like No Other	Have a total of 20 or more 5-star rated matches in your overall match history.	50
Mickie James Story	Complete the MICKIE JAMES story in ROAD TO WRESTLEMANIA mode.	20
Edge Story	Complete the EDGE story in ROAD TO WRESTLEMANIA mode.	20
HBK Story	Complete the HBK story in ROAD TO WRESTLEMANIA mode.	20
Orton Story	Complete the ORTON story in ROAD TO WRESTLEMANIA mode.	20
Brand Warfare Story	Complete the BRAND WARFARE story in ROAD TO WRESTLEMANIA mode.	20
Created Superstar Story	Complete the CREATE A SUPERSTAR story in ROAD TO WRESTLEMANIA mode.	20
Nothing More to Collect	Unlock all the playable characters and bonus items.	100
Face on the Big Screen	Convert a HIGHLIGHT REEL into an entrance movie.	15
Developmental Graduate	Complete the TRAINING CHECKLIST.	50
Career Growth	Increase the overall rating of a CREATED SUPERSTAR character to a 90 or above.	50
Check Out the New Threads	Create ALTERNATE ATTIRE for a CREATED SUPERSTAR and new THREADS for a WWE SUPERSTAR.	15
Finisher of the Year Candidate	Create a dive finisher, in Create A Finisher mode, and use it in a match (single player only).	20
Ask Him Ref!	Win 10 matches by submission (single player only).	20
Ahead of the Pack	Win as tentative Champion from start to end in CHAMPIONSHIP SCRAMBLE. (single player only)	50
Royal Rumble Specialist	Win a 30-Man ROYAL RUMBLE as the first entrant without changing Superstars (single player only).	100
And STILL Champion...	Defend a Title in a Championship Scramble match on Legend difficulty (single player only).	100
Shoulders to the Mat	Win 50 matches by pinfall (single player only).	20
A Grappling Machine	In one match, perform all 16 STRONG GRAPPLE moves on your opponent (single player only).	20

SECRET ACHIEVEMENTS

NAME	GOAL/REQUIREMENT	POINT VALUE
New Superstar Initiative	Create a SUPERSTAR in CREATE A SUPERSTAR Mode.	15
An Original Design	Create an original image using the PAINT TOOL.	15
Intermediate Technician	Succeed at a cumulative total of 50 reversals (single player only).	20
Technical Wizardry	Succeed at a cumulative total of 100 reversals (single player only).	100

X-MEN ORIGINS: WOLVERINE

ACHIEVEMENTS

NAME	GOAL/REQUIREMENT	POINT VALUE
Getting Started	Killed 100 enemies	10
A Day's Work	Killed 500 enemies	20
What I Do Best	Killed 2000 enemies	30
You Can't Hide	Lunged to 250 enemies	20
Lunge	Lunged to 25 enemies	10
Pounce	Lunged to 100 enemies	15
Piggy Back Ride	Lunged to a W.E.N.D.I.G.0 prototype's back	10

XBOX 360 ACHIEVEMENTS

NAME	GOAL/REQUIREMENT	POINT VALUE
Quick Killer	Quick Killed 1 enemy	10
Efficient Killer	Quick Killed 20 enemies	15
Perfect Killer	Quick Killed 3 enemies in a row	20
Drop Dead	Killed 10 enemies by throwing them off high areas	10
Apprentice	Raised One Combat Reflex to Master Level	10
Samurai	Raised All Combat Reflexes to Master Level	25
Mutant Lover	Raised one Mutagen to level 3	15
Astonishing	Found 1/2 of all Dog Tags in the game	20
Devil's Brigade	Found all Dog Tags in the game	30
Defensive	Performed 1 Counter move	10
Untouchable	Performed 25 Counter moves	20
Catch!	Killed 1 enemy with a reflected projectile	10
Boomerang	Killed 25 enemies with a reflected projectile	20
Aerial Assault	Performed 10 Air Grabs	10
Ultimate Wolverine	Fought 4 W.E.N.D.I.G.0 prototypes at the same time and defeated them at Alkali lake.	15
Hot Potato	Light 20 enemies on fire	20
Shotgun Epic Fail	Killed 25 Ghosts with their own weapon	15
James Howlett	Performed a Wolverine to Wolverine Lunge	15
WoW!	You feel cold as you examine the skeleton and read the name "Arthas" etched into the nearby sword	15
Aerial Master	Got 6 enemies airborne at once	15
Fully Loaded	Maxed out all upgrades	35
Slice n' Dice	Killed 6 enemies with a single attack	15
Found!	You found a mysterious hatch!	15
Slaughter House	Dismembered 100 enemies	15
Blender	Killed 200 enemies with Claw Spin	25
Walking Death	Beat the game on Hard Difficulty	50
Heightened Senses	Killed 200 enemies in Feral Sense	20
Environmentally Friendly	Killed 10 enemies using objects in the environment	15
Whatever it Takes	Killed 30 enemies using objects in the environment	20
Bloodlust	Killed 50 enemies while in Berserker mode	20
Weapon X	Killed 150 enemies while in Berserker mode	25
The Cake	You found the cake, yummy!	15

SECRET ACHIEVEMENTS

NAME	GOAL/REQUIREMENT	POINT VALUE
Bar Fight	Defeated Victor Creed (Sabretooth)	30
Spillway Escape	Escapes from Weapon X	30
Helicopter Ride	Defeated David Nord (Agent Zero)	30

NINTENDO Wii™

GAMES

2010 FIFA WORLD CUP SOUTH AFRICA

WORLD CLASSIC XI TEAM

Earn at least Bronze against each team in Kazumi's Dream Team to play the World Classic XI Team. Defeat them in a best of three match to play as the team in Hit the Pitch.

ASTRO BOY: THE VIDEO GAME

INVULNERABLE

Pause the game and press Up, Down, Down, Up, 1, 2.

MAX STATS

Pause the game and press Left, Left, 2, Down, Down, 1.

INFINITE SUPERS

Pause the game and press Left, 1, Right, 1, Up, Down.

INFINITE DASHES

Pause the game and press 2, 2, 1, 2, Left, Up.

DISABLE SUPERS
Pause the game and press 1, 1, 2, 2, 1, Left.

COSTUME SWAP (ARENA AND CLASSIC COSTUMES)
Pause the game and press 2, Up, 1, Up, Down, 2.

UNLOCK LEVELS
Pause the game and press Up, 1, Right, 1, Down, 1. This allows you to travel to any level from the Story menu.

AVATAR: THE LAST AIRBENDER

UNLIMITED HEALTH
Select Code Entry from Extras and enter 94677.

UNLIMITED CHI
Select Code Entry from Extras and enter 24463.

UNLIMITED COPPER
Select Code Entry from Extras and enter 23637.

NEVERENDING STEALTH
Select Code Entry from Extras and enter 53467.

ONE-HIT DISHONOR
Select Code Entry from Extras and enter 54641.

DOUBLE DAMAGE
Select Code Entry from Extras and enter 34743.

ALL TREASURE MAPS
Select Code Entry from Extras and enter 37437.

THE CHARACTER CONCEPT ART GALLERY
Select Code Entry from Extras and enter 97831.

AVATAR: THE LAST AIRBENDER— THE BURNING EARTH

DOUBLE DAMAGE
Go to the code entry section and enter 90210.

INFINITE LIFE
Go to the code entry section and enter 65049.

INFINITE SPECIAL ATTACKS
Go to the code entry section and enter 66206.

MAX LEVEL
Go to the code entry section and enter 89121.

ONE-HIT DISHONOR
Go to the code entry section and enter 28260.

ALL BONUS GAMES
Go to the code entry section and enter 99801.

ALL GALLERY ITEMS
Go to the code entry section and enter 85061.

AVATAR: THE LAST AIRBENDER— INTO THE INFERNO

After you have defeated the first level, The Awakening, go to Ember Island. Walk to the left, past the volleyball net, to a red and yellow door. Select Game Secrets and then Code Entry. Now you can enter the following cheats:

MAX COINS
Enter 66639224.

ALL ITEMS AVAILABLE FROM SHOP
Enter 34737253.

ALL CHAPTERS
Enter 52993833.

UNLOCK CONCEPT ART IN GALLERY
Enter 27858343.

BAKUGAN BATTLE BRAWLERS

1,000 BP
Enter 33204429 as your name.

5,000 BP
Enter 42348294 as your name.

10,000 BP
Enter 46836478 as your name.

100,000 BP
Enter 18499753 as your name.

500,000 BP
Enter 26037947 as your name.

BRONZE WARIUS
Enter 44982493 as your name.

BAND HERO

MOST CHARACTERS UNLOCKED
Select Input Cheats from the options and enter Blue, Yellow, Green, Yellow, Red, Green, Red, Yellow.

ELECTRIKA STEEL UNLOCKED
Select Input Cheats from the options and enter Blue, Blue, Red, Yellow, Red, Yellow, Blue, Blue.

ALL HOPO MODE
Select Input Cheats from the options and enter Red, Green, Blue, Green, Blue, Green, Red, Green.

ALWAYS SLIDE
Select Input Cheats from the options and enter Yellow, Green, Yellow, Yellow, Yellow, Red, Blue, Red.

AUTO KICK
Select Input Cheats from the options and enter Yellow, Green, Yellow, Blue, Blue, Red, Blue, Red.

FOCUS MODE
Select Input Cheats from the options and enter Yellow, Yellow, Green, Green, Red, Red, Blue, Blue.

HUD FREE MODE
Select Input Cheats from the options and enter Green, Red, Green, Red, Yellow, Blue, Green, Red.

PERFORMANCE MODE
Select Input Cheats from the options and enter Yellow, Yellow, Blue, Green, Blue, Red, Red, Red.

AIR INSTRUMENTS
Select Input Cheats from the options and enter Blue, Yellow, Blue, Red, Red, Yellow, Green, Yellow.

INVISIBLE ROCKER
Select Input Cheats from the options and enter Green, Red, Yellow, Green, Yellow, Blue, Yellow, Green.

THE BEATLES: ROCK BAND

BONUS PHOTOS
At the title screen, press Blue, Yellow, Orange, Orange, Orange, Blue, Blue, Blue, Yellow, Orange.

BEN 10: ALIEN FORCE VILGAX ATTACKS

LEVEL SKIP
Pause the game and enter Portal in the Cheats menu.

UNLOCK ALL SPECIAL ATTACKS (ALL FORMS)
Pause the game and enter Everythingproof in the Cheats menu.

UNLOCK ALL ALIEN FORMS
Pause the game and enter Primus in the Cheats menu.

TOGGLE INVULNERABILITY ON AND OFF
Pause the game and enter Xlmrsmoothy in the Cheats menu.

FULL HEALTH
Pause the game and enter Herotime in the Cheats menu.

QUICK ENERGY REGENERATION
Pause the game and enter Generator in the Cheats menu.

BEN 10: PROTECTOR OF EARTH

INVINCIBILITY
Select a game from the Continue option. Go to the Map Selection screen, press Plus and choose Extras. Select Enter Secret Code and enter XLR8, Heatblast, Wildvine, Fourarms.

ALL COMBOS
Select a game from the Continue option. Go to the Map Selection screen, press Plus and choose Extras. Select Enter Secret Code and enter Cannonblot, Heatblast, Fourarms, Heatblast.

ALL LOCATIONS
Select a game from the Continue option. Go to the Map Selection screen, press Plus and choose Extras. Select Enter Secret Code and enter Heatblast, XLR8, XLR8, Cannonblot.

DNA FORCE SKINS
Select a game from the Continue option. Go to the Map Selection screen, press Plus and choose Extras. Select Enter Secret Code and enter Wildvine, Fourarms, Heatblast, Cannonbolt.

DARK HEROES SKINS

Select a game from the Continue option. Go to the Map Selection screen, press Plus and choose Extras. Select Enter Secret Code and enter Cannonbolt, Cannonbolt, Fourarms, Heatblast.

ALL ALIEN FORMS

Select a game from the Continue option. Go to the Map Selection screen, press Plus and choose Extras. Select Enter Secret Code and enter Wildvine, Fourarms, Heatblast, Wildvine.

MASTER CONTROL

Select a game from the Continue option. Go to the Map Selection screen, press Plus and choose Extras. Select Enter Secret Code and enter Cannonbolt, Heatblast, Wildvine, Fourarms.

BEN 10 ULTIMATE ALIEN: COSMIC DESTRUCTION

To remove the following cheats, you must start a new game.

1,000,000 DNA

Pause the game, select Cheats, and enter Cash.

REGENERATE HEALTH

Pause the game, select Cheats, and enter Health.

REGENERATE ENERGY

Pause the game, select Cheats, and enter Energy.

UPGRADE EVERYTHING

Pause the game, select Cheats, and enter Upgrade.

ALL LEVELS

Pause the game, select Cheats, and enter Levels.

DAMAGE

Pause the game, select Cheats, and enter Hard. With this code, enemies cause double damage while you cause half damage.

BLAZING ANGELS: SQUADRONS OF WWII

ALL AIRCRAFT AND CAMPAIGNS

After you have chosen a pilot, hold Minus + Plus and press Left, Right, 1, 2, 2, 1.

GOD MODE

Pause the game, hold Minus and press 1, 2, 1, 2.

WEAPON DAMAGE INCREASED

Pause the game, hold Minus and press 2, 1, 1, 2.

BOOM BLOX

ALL TOYS IN CREATE MODE

At the Title screen, press Up, Right, Down, Left to bring up a cheats menu. Enter Tool Pool.

SLOW-MO IN SINGLE PLAYER

At the Title screen, press Up, Right, Down, Left to bring up a cheats menu. Enter Blox Time.

CHEERLEADERS BECOME PROFILE CHARACTER

At the Title screen, press Up, Right, Down, Left to bring up a cheats menu. Enter My Team.

FLOWER EXPLOSIONS

At the Title screen, press Up, Right, Down, Left to bring up a cheats menu. Enter Flower Power.

JINGLE BLOCKS

At the Title screen, press Up, Right, Down, Left to bring up a cheats menu. Enter Maestro.

BOOM BLOX BASH PARTY

At the title screen, press Up, Right, Down, Left. Now you can enter the following codes:

UNLOCK EVERYTHING

Enter Nothing But Hope.

1 MILLION BOOM BUX

Enter Bailout.

TURN ON BLOX TIME

Enter Freeze Frame.

TURNS ALL SOUND EFFECTS INTO VIRUS BLOX SOUND EFFECTS

Enter Musical Fruit.

ALL COLORED BLOX

Enter Rainbow Blox.

BRATZ: MOVIE STARZ

FEELIN' PRETTY CLOTHING LINE
At the Cheat Computer enter PRETTY.

HIGH SCHOOL CLOTHING LINE
At the Cheat Computer enter SCHOOL.

HOLLYWOOD CLOTHING LINE
At the Cheat Computer enter MOVIES

PASSION FOR FASHION CLOTHING LINE
At the Cheat Computer enter ANGELZ.

PRINCESS CLOTHING LINE
At the Cheat Computer enter SPARKL.

BUILD-A-BEAR WORKSHOP: A FRIEND FUR ALL SEASONS

ALL ISLANDS, MINIGAMES, OUTFITS, AND ACCESSORIES
At the Main menu, press Up, Down, Left, Right, A, B.

CABELA'S DANGEROUS HUNTS 2009

.470 NITRO EXPRESS HIGH CALIBER RIFLE
Select Enter Special Code from the Extras menu and enter 101987.

CARS MATER-NATIONAL

ALL ARCADE RACES, MINI-GAMES, AND WORLDS
Select Codes/Cheats from the options and enter PLAYALL.

ALL CARS
Select Codes/Cheats from the options and enter MATTEL07.

ALTERNATE LIGHTNING MCQUEEN COLORS
Select Codes/Cheats from the options and enter NCEDUDZ.

ALL COLORS FOR OTHERS
Select Codes/Cheats from the options and enter PAINTIT.

UNLIMITED TURBO
Select Codes/Cheats from the options and enter ZZOOOOM.

EXTREME ACCELERATION
Select Codes/Cheats from the options and enter 0TO200X.

EXPERT MODE
Select Codes/Cheats from the options and enter VRYFAST.

ALL BONUS ART
Select Codes/Cheats from the options and enter BUYTALL.

CARS RACE-O-RAMA

ALL ARCADE MODE EVENTS
Select Cheats from the Options menu and enter SLVRKEY.

ALL STORY MODE EVENTS
Select Cheats from the Options menu and enter GOLDKEY.

ALL OF LIGHTNING MCQUEEN'S FRIENDS
Select Cheats from the Options menu and enter EVRYBDY.

ALL LIGHTNING MCQUEEN CUSTOM KIT PARTS
Select Cheats from the Options menu and enter GR8MODS.

ALL PAINT JOBS FOR ALL NON-LIGHTNING MCQUEEN CHARACTERS
Select Cheats from the Options menu and enter CARSHOW.

CASTLEVANIA THE ADVENTURE REBIRTH

LEVEL SELECT
Select Game Start and hold Right for a few seconds. You can play any level you have already played.

CODE LYOKO: QUEST FOR INFINITY

UNLOCK EVERYTHING
Pause the game and press 2, 1, C, Z, 2, 1.

UNLIMITED HEALTH AND POWER
Pause the game and press 2, 2, Z, Z, 1, 1.

INCREASE SPEED
Pause the game and press Z, 1, 2, 1 (x3).

INCREASE DAMAGE
Pause the game and press 1, Z, Z, C (x3).

CONFIGURATION A
Pause the game and press 2, Z, 1, Z, C, Z.

CONFIGURATION B
Pause the game and press C, C, 1, C, Z, C.

ALL ABILITIES
Pause the game and press Z, C, Z, C (x3).

ALL BONUSES
Pause the game and press 1, 2, C, 2 (x3).

ALL GOODIES
Pause the game and press C, 2, 2, Z, C, Z.

THE CONDUIT

SECRET AGENT MODEL, MULTIPLAYER
Enter SuitMP13 at the Cheat menu.

SPECIAL ASE TEXTURE
Enter NewASE11 at the Cheat menu.

PLAY AS DRONE, SINGLE PLAYER
Enter Drone4SP at the Cheat menu.

CONTRA REBIRTH

DEBUG MENU
At the title screen, press Plus + 1 + 2.

CORALINE

UNLIMITED LEVEL SKIP
Select Cheats from the Options menu and enter beldam.

UNLIMITED HEALTH
Select Cheats from the Options menu and enter beets.

UNLIMITED FIREFLIES
Select Cheats from the Options menu and enter garden.

FREE HALL PASSES
Select Cheats from the Options menu and enter well.

BUTTON EYE CORALINE
Select Cheats from the Options menu and enter cheese.

CRASH: MIND OVER MUTANT

FREEZE ENEMIES WITH TOUCH
Pause the game, hold guard and press Down, Down, Down, Up.

ENEMIES DROP X4 DAMAGE
Pause the game, hold guard and press Up, Up, Up, Left.

ENEMIES DROP PURPLE FRUIT
Pause the game, hold guard and press Up, Down, Down, Up.

ENEMIES DROP SUPER KICK
Pause the game, hold guard and press Up, Right, Down, Left.

ENEMIES DROP WUMPA FRUIT
Pause the game, hold guard and press Right, Right, Right, Up.

SHADOW CRASH
Pause the game, hold guard and press Left, Right, Left, Right.

NINTENDO Wii

OVERLOAD

DEFORMED CRASH

Pause the game, hold guard and press Left, Left, Left, Down.

COSTUMES

Complete all of the following character's mini-games to unlock each costume.

COSTUME	CHARACTER
Magmadon	Little Bear
Ratcicle	Ratcicle Kid
Skeleton	Sludge Brother
Snipe	Crunch
Spike	Uka Uka

DE BLOB

INVULNERABILITY

During a game, hold C and press 1, 1, 1, 1. Re-enter the code to disable.

LIFE UP

During a game, hold C and press 1, 1, 2, 2.

TIME BONUS

During a game, hold C and press 1, 2, 1, 2. This adds 10 minutes to your time.

ALL MOODS

At the Main menu, hold C and press B, B, 1, 2, 1, 2, B, B.

ALL MULTIPLAYER LEVELS

At the Main menu, hold C and press 2, 2, B, B, 1, 1, B, B.

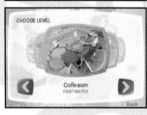

DEAD SPACE EXTRACTION

4 CHALLENGE MODE LEVELS

At the title screen, press Down, Up, Left, Right, Right, Left.

DEADLY CREATURES

ALL CHAPTERS

At the chapter select, press Right, Right, Up, Down, 2, 1, 1, 2. When you jump to a later chapter, you get any move upgrades you would have, but not health upgrades.

DEFEND YOUR CASTLE

GIANT ENEMIES

Select Credits and click SMB3W4 when it appears.

TINY UNITS

Select Credits and click Chuck Norris when it appears.

EASY LEVEL COMPLETE

Pause the game and wait for the sun to set. Unpause to complete the level.

DESTROY ALL HUMANS! BIG WILLY UNLEASHED

Pause the game and go to the Unlockables screen. Hold the analog stick Up until a Enter Unlock Code window appears. You can now enter the following cheats with the directional-pad. Press A after entering a code.

Use this menu to toggle cheats on and off.

UNLOCK ALL GAME WORLDS
Up, Right, Down, Right, Up

CAN'T BE KILLED
Left, Down, Up, Right, Up

LOTS OF GUNS
Right, Left, Down, Left, Up

INFINITE AMMO
Right, Up, Up, Left, Right

UNLIMITED BIG WILLY BATTERY
Left, Left, Up, Right, Down

UNLIMITED JETPACK FUEL
Right, Right, Up, Left, Left

PICK UP HEAVY THINGS
Down, Up, Left, Up, Right

STEALTH SPACE NINJA
Up, Right, Down, Down, Left

CRYPTO DANCE FEVER SKIN
Right, Left, Right, Left, Up

KLUCKIN'S CHICKEN BLIMP SKIN
Left, Up, Down, Up, Down

LEISURE SUIT SKIN
Left, Down, Right, Left, Right

PIMP MY BLIMP SKIN
Down, Up, Right, Down, Right

DISNEY PRINCESS: ENCHANTED JOURNEY

BELLE'S KINGDOM
Select Secrets and enter GASTON.

GOLDEN SET
Select Secrets and enter BLUEBIRD.

FLOWER WAND
Select Secrets and enter SLEEPY.

HEART WAND
Select Secrets and enter BASHFUL.

SHELL WAND
Select Secrets and enter RAJAH.

SHIELD WAND
Select Secrets and enter CHIP.

STAR WAND
Select Secrets and enter SNEEZY.

DISNEY'S CHICKEN LITTLE: ACE IN ACTION

ALL LEVELS
Select the Cheats option and enter Right, Up, Left, Right, Up.

ALL WEAPONS
Select the Cheats option and enter Right, Down, Right, Left.

UNLIMITED SHIELD
Select the Cheats option and enter Right, Down, Right, Down, Right.

DJ HERO

Select Cheats from Options and enter the following. Some codes will disable high scores and progress. Cheats cannot be used in tutorials and online.

UNLOCK ALL CONTENT
Enter tol0.

ALL CHARACTER ITEMS
Enter uNA2.

ALL VENUES
Enter Wv1u.

ALL DECKS
Enter LAuP.

ALL HEADPHONES
Enter 62Db.

ALL MIXES
Enter 82xl.

AUTO SCRATCH
Enter IT6j.

AUTO EFFECTS DIAL
Enter ab1L.

AUTO FADER
Enter SL5d.

AUTO TAPPER
Enter ZitH.

AUTO WIN EUPHORIA
Enter r3a9.

BLANK PLINTHS
Enter ipr0.

HAMSTER SWITCH
Enter 7geo.

HYPER DECK MODE
Enter 76st.

SHORT DECK
Enter 51uC.

INVISIBLE DJ
Enter oh5T.

PITCH BLACK OUT
Enter d4kR.

PLAY IN THE BEDROOM
Enter g7nH.

ANY DJ, ANY SETLIST
Enter 0jj8.

DAFT PUNK'S CONTENT
Enter d1g?.

DJ AM'S CONTENT
Enter k07u.

DJ JAZZY JEFF'S CONTENT
Enter n1fz.

DJ SHADOW'S CONTENT
Enter oMxV.

DJ Z-TRIP'S CONTENT
Enter 5rtg.

GRANDMASTER FLASH'S CONTENT
Enter ami8.

NINTENDO Wii

DRAGON BALL Z: BUDOKAI TENKAICHI 2

DOUBLE FIST POWER
At the Stage Select screen in Vs. Mode, hold Z + Plus to start the code input. Swing the Nunchuk Right, Wiimote Left, Wiimote Left + Nunchuk Right, Wiimote and Nunchuk Down. Hold Z + Minus to clear codes.

TAIL POWER
At the Stage Select screen in Vs. Mode, hold Z + Plus to start the code input. Swing the Wiimote Down, Up, Left, Right. Hold Z + Minus to clear codes.

DRAGON BALL Z: BUDOKAI TENKAICHI 3

SURVIVAL MODE
Clear 30 missions in Mission 100 mode.

DRAGON BLADE: WRATH OF FIRE

ALL LEVELS
At the Title screen, hold Plus + Minus and select New Game or Load game. Hold the buttons until the stage select appears.

EASY DIFFICULTY
At the Title screen, hold Z + 2 when selecting "New Game."

HARD DIFFICULTY
At the Title screen, hold C + 2 when selecting "New Game."

To clear the following codes, hold Z at the stage select.

DRAGON HEAD
At the stage select, hold Z and press Plus. Immediately Swing Wii-mote Right, swing Wii-mote Down, swing Nunchuck Left, swing Nunchuck Right.

DRAGON WINGS
At the stage select, hold Z and press Plus. Immediately Swing Nunchuck Up + Wii-mote Up, swing Nunchuck Down + Wii-mote Down, swing Nunchuck Right + Wii-mote Left, swing Nunchuck Left + Wii-mote Right.

TAIL POWER
At the stage select, hold Z and press Plus. Immediately Swing your Wii-mote Down, Up, Left, and Right

DOUBLE FIST POWER
At the stage select, hold Z and press Plus. Immediately swing your Nunchuck Right, swing your Wii-mote left, swing your Nunchuck right while swinging your Wii-mote left, then swing both Wii-mote and Nunchuck down

DRIVER: PARALLEL LINES

ALL VEHICLES
Pause the game, select cheats and enter carshow.

ALL WEAPONS
Pause the game, select cheats and enter gunrange.

INVINCIBILITY
Pause the game, select cheats and enter steelman.

INFINITE AMMUNITION
Pause the game, select cheats and enter gunbelt.

INFINITE NITROUS
Pause the game, select cheats and enter zoomzoom.

INDESTRUCTIBLE CARS
Pause the game, select cheats and enter rollbar.

WEAKER COPS
Pause the game, select cheats and enter keystone.

ZERO COST
Pause the game, select cheats and enter tooledup. This gives you free upgrades.

EARTHWORM JIM

CHEAT MENU
Pause the game and press Y + Left, B, B, Y, Y + Right, B, B, Y. Notes that these are the button presses for the classic controller.

EA SPORTS NBA JAM

Hold the Wii Remote vertically when entering the following codes. To access the teams, press + at the Team Select screen.

BEASTIE BOYS
At the Title screen, press Up, Up, Down, Down, Left, Right, Left, Right, B, +. This team includes Ad Rock, MCA, and Mike D.

J.COLE & 9TH WONDER
At the Title screen, press Up, Left, Down, Right, Up, Left, Down, Right, 1, 2.

DEMOCRAT TEAM
At the Title screen, press Left (x13), +. This team includes Barack Obama, Joe Biden, Bill Clinton, and Hillary Clinton.

REPUBLICAN TEAM
At the Title screen, press Right (x13), +. The team includes George W. Bush, Sarah Palin, and John McCain.

ESPN'S SPORTSNATION
Select Play Now. When entering the initials, enter ESP for P1 and NSN for P2. Advance to the Choose Teams screen and use + to find the team. This team includes the hosts of the show, Colin Cowherd and Michelle Beadle.

NBA MASCOTS
Select Play Now. When entering the initials, enter MAS for P1 and COT for P2. Advance to the Choose Teams screen and use + to find the team.

ORIGINAL JAM
Select Play Now. When entering the initials, enter MJT for P1. Advance to the Choose Teams screen and use + to find the team. This team includes Mark Turmell and Tim Kitzrow.

FAMILY FEUD 2010 EDITION

NEW WARDROBE
Select the lock tab from the Wardrobe screen and enter FAMILY.

FAR CRY VENGEANCE

ALL MAPS
Select Cheats Menu from the Options menu and enter GiveMeTheMaps.

FATAL FURY SPECIAL

SOUND TEST
Pause the game and press A, B, C, D, A.

FIGHTING STREET

+4 CREDITS, SIMPLIFIED SPECIAL MOVES, AND STAGE SELECT
After getting a high score, enter .SD as your initials. Then, at the title screen, hold Left + 1 + 2, and press Minus.

+4 CREDITS
After getting a high score, enter .HU as your initials. Then, at the title screen, hold Left + 1 + 2, and press Minus.

SIMPLIFIED SPECIAL MOVES
After getting a high score, enter .LK as your initials. Then, at the title screen, hold Left + 1 + 2, and press Minus.

STAGE SELECT
After getting a high score, enter .AS as your initials. Then, at the title screen, hold Left + 1 + 2, and press Minus.

GHOST SQUAD

COSTUMES

Reach the following levels in single player to unlock the corresponding costume.

LEVEL	COSTUME	LEVEL	COSTUME
07	Desert Camouflage	30	Urban Camouflage
10	Policeman	34	Virtua Cop
15	Tough Guy	38	Future Warrior
18	Sky Camouflage	50	Ninja
20	World War II	60	Panda Suit
23	Cowboy	99	Gold Uniform

NINJA MODE
Play through Arcade Mode.

PARADISE MODE
Play through Ninja Mode.

GHOUL PATROL

PASSWORDS

LEVEL	PASSWORD	LEVEL	PASSWORD
5	CP4V	13	KVCY
9	7LBR		

GI JOE: THE RISE OF COBRA

CLASSIC DUKE
At the Title screen, press Left, Up, Minus, Up, Right, Plus.

CLASSIC SCARLETT
At the Title screen, press Right, Up, Down, Down, Plus.

THE GODFATHER: BLACKHAND EDITION

The following pause screen codes can be used only once every five minutes.

$5000
Pause the game and press Minus, 2, Minus, Minus, 2, Up.

FULL HEALTH
Pause the game and press Left, Minus, Right, 2, Right, Up.

FULL AMMO
Pause the game and press 2, Left, 2, Right, Minus, Down.

FILM CLIPS
After loading your game, before selecting Play Game, press 2, Minus, 2, Minus, Minus, Up.

GODZILLA UNLEASHED

UNLOCK ALL
At the Main menu, press A + Up to bring up the cheat entry screen. Enter 204935.

SHOW MONSTER MOVES
At the Main menu, press A + Up to bring up the cheat entry screen. Enter 411411.

90000 STORE POINTS
At the Main menu, press A + Up to bring up the cheat entry screen. Enter 031406.

VERSION NUMBER
At the Main menu, press A + Up to bring up the cheat entry screen. Enter 787321.

SET DAY
At the Main menu, press A + Up to bring up the cheat entry screen. Enter 0829XX, where XX represents the day. Use 00 for day one.

MOTHERSHIP LEVEL
Playing as the Aliens, destroy the mothership in the Invasion level.

GRADIUS REBIRTH

4 OPTIONS
Pause the game and press Up, Up, Down, Down, Left, Right, Left, Right, Fire, Powerup. This code can be used once for each stage you have attempted.

GRAVITRONIX

VERSUS OPTIONS AND LEVEL SELECT
At the Options menu, press 1, 2, 2, 2, 1.

GREG HASTINGS PAINTBALL 2

PRO & NEW GUN
Select Career, hold C, and press Up, Up, Down, Right, Left, Left, Right, Up.

THE GRIM ADVENTURES OF BILLY & MANDY

CONCEPT ART
At the Main menu, hold 1 and press Up, Up, Down, Down, Left, Right, Left, Right.

GUITAR HERO III: LEGENDS OF ROCK

To enter the following cheats, strum the guitar with the given buttons held. For example, if it says Yellow + Orange, hold Yellow and Orange as you strum. Air Guitar, Precision Mode and Performance Mode can be toggled on and off from the Cheats menu. You can also change between five different levels of Hyperspeed at this menu.

UNLOCK EVERYTHING
Select Cheats from the Options. Choose Enter Cheat and enter Green + Red + Blue + Orange, Green + Red + Yellow + Blue, Green + Red + Yellow + Orange, Green + Yellow + Blue + Orange, Green + Red + Yellow + Blue, Red + Yellow + Blue + Orange, Green + Red + Yellow + Blue, Green + Yellow + Blue + Orange, Green + Red + Yellow + Blue, Green + Red + Yellow + Orange, Green + Red + Yellow + Orange, Green + Red + Yellow + Blue, Green + Red + Yellow + Orange. No sounds play while this code is entered.

An easier way to show this code is by representing Green as 1 down to Orange as 5. For example, if you have 1345, you would hold down Green + Yellow + Blue + Orange while strumming. 1245 + 1234 + 1235 + 1345 + 1234 + 2345 + 1234 + 1345 + 1234 + 1235 + 1235 + 1234 + 1235.

ALL SONGS
Select Cheats from the Options. Choose Enter Cheat and enter Yellow + Orange, Red + Blue, Red + Orange, Green + Blue, Red + Yellow, Yellow + Orange, Red + Yellow, Red + Blue, Green + Yellow, Green + Yellow, Yellow + Blue, Yellow + Blue, Yellow + Orange, Yellow + Orange, Yellow + Blue, Yellow, Red, Red + Yellow, Red, Yellow, Orange.

NO FAIL
Select Cheats from the Options. Choose Enter Cheat and enter Green + Red, Blue, Green + Red, Green + Yellow, Blue, Green + Yellow, Red + Yellow, Orange, Red + Yellow, Green + Yellow, Yellow, Green + Yellow, Green + Red.

AIR GUITAR
Select Cheats from the Options. Choose Enter Cheat and enter Blue + Yellow, Green + Yellow, Green + Yellow, Red + Blue, Red + Blue, Red + Yellow, Red + Yellow, Blue + Yellow, Green + Yellow, Green + Yellow, Red + Blue, Red + Blue, Red + Yellow, Red + Yellow, Green + Yellow, Green + Yellow, Red + Yellow, Red + Yellow.

HYPERSPEED
Select Cheats from the Options. Choose Enter Cheat and enter Orange, Blue, Orange, Yellow, Orange, Blue, Orange, Yellow.

PERFORMANCE MODE
Select Cheats from the Options. Choose Enter Cheat and enter Red + Yellow, Red + Blue, Red + Orange, Red + Blue, Red + Yellow, Green + Blue, Red + Yellow, Red + Blue.

EASY EXPERT
Select Cheats from the Options. Choose Enter Cheat and enter Green + Red, Green + Yellow, Yellow + Blue, Red + Blue, Blue + Orange, Yellow + Orange, Red + Yellow, Red + Blue.

OVERLOAD

NINTENDO Wii

PRECISION MODE

Select Cheats from the Options. Choose Enter Cheat and enter Green + Red, Green + Red, Green + Red, Red + Yellow, Red + Yellow, Red + Blue, Red + Blue, Yellow + Blue, Yellow + Orange, Yellow + Orange, Green + Red, Green + Red, Green + Red, Red + Yellow, Red + Yellow, Red + Blue, Red + Blue, Yellow + Blue, Yellow + Orange, Yellow + Orange.

LARGE GEMS

Select Cheats from the Options. Choose Enter Cheat and enter Green, Red, Green, Yellow, Green, Blue, Green, Orange, Green, Blue, Green, Yellow, Green, Red, Green, Green + Red, Red + Yellow, Green + Red, Yellow + Blue, Green + Red, Blue + Orange, Green + Red, Yellow + Blue, Green + Red, Red + Yellow, Green + Red, Green + Yellow.

GUITAR HERO 5

ALL HOPOS

Select Input Cheats from the Options menu and enter Green, Green, Blue, Green, Green, Green, Yellow, Green.

ALWAYS SLIDE

Select Input Cheats from the Options menu and enter Green, Green, Red, Red, Yellow, Blue, Yellow, Blue.

AUTO KICK

Select Input Cheats from the Options menu and enter Yellow, Green, Red, Blue, Blue, Blue, Blue, Red.

FOCUS MODE

Select Input Cheats from the Options menu and enter Yellow, Green, Red, Green, Yellow, Blue, Green, Green.

HUD FREE MODE

Select Input Cheats from the Options menu and enter Green, Red, Green, Green, Yellow, Green, Green, Green.

PERFORMANCE MODE

Select Input Cheats from the Options menu and enter Yellow, Yellow, Blue, Red, Blue, Green, Red, Red.

AIR INSTRUMENTS

Select Input Cheats from the Options menu and enter Red, Red, Blue, Yellow, Green, Green, Green, Yellow.

INVISIBLE ROCKER

Select Input Cheats from the Options menu and enter Green, Red, Yellow, Yellow, Yellow, Blue, Blue, Green.

ALL CHARACTERS

Select Input Cheats from the Options menu and enter Blue, Blue, Green, Green, Red, Green, Red, Yellow.

CONTEST WINNER 1

Select Input Cheats from the Options menu and enter Green, Green, Red, Red, Yellow, Red, Yellow, Blue.

GUITAR HERO: METALLICA

METALLICA COSTUMES

Select Cheats from Settings and enter Green, Red, Yellow, Blue, Blue, Yellow, Red, Green.

HYPERSPEED

Select Cheats from Settings and enter Green, Blue, Red, Yellow, Yellow, Red, Green, Green.

PERFORMANCE MODE

Select Cheats from Settings and enter Yellow, Yellow, Blue, Red, Blue, Green, Red, Red.

INVISIBLE ROCKER

Select Cheats from Settings and enter Green, Red, Yellow (x3), Blue, Blue, Green.

AIR INSTRUMENTS

Select Cheats from Settings and enter Red, Red, Blue, Yellow, Green (x3), Yellow.

ALWAYS DRUM FILL

Select Cheats from Settings and enter Red (x3), Blue, Blue, Green, Green, Yellow.

AUTO KICK

Select Cheats from Settings and enter Yellow, Green, Red, Blue (x4), Red. With this cheat activated, the bass pedal is automatically hit.

ALWAYS SLIDE

Select Cheats from Settings and enter Green, Green, Red, Red, Yellow, Red, Yellow, Blue. All Guitar Notes Become Touch Pad Sliding Notes.

BLACK HIGHWAY

Select Cheats from Settings and enter Yellow, Red, Green, Red, Green, Red, Red, Blue.

FLAME COLOR

Select Cheats from Settings and enter Green, Red, Green, Blue, Red, Red, Yellow, Blue.

GEM COLOR

Select Cheats from Settings and enter Blue, Red, Red, Green, Red, Green, Red, Yellow.

STAR COLOR

Select Cheats from Settings and enter Press Red, Red, Yellow, Red, Blue, Red, Red, Blue.

ADDITIONAL LINE 6 TONES

Select Cheats from Settings and enter Green, Red, Yellow, Blue, Red, Yellow, Blue, Green.

VOCAL FIREBALL

Select Cheats from Settings and enter Red, Green, Green, Yellow, Blue, Green, Yellow, Green.

GUITAR HERO: SMASH HITS

ALWAYS DRUM FILL

Select Cheats from the Options menu and enter Green, Green, Red, Red, Blue, Blue, Yellow, Yellow.

ALWAYS SLIDE

Select Cheats from the Options menu and enter Blue, Yellow, Red, Green, Blue, Green, Green, Yellow.

AIR INSTRUMENTS

Select Cheats from the Options menu and enter Yellow, Red, Blue, Green, Yellow, Red, Red, Red.

INVISIBLE ROCKER

Select Cheats from the Options menu and enter Blue, Red, Red, Red, Red, Yellow, Blue, Green.

PERFORMANCE MODE

Select Cheats from the Options menu and enter Blue, Red, Yellow, Yellow, Red, Red, Yellow, Yellow.

HYPERSPEED

Select Cheats from the Options menu and enter Red, Green, Blue, Yellow, Green, Yellow, Red, Red. This unlocks the HyperGuitar, HyperBass, and HyperDrums cheats.

AUTO KICK

Select Cheats from the Options menu and enter Blue, Green, Red, Yellow, Red, Yellow, Red, Yellow.

GEM COLOR

Select Cheats from the Options menu and enter Red, Red, Red, Blue, Blue, Blue, Yellow, Green.

FLAME COLOR

Select Cheats from the Options menu and enter Yellow, Blue, Red, Green, Yellow, Red, Green, Blue.

STAR COLOR

Select Cheats from the Options menu and enter Green, Red, Green, Yellow, Green, Blue, Yellow, Red.

VOCAL FIREBALL

Select Cheats from the Options menu and enter Green, Blue, Red, Red, Yellow, Yellow, Blue, Blue.

GUITAR HERO: WARRIORS OF ROCK

Select Extras from the Options menu to toggle the following on and off.

ALL CHARACTERS

Select Cheats from the Options menu and enter Blue, Green, Green, Red, Green, Red, Yellow, Blue.

ALL VENUES

Select Cheats from the Options menu and enter Red, Blue, Blue, Red, Red, Blue, Blue, Red.

ALWAYS SLIDE

Select Cheats from the Options menu and enter Blue, Green, Green, Red, Red, Yellow, Blue, Yellow.

ALL HOPOS

Select Cheats from the Options menu and enter Green (x3), Blue, Green (x3), Yellow. Most notes become hammer-ons or pull-offs.

INVISIBLE ROCKER

Select Cheats from the Options menu and enter Green, Green, Red, Yellow (x3), Blue, Blue.

AIR INSTRUMENTS

Select Cheats from the Options menu and enter Yellow, Red, Red, Blue, Yellow, Green (x3).

NINTENDO Wii

FOCUS MODE
Select Cheats from the Options menu and enter Green, Yellow, Green, Red, Green, Yellow, Blue, Green. This removes the busy background.

NO HUD MODE
Select Cheats from the Options menu and enter Green, Green, Red, Green, Green, Yellow, Green, Green.

PERFORMANCE MODE
Select Cheats from the Options menu and enter Red, Yellow, Yellow, Blue, Red, Blue, Green, Red.

COLOR SHUFFLE
Select Cheats from the Options menu and enter Blue, Green, Blue, Red, Yellow, Green, Red, Yellow.

MIRROR GEMS
Select Cheats from the Options menu and enter Blue, Blue, Red, Blue, Green, Green, Red, Green.

RANDOM GEMS
Select Cheats from the Options menu and enter Green, Green, Red, Red, Yellow, Red, Yellow, Blue.

GUITAR HERO WORLD TOUR

The following cheats can be toggled on and off at the Cheats menu.

QUICKPLAY SONGS
Select Cheats from the Options menu, choose Enter New Cheat and press Blue, Blue, Red, Green, Green, Blue, Blue, Yellow.

ALWAYS SLIDE
Select Cheats from the Options menu, choose Enter New Cheat and press Green, Green, Red, Red, Yellow, Red, Yellow, Blue.

AT&T BALLPARK
Select Cheats from the Options menu, choose Enter New Cheat and press Yellow, Green, Red, Red, Green, Blue, Red, Yellow.

AUTO KICK
Select Cheats from the Options menu, choose Enter New Cheat and press Yellow, Green, Red, Blue (x4), Red.

EXTRA LINE 6 TONES
Select Cheats from the Options menu, choose Enter New Cheat and press Green, Red, Yellow, Blue, Red, Yellow, Blue, Green.

FLAME COLOR
Select Cheats from the Options menu, choose Enter New Cheat and press Green, Red, Green, Blue, Red, Red, Yellow, Blue.

GEM COLOR
Select Cheats from the Options menu, choose Enter New Cheat and press Blue, Red, Red, Green, Red, Green, Red, Yellow.

STAR COLOR
Select Cheats from the Options menu, choose Enter New Cheat and press Red, Red, Yellow, Red, Blue, Red, Red, Blue.

AIR INSTRUMENTS
Select Cheats from the Options menu, choose Enter New Cheat and press Red, Red, Blue, Yellow, Green (x3), Yellow.

HYPERSPEED
Select Cheats from the Options menu, choose Enter New Cheat and press Green, Blue, Red, Yellow, Yellow, Red, Green, Green. These show up in the menu as HyperGuitar, HyperBass, and HyperDrums.

PERFORMANCE MODE
Select Cheats from the Options menu, choose Enter New Cheat and press Yellow, Yellow, Blue, Red, Blue, Green, Red, Red.

INVISIBLE ROCKER
Select Cheats from the Options menu, choose Enter New Cheat and press Green, Red, Yellow (x3), Blue, Blue, Green.

VOCAL FIREBALL
Select Cheats from the Options menu, choose Enter New Cheat and press Red, Green, Green, Yellow, Blue, Yellow, Green.

AARON STEELE!
Select Cheats from the Options menu, choose Enter New Cheat and press Blue, Red, Yellow (x5), Green.

JONNY VIPER
Select Cheats from the Options menu, choose Enter New Cheat and press Blue, Red, Blue, Blue, Yellow (x3), Green.

NICK
Select Cheats from the Options menu, choose Enter New Cheat and press Green, Red, Blue, Green, Red, Blue, Blue, Green.

RINA
Select Cheats from the Options menu, choose Enter New Cheat and press Blue, Red, Green, Green, Yellow (x3), Green.

HARRY POTTER AND THE HALF-BLOOD PRINCE

BONUS TWO-PLAYER DUELING ARENA CASTLE GATES
At the Rewards menu, press Right, Right, Down, Down, Left, Right, Left, Right, Left, Right, +.

HASBRO FAMILY GAME NIGHT 2

SECRET PRIZE
Have a saved file from the first Hasbro Family Game Night.

ICE AGE 2: THE MELTDOWN

INFINITE PEBBLES
Pause the game and press Down, Down, Left, Up, Up, Right, Up, Down.

INFINITE ENERGY
Pause the game and press Down, Left, Right, Down, Down, Right, Left, Down.

INFINITE HEALTH
Pause the game and press Up, Right, Down, Up, Left, Down, Right, Left.

INDIANA JONES AND THE STAFF OF KINGS

FATE OF ATLANTIS GAME
At the Extras menu, hold Z and press A, Up, Up, B, Down, Down, Left, Right, Left, B.

IRON MAN

ARMOR SELECTION
Iron Man's different armor suits are unlocked by completing certain missions. Refer to the following tables for when each is unlocked. After selecting a mission to play, you get the opportunity to pick the armor you wish to use.

COMPLETE MISSION	SUIT UNLOCKED
1: Escape	Mark I
2: First Flight	Mark II
3: Fight Back	Mark III
6: Flying Fortress	Comic Tin Can
9: Home Front	Classic
13: Showdown	Silver Centurion

CONCEPT ART
Concept Art is unlocked after finding certain numbers of Weapon Crates.

CONCEPT ART UNLOCKED	NUMBER OF WEAPON CRATES FOUND
Environments Set 1	6
Environments Set 2	12
Iron Man	18
Environments Set 3	24
Enemies	30
Environments Set 4	36
Villains	42
Vehicles	48
Covers	50

IVY THE KIWI?

BONUS MODE & PICTURE BOOK
Finish the main game.

DOG COSTUME
Collect 100 red feathers (50 from the main game and 50 from Bonus Mode).

KUNG FU PANDA

INFINITE CHI
Select Cheats from the Extra menu and press Down, Right, Left, Up, Down.

INVINCIBILITY
Select Cheats from the Extra menu and press Down, Down, Right, Up, Left.

4X DAMAGE MULTIPLIER
Select Cheats from the Extra menu and press Up, Down, Up, Right, Left.

ALL MULTIPLAYER CHARACTERS
Select Cheats from the Extra menu and press Left, Down, Left, Right, Down.

DRAGON WARRIOR OUTFIT IN MULTIPLAYER
Select Cheats from the Extra menu and press Left, Down, Right, Left, Up.

THE LEGEND OF SPYRO: DAWN OF THE DRAGON

INFINITE HEALTH
Pause the game, hold Z and move the Nunchuk Right, Right, Down, Down, Left.

INFINITE MANA
Pause the game, hold Z and move the Nunchuk Up, Right, Up, Left, Down.

MAX XP
Pause the game, hold Z and move the Nunchuk Up, Left, Left, Down, Up.

ALL ELEMENTAL UPGRADES
Pause the game, hold Z and move the Nunchuk Left, Up, Down, Up, Right.

LEGO BATMAN

BATCAVE CODES
Using the computer in the Batcave, select Enter Code and enter the following codes.

CHARACTERS

CHARACTER	CODE	CHARACTER	CODE
Alfred	ZAQ637	Penguin Henchman	BJH782
Batgirl	JKR331	Penguin Minion	KJP748
Bruce Wayne	BDJ327	Poison Ivy Goon	GTB899
Catwoman (Classic)	M1AAWW	Police Marksman	HKG984
Clown Goon	HJK327	Police Officer	JRY983
Commissioner Gordon	DDP967	Riddler Goon	CRY928
Fishmonger	HGY748	Riddler Henchman	XEU824
Freeze Girl	XVK541	S.W.A.T.	HTF114
Joker Goon	UTF782	Sailor	NAV592
Joker Henchman	YUN924	Scientist	JFL786
Mad Hatter	JCA283	Security Guard	PLB946
Man-Bat	NYU942	The Joker (Tropical)	CCB199
Military Policeman	MKL382	Yeti	NJL412
Nightwing	MVY759	Zoo Sweeper	DWR243
Penguin Goon	NKA238		

VEHICLES

VEHICLE	CODE	VEHICLE	CODE
Bat-Tank	KNTT4B	Mad Hatter's Steamboat	M4DM4N
Bruce Wayne's Private Jet	LEA664	Mr. Freeze's Iceberg	ICYICE
Catwoman's Motorcycle	HPL826	The Joker's Van	JUK657
Garbage Truck	DUS483	Mr. Freeze's Kart	BCT229
Goon Helicopter	GCH328	Penguin Goon Submarine	BTN248
Harbor Helicopter	CHP735	Police Bike	LJP234
Harley Quinn's Hammer Truck	RDT637	Police Boat	PLC999
Mad Hatter's Glider	HS000W	Police Car	KJL832
		Police Helicopter	CWR732

OVERLOAD

VEHICLE	CODE
Police Van	MAC788
Police Watercraft	VJD328
Riddler's Jet	HAHAHA

VEHICLE	CODE
Robin's Submarine	TTF453
Two-Face's Armored Truck	EFE933

CHEATS

CHEAT	CODE
Always Score Multiply	9LRGNB
Fast Batarangs	JRBDCB
Fast Walk	ZOLM6N
Flame Batarang	D8NYWH
Freeze Batarang	XPN4NG
Extra Hearts	ML3KHP
Fast Build	EVG26J
Immune to Freeze	JXUDY6
Invincibility	WYD5CP
Minikit Detector	ZXGH9J

CHEAT	CODE
More Batarang Targets	XWP645
Piece Detector	KHJ554
Power Brick Detector	MMN786
Regenerate Hearts	HJH7HJ
Score x2	N4NR3E
Score x4	CX9MAT
Score x6	MLVNF2
Score x8	WCCDB9
Score x10	18HW07

LEGO HARRY POTTER: YEARS 1-4

RED BRICK EXTRAS

After gaining access to The Leaky Cauldron, enter Wiseacre's Wizarding Supplies from Diagon Alley. Go upstairs to enter the following codes. Pause the game and select Extras to toggle the cheats on/off.

CODE	ENTER
Carrot Wands	AUC8EH
Character Studs	H27KGC
Character Token Detector	HA79V8
Christmas	T7PVVN
Disguise	4DMK2R
Fall Rescue	ZEX7MV
Extra Hearts	J9U6Z9
Fast Dig	Z9BFAD
Fast Magic	FA3GQA
Gold Brick Detector	84QNQN
Hogwarts Crest Detector	TTMC6D
Ice Rink	F88VUW
Invincibility	QQWC6B
Red Brick Detector	7AD7HE
Regenerate Hearts	89ML2W

CODE	ENTER
Score x2	74YKR7
Score x4	J3WHNK
Score x6	XK9ANE
Score x8	HUFV2H
Score x10	H8X69Y
Silhouettes	HZBVX7
Singing Mandrake	BMEU6X
Stud Magnet	67FKWZ

NINTENDO Wii

WISEACRE SPELLS

After gaining access to The Leaky Cauldron, enter Wiseacre's Wizarding Supplies from Diagon Alley. Go upstairs to enter the following codes. You need to learn Wingardium Leviosa before you can use these cheats.

SPELL	ENTER
Accio	VE9VV7
Anteoculatia	QFB6NR
Calvorio	6DNR6L
Colovaria	9GJ442
Engorgio Skullus	CD4JLX
Entomorphis	MYN3NB
Flipendo	ND2L7W
Glacius	ERA9DR
Herbifors	H8FTHL
Incarcerous	YEB9Q9
Locomotor Mortis	2M2XJ6
Multicorfors	JK6QRM
Redactum Skullus	UW8LRH

SPELL	ENTER
Rictusempra	2UCA3M
Slugulus Eructo	U6EE8X
Stupefy	UWDJ4Y
Tarantallegra	KWWQ44
Trip Jinx	YZNRF6

EEYLOPS GOLD BRICKS

After gaining access to The Leaky Cauldron, enter Wiseacre's Wizarding Supplies from Diagon Alley. Go upstairs to enter the following codes. To access the LEGO Builder, visit Gringott's Bank at the end of Diagon Alley.

GOLD BRICK	ENTER
1	QE4VC7
2	FY8H97
3	3MQT4P
4	PQPM7Z
5	ZY2CPA
6	3GMTP6

GOLD BRICK	ENTER
7	XY6VYZ
8	TUNC4W
9	EJ42Q6
10	GFJCV9
11	DZCY6G

LEGO INDIANA JONES: THE ORIGINAL ADVENTURES

EXTRAS

Approach the blackboard in the Classroom and enter the following codes. Pause the game and select Extras. Here you can enable the cheat.

EXTRA	CODE
Artifact Detector	VIKED7
Beep Beep	VNF59Q
Character Treasure	VIES2R
Disarm Enemies	VKRNS9
Disguises	4ID1N6
Fast Build	V83SLO
Fast Dig	378RS6
Fast Fix	FJ59WS
Fertilizer	B1GW1F
Ice Rink	33GM7J
Parcel Detector	VUT673
Poo Treasure	WWQ1SA

EXTRA	CODE
Regenerate Hearts	MDLP69
Secret Characters	3X44AA
Silhouettes	3HE85H
Super Scream	VN3R7S
Super Slap	0P1TA5
Treasure Magnet	H86LA2
Treasure x2	VM4TS9
Treasure x4	VLWEN3
Treasure x6	V84RYS
Treasure x8	A72E1M
Treasure x10	VI3PS8

OVERLOAD

CHARACTERS

Approach the blackboard in the Classroom and enter the following codes.

CHARACTER	CODE
Bandit	12N68W
Bandit Swordsman	1MK4RT
Barranca	04EM94
Bazooka Trooper (Crusade)	MK83R7
Bazooka Trooper (Raiders)	S93Y5R
Belloq	CHN3YU
Belloq (Jungle)	TDR197
Belloq (Robes)	VEO29L
British Commander	B73EUA
British Officer	VJ5TI9
British Soldier	DJ5I2W
Captain Katanga	VJ3TT3
Chatter Lal	ENW936
Chatter Lal (Thuggee)	CNH4RY
Chen	3NK48T
Colonel Dietrich	2K9RKS
Colonel Vogel	8EAL4H
Dancing Girl	C7EJ21
Donovan	3NFTU8
Elsa (Desert)	JSNRT9
Elsa (Officer)	VMJ5US
Enemy Boxer	8246RB
Enemy Butler	VJ48W3
Enemy Guard	VJ7R51
Enemy Guard (Mountains)	YR47WM
Enemy Officer	572E61
Enemy Officer (Desert)	2MK45O
Enemy Pilot	B84ELP
Enemy Radio Operator	1MF94R

CHARACTER	CODE
Enemy Soldier (Desert)	4NSU7Q
Fedora	V75YSP
First Mate	0GIN24
Grail Knight	NE6THI
Hovitos Tribesman	H0V1SS
Indiana Jones (Desert Disguise)	4J8S4M
Indiana Jones (Officer)	VJ85OS
Jungle Guide	24PF34
Kao Kan	WMO46L
Kazim	NRH23J
Kazim (Desert)	3M29TJ
Lao Che	2NK479
Maharajah	NFK5N2
Major Toht	13NS01
Masked Bandit	N48SF0
Mola Ram	FJUR31
Monkey Man	3RF6YJ
Pankot Assassin	2NKT72
Pankot Guard	VN28RH
Sherpa Brawler	VJ37WJ
Sherpa Gunner	ND762W
Slave Child	0E3ENW
Thuggee	VM683E
Thuggee Acolyte	T2R3F9
Thuggee Slave Driver	VBS7GW
Village Dignitary	KD48TN
Village Elder	4682E1
Willie (Dinner Suit)	VK93R7
Willie (Pajamas)	MEN4IP
Wu Han	3NSLT8

EXTRAS

Approach the blackboard in the Classroom and enter the following codes. Some cheats must be enabled by selecting Extras from the Pause menu.

CHEAT	CODE
Artifact Detector	VIKED7
Beep Beep	VNF59Q
Character Treasure	VIES2R
Disarm Enemies	VKRNS9
Disguises	4ID1N6
Fast Build	V83SLO
Fast Dig	378RS6
Fast Fix	FJ59WS
Fertilizer	B1GW1F
Ice Rink	33GM7J
Parcel Detector	VUT673
Poo Treasure	WWQ1SA

CHEAT	CODE
Regenerate Hearts	MDLP69
Secret Characters	3X44AA
Silhouettes	3HE85H
Super Scream	VN3R7S
Super Slap	0P1TA5
Treasure Magnet	H86LA2
Treasure x10	VI3PS8
Treasure x2	VM4TS9
Treasure x4	VLWEN3
Treasure x6	V84RYS
Treasure x8	A72E1M

NINTENDO Wii

LEGO INDIANA JONES 2: THE ADVENTURE CONTINUES

Pause the game, select Enter Secret Code from the Extras menu, and enter the following.

CHARACTERS

CHARACTER	CODE
Belloq (Priest)	FTL48S
Dovchenko	WL4T6N
Enemy Boxer	7EQF47
Henry Jones	4CSAKH
Indiana Jones	PGWSEA
Indiana Jones: 2	FGLKYS
Indiana Jones (Collect)	DZFY9S
Indiana Jones (Desert)	M4C34K
Indiana Jones (Desert Disguise)	2W8QR3
Indiana Jones (Dinner Suit)	QUNZUT
Indiana Jones (Kali)	J2XS97
Indiana Jones (Officer)	3FQFKS
Interdimensional Being	PXT4UP
Lao Che	7AWX3J

CHARACTER	CODE
Mannequin (Boy)	2UJQWC
Mannequin (Girl)	3PGSEL
Mannequin (Man)	QPWDMM
Mannequin (Woman)	U7SMVK
Mola Ram	82RMC2
Mutt	2GKS62
Salah	E88YRP
Willie	94RUAJ

EXTRAS

EFFECT	CODE
Beep Beep	UU3VSC
Disguise	Y9TE98
Fast Build	SNXC2F
Fast Dig	XYAN83
Fast Fix	3Z7PJX
Fearless	TUXNZF
Ice Rink	TY9P4U
Invincibility	6JBB65
Poo Money	SZFAAE
Score x3	PEHHPZ
Score x4	UXGTB3
Score X6	XWLJEY

EFFECT	CODE
Score x8	S5UZCP
Score x10	V7JYBU
Silhouettes	FQGPYH
Snake Whip	2U7YCV
Stud Magnet	EGSM5B

LEGO STAR WARS: THE COMPLETE SAGA

The following must still be purchased after entering the codes.

CHARACTERS

ADMIRAL ACKBAR
At the bar in Mos Eisley Cantina, select Enter Code and enter ACK646.

BATTLE DROID (COMMANDER)
At the bar in Mos Eisley Cantina, select Enter Code and enter KPF958.

BOBA FETT (BOY)
At the bar in Mos Eisley Cantina, select Enter Code and enter GGF539.

BOSS NASS
At the bar in Mos Eisley Cantina, select Enter Code and enter HHY697.

CAPTAIN TARPALS
At the bar in Mos Eisley Cantina, select Enter Code and enter QRN714.

COUNT DOOKU
At the bar in Mos Eisley Cantina, select Enter Code and enter DDD748.

DARTH MAUL
At the bar in Mos Eisley Cantina, select Enter Code and enter EUK421.

EWOK
At the bar in Mos Eisley Cantina, select Enter Code and enter EWK785.

GENERAL GRIEVOUS
At the bar in Mos Eisley Cantina, select Enter Code and enter PMN576.

GREEDO
At the bar in Mos Eisley Cantina, select Enter Code and enter ZZR636.

IG-88
At the bar in Mos Eisley Cantina, select Enter Code and enter GIJ989.

IMPERIAL GUARD
At the bar in Mos Eisley Cantina, select Enter Code and enter GUA850.

JANGO FETT
At the bar in Mos Eisley Cantina, select Enter Code and enter KLJ897.

KI-ADI MUNDI
At the bar in Mos Eisley Cantina, select Enter Code and enter MUN486.

LUMINARA
At the bar in Mos Eisley Cantina, select Enter Code and enter LUM521.

PADMÉ
At the bar in Mos Eisley Cantina, select Enter Code and enter VBJ322.

R2-Q5
At the bar in Mos Eisley Cantina, select Enter Code and enter EVILR2.

STORMTROOPER
At the bar in Mos Eisley Cantina, select Enter Code and enter NBN431.

TAUN WE
At the bar in Mos Eisley Cantina, select Enter Code and enter PRX482.

VULTURE DROID
At the bar in Mos Eisley Cantina, select Enter Code and enter BDC866.

WATTO
At the bar in Mos Eisley Cantina, select Enter Code and enter PLL967.

ZAM WESELL
At the bar in Mos Eisley Cantina, select Enter Code and enter 584HJF.

SKILLS

DISGUISE
At the bar in Mos Eisley Cantina, select Enter Code and enter BRJ437.

FORCE GRAPPLE LEAP
At the bar in Mos Eisley Cantina, select Enter Code and enter CLZ738.

VEHICLES

DROID TRIFIGHTER
At the bar in Mos Eisley Cantina, select Enter Code and enter AAB123.

IMPERIAL SHUTTLE
At the bar in Mos Eisley Cantina, select Enter Code and enter HUT845.

TIE INTERCEPTOR
At the bar in Mos Eisley Cantina, select Enter Code and enter INT729.

TIE FIGHTER
At the bar in Mos Eisley Cantina, select Enter Code and enter DBH897.

ZAM'S AIRSPEEDER
At the bar in Mos Eisley Cantina, select Enter Code and enter UUU875.

LOST IN SHADOW

GOBLIN HAND
While the game is loading, press and hold Z.

KNIFE
While the game is loading, press and hold C.

MADDEN NFL 10

UNLOCK EVERYTHING
Select Enter Game Code from the Extras menu and enter THEWORKS.

FRANCHISE MODE
Select Enter Game Code from the Extras menu and enter TEAMPLAYER.

SITUATION MODE
Select Enter Game Code from the Extras menu and enter YOUCALLIT.

SUPERSTAR MODE
Select Enter Game Code from the Extras menu and enter EGOBOOST.

PRO BOWL STADIUM
Select Enter Game Code from the Extras menu and enter ALLSTARS.

SUPER BOWL STADIUM
Select Enter Game Code from the Extras menu and enter THEBIGSHOW.

NINTENDO Wii

MADSTONE

HIGH GRAVITY
At the Main menu, press Down, Down, Down, Down, Right, Left, Right, Left.

LOW GRAVITY
At the Main menu, press Up, Up, Left, Left, Up, Up, Right, Right.

PLAYER SKULLS, ARCADE MODE
At the Difficulty Select screen, press Up, Right, Down, Left, Up, Right, Down, Left.

SAVANT MODE, ARCADE MODE
At the Difficulty Select screen, press Down (x10).

MANHUNT 2

INFINITE AMMO
At the Main menu, press Up, Up, Down, Down, Left, Right, Left, Right.

LEVEL SELECT
At the Main menu, press Up, Down, Left, Right, Up, Down, Left, Right.

MARBLE SAGA: KORORINPA

MASTER HIGGINS BALL
Select ??? from the Options. Press A on the right lamp, the left lamp twice, and the right lamp again. Now select the right icon and enter TV, Car, Sunflower, Bike, Helicopter, Strawberry.

MIRROR MODE
Select ??? from the Options. Press A on the right lamp, the left lamp twice, and the right lamp again. Now select the right icon and enter Beetle, Clover, Boy, Plane, Car, Bike.

MARIO & SONIC AT THE OLYMPIC GAMES

UNLOCK 4X100M RELAY EVENT
Medal in Mercury, Venus, Jupiter, and Saturn.

UNLOCK SINGLE SCULLS EVENT
Medal in Mercury, Venus, Jupiter, and Saturn.

UNLOCK DREAM RACE EVENT
Medal in Mercury, Venus, Jupiter, and Saturn.

UNLOCK ARCHERY EVENT
Medal in Moonlight Circuit.

UNLOCK HIGH JUMP EVENT
Medal in Stardust Circuit.

UNLOCK 400M EVENT
Medal in Planet Circuit.

UNLOCK DREAM FENCING EVENT
Medal in Comet Circuit.

UNLOCK DREAM TABLE TENNIS EVENT
Medal in Satellite Circuit.

UNLOCK 400M HURDLES EVENT
Medal in Sunlight Circuit.

UNLOCK POLE VAULT EVENT
Medal in Meteorite Circuit.

UNLOCK VAULT EVENT
Medal in Meteorite Circuit.

UNLOCK DREAM PLATFORM EVENT
Medal in Cosmos Circuit.

CROWNS
Get all gold medals in all events with a character to unlock their crown.

MARIO KART WII

CHARACTERS

CHARACTER	UNLOCK BY...
Baby Daisy	Earn 1 Star in 50cc for Mushroom, Flower, Star, and Special Cups.
Baby Luigi	Unlock 8 Expert Staff Ghost Data in Time Trials.
Birdo	Race 16 different courses in Time Trials or win 250 versus races.
Bowser Jr.	Earn 1 Star in 100cc for Shell, Banana, Leaf, and Lightning Cups.
Daisy	Win 150cc Special Cup.
Diddy Kong	Win 50cc Lightning Cup.
Dry Bones	Win 100cc Leaf Cup.
Dry Bowser	Earn 1 Star in 150cc for Mushroom, Flower, Star, and Special Cups.
Funky Kong	Unlock 4 Expert Staff Ghost Data in Time Trials.
King Boo	Win 50cc Star Cup.

Mii Outfit A	Win 100cc Special Cup.
Mii Outfit B	Unlock all 32 Expert Staff Ghost Data in Time Trials.
Mii Outfit C	Get 15,000 points in Versus Mode.
Rosalina	Have a Super Mario Galaxy save file and she is unlocked after 50 races or earn 1 Star in all Mirror Cups.
Toadette	Race 32 different courses in Time Trials.

KARTS

KART	UNLOCK BY...
Blue Falcon	Win Mirror Lightning Cup.
Cheep Charger	Earn 1 Star in 50cc for Mushroom, Flower, Star, and Special Cups.
Rally Romper	Unlock an Expert Staff Ghost Data in Time Trials.
B Dasher Mk. 2	Unlock 24 Expert Staff Ghost Data in Time Trials.
Royal Racer	Win 150cc Leaf Cup.
Turbo Blooper	Win 50cc Leaf Cup.
Aero Glider	Earn 1 Star in 150cc for Mushroom, Flower, Star, and Special Cups.
Dragonetti	Win 150cc Lightning Cup.
Piranha Prowler	Win 50cc Special Cup.

BIKES

BIKE	UNLOCK BY...
Bubble Bike	Win Mirror Leaf Cup.
Magikruiser	Race 8 different courses in Time Trials.
Quacker	Win 150cc Star Cup.
Dolphin Dasher	Win Mirror Star Cup.
Nitrocycle	Earn 1 Star in 100cc for all cups.
Rapide	Win 100cc Lightning Cup.
Phantom	Win Mirror Special Cup.
Torpedo	Unlock 12 Expert Staff Ghost Data in Time Trials.
Twinkle Star	Win 100cc Star Cup.

MARVEL SUPER HERO SQUAD

IRON MAN BONUS COSTUME
Select Enter Code from the Options menu and enter 111111. This unlocks the bonus costume "War Machine."

HULK BONUS COSTUMES
Select Enter Code from the Options menu and enter 222222. This unlocks the bonus costumes "Grey Hulk and "Red Hulk."

WOLVERINE BONUS COSTUMES
Select Enter Code from the Options menu and enter 333333. This unlocks the bonus costumes "Wolverine (Brown Costume)" and "Feral Wolverine."

THOR BONUS COSTUMES
Select Enter Code from the Options menu and enter 444444. This unlocks the bonus costumes "Thor (Chain Armor)" and "Loki-Thor."

SILVER SURFER BONUS COSTUMES
Select Enter Code from the Options menu and enter 555555. This unlocks the bonus costumes "Anti-Surfer" and "Gold Surfer."

FALCON BONUS COSTUME
Select Enter Code from the Options menu and enter 666666. This unlocks the bonus costume "Ultimates Falcon."

DOCTOR DOOM BONUS COSTUMES
Select Enter Code from the Options menu and enter 999999. This unlocks the bonus costumes "Ultimates Doctor Doom" and "Professor Doom."

NINTENDO Wii

CAPTAIN AMERICA BONUS COSTUME
Select Enter Code from the Options menu and enter 177674. This unlocks the bonus costume "Ultimate Captain America."

A.I.M. AGENT BONUS COSTUME
Select Enter Code from the Options menu and enter 246246. This unlocks the bonus costume "Blue Suit A.I.M."

SUPER KNOCKBACK
Select Enter Code from the Options menu and enter 777777.

NO BLOCK MODE
Select Enter Code from the Options menu and enter 888888.

GROUNDED
Select Enter Code from the Options menu and enter 476863

ONE-HIT TAKEDOWN
Select Enter Code from the Options menu and enter 663448

INFINITE SHARD DURATION
Select Enter Code from the Options menu and enter 742737

THROWN OBJECT TAKEDOWN
Select Enter Code from the Options menu and enter 847936

MARVEL ULTIMATE ALLIANCE

UNLOCK ALL SKINS
At the Team menu, press Up, Down, Left, Right, Left, Right, Plus.

UNLOCKS ALL HERO POWERS
At the Team menu, press Left, Right, Up, Down, Up, Down, Plus.

ALL HEROES TO LEVEL 99
At the Team menu, press Up, Left, Up, Left, Down, Right, Down, Right, Plus.

UNLOCK ALL HEROES
At the Team menu, press Up, Up, Down, Down, Left, Left, Left, Plus.

UNLOCK DAREDEVIL
At the Team menu, press Left, Left, Right, Right, Up, Down, Up, Down, Plus.

UNLOCK SILVER SURFER
At the Team menu, press Down, Left, Left, Up, Right, Up, Down, Left, Plus.

GOD MODE
During gameplay, press Up, Down, Up, Down, Up, Left, Down, Right, Plus.

TOUCH OF DEATH
During gameplay, press Left, Right, Down, Down, Right, Left, Plus.

SUPER SPEED
During gameplay, press Up, Left, Up, Right, Down, Right, Plus.

FILL MOMENTUM
During gameplay, press Left, Right, Right, Left, Up, Down, Down, Up, Plus.

UNLOCK ALL COMICS
At the Review menu, press Left, Right, Right, Left, Up, Up, Right, Plus.

UNLOCK ALL CONCEPT ART
At the Review menu, press Down, Down, Down, Right, Right, Left, Down, Plus.

UNLOCK ALL CINEMATICS
At the Review menu, press Up, Left, Left, Up, Right, Right, Up, Plus.

UNLOCK ALL LOAD SCREENS
At the Review menu, press Up, Down, Right, Left, Up, Up Down, Plus.

UNLOCK ALL COURSES
At the Comic Missions menu, press Up, Right, Left, Down, Up, Right, Left, Down, Plus.

MARVEL ULTIMATE ALLIANCE 2

GOD MODE
At any point during a game, press Up, Up, Down, Down, Left, Right, Down.

GIVE MONEY
At the Team Select or Hero Details screen press Up, Up, Down, Down, Up, Up, Up, Down.

UNLOCK ALL POWERS
At the Team Select or Hero Details screen press Up, Up, Down, Down, Left, Right, Right, Left.

ADVANCE ALL CHARACTERS TO L99
At the Hero Details screen press Down, Up, Left, Up, Right, Up, Left, Down.

UNLOCK ALL BONUS MISSIONS
While using the Bonus Mission Simulator, press Up, Right, Down, Left, Left, Right, Up, Up.

ADD 1 CHARACTER LEVEL
During a game, press Down, Up, Right, Up, Right, Up, Right, Down.

ADD 10 CHARACTER LEVELS
During a game, press Down, Up, Left, Up, Left, Up, Left, Down.

MEDAL OF HONOR: VANGUARD

EXTRA ARMOR

Pause the game and press Up, Down, Up, Down to display the words Enter Cheat Code. Then press Right, Left, Right, Down, Up, Right.

DECREASE ENEMY ACCURACY

Pause the game and press Up, Down, Up, Down to display the words Enter Cheat Code. Then press Right, Left, Right, Down, Up, Right.

INVISIBLE

Pause the game and press Up, Down, Up, Down to display the words Enter Cheat Code. Then press Up, Right, Left, Down, Down, Up.

METROID OTHER M

HARD MODE

Finish the game with all items.

THEATER MODE

Defeat the final boss.

GALLERY MODE

Defeat the final boss.

CHAPTERS	HOW TO UNLOCK
Unlock Chapters 1-26	Defeat the final boss.
Unlock Chapters 27-30	After the credits, finish the bonus area and defeat the boss.

GALLERY PAGES	HOW TO UNLOCK
1-4	Defeat the final boss.
5-7	After the credits, finish the bonus area and defeat the boss.
8	Finish the game with all items.

MLB POWER PROS

EXTRA FORMS

At the Main menu, press Right, Left, Up, Down, Down, Right, Right, Up, Up, Left, Down, Left.

VIEW MLB PLAYERS AT CUSTOM PLAYER MENU

Select View or Delete Custom Players/Password Display from My Data and press Up, Up, Down, Down, Left, Right, Left, Right, 1, 2.

MONSTER JAM

TRUCKS

As you collect monster points, they are tallied toward your Championship Score. Trucks are unlocked when you reach certain point totals.

TRUCK	POINTS
Destroyer	10,000
Blacksmith	50,000
El Toro Loco	70,000

TRUCK	POINTS
Suzuki	110,000
Maximum Destruction	235,000

MONSTER LAIR

CONTINUE

At the Game Over screen, press Left, Right, Down, Up, Select + Left.

SOUND TEST

At the Title screen, press and hold 1 + 2 and then press Run.

UNLIMITED CONTINUES

Enter 68K as your initials.

MORTAL KOMBAT: ARMAGEDDON

The following codes are for the Wii Remote and Nunchuck. Directions are input with the Nunchuck stick, except where noted to use the Wii Remote's D-pad. You need to use a Classic Controller to input ZL and ZR where called for.

You can also use the Classic Controller alone to input the codes with the following chart:

REMOTE/NUNCHUCK	CLASSIC CONTROLLER
Nunchuck Directions	D-pad
Down on Wii Remote D-pad	B
Up on Wii Remote D-pad	X
Left on Wii Remote D-pad	Y

REMOTE/NUNCHUCK	CLASSIC CONTROLLER
Right on Wii Remote D-pad	A
A	R
C	L
ZL on Classic Controller	Same
ZR on Classic Controller	Same

BLAZE CHARACTER

While in The Krypt, select the "?" and press Up on D-pad, Left on D-pad, Left, C, Left, Right on D-pad.

DAEGON CHARACTER

While in The Krypt, select the "?" and press A, C, Up on D-pad, Down, Down, Left on D-pad.

MEAT CHARACTER

While in The Krypt, select the "?" and press Up, Left on D-pad, Left on D-pad, Right on D-pad, Right on D-pad, Up.

TAVEN CHARACTER

While in The Krypt, select the "?" and press C, Left, ZR, Up, Right on D-pad, Down.

DRAHMIN'S ALTERNATE COSTUME

While in The Krypt, select the "?" and press C, Right, Down on D-pad, A, Up, Up.

FROST'S ALTERNATE COSTUME

While in The Krypt, select the "?" and press Down, A, A, C, Right on D-pad, C.

NITARA'S ALTERNATE COSTUME

While in The Krypt, select the "?" and press Down, C, Up, C, C, Right.

SHANG TSUNG'S ALTERNATE COSTUME

While in The Krypt, select the "?" and press C, Left, Up, Right on D-pad, Up, L (or ZL).

FALLING CLIFFS ARENA

While in The Krypt, select the "?" and press ZR, Right on D-pad, Left on D-pad, Down on D-pad, Right on D-pad, Up on D-pad.

KRIMSON FOREST ARENA

While in The Krypt, select the "?" and press Right on D-pad, C, Up, Left on D-pad, Right on D-pad, Down.

NETHERSHIP INTERIOR ARENA

While in The Krypt, select the "?" and press A, Left, Left, Down, C, Left on D-pad.

THE PYRAMID OF ARGUS ARENA

While in The Krypt, select the "?" and press A, C, Left on D-pad, Down on D-pad, A, Up.

REIKO'S WAR ROOM ARENA

While in The Krypt, select the "?" and press A, Up on D-pad, A, Up, Down on D-pad, Down on D-pad.

SHINNOK'S SPIRE ARENA

While in The Krypt, select the "?" and press Left, Left, Right on D-pad, Up, Up on D-pad, C.

ARMAGEDDON PROMO MOVIE

While in The Krypt, select the "?" and press Up, Up, Down, Up, ZL, Right on D-pad.

CYRAX FATALITY BLOOPER MOVIE

While in The Krypt, select the "?" and press Right, C, ZR, Down, Up, C.

MOTOR GAMEPLAY MOVIE

While in The Krypt, select the "?" and press Up on D-pad, Up, ZR, L (or ZL), A, ZR.

BLAZE BOSS SKETCH KONCEPT ART

While in The Krypt, select the "?" and press C, Up on D-pad, C, C, A, Left on D-pad.

COLOR STUDY FOR OPENING MOVIE 3 KONCEPT ART

While in The Krypt, select the "?" and press Up on D-pad, Left, Left, Down on D-pad, Down, Right on D-pad.

FIREWELL SKETCH 3 KONCEPT ART

While in The Krypt, select the "?" and press Up, Left on D-pad, R (or ZR), L (or ZL), Right on D-pad, C.

GAUNTLET TRAP SKETCH KONCEPT ART

While in The Krypt, select the "?" and press Right on D-pad, RZ, Up on D-pad, Down, Right on D-pad, Left.

HERO SKETCHES 1 KONCEPT ART

While in The Krypt, select the "?" and press Up, Down on D-pad, RZ, Down, L (or LZ), Down on D-pad.

MILEENA'S CAR SKETCH KONCEPT ART

While in The Krypt, select the "?" and press R (or ZR), Right, Up, R (or ZR), Up on D-pad, Up.

SCORPION THROW SKETCH KONCEPT ART

While in The Krypt, select the "?" and press L (or ZL), Left, Up, Right on D-pad, R (or ZR), C.

SEKTOR'S 2-HAND PULSE BLADE SKETCH KONCEPT ART

While in The Krypt, select the "?" and press A, C, Left, Down on D-pad, Up, A.

ARMORY FIGHT TUNE

While in The Krypt, select the "?" and press Down on D-pad, Left on D-pad, Left, Up on D-pad, Left on D-pad, Down on D-pad.

LIN KUEI PALACE TUNE

While in The Krypt, select the "?" and press L (or ZL), Left, Right on D-pad, Down on D-pad, RZ, Right.

PYRAMID OF ARGUS TUNE

While in The Krypt, select the "?" and press Down, Left, A, C, Up, C.

TEKUNIN WARSHIP TUNE

While in The Krypt, select the "?" and press Up, Right on D-pad, C, A, A, Down on D-pad.

MYSIMS

PASSWORD SCREEN

Press the Minus Button to bring up the pause screen. Then enter the following with the Wii Remote: 2, 1, Down, Up, Down, Up, Left, Left, Right, Right. Now you can enter the following passwords:

OUTFITS	PASSWORD
Diamond vest	Tglg0ca
Genie outfit	Gvsb3k1
Kimono dress	l3hkdvs
White jacket	R705aan

FURNITURE	PASSWORD
Bunk bed	F3nevr0
Hourglass couch	Ghtymba
Modern couch	T7srhca
Racecar bed	Ahvmrva
Rickshaw bed	Itha7da

MYSIMS AGENTS

ASTRONAUT SUIT

At the Create-a-Sim screen, press Up, Down, Up, Down, Left, Right, Left, Right.

BLACK NINJA OUTFIT

At the Create-a-Sim screen, press Right, Up, Right, Up, Down, Left, Down, Left.

STEALTH SUIT

At the Create-a-Sim screen, press Left, Right, Left, Right, Up, Down, Up, Down.

MYSIMS KINGDOM

DETECTIVE OUTFIT

Pause the game and press Left, Right, Left, Right, Left, Right.

SWORDSMAN OUTFIT

Pause the game and press Down, Up, Down, Up, Down, Up, Down, Up.

TATTOO VEST OUTFIT

Pause the game and press C, Z, C, Z, B, A, B, A.

NARUTO SHIPPUDEN: CLASH OF NINJA REVOLUTION III

RYO BONUS

A 50,00 starting Ryo bonus is given if you have a saved data from Naruto Shippuden: Clash of Ninja Revolution 1 or 2 on your Nintendo Wii.

NASCAR KART RACING

JOEY LOGANO

Select Enter Cheat from the Profile Info menu and enter 426378.

NBA LIVE 08

AGENT ZERO SHOES
At the Extras menu, enter ADGILLIT6BE as a code.

CUBA SHOES
At the Extras menu, enter ADGILLIT4BC as a code.

CUSTOMIZE SHOES
At the Extras menu, enter ADGILLIT5BD as a code.

DUNCAN ALL STAR SHOES
At the Extras menu, enter FE454DFJCC as a code.

GIL WOOD SHOES
At the Extras menu, enter ADGILLIT1B9 as a code.

GIL ZERO ALL STAR SHOES
At the Extras menu, enter 23DN1PPOG4 as a code.

TS LIGHTSWITCH AWAY SHOES
At the Extras menu, enter ADGILLIT0B8 as a code.

TS LIGHTSWITCH HOME SHOES
At the Extras menu, enter ADGILLIT2BA as a code.

NBA 2K10

ABA BALL
Select Codes from the Options menu. Then select Enter Code and enter payrespect.

NBA 2K TEAM
Select Codes from the Options menu. Then select Enter Code and enter nba2k.

2K SPORTS TEAM
Select Codes from the Options menu. Then select Enter Code and enter 2ksports.

VISUAL CONCEPTS TEAM
Select Codes from the Options menu. Then select Enter Code and enter vcteam.

2010 ALL-STAR UNIFORMS
Select Codes from the Options menu. Then select Enter Code and enter otnresla.

HARDWOOD CLASSIC UNIFORMS
Select Codes from the Options menu. Then select Enter Code and enter wasshcicsl. This code gives Hardwood Classic Uniforms for the Cavaliers, Jazz, Magic, Raptors, timberwolves, Trail Blazers, and Warriors.

2K CHINA TEAM
Select Codes from the Options menu. Then select Enter Code and enter 2kchina.

LATIN NIGHTS UNIFORMS
Select Codes from the Options menu. Then select Enter Code and enter aihinntslgt. This code gives Latin Nights jerseys for Bulls, Heat, Knicks, Lakers, Mavericks, Rockets, Spurs, and Suns.

NBA GREEN UNIFORMS
Select Codes from the Options menu. Then select Enter Code and enter nreogge. This code gives green uniforms for the Bobcats, Bulls, and Nuggets.

SECONDARY ROAD UNIFORMS
Select Codes from the Options menu. Then select Enter Code and enter eydonscar. This code gives Second Road Uniforms for the Grizzlies, Hawks, Mavericks, and Rockets.

ST. PATRICK'S DAY UNIFORMS
Select Codes from the Options menu. Then select Enter Code and enter riiasgerh. This code gives St. Patrick's Day jerseys for the Bulls, Celtics, Knicks, and Raptors.

BOBCATS RACING UNIFORM
Select Codes from the Options menu. Then select Enter Code and enter agsntrccai.

CAVALIERS CAVFANATICS UNIFORM
Select Codes from the Options menu. Then select Enter Code and enter aifnaatccv.

HORNETS MARDI GRAS UNIFORM
Select Codes from the Options menu. Then select Enter Code and enter asrdirmga.

TRAIL BLAZERS RIP CITY UNIFORM
Select Codes from the Options menu. Then select Enter Code and enter ycprtii.

NBA 2K11

MJ: CREATING A LEGEND
In Features, select Codes from the Extras menu. Choose Enter Code and input icanbe23.

2K CHINA TEAM
In Features, select Codes from the Extras menu. Choose Enter Code and input 2kchina.

2K SPORTS TEAM
In Features, select Codes from the Extras menu. Choose Enter Code and input 2Ksports.

NBA 2K TEAM
In Features, select Codes from the Extras menu. Choose Enter Code and input nba2k.

VC TEAM
In Features, select Codes from the Extras menu. Choose Enter Code and input vcteam.

ABA BALL
In Features, select Codes from the Extras menu. Choose Enter Code and input payrespect.

NEED FOR SPEED CARBON

CASTROL CASH
At the Main menu, press Down, Up, Left, Down, Right, Up, Button 1, B. This gives you 10,000 extra cash.

INFINITE CREW CHARGE
At the Main menu, press Down, Up, Up, Right, Left, Left, Right, Button 1.

INFINITE NITROUS
At the Main menu, press Left, Up, Left, Down, Left, Down, Right, Button 1.

INFINITE SPEEDBREAKER
At the Main menu, press Down, Right, Right, Left, Right, Up, Down, Button 1.

NEED FOR SPEED CARBON LOGO VINYLS
At the Main menu, press Right, Up, Down, Up, Down, Left, Right, Button 1.

NEED FOR SPEED CARBON SPECIAL LOGO VINYLS
At the Main menu, press Up, Up, Down, Down, Down, Down, Up, Button 1.

NEED FOR SPEED PROSTREET

$2,000
Select Career and then choose Code Entry. Enter 1MA9X99.

$4,000
Select Career and then choose Code Entry. Enter W2IOLL01.

$8,000
Select Career and then choose Code Entry. Enter L1IS97A1.

$10,000
Select Career and then choose Code Entry. Enter 1MI9K7E1.

$10,000
Select Career and then choose Code Entry. Enter CASHMONEY.

$10,000
Select Career and then choose Code Entry. Enter REGGAME.

AUDI TT
Select Career and then choose Code Entry. Enter ITSABOUTYOU.

CHEVELLE SS
Select Career and then choose Code Entry. Enter HORSEPOWER.

OVERLOAD

NINTENDO Wii

COKE ZERO GOLF GTI
Select Career and then choose
Code Entry. Enter COKEZERO.

DODGE VIPER
Select Career and then
choose Code Entry. Enter
WORLDSLONGESTLASTING.

MITSUBISHI LANCER EVOLUTION
Select Career and then
choose Code Entry. Enter
MITSUBISHIGOFAR.

UNLOCK ALL BONUSES
Select Career and then
choose Code Entry. Enter
UNLOCKALLTHINGS.

5 REPAIR MARKERS
Select Career and then choose
Code Entry. Enter SAFETYNET.

ENERGIZER VINYL
Select Career and then
choose Code Entry. Enter
ENERGIZERLITHIUM.

CASTROL SYNTEC VINYL
Select Career and then choose Code
Entry. Enter CASTROLSYNTEC. This
also gives you $10,000.

NERF: N-STRIKE

BLACK HEART VENGEANCE
Select Codes from the Main menu
and enter BHDETA8.

CRUSHER SAD-G
Select Codes from the Main menu
and enter CRUSH14.

FIREFLY ELITE
Select Codes from the Main menu
and enter HELIOX6.

GOLIATHAN NITRO
Select Codes from the Main menu
and enter FIERO2.

HABANERO
Select Codes from the Main menu
and enter 24KGCON4.

HYDRA
Select Codes from the Main menu
and enter HRANGEL3.

LONGSHOT STREET
Select Codes from the Main menu
and enter LONGST5.

MAVERICK CRYSTAL
Select Codes from the Main menu
and enter CRISTOL10.

MAVERICK MIDNIGHT
Select Codes from the Main menu
and enter MAVMID7.

MERCURIO
Select Codes from the Main menu
and enter RSMERC9.

SEMPER FIRE ULTRA
Select Codes from the Main menu
and enter CROMO1.

SPARTAN NCS-12
Select Codes from the Main menu
and enter THISIS12.

STAMPEDE
Select Codes from the Main menu
and enter DOGIE15.

VULCAN MAGMA
Select Codes from the Main menu
and enter MAGMA3.

NERF: N-STRIKE ELITE

Select Codebook and enter the following codes.

10 CANISTERS
Enter NERF.

UNLIMITED AMMO
Enter DART. This
can be toggled on
and off.

CERBERUS CS-12
Enter DUDE.

CRUSHER SAD-G
Enter RUSH.

GOLITHUN UB-1
Enter ROCK.

HAMMERHEAD GL-1
Enter PONG.

HYDRA SG-7
Enter WIDE.

ICARUS HM-7
Enter DOOM.

LONGSHOT CS-6
Enter IDOL.

LONGSTRIKE CS-6
Enter PING.

RECON CS-6
Enter DIRT.

SEMPERFIRE RF-100
Enter FLEX.

SPARTAN NCS-12
Enter ICON.

VULCAN EBF-25
Enter LOTS.

NHL 2K9

3RD JERSEYS
At the Codes menu enter R6y34bsH52.

NHL 2K10

THIRD JERSEYS
Select Cheats from the Extras menu and enter G8r23Bty56.

VISUAL CONCEPTS TEAM
Select Cheats from the Extras menu and enter vcteam.

NICKTOONS: ATTACK OF THE TOYBOTS

DAMAGE BOOST
Select Cheats from the Extras menu. Choose Enter Cheat Code and enter 456645.

UNLIMITED LOBBER GOO
Select Cheats from the Extras menu. Choose Enter Cheat Code and enter 118147.

INVULNERABILITY
Select Cheats from the Extras menu. Choose Enter Cheat Code and enter 313456.

UNLIMITED SCATTER GOO
Select Cheats from the Extras menu. Choose Enter Cheat Code and enter 971238.

UNLOCK EXO-HUGGLES 9000
Select Cheats from the Extras menu. Choose Enter Cheat Code and enter 691427.

UNLIMITED SPLITTER GOO
Select Cheats from the Extras menu. Choose Enter Cheat Code and enter 854511.

UNLOCK MR. HUGGLES
Select Cheats from the Extras menu. Choose Enter Cheat Code and enter 654168.

PINBALL HALL OF FAME - THE GOTTLIEB COLLECTION

UNLOCK TABLES IN FREEPLAY, EXTRA OPTIONS, AND PAYOUT MODE
Select Enter Code from the Main Menu and enter the following:

EFFECTS	CODE
Aces High Freeplay	UNO
Big Shot Freeplay	UJP
Black Hole Freeplay	LIS
Central Park Freeplay	NYC
Goin' Nuts Freeplay	PHF
Love Machine Freeplay	HOT
Playboy Freeplay	HEF

EFFECTS	CODE
Strikes 'N Spares Freeplay	PBA
Tee'd Off Freeplay	PGA
Xolten Freeplay	BIG
Custom Balls in Options	CKF
Optional Tilt in Options	BZZ
Payout Mode	WGR

PIRATES PLUNDARRR

CHEAT MENU
Press + to pause the game. Press Up, Up, Down, Down, Left, Right, Left, Right, 2, 1 to make a new Cheat option appear at the bottom of the menu.

AMAZON
Defeat Tecciztecatl, Witch Doctor.

SPECTRAL
Defeat Nanauatl, Hero of the Sun.

POKÉMON RUMBLE

POKÉMON PASSWORDS
Go to the recruitment building in the terminal and enter the following passwords to get the corresponding Pokémon.

POKÉMON	PASSWORD
Blastoise	9580-1423
Charizard	7968-4528
Charmander	7927-6161
Cherrim Positive Forme	7540-5667
Chimchar	8109-8384
Eevee	0511-0403
Giratina (Origin Form)	8322-3706

POKÉMON	PASSWORD
Mew	9561-8808
Piplup	9900-2455
Shaymin (Sky Form)	5468-6284
Shiny Bidoof	5575-2435
Shiny Rattata	9849-3731
Squirtle	6824-2045
Turtwig	8672-1076
Venusaur	1589-3955

NINTENDO Wii

OVERLOAD

PRESS YOUR LUCK 2010 EDITION

WARDROBE PIECES FOR AVATAR
Select the lock tab from the Wardrobe screen and enter SECRET.

THE PRICE IS RIGHT 2010 EDITION

AVATAR UPGRADES
Select the lock tab from the Wardrobe screen and enter PRIZES.

PRINCE OF PERSIA RIVAL SWORDS

BABY TOY WEAPON
Pause the game and enter the following code. Use the D-pad for the directions.
Left, Left, Right, Right, Z, Nunchuck down, Nunchuck down, Z, Up, Down

CHAINSAW
Pause the game and enter the following code. Use the D-pad for the directions.
Up, Up, Down, Down, Left, Right, Left, Right, Z, Nunchuck down, Z, Nunchuck down

SWORDFISH
Pause the game and enter the following code. Use the D-pad for the directions.
Up, Down, Up, Down, Left, Right, Left, Right, Z, Nunchuck down, Z, Nunchuck down

TELEPHONE SWORD
Pause the game and enter the following code. Use the D-pad for the directions.
Right, Left, Right, Left, Down, Down, Up, Up, Z, Nunchuck Down, Z, Z, Nunchuck Down, Nunchuck Down

PRINCESS TOMATO IN THE SALAD KINGDOM

DEBUG BATTLE PASSWORD
Enter GG62 as a password.

PUNCH-OUT!!

REGAIN HEALTH IN BETWEEN ROUNDS
Press the Minus button between rounds to regain health at the start of the next round.

DONKEY KONG, EXHIBITION MODE
Fight Donkey Kong in Last Stand mode.

CHAMPIONS MODE
Win 10 bouts in Mac's Last Stand.

RABBIDS GO HOME

ASSASSIN RABBID
Finish Nick of Time to unlock the Rabbid customization option. Enter this option and select a Rabbid. Go to the menu and select Manage Figurines from the Figurines screen. Hold C + Z and press 2, 2, 1, 1, A, A, 1, 1.

BEST BUY RABBID
Finish Nick of Time to unlock the Rabbid customization option. Enter this option and select a Rabbid. Go to the menu and select Manage Figurines from the Figurines screen. Hold C + Z and press B, 1, 1, B, A, 2, 2, A.

GEEK SQUAD RABBID

Finish Nick of Time to unlock the Rabbid customization option. Enter this option and select a Rabbid. Go to the menu and select Manage Figurines from the Figurines screen. Hold C + Z and press A, A, 1, 1, 1, 1, 2, 2.

LEONARDO RABBID

Finish Nick of Time to unlock the Rabbid customization option. Enter this option and select a Rabbid. Go to the menu and select Manage Figurines from the Figurines screen. Hold C + Z and press 1, 1, 2, 2, A, A, 1, 1.

KANGAROO RABBID

Finish Nick of Time to unlock the Rabbid customization option. Enter this option and select a Rabbid. Go to the menu and select Manage Figurines from the Figurines screen. Hold C + Z and press 1, 1, 1, 1, 1, 2, 1, 2.

PRINCE RABBID

Finish Nick of Time to unlock the Rabbid customization option. Enter this option and select a Rabbid. Go to the menu and select Manage Figurines from the Figurines screen. Hold C + Z and press 1, 2, 1, 2, 1, 2, A, A.

SPLINTER CELL RABBID

Finish Nick of Time to unlock the Rabbid customization option. Enter this option and select a Rabbid. Go to the menu and select Manage Figurines from the Figurines screen. Hold C + Z and press B, B, B, B, A, A, A, A.

RAMPAGE: TOTAL DESTRUCTION

ALL MONSTERS

At the Main menu, press Minus + Plus to access the Cheat menu and enter 141421.

INVULNERABLE TO ATTACKS

At the Main menu, press Minus + Plus to access the Cheat menu and enter 986960.

ALL SPECIAL ABILITIES

At the Main menu, press Minus + Plus to access the Cheat menu and enter 011235.

ALL LEVELS

At the Main menu, press Minus + Plus to access the Cheat menu and enter 271828.

CPU VS CPU DEMO

At the Main menu, press Minus + Plus to access the cheat menu and enter 082864.

FAST CPU VS CPU DEMO

At the Main menu, press Minus + Plus to access the Cheat menu and enter 874098.

ONE-HIT DESTROYS BUILDINGS

At the Main menu, press Minus + Plus to access the Cheat menu and enter 071767.

OPENING MOVIE

At the Main menu, press Minus + Plus to access the Cheat menu and enter 667300.

OVERLOAD

NINTENDO Wii

ENDING MOVIE

At the Main menu, press Minus + Plus to access the Cheat menu and enter 667301.

CREDITS

At the Main menu, press Minus + Plus to access the Cheat menu and enter 667302.

VERSION INFORMATION

At the Main menu, press Minus + Plus to access the Cheat menu and enter 314159.

CLEAR CHEATS

At the Main menu, press Minus + Plus to access the Cheat menu and enter 000000.

RATATOUILLE

Select Gusteau's Shop from the Extras menu. Choose Secrets, select the appropriate code number, and then enter the code. Once the code is entered, select the cheat you want to activate it.

CODE NUMBER	CODE	EFFECT
1	Pieceocake	Very Easy difficulty mode
2	Myhero	No impact and no damage from enemies
3	Shielded	No damage from enemies
4	Spyagent	Move undetected by any enemy
5	Ilikeonions	Fart every time Remy jumps
6	Hardfeelings	Head butt when attacking instead of tailswipe
7	Slumberparty	Multiplayer mode
8	Gusteauart	All Concept Art
9	Gusteauship	All four championship modes
10	Mattelme	All single player and multiplayer minigames
11	Gusteauvid	All Videos
12	Gusteaures	All Bonus Artworks
13	Gusteaudream	All Dream Worlds in Gusteau's Shop
14	Gusteauslide	All Slides in Gusteau's Shop
15	Gusteaulevel	All single player minigames
16	Gusteaucombo	All items in Gusteau's Shop
17	Gusteaupot	5,000 Gusteau points
18	Gusteaujack	10,000 Gusteau points
19	Gusteauomni	50,000 Gusteau points

RAYMAN RAVING RABBIDS 2

FUNKYTOWN

Play each game at least once.

RABBID COSTUMES

Costumes are unlocked as you score 12,000 points in certain games, as well as when you shoot the correct rabbid in the shooting games.

COSTUME	MINIGAME	HOW TO UNLOCK
Cossack	Chess	Earn 12,000 points
Crash Test Dummy	Shopping Cart Downhill	Earn 12,000 points
Cupid	Burgerinnii	Earn 12,000 points
Doctor	Anesthetics	Earn 12,000 points
Fireman	Paris, Pour Troujours	Shoot fireman rabbid
French Maid	Little Chemist	Earn 12,000 points
Fruit-Hat Dancer	Year of the Rabbids	Shoot rabbid wearing fruit hat
Gingerbread	Hot Cake	Earn 12,000 points
HAZE Armor	Big City Fights	Shoot rabbid with armor
Indiana Jones	Rolling Stone	Earn 12,000 points
Jet Trooper	Greatest Hits	Earn 12,000 points
Ken	RRR Xtreme Beach Volleyball	Earn 12,000 points
Martian	Bumper Cars	Earn 12,000 points
Party Girl	Paris, Mon Amour	Once inside boat, shoot girl rabbid
Raider's	American Football	Earn 12,000 points
Sam Fisher	Rabbid School	Earn 12,000 points
Samurai	The Office	Earn 12,000 points
Space	Year of the Rabbids	Earn 12,000 points

COSTUME	MINIGAME	HOW TO UNLOCK
Spider-	Spider Rabbid	Play the "Spider Rabbid" Game
TMNT, Leonardo	Usual Rabbids	Earn 12,000 points
Transformer	Plumber Rabbids	Earn 12,000 points
Vegas Showgirl	Burp	Earn 12,000 points
Voodoo	Voodoo Rabbids	Earn 12,000 points
Wrestler	Greatest Hits	Shoot rabbid in green outfit

RED STEEL 2

.357 MAGNUM, THE TATARO
Select Preorder from Extras and enter 370402.

BARRACUDA
Select Preorder from Extras and enter 3582880.

THE LOST BLADE OF THE KUSAGARI CLAN
Select Preorder from Extras and enter 360378.

NIHONTO HANA SWORD
Select Preorder from Extras and enter 58855558.

SORA KATANA OF THE KATAKARA CLAN
Select Preorder from Extras and enter 360152.

RESIDENT EVIL: THE UMBRELLA CHRONICLES

UNLIMITED AMMO
Earn S rank in all scenarios on hard difficulty.

ARCHIVE ITEMS
Defeat the following scenarios with the indicated rank to earn that item. Get an S rank to get both A and S items.

SCENARIO	A RANK	S RANK
Train Derailment 1	Mixing Set	Briefcase
Train Derailment 2	Statue of Evil/Good	Relief of Discipline/Obedience/Unity
Train Derailment 3	Blue/Green Leech Charm	Sterilizing Agent
Beginnings 1	Motherboard	Valve Handle
Beginnings 2	Fire/Water Key	Microfilm A/B
Mansion Incident 1	Lighter/Lockpick	Great Eagle/Wolf Medal
Mansion Incident 2	Sun/Star/Moon Crest	V-Jolt
Mansion Incident 3	MO Disc	Fuel Canteen
Nightmare 1	Cylinder Shaft	Hex Crank
Nightmare 2	Last Book, Vol. 1/2	Emblem/Gold Emblem
Rebirth 1	Clark/Gail X-Ray	Slide Cartridge
Rebirth 2	Blue/Red/Yellow Gemstone	Death Mask
Raccoon's Destruction 1	S.T.A.R.S. Card (Jill's)	Book of Wisdom/Future Compass
Raccoon's Destruction 2	Joint N/S Plug	Lighter Fluid
Raccoon's Destruction 3	Crystal/Obsidian/Amber Ball	Chronos Key
Death's Door	Picture (Ada and Jon)	S.T.A.R.S. Card (Brad's)
Fourth Survivor	G-virus	Eagle/Serpent/Jaguar Stone
Umbrella's End 1	Plastic Bomb/Detonator	Square Crank
Umbrella's End 2	Blue/Red/Green Chemical	Ink Ribbon
Umbrella's End 3	Vaccine	Medium Base
Dark Legacy 1	King/Knight/Bishop/Rook Plug	Battery
Dark Legacy 2	Film A/B/D/C	Spade/Diamond/Club/Heart Key

ROCK BAND

UNLOCK ALL SONGS
At the Title screen, press Red, Yellow, Blue, Red, Red, Blue, Blue, Red, Yellow, Blue. This code disables saving.

RUBIK'S PUZZLE WORLD

ALL LEVELS AND CUBIES
At the Main menu, press A, B, B, A, A.

RUGBY LEAGUE 3

$100,000,000 SALARY CAP
Go to Create a Player and enter SOMBRERO as the name.

PRESS Z FOR MAX SPEED
Go to Create a Player and enter RSI as the name.

UNLIMITED FUNDING
Go to Create a Player and enter Sugar Daddy as the name.

STRONG WIND
Go to Create a Player and enter Beans & Eggs as the name.

HUGE MUSCLES
Go to Create a Player and enter i'll be back as the name.

ONE TACKLE THEN HANDOVER
Go to Create a Player and enter Force Back as the name.

SAKURA WARS: SO LONG, MY LOVE

ALL 3 EVENTS
In Free & Easy Day in N.Y., visit Romando and enter 928993363528 as a password.

ALL 6 RINGTONES
In Free & Easy Day in N.Y., visit Romando and enter 924005530128 as a password.

ALL 30 PHOTOS
In Free & Easy Day in N.Y., visit Romando and enter 837871465578 as a password.

PASSWORDS IN FREE & EASY DAY IN N.Y.
In Free & Easy Day in N.Y., visit Romando and enter the following as a password.

NAME	PASSWORD	NAME	PASSWORD
Photograph 1	945476282278	Photograph 22	363919657658
Photograph 2	909316867958	Photograph 23	329209358788
Photograph 3	511006563288	Photograph 24	347549954628
Photograph 4	510846764928	Photograph 25	340029139708
Photograph 5	574728027208	Photograph 26	304867438278
Photograph 6	596268228578	Photograph 27	812787630958
Photograph 7	558588824458	Photograph 28	878237389288
Photograph 8	535038549588	Photograph 29	893557986928
Photograph 9	589858748428	Photograph 30	859097180208
Photograph 10	567793040508	Ringtone: Gemini	922566130958
Photograph 11	560273209078	Ringtone: Cheiron	926906817278
Photograph 12	524513806358	Ringtone: Rosita	928267292088
Photograph 13	546403500088	Ringtone: Diana	928935668428
Photograph 14	508343915328	Ringtone: Subaru	928974804588
Photograph 15	313123116008	Ringtone: Ratchet	928993468958
Photograph 16	379665471878	Special Event 1	928996495658
Photograph 17	397985673158	Special Event 2	928993482128
Photograph 18	390435372888	Special Event 3	928996609188
Photograph 19	354355997128	Unlock Shinjiro's Girl Costume	928996605128
Photograph 20	332195193808		
Photograph 21	388679494778		

SAMBA DE AMIGO

UNLOCK EVERYTHING
At the Title screen, press 1, 1, 1, B, A, 1, 1, 1, B, A.

SCARFACE: THE WORLD IS YOURS

MAX AMMO
Pause the game, select Cheats and enter AMMO.

REFILL HEALTH
Pause the game, select Cheats and enter MEDIK.

BULLDOZER
Pause the game, select Cheats and enter DOZER.

INCREASE GANG HEAT
Pause the game, select Cheats and enter GOBALLS.

DECREASE GANG HEAT
Pause the game, select Cheats and enter NOBALLS.

INCREASE COP HEAT
Pause the game, select Cheats and enter DONUT.

DECREASES COP HEAT
Pause the game, select Cheats and enter FLYSTRT.

FILL BALLS METER
Pause the game, select Cheats and enter FPATCH.

GRAY SUIT TONY WITH SUNGLASSES
Pause the game, select Cheats and enter GRAYSH.

TOGGLE RAIN
Pause the game, select Cheats and enter RAINY.

SCOOBY-DOO! FIRST FRIGHTS

DAPHNE'S SECRET COSTUME
Select Codes from the Extras menu and enter 2839.

FRED'S SECRET COSTUME
Select Codes from the Extras menu and enter 4826.

SCOOBY DOO'S SECRET COSTUME
Select Codes from the Extras menu and enter 1585.

SHAGGY'S SECRET COSTUME
Select Codes from the Extras menu and enter 3726.

VELMA'S SECRET COSTUME
Select Codes from the Extras menu and enter 6588.

SCOOBY-DOO! AND THE SPOOKY SWAMP

BIG HEAD
Enter the clubhouse and select Codes from the Extras menu. Enter 2654.

CHIPMUNK TALK
Enter the clubhouse and select Codes from the Extras menu. Enter 3293.

DOUBLE DAMAGE
Enter the clubhouse and select Codes from the Extras menu. Enter 9991.

SLOW MOTION
Enter the clubhouse and select Codes from the Extras menu. Enter 1954.

THE SECRET SATURDAYS: BEASTS OF THE 5TH SUN

ALL LEVELS
Select Enter Secret Code from the Secrets menu and input Zon, Zon, Zon, Zon.

UNLOCK AMAROK TO BE SCANNED IN LEVEL 2
Select Enter Secret Code from the Secrets menu and input Fiskerton, Zak, Zon, Komodo.

UNLOCK BISHOPVILLE LIZARDMAN TO BE SCANNED IN LEVEL 3
Select Enter Secret Code from the Secrets menu and input Komodo, Zon, Zak, Komodo.

UNLOCK NAGA TO BE SCANNED IN LEVEL 7
Select Enter Secret Code from the Secrets menu and input Zak, Zak, Zon, Fiskerton.

UNLOCK RAKSHASA TO BE SCANNED IN LEVEL 8
Select Enter Secret Code from the Secrets menu and input Zak, Komodo, Fiskerton, Fiskerton.

UNLOCK BILOKO TO BE SCANNED IN LEVEL 9
Select Enter Secret Code from the Secrets menu and input Zon, Zak, Zon, Fiskerton.

SHREK THE THIRD

10,000 GOLD COINS
At the gift shop, press Up, Up, Down, Up, Right, Left.

SHOCKMAN

REFILL ENERGY
Pause the game and press Left + Select + 2

SOUND TEST
After completing the game and at the To Be Continued screen, hold Select and press Up or Down.

SIMANIMALS

FERRET
Begin a game in an unlocked forest area, press 2 to pause, and select Enter Codes. Enter Ferret.

PANDA
Begin a game in an unlocked forest area, press 2 to pause, and select Enter Codes. Enter PANDA.

RED PANDA
Begin a game in an unlocked forest area, press 2 to pause, and select Enter Codes. Enter Red Panda.

SIMCITY CREATOR

EGYPTIAN BUILDING SET
Name your city Mummy's desert.

GREEK BUILDING SET
Name your city Ancient culture.

JUNGLE BUILDING SET
Name your city Become wild.

SCI-FI BUILDING SET
Name your city Future picture.

THE SIMPSONS GAME

UNLIMITED POWER FOR ALL CHARACTERS
At the Extras menu, press Plus, Left, Right, Plus, Minus, Z.

ALL MOVIES
At the Extras menu, press Minus, Left, Minus, Right, Plus, C.

ALL CLICHÉS
At the Extras menu, press Left, Minus, Right, Plus, Right, Z.

THE SIMS 2: CASTAWAY

CHEAT GNOME
During a game, press B, Z, Up, Down, B. You can now use this Gnome to get the following:

MAX ALL MOTIVES
During a game, press Minus, Plus, Z, Z, A.

MAX CURRENT INVENTORY
During a game, press Left, Right, Left, Right, A.

MAX RELATIONSHIPS
During a game, press Z, Plus, A, B, 2.

ALL RESOURCES
During a game, press A, A, Down, Down, A.

ALL CRAFTING PLANS
During a game, press Plus, Plus, Minus, Minus, Z.

ADD 1 TO SKILL
During a game, press 2, Up, Right, Z, Right.

SIN AND PUNISHMENT: STAR SUCCESSOR

ISA & KACHI MODE
Defeat the game as Isa and as Kachi. Use the – (minus) button to switch between the two.

SPACE HARRIER

CONTINUE AFTER GAME OVER
At the Game Over screen, press Up, Up, Down, Down, Left, Right, Left, Right, Down, Up, Down, Up.

SPECTROBES: ORIGINS

METALLIC LEO AND RYZA
At the Title screen and before creating a game save, press Up, Down, Left, Right, A.

SPEED RACER

INVULNERABILITY
Select Enter Code from the Options menu and enter A, B, A, Up, Left, Down, Right.

UNLIMITED BOOST
Select Enter Code from the Options menu and enter B, A, Down, Up, B, A, Down.

LAST 3 CARS
Select Enter Code from the Options menu and enter 1, 2, 1, 2, B, A, Plus.

GRANITE CAR
Select Enter Code from the Options menu and enter B, Up, Minus, Plus, 1, Up, Plus.

MONSTER TRUCK
Select Enter Code from the Options menu and enter B, Up, Minus, 2, B, Up, Minus.

AGGRESSIVE OPPONENTS
Select Enter Code from the Options menu and enter Up, Left, Down, Right, Up, Left, Down.

PACIFIST OPPONENTS
Select Enter Code from the Options menu and enter Up, Right, Down, Left, Up, Right, Down.

TINY OPPONENTS
Select Enter Code from the Options menu and enter B, A, Left, Down, Minus, Up, Minus.

HELIUM
Select Enter Code from the Options menu and enter Minus, Up, Minus, 2, Minus, Up, Minus.

MOON GRAVITY
Select Enter Code from the Options menu and enter Up, Plus, Up, Right, Minus, Up, Minus.

OVERKILL
Select Enter Code from the Options menu and enter A, Minus, Plus, Down, Up, Plus, 1.

PSYCHEDELIC
Select Enter Code from the Options menu and enter Left, A, Right, Down, B, Up, Minus.

SPIDER-MAN: FRIEND OR FOE

NEW GREEN GOBLIN AS A SIDEKICK
While standing in the Helicarrier between levels, press Left, Down, Right, Right, Down, Left.

SANDMAN AS A SIDEKICK
While standing in the Helicarrier between levels, press Right, Right, Right, Up, Down, Left.

VENOM AS A SIDEKICK
While standing in the Helicarrier between levels, press Left, Left, Right, Up, Down, Down.

5000 TECH TOKENS
While standing in the Helicarrier between levels, press Up, Up, Down, Down, Left, Right.

SPIDER-MAN: SHATTERED DIMENSIONS

The following can be entered after completing the tutorial.

IRON SPIDER SUIT
After completing the tutorial and at the Main menu, press Up, Right, Right, Right, Left, Left, Left, Down, Up.

NEGATIVE ZONE SUIT
After completing the tutorial and at the Main menu, press Left, Right, Right, Down, Right, Down, Up, Left.

SCARLET SPIDER SUIT
After completing the tutorial and at the Main menu, press Right, Up, Left, Right, Up, Left, Right, Up, Left, Right.

SPONGEBOB SQUAREPANTS: CREATURE FROM THE KRUSTY KRAB

30,000 EXTRA Z'S
Select Cheat Codes from the Extras menu and enter ROCFISH.

PUNK SPONGEBOB IN DIESEL DREAMING
Select Cheat Codes from the Extras menu and enter SPONGE. Select Activate Bonus Items to enable this bonus item.

HOT ROD SKIN IN DIESEL DREAMING
Select Cheat Codes from the Extras menu and enter HOTROD. Select Activate Bonus Items to enable this bonus item.

PATRICK TUX IN STARFISHMAN TO THE RESCUE
Select Cheat Codes from the Extras menu and enter PATRICK. Select Activate Bonus Items to enable this bonus item.

SPONGEBOB PLANKTON IN SUPER-SIZED PATTY
Select Cheat Codes from the Extras menu and enter PANTS. Select Activate Bonus Items to enable this bonus item.

PATRICK LASER COLOR IN ROCKET RODEO
Select Cheat Codes from the Extras menu and enter ROCKET. Select Activate Bonus Items to enable this bonus item.

PATRICK ROCKET SKIN COLOR IN ROCKET RODEO
Select Cheat Codes from the Extras menu and enter SPACE. Select Activate Bonus Items to enable this bonus item.

PLANKTON ASTRONAUT SUIT IN REVENGE OF THE GIANT PLANKTON MONSTER
Select Cheat Codes from the Extras menu and enter ROBOT. Select Activate Bonus Items to enable this bonus item.

PLANKTON EYE LASER COLOR IN REVENGE OF THE GIANT PLANKTON MONSTER

Select Cheat Codes from the Extras menu and enter LASER. Select Activate Bonus Items to enable this bonus item.

PIRATE PATRICK IN ROOFTOP RUMBLE

Select Cheat Codes from the Extras menu and enter PIRATE. Select Activate Bonus Items to enable this bonus item.

HOVERCRAFT VEHICLE SKIN IN HYPNOTIC HIGHWAY - PLANKTON

Select Cheat Codes from the Extras menu and enter HOVER. Select Activate Bonus Items to enable this bonus item.

SPONGEBOB SQUAREPANTS FEATURING NICKTOONS: GLOBS OF DOOM

When entering the following codes, the order of the characters going down is: SpongeBob SquarePants, Nicolai Technus, Danny Phantom, Dib, Zim, Tlaloc, Tak, Beautiful Gorgeous, Jimmy Neutron, Plankton. These names are shortened to the first name in the following.

ATTRACT COINS

Using the Upgrade Machine on the bottom level of the lair, select "Input cheat codes here". Enter Tlaloc, Plankton, Danny, Plankton, Tak. Coins are attracted to you making them much easier to collect.

DON'T LOSE COINS

Using the Upgrade Machine on the bottom level of the lair, select "Input cheat codes here." Enter Plankton, Jimmy, Beautiful, Jimmy, Plankton. You don't lose coins when you get knocked out.

GOO HAS NO EFFECT

Using the Upgrade Machine on the bottom level of the lair, select "Input cheat codes here". Enter Danny, Danny, Danny, Nicolai, Nicolai. Goo does not slow you down.

MORE GADGET COMBO TIME

Using the Upgrade Machine on the bottom level of the lair, select "Input cheat codes here". Enter SpongeBob, Beautiful, Danny, Plankton, Nicolai. You have more time to perform gadget combos.

SSX BLUR

ALL CHARACTERS

Select Cheats from the Options menu and enter NoHolds.

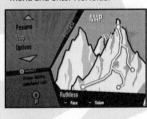

ENTIRE MOUNTAIN UNLOCKED

Select Cheats from the Options menu and enter MasterKey.

ALL OUTFITS

Select Cheats from the Options menu and enter ClothShop.

YETI OUTFIT

Select Cheats from the Options menu and enter WildFur.

STAR WARS: THE FORCE UNLEASHED

CHEATS

Once you have accessed the Rogue Shadow, select Enter Code from the Extras menu. Now you can enter the following codes:

CHEAT	CODE
Invincibility	CORTOSIS
Unlimited Force	VERGENCE
1,000,000 Force Points	SPEEDER
All Force Powers	TYRANUS
Max Force Power Level	KATARN
Max Combo Level	COUNTDOOKU
Stronger Lightsaber	LIGHTSABER

COSTUMES

Once you have accessed the Rogue Shadow, select Enter Code from the Extras menu. Now you can enter the following codes:

COSTUME	CODE	COSTUME	CODE
All Costumes	GRANDMOFF	Heavy trooper	SHOCKTROOP
501st Legion	LEGION	Juno Eclipse	ECLIPSE
Aayla Secura	AAYLA	Kento's Robe	WOOKIEE
Admiral Ackbar	ITSATWAP	Kleef	KLEEF
Anakin Skywalker	CHOSENONE	Lando Calrissian	SCOUNDREL
Asajj Ventress	ACOLYTE	Luke Skywalker	T16WOMPRAT
Ceremonial Jedi Robes	DANTOOINE	Luke Skywalker (Yavin)	YELLOWJCKT
Chop'aa Notimo	NOTIMO	Mace Windu	JEDIMASTER
Classic stormtrooper	TK421	Mara Jade	MARAJADE
Count Dooku	SERENNO	Maris Brook	MARISBROOD
Darth Desolous	PAUAN	Navy commando	STORMTROOP
Darth Maul	ZABRAK	Obi Wan Kenobi	BENKENOBI
Darth Phobos	HIDDENFEAR	Proxy	HOLOGRAM
Darth Vader	SITHLORD	Qui Gon Jinn	MAVERICK
Drexl Roosh	DREXLROOSH	Shaak Ti	TOGRUTA
Emperor Palpatine	PALPATINE	Shadow trooper	INTHEDARK
General Rahm Kota	MANDALORE	Sith Robes	HOLOCRON
Han Solo	NERFHERDER	Sith Stalker Armor	KORRIBAN
		Twi'lek	SECURA

STREET FIGHTER ALPHA 2

AUSTRALIA STAGE
In versus mode, highlight Sagat, hold Start, and press any button.

CHUN-LI'S HIDDEN COSTUME
At the character select, highlight Chun-li, hold Start and press any button.

STRONG BAD'S COOL GAME FOR ATTRACTIVE PEOPLE EPISODE 1: HOMESTAR RUINER

COBRA MODE IN SNAKE BOXER 5
At the Snake Boxer 5 title screen, press Up, Up, Down, Up, Plus.

SUPER C

RETAIN LIVES AND SCORE ON NEW GAME
After defeating the game, press A and then Start.

RETAIN SCORE ON NEW GAME
After defeating the game, press A, B, and then Start.

10 LIVES
At the Title screen, press Right, Left, Down, Up, A, B, Start.

SOUND TEST
At the Title screen, hold A + B and press Start.

SUPER MARIO GALAXY

PLAY AS LUIGI
Collect all 120 stars and fight Bowser. After the credits you will get a message that Luigi is playable.

GRAND FINALE GALAXY
Collect all 120 stars with Luigi and beat Bowser.

STAR 121
Collect 100 purple coins.

SUPER MARIO GALAXY 2

ALL LUIGI GHOSTS
Collect 9999 coins.

BANKER TOAD
Depositing star bits with Banker Toad changes his outfit as indicated in the following table.

ITEM	# OF STAR BITS
Glasses	1000
Spear/Shield	2000
Pickaxe	4000
Scuba Suit	6000
Explorer Outfit	8000

GREEN STARS
Collect 120 stars to unlock 120 green stars.

WORLD S
After completing the game and watching the game ending, you'll unlock World S.

GRANDMASTER GALAXY
Collect 120 stars and 120 green stars.

GRANDMASTER GALAXY COMET—THE PERFECT RUN
Deposit 9999 star bits with Banker Toad.

SURF'S UP

ALL CHAMPIONSHIP LOCATIONS
Select Cheat Codes from the Extras menu and enter FREEVISIT.

ALL LEAF SLIDE STAGES
Select Cheat Codes from the Extras menu and enter GOINGDOWN.

ALL MULTIPLAYER LEVELS
Select Cheat Codes from the Extras menu and enter MULTIPASS.

ALL BOARDS
Select Cheat Codes from the Extras menu and enter MYPRECIOUS.

ASTRAL BOARD
Select Cheat Codes from the Extras menu and enter ASTRAL.

MONSOON BOARD
Select Cheat Codes from the Extras menu and enter MONSOON.

TINE SHOCKWAVE BOARD
Select Cheat Codes from the Extras menu and enter TINYSHOCKWAVE.

ALL CHARACTER CUSTOMIZATIONS
Select Cheat Codes from the Extras menu and enter TOPFASHION.

PLAY AS ARNOLD
Select Cheat Codes from the Extras menu and enter TINYBUTSTRONG.

PLAY AS ELLIOT
Select Cheat Codes from the Extras menu and enter SURPRISEGUEST.

PLAY AS GEEK
Select Cheat Codes from the Extras menu and enter SLOWANDSTEADY.

PLAY AS TANK EVANS
Select Cheat Codes from the Extras menu and enter IMTHEBEST.

PLAY AS TATSUHI KOBAYASHI
Select Cheat Codes from the Extras menu and enter KOBAYASHI.

PLAY AS ZEKE TOPANGA
Select Cheat Codes from the Extras menu and enter THELEGEND.

ALL VIDEOS AND SPEN GALLERY
Select Cheat Codes from the Extras menu and enter WATCHAMOVIE.

ART GALLERY
Select Cheat Codes from the Extras menu and enter NICEPLACE.

SWORDS AND SOLDIERS

ALL LEVELS & MODES
Pause the game and press Down, Up, B, Left, B, Up, Right, B.

10,000 MANA
Pause the game and press B, Left, Up, B, B, Left, Up, B.

OVERLOAD

NINTENDO Wii

10,000 MONEY
Pause the game and press Right, Up, B, B, B, Left, Up, Down.

LOSE LEVEL
Pause the game and press Down, Up, Left, Left, B, Up, Left, Left.

WIN LEVEL
Pause the game and press B, Right, Up, Left, B, Up, Left, Left.

TEENAGE MUTANT NINJA TURTLES: SMASH-UP

NINJA RABBID AND UNDERGROUND STAGE
At the Bonus Content menu, press Up, Up, Down, Down, Down, Right, Up, Left, Right, Left.

SHREDDER AND CYBER SHREDDER OUTFIT
At the Bonus Content menu, press Up, Down, Right, Up, Down, Right, Left, Up, Right, Down.

TENCHU: SHADOW ASSASSINS

ALL NORMAL ITEMS
At the Title screen, hold C + Z and quickly press Up, Left, Down, Right, Up, Left, Down, Right, Right, 1, 2.

ALL SECRET ITEMS
At the Title screen, hold C + Z and quickly press Up, Right, Down, Left, Up, Right, Down, Left, Left, 1, 2.

MAX ITEMS
At the Title screen, hold C + Z and quickly press Down, Up, Down, Up, Right, Left, Right, Left, Left, 1.

ALL MISSIONS/ASSIGNMENTS
At the Title screen, hold C + Z and quickly press Left, Left, Left, Left, Right, Right, Right, Right, 1, 2.

FULL SWORD GAUGE
At the Title screen, hold C + Z and quickly press Up, Down, Up, Down, Left, Right, Left, Right, 1, 2.

THRILLVILLE: OFF THE RAILS

$50,000
During a game, press C, Z, B, C, Z, B, A.

500 THRILL POINTS
During a game, press Z, C, B, Z, C, B, C.

ALL MISSIONS
During a game, press C, Z, B, C, Z, B, Z.

ALL PARKS
During a game, press C, Z, B, C, Z, B, C.

ALL RIDES
During a game, press C, Z, B, C, Z, B, B.

ALL MINIGAMES
During a game, press C, Z, B, C, Z, B, Right.

TIGER WOODS PGA TOUR 08

ALL CLUBS
Select Passwords from the Options and enter PROSHOP.

ALL GOLFERS
Select Passwords from the Options and enter GAMEFACE.

BRIDGESTONE ITEMS
Select Passwords from the Options and enter NOTJUSTTIRES.

BUICK ITEMS
Select Passwords from the Options and enter THREESTRIPES.

CLEVELAND GOLF ITEMS
Select Passwords from the Options and enter CLEVELAND.

COBRA ITEMS
Select Passwords from the Options and enter SNAKEKING.

EA ITEMS
Select Passwords from the Options and enter INTHEGAME.

GRAFALLOY ITEMS
Select Passwords from the Options and enter JUSTSHAFTS.

MIZUNO ITEMS
Select Passwords from the Options and enter RIHACHINRIZO.

NIKE ITEMS
Select Passwords from the Options and enter JUSTDOIT.

PRECEPT ITEMS
Select Passwords from the Options and enter GUYSAREGOOD.

TIGER WOODS PGA TOUR 09 ALL-PLAY

SPECTATORS BIG HEAD MODE
Select EA SPORTS Extras from My Tiger '09, choose Password and enter cephalus.

TIGER WOODS PGA TOUR 10

TIGER WOODS ITEMS IN PRO SHOP
Select Password from the Options menu and enter eltigre.

TMNT

CHALLENGE MAP 2
At the Main menu, hold Z and press A, A, A, 1, A.

DON'S BIG HEAD GOODIE
At the Main menu, hold Z and press 1, A, C, 2.

TONY HAWK RIDE

RYAN SHECKLER
Select Cheats from the Options menu and enter SHECKLERSIG.

QUICKSILVER 80S LEVEL
Select Cheats from the Options menu and enter FEELINGEIGHTIES.

TONY HAWK'S DOWNHILL JAM

BOARDS

BOARD	COMPLETE EVENT
Street Issue	Street Issue Slalom (Tier 1)
Solar	Tourist Trap (Tier 1)
Chaos	Vista Point Race (Random)
Kuni	Hong Kong Race (Tier 2)
Red Rascal	San Francisco Elimination (Tier 3)
Cruiser	Grind Time (Tier 4)
Illuminate	Machu Pichu Top to Bottom Tricks (Tier 4)
Dark Sign	He-Man Club/Girl Power (Tier 5)
Spooky	Clearance Sale (Tier 6)
Black Icer	Precision Shopping Slalom (Tier 7)
Ripper	Del Centro Slalom (Tier 7)
Dispersion	Machu Picchu Top to Bottom Race (Tier 7)
Makonga	Mall Rats (Tier 8)
Goddess of Speed	The Hills Are Alive Tricks (Tier 9)
Dragon	Swiss Elimination (Tier 9)

OUTFITS

CHARACTER	OUTFIT	COMPLETE EVENT
Gunnar	High-G Armor	Gunnar's Threads (Tier 1)
Kyla	Shooting Star	Cuzco Challenge Race (Tier 2)
Tony	Business Camouflage	Mountain High Race (Random)
Budd	The Bohemian	Catacombs Slalom (Tier 2)
Tiffany	Baby Blue	Tourist Spot Slalom (Tier 2)
Ammon	Money Suit	Edinburgh Full Tricks (Tier 3)
Jynx	Black Tuesday	Road to Cuzco Race (Tier 3)
Jynx	Graveyard Casual	Cable Car Tricks (Random)
Crash	Bombs Away	Fallen Empire Race (Tier 4)
MacKenzie	Spitfire Squadron	Edinburgh Full Race (Tier 4)
Gunnar	Street Creds	Favela Rush (Tier 4)
Crash	Brace for Impact	Out of the Woods Race (Tier 5)
Kyla	Touchdown	Clear the Streets (Tier 5)
Tony	Mariachi Loco	Out of the Woods Tricks (Random)
MacKenzie	Killer Bee	High Street Slalom (Tier 6)
Ammon	Tommy T	Seaside Village Race (Tier 6)
Budd	Power of Chi	Rome Elimination (Tier 6)
Crash	Space Monkey	Lift Off (Tier 7)
Jynx	Funeral Fun	Del Centro Race (Tier 7)
Budd	Toys for Bob	Waterfront Race (Random)

OVERLOAD

NINTENDO Wii

CHARACTER	OUTFIT	COMPLETE EVENT
MacKenzie	Street Combat	Parking Lot Shuffle (Tier 7)
Gunnar	Black Knight	Park It Anywhere (Tier 7)
Tiffany	Nero Style	Rome Burning (Tier 7)
Tiffany	Military Chic	Shopping Spree (Tier 8)
Ammon	Tan Suit	Saturday Matinee (Tier 9)
Tony	Downhill Jam	Hills Are Alive Race (Tier 9)
Kyla	Alpine Red	San Francisco Full Slalom (Tier 9)

SKATERS

SKATER	COMPLETE EVENT
Kevin Staab	Kevin's Challenge (Random)
MacKenzie	MacKenzie's Challenge (Tier 2)
Crash	Crash Test (Tier 3)
Armando Gnutbagh	Unknown Skater (Tier 10)

CHEAT CODES

Select Cheat Codes from the Options menu and enter the following cheats. Select Toggle Cheats to enable/disable them.

FREE BOOST
Enter OOTBAGHFOREVER.

ALWAYS SPECIAL
Enter POINTHOGGER.

UNLOCK MANUALS
Enter IMISSMANUALS.

PERFECT RAIL
Enter LIKETILTINGAPLATE.

PERFECT MANUAL
Enter TIGHTROPEWALKER.

PERFECT STATS
Enter IAMBOB.

EXTREME CAR CRASHES
Enter WATCHFORDOORS.

FIRST-PERSON SKATER
Enter FIRSTPERSONJAM.

SHADOW SKATER
Enter CHIMNEYSWEEP.

DEMON SKATER
Enter EVILCHIMNEYSWEEP.

MINI SKATER
Enter DOWNTHERABBITHOLE.

GIGANTO-SKATER
Enter IWANNABETALLTALL.

INVISIBLE BOARD
Enter LOOKMANOBOARD.

INVISIBLE SKATER
Enter NOWYOUSEEME.

PICASSO SKATER
Enter FOURLIGHTS.

CHIPMUNK VOICES
Enter HELLOHELIUM.
Enter DISPLAYCOORDINATES.

LARGE BIRDS
Enter BIRDBIRDBIRDBIRD.

REALLY LARGE BIRDS
Enter BIRDBIRDBIRDBIRDBIRD.

TINY PEOPLE
Enter SHRINKTHEPEOPLE.
*There is no need to toggle on the following cheats. They take effect after entering them.

ALL EVENTS
Enter ADVENTURESOFKWANG.

ALL SKATERS
Enter IMINTERFACING.

ALL BOARDS/OUTFITS
Enter RAIDTHEWOODSHED.

ALL MOVIES
Enter FREEBOZZLER.

TONY HAWK'S PROVING GROUND

Select Cheat Codes from the Options and enter the following cheats. Some codes need to be enabled by selecting Cheats from the Options during a game.

UNLOCK	CHEAT
Bosco	MOREMILK
Cam	NOTACAMERA
Cooper	THECOOP
Eddie X	SKETCHY
El Patinador	PILEDRIVER
Eric	FLYAWAY
Judy Nails	LOVEROCKNROLL
Mad Dog	RABBIES
MCA	INTERGALACTIC
Mel	NOTADUDE

UNLOCK	CHEAT
Rube	LOOKSSMELLY
Spence	DAPPER
Shayne	MOVERS
TV Producer	SHAKER
FDR	THEPREZPARK
Lansdowne	THELOCALPARK
Air & Space Museum	THEINDOORPARK
All Fun Items	OVERTHETOP
All Game Movies	WATCHTHIS

UNLOCK	CHEAT
All Rigger Pieces	IMGONNABUILD
All specials unlocked and in player's special list	LOTSOFTRICKS

UNLOCK	CHEAT
Full Stats	BEEFEDUP
Give player +50 skill points	NEEDSHELP

The following cheats lock you out of the Leaderboards:

UNLOCK	CHEAT
Perfect Manual	STILLAINTFALLIN
Perfect Rail	AINTFALLIN
Unlimited Focus	MYOPIC

You can not use the Video Editor with the following cheats:

UNLOCK	CHEAT
Invisible Man	THEMISSING
Mini Skater	TINYTATER

TRANSFORMERS: THE GAME

INFINITE HEALTH
At the Main menu, press Left, Left, Up, Left, Right, Down, Right.

INFINITE AMMO
At the Main menu, press Up, Down, Left, Right, Up, Up, Down.

NO MILITARY OR POLICE
At the Main menu, press Right, Left, Right, Left, Right, Left, Right.

ALL MISSIONS
At the Main menu, press Down, Up, Left, Right, Right, Right, Up, Down.

BONUS CYBERTRON MISSIONS
At the Main menu, press Right, Up, Up, Down, Right, Left, Left.

GENERATION 1 SKIN: JAZZ
At the Main menu, press Left, Up, Down, Down, Left, Up, Right.

GENERATION 1 SKIN: MEGATRON
At the Main menu, press Down, Left, Left, Down, Right, Right, Up.

GENERATION 1 SKIN: OPTIMUS PRIME
At the Main menu, press Down, Right, Left, Up, Down, Down, Left.

GENERATION 1 SKIN: ROBOVISION OPTIMUS PRIME
At the Main menu, press Down, Down, Up, Up, Right, Right, Right.

GENERATION 1 SKIN: STARSCREAM
At the Main menu, press Right, Down, Left, Left, Down, Up, Up.

GENERATION 1 SKIN: MEGATRON
At the Main menu, press Down, Left, Left, Down, Right, Right, Up.

GENERATION 1 SKIN: OPTIMUS PRIME
At the Main menu, press Down, Right, Left, Up, Down, Down, Left.

GENERATION 1 SKIN: ROBOVISION OPTIMUS PRIME
At the Main menu, press Down, Down, Up, Up, Right, Right, Right.

GENERATION 1 SKIN: STARSCREAM
At the Main menu, press Right, Down, Left, Left, Down, Up, Up.

ULTIMATE SHOOTING COLLECTION

ROTATE DISPLAY ON SIDE IN TATE MODE
At the Main menu, press Left, Right, Left, Right, Up, Up, 1, 2.

WALL-E

The following cheats will disable saving. The five possible characters starting with Wall-E and going down are: Wall-E, Auto, EVE, M-O, GEL-A Steward.

ALL BONUS FEATURES UNLOCKED
Select Cheats from the Bonus Features menu and enter Wall-E, Auto, EVE, GEL-A Steward.

ALL GAME CONTENT UNLOCKED
Select Cheats from the Bonus Features menu and enter M-O, Auto, GEL-A Steward, EVE.

ALL SINGLE PLAYER LEVELS UNLOCKED
Select Cheats from the Bonus Features menu and enter Auto, GEL-A Steward, M-O, Wall-E.

ALL MULTIPLAYER MAPS UNLOCKED
Select Cheats from the Bonus Features menu and enter EVE, M-O, Wall-E, Auto.

ALL HOLIDAY COSTUMES UNLOCKED
Select Cheats from the Bonus Features menu and enter Auto, Auto, GEL-A Steward, GEL-A Steward.

ALL MULTIPLAYER COSTUMES UNLOCKED
Select Cheats from the Bonus Features menu and enter GEL-A Steward, Wall-E, M-O, Auto.

UNLIMITED HEALTH UNLOCKED
Select Cheats from the Bonus Features menu and enter Wall-E, M-O, Auto, M-O.

WALL-E: MAKE ANY CUBE AT ANY TIME
Select Cheats from the Bonus Features menu and enter Auto, M-O, Auto, M-O.

WALL-EVE: MAKE ANY CUBE AT ANY TIME
Select Cheats from the Bonus Features menu and enter M-O, GEL-A Steward, EVE, EVE.

WALL-E WITH A LASER GUN AT ANY TIME
Select Cheats from the Bonus Features menu and enter Wall-E, EVE, EVE, Wall-E.

WALL-EVE WITH A LASER GUN AT ANY TIME
Select Cheats from the Bonus Features menu and enter GEL-A Steward, EVE, M-O, Wall-E.

WALL-E: PERMANENT SUPER LASER UPGRADE
Select Cheats from the Bonus Features menu and enter Wall-E, Auto, EVE, M-O.

EVE: PERMANENT SUPER LASER UPGRADE
Select Cheats from the Bonus Features menu and enter EVE, Wall-E, Wall-E, Auto.

CREDITS
Select Cheats from the Bonus Features menu and enter Auto, Wall-E, GEL-A Steward, M-O.

WII PARTY

SPOT THE SNEAK IN MINI-GAMES
Play all of the 4-player mini-games.

WII SPORTS

BOWLING BALL COLOR
After selecting your Mii, hold the following direction on the D-pad and press A at the warning screen:

DIRECTION	COLOR
Up	Blue
Right	Gold
Down	Green
Left	Red

NO HUD IN GOLF
Hold 2 as you select a course to disable the power meter, map, and wind speed meter.

BLUE TENNIS COURT
After selecting your Mii, hold 2 and press A at the warning screen.

WII SPORTS RESORT

MODIFY EVENTS
At the Select a Mii screen, hold 2 while pressing A while on "OK." This will make the following modifications to each event.

EVENT	MODIFICATION
Air Sports Island Flyover	No balloons or I points
Air Sports Skydiving	Play intro event
Archery	More difficult; no aiming reticule
Basketball Pickup Game	Nighttime

EVENT	MODIFICATION
Frisbee Golf	No wind display or distance
Golf	No wind display or distance
Swordplay Duel	Evening
Table Tennis Match	11-point match

WIPEOUT: THE GAME

JOHN ANDERSON ALTERNATE OUTFIT
Play a single player game.

MAD COWGIRL, VALLEY GIRL (SECOND OUTFIT) AND GRASSHOPPER
Play a multiplayer game.

CHEF MUTTEN
Defeat Wipeout Zone within 1:00.

WWE SMACKDOWN! VS. RAW 2008

HBK AND HHH'S DX OUTFIT
Select Cheat Codes from the Options and enter DXCostume69K2.

KELLY KELLY'S ALTERNATE OUTFIT
Select Cheat Codes from the Options and enter KellyKG12R.

WWE SMACKDOWN VS. RAW 2010

THE ROCK
Select Cheat Codes from the Options and enter The Great One.

VINCE'S OFFICE AND DIRT SHEET FOR BACKSTAGE BRAWL
Select Cheat Codes from the Options menu and enter BonusBrawl.

HBK/SHAWN MICHAEL'S ALTERNATE COSTUME
Select Cheat Codes from the Options menu and enter Bow Down.

JOHN CENA'S ALTERNATE COSTUME
Select Cheat Codes from the Options menu and enter CENATION.

RANDY ORTON'S ALTERNATE COSTUME
Select Cheat Codes from the Options menu and enter ViperRKO.

SANTINO MARELLA'S ALTERNATE COSTUME
Select Cheat Codes from the Options menu and enter Milan Miracle.

TRIPLE H'S ALTERNATE COSTUME
Select Cheat Codes from the Options menu and enter Suck IT!.

WWE SMACKDOWN VS. RAW 2011

JOHN CENA (ENTRANCE/CIVILIAN)
In My WWE, select Cheat Codes from the Options and enter SLURPEE.

RANDY ORTON'S COSTUMES
In My WWE, select Cheat Codes from the Options and enter apexpredator.

TRIBUTE TO THE TROOPS ARENA
In My WWE, select Cheat Codes from the Options and enter 8thannualtribute.

OVERLORD

NINTENDO Wii

PLAYSTATION 3

2010 FIFA WORLD CUP SOUTH AFRICA

PLAYSTATION

ADIDAS U11 TEAM
Go to EA Extras in My 2010 FIFA World Cup. Select Unlockable Code Entry and enter WSBJPJYODFYQIIGK.

FINAL MATCH BALL
Go to EA Extras in My 2010 FIFA World Cup. Select Unlockable Code Entry and enter FGWIXGFXTNSICLSS.

ADIDAS ADIPURE III TRX (BLACK/SUN)
Go to EA Extras in My 2010 FIFA World Cup. Select Unlockable Code Entry and enter HHDOPWPMIXZQOJOZ.

ADIDAS F50 ADIZERO (BLACK/SUN/SUN)
Go to EA Extras in My 2010 FIFA World Cup. Select Unlockable Code Entry and enter SGFSTZPPXCHHMJMH.

ADIDAS F50 ADIZERO (CHAMELEON)
Go to EA Extras in My 2010 FIFA World Cup. Select Unlockable Code Entry and enter VOKMNEZTJOQPULUT.

ADIDAS F50 ADIZERO (SUN/BLACK/GOLD)
Go to EA Extras in My 2010 FIFA World Cup. Select Unlockable Code Entry and enter YOZCCVIFJGKQJWTW.

ADIDAS PREDATOR X (BLACK/SUN)
Go to EA Extras in My 2010 FIFA World Cup. Select Unlockable Code Entry and enter OCEGZCUHXOBSBNFU.

COCA-COLA CELEBRATIONS
Go to EA Extras in My 2010 FIFA World Cup. Select Unlockable Code Entry and enter one of the following:

CODE	CELEBRATION
UGSIMLBHLFPUBFJY	Baby Cradle (L2 + ✖)
KBRRWKUIRSTWUJQW	Dance (L2 + ●)
DVMNJPBTLHJZGECP	Dying Fly (L2 + ■)
DBQDUXQTRWTVXYDC	Flying Dive (L2 + ▲)
TWVBIXYACAOLGOWO	Prancing Bird (R1 + ●)
MIKAKPUMEEWNTQVE	River Dance (R1 + ■)
VNDWDUDLMGRNHDNV	Side Slide (R1 + ▲)
LHEHJZTPYYQDJQXB	Speed Skating (R1 + ✖)

3D DOT GAME HEROES

HIDE SHIELD
Pause the game and press Up, Up, Down, Down, Left, Right, Left, Right, ●, ▲. Re-enter the code to reveal the shield again.

TOGGLE SWAY IN WALKING
Pause the game and press L1, R1, L1, R1, L1, L1, R1, R1, ●. Re-enter to turn the code back on.

SPELUNKER MODE
Enter your name as SPELUNKER. In this mode, you will die with one hit.

BAJA: EDGE OF CONTROL

CAREER COMPLETE 100%
Select Cheat Codes from the Options menu and enter SHOWTIME.

INSTALL ALL PARTS
Select Cheat Codes from the Options menu and enter SUPERMAX.

BAKUGAN BATTLE BRAWLERS

1,000 BP
Enter 33204429 as your name.

10,000 BP
Enter 46836478 as your name.

100,000 BP
Enter 18499753 as your name.

5,000 BP
Enter 42348294 as your name.

500,000 BP
Enter 26037947 as your name.

BATTLEFIELD: BAD COMPANY

M60
Select Unlocks from the Multiplayer menu, press Start and enter try4ndrunf0rcov3r.

QBU88
Select Unlocks from the Multiplayer menu, press Start and enter your3mynextt4rget.

UZI
Select Unlocks from the Multiplayer menu, press Start and enter cov3r1ngthecorn3r.

BAYONETTA

In Chapter 2 after Verse 3, find the phones in the plaza area. Stand in front of the appropriate phone and enter the following codes. The left phone is used for Weapons, the right phone is for Accessories, and the far phone is for Characters.

These codes require a certain amount of halos to be used. You will lose these halos immediately after entering the code.

WEAPONS

BAZILLIONS
Required Halos: 1 Million
Up, Up, Up, Up, Down, Down, Down, Down, Left, Right, Left, Right, ▲

PILLOW TALK
Required Halos: 1 Million
Up, Up, Up, Up, Down, Down, Down, Down, Left, Right, Left, Right, X

RODIN
Required Halos: 5 Million
Up, Up, Up, Up, Down, Down, Down, Down, Left, Right, Left, Right, L1

ACCESSORIES

BANGLE OF TIME
Required Halos: 3 Million
Up, Up, Up, Up, Down, Down, Down, Down, Left, Right, Left, Right, L2

CLIMAX BRACELET
Required Halos: 5 Million
Up, Up, Up, Up, Down, Down, Down, Down, Left, Right, Left, Right, R2

ETERNAL TESTIMONY
Required Halos: 2 Million
Up, Up, Up, Up, Down, Down, Down, Down, Left, Right, Left, Right, R1

CHARACTERS

JEANNE
Required Halos: 1 Million
Up, Up, Up, Up, Down, Down, Down, Down, Left, Right, Left, Right, ●

LITTLE ZERO
Required Halos: 5 Million
Up, Up, Up, Up, Down, Down, Down, Down, Left, Right, Left, Right, ●

THE BEATLES: ROCK BAND

BONUS PHOTOS
At the title screen, press Blue, Yellow, Orange, Orange, Orange, Blue, Blue, Blue, Yellow, Orange.

BEJEWELED 2

TOGGLE CLASSIC STYLE GEMS
During a game, hold L1 + L2 + R1 + R2 and press ✕.

TOGGLE GAME BORDERS
During a game, hold L1 + L2 + R1 + R2 and press ●.

BEN 10 ULTIMATE ALIEN: COSMIC DESTRUCTION

Note that these cheats will disable Trophies! To remove the cheats, you will need to start a new game.

1,000,000 DNA
Pause the game, select Cheats, and enter Cash.

REGENERATE HEALTH
Pause the game, select Cheats, and enter Health.

REGENERATE ENERGY
Pause the game, select Cheats, and enter Energy.

UPGRADE EVERYTHING
Pause the game, select Cheats, and enter Upgrade.

ALL LEVELS
Pause the game, select Cheats, and enter Levels.

DAMAGE
Pause the game, select Cheats, and enter Hard. When entered, the enemies cause double damage while the player inflicts about half damage.

UNLOCK FOUR ARMS
Pause the game, select Cheats, and enter Classic.

THE BIGS

START A ROOKIE WITH HIGHER STATS
When you create a rookie, name him HOT DOG. His stats will be higher than when you normally start.

BIONIC COMMANDO REARMED

The following challenge rooms can be found in the Challenge Room list. Only one code can be active at a time.

AARON SEDILLO'S CHALLENGE ROOM (CONTEST WINNER)
At the Title screen, Right, Down, Left, Up, L1, R1, ●, ●, ●, ●, ●, Start.

EUROGAMER CHALLENGE ROOM
At the Title screen, press Down, Up, Down, Up, Left, L1, ●, L1, ●, ●, Start.

GAMESRADAR CHALLENGE ROOM
At the Title screen, R1, ●, ●, ●, Up, Down, L1, L1, Up, Down, Start.

IGN CHALLENGE ROOM
At the Title screen, Up, Down, ●, ●, ●, ●, Down, Up, L1, L1, Start.

BLACKLIGHT: TANGO DOWN

UNLOCK CODES
Select Unlock Code from the Help & Options menu, then enter the following. These tags can be used on your customized weapons.

TAG	UNLOCK CODE
Alienware Black	Alienwarec8pestU
Alienware	Al13nwa4re5acasE
AMD VISION	4MDB4quprex
AMD VISION	AMD3afrUnap
ATi	AT1hAqup7Su
Australian Flag	AUS9eT5edru
Austria Flag	AUTF6crAS5u
Belgium Flag	BELS7utHAsP
Blacklight	R41nB0wu7p3
Blacklight	Ch1pBLuS9PR
Canada Flag	CANfeprUtr5
Denmark Flag	DENdathe8HU
E3 Dog Tags	E3F6crAS5u
Famitsu Magazine	Fam1tsuprusWe2e
Finland Flag	FINw3uthEfe
France Flag	FRApRUyUT4a
Germany Flag	GERtRE4a4eS
Holland Flag	HOLb8e6UWuh
Hong Kong Flag	HOKYeQuKuw3
India Flag	INDs4u8RApr
Ireland Flag	IRE8ruGejec
Italy Flag	ITAQ7Swu9re
Jace Hall Show	J4ceH4llstuFaCh4
Japan Flag	JPNj7fazebR
Korea Flag	KORpaphA9uK
Mexico Flag	MEX5Usw2YAd
New Zealand Flag	NZLxut32eSA
Norway Flag	NOR3Waga8wa

TAG	UNLOCK CODE
Orange Scorpion	Ch1pMMRSc0rp
Order Logo Chip	Ch1p0RD3Ru02
Pink Brass Knuckles	H4rtBr34kerio4u
Portugal Flag	PORQ54aFrEY
Razer	R4z3erzu8habuC
Russia Flag	RUS7rusteXe
Singapore Flag	SINvuS8E2aC
Spain Flag	ESPChE4At5p
Storm Lion Comics	StormLion9rAVaZ2
Storm Lion Comics	St0rmLi0nB4qupre
Sweden Flag	SWEt2aPHutr
Switzerland Flag	SWIsTE8tafU
Taiwan Flag	TAW8udukUP2
United Kingdom Flag	UKv4D3phed
United States Flag	USAM3spudre
Upper Playground	UPGr0undv2FUDame
Upper Playground	UPGr0undWupraf4u
UTV Lightning Logo chip	Ch1p1GN1u0S
Yellow Teddy Bear	Denek1Ju3aceH7
Zombie Studios Logo Chip	Ch1pZ0MB1Et7

BLAZING ANGELS: SQUADRONS OF WWII

ALL MISSIONS AND PLANES UNLOCKED
At the Main menu, hold L2 + R2, and press ●, L1, R1, ▲, ▲, R1, L1, ●.

GOD MODE
Pause the game, hold L2, and press ●, ▲, ▲, ●. Release L2, hold R2 and press ▲, ●, ●, ▲. Re-enter the code to disable it.

INCREASED DAMAGE WITH ALL WEAPONS
Pause the game, hold L2, and press L1, L1, R1. Release L2, hold R2, and press R1, R1, L1. Re-enter the code to disable it.

BLUR

CONCEPT 1 SERIES TII CHROME
In the Multiplayer Showroom, highlight the BMW Concept 1 Series tii and press L2, R2, L2, R2.

FORD BRONCO FULLY UPGRADED
In the Multiplayer Showroom, highlight the Ford Bronco and press L2, R2, L2, R2.

BOLT

Many of the following cheats can be toggled on/off by pausing the game and selecting Cheats.

LEVEL SELECT
Select Cheats from the Extras menu and enter Right, Up, Left, Right, Up, Right.

ALL MINIGAMES
Select Cheats from the Extras menu and enter Right, Up, Right, Right.

UNLIMITED ENHANCED VISION
Select Cheats from the Extras menu and enter Left, Right, Up, Down.

UNLIMITED GROUND POUND
Select Cheats from the Extras menu and enter Right, Up, Right, Up, Left, Down.

UNLIMITED INVULNERABILITY
Select Cheats from the Extras menu and enter Down, Down, Up, Left.

UNLIMITED GAS MINES
Select Cheats from the Extras menu and enter Right, Left, Left, Up, Down, Right.

UNLIMITED LASER EYES
Select Cheats from the Extras menu and enter Left, Left, Up, Right.

UNLIMITED STEALTH CAMO
Select Cheats from the Extras menu and enter Left, Down (x3).

UNLIMITED SUPERBARK
Select Cheats from the Extras menu and enter Right, Left, Left, Up, Down, Up.

BROTHERS IN ARMS: HELL'S HIGHWAY

ALL CHAPTERS
Select Enter Code from the Options and enter gimmechapters.

ALL RECON POINTS
Select Enter Code from the Options and enter 0zndrbicra.

KILROY DETECTOR
Select Enter Code from the Options and enter sh2vyivnzf.

TWO MULTIPLAYER SKINS
Select Enter Code from the Options and enter hi9wtpxsuk.

BURNOUT PARADISE

BEST BUY CAR
Pause the game and select Sponsor Product Code from the Under the Hood menu. Enter Bestbuy. Need the A License to use this car offline.

CIRCUIT CITY CAR
Pause the game and select Sponsor Product Code from the Under the Hood menu. Enter Circuitcity. Need the Burnout Paradise License to use this car offline.

GAMESTOP CAR
Pause the game and select Sponsor Product Code from the Under the Hood menu. Enter Gamestop. Need the A License to use this car offline.

WALMART CAR
Pause the game and select Sponsor Product Code from the Under the Hood menu. Enter Walmart. Need the Burnout Paradise License to use this car offline.

"STEEL WHEELS" GT
Pause the game and select Sponsor Product Code from the Under the Hood menu. Enter G23X 5K8Q GX2V 04B1 or E60J 8Z7T MS8L 51U6.

LICENSES

LICENSE	NUMBER OF WINS NEEDED
D	2
C	7
B	16

LICENSE	NUMBER OF WINS NEEDED
A	26
Burnout Paradise	45
Elite License	All events

CABELA'S DANGEROUS HUNTS 2009

.470 NITRO EXPRESS HIGH CALIBER RIFLE
Select Enter Special Code from Extras and enter 101987.

ARCADE MODE
After a complete playthrough of the game, Arcade Mode becomes available from the Main menu.

UNLOCKABLE CHEATS
After completing the game, cheats are unlocked based on how many intelligence pieces were gathered. These cheats cannot be used during Arcade Mode. These cheats may also disable the ability to earn Achievements.

CHEAT	INTEL ITEMS	DESCRIPTION
CoD Noir	2	Black and white
Photo-Negative	4	Inverses colors
Super Contrast	6	Increases contrast
Ragtime Warfare	8	Black and white, scratches fill screen, double speed, piano music
Cluster Bombs	10	Four extra grenade explosions after frag grenade explodes.
A Bad Year	15	Enemies explode into a bunch of old tires when killed.
Slow-Mo Ability	20	Melee button enables/disables slow-motion mode.
Infinite Ammo	30	Unlimited ammo and no need to reload. Doesn't work for single-shot weapons such as RPG.

CALL OF DUTY: WORLD AT WAR

ZOMBIE MODE
Complete Campaign mode.

CALL OF JUAREZ: BOUND IN BLOOD

EXCLUSIVE CONTENT
Select Enter Code from Exclusive Content and enter 735S653J. This code unlocks extra money for equipment in single-player mode, a silver weapon in multiplayer, and an exclusive weapon for the first two chapters.

CARS MATER-NATIONAL

ALL ARCADE RACES, MINI-GAMES, AND WORLDS
Select Codes/Cheats from the options and enter PLAYALL.

ALL CARS
Select Codes/Cheats from the options and enter MATTEL07.

ALTERNATE LIGHTNING MCQUEEN COLORS
Select Codes/Cheats from the options and enter NCEDUDZ.

ALL COLORS FOR OTHERS
Select Codes/Cheats from the options and enter PAINTIT.

UNLIMITED TURBO
Select Codes/Cheats from the options and enter ZZOOOOM.

EXTREME ACCELERATION
Select Codes/Cheats from the options and enter 0TO200X.

EXPERT MODE
Select Codes/Cheats from the options and enter VRYFAST.

ALL BONUS ART
Select Codes/Cheats from the options and enter BUYTALL.

CASTLEVANIA: LORDS OF SHADOW

CHEAT MENU
At the loading screen, press Up, Up, Down, Down, Left, Right, Left, Right, ●, ✖. Note, however, that using this cheat disables Trophies and saving.

SNAKE OUTFIT
After completing the game, go to the Extras menu and toggle on Solid Eye and Bandanna.

VAMPIRE WARGAME
During Chapter 6-3, Castle Hall, complete the Vampire Wargame to unlock this mini-game in the Extras menu.

CONAN

PROMOTIONAL UNLOCKABLE #1 CONCEPT ART

Go to the Concept Art menu in Extras and press Up, Down, Up, Down, Left, Right, Left, Right, ●, ▲.

PROMOTIONAL UNLOCKABLE #2 CONCEPT ART

Go to the Concept Art menu in Extras and press Up, Down, Left, Left, ●, ●, ●.

PROMOTIONAL UNLOCKABLE #3 CONCEPT ART

Go to the Concept Art menu in Extras and press L3, L3, ▲, ▲, ●, R3.

PROMOTIONAL UNLOCKABLE #4 CONCEPT ART

Go to the Concept Art menu in Extras and press Left, ●, Left, ▲, Down, R3, R3.

PROMOTIONAL UNLOCKABLE #5 CONCEPT ART

Go to the Concept Art menu in Extras and press Right, Right, Left, Left, Up, Down, Up, Down, ●, ●.

PROMOTIONAL UNLOCKABLE #6 CONCEPT ART

Go to the Concept Art menu in Extras and press ▲, ▲, L3, ●, ●, R3, Up, Down.

DAMNATION

INSANE DIFFICULTY

Select Enter Code from Unlockables and enter Revenant.

VORPAL MECHANICAL REPEATER

Select Enter Code from Unlockables and enter BlowOffSomeSteam.

BIG HEAD MODE

Select Enter Code from Unlockables and enter LincolnsTopHat.

CUSTOM CHARACTERS

Select Enter Code from Unlockables and enter PeoplePerson.

CUSTOM LOADOUT

Select Enter Code from Unlockables and enter LockNLoad.

THE DARKNESS

DARKLING OUTFITS

Even Darklings can make a fashion statement. Support your mini minions with an ensemble fit for murderous monsters by collecting these fun and colorful outfits.

OUTFIT	MENTIONED IN	AREA	LOCATION
Potato Sack	Chapter 1	Chinatown	Sitting against alley wall near metro exit
Jungle	Chapter 1	Hunters Point Alley	Inside hidden room
Roadworker	Chapter 3	City Hall station	Inside train car
Lumberjack	Side Objectives	Cutrone objective	Inside Cutrone's apartment
Fireman	Side Objectives	Pajamas objective	Inside room 261
Construction	Side Objectives	Mortarello objective	Inside room of last mission
Baseball	N/A	Dial: 555-4263	N/A
Golfshirt	N/A	Dial: 555-5664	N/A

PHONE NUMBERS

Dialing 'D' for Darkness isn't the only number to punch on a telephone. Sure, you called every number you found on those hard-to-get Collectibles, but you certainly haven't found *all* of the phone numbers. Pay close to attention to the environment as you hunt down Uncle Paulie. Chances are, you overlooked a phone number or two without even knowing it as you ripped out a goon's heart. All 25 'secret' phone numbers are scattered throughout New York and can be seen on anywhere from flyers and storefronts to garbage cans and posters. Dial 18 of the 25 numbers on a phone—in no specific order—to unlock the final secret of the game.

PHONE NUMBERS	PHONE NUMBERS	PHONE NUMBERS	PHONE NUMBERS
555-6118	555-4569	555-1206	555-5723
555-1847	555-9985	555-9528	555-8024
555-6667	555-1037	555-3285	555-6322

OVERLOAD

PHONE NUMBERS	PHONE NUMBERS	PHONE NUMBERS	PHONE NUMBERS
555-9132	555-9723	555-9562	555-2349
555-6893	555-5289	555-7934	555-6325
555-2402	555-6205	555-7892	555-4565
555-6557	555-7658	555-8930	555-9898
555-2309	555-1233	555-3243	555-7613
555-4372	555-3947	555-3840	555-6969

DARKSIDERS

HARVESTER FOR 0 SOULS

Pause the game and select Enter Code from the Options.
Enter The Hollow Lord.

DEAD RISING 2

KNIGHT ARMOR

Wearing this armor doubles Chuck's health. When his health falls below half, though, the armor is destroyed.

ARMOR NAME	OBTAIN
Full Beard Moustache	Found in the back of Wave of Style, located in Royal Flush Plaza.
Knight Armor	Finish the game with an "S" ending.
Knight Boots	Purchase for $2,000,000 at Moe's Maginations pawnshop on the Platinum Strip.
Knight Helmet	Rescue Jack in "Meet the Family" and win at poker in "Ante Up."

UNLOCKABLE OUTFITS

The following items are unlocked by performing the corresponding task.

ITEM	OBTAINED BY
Bowling Shirt, Diner Waitress, Hunting Jacket, and Overalls	Import a save game from Case Zero.
Champion Jacket	Earn the Win Big! Trophy. Get this by finishing in first place in a TIR Episode.
Dealer Outfit	Earn Chuck Greene: Cross Dresser? Trophy. Get this by changing into all the clothes in the game.
Hockey Mask	Earn the Head Trauma Trophy. Get this by using every type of melee weapon on a zombie.
Orange Prison Outfit	Earn the Judge, Jury and Executioner Trophy. Get this by killing 10 psychos.
Tattered Clothes	Earn the Zombie Fu Trophy. Get this by killing 1000 zombies barehanded.
TIR Helmet	Earn $1,000,000 in Terror is Reality.
TIR Outfit	Earn $5,000,000 in Terror is Reality.
Willamette Mall Security Uniform	Earn Hero of Fortune City Trophy. Get this by rescuing 50 survivors.

DEAD SPACE

REFILL STASIS AND KINESIS ENERGY

Pause the game and press ●, ▲, ▲, ●, ▲.

REFILL OXYGEN

Pause the game and press ●, ●, ▲ (x3).

ADD 2 POWER NODES

Pause the game and press ▲, ● (x3), ▲. This code can only be used once.

ADD 5 POWER NODES

Pause the game and press ▲, ●, ▲, ●, ●, ▲, ●, ▲, ●, ●, ▲. This code can only be used once.

1,000 CREDITS

Pause the game and press ● (x3), ▲, ●. This code can only be used once.

2,000 CREDITS

Pause the game and press ● (x3), ▲, ▲. This code can only be used once.

5,000 CREDITS

Pause the game and press ● (x3), ▲, ●, ▲. This code can only be used once.

10,000 CREDITS

Pause the game and press ●, ▲ (x3), ●, ●, ▲. This code can only be used once.

PLAYSTATION 3

DEAD SPACE IGNITION

HACKER SUIT
Complete the game in single-player mode.

DEADLIEST WARRIOR: THE GAME

Enabling the following cheats will not affect Trophies, but they are disabled when going online.

GOD MODE, PLAYER 1
At the Main menu, press Up, ✕, ■, ●, ▲, Down.

GOD MODE, PLAYER 2
At the Main menu, press Down, ●, ■, ✕, ▲, Up.

SLICE MODE
At the Main menu, press L2, ■, ✕, ■, ✕, R2.

SUDDEN DEATH
At the Main menu, press ●, R1, Up, Down, L1, ✕.

ZOMBIE MODE
At the Main menu, press ▲, ✕, ✕, ✕, ■, ●.

DEF JAM: ICON

IT'S GOING DOWN BY YUNG JOC
At the Title Screen, after "Press Start Button" appears, press Down, ●, ✕, Right.

MAKE IT RAIN BY FAT JOE AND FIGHT AS FAT JOE
At the Title Screen, after "Press Start Button" appears, press ●, Up, Right, Left, ■.

DESTROY ALL HUMANS! PATH OF THE FURON

After entering the following codes, select Customize from the Options to activate them.

60S APPEARANCE
Select Unlock Content from Extras and enter M13Ni95L.

70S APPEARANCE
Select Unlock Content from Extras and enter S63bf2kd.

BIKER OUTFIT
Select Unlock Content from Extras and enter 1gb57M2x.

CHEF OUTFIT
Select Unlock Content from Extras and enter 51c24KiW.

GANGSTER OUTFIT
Select Unlock Content from Extras and enter J5d99bPz.

KUNG FU OUTFIT
Select Unlock Content from Extras and enter Ly11r98H.

MIME OUTFIT
Select Unlock Content from Extras and enter 7qd33J1n.

VELVET OUTFIT
Select Unlock Content from Extras and enter F9sT5v88.

SAUCER ATTACHMENTS
Select Unlock Content from Extras and enter V81fvUW3.

SAUCER SKINS
Select Unlock Content from Extras and enter X91mw7zp.

DIRT 2

Win the given events to earn the following cars:

VEHICLE	EVENT
Ford RS200 Evolution	Rally Cross World Tour
Toyota Stadium Truck	Landrush World Tour
Mitsubishi Pajero Dakar 1993	Raid World Tour
Dallenbach Special	Trailblazer World Tour
1995 Subaru Impreza WRX STi	Colin McRae Challenge
Colin McRae R4 [X Games]	X Games Europe

PLAYSTATION 3

VEHICLE	EVENT
Mitsubishi Lancer Evolution X [X Games]	X Games Asia
Subaru Impreza WRX STi [X Games]	X Games America
Ford Escort MKII and MG Metro 6R4	All X Games events

DJ HERO

Select Cheats from Options and enter the following. Some codes will disable high scores and progress. Cheats cannot be used in tutorials and online.

UNLOCK ALL CONTENT
Enter tol0.

ALL CHARACTER ITEMS
Enter uNA2.

ALL VENUES
Enter Wv1u.

ALL DECKS
Enter LAuP.

ALL HEADPHONES
Enter 62Db.

ALL MIXES
Enter 82xl.

AUTO SCRATCH
Enter it6j.

AUTO EFFECTS DIAL
Enter ab1l.

AUTO FADER
Enter sl5d.

AUTO TAPPER
Enter zith.

AUTO WIN EUPHORIA
Enter r3a9.

BLANK PLINTHS
Enter ipr0.

HAMSTER SWITCH
Enter 7geo.

HYPER DECK MODE
Enter 76st.

SHORT DECK
Enter 51uc.

BLACK AND WHITE
Enter b!99.

EDGE EFFECT
Enter 2u4u.

INVISIBLE DJ
Enter oh5t.

MIDAS
Enter 4pe5.

PITCH BLACK OUT
Enter d4kr.

PLAY IN THE BEDROOM
Enter g7nh.

RAINBOW
Enter ?jy!.

ANY DJ, ANY SETLIST
Enter 0jj8.

DAFT PUNK'S CONTENT
Enter d1g?.

DJ AM'S CONTENT
Enter k07u.

DJ JAZZY JEFF'S CONTENT
Enter n1fz.

DJ SHADOW'S CONTENT
Enter omxv.

DJ Z-TRIP'S CONTENT
Enter 5rtg.

GRANDMASTER FLASH'S CONTENT
Enter ami8.

DJ HERO 2

ALL BONUS CONTENT
Select Cheats from the Options menu, then choose Retail Cheats and enter VIP Pass.

DAVID GUETTA
Select Cheats from the Options menu, then choose Retail Cheats and enter Guetta Blaster.

DEADMAU5
Select Cheats from the Options menu, then choose Retail Cheats and enter Open The Trap.

EAT LEAD: THE RETURN OF MATT HAZARD

MAXIMUM HAZARD DIFFICULTY
At the difficulty select, press Up, Up, Down, Down, Left, Right, Left, Right.

FAR CRY 2

BONUS MISSIONS
Select Promotional Content from the Additional Content menu and enter the following codes. Each code gives four or six extra missions.

6aPHuswe
Cr34ufrE
2Eprunef

JeM8SpaW
tr99pUkA

F.E.A.R.

ALL MISSIONS
Enter F3ARDAY1 as your profile name.

PLAYSTATION 3

FIGHT NIGHT ROUND 3

ALL VENUES
Create a champ with a first name of NEWVIEW.

FRACTURE

EXCLUSIVE PRE-ORDER SKIN
Pause the game and press Up, Right, Left, Down, Up, Left, Right, Down.

FULL AUTO 2: BATTLELINES

ALL CARS
Select Cheat Codes from Extras and enter 47GIV3MECARS.

ALL MISSIONS
Select Cheat Codes from Extras and enter IMFEDUPWITHTHIS.

SCEPTRE AND MINI-ROCKETS
Select Cheat Codes from Extras and enter 10E6CUSTOMER. This vehicle and weapon become available in Arcade Mode and Head to Head.

GI JOE: THE RISE OF COBRA

CLASSIC DUKE
At the Main menu, press Left, Up, ⬤, Up, Right, ▲.

CLASSIC SCARLETT
At the Main menu, press Right, Up, Down, Down, ▲.

GOD OF WAR III

TREASURES OF THE GODS
These items can be turned on and off after you've completed the game. Note, however, that using these items disables Trophies.

TREASURE	DESCRIPTION	LOCATION
Zeus' Eagle	Grants infinite Rage of Sparta.	Climb the vines on the wall east of Gaia's heart. The treasure is located beneath an ancient mural.
Hades' Helm	Maxes Health, Magic, and Item Meters.	After defeating Hades and diving into the River Styx, search the bottom for this treasure.
Helios' Shield	Triples the number on the Hits Counter.	After defeating Helios, search the area to the right.
Hermes' Coin	Kratos collects 10 times the amount of Red Orbs.	After Kratos and Hermes fall and land in the damaged room, search behind the head of the demolished Athena Statue.
Hercules' Shoulder Guard	Decreases damage taken by one-third.	After defeating Hercules, search the bottom of the pool beneath his body.
Poseidon's Conch Shell	Grants infinite Magic.	After freeing the frightened Princess, this treasure is near an item chest.
Aphrodite's Garter	Lets Kratos continue to use Athena's Blades.	Fly behind Aphrodite's bed to find this rare treasure.
Hephaestus' Ring	Kratos automatically wins all context-sensitive attacks.	Finish off Hephaestus and search his cooling pool for the ring.
Daedalus' Schematics	Grants infinite item use.	Found in Daedalus' Workshop after lowering two item chests with a pull of a lever.
Hera's Chalice	Causes your Health Meter to slowly drain over time; it never completely empites.	It's located to the left of where Kratos enters Hera's Garden and a Save Altair.

CHAOS DIFFICULTY, CHALLENGES OF OLYMPUS, & FEAR KRATOS COSTUME
Complete the game on any difficulty.

COMBAT ARENA
Complete the Challenges of Olympus.

THE GODFATHER: THE DON'S EDITION

The following codes can be used only once every five minutes.

$5,000
Pause the game and press ●, ▲, ●, ●, ▲, L3.

FULL HEALTH
Pause the game and press Left, ●, Right, ▲, Right, L3.

FULL AMMO
Pause the game and press ▲, Left, ▲, Right, ●, R3.

ALL MOVIES
At the Main menu, press ▲, ●, ▲, ●, ●, L3.

THE GODFATHER II

These codes can only be used once every few minutes.

$5,000
While in Don view, press ●, ▲, ●, ●, ▲, L3.

FULL AMMO
While in Don view, press ▲, Left, ▲, Right, ●, R3.

FULL HEALTH
While in Don view, press Left, ●, Right, ▲, Right, L3.

GRAND THEFT AUTO IV

CHEATS

Call the following phone numbers with Niko's phone to activate the cheats. Some cheats may affect the missions and achievements.

VEHICLE	PHONE NUMBER
Change weather	468-555-0100
Get weapons	486-555-0100
Get different weapons	486-555-0150
Raise wanted level	267-555-0150
Remove wanted level	267-555-0100
Restore armor	362-555-0100
Restore health	482-555-0100
Restore armor, health, and ammo	482-555-0100

SPAWN VEHICLES

Call the following phone numbers with Niko's phone to spawn the corresponding vehicle.

VEHICLE	PHONE NUMBER	VEHICLE	PHONE NUMBER
Annihilator	359-555-0100	NRG-900	625-555-0100
Cognoscenti	227-555-0142	Sanchez	625-555-0150
Comet	227-555-0175	SuperGT	227-555-0168
FIB Buffalo	227-555-0100	Turismo	227-555-0147
Jetmax	938-555-0100		

MAP LOCATIONS

Access a computer in-game and enter the following URL: www.whattheydonotwantyoutoknow.com.

GRAND THEFT AUTO IV: THE BALLAD OF GAY TONY

CHEATS

Call the following phone numbers with your phone to activate the cheats. Some cheats may affect the missions and achievements.

CHEAT	PHONE NUMBER	CHEAT	PHONE NUMBER
Get weapons	486-555-0100	Restore armor, health, and ammo	482-555-0100
Get different weapons	486-555-0150	Sniper uses exploding bullets	486-555-2526
Raise wanted level	267-555-0150	Super Punch	276-555-2666
Remove wanted level	267-555-0100	Parachute	359-555-7272
Restore armor	362-555-0100	Change Weather	468-555-0100

SPAWN VEHICLES

Call the following phone numbers with your phone to spawn the corresponding vehicle.

VEHICLE	PHONE NUMBER
Akuma	625-555-0200
Annihilator	359-555-0100
APC	272-555-8265
Bullet GT	227-555-9666
Buzzard	359-555-2899
Cognoscenti	227-555-0142
Comet	227-555-0175
FIB Buffalo	227-555-0100

VEHICLE	PHONE NUMBER
Floater	938-555-0150
Jetmax	938-555-0100
NRG-900	625-555-0100
Sanchez	625-555-0150
Super GT	227-555-0168
Turismo	227-555-0147
Vader	625-555-3273

GRAND THEFT AUTO IV: THE LOST AND DAMNED

SPAWN VEHICLES

Call the following phone numbers with your phone to spawn the corresponding vehicle.

VEHICLE	PHONE NUMBER
Annihilator	359-555-0100
Burrito	826-555-0150
Cognoscenti	227-555-0142
Comet	227-555-0175
Double T	245-555-0125
FIB Buffalo	227-555-0100
Hakuchou	245-555-0199

VEHICLE	PHONE NUMBER
Hexer	245-555-0150
Innovation	245-555-0100
Jetmax	938-555-0100
NRG-900	625-555-0100
Sanchez	625-555-0150
Slamvan	826-555-0100
Turismo	227-555-0147

GRID

ALL DRIFT CARS
Select Bonus Codes from the Options. Then choose Enter Code and enter TUN58396.

ALL MUSCLE CARS
Select Bonus Codes from the Options. Then choose Enter Code and enter MUS59279.

BUCHBINDER EMOTIONAL ENGINEERING BMW 320SI
Select Bonus Codes from the Options. Then choose Enter Code and enter F93857372. You can use this in Race Day or in GRID World once you've started your own team.

EBAY MOTORS MUSTANG
Select Bonus Codes from the Options. Then choose Enter Code and enter DAFJ55E01473M0. You can use this in Race Day or in GRID World once you've started your own team.

GAMESTATION BMW 320SI
Select Bonus Codes from the Options. Then choose Enter Code and enter G29782655. You can use this in Race Day or in GRID World once you've started your own team.

MICROMANIA PAGANI ZONDA R
Select Bonus Codes from the Options. Then choose Enter Code and enter M38572343. You can use this in Race Day or in GRID World once you've started your own team.

PLAY.COM ASTON MARTIN DBR9
Select Bonus Codes from the Options. Then choose Enter Code and enter P47203845. You can use this in Race Day or in GRID World once you've started your own team.

GUITAR HERO III: LEGENDS OF ROCK

To enter the following cheats, strum the guitar with the given buttons held. For example, if it says Yellow + Orange, hold Yellow and Orange as you strum. Air Guitar, Precision Mode, and Performance Mode can be toggled on and off from the Cheats menu. You can also change between five different levels of Hyperspeed at this menu.

UNLOCK EVERYTHING

Select Cheats from the Options. Choose Enter Cheat and enter Green + Red + Blue + Orange, Green + Red + Yellow + Blue, Green + Red + Yellow + Orange, Green + Yellow + Blue + Orange, Green + Red + Yellow + Blue, Red + Yellow + Blue + Orange, Green + Red + Yellow + Blue, Green + Yellow + Blue + Orange, Green + Red + Yellow + Blue, Green + Red + Yellow + Orange, Green + Red + Yellow + Orange, Green + Red + Yellow + Blue, Green + Red + Yellow + Orange. No sounds play while this code is entered.

An easier way to show this code is by representing Green as 1 down to Orange as 5. For example, if you have 1345, you would hold down Green + Yellow + Blue + Orange while strumming. 1245 + 1234 + 1235 + 1345 + 1234 + 2345 + 1234 + 1345 + 1234 + 1235 + 1235 + 1234 + 1235.

ALL SONGS

Select Cheats from the Options. Choose Enter Cheat and enter Yellow + Orange, Red + Blue, Red + Orange, Green + Blue, Red + Yellow, Yellow + Orange, Red + Yellow, Red + Blue, Green + Yellow, Green + Yellow, Yellow + Blue, Yellow + Blue, Yellow + Orange, Yellow + Orange, Yellow + Blue, Yellow, Red, Red + Yellow, Red, Yellow, Orange.

NO FAIL

Select Cheats from the Options. Choose Enter Cheat and enter Green + Red, Blue, Green + Red, Green + Yellow, Blue, Green + Yellow, Red + Yellow, Orange, Red + Yellow, Green + Yellow, Yellow, Green + Yellow, Green + Red.

AIR GUITAR

Select Cheats from the Options. Choose Enter Cheat and enter Blue + Yellow, Green + Yellow, Green + Yellow, Red + Blue, Red + Blue, Red + Yellow, Red + Yellow, Blue + Yellow, Green + Yellow, Green + Yellow, Red + Blue, Red + Blue, Red + Yellow, Red + Yellow, Green + Yellow, Green + Yellow, Red + Yellow, Red + Yellow.

HYPERSPEED

Select Cheats from the Options. Choose Enter Cheat and enter Orange, Blue, Orange, Yellow, Orange, Blue, Orange, Yellow.

PERFORMANCE MODE

Select Cheats from the Options. Choose Enter Cheat and enter Red + Yellow, Red + Blue, Red + Orange, Red + Blue, Red + Yellow, Green + Blue, Red + Yellow, Red + Blue.

EASY EXPERT

Select Cheats from the Options. Choose Enter Cheat and enter Green + Red, Green + Yellow, Yellow + Blue, Red + Blue, Blue + Orange, Yellow + Orange, Red + Yellow, Red + Blue.

PRECISION MODE

Select Cheats from the Options. Choose Enter Cheat and enter Green + Red, Green + Red, Green + Red, Red + Yellow, Red + Yellow, Red + Blue, Red + Blue, Yellow + Blue, Yellow + Orange, Yellow + Orange, Green + Red, Green + Red, Green + Red, Red + Yellow, Red + Yellow, Red + Blue, Red + Blue, Yellow + Blue, Yellow + Orange, Yellow + Orange.

BRET MICHAELS SINGER

Select Cheats from the Options. Choose Enter Cheat and enter Green + Red, Green + Red, Green + Red, Green + Blue, Green + Blue, Green + Blue, Red + Blue, Red, Red, Red + Blue, Red, Red, Red + Blue, Red, Red, Red.

GUITAR HERO 5

ALL HOPOS

Select Input Cheats from the Options menu and enter Green, Green, Blue, Green, Green, Green, Yellow, Green.

ALWAYS SLIDE

Select Input Cheats from the Options menu and enter Green, Green, Red, Red, Yellow, Blue, Yellow, Blue.

AUTO KICK

Select Input Cheats from the Options menu and enter Yellow, Green, Red, Blue, Blue, Blue, Blue, Red.

FOCUS MODE

Select Input Cheats from the Options menu and enter Yellow, Green, Red, Green, Yellow, Blue, Green, Green.

HUD FREE MODE
Select Input Cheats from the Options menu and enter Green, Red, Green, Green, Yellow, Green, Green, Green.

PERFORMANCE MODE
Select Input Cheats from the Options menu and enter Yellow, Yellow, Blue, Red, Blue, Green, Red, Red.

AIR INSTRUMENTS
Select Input Cheats from the Options menu and enter Red, Red, Blue, Yellow, Green, Green, Green, Yellow.

INVISIBLE ROCKER
Select Input Cheats from the Options menu and enter Green, Red, Yellow, Yellow, Yellow, Blue, Blue, Green.

ALL CHARACTERS
Select Input Cheats from the Options menu and enter Blue, Blue, Green, Green, Red, Green, Red, Yellow.

CONTEST WINNER 1
Select Input Cheats from the Options menu and enter Green, Green, Red, Red, Yellow, Red, Yellow, Blue.

GUITAR HERO: AEROSMITH

Select Cheats from the Options menu and enter the following. To do this, strum the guitar with the given buttons held. For example, if it says Yellow + Orange, hold Yellow and Orange as you strum. Air Guitar, Precision Mode, and Performance Mode can be toggled on and off from the Cheats menu. You can also change between five different levels of Hyperspeed at this menu.

ALL SONGS
Red + Yellow, Green + Red, Green + Red, Red + Yellow, Red + Yellow, Green + Red, Red + Yellow, Red + Yellow, Green + Red, Green + Red, Red + Yellow, Red + Yellow, Green + Red, Red + Yellow, Red + Blue. This code does not unlock Pandora's Box.

AIR GUITAR
Red + Yellow, Green + Red, Red + Yellow, Red + Yellow, Red + Blue, Red + Blue, Red + Blue, Red + Blue, Red + Blue, Yellow + Blue, Yellow + Blue, Yellow + Orange

HYPERSPEED
Yellow + Orange, Yellow + Orange, Yellow + Orange, Yellow + Orange, Yellow + Orange, Red + Yellow, Red + Yellow, Red + Yellow, Red + Yellow, Red + Blue, Red + Blue, Red + Blue, Red + Blue, Yellow + Blue, Yellow + Orange, Yellow + Orange.

NO FAIL
Select Cheats from the Options. Choose Enter Cheat and enter Green + Red, Blue, Green + Red, Green + Yellow, Blue, Green + Yellow, Red + Yellow, Orange, Red + Yellow, Green + Yellow, Yellow, Green + Yellow, Green + Red.

PERFORMANCE MODE
Green + Red, Green + Red, Red + Orange, Red + Blue, Green + Red, Green + Red, Red + Orange, Red + Blue.

PRECISION MODE
Red + Yellow, Red + Blue, Red + Blue, Red + Yellow, Red + Yellow, Yellow + Blue, Yellow + Blue, Yellow + Blue, Red + Blue, Red + Yellow, Red + Blue, Red + Blue, Red + Yellow, Red + Yellow, Yellow + Blue, Yellow + Blue, Yellow + Blue, Red + Blue.

GUITAR HERO: METALLICA

Once entered, the cheats must be activated in the Cheats menu.

METALLICA COSTUMES
Select Cheats from Settings and enter Green, Red, Yellow, Blue, Blue, Yellow, Red, Green.

HYPERSPEED
Select Cheats from Settings and enter Green, Blue, Red, Yellow, Yellow, Red, Green, Green.

PERFORMANCE MODE
Select Cheats from Settings and enter Yellow, Yellow, Blue, Red, Blue, Green, Red, Red.

INVISIBLE ROCKER
Select Cheats from Settings and enter Green, Red, Yellow (x3), Blue, Blue, Green.

AIR INSTRUMENTS
Select Cheats from Settings and enter Red, Red, Blue, Yellow, Green (x3), Yellow.

ALWAYS DRUM FILL
Select Cheats from Settings and enter Red (x3), Blue, Blue, Green, Green, Yellow.

AUTO KICK
Select Cheats from Settings and enter Yellow, Green, Red, Blue (x4), Red. With this cheat activated, the bass pedal is automatically hit.

ALWAYS SLIDE
Select Cheats from Settings and enter Green, Green, Red, Red, Yellow, Red, Yellow, Blue. All Guitar Notes Become Touch Pad Sliding Notes.

BLACK HIGHWAY
Select Cheats from Settings and enter Yellow, Red, Green, Red, Green, Red, Red, Blue.

FLAME COLOR
Select Cheats from Settings and enter Green, Red, Green, Blue, Red, Red, Yellow, Blue.

GEM COLOR
Select Cheats from Settings and enter Blue, Red, Red, Green, Red, Green, Red, Yellow.

STAR COLOR
Select Cheats from Settings and enter Press Red, Red, Yellow, Red, Blue, Red, Red, Blue.

ADDITIONAL LINE 6 TONES
Select Cheats from Settings and enter Green, Red, Yellow, Blue, Red, Yellow, Blue, Green.

VOCAL FIREBALL
Select Cheats from Settings and enter Red, Green, Green, Yellow, Blue, Green, Yellow, Green.

GUITAR HERO: SMASH HITS

ALWAYS DRUM FILL
Select Cheats from the Options menu and enter Green, Green, Red, Red, Blue, Blue, Yellow, Yellow.

ALWAYS SLIDE
Select Cheats from the Options menu and enter Blue, Yellow, Red, Green, Blue, Green, Green, Yellow.

AIR INSTRUMENTS
Select Cheats from the Options menu and enter Yellow, Red, Blue, Green, Yellow, Red, Red, Red.

INVISIBLE ROCKER
Select Cheats from the Options menu and enter Blue, Red, Red, Red, Red, Yellow, Blue, Green.

PERFORMANCE MODE
Select Cheats from the Options menu and enter Blue, Red, Yellow, Yellow, Red, Red, Yellow, Yellow.

HYPERSPEED
Select Cheats from the Options menu and enter Red, Green, Blue, Yellow, Green, Yellow, Red, Red. This unlocks the Hyperguitar, Hyperbass, and Hyperdrums cheats.

AUTO KICK
Select Cheats from the Options menu and enter Blue, Green, Red, Yellow, Red, Yellow, Red, Yellow.

GEM COLOR
Select Cheats from the Options menu and enter Red, Red, Red, Blue, Blue, Blue, Yellow, Green.

FLAME COLOR
Select Cheats from the Options menu and enter Yellow, Blue, Red, Green, Yellow, Red, Green, Blue.

STAR COLOR
Select Cheats from the Options menu and enter Green, Red, Green, Yellow, Green, Blue, Yellow, Red.

VOCAL FIREBALL
Select Cheats from the Options menu and enter Green, Blue, Red, Red, Yellow, Yellow, Blue, Blue.

EXTRA LINE 6 TONES
Select Cheats from the Options menu and enter Green, Red, Yellow, Blue, Red, Yellow, Blue, Green.

GUITAR HERO: WARRIORS OF ROCK

Select Extras from Options menu to toggle the following on and off. Note, however, that some cheats will disable Trophies.

ALL CHARACTERS
Select Cheats from the Options menu and enter Blue, Green, Green, Red, Green, Red, Yellow, Blue.

ALL VENUES
Select Cheats from the Options menu and enter Red, Blue, Blue, Red, Red, Blue, Blue, Red.

ALWAYS SLIDE
Select Cheats from the Options menu and enter Blue, Green, Green, Red, Red, Yellow, Blue, Yellow.

ALL HOPOS
Select Cheats from the Options menu and enter Green (x3), Blue, Green (x3), Yellow. With this code, most notes become hammer-ons (HO) or pull-offs (PO).

INVISIBLE ROCKER
Select Cheats from the Options menu and enter Green, Green, Red, Yellow (x3), Blue, Blue.

AIR INSTRUMENTS
Select Cheats from the Options menu and enter Yellow, Red, Red, Blue, Yellow, Green (x3).

FOCUS MODE
Select Cheats from the Options menu and enter Green, Yellow, Green, Red, Green, Yellow, Blue, Green. This code removes the busy background.

NO HUD MODE
Select Cheats from the Options menu and enter Green, Green, Red, Green, Green, Yellow, Green, Green.

PERFORMANCE MODE
Select Cheats from the Options menu and enter Red, Yellow, Yellow, Blue, Red, Blue, Green, Red.

COLOR SHUFFLE
Select Cheats from the Options menu and enter Blue, Green, Blue, Red, Yellow, Green, Red, Yellow.

MIRROR GEMS
Select Cheats from the Options menu and enter Blue, Blue, Red, Blue, Green, Green, Red, Green.

RANDOM GEMS
Select Cheats from the Options menu and enter Green, Green, Red, Red, Yellow, Red, Yellow, Blue.

GUITAR HERO WORLD TOUR

The following cheats can be toggled on and off at the Cheats menu.

QUICKPLAY SONGS
Select Cheats from the Options menu, choose Enter New Cheat and press Blue, Blue, Red, Green, Green, Blue, Blue, Yellow.

ALWAYS SLIDE
Select Cheats from the Options menu, choose Enter New Cheat and press Green, Green, Red, Red, Yellow, Red, Yellow, Blue.

AT&T BALLPARK
Select Cheats from the Options menu, choose Enter New Cheat and press Yellow, Green, Red, Red, Green, Blue, Red, Yellow.

AUTO KICK
Select Cheats from the Options menu, choose Enter New Cheat and press Yellow, Green, Red, Blue (x4), Red.

EXTRA LINE 6 TONES
Select Cheats from the Options menu, choose Enter New Cheat and press Green, Red, Yellow, Blue, Red, Yellow, Blue, Green.

FLAME COLOR
Select Cheats from the Options menu, choose Enter New Cheat and press Green, Red, Green, Blue, Red, Red, Yellow, Blue.

GEM COLOR
Select Cheats from the Options menu, choose Enter New Cheat and press Blue, Red, Red, Green, Red, Green, Red, Yellow.

STAR COLOR
Select Cheats from the Options menu, choose Enter New Cheat and press Red, Red, Yellow, Red, Blue, Red, Red, Blue.

AIR INSTRUMENTS
Select Cheats from the Options menu, choose Enter New Cheat and press Red, Red, Blue, Yellow, Green (x3), Yellow.

HYPERSPEED
Select Cheats from the Options menu, choose Enter New Cheat and press Green, Blue, Red, Yellow, Yellow, Red, Green, Green. These show up in the menu as HyperGuitar, HyperBass, and HyperDrums.

PERFORMANCE MODE
Select Cheats from the Options menu, choose Enter New Cheat and press Yellow, Yellow, Blue, Red, Blue, Green, Red, Red.

INVISIBLE ROCKER
Select Cheats from the Options menu, choose Enter New Cheat and press Green, Red, Yellow (x3), Blue, Blue, Green.

VOCAL FIREBALL
Select Cheats from the Options menu, choose Enter New Cheat and press Red, Green, Green, Yellow, Blue, Green, Yellow, Green.

AARON STEELE!
Select Cheats from the Options menu, choose Enter New Cheat and press Blue, Red, Yellow (x5), Green.

JONNY VIPER
Select Cheats from the Options menu, choose Enter New Cheat and press Blue, Red, Blue, Blue, Yellow (x3), Green.

NICK
Select Cheats from the Options menu, choose Enter New Cheat and press Green, Red, Blue, Green, Red, Blue, Blue, Green.

RINA
Select Cheats from the Options menu, choose Enter New Cheat and press Blue, Red, Green, Green, Yellow (x3), Green.

IRON MAN

CLASSIC ARMOR
Clear One Man Army vs. Mercs.

EXTREMIS ARMOR
Clear One Man Army vs. Maggia.

MARK II ARMOR
Clear One Man Army vs. Ten Rings.

HULKBUSTER ARMOR
Clear One Man Army vs. AIM-X. Can also be unlocked when clear game save data from Incredible Hulk is stored on the same console.

CLASSIC MARK I ARMOR
Clear One Man Army vs. AIM.

ULTIMATE ARMOR
Clear Mission 13: Showdown.

JUICED 2: HOT IMPORT NIGHTS

ASCARI KZ1
Select Cheats and Codes from the DNA Lab menu and enter KNOX. Defeat the challenge to earn the car.

AUDI TT 1.8L QUATTRO
Select Cheats and Codes from the DNA Lab menu and enter YTHZ. Defeat the challenge to earn the car.

BMW Z4 ROADSTER
Select Cheats and Codes from the DNA Lab menu and enter GVDL. Defeat the challenge to earn the car.

FRITO-LAY INFINITI G35
Select Cheats and Codes from the DNA Lab menu and enter MNCH. Defeat the challenge to earn the car.

HOLDEN MONARO
Select Cheats and Codes from the DNA Lab menu and enter RBSG. Defeat the challenge to earn the car.

HYUNDAI COUPE 2.7L V6
Select Cheats and Codes from the DNA Lab menu and enter BSLU. Defeat the challenge to earn the car.

INFINITI G35
Select Cheats and Codes from the DNA Lab menu and enter MRHC. Defeat the challenge to earn the car.

KOENIGSEGG CCX
Select Cheats and Codes from the DNA Lab menu and enter KDTR. Defeat the challenge to earn the car.

MITSUBISHI PROTOTYPE X
Select Cheats and Codes from the DNA Lab menu and enter DOPX. Defeat the challenge to earn the car.

NISSAN 350Z
Select Cheats and Codes from the DNA Lab menu and enter PRGN. Defeat the challenge to earn the car.

NISSAN SKYLINE R34 GT-R
Select Cheats and Codes from the DNA Lab menu and enter JWRS. Defeat the challenge to earn the car.

SALEEN S7
Select Cheats and Codes from the DNA Lab menu and enter WIKF. Defeat the challenge to earn the car.

SEAT LEON CUPRA R
Select Cheats and Codes from the DNA Lab menu and enter FAMQ. Defeat the challenge to earn the car.

KUNG FU PANDA

UNLIMITED CHI
Select Cheats from the Extra menu and enter Down, Right, Left, Up, Down.

INVULNERABILITY
Select Cheats from the Extra menu and enter Down, Down, Right, Up, Left.

FULL UPGRADES
Select Cheats from the Extra menu and enter Left, Right, Down, Left, Up.

FULL AWESOME METER
Select Cheats from the Extra menu and enter Up, Down, Up, Right, Left. This gives Po 4X damage.

MULTIPLAYER CHARACTERS
Select Cheats from the Extra menu and enter Left, Down, Left, Right, Down.

OUTFITS
Select Cheats from the Extra menu and enter Right, Left, Down, Up, Right.

LAIR

CHICKEN VIDEO
At the Cheat menu, enter chicken.

COFFEE VIDEO
At the Cheat menu, enter 686F7420636F66666565.

UNLOCKS STABLE OPTION FOR ALL LEVELS
At the Cheat menu, enter koelsch. Saving is disabled with this code.

LARA CROFT AND THE GUARDIAN OF LIGHT

HEAVY JUNGLE OUTFIT
Complete the game.

JUNGLE OUTFIT
Score 1,410,000 points.

BIKER OUTFIT
Score 1,900,000 points.

LEGEND OUTFIT
Defeat Xolotl.

DOPPELGANGER OUTFIT
Score 2,400,000 points.

THE LEGEND OF SPYRO: DAWN OF THE DRAGON

UNLIMITED LIFE
Pause the game, hold L1 and press Right, Right, Down, Down, Left with the Left Analog Stick.

UNLIMITED MANA
Pause the game, hold R1 and press Up, Right, Up, Left, Down with the Left Analog Stick.

MAXIMUM XP
Pause the game, hold R1 and press Left, Right, Right, Up, Up with the Left Analog Stick.

ALL ELEMENTAL UPGRADES
Pause the game, hold L1 and press Left, Up, Down, Up, Right with the Left Analog Stick.

LEGENDS OF WRESTLEMANIA

ANIMAL'S SECOND COSTUME
Select Cheat Codes from the Options menu and enter TheRoadWarriorAnimal.

BRUTUS BEEFCAKE'S SECOND COSTUME
Select Cheat Codes from the Options menu and enter BrutusTheBarberShop!.

IRON SHEIK'S SECOND COSTUME
Select Cheat Codes from the Options menu and enter IronSheikCamelClutch.

JIMMY HART'S SECOND COSTUME
Select Cheat Codes from the Options menu and enter WithManagerJimmyHart.

KOKO B WARE'S SECOND COSTUME
Select Cheat Codes from the Options menu and enter TheBirdmanKokoBWare!.

THE ROCK'S SECOND COSTUME
Select Cheat Codes from the Options menu and enter UnlockTheRockBottom!.

SGT. SLAUGHTER'S SECOND COSTUME
Select Cheat Codes from the Options menu and enter CobraClutchSlaughter.

SHAWN MICHAELS'S SECOND COSTUME
Select Cheat Codes from the Options menu and enter ShawnsSweetChinMusic.

UNDERTAKER'S SECOND COSTUME
Select Cheat Codes from the Options menu and enter UndertakersTombstone.

LEGO BATMAN

BATCAVE CODES

Using the computer in the Batcave, select Enter Code and enter the following:

CHARACTERS

CHARACTER	CODE	CHARACTER	CODE
Alfred	ZAQ637	Penguin Henchman	BJH782
Batgirl	JKR331	Penguin Minion	KJP748
Bruce Wayne	BDJ327	Poison Ivy Goon	GTB899
Catwoman (Classic)	M1AAWW	Police Marksman	HKG984
Clown Goon	HJK327	Police Officer	JRY983
Commissioner Gordon	DDP967	Riddler Goon	CRY928
Fishmonger	HGY748	Riddler Henchman	XEU824
Freeze Girl	XVK541	S.W.A.T.	HTF114
Joker Goon	UTF782	Sailor	NAV592
Joker Henchman	YUN924	Scientist	JFL786
Mad Hatter	JCA283	Security Guard	PLB946
Man-Bat	NYU942	The Joker (Tropical)	CCB199
Military Policeman	MKL382	Yeti	NJL412
Nightwing	MVY759	Zoo Sweeper	DWR243
Penguin Goon	NKA238		

VEHICLES

VEHICLE	CODE	VEHICLE	CODE
Bat-Tank	KNTT4B	The Joker's Van	JUK657
Bruce Wayne's Private Jet	LEA664	Mr. Freeze's Kart	BCT229
Catwoman's Motorcycle	HPL826	Penguin Goon Submarine	BTN248
Garbage Truck	DUS483	Police Bike	LJP234
Goon Helicopter	GCH328	Police Boat	PLC999
Harbor Helicopter	CHP735	Police Car	KJL832
Harley Quinn's Hammer Truck	RDT637	Police Helicopter	CWR732
Mad Hatter's Glider	HS000W	Police Van	MAC788
		Police Watercraft	VJD328
Mad Hatter's Steamboat	M4DM4N	Riddler's Jet	HAHAHA
		Robin's Submarine	TTF453
Mr. Freeze's Iceberg	ICYICE	Two-Face's Armored Truck	EFE933

CHEATS

CHEAT	CODE	CHEAT	CODE
Always Score Multiply	9LRGNB	More Batarang Targets	XWP645
Fast Batarangs	JRBDCB	Piece Detector	KHJ554
Fast Walk	ZOLM6N	Power Brick Detector	MMN786
Flame Batarang	D8NYWH	Regenerate Hearts	HJH7HJ
Freeze Batarang	XPN4NG	Score x2	N4NR3E
Extra Hearts	ML3KHP	Score x4	CX9MAT
Fast Build	EVG26J	Score x6	MLVNF2
Immune to Freeze	JXUDY6	Score x8	WCCDB9
Invincibility	WYD5CP	Score x10	18HW07
Minikit Detector	ZXGH9J		

RED BRICK EXTRAS

After gaining access to the Leaky Cauldron, enter Wiseacre's Wizarding Supplies from Diagon Alley. Go upstairs to enter the following. Pause the game and select Extras to toggle the cheats on and off.

NAME	ENTER	NAME	ENTER
Carrot Wands	AUC8EH	Ice Rink	F88VUW
Character Studs	H27KGC	Invincibility	QQWC6B
Character Token Detector	HA79V8	Red Brick Detector	7AD7HE
Christmas	T7PVVN	Regenerate Hearts	89ML2W
Disguise	4DMK2R	Score x2	74YKR7
Fall Rescue	ZEX7MV	Score x4	J3WHNK
Extra Hearts	J9U6Z9	Score x6	XK9ANE
Fast Dig	Z9BFAD	Score x8	HUFV2H
Fast Magic	FA3GQA	Score x10	H8X69Y
Gold Brick Detector	84QNQN	Silhouettes	HZBVX7
Hogwarts Crest Detector	TTMC6D	Singing Mandrake	BMEU6X
		Stud Magnet	67FKWZ

WISEACRE SPELLS

After gaining access to the Leaky Cauldron, enter Wiseacre's Wizarding Supplies from Diagon Alley. Go upstairs to enter the following. Note that you must learn Wingardium Leviosa before you can use these cheats.

NAME	ENTER	NAME	ENTER
Accio	VE9VV7	Locomotor Mortis	2M2XJ6
Anteoculatia	QFB6NR	Multicorfors	JK6QRM
Calvorio	6DNR6L	Redactum Skullus	UW8LRH
Colovaria	9GJ442	Rictusempra	2UCA3M
Engorgio Skullus	CD4JLX	Slugulus Eructo	U6EE8X
Entomorphis	MYN3NB	Stupefy	UWDJ4Y
Flipendo	ND2L7W	Tarantallegra	KWWQ44
Glacius	ERA9DR	Trip Jinx	YZNRF6
Herbifors	H8FTHL		
Incarcerous	YEB9Q9		

EEYLOPS GOLD BRICKS

After gaining access to the Leaky Cauldron, enter Wiseacre's Wizarding Supplies from Diagon Alley. Go upstairs to enter the following. To access the LEGO Builder, visit Gringott's Bank at the end of Diagon Alley.

GOLD BRICK	ENTER	GOLD BRICK	ENTER
1	QE4VC7	7	XY6VYZ
2	FY8H97	8	TUNC4W
3	3MQT4P	9	EJ42Q6
4	PQPM7Z	10	GFJCV9
5	ZY2CPA	11	DZCY6G
6	3GMTP6		

LEGO INDIANA JONES: THE ORIGINAL ADVENTURES

CHARACTERS

Approach the blackboard in the Classroom and enter the following codes.

CHARACTER	CODE	CHARACTER	CODE
Bandit	12N68W	British Commander	B73EUA
Bandit Swordsman	1MK4RT	British Officer	VJ5TI9
Barranca	04EM94	British Soldier	DJ5I2W
Bazooka Trooper (Crusade)	MK83R7	Captain Katanga	VJ3TT3
Bazooka Trooper (Raiders)	S93Y5R	Chatter Lal	ENW936
		Chatter Lal (Thuggee)	CNH4RY
Belloq	CHN3YU	Chen	3NK48T
Belloq (Jungle)	TDR197	Colonel Dietrich	2K9RKS
Belloq (Robes)	VEO29L	Colonel Vogel	8EAL4H

CHARACTER	CODE
Dancing Girl	C7EJ21
Donovan	3NFTU8
Elsa (Desert)	JSNRT9
Elsa (Officer)	VMJ5US
Enemy Boxer	8246RB
Enemy Butler	VJ48W3
Enemy Guard	VJ7R51
Enemy Guard (Mountains)	YR47WM
Enemy Officer	572E61
Enemy Officer (Desert	2MK45O
Enemy Pilot	B84ELP
Enemy Radio Operator	1MF94R
Enemy Soldier (Desert)	4NSU7Q
Fedora	V75YSP
First Mate	0GIN24
Grail Knight	NE6THI
Hovitos Tribesman	H0V1SS
Indiana Jones (Desert Disguise)	4J8S4M
Indiana Jones (Officer)	VJ85OS
Jungle Guide	24PF34

CHARACTER	CODE
Kao Kan	WMO46L
Kazim	NRH23J
Kazim (Desert)	3M29TJ
Lao Che	2NK479
Maharajah	NFK5N2
Major Toht	13NS01
Masked Bandit	N48SF0
Mola Ram	FJUR31
Monkey Man	3RF6YJ
Pankot Assassin	2NKT72
Pankot Guard	VN28RH
Sherpa Brawler	VJ37WJ
Sherpa Gunner	ND762W
Slave Child	0E3ENW
Thuggee	VM683E
Thuggee Acolyte	T2R3F9
Thuggee Slave Driver	VBS7GW
Village Dignitary	KD48TN
Village Elder	4682E1
Willie (Dinner Suit)	VK93R7
Willie (Pajamas)	MEN4IP
Wu Han	3NSLT8

EXTRAS

Approach the blackboard in the Classroom and enter the following codes. Some cheats need to be enabled by selecting Extras from the Pause menu.

CHEAT	CODE
Artifact Detector	VIKED7
Beep Beep	VNF59Q
Character Treasure	VIES2R
Disarm Enemies	VKRNS9
Disguises	4ID1N6
Fast Build	V83SLO
Fast Dig	378RS6
Fast Fix	FJ59WS
Fertilizer	B1GW1F
Ice Rink	33GM7J
Parcel Detector	VUT673
Poo Treasure	WWQ1SA

CHEAT	CODE
Regenerate Hearts	MDLP69
Secret Characters	3X44AA
Silhouettes	3HE85H
Super Scream	VN3R7S
Super Slap	0P1TA5
Treasure Magnet	H86LA2
Treasure x10	VI3PS8
Treasure x2	VM4TS9
Treasure x4	VLWEN3
Treasure x6	V84RYS
Treasure x8	A72E1M

LEGO INDIANA JONES 2: THE ADVENTURE CONTINUES

Pause the game, select Enter Secret Code from the Extras menu, and enter the following.

CHARACTERS

CHARACTER	CODE
Belloq (Priest)	FTL48S
Dovchenko	WL4T6N
Enemy Boxer	7EQF47
Henry Jones	4CSAKH
Indiana Jones	PGWSEA
Indiana Jones: 2	FGLKYS
Indiana Jones (Collect)	DZFY9S
Indiana Jones (Desert)	M4C34K
Indiana Jones (Desert Disguise)	2W8QR3
Indiana Jones (Dinner Suit)	QUNZUT

CHARACTER	CODE
Indiana Jones (Kali)	J2XS97
Indiana Jones (Officer)	3FQFKS
Interdimensional Being	PXT4UP
Lao Che	7AWX3J
Mannequin (Boy)	2UJQWC
Mannequin (Girl)	3PGSEL
Mannequin (Man)	QPWDMM
Mannequin (Woman)	U7SMVK
Mola Ram	82RMC2
Mutt	2GKS62
Salah	E88YRP
Willie	94RUAJ

PLAYSTATION 3

EXTRAS

EFFECT	CODE
Beep Beep	UU3VSC
Disguise	Y9TE98
Fast Build	SNXC2F
Fast Dig	XYAN83
Fast Fix	3Z7PJX
Fearless	TUXNZF
Ice Rink	TY9P4U
Invincibility	6JBB65
Poo Money	SZFAAE

EFFECT	CODE
Score x3	PEHHPZ
Score x4	UXGTB3
Score X6	XWLJEY
Score x8	S5UZCP
Score x10	V7JYBU
Silhouettes	FQGPYH
Snake Whip	2U7YCV
Stud Magnet	EGSM5B

LEGO STAR WARS: THE COMPLETE SAGA

The following still need to be purchased after entering the codes.

CHARACTERS

ADMIRAL ACKBAR
At the bar in Mos Eisley Cantina, select Enter Code and enter ACK646.

BATTLE DROID (COMMANDER)
At the bar in Mos Eisley Cantina, select Enter Code and enter KPF958.

BOBA FETT (BOY)
At the bar in Mos Eisley Cantina, select Enter Code and enter GGF539.

BOSS NASS
At the bar in Mos Eisley Cantina, select Enter Code and enter HHY697.

CAPTAIN TARPALS
At the bar in Mos Eisley Cantina, select Enter Code and enter QRN714.

COUNT DOOKU
At the bar in Mos Eisley Cantina, select Enter Code and enter DDD748.

DARTH MAUL
At the bar in Mos Eisley Cantina, select Enter Code and enter EUK421.

EWOK
At the bar in Mos Eisley Cantina, select Enter Code and enter EWK785.

GENERAL GRIEVOUS
At the bar in Mos Eisley Cantina, select Enter Code and enter PMN576.

GREEDO
At the bar in Mos Eisley Cantina, select Enter Code and enter ZZR636.

IG-88
At the bar in Mos Eisley Cantina, select Enter Code and enter GIJ989.

IMPERIAL GUARD
At the bar in Mos Eisley Cantina, select Enter Code and enter GUA850.

JANGO FETT
At the bar in Mos Eisley Cantina, select Enter Code and enter KLJ897.

KI-ADI MUNDI
At the bar in Mos Eisley Cantina, select Enter Code and enter MUN486.

LUMINARA
At the bar in Mos Eisley Cantina, select Enter Code and enter LUM521.

PADMÉ
At the bar in Mos Eisley Cantina, select Enter Code and enter VBJ322.

R2-Q5
At the bar in Mos Eisley Cantina, select Enter Code and enter EVILR2.

STORMTROOPER
At the bar in Mos Eisley Cantina, select Enter Code and enter NBN431.

TAUN WE
At the bar in Mos Eisley Cantina, select Enter Code and enter PRX482.

VULTURE DROID
At the bar in Mos Eisley Cantina, select Enter Code and enter BDC866.

WATTO
At the bar in Mos Eisley Cantina, select Enter Code and enter PLL967.

ZAM WESELL
At the bar in Mos Eisley Cantina, select Enter Code and enter 584HJF.

SKILLS

DISGUISE
At the bar in Mos Eisley Cantina, select Enter Code and enter BRJ437.

FORCE GRAPPLE LEAP
At the bar in Mos Eisley Cantina, select Enter Code and enter CLZ738.

VEHICLES

DROID TRIFIGHTER
At the bar in Mos Eisley Cantina, select Enter Code and enter AAB123.

IMPERIAL SHUTTLE
At the bar in Mos Eisley Cantina, select Enter Code and enter HUT845.

TIE INTERCEPTOR
At the bar in Mos Eisley Cantina, select Enter Code and enter INT729.

TIE FIGHTER
At the bar in Mos Eisley Cantina, select Enter Code and enter DBH897.

ZAM'S AIRSPEEDER
At the bar in Mos Eisley Cantina, select Enter Code and enter UUU875.

LINGER IN SHADOWS

CREDITS AND HIDDEN PART
At the Title screen, press L3 + R3.

LITTLEBIGPLANET

BYPASS THE CREATE MODE TUTORIALS
As the credits roll press Down, Up, L1, L2, R2, R1, ▲, ✕.

LOST PLANET 2

Go to the Customization screen from My Page and select Character Parts. Press ▲ to access the LP2 Slot Machine and then press ● to enter the following passwords.

T-SHIRT 1
Enter 73154986.

T-SHIRT 4
Enter 40358056.

T-SHIRT 5
Enter 96725729.

T-SHIRT 6
Enter 21899787.

T-SHIRT 7
Enter 52352345.

T-SHIRT 8
Enter 63152256.

T-SHIRT 9
Enter 34297758.

T-SHIRT 10
Enter 88020223.

T-SHIRT 11
Enter 25060016.

T-SHIRT 12
Enter 65162980.

T-SHIRT 13
Enter 56428338.

T-SHIRT 14
Enter 18213092.

T-SHIRT 15
Enter 26797358.

T-SHIRT 16
Enter 71556463.

T-SHIRT 17
Enter 31354816.

T-SHIRT 18
Enter 12887439.

ALBERT WESKER
To unlock Albert Wesker, you need a save game from Resident Evil 5. Alternately, you can unlock him from the LP2 Slot Machine by entering 72962792. This character model can be found in Customization under Preset Models.

FRANK WEST
To unlock Frank West, you need a save game from Lost Planet. Alternately, you can unlock him from the LP2 Slot Machine by entering 83561942. This character model can be found in Customization under Preset Models.

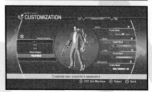

LUCHA LIBRE AAA: HEROES DEL RING

LITTLE ONES
At the Character Select screen, press Up, Up, Down, Down, Left, Right, Left, Right. To obtain the Little Ones Can Too Trophy, simply play with them.

MARVEL ULTIMATE ALLIANCE

UNLOCK ALL SKINS
At the Team menu, press Up, Down, Left, Right, Left, Right, Start.

UNLOCKS ALL HERO POWERS
At the Team menu, press Left, Right, Up, Down, Up, Down, Start.

ALL HEROES TO LEVEL 99
At the Team menu, press Up, Left, Up, Left, Down, Right, Down, Right, Start.

UNLOCK ALL HEROES
At the Team menu, press Up, Up, Down, Down, Left, Left, Left, Start.

UNLOCK DAREDEVIL
At the Team menu, press Left, Left, Right, Right, Up, Down, Up, Down, Start.

UNLOCK SILVER SURFER
At the Team menu, press Down, Left, Left, Up, Right, Up, Down, Left, Start.

GOD MODE
During gameplay, press Up, Down, Up, Down, Up, Left, Down, Right, Start.

TOUCH OF DEATH
During gameplay, press Left, Right, Down, Down, Right, Left, Start.

SUPER SPEED
During gameplay, press Up, Left, Up, Right, Down, Right, Start.

FILL MOMENTUM
During gameplay, press Left, Right, Right, Left, Up, Down, Down, Up, Start.

UNLOCK ALL COMICS
At the Review menu, press Left, Right, Right, Left, Up, Up, Right, Start.

UNLOCK ALL CONCEPT ART
At the Review menu, press Down, Down, Down, Right, Right, Left, Down, Start.

UNLOCK ALL CINEMATICS
At the Review menu, press Up, Left, Left, Up, Right, Right, Up, Start.

UNLOCK ALL LOAD SCREENS
At the Review menu, press Up, Down, Right, Left, Up, Up Down, Start.

UNLOCK ALL COURSES
At the Comic Missions menu, press Up, Right, Left, Down, Up, Right, Left, Down, Start.

MARVEL: ULTIMATE ALLIANCE 2

These codes will disable the ability to save.

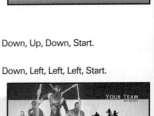

GOD MODE
During a game, press Up, Down, Up, Down, Up, Left, Down, Right, Start.

UNLIMITED FUSION
During a game, press Right, Right, Up, Down, Up, Up, Left, Start.

UNLOCK ALL POWERS
During a game, press Left, Right, Up, Down, Up, Down, Start.

UNLOCK ALL HEROES
During a game, press Up, Up, Down, Down, Left, Left, Left, Start.

UNLOCK ALL SKINS
During a game, press Up, Down, Left, Right, Left, Right, Start.

UNLOCK JEAN GREY
During a game, press Left, Left, Right, Right, Up, Down, Up, Down, Start.

UNLOCK HULK
During a game, press Down, Left, Left, Up, Right, Up, Down, Left, Start.

UNLOCK THOR
During a game, press Up, Right, Right, Down, Right, Down, Left, Right, Start.

UNLOCK ALL AUDIO LOGS
At the main menu, press Left, Right, Right, Left, Up, Up, Right, Start.

UNLOCK ALL DOSSIERS
At the main menu, press Down, Down, Down, Right, Right, Left, Down, Start.

UNLOCK ALL MOVIES
At the main menu, press Up, Left, Left, Up, Right, Right, Up, Start.

MEDAL OF HONOR: AIRBORNE

Using the following cheats disables saves. During a game, hold L1 + R1, and press ●, ●, ▲, ✖, ✖. This brings up an Enter Cheat screen. Now you can enter the following:

FULL AMMO
Hold L1 + R1 and press ●, ●, ▲, ●, ✖, ▲.

FULL HEALTH
Hold L1 + R1 and press ▲, ●, ●, ▲, ✖, ●.

MERCENARIES 2: WORLD IN FLAMES

To use Cheat Mode, you must update the game by being online when the game is started. The cheats will keep you from earning trophies, but anything earned up to that point remains. You can still save with the cheats, but be careful if you want to earn trophies. Quit the game without saving to return to normal.

CHEAT MODE
Access your PDA by pressing Select. Press L2, R2, R2, L2, R2, L2, L2, R2, R2, R2, L2 and close the PDA. You then need to accept the agreement that says trophies are disabled. Now you can enter the following cheats.

INVINCIBILITY
Access your PDA and press Up, Down, Left, Down, Right, Right. This activates invincibility for you and anyone that joins your game.

INFINITE AMMO
Access your PDA and press Up, Down, Left, Right, Left, Left.

OVERLOAD

PLAYSTATION 3

GIVE ALL VEHICLES
Access your PDA and press Up, Down, Left, Right, Right, Left.

GIVE ALL SUPPLIES
Access your PDA and press Left, Right, Right, Left, Up, Up, Left, Up.

GIVE ALL AIRSTRIKES (EXCEPT NUKE)
Access your PDA and press Right, Left, Down, Up, Right, Left, Down, Up.

GIVE NUKE
Access your PDA and press Up, Up, Down, Down, Left, Right, Left, Right.

FILL FUEL
Access your PDA and press Up, Up, Up, Down, Down, Down.

ALL COSTUMES
Access your PDA and press Up, Right, Down, Left, Up.

GRAPPLING HOOK
Access your PDA and press Up, Left, Down, Right, Up.

METAL GEAR SOLID 4: GUNS OF THE PATRIOTS

100,000 DREBIN POINTS
At Otacon's computer in Shadow Moses, enter 14893.

OPENING – OLD L.A. 2040 IPOD SONG
At Otacon's computer in Shadow Moses, enter 78925.

POLICENAUTS END TITLE IPOD SONG
At Otacon's computer in Shadow Moses, enter 13462.

You must first defeat the game to use the following passwords.

DESPERATE CHASE IPOD SONG
Select password from the Extras menu and enter thomas.

GEKKO IPOD SONG
Select password from the Extras menu and enter george.

MIDNIGHT SHADOW IPOD SONG
Select password from the Extras menu and enter theodore.

MOBS ALIVE IPOD SONG
Select password from the Extras menu and enter abraham.

DESERT EAGLE—LONG BARREL
Select password from the Extras menu and enter deskyhstyl.

MK. 23 SOCOM PISTOL
Select password from the Extras menu and enter mekakorkkk.

MOSIN NAGANT
Select password from the Extras menu and enter mnsoymsyhn.

TYPE 17 PISTOL
Select password from the Extras menu and enter jmsotsynrn.

ALTAIR COSTUME
Select password from the Extras menu and enter aottrykmyn.

MLB 08: THE SHOW

ALL CLASSIC STADIUMS
At the Main menu, press Down, Right, ●, ●, Left, ▲, Up, L1. The controller will vibrate if entered correctly.

MLB 10: THE SHOW

SILENCE DAVE CAMPBELL
Pause the game and press Up, Up, Down, Down, Left, Right, Left, Up.

SILENCE MATT VASGERSIAN
Pause the game and press Up, Up, Down, Down, Left, Right, Left, Right.

SILENCE REX HUDLER
Pause the game and press Up, Up, Down, Down, Left, Right, Left, Left.

MODNATION RACERS

BOOST START
Press L1 when the word GO appears on-screen.

MOTOSTORM

UNLOCK EVERYTHING
At the Main menu, hold L1 + L2 + R1 + R2 + R3 (while pressed Up) + L3 (while pressed Down).

BIG HEADS ON ATVS AND BIKES
Pause the game and hold L1 + L2 + R1 + R2 + R3 (while pressed Right), + L3 (while pressed Left).

MX VS. ATV REFLEX

MX VEHICLES FOR PURCHASE
Select Enter Cheat Code from the Options and enter brapbrap.

JUSTIN BRAYTON, KTM MX BIKES AND ATVS IN ARCADE MODE
Select Enter Cheat Code from the Options and enter readytorace.

ALL EVENT LOCATIONS IN ARCADE MODE
Select Enter Cheat Code from the Options and enter whereto.

ALL AI OPPONENTS
Select Enter Cheat Code from the Options and enter allai.

ATV VEHICLES FOR PURCHASE
Select Enter Cheat Code from the Options and enter couches.

ALL AVAILABLE RIDER GEAR
Select Enter Cheat Code from the Options and enter gearedup.

ALL AVAILABLE HELMETS
Select Enter Cheat Code from the Options and enter skullcap.

ALL AVAILABLE BOOTS
Select Enter Cheat Code from the Options and enter kicks.

ALL AVAILABLE GOGGLES
Select Enter Cheat Code from the Options and enter windows.

MX VS. ATV UNTAMED

ALL RIDING GEAR
Select Cheat Codes from the Options and enter crazylikea.

ALL HANDLEBARS
Select Cheat Codes from the Options and enter nohands.

NASCAR 08

ALL CHASE MODE CARS
Select cheat codes from the Options menu and enter checkered flag.

EA SPORTS CAR
Select cheat codes from the Options menu and enter ea sports car.

FANTASY DRIVERS
Select cheat codes from the Options menu and enter race the pack.

WALMART CAR AND TRACK
Select cheat codes from the Options menu and enter walmart everyday.

NASCAR 09

ALL FANTASY DRIVERS
Select EA Extras from My Nascar, choose Cheat Codes and enter CHECKERED FLAG.

WAL-MART CAR & CHICAGO PIER RACETRACK
Select EA Extras from My Nascar, then choose Cheat Codes and enter WALMART EVERYDAY.

PLAYSTATION 3

NBA 09: THE INSIDE

EASTERN ALL-STARS 09 JERSEY
Select Extras from the Progression menu. Then choose nba.com from the Jerseys menu. Press ● and enter SHPNV2K699.

WESTERN ALL-STARS 09 JERSEY
Select Extras from the Progression menu. Then choose nba.com from the Jerseys menu. Press ● and enter K8AV6YMLNF.

L.A. LAKERS LATIN NIGHT JERSEY
Select Extras from the Progression menu. Then choose nba.com from the Jerseys menu. Press ● and enter NMTWCTC84S.

MIAMI HEAT LATIN NIGHT JERSEY
Select Extras from the Progression menu. Then choose nba.com from the Jerseys menu. Press ● and enter WCTGSA8SPD.

PHOENIX SUNS LATIN NIGHT JERSEY
Select Extras from the Progression menu. Then choose nba.com from the Jerseys menu. Press ● and enter LKUTSENFJH.

SAN ANTONIO SPURS LATIN NIGHT JERSEY
Select Extras from the Progression menu. Then choose nba.com from the Jerseys menu. Press ● and enter JFHSY73MYD.

ST. PATRICK'S DAY JERSEYS
Select Codes from the Features menu and enter uclerehanp.

VALENTINE'S DAY JERSEYS
Select Codes from the Features menu and enter amcnreo.

NBA 2K8

ABA BALL
Select Codes from the Features menu and enter Payrespect.

2KSPORTS TEAM
Select Codes from the Features menu and enter 2ksports.

NBA DEVELOPMENT TEAM
Select Codes from the Features menu and enter nba2k.

SUPERSTARS TEAM
Select Codes from the Features menu and enter llmohffaae.

VISUAL CONCEPTS TEAM
Select Codes from the Features menu and enter Vcteam.

2008 ALL STAR NBA JERSEYS
Select Codes from the Features menu and enter haeitgyebs.

BOBCATS RACING JERSEY
Select Codes from the Features menu and enter agtaccsinr.

PACERS SECOND ROAD JERSEY
Select Codes from the Features menu and enter cpares.

NBA 2K9

2K SPORTS TEAM
Select Codes from the Features menu and enter 2ksports.

NBA 2K TEAM
Select Codes from the Features menu and enter nba2k.

SUPERSTARS
Select Codes from the Features menu and enter llmohffaae.

VC TEAM
Select Codes from the Features menu and enter vcteam.

ABA BALL
Select Codes from the Features menu and enter payrespect.

ABA BALL

Select Codes from the Options menu. Then select Enter Code and enter payrespect.

2K CHINA TEAM

Select Codes from the Options menu. Then select Enter Code and enter 2kchina.

NBA 2K TEAM

Select Codes from the Options menu. Then select Enter Code and enter nba2k.

2K SPORTS TEAM

Select Codes from the Options menu. Then select Enter Code and enter 2ksports.

VISUAL CONCEPTS TEAM

Select Codes from the Options menu. Then select Enter Code and enter vcteam.

2010 ALL-STAR UNIFORMS

Select Codes from the Options menu. Then select Enter Code and enter otnresla.

HARDWOOD CLASSIC UNIFORMS

Select Codes from the Options menu. Then select Enter Code and enter wasshcicsl. This code gives Hardwood Classic Uniforms for the Cavaliers, Jazz, Magic, Raptors, timberwolves, Trail Blazers, and Warriors.

LATIN NIGHTS UNIFORMS

Select Codes from the Options menu. Then select Enter Code and enter aihinntslgt. This code gives Latin Nights jerseys for Bulls, Heat, Knicks, Lakers, Mavericks, Rockets, Spurs, and Suns.

NBA GREEN UNIFORMS

Select Codes from the Options menu. Then select Enter Code and enter nreogge. This code gives green uniforms for the Bobcats, Bulls, and Nuggets.

SECONDARY ROAD UNIFORMS

Select Codes from the Options menu. Then select Enter Code and enter eydonscar. This code gives Second Road Uniforms for the Grizzlies, Hawks, Mavericks, and Rockets.

ST. PATRICK'S DAY UNIFORMS

Select Codes from the Options menu. Then select Enter Code and enter riiasgerh. This code gives St. Patrick's Day jerseys for the Bulls, Celtics, Knicks, and Raptors.

BOBCATS RACING UNIFORM

Select Codes from the Options menu. Then select Enter Code and enter agsntrccai.

CAVALIERS CAVFANATICS UNIFORM

Select Codes from the Options menu. Then select Enter Code and enter aifnaatccv.

HORNETS MARDI GRAS UNIFORM

Select Codes from the Options menu. Then select Enter Code and enter asrdirmga.

TRAIL BLAZERS RIP CITY UNIFORM

Select Codes from the Options menu. Then select Enter Code and enter ycprtii.

OVERLOAD

PLAYSTATION 3

NBA 2K11

MJ: CREATING A LEGEND
In Features, select Codes from the Extras menu. Choose Enter Code and input icanbe23.

2K CHINA TEAM
In Features, select Codes from the Extras menu. Choose Enter Code and input 2kchina.

2K SPORTS TEAM
In Features, select Codes from the Extras menu. Choose Enter Code and input 2Ksports.

NBA 2K TEAM
In Features, select Codes from the Extras menu. Choose Enter Code and input nba2k.

VC TEAM
In Features, select Codes from the Extras menu. Choose Enter Code and input vcteam.

ABA BALL
In Features, select Codes from the Extras menu. Choose Enter Code and input payrespect.

NBA LIVE 08

ADIDAS GIL-ZERO—ALL-STAR EDITION
Select NBA Codes from My NBA and enter 23DN1PPOG4.

ADIDAS TIM DUNCAN STEALTH—ALL-STAR EDITION
Select NBA Codes from My NBA and enter FE454DFJCC.

NBA LIVE 09

SUPER DUNKS MODE
Use the Sprite vending machine in the practice area and enter spriteslam.

CHARLOTTE BOBCATS' 2009/2010 RACE DAY ALTERNATE JERSEYS
Select Options from My NBA Live and go to Select Codes. Enter ceobdabacarstcy.

NEW ORLEANS HORNETS' 2009/2010 MARDI GRAS ALTERNATE JERSEYS
Select Options from My NBA Live and go to Select Codes. Enter nishrag1rosmad0.

ALTERNATE JERSEYS
Select Options from My NBA Live and go to Select Codes. Enter ndnba1rooaesdc0. This unlocks alternate jerseys for Atlanta Hawks, Dallas Mavericks, Houston Rockets, and Memphis Grizzlies.

MORE HARDWOOD CLASSICS NIGHTS JERSEYS
Select Options from My NBA Live and go to Select Codes. Enter hdogdrawhoticns. This unlocks Hardwood Classics Nights jerseys for Cleveland Cavaliers, Golden State Warriors, Minnesota Timberwolves, Orlando Magic, Philadelphia 76ers.

ADIDAS EQUATIONS
Select Options from My NBA Live and go to Select Codes. Enter adaodqauieints1.

ADIDAS TS CREATORS WITH ANKLE BRACES
Select Options from My NBA Live and go to Select Codes. Enter atciadsstsdhecf.

ADIDAS TS SUPERNATURAL COMMANDERS
Select Options from My NBA Live and go to Select Codes. Enter andsicdsmatdnsr.

ADIDAS TS SUPERNATURAL CREATORS
Select Options from My NBA Live and go to Select Codes. Enter ard8siscdnatstr.

AIR MAX LEBRON VII
Select Options from My NBA Live and go to Select Codes. Enter ere1nbvlaoeknii, 2ovnaebnkrielei, 3rioabeneikenvl, ri4boenanekilve, ivl5brieekaeonn, or n6ieirvalkeeobn.

KOBE V
Select Options from My NBA Live and go to Select Codes. Enter ovze1bimenkoko0, m0kveokoiebozn2, eev0nbimokk3ozo, or bmo4inozeeo0kvk.

JORDAN CP3 IIIS
Select Options from My NBA Live and go to Select Codes. Enter iaporcdian3ejis.

JORDAN MELO M6S
Select Options from My NBA Live and go to Select Codes. Enter emlarmeoo6ajdsn.

JORDAN SIXTY PLUSES
Select Options from My NBA Live and go to Select Codes. Enter aondsuilyjrspxt.

NIKE HUARACHE LEGIONS
Select Options from My NBA Live and go to Select Codes. Enter aoieuchrahelgn.

NIKE KD 2S
Select Options from My NBA Live and go to Select Codes. Enter kk2tesaosepinrd.

NIKE ZOOM FLIP'NS
Select Options from My NBA Live and go to Select Codes. Enter epfnozaeminolki.

NBA STREET HOMECOURT

ALL TEAMS
At the Main menu, hold R1 + L1 and press Left, Right, Left, Right.

ALL COURTS
At the Main menu, hold R1 + L1 and press Up, Right, Down, Left.

BLACK/RED BALL
At the Main menu, hold R1 + L1 and press Up, Down, Left, Right.

NEED FOR SPEED PROSTREET

$2,000
Select Career and then choose Code Entry. Enter 1MA9X99.

$4,000
Select Career and then choose Code Entry. Enter W2IOLL01.

$8,000
Select Career and then choose Code Entry. Enter L1IS97A1.

$10,000
Select Career and then choose Code Entry. Enter 1MI9K7E1.

$10,000
Select Career and then choose Code Entry. Enter CASHMONEY.

$10,000
Select Career and then choose Code Entry. Enter REGGAME.

AUDI TT
Select Career and then choose Code Entry. Enter ITSABOUTYOU.

CHEVELLE SS
Select Career and then choose Code Entry. Enter HORSEPOWER.

COKE ZERO GOLF GTI
Select Career and then choose Code Entry. Enter COKEZERO.

DODGE VIPER
Select Career and then choose Code Entry. Enter WORLDSLONGESTLASTING.

MITSUBISHI LANCER EVOLUTION
Select Career and then choose Code Entry. Enter MITSUBISHIGOFAR.

UNLOCK ALL BONUSES
Select Career and then choose Code Entry. Enter UNLOCKALLTHINGS.

5 REPAIR MARKERS
Select Career and then choose Code Entry. Enter SAFETYNET.

ENERGIZER VINYL
Select Career and then choose Code Entry. Enter ENERGIZERLITHIUM.

CASTROL SYNTEC VINYL
Select Career and then choose Code Entry. Enter CASTROLSYNTEC. This also gives you $10,000.

NEED FOR SPEED UNDERCOVER

$10,000
Select Secret Codes from the Options menu and enter %%$3/".

DIE-CAST BMW M3 E92
Select Secret Codes from the Options menu and enter)B7@B=.

DIE-CAST LEXUS IS F
Select Secret Codes from the Options menu and enter 0;5M2;.

NEEDFORSPEED.COM LOTUS ELISE
Select Secret Codes from the Options menu and enter -KJ3=E.

DIE-CAST NISSAN 240SX (S13)
Select Secret Codes from the Options menu and enter ?P:COL.

DIE-CAST PORSCHE 911 TURBO
Select Secret Codes from the Options menu and enter >8P:I;.

SHELBY TERLINGUA
Select Secret Codes from the Options menu and enter NeedForSpeedShelbyTerlingua.

DIE-CAST VOLKSWAGEN R32
Select Secret Codes from the Options menu and enter!2ODBJ:.

NHL 08

ALL RBK EDGE JERSEYS
At the RBK Edge Code option, enter h3oyxpwksf8ibcgt.

NHL 10

THIRD JERSEYS
At the EA Extras screen, enter rwyhafwh6ekyjcmr

NHL 2K9

3RD JERSEYS
From the Features menu, enter R6y34bsH52 as a code.

NINJA GAIDEN SIGMA

5 EXTRA MISSIONS IN MISSION MODE.
At the mission mode screen, press Up, Down, Left, Down, Right, Up, ⬤.

OPERATION FLASHPOINT: DRAGON RISING

AMBUSH BONUS MISSION
Select Cheats from the Options menu and enter AmbushU454.

CLOSE QUARTERS BONUS MISSION
Select Cheats from the Options menu and enter CloseQ8M3

COASTAL STRONGHOLD BONUS MISSION
Select Cheats from the Options menu and enter StrongM577

DEBRIS FIELD BONUS MISSION
Select Cheats from the Options menu and enter OFPWEB2

ENCAMPMENT BONUS MISSION
Select Cheats from the Options menu and enter OFPWEB1

NIGHT RAID BONUS MISSION
Select Cheats from the Options menu and enter RaidT18Z

THE ORANGE BOX

HALF-LIFE 2
The following codes work for Half-Life 2, Half-Life 2: Episode One, and Half-Life 2: Episode Two.

CHAPTER SELECT
While playing, press Left, Left, Left, Left, L1, Right, Right, Right, Right, R1. Pause the game and select New Game to skip to another chapter.

RESTORE HEALTH (25 POINTS)
While playing, press Up, Up, Down, Down, Left, Right, Left, Right, ⬤, ❌.

RESTORE AMMO FOR CURRENT WEAPON
While playing, press R1, ⬤, ⬤, ❌, ⬤, R1, ⬤, ⬤, ❌, ⬤, R1.

PORTAL

CHAPTER SELECT
While playing, press Left, Left, Left, Left, L1, Right, Right, Right, Right, R1. Pause the game and select New Game to skip to another chapter.

GET A BOX
While playing, press Down, ⬤, ❌, ⬤, ⬤, Down, ⬤, ❌, ⬤, ⬤.

ENERGY BALL
While playing, press Up, ⬤, ⬤, ⬤, ⬤, ❌, ❌, ⬤, ⬤, Up.

PORTAL PLACEMENT ANYWHERE
While playing, press ⬤, ❌, ⬤, ❌, ⬤, ⬤, ⬤, ❌, Left, Right.

PORTALGUN ID 0
While playing, press Up, Left, Down, Right, Up, Left, Down, Right, ⬤, ⬤.

PORTALGUN ID 1
While playing, press Up, Left, Down, Right, Up, Left, Down, Right, ⬤, ⬤.

PORTALGUN ID 2
While playing, press Up, Left, Down, Right, Up, Left, Down, Right, ❌, ❌.

PORTALGUN ID 3
While playing, press Up, Left, Down, Right, Up, Left, Down, Right, ⬤, ⬤.

UPGRADE PORTALGUN
While playing, press ⬤, ⬤, L1, R1, Left, Right, L1, R1, L2, R2.

PRINCE OF PERSIA

SANDS OF TIME PRINCE/FARAH SKINS
Select Skin Manager from the Extras menu. Press ⬤ and enter 52585854. This gives you the Sands of Time skin for the Prince and Farah from Sands of Time for the Princess. Access them from the Skin Manager

PRINCE ALTAIR IBN LA-AHAD SKIN
Create an Ubisoft account. Then select "Altair Skin for Prince" to unlock.

PROTOTYPE

BODY SURFING ABILITY
Select Cheats from the Extras menu and enter Right, Right, Left, Down, Up, Up, Up, Down.

OVERLOAD

PLAYSTATION 3

RATATOUILLE

Select Gusteau's Shop from the Extras menu. Choose Secrets, select the appropriate code number, and then enter the code. Once the code is entered, select the cheat you want to activate it.

CODE NUMBER	CODE	EFFECT
1	Pieceocake	Very Easy difficulty mode.
2	Myhero	No impact and no damage from enemies.
3	Shielded	No damage from enemies.
4	Spyagent	Move undetected by any enemy.
5	Ilikeonions	Fart every time Remy jumps.
6	Hardfeelings	Head butt when attacking instead of tailswipe.
7	Slumberparty	Multiplayer mode.
8	Gusteauart	All Concept Art.
9	Gusteauship	All four championship modes.
10	Mattelme	All single player and multiplayer minigames.
11	Gusteauvid	All Videos.
12	Gusteaures	All Bonus Artworks.
13	Gusteaudream	All Dream Worlds in Gusteau's Shop.
14	Gusteauslide	All Slides in Gusteau's Shop.
15	Gusteaulevel	All single player minigames.
16	Gusteaucombo	All items in Gusteau's Shop.
17	Gusteaupot	5,000 Gusteau points.
18	Gusteaujack	10,000 Gusteau points.
19	Gusteauomni	50,000 Gusteau points.

RATCHET & CLANK FUTURE: A CRACK IN TIME

DISCOUNT AT WEAPON VENDORS
Have a save game for Ratchet and Clank Future: Tools of Destruction.

PIRATE HAT SKIN
Have a save game for Ratchet and Clank Future: Quest for Booty.

BANCHO RATCHET SKIN
Pause the game and enter Up, Right, Down, Left, ▲, ●, ✖, ●, R3.

RATCHET & CLANK FUTURE: TOOLS OF DESTRUCTION

CHALLENGE MODE
After defeating the game, you can replay it in Challenge Mode with all of Ratchet's current upgraded weapons and armor.

SKILL POINTS
Complete the following objectives to earn skill points. Each one is worth 10 to 40 points and you can use these points to unlock Cheats in the Cheats menu. The list below lists the skill points with a location and description.

SKILL POINT	LOCATION	DESCRIPTION
Smashing Good Time	Cobalia	Destroy all crates and consumer bots in the trade port and gel factory.
I Should Have Gone Down in a Barrel	Cobalia	Jump into each of the two gel waterfall areas in Cobalia gel factory.
Giant Hunter	Cobalia	Kill several Basilisk Leviathans in the Cobalia wilderness.
Wrench Ninja 3	Stratus City	Use only the Omniwrench to get through the level to the Robo-Wings segment.

SKILL POINT	LOCATION	DESCRIPTION
We Don't Need No Stinkin' Bridges!	Stratus City	Cross the tri-pad sequence using gel-cube bounces.
Surface-to-Air Plasma Beasts	Stratus City	Take out several flying targets using a specific weapon.
Been Around	Stratus City	Take off from every Robo-wing launch pad in Stratus City.
Collector's Addition	Voron	Be very thorough in your collection of goodies.
Minesweeper	Voron	Clear out a bunch of mines.
What's That, R2?	Voron	Barrel roll multiple times.
I Think I'm Gonna Be Sick	IFF	Ride the ferris wheel for 5 loops without getting off or taking damage.
Fast and the Fire-ious	IFF	Use the Charge Boots to cross the bridge to the arena without being burned.
One Heckuva Peephole	IFF	Return after receiving the Geo-laser and complete the Geo-laser setup.
Alphabet City	Apogee	Teleport to each of the six asteroids in alphabetical order.
Knock You Down to Size	Apogee	Wrench Slam 5 centipedes.
Dancin' with the Stars	Apogee	Make 5 enemies dance at once on an asteroid.
Taste o' Yer Own Medicine	Pirate Base	Destroy all of the Shooter Pirates with the Combuster.
Preemptive Strike	Pirate Base	Destroy all of the "sleeping bats" while they are still sleeping.
It's Mutant-E Cap'n!	Pirate Base	Change 5 pirates into penguins in one blast.
You Sunk My Battleship!	Rakar	Shoot down a large percentage of the big destroyers.
Pretty Lights	Rakar	Complete the level without destroying any of the snatchers that fire beams at Ratchet.
I've Got Places To Be	Rakar	Destroy the boss in under 2:30.
The Consumer Is Not (Always) Right	Rykan V	Destroy a bunch of consumer bots in the level.
Live Strong	Rykan V	Complete the Gryo Cycle in 1:45.
Untouchable	Rykan V	Don't take damage in the Gyro-Cycle.
It Sounded Like a Freight Train	Sargasso	Get 10 Swarmers in one tornado.
Head Examiner	Sargasso	Land on all of the dinosaur heads in Sargasso.
Extinction	Sargasso	Kill all of the Sargasso Predators.
Lombaxes Don't Like Cold	Iris	Break all the breakable icicles.
Mow Down Ho-Down	Iris	Use turrets to destroy 10 dancing pirates.
Dancin' on the Ceiling	Zordoom	Successfully use a Groovitron while on a Magboot surface.
Seared Ahi	Zordoom	Use the Pyroblaster on 3 Drophid creatures after freeing them from their robotic suits.
Shocking Ascent	Zordoom	Destroy all enemies on the elevator using just the Shock Ravager.
Expert Marksman	Borag	Kill 75% of all of the enemies.
Can't Touch This	Borag	Don't take damage before fighting the boss.
Pyoo, Pyoo!	Borag	Complete the level without secondary fire.
Dead Aim	Kerchu	Destroy several destructible towers while on the pirate barge.
Fire With Fire	Kerchu	Kill a few Kerchu Flamethrowers with the Pyro Blaster.
Rocket Jump	Kerchu	Successfully jump over a row of three rockets while on the grindrail during the boss fight in Kerchu City.
Your Friendly Neighborhood...	Slag Fleet	Destroy 5 enemies while on the grav ramp before Slag's ship.

OVERLOAD

PLAYSTATION 3

SKILL POINT	LOCATION	DESCRIPTION
Turret Times Two	Slag Fleet	Destroy at least 2 pirates with each turret in the level.
Six Gun Salute	Slag Fleet	Get six pirates in a row to salute Ratchet while in the Pirate Disguise.
Gotta Catch 'Em All	Cragmite Ruins	Hit all Cragmite soldiers with the Mag-Net Launcher.
Ratchet and Goliath	Cragmite Ruins	Destroy multiple walkers using just the Nano-Swarmers.
Ratchet &...Not Clank?!	Cragmite Ruins	Use Mr. Zurkon in Cragmite's Ratchet-only segment.
Stay Still So I Can Shoot You!	Meridian	Use strafe-flip 10 times while fighting the Cragmite soldiers.
Now Boarding...	Meridian	Complete the Gyro-Cycle in 55 seconds.
Low Flying Howls	Meridian	Fly under an electrified barrier in the Robo-wings segment.
Extreme Alien Makeover	Fastoon2	Turn 10 Cragmites into penguins.
Empty Bag o' Tricks	Fastoon2	Complete the level without using any devices.
Nowhere to Hide	Fastoon2	Destroy every piece of breakable cover.
No, Up Your Arsenal	Global	Upgrade every weapon to the max.
Roflcopter	Global	Turn enemies into penguins, then use the Visicopter to destroy the penguins.
Stir Fry	Global	Kill 2 different enemy types using the Shock Ravager while they are trapped in a tornado.
Golden Children	Overall	Find all of the Gold Bolts.
Sacagawea	Global	Complete all of the maps 100%, leaving no area undiscovered.
Cheapskate	Global	Purchase a single Combustor round.
Everybody Dance Now	Global	Make every type of enemy in the game dance.
F5 on the Fujita Scale	Global	Pick up more than 10 enemies with one tornado.
Chorus line	Global	Get 10+ enemies to dance together.
Happy Feet	Global	Get several penguins to dance on-screen.
Disco Inferno	Global	Use the Groovitron followed by the Pyro Blaster.
Bolts in the Bank	Global	Sell a bunch of Leviathan Souls to the Smuggler.
It's Like the North Pole Here	Global	Have at least 12-15 enemies and/or citizens turned into penguins at one time.
Say Hello to My Little Friend	Global	Kill 15 enemies with one RYNO shot.
For the Hoard!	Global	Get every item.
Promoted to Inspector	Global	Get every gadget.
Global Thermonuclear War	Global	Get every weapon.
It's Even Better the Second Time!	Global	Complete Challenge Mode.
The Hardest of Core	Global	Get all skill points and everything else in the game.

RED DEAD REDEMPTION

CHEATS

Select Cheats from Options menu and enter the following codes. Note, though, that entering cheats will disable Trophies and saving.

NAME	ENTER
Invincibility	HE GIVES STRENGTH TO THE WEAK
Infinite Dead Eye	I DON'T UNDERSTAND IMNFINITY
Infinite Horse Stamina	MAKE HAY WHILE THE SUN SHINES

Infinite Ammo	ABUNDANCE IS EVERYWHERE
Money ($500)	THE ROOT OF ALL EVIL, WE THANK YOU!
Coach	NOW WHO PUT THAT THERE?
Horse	BEASTS AND MAN TOGETHER
Good Guy	IT AINT PRIDE. IT'S HONOR
Famous	I AM ONE OF THEM FAMOUS FELLAS
Diplomatic Immunity	I WISH I WORKED FOR UNCLE SAM
Decrease Bounty	THEY SELL SOULS CHEAP HERE
Gun Set 1	IT'S MY CONSTITUTIONAL RIGHT
Gun Set 2	I'M AN AMERICAN. I NEED GUNS
Who?	HUMILITY BEFORE THE LORD
Old School (Sepia)	THE OLD WAYS IS THE BEST WAYS
Man in Uniform (Bureau, US Army, and US Marshal uniforms)	I LOVE A MAN IN UNIFORM
Sharp Dressed Man (Gentleman's Suit)	DON'T YOU LOOK FINE AND DANDY
Lewis and Clark (All areas)	YOU GOT YOURSELF A FINE PAIR OF EYES
Gang Chic (Treasure Hunter outfit)	YOU THINK YOU TOUGH, MISTER?
Jack Attack (Play as Jack)	OH MY SON, MY BLESSED SON
Hic (Drunk)	I'M DRUNK AS A SKUNK AND TWICE AS SMELLY

PLAYSTATION HOME AVATAR ITEMS

ITEM	EARNED BY
Sombrero	Shooting the hat off an enemy.
Black on red RDR logo T-shirt (male & female)	Opening the chest in the burned out house in Riley's Charge.
Yellow Rockstar logo T-shirt (male & female)	Opening the chest in the attic of John Marston's Beechers Hope house.
Gentleman's attire/lady's finest	Completing Skin It To Win It Social Club Challenge
Posse T-shirt (male & female)	Getting the high score in Strike It Rich Social Club Challenge

RED FACTION: GUERRILLA

WRECKING CREW MAPS
Select Extras from the Options menu, choose Enter Code, and enter MAPMAYHEM.

GOLDEN SLEDGEHAMMER, SINGLE-PLAYER MODE
Select Extras from the Options menu, choose Enter Code, and enter HARDHITTER.

RESIDENT EVIL 5

MERCENARY CHARACTERS
Complete the following stages in The Mercenaries with at least an A-rank to unlock the corresponding character.

CHARACTER (OUTFIT)	STAGE
Jill (BSAA)	Public Assembly
Wesker (Midnight)	The Mines
Chris (Safari)	The Village
Sheva (Clubbin')	Ancient Ruins
Chris (S.T.A.R.S.)	Experimental Facility
Sheva (Tribal)	Missile Area
Jill (Battle Suit)	Ship Deck
Wesker (S.T.A.R.S.)	Prison

PLAYSTATION 3

RESISTANCE: FALL OF MAN

HARD DIFFICULTY
Complete the game on Medium difficulty.

SUPERHUMAN DIFFICULTY
Complete the game on Hard difficulty.

SKILL POINTS
You can access the Skill Points and Rewards menus during gameplay by pressing START to access the Pause Menu, then selecting EXTRAS.

ENEMIES

NAME	LEVEL ACQUIRED	DESCRIPTION
Hybrid	The Gauntlet	After defeating first set of Hybrids.
Leaper	A Lone Survivor	After defeating first few Leapers.
Crawler	A Lone Survivor	After the cinematic and FPNICS.
Menial	Fate Worse Than Death	After the first room.
Cocoon	Conversion	At the third checkpoint.
Carrier	Fate Worse Than Death	At the window when you first see the Carriers.
Howler	Path of Least Resistance	After defeating the Howlers at the end of the level.
Steelhead	Cathedral	After defeating the first two Steelheads in the church.
Titan	Conduits	After defeating the Titan at the beginning of Conduits.
Slipskull	No Way Out	After defeating all three Slipskulls in the burrower room.
Leaper Pod	No Way Out or 61	After finding the Leaper Pods for the first time.
Gray Jack	Angel	After the cryo room.
Hardfang	Evacuation	After defeating the first Hardfang in the cafeteria.
Roller	Into the Depths	After defeating the Rollers in the room with the tunnel in the floor.
Widowmaker	Ice and Iron	After defeating the first Widowmaker.
Hybrid 2.0	Angel's Lair	After the first wave of Hybrids in the node.
Angel	Angel's Lair	After defeating the first Angel on the bridge.

VEHICLES

NAME	LEVEL ACQUIRED	DESCRIPTION
Hawk	The Gauntlet	Player automatically starts with this.
Kingfisher	Path of Least Resistance	At the start of the level.
Sabertooth	A Lone Survivor	After getting inside the tank.
Dropship	Hunted Down	After spotting a Dropship in the parking lot area.
Stalker	Outgunned	After spotting the first one in Outgunned.
Burrower	No Way Out	After spotting the first one in No Way Out.
Lynx	Common Ground	After getting inside the Lynx.
Goliath	Giant Slayer	After spotting the first one.

WEAPONS—1ST PLAYTHROUGH

NAME	LEVEL ACQUIRED	DESCRIPTION
M5A2 Carbine	The Gauntlet	Automatically unlocked at start of the game.
Frag Grenade	The Gauntlet	Automatically unlocked at start of the game.
Bullseye	The Gauntlet	In the alleyway after checkpoint 2.
Shotgun	Fate Worse Than Death or 32 or 40	Fate Worse Than Death: Behind the stairs in the outdoor area. Hunted Down: Behind the bar. Hunted Down: In the docks area. Path of Least Resistance: Forced here on the stairs between hill 1 and 2.

NAME	LEVEL ACQUIRED	DESCRIPTION
Auger	Cathedral	After defeating the first two advanced Hybrids.
Fareye	Conduits	After defeating the large Hybrid and reaching checkpoint 1.
Hailstorm	Search and Rescue	After leaving the first area.
Sapper	A Disturbing Discovery	At the back of the first mech factory.
LAARK	In a Darker Place	On the ground in the first room.
Bullseye Mark 2	Angel's Lair	After leaving the first room and going into the node.

WEAPONS—2ND PLAYTHROUGH

NAME	LEVEL ACQUIRED	DESCRIPTION
Reapers	The Gauntlet	Inside the house at the bottom of the hill.
Backlash Grenade	Cathedral	After crossing alley just past the cathedral; it's the first room on the left.
Arc Charger	No Way Out	At the end of the long hallway prior to the burrower.
L11-Dragon	Evacuation	Before the first elevator leading to the hangar.
Splitter	A Desperate Gambit	At checkpoint 1, near the big windows.

LOCATIONS

NAME	LEVEL ACQUIRED	DESCRIPTION
York	The Gauntlet	Unlocked at the start of the level.
Grimsby	Fate Worse Than Death	Unlocked at the start of the level.
Manchester	Path of Least Resistance	Unlocked at the start of the level.
Nottingham	Into the Fire	Unlocked at the start of the level.
Cheshire	No Way Out	Unlocked at the start of the level.
Somerset	Search and Rescue	Unlocked at the start of the level.
Bristol	Devil at the Door	Unlocked at the start of the level.
Bracknell	Into the Depths	Unlocked at the start of the level.
London	A Desperate Gambit	Unlocked at the start of the level.
Thames	Burning Bridges	Unlocked at the start of the level.
Tower	Angel's Lair	Unlocked at the start of the level.

REWARDS

NAME	HOW TO UNLOCK
Concept Art Pack 1	10 points
Concept Art Pack 2	20 points
The Mighty Wrench - Gives allies wrench	40 points
Flip Levels	70 points
Clank Backpacks	100 points
MP Mechanic Skin	126 points
MP Soldier Skin	Beat game on Superhuman mode.
MP Soldier head skin	Beat game on Superhuman mode and collect all Skill Points.
Movie player	Beat game once.

RESONANCE OF FATE

Once you have reached Chapter 7, search Leanne's closet. As she speaks her first line enter the following codes to unlock more outfits.

8-BIT GIRL SHIRT
Up, Up, Down, Down, Left, Right, Left, Right, ▲, ●

CLUB FAMITSU SHIRT
▲, ▲, Up, Up, ●, ●, Left, Left, L1, R1

GEMAGA SHIRT
R2, L2, L1, R1, ▲, ▲, ▲, ●, ●, Up

HIRAKOU SHIRT
●, ▲, L1, L1, R1, R1, L3, L3, Up, Down

PLATFORM LOGO SHIRT
R2, R1, R3, L3, L1, L2, Right, Left, ●, ▲

POLITAN SUIT
R3, R3, R3, Right, Left, ▲, ●, L2, R2, L1. This requires you to have the Reindeer Suit first.

ROBERT LUDLUM'S THE BOURNE CONSPIRACY

AUTOMATIC SHOTGUNS REPLACE SIMI-AUTOS
Select Cheats from the Main menu, press ●, and then enter alwaysanobjective.

LIGHT MACHINE GUNS HAVE SILENCERS
Select Enter Code from the Cheats screen and enter whattheymakeyougive.

EXTRAS UNLOCKED – CONCEPT ART
Select Enter Code from the Cheats screen and enter lastchancemarie. Select Concept Art from the Extras menu.

EXTRAS UNLOCKED – MUSIC TRACKS
Select Enter Code from the Cheats screen and enter jasonbourneisdead. This unlocks Treadstone Appointment and Manheim Suite in the Music Selector found in the Extras menu.

ROCK BAND

ALL SONGS
At the Title screen, press Red, Yellow, Blue, Red, Red, Blue, Blue, Red, Yellow, Blue. Saving and all network features are disabled with this code.

TRANSPARENT INSTRUMENTS
Complete the hall of fame concert with that instrument.

GOLD INSTRUMENT
Complete the solo tour with that instrument.

SILVER INSTRUMENT
Complete the bonus tour with that instrument.

ROCK BAND 2

Most of these codes disable saving, achievements, and Xbox LIVE play. The first code listed is with the guitar and the second is an alternative using a controller.

UNLOCK ALL SONGS
Select Modify Game from the Extras menu, choose Enter Unlock Code and press Red, Yellow, Blue, Red, Red, Blue, Blue, Red, Yellow, Blue or ●, ▲, ■, ●, ●, ■, ■, ●, ▲, ●. Toggle this cheat on or off from the Modify Game menu.

SELECT VENUE SCREEN
Select Modify Game from the Extras menu, choose Enter Unlock Code and press Blue, Orange, Orange, Blue, Yellow, Blue, Orange, Orange, Blue, Yellow or ■, L1, L1, ■, ▲, ■, L1, L1, ■, ▲. Toggle this cheat on or off from the Modify Game menu.

NEW VENUES ONLY
Select Modify Game from the Extras menu, choose Enter Unlock Code and press Red, Red, Red, Red, Yellow, Yellow, Yellow, Yellow or ● (x4), ▲ (x4). Toggle this cheat on or off from the Modify Game menu.

PLAY THE GAME WITHOUT A TRACK
Select Modify Game from the Extras menu, choose Enter Unlock Code and press Blue, Blue, Red, Red, Yellow, Yellow, Blue, Blue or ■, ■, ●, ●, ▲, ▲, ■, ■. Toggle this cheat on or off from the Modify Game menu.

AWESOMENESS DETECTION
Select Modify Game from the Extras menu, choose Enter Unlock Code and press Yellow, Blue, Orange, Yellow, Blue, Orange, Yellow, Blue, Orange or ▲, ■, L1, ▲, ■, L1, ▲, ■, L1. Toggle this cheat on or off from the Modify Game menu.

STAGE MODE
Select Modify Game from the Extras menu, choose Enter Unlock Code and press Blue, Yellow, Red, Blue, Yellow, Red or ■, ▲, ●, ■, ▲, ●. Toggle this cheat on or off from the Modify Game menu.

ROCK BAND 3

GUILD X-79 GUITAR
At the Main menu, press Blue, Orange, Orange, Blue, Orange, Orange, Blue, Blue.

OVATION D-2010 GUITAR
At the Main menu, press Orange, Blue, Orange, Orange, Blue, Blue, Orange, Blue.

ROCK REVOLUTION

ALL CHARACTERS
At the Main menu, press ●, ■, ●, ■, ●, ■, ●, ▲, ■.

ALL VENUES
At the Main menu, press ■, ●, ▲, ●, ■, ●, ▲, ■, ▲.

ROCKET KNIGHT

ALL CHARACTER SKINS
At the Title screen, press Up, Up, Down, Down, Left, Right, Left, Right, ●, ✕, Start.

SAINTS ROW 2

CHEAT CODES
Select Dial from the Phone menu and enter these numbers followed by the Call button. Activate the cheats by selecting Cheats from the Phone menu. Enabling a cheat prevents the acquisition of Achievements

PLAYER ABILITY

CHEAT	CODE	CHEAT	CODE
Give Cash	#2274666399	Car Mass Hole	#2
No Cop Notoriety	#50	Infinite Ammo	#11
No Gang Notoriety	#51	Heaven Bound	#12
Infinite Sprint	#6	Add Police Notoriety	#4
Full Health	#1	Add Gang Notoriety	#35
Player Pratfalls	#5	Never Die	#36
Milk Bones	#3	Unlimited Clip	#9

VEHICLES

CHEAT	CODE	CHEAT	CODE
Repair Car	#1056	Titan	#1076
Venom Classic	#1079	Varsity	#1078
Five-0	#1055	Anchor	#1041
Stilwater Municipal	#1072	Blaze	#1044
Baron	#1047	Sabretooth	#804
Attrazione	#1043	Sandstorm	#805
Zenith	#1081	Kaneda	#801
Vortex	#1080	Widowmaker	#806
Phoenix	#1064	Kenshin	#802
Bootlegger	#1049	Melbourne	#803
Raycaster	#1068	Miami	#826
Hollywood	#1057	Python	#827
Justice	#1058	Hurricane	#825
Compton	#1052	Shark	#828
Eiswolf	#1053	Skipper	#829
Taxi	#1074	Mongoose	#1062
Ambulance	#1040	Superiore	#1073
Backhoe	#1045	Tornado	#713
Bagboy	#1046	Horizon	#711
Rampage	#1067	Wolverine	#714
Reaper	#1069	Snipes 57	#712
The Job	#1075	Bear	#1048
Quota	#1066	Toad	#1077
FBI	#1054	Kent	#1059
Mag	#1060	Oring	#1063
Bulldog	#1050	Longhauler	#1061
Quasar	#1065	Atlasbreaker	#1042

OVERLOAD

CHEAT	CODE
Septic Avenger	#1070
Shaft	#1071

CHEAT	CODE
Bulldozer	#1051

WEAPONS

CHEAT	CODE
AR-50	#923
K6	#935
GDHC	#932
NR4	#942
44	#921
Tombstone	#956
T3K	#954
VICE9	#957
AS14 Hammer	#925
12 Gauge	#920
SKR-9	#951
McManus 2010	#938
Baseball Bat	#926
Knife	#936
Molotov	#940
Grenade	#933
Nightstick	#941
Pipebomb	#945
RPG	#946
Crowbar	#955
Pimp Cane	#944

CHEAT	CODE
AR200	#922
AR-50/Grenade Launcher	#924
Chainsaw	#927
Fire Extinguisher	#928
Flamethrower	#929
Flashbang	#930
GAL43	#931
Kobra	#934
Machete	#937
Mini-gun	#939
Pepperspray	#943
Annihilator RPG	#947
Samurai Sword	#948
Satchel Charge	#949
Shock Paddles	#950
Sledgehammer	#952
Stungun	#953
XS-2 Ultimax	#958
Pimp Slap	#969

WEATHER

CHEAT	CODE
Clear Skies	#78669
Heavy Rain	#78666
Light Rain	#78668
Overcast	#78665

CHEAT	CODE
Time Set Midnight	#2400
Time Set Noon	#1200
Wrath Of God	#666

WORLD

CHEAT	CODE
Super Saints	#8
Super Explosions	#7
Evil Cars	#16
Pedestrian War	#19

CHEAT	CODE
Drunk Pedestrians	#15
Raining Pedestrians	#20
Low Gravity	#18

SCOTT PILGRIM VS THE WORLD: THE GAME

PLAY AS SAME CHARACTER
At the Title screen, press Down, R1, Up, L1, ▲, ●.

HEART SWORD
At the Title screen, press ●, ●, ●, ✕, ●, ✕, ▲.

BLOOD MODE
At the Title screen, press ✕, ●, ✕, ●, ✕, ●, ●.

BOSS RUSH MODE
Pause the game on the overworld and press Right, Right, ●, R1, Right, Right, ●, R1.

ZOMBIE MODE
At the Title screen, press Down, Up, Right, Down, Up, Right, Down, Up, Right, Right, Right.

SOUND CHECK BONUS LEVEL
Pause the game on the overworld and press L1, L1, R1, R1, L1, L1, L1, R1, R1, R1, L1, R1.

CHANGE MONEY TO ANIMALS
At the Title screen, press Up, Up, Down, Down, Up, Up, Up, Up.

SEGA SUPERSTARS TENNIS

UNLOCK CHARACTERS

Complete the following missions to unlock the corresponding character.

CHARACTER	COMPLETE THIS MISSION
Alex Kidd	Mission 1 of Alex Kidd's World
Amy Rose	Mission 2 of Sonic the Hedgehog's World
Gilius	Mission 1 of Golden Axe's World
Gum	Mission 12 of Jet Grind Radio's World
Meemee	Mission 8 of Super Monkey Ball's World
Pudding	Mission 1 of Space Channel 5's World
Reala	Mission 2 of NiGHTs' World
Shadow The Hedgehog	Mission 14 of Sonic the Hedgehog's World

SHANK

KUNG FU SHANK
Reach 1000 kills. Press Start to view your tally.

SHANK THE GIMP
Kill 500 creatures.

HORROR SHANK
Get 100 kills with the Chainsaw.

WHITE PAJAMAS SHANK
Perform a 100-hit combo.

RED PAJAMAS SHANK
Perform a 150-hit combo.

DANCE SHANK
Complete the single-player campaign on Normal mode.

WILDMAN SHANK
Complete the single-player campaign on Hard mode.

SHANK THE SPARTAN
Complete the Backstory Co-op mode.

ANY-S
After completing the single-player campaign, pause a game and press Up, Up, Down, Down, Left, Right, Left, Right, ◉, ✖.

DEATHSPANK
After completing the single-player campaign, pause a game and press Up, ◉, Down, ◉, Left, ▲, Right, ✖

SILENT HILL: HOMECOMING

YOUNG ALEX COSTUME
At the Title screen, press Up, Up, Down, Down, Left, Right, Left, Right, ◉.

THE SIMPSONS GAME

After unlocking the following, the outfits can be changed at the downstairs closet in the Simpson's house. The Trophies can be viewed at different locations in the house: Bart's room, Lisa's room, Marge's room, and the garage.

BART'S OUTFITS AND TROPHIES (POSTER COLLECTION)
At the Main menu, press Right, Left, ◉, ◉, ▲, R3.

HOMER'S OUTFITS AND TROPHIES (BEER BOTTLE COLLECTION)
At the Main menu, press Left, Right, ▲, ◉, ◉, L3.

LISA'S OUTFITS AND TROPHIES (DOLLS)
At the Main menu, press ◉, ▲, ◉, ◉, ◉, ▲, L3.

MARGE'S OUTFITS AND TROPHIES (HAIR PRODUCTS)
At the Main menu, press ▲, ◉, ▲, ▲, ◉, R3.

THE SIMS 3

CHEATS
Load your family, press Start, and hold L1 + L2 + R1 + R2. The game will then prompt you to save another file before activating the cheats. After doing so, Spoot the Llama will be available in Misc Décor. Place it in your lot and click it to access the cheats. Note, however, that this disables Trophies and challenges.

PLAYSTATION 3

OVERLOAD

SKATE

BEST BUY CLOTHES
At the Main menu, press Up, Down, Left, Right, ●, R1, ▲, L1.

SKATE 2

BIG BLACK
Select Enter Cheat from the Extras menu and enter letsdowork.

3D MODE
Select Enter Cheat from the Extras menu and enter strangeloops. Use glasses to view in 3D.

SKATE 3

HOVERBOARD MODE
In Free Play, select Extras from the Options menu. Choose Enter Cheat Code and input mcfly.

MINI SKATER MODE
In Free Play, select Extras from the Options menu. Choose Enter Cheat Code and input miniskaters.

ZOMBIE MODE
In Free Play, select Extras from the Options menu. Choose Enter Cheat Code and input zombie.

ISAAC CLARK FROM DEADSPACE
In Free Play, select Extras from the Options menu. Choose Enter Cheat Code and input deadspacetoo.

DEM BONES
Defeat most of the Hall of Meat Challenges.

MEAT MAN
Complete all Hall of Meat Challenges.

RESET OBJECTS TO ORIGINAL POSITIONS
In Free Play, select Extras from the Options menu. Choose Enter Cheat Code and input streetsweeper.

SOCOM: U.S. NAVY SEALS CONFRONTATION

AMELI MACHINE GUN
Select Spain as your clan country.

FAMAS G2 ASSAULT RIFLE
Select France as your clan country.

GMP SUBMACHINE GUN
Select Germany as your clan country.

IW-80 A2 ASSAULT RIFLE
Select U.K. as your clan country.

SCFR-LW ASSAULT RIFLE
Select U.S. as your clan country.

SOLDIER OF FORTUNE: PAYBACK

ACR-2 SNIPER RIFLE
At the difficulty select, press Up, Up, Down, Left, Right, Right, Down.

SPIDER-MAN: SHATTERED DIMENSIONS

The following codes can be entered after completing the tutorial. All the suits are found in the Bonus Gallery under Alternate Suits.

IRON SPIDER SUIT
At the Main menu, press Up, Right, Right, Right, Left, Left, Left, Down, Up.

NEGATIVE ZONE SUIT

At the Main menu, press Left, Right, Right, Down, Right, Down, Up, Left.

SCARLET SPIDER SUIT

At the Main menu, press Right, Up, Left, Right, Up, Left, Right, Up, Left, Right.

SPLIT/ SECOND

HANZO FX350 CX (QUICK PLAY)
At the Options menu, press ✖, Up, ✖, Up, ✖, Up.

RYBACK COYOTE AMX (QUICK PLAY)
At the Options menu, press Left, ✖, Left, ✖, Left, ✖, Left, ✖, Left, ✖, Right.

RYBACK MOHAWK XDX (QUICK PLAY)
At the Options menu, press ✖, Down, ✖, Down, ✖, Down.

STAR WARS THE CLONE WARS: REPUBLIC HEROES

BIG HEAD MODE

Pause the game, select Shop, and enter the following in Cheats: Up, Down, Left, Right, Left, Down, Up.

MINI-GUN

Pause the game, select Shop, and enter the following in Cheats: Down, Left, Right, Up, Right, Up, Left, Down.

ULTIMATE LIGHTSABER

Pause the game, select Shop, and enter the following in Cheats: Right, Down, Down, Up, Left, Up, Up, Down.

LIGHTSABER THROW UPGRADE

Pause the game, select Shop, and enter the following in Combat Upgrades: Left, Left, Right, Right, Up, Down, Down, Up.

SPIDER DROID UPGRADE

Pause the game, select Shop, and enter the following in Droid-Jak Upgrades: Up, Left, Down, Left, Right, Left, Left, Left.

STAR WARS: THE FORCE UNLEASHED II

BOBA FETT COSTUME

Pause the game, select Cheat Codes from the Options menu, and enter MANDALORE.

DARK APPRENTICE COSTUME

Pause the game, select Cheat Codes from the Options menu, and enter VENTRESS.

GENERAL KOTA COSTUME

Pause the game, select Cheat Codes from the Options menu, and enter RAHM.

NEIMOIDIAN COSTUME

Pause the game, select Cheat Codes from the Options menu, and enter GUNRAY.

REBEL COMMANDO COSTUME

Pause the game, select Cheat Codes from the Options menu, and enter SPECFORCE.

REBEL SOLDIER COSTUME

Pause the game, select Cheat Codes from the Options menu, and enter REBELSCUM.

SABER GUARD COSTUME

Pause the game, select Cheat Codes from the Options menu, and enter MORGUKAI.

SITH ACOLYTE COSTUME

Pause the game, select Cheat Codes from the Options menu, and enter HAAZEN.

STORMTROOPER COSTUME

Pause the game, select Cheat Codes from the Options menu, and enter TK421.

TERROR TROOPER COSTUME

Pause the game, select Cheat Codes from the Options menu, and enter SHADOW.

PLAYSTATION 3

TRAINING DROID COSTUME
Pause the game, select Cheat Codes from the Options menu, and enter HOLODROID.

REPULSE FORCE POWER
Pause the game, select Cheat Codes from the Options menu, and enter MAREK.

SABRE THROW
Pause the game, select Cheat Codes from the Options menu, and enter TRAYA.

WISDOM LIGHTSABER CRYSTALS
Pause the game, select Cheat Codes from the Options menu, and enter SOLARI.

TRAINING GEAR
Have a save game from Star Wars: The Force Unleashed.

CEREMONIAL ROBES
Have a save game from Star Wars: The Force Unleashed with the Light Side ending.

SITH STALKER ARMOR
Have a save game from Star Wars: The Force Unleashed with the Dark Side ending.

STAR WARS THE FORCE UNLEASHED: ULTIMATE SITH EDITION

CHEAT CODES
Pause the game and select Input Code. Here you can enter the following codes. Activating any of the following cheat codes will disable some unlockables, and you will be unable to save your progress.

CHEAT	CODE
All Force Powers at Max Power	KATARN
All Force Push Ranks	EXARKUN
All Saber Throw Ranks	ADEGAN

CHEAT	CODE
All Repulse Ranks	DATHOMIR
All Saber Crystals	HURRIKANE
All Talents	JOCASTA
Deadly Saber	LIGHTSABER

COMBOS
Pause the game and select Input Code. Here you can enter the following codes. Activating any of the following cheat codes will disable some unlockables, and you will be unable to save your progress.

COMBO	CODE
All Combos	MOLDYCROW
Aerial Ambush	VENTRESS
Aerial Assault	EETHKOTH
Aerial Blast	YADDLE
Impale	BRUTALSTAB
Lightning Bomb	MASSASSI
Lightning Grenade	RAGNOS

COMBO	CODE
Saber Slam	PLOKOON
Saber Sling	KITFISTO
Sith Saber Flurry	LUMIYA
Sith Slash	DARAGON
Sith Throw	SAZEN
New Combo	FREEDON
New Combo	MARAJADE

ALL DATABANK ENTRIES
Pause the game and select Input Code. Enter OSSUS.

MIRRORED LEVEL
Pause the game and select Input Code. Enter MINDTRICK. Re-enter the code to return level to normal.

SITH MASTER DIFFICULTY
Pause the game and select Input Code. Enter SITHSPAWN.

COSTUMES
Pause the game and select Input Code. Here you can enter the following codes.

COSTUME	CODE
All Costumes	SOHNDANN
Bail Organa	VICEROY
Ceremonial Jedi Robes	DANTOOINE
Drunken Kota	HARDBOILED
Emperor	MASTERMIND
Incinerator Trooper	PHOENIX
Jedi Adventure Robe	HOLOCRON
Kashyyyk Trooper	TK421GREEN

COSTUME	CODE
Kota	MANDALORE
Master Kento	WOOKIEE
Proxy	PROTOTYPE
Scout Trooper	FERRAL
Shadow Trooper	BLACKHOLE
Sith Stalker Armor	KORRIBAN
Snowtrooper	SNOWMAN
Stormtrooper	TK421WHITE
Stormtrooper Commander	TK421BLUE

OVERLOAD

SUPER STREET FIGHTER IV

BARREL BUSTER & CAR CRUSHER BONUS STAGES
Complete Arcade Mode in any difficulty.

COLORS & TAUNTS
Colors 1 and 2 plus the first taunt for each fighter are available from the start. For colors 11 and 12, start a game with a Street Fighter IV save game on your system. To earn the rest of the colors and taunts, you must fight a certain number of matches with that character.

COLOR	# OF MATCHES	COLOR	# OF MATCHES	COLOR	# OF MATCHES
3	2	6	8	9	14
4	4	7	10	10	16
5	6	8	12		

TAUNT	# OF MATCHES	TAUNT	# OF MATCHES	TAUNT	# OF MATCHES
2	1	5	7	8	13
3	3	6	9	9	15
4	5	7	11	10	16

STUNTMAN IGNITIO

3 PROPS IN STUNT CREATOR MODE
Select Cheats from Extras and enter COOLPROP.

ALL ITEMS UNLOCKED FOR CONSTRUCTION MODE
Select Cheats from Extras and enter NOBLEMAN.

MVX SPARTAN
Select Cheats from Extras and enter fastride.

ALL CHEATS
Select Cheats from Extras and enter Wearefrozen. This unlocks the following cheats: Slo-mo Cool, Thrill Cam, Vision Switcher, Nitro Addiction, Freaky Fast, and Ice Wheels.

ALL CHEATS
Select Cheats from Extras and enter Kungfoopete.

ICE WHEELS CHEAT
Select Cheats from Extras and enter IceAge.

NITRO ADDICTION CHEAT
Select Cheats from Extras and enter TheDuke.

VISION SWITCHER CHEAT
Select Cheats from Extras and enter GFXMODES.

SUPER PUZZLE FIGHTER II TURBO HD REMIX

PLAY AS AKUMA
At the character select, highlight Hsien-Ko and press Down.

PLAY AS DAN
At the character select, highlight Donovan and press Down.

PLAY AS DEVILOT
At the character select, highlight Morrigan and press Down.

PLAY AS ANITA
At the character select, hold L1 + R1 and choose Donovan.

PLAY AS HSIEN-KO'S TALISMAN
At the character select, hold L1 + R1 and choose Hsien-Ko.

PLAY AS MORRIGAN AS A BAT
At the character select, hold L1 + R1 and choose Morrigan.

SUPER STREET FIGHTER II TURBO HD REMIX

The following codes give you the classic fighters in Classic Arcade Mode. Select the character, quickly enter the given code, and select him/her again.

CLASSIC BALROG
Right, Left, Left, Right

CLASSIC BLANKA
Left, Right (x3)

CLASSIC CAMMY
Up, Up, Down, Down

CLASSIC CHUN-LI
Down (x3), Up

CLASSIC DEE JAY
Down, Down, Up, Up

CLASSIC DHALSIM
Down, Up (x3)

CLASSIC E. HONDA Up (x3), Down	**CLASSIC M. BISON** Down, Up, Up, Down	**CLASSIC VEGA** Left, Right, Right, Left
CLASSIC FEI LONG Left, Left, Right, Right	**CLASSIC RYU** Right (x3), Left	**CLASSIC ZANGIEF** Left, Right (x3)
CLASSIC GUILE Up, Down (x3)	**CLASSIC SAGAT** Up, Down (x3), Up	
CLASSIC KEN Left (x3), Right	**CLASSIC T. HAWK** Right, Right, Left, Left	

SURF'S UP

ALL CHAMPIONSHIP LOCATIONS
Select Cheat Codes from the Extras menu and enter FREEVISIT.

ALL LEAF SLIDE STAGES
Select Cheat Codes from the Extras menu and enter GOINGDOWN.

ALL MULTIPLAYER LEVELS
Select Cheat Codes from the Extras menu and enter MULTIPASS.

ALL BOARDS
Select Cheat Codes from the Extras menu and enter MYPRECIOUS.

ASTRAL BOARD
Select Cheat Codes from the Extras menu and enter ASTRAL.

MONSOON BOARD
Select Cheat Codes from the Extras menu and enter MONSOON.

TINE SHOCKWAVE BOARD
Select Cheat Codes from the Extras menu and enter TINYSHOCKWAVE.

ALL CHARACTER CUSTOMIZATIONS
Select Cheat Codes from the Extras menu and enter TOPFASHION.

PLAY AS ARNOLD
Select Cheat Codes from the Extras menu and enter TINYBUTSTRONG.

PLAY AS ELLIOT
Select Cheat Codes from the Extras menu and enter SURPRISEGUEST.

PLAY AS GEEK
Select Cheat Codes from the Extras menu and enter SLOWANDSTEADY.

PLAY AS TANK EVANS
Select Cheat Codes from the Extras menu and enter IMTHEBEST.

PLAY AS TATSUHI KOBAYASHI
Select Cheat Codes from the Extras menu and enter KOBAYASHI.

PLAY AS ZEKE TOPANGA
Select Cheat Codes from the Extras menu and enter THELEGEND.

ALL VIDEOS AND SPEN GALLERY
Select Cheat Codes from the Extras menu and enter WATCHAMOVIE.

ART GALLERY
Select Cheat Codes from the Extras menu and enter NICEPLACE.

TIGER WOODS PGA TOUR 08

ALL COURSES
Select Password from EA Sports Extras and enter greensfees.

ALL GOLFERS
Select Password from EA Sports Extras and enter allstars.

TIMESHIFT

KRONE IN MULTIPLAYER
Select Multiplayer from the Options menu. Highlight Model and press ⬛ to get to Krone. Press Y and enter RXYMCPENCJ.

TOMB RAIDER UNDERWORLD

BULLETPROOF LARA
During a game, hold L2 and press ✖, R2, ▲, R2, ⬤, L1.

ONE-SHOT KILL
During a game, hold L2 and press ▲, ✖, ▲, ⬤, L1, ⬤.

SHOW ENEMY HEALTH
During a game, hold L2 and press ⬤, ⬤, ✖, L1, R2, ▲.

TOM CLANCY'S ENDWAR

EUROPEAN ENFORCER CORPS
Go to Community and Extras, highlight VIP and press ⬤. Enter EUCA20.

RUSSIAN SPETZNAZ GUARD BRIGADE
Go to Community and Extras, highlight VIP and press ⬤. Enter SPZA39.

RUSSIAN SPETZNAZ BATTALION
Go to Community and Extras, highlight VIP and press ⬤. Enter SPZT17.

US JOINT STRIKE FORCE BATTALION
Go to Community and Extras, highlight VIP and press ⬤. Enter JSFA35.

TOM CLANCY'S HAWX

A-12 AVENGER II
At the hangar, hold L2 and press ⬤, L1, ⬤, R1, ⬤, ⬤.

F-18 HARV
At the hangar, hold L2 and press L1, ⬤, L1, ⬤, L1, ⬤.

FB-22 STRIKE RAPTOR
At the hangar, hold L2 and press R1, ⬤, R1, ⬤, R1, ⬤.

TOM CLANCY'S RAINBOW SIX VEGAS

SUPER RAGDOLL
Pause the game, hold L2 and press ✕, ✕, ⬤, ⬤, ⬤, ⬤, ⬤, ⬤, ✕, ⬤, ⬤, ⬤.

THIRD PERSON MODE
Pause the game, hold L2 and press ⬤, ⬤, ⬤, ⬤, L3, L3, ⬤, ✕, ⬤, ✕, R3, R3.

BIG HEAD
Pause the game, hold L2 and press ⬤, ⬤, ✕, ⬤, L3, ⬤, ✕, ⬤, ⬤, R3.

ONE-HIT KILLS
Pause the game, hold L2 and press L3, R3, L3, R3, ✕, ⬤, L3, R3, L3, R3 ⬤, ⬤.

TOM CLANCY'S RAINBOW SIX VEGAS 2

GI JOHN DOE MODE
Pause the game, hold the R1 and press L3, L3, ✕, R3, R3, ⬤, L3, L3, ⬤, R3, R3, ⬤.

SUPER RAGDOLL
Pause the game, hold the R1 and press ✕, ✕, ⬤, ⬤, ⬤, ⬤, ⬤, ⬤, ⬤, ✕, ⬤, ⬤, ⬤.

THIRD-PERSON MODE
Pause the game, hold the R1 and press ⬤, ⬤, ⬤, ⬤, L3, L3, ⬤, ✕, ⬤, ✕, R3, R3.

TAR-21 ASSAULT RIFLE
At the Character Customization screen, hold R1 and press Down, Down, Up, Up, ⬤, ⬤, ⬤, ⬤, ⬤, Up, Up, ⬤.

MULTIPLAYER MAP: COMCAST EVENT
Select Extras from the Main menu. Choose Comcast Gift and enter Comcast Faster.

TONY HAWK RIDE

RYAN SHECKLER
Select Cheats from the Options menu and enter SHECKLERSIG.

QUICKSILVER 80'S LEVEL
Select Cheats from the Options menu and enter FEELINGEIGHTIES.

SPONSOR ITEMS

As you progress through Career mode and move up the rankings, you gain sponsors and each comes with its own Create-a-skater item.

RANK REQUIRED	CAS ITEM UNLOCKED
Rank 040	Adio Kenny V2 Shoes
Rank 050	Quiksilver Hoody 3
Rank 060	Birdhouse Tony Hawk Deck
Rank 080	Vans No Skool Gothic Shoes
Rank 100	Volcom Scallero Jacket
Rank 110	eS Square One Shoes
Rank 120	Almost Watch What You Say Deck
Rank 140	DVS Adage Shoe
Rank 150	Element Illuminate Deck
Rank 160	Etnies Sheckler White Lavender Shoes
Complete Skateshop Goal	Stereo Soundwave Deck

SKATERS

All of the skaters, except for Tony Hawk, must be unlocked by completing challenges in the Career Mode. They are useable in Free Skate and 2 Player modes.

SKATER	HOW TO UNLOCK
Tony Hawk	Always Unlocked
Lyn-z Adams Hawkins	Complete Pro Challenge
Bob Burquist	Complete Pro Challenge
Dustin Dollin	Complete Pro Challenge
Nyjah Huston	Complete Pro Challenge
Bam Margera	Complete Pro Challenge
Rodney Mullen	Complete Pro Challenge
Paul Rodriguez	Complete Pro Challenge
Ryan Sheckler	Complete Pro Challenge
Daewon Song	Complete Pro Challenge
Mike Vallely	Complete Pro Challenge
Stevie Willams	Complete Pro Challenge
Travis Barker	Complete Pro Challenge
Kevin Staab	Complete Pro Challenge
Zombie	Complete Pro Challenge
Christaian Hosoi	Rank #1
Jason Lee	Complete Final Tony Hawk Goal
Photographer	Unlock Shops
Security Guard	Unlock School
Bum	Unlock Car Factory
Beaver Mascot	Unlock High School
Real Estate Agent	Unlock Downtown
Filmer	Unlock High School
Skate Jam Kid	Rank #4
Dad	Rank #1
Colonel	All Gaps
Nerd	Complete School Spirit Goal

CHEAT CODES

Select Cheat Codes from the Options and enter the following codes. In game you can access some codes from the Options menu.

CHEAT CODE	RESULTS
plus44	Unlocks Travis Barker
hohohosoi	Unlocks Christian Hosoi
notmono	Unlocks Jason Lee
mixitup	Unlocks Kevin Staab
strangefellows	Unlocks Dad & Skater Jam Kid
themedia	Unlocks Photog Girl & Filmer
militarymen	Unlocks Colonel & Security Guard
Cheat Code	Results
jammypack	Unlocks Always Special

balancegalore	Unlocks Perfect Rail
frontandback	Unlocks Perect Manual
shellshock	Unlocks Unlimited Focus
shescaresme	Unlocks Big Realtor
birdhouse	Unlocks Inkblot deck
allthebest	Full stats
needaride	All decks unlocked and free, except for Inkblot Deck and Gamestop Deck
yougotitall	All specials unlocked and in player's special list and set as owned in skate shop
wearelosers	Unlocks Nerd and a Bum
manineedadate	Unlocks Beaver Mascot
suckstobedead	Unlocks Officer Dick
HATEDANDPROUD	Unlocks the Vans item

TONY HAWK'S PROVING GROUND

Select Cheat Codes from the Options and enter the following cheats. Some codes need to be enabled by selecting Cheats from the Options during a game.

UNLOCK	CHEAT
Unlocks Boneman	CRAZYBONEMAN
Unlocks Bosco	MOREMILK
Unlocks Cam	NOTACAMERA
Unlocks Cooper	THECOOP
Unlocks Eddie X	SKETCHY
Unlocks El Patinador	PILEDRIVER
Unlocks Eric	FLYAWAY
Unlocks Mad Dog	RABBIES
Unlocks MCA	INTERGALACTIC
Unlocks Mel	NOTADUDE
Unlocks Rube	LOOKSSMELLY
Unlocks Spence	DAPPER
Unlocks Shayne	MOVERS
Unlocks TV Producer	SHAKER
Unlock FDR	THEPREZPARK
Unlock Lansdowne	THELOCALPARK
Unlock Air & Space Museum	THEINDOORPARK
Unlocks all Fun Items	OVERTHETOP
Unlocks all CAS items	GIVEMESTUFF
Unlocks all Decks	LETSGOSKATE
Unlock all Game Movies	WATCHTHIS
Unlock all Lounge Bling Items	SWEETSTUFF
Unlock all Lounge Themes	LAIDBACKLOUNGE
Unlock all Rigger Pieces	IMGONNABUILD
Unlock all Video Editor Effects	TRIPPY
Unlocks all Video Editor Overlays	PUTEMONTOP
All specials unlocked and in player's special list	LOTSOFTRICKS
Full Stats	BEEFEDUP
Give player +50 skill points	NEEDSHELP

The following cheats lock you out of the Leaderboards:

UNLOCK	CHEAT
Unlocks Perfect Manual	STILLAINTFALLIN
Unlocks Perfect Rail	AINTFALLIN
Unlock Super Check	BOOYAH
Unlocks Unlimited Focus	MYOPIC
Unlock Unlimited Slash Grind	SUPERSLASHIN
Unlocks 100% branch completion in NTT	FOREVERNAILED
No Bails	ANDAINTFALLIN

You can not use the Video Editor with the following cheats:

UNLOCK	CHEAT
Invisible Man	THEMISSING
Mini Skater	TINYTATER

UNLOCK	CHEAT
No Board	MAGICMAN

TRANSFORMERS: THE GAME

INFINITE HEALTH
At the Main menu, press Left, Left, Up, Left, Right, Down, Right.

INFINITE AMMO
At the Main menu, press Up, Down, Left, Right, Up, Up, Down.

NO MILITARY OR POLICE
At the Main menu, press Right, Left, Right, Left, Right, Left, Right.

ALL MISSIONS
At the Main menu, press Down, Up, Left, Right, Right, Right, Up, Down.

BONUS CYBERTRON MISSIONS
At the Main menu, press Right, Up, Up, Down, Right, Left, Left.

GENERATION 1 SKIN: JAZZ
At the Main menu, press Left, Up, Down, Down, Left, Up, Right.

GENERATION 1 SKIN: MEGATRON
At the Main menu, press Down, Left, Left, Down, Right, Right, Up.

GENERATION 1 SKIN: OPTIMUS PRIME
At the Main menu, press Down, Right, Left, Up, Down, Down, Left.

GENERATION 1 SKIN: ROBOVISION OPTIMUS PRIME
At the Main menu, press Down, Down, Up, Up, Right, Right, Right.

GENERATION 1 SKIN: STARSCREAM
At the Main menu, press Right, Down, Left, Left, Down, Up, Up.

TRANSFORMERS: REVENGE OF THE FALLEN

LOW GRAVITY MODE
Select Cheat Code and enter ✕, ●, ▲, L3, ▲, L3.

NO WEAPON OVERHEAT
Select Cheat Code and enter L3, ●, ✕, L3, ▲, L1.

ALWAYS IN OVERDRIVE MODE
Select Cheat Code and enter L1, ●, L1, ✕, ●, R3.

UNLIMITED TURBO
Select Cheat Code and enter ●, L3, ●, R3, ✕, ▲

NO SPECIAL COOLDOWN TIME
Select Cheat Code and enter R3, ●, R3, R3, ●, ✕.

INVINCIBILITY
Select Cheat Code and enter R3, ✕, ●, L3, ●, ●.

4X ENERGON FROM DEFEATED ENEMIES
Select Cheat Code and enter ▲, ●, ●, R3, ✕, ▲.

INCREASED WEAPON DAMAGE (ROBOT FORM)
Select the Cheat Code option and enter ▲, ▲, R3, ✕, L1, ▲.

INCREASED WEAPON DAMAGE (VEHICLE FORM)
Select Cheat Code and enter ▲, ●, R1, ✕, R3, L3.

MELEE INSTANT KILLS
Select the Cheat Code option and enter R3, ✕. L1, ●, R3, L1.

LOWER ENEMY ACCURACY
Select Cheat Code and enter ✕, L3, R3, L3, R3, R1.

INCREASED ENEMY HEALTH
Select Cheat Code and enter ●, ✕, L1, ●, R3, ▲.

INCREASED ENEMY DAMAGE
Select Cheat Code and enter L1, ▲, ✕, ▲, R3, R3.

INCREASED ENEMY ACCURACY
Select Cheat Code and enter ▲, ▲, ●, ✕, A, L1.

SPECIAL KILLS ONLY MODE
Select Cheat Code and enter ●, ●, R1, ●, ✕, L3.

UNLOCK ALL SHANGHAI MISSIONS & ZONES
Select Cheat Code and enter ▲, L3, R3, L1, ▲, ✕.

UNLOCK ALL WEST COAST MISSIONS & ZONES
Select Cheat Code and enter L1, R1, R3, ▲, R3, ●.

UNLOCK ALL DEEP SIX MISSIONS & ZONES
Select Cheat Code and enter ✕, R1, ▲, ●, ✕, L1.

UNLOCK ALL EAST COAST MISSIONS & ZONES
Select Cheat Code and enter R3, L3, R1, ✕, ●, ✕.

UNLOCK ALL CAIRO MISSIONS & ZONES
Select Cheat Code and enter R3, ▲, ✕, ▲, L3, L1.

UNLOCK & ACTIVATE ALL UPGRADES
Select Cheat Code and enter L1, ▲, L1, ●, ✕, ✕.

UFC 2009 UNDISPUTED

MASK
Win three consecutive fights by submission in Career Mode.

PUNKASS
Earn the TapouT sponsorship in Career Mode.

SKYSKRAPE
At the Title screen, enter Up, Up, Up, Down, Left, Right, Up, Start.

UFC UNDISPUTED 2010

BJ PENN (BLACK SHORTS)
At the Main menu, press L1, R1, L2, R2, R2, L2, R1, L1, ●, ●, ●, ●, Start.

SHAQUILLE O'NEAL
At the Main menu, press Right, Up, Left, Right, Down, Left, Up, Right, Down, Left, ●, ▲, ▲, ●, Start.

TAPOUT CREW
At the Main menu, press Down, Down, Up, Right, Left, Down, Select, Start.

UNCHARTED: DRAKE'S FORTUNE

DRAKE'S BASEBALL T-SHIRT
At the costume select, press Left, Right, Down, Up, ▲, R1, L1, ●.

MAKING A CUTSCENE—GRAVE ROBBING
At the rewards screen, highlight Making a Cutscene—Grave Robbing and press Left, R2, Right, Up, L2, ▲, ●, Down.

MAKING A CUTSCENE—TIME'S UP
At the rewards screen, highlight Making a Cutscene—Time's Up and press L1, Right, ●, Down, Left, ▲, R1, Up.

CONCEPT ART—BONUS 1
At the rewards screen, highlight Concept Art—Bonus 1 and press L2, Right, Up, ●, Left, ▲, R1, Down.

CONCEPT ART—BONUS 2
At the rewards screen, highlight Concept Art—Bonus 2 and press ●, L1, Right, Left, Down, R2, ▲, Up.

UNCHARTED 2: AMONG THIEVES

In Uncharted 2: Among Thieves, upon opening the store you'll have the option to hit the Square button to check for Uncharted: Drake's Fortune save data. You'll obtain cash for having save data! This cash can be used in the single and multiplayer stores. Could be useful if you want a head start online!

$20,000
Have a saved game of Uncharted: Drake's Fortune.

$80,000
Have a saved game of Uncharted: Drake's Fortune with the story completed at least once.

WALL-E

The following cheats will disable saving. The five possible characters starting with Wall-E and going down are: Wall-E, Auto, EVE, M-O, GEL-A Steward.

ALL BONUS FEATURES UNLOCKED
Select Cheats from the Bonus Features menu and enter Wall-E, Auto, EVE, GEL-A Steward.

ALL GAME CONTENT UNLOCKED
Select Cheats from the Bonus Features menu and enter M-O, Auto, GEL-A Steward, EVE.

ALL SINGLE PLAYER LEVELS UNLOCKED
Select Cheats from the Bonus Features menu and enter Auto, GEL-A Steward, M-O, Wall-E.

ALL MULTIPLAYER MAPS UNLOCKED
Select Cheats from the Bonus Features menu and enter EVE, M-O, Wall-E, Auto.

ALL HOLIDAY COSTUMES UNLOCKED
Select Cheats from the Bonus Features menu and enter Auto, Auto, GEL-A Steward, GEL-A Steward.

ALL MULTIPLAYER COSTUMES UNLOCKED
Select Cheats from the Bonus Features menu and enter GEL-A Steward, Wall-E, M-O, Auto.

OVERLOAD

PLAYSTATION 3

UNLIMITED HEALTH UNLOCKED
Select Cheats from the Bonus Features menu and enter Wall-E, M-O, Auto, M-O.

WALL-E: MAKE ANY CUBE AT ANY TIME
Select Cheats from the Bonus Features menu and enter Auto, M-O, Auto, M-O.

WALL-EVE: MAKE ANY CUBE AT ANY TIME
Select Cheats from the Bonus Features menu and enter M-O, GEL-A Steward, EVE, EVE.

WALL-E WITH A LASER GUN AT ANY TIME
Select Cheats from the Bonus Features menu and enter Wall-E, EVE, EVE, Wall-E.

WALL-EVE WITH A LASER GUN AT ANY TIME
Select Cheats from the Bonus Features menu and enter GEL-A Steward, EVE, M-O, Wall-E.

WALL-E: PERMANENT SUPER LASER UPGRADE
Select Cheats from the Bonus Features menu and enter Wall-E, Auto, EVE, M-O.

EVE: PERMANENT SUPER LASER UPGRADE
Select Cheats from the Bonus Features menu and enter EVE, Wall-E, Wall-E, Auto.

CREDITS
Select Cheats from the Bonus Features menu and enter Auto, Wall-E, GEL-A Steward, M-O.

WANTED: WEAPONS OF FATE

HEALTH IMPROVEMENT
Select Secret Codes and enter 0100 1100.

ONE SHOT ONE KILL
Select Secret Codes and enter 0111 0010.

PLAY WITH SPECIAL SUIT
Select Secret Codes and enter 0110 0001.

SUPER WEAPONS
Select Secret Codes and enter 0100 1111.

UNLIMITED ADRENALINE
Select Secret Codes and enter 0110 1101.

UNLIMITED AMMO
Select Secret Codes and enter 0110 1111.

PLAY AS AIRPLANE BODYGUARD
Select Secret Codes and enter 0101 0111.

WOLFENSTEIN

$1000
Purchase and play Wolfenstein 3D from the PSN store. At the start of Train Yard, you will earn $1000.

WORLD OF OUTLAWS: SPRINT CARS

$5,000,000
Enter your name as CHICMCHIM.

ALL DRIVERS
Enter your name as MITYMASTA.

ALL TRACKS
Enter your name as JOEYJOEJOE.

WORLD SERIES OF POKER 2008: BATTLE FOR THE BRACELETS

PHILLIP J. HELLMUTH
Enter BEATTHEBRAT as the player name.

WWE SMACKDOWN! VS RAW 2008

HBK AND HHH'S DX OUTFIT
Select Cheat Codes from the Options and enter DXCostume69K2.

KELLY KELLY'S ALTERNATE OUTFIT
Select Cheat Codes from the Options and enter KellyKG12R.

BRET HART
Complete the March 31, 1996 Hall of Fame challenge by defeating Bret Hart with Shawn Michaels in a One-On-One 30-Minute Iron Man Match on Legend difficulty. Purchase from WWE Shop for $210,000.

MICK FOLEY
Complete the June 28, 1998 Hall of Fame challenge by defeating Mick Foley The Undertaker in a Hell In a Cell Match on Legend difficulty. Purchase from WWE Shop for $210,000.

MR. MCMAHON
Win or successfully defend a championship (WWE or World Heavyweight) at WrestleMania in WWE 24/7 GM Mode. Purchase from WWE Shop for $110,000.

THE ROCK
Complete the April 1, 2001 Hall of Fame challenge by defeating The Rock with Steve Austin in a Single Match on Legend Difficulty. Purchase from WWE Shop for $210,000.

STEVE AUSTIN
Complete the March 23, 1997 Hall of Fame challenge by defeating Steve Austin with Bret Hart in a Submission Match on Legend Difficulty. Purchase from WWE Shop for $210,000.

TERRY FUNK
Complete the April 13, 1997 Hall of Fame challenge by defeating Tommy Dreamer, Sabu and Sandman with any Superstar in an ECW Extreme Rules 4-Way Match on Legend difficulty. Purchase from WWE Shop for $210,000.

MR. MCMAHON BALD
Must unlock Mr. McMahon as a playable character first. Purchase from WWE Shop for $60,000.

WWE SMACKDOWN VS. RAW 2009

BOOGEYMAN
Select Cheat Codes from My WWE and enter BoogeymanEatsWorms!!.

GENE SNITSKY
Select Cheat Codes from My WWE and enter UnlockSnitskySvR2009.

HAWKINS & RYDER
Select Cheat Codes from My WWE and enter Ryder&HawkinsTagTeam.

JILLIAN HALL
Select Cheat Codes from My WWE and enter PlayAsJillianHallSvR.

LAYLA
Select Cheat Codes from My WWE and enter UnlockECWDivaLayla09.

RIC FLAIR
Select Cheat Codes from My WWE and enter FlairWooooooooooooooo.

TAZZ
Select Cheat Codes from My WWE and enter UnlockECWTazzSvR2009.

VINCENT MCMAHON
Select Cheat Codes from My WWE and enter VinceMcMahonNoChance.

HORNSWOGGLE AS MANAGER
Select Cheat Codes from My WWE and enter HornswoggleAsManager.

CHRIS JERICHO COSTUME B
Select Cheat Codes from My WWE and enter AltJerichoModelSvR09.

CM PUNK COSTUME B
Select Cheat Codes from My WWE and enter CMPunkAltCostumeSvR!.

REY MYSTERIO COSTUME B
Select Cheat Codes from My WWE and enter BooyakaBooyaka619SvR.

SATURDAY NIGHT'S MAIN EVENT ARENA
Select Cheat Codes from My WWE and enter SatNightMainEventSvR.

WWE SMACKDOWN VS. RAW 2010

THE ROCK
Select Cheat Codes from the Options and enter The Great One.

VINCE'S OFFICE AND DIRT SHEET FOR BACKSTAGE BRAWL
Select Cheat Codes from the Options menu and enter BonusBrawl.

SHAWN MICHAEL'S ALTERNATE COSTUME
Select Cheat Codes from the Options menu and enter Bow Down.

JOHN CENA'S ALTERNATE COSTUME
Select Cheat Codes from the Options menu and enter CENATION.

RANDY ORTON'S ALTERNATE COSTUME
Select Cheat Codes from the Options menu and enter ViperRKO.

SANTINO MARELLA'S ALTERNATE COSTUME
Select Cheat Codes from the Options menu and enter Milan Miracle.

TRIPLE H'S ALTERNATE COSTUME
Select Cheat Codes from the Options menu and enter Suck IT!.

OVERLORD

PLAYSTATION 3

PLAYSTATION

JOHN CENA (ENTRANCE/CIVILIAN)
In My WWE, select Cheat Codes from the Options menu and enter SLURPEE.

ALL OF RANDY ORTON'S COSTUMES
In My WWE, select Cheat Codes from the Options menu and enter apexpredator.

TRIBUTE TO THE TROOPS ARENA
In My WWE, select Cheat Codes from the Options menu and enter 8thannualtribute.

X-MEN ORIGINS: WOLVERINE

CLASSIC WOLVERINE UNIFORM
During a game, press ✕, ●, ●, ●, ✕, ●, ●, ✕, ●, ●, ●, ●, R3. Note that this code disables trophies.

INVINCIBLE
During a game, press ●, ✕, ✕, ●, ●, ●, ●, ●, ●, R3. Note that this code disables trophies.

INFINITE RAGE
During a game, press ●, ●, ●, ●, ●, ●, ●, ✕, ✕, ●, R3. Note that this code disables trophies.

DOUBLES ENEMY REFLEX POINTS
During a game, press ✕, ✕, ●, ●, ●, ●, ●, ●, ●, ●, ●, ●, ✕, ✕, R3. Note that this code disables trophies.

CLASSIC WOLVERINE CHALLENGE/OUTFIT
Find any two Classic Wolverine action figures to unlock this challenge. Defeat Classic Wolverine in combat to unlock the Classic Wolverine outfit. Note that this code disables trophies.

ORIGINAL WOLVERINE CHALLENGE/OUTFIT
Find any two Original Wolverine action figures to unlock this challenge. Defeat Original Wolverine in combat to unlock the Original Wolverine outfit. Note that this code disables trophies.

X-FORCE WOLVERINE CHALLENGE/OUTFIT
Find any two X-Force Wolverine action figures to unlock this challenge. Defeat X-Force Wolverine in combat to unlock the X-Force Wolverine outfit. Note that this code disables trophies.

ZOMBIE APOCALYPSE

7 DAYS OF HELL MODE
Complete Day 55.

CHAINSAW ONLY MODE
Complete a day only using the chainsaw.

HARDCORE MODE
Survive for seven straight days.

TURBO MODE
Get a 100 multiplier.

SONY PLAYSTATION® 2

GAMES

PLAYSTATION 2

AMPLITUDE

BLUR
During a game, press R3 (x4), L3 (x4), then R3.

MONKEY NOTES
During a game, press L3 (x4), R3 (x4), then L3. Quit the game and go back into the song to see the effect. Re-enter the code to disable it.

RANDOM NOTE PLACEMENT
During a game, press ✪, ✪, Left, Left, R3, R3, Right, Right. Quit the game and go back into the song to see the effect. Re-enter the code to disable it.

CHANGE SHAPE OF TRACK LAYOUT
During the game, press L3 (x3), R3 (x3), L3, R3, and L3. Quit the game and go back into the song to see the effect. Enter it once for a tunnel appearance and a second time for a Tempest-style look. Enter the code a third time to disable it.

APE ESCAPE: PUMPED & PRIMED

ALL GADGETS
Complete Story Mode. At the mode select, hold R1 + L1 + R2 + L2 to access the password screen. Enter Go Wild!.

DISABLE ALL GADGETS CHEAT
Complete Story Mode. At the mode select, hold R1 + L1 + R2 + L2 to access the password screen. Enter Limited!.

NORMAL DIFFICULTY
Complete Story Mode. At the mode select, hold R1 + L1 + R2 + L2 to access the password screen. Enter NORMAL!.

HARD DIFFICULTY
Complete Story Mode. At the mode select, hold R1 + L1 + R2 + L2 to access the password screen. Enter HARD!.

ASTRO BOY: THE VIDEO GAME

INVULNERABLE
Pause the game and press Up, Down, Down, Up, L1, R1.

DISABLE SUPERS
Pause the game and press L1, L1, R1, R1, L1, Left.

MAX STATS
Pause the game and press Left, Left, R1, Down, Down, L1.

COSTUME SWAP (ARENA AND CLASSIC COSTUMES)
Pause the game and press R1, Up, L1, Up, Down, R1.

INFINITE SUPERS
Pause the game and press Left, L1, Right, L1, Up, Down.

UNLOCK LEVELS
Pause the game and press Up, L1, Right, L1, Down, L1. This allows you to travel to any level from the Story menu.

INFINITE DASHES
Pause the game and press R1, R1, L1, R1, Left, Up.

AVATAR: THE LAST AIRBENDER—THE BURNING EARTH

1-HIT DISHONOR
At the Main menu, press L1 and select Code Entry. Enter 28260.

INFINITE HEALTH
At the Main menu, press L1 and select Code Entry. Enter 65049.

ALL BONUS GAME
At the Main menu, press L1 and select Code Entry. Enter 99801.

MAX LEVEL
At the Main menu, press L1 and select Code Entry. Enter 89121.

ALL GALLERY ITEMS
At the Main menu, press L1 and select Code Entry. Enter 85061.

UNLIMITED SPECIAL ATTACKS
At the Main menu, press L1 and select Code Entry. Enter 66206.

DOUBLE DAMAGE
At the Main menu, press L1 and select Code Entry. Enter 90210.

AVATAR: THE LAST AIRBENDER—INTO THE INFERNO

ALL CHAPTERS
Select Game Secrets at Ember Islands and enter 52993833.

ALL ITEMS AVAILABLE AT SHOP
Select Game Secrets at Ember Islands and enter 34737253.

MAX COINS
Select Game Secrets at Ember Islands and enter 66639224.

ALL CONCEPT ART
Select Game Secrets at Ember Islands and enter 27858343.

BAKUGAN BATTLE BRAWLERS

1,000 BP
Enter 33204429 as your name.

100,000 BP
Enter 18499753 as your name.

5,000 BP
Enter 42348294 as your name.

500,000 BP
Enter 26037947 as your name.

10,000 BP
Enter 46836478 as your name.

BEN 10: ALIEN FORCE: THE GAME

LEVEL LORD
Enter Gwen, Kevin, Big Chill, Gwen as a code.

INVINCIBILITY
Enter Kevin, Big Chill, Swampfire, Kevin as a code.

ALL COMBOS
Enter Swampfire, Gwen, Kevin, Ben as a code.

INFINITE ALIENS
Enter Ben, Swampfire, Gwen, Big Chill as a code.

BEN 10: ALIEN FORCE VILGAX ATTACKS

LEVEL SKIP
Pause the game and enter Portal at the Cheats menu.

UNLOCK ALL SPECAL ATTACKS FOR ALL FORMS
Pause the game and enter Everythingproof at the Cheats menu.

UNLOCK ALL ALIEN FORMS
Pause the game and enter Primus at the Cheats menu.

TOGGLE INVULNERABILITY
Pause the game and enter Xlmrsmoothy at the Cheats menu.

FULL HEALTH
Pause the game and enter Herotime at the Cheats menu.

QUICK ENERGY REGENERATION
Pause the game and enter Generator at the Cheats menu.

BEN 10: PROTECTOR OF EARTH

INVINCIBILITY
Select a game from the Continue option. Go to the Map Selection screen, press Start and choose Extras. Select Enter Secret Code and enter XLR8, Heatblast, Wildvine, Fourarms.

ALL COMBOS
Select a game from the Continue option. Go to the Map Selection screen, press Start and choose Extras. Select Enter Secret Code and enter Cannonblot, Heatblast, Fourarms, Heatblast.

ALL LOCATIONS
Select a game from the Continue option. Go to the Map Selection screen, press Start and choose Extras. Select Enter Secret Code and enter Heatblast, XLR8, XLR8, Cannonblot.

DNA FORCE SKINS
Select a game from the Continue option. Go to the Map Selection screen, press Start and choose Extras. Select Enter Secret Code and enter Wildvine, Fourarms, Heatblast, Cannonbolt.

DARK HEROES SKINS
Select a game from the Continue option. Go to the Map Selection screen, press Start and choose Extras. Select Enter Secret Code and enter Cannonbolt, Cannonbolt, Fourarms, Heatblast.

ALL ALIEN FORMS
Select a game from the Continue option. Go to the Map Selection screen, press Start and choose Extras. Select Enter Secret Code and enter Wildvine, Fourarms, Heatblast, Wildvine.

MASTER CONTROL
Select a game from the Continue option. Go to the Map Selection screen, press Start and choose Extras. Select Enter Secret Code and enter Cannonbolt, Heatblast, Wildvine, Fourarms.

BEN 10 ULTIMATE ALIEN: COSMIC DESTRUCTION

To remove these cheats, simply start a new game.

1,000,000 DNA
Pause the game, select Cheats, and enter Cash.

REGENERATE HEALTH
Pause the game, select Cheats, and enter Health.

REGENERATE ENERGY
Pause the game, select Cheats, and enter Energy.

UPGRADE EVERYTHING
Pause the game, select Cheats, and enter Upgrade.

ALL LEVELS
Pause the game, select Cheats, and enter Levels.

DAMAGE
Pause the game, select Cheats, and enter Hard. Once activated, enemies will cause double damage while you will inflict approximately half damage

BOLT

Some of the following cheats can be toggled on/off by selecting Cheats from the Pause menu.

ALL GAME LEVELS
Select Cheats from the Extras menu and enter Right, Up, Left, Right, Up, Right.

ALL MINI-GAMES
Select Cheats from the Extras menu and enter Right, Up, Right, Right.

ENHANCED VISION
Select Cheats from the Extras menu and enter Left, Right, Up, Down.

UNLIMITED GAS MINES
Select Cheats from the Extras menu and enter Right, Left, Left, Up, Down, Right.

UNLIMITED GROUND POUND
Select Cheats from the Extras menu and enter Right, Up, Right, Up, Left, Down.

UNLIMITED INVULNERABILITY
Select Cheats from the Extras menu and enter Down, Down, Up, Left.

UNLIMITED LASER EYES
Select Cheats from the Extras menu and enter Left, Left, Up, Right.

UNLIMITED STEALTH CAMO
Select Cheats from the Extras menu and enter Left, Down, Down, Down.

UNLIMITED SUPERBARK
Select Cheats from the Extras menu and enter Right, Left, Left, Up, Down, Up.

BRATZ: FOREVER DIAMONDZ

1000 BLINGZ
While in the Bratz Office, use the Cheat computer to enter SIZZLN.

2000 BLINGZ
While in the Bratz Office, use the Cheat computer to enter FLAUNT.

PET TREATS
While in the Bratz Office, use the Cheat computer to enter TREATZ.

GIFT SET A
While in the Bratz Office, use the Cheat computer to enter STYLIN.

GIFT SET B
While in the Bratz Office, use the Cheat computer to enter SKATIN.

GIFT SET C
While in the Bratz Office, use the Cheat computer to enter JEWELZ.

GIFT SET E
While in the Bratz Office, use the Cheat computer to enter DIMNDZ.

BROTHERS IN ARMS: EARNED IN BLOOD

ALL LEVELS AND REWARDS
Create a profile with the name 2ndsquad.

BULLY

The following codes must be entered with a controller plugged into port 2:

FULL HEALTH
During a game, hold L1 and press R2, R2, R2.

ALL WEAPONS
During a game, hold L1 and press Up, Up, Up, Up.

INFINITE AMMO
During a game, hold L1 and press Up, Down, Up, Down.

MAX AMMO
During a game, hold L1 and press Up, Up.

MONEY
During a game, hold L1 and press ▲, ●, ●, ✕.

ALL CLOTHES
During a game, press L1, L1, R1, L1, L1, L1, R1, R1.

ALL GYM GRAPPLE MOVES
During a game, hold L1 and press Up, Left, Down, Down, ▲, ●, ✕, ✕.

ALL HOBO FIGHTING MOVES
During a game, hold L1 and press Up, Left, Down, Right, ▲, ●, ✕, ●.

PLAYSTATION 2

CAPCOM CLASSICS COLLECTION VOL. 2

UNLOCK EVERYTHING
At the Title screen, press Left, Right, Up, Down, L1, R1, L1, R1. This code unlocks Cheats, Tips, Art, and Sound Tests.

CARS MATER-NATIONAL

ALL ARCADE RACES, MINI-GAMES, AND WORLDS
Select Codes/Cheats from the options and enter PLAYALL.

ALL CARS
Select Codes/Cheats from the options and enter MATTEL07.

ALTERNATE LIGHTNING MCQUEEN COLORS
Select Codes/Cheats from the options and enter NCEDUDZ.

ALL COLORS FOR OTHERS
Select Codes/Cheats from the options and enter PAINTIT.

UNLIMITED TURBO
Select Codes/Cheats from the options and enter ZZOOOOM.

EXTREME ACCELERATION
Select Codes/Cheats from the options and enter 0TO200X.

EXPERT MODE
Select Codes/Cheats from the options and enter VRYFAST.

ALL BONUS ART
Select Codes/Cheats from the options and enter BUYTALL.

CARS RACE-O-RAMA

ALL ARCADE MODE EVENTS
Select Cheats from the Options menu and enter SLVRKEY.

ALL STORY MODE EVENTS
Select Cheats from the Options menu and enter GOLDKEY.

ALL OF LIGHTNING MCQUEEN'S FRIENDS
Select Cheats from the Options menu and enter EVRYBDY.

ALL LIGHTNING MCQUEEN CUSTOM KIT PARTS
Select Cheats from the Options menu and enter GR8MODS.

ALL PAINT JOBS FOR ALL NON-LIGHTNING MCQUEEN CHARACTERS
Select Cheats from the Options menu and enter CARSHOW.

CORALINE

BUTTON EYE CORALINE
Select Cheats from Options and enter Cheese.

CRASH OF THE TITANS

BIG HEAD CRASH
Pause the game, hold R1, and press ●, ●, ▲, ✖. Re-enter the code to disable.

SHADOW CRASH
Pause the game, hold R1, and press ▲, ●, ▲, ●. Re-enter the code to disable.

DESTROY ALL HUMANS! 2

SALAD DAYS WITH POX & CRYPTO
Pause the game and select Archives. Then press and hold L3 and press ✖, ●, ▲, ●, ●, ▲, ✖, ✖.

DJ HERO

Select Cheats from Options and enter the following. Some codes will disable high scores and progress. Cheats cannot be used in tutorials and online.

UNLOCK ALL CONTENT
Enter tol0.

ALL CHARACTER ITEMS
Enter uNA2.

ALL VENUES
Enter Wv1u.

ALL DECKS
Enter LAuP.

ALL HEADPHONES
Enter 62Db.

ALL MIXES
Enter 82xl.

AUTO SCRATCH
Enter IT6j.

AUTO EFFECTS DIAL
Enter ab1L.

AUTO FADER
Enter SL5d.

AUTO TAPPER
Enter ZitH.

AUTO WIN EUPHORIA
Enter r3a9.

BLANK PLINTHS
Enter ipr0.

HAMSTER SWITCH
Enter 7geo.

HYPER DECK MODE
Enter 76st.

SHORT DECK
Enter 51uC.

INVISIBLE DJ
Enter oh5T.

PITCH BLACK OUT
Enter d4kR.

PLAY IN THE BEDROOM
Enter g7nH.

ANY DJ, ANY SETLIST
Enter 0jj8.

DAFT PUNK'S CONTENT
Enter d1g?.

DJ AM'S CONTENT
Enter k07u.

**DJ JAZZY JEFF'S
CONTENT**
Enter n1fz.

DJ SHADOW'S CONTENT
Enter oMxV.

DJ Z-TRIP'S CONTENT
Enter 5rtg.

**GRANDMASTER FLASH'S
CONTENT**
Enter ami8.

DRAGON BALL Z: SAGAS

PENDULUM ROOMS
Select Options from the Main menu and press Up, Down, Up, Down,
Left, Right, Left, Right, Select, Start, Select, Start, ●, ●, ●, ●, ✖, ✖, Start.
When entered correctly, the message "Pendulum Rooms Unlocked" will
appear on-screen. This unlocks the Pendulum mode, all Extras, all Sagas,
and all Upgrades.

INVINCIBILITY
Pause the game, select Controller
and press Down, ✖, Select, Start,
Right, ●, Left, ●, Up, ▲.

ALL UPGRADES
Pause the game, select Controller
and press Up, Left, Down, Right,
Select, Start, ●, ✖, ●, ▲.

DUEL MASTERS

ALL LOCATIONS
At the Map screen, hold R3 and
press ● (x3).

**4 OF EVERY CARD & UNLOCK CHUCK IN
ARCADE MODE**
At the Deck Building screen, hold
R3 and press L1, L1, L1.

PLAYER 1 LOSES SHIELD
During a duel, hold R3 and press
▲, ●, ✖. Release R3.

PLAYER 2 LOSES SHIELD
During a duel, hold R3 and press
▲, ●, ✖. Release R3.

PLAYER 1 GAINS SHIELD
During a duel, hold R3 and press
✖, ●, ▲. Release R3.

PLAYER 2 GAINS SHIELD
During a duel, hold R3 and press
✖, ●, ▲. Release R3.

PLAYER 1 WINS
During a duel, hold R3 and press
L1, R1, L1.

PLAYER 2 WINS
During a duel, hold R3 and press
R1, L1, R1.

TURN OFF DECK OUTS
During a duel, hold R3 and press
● (x3).

PLAYSTATION 2

ERAGON

FURY MODE
Pause the game, hold L1 + L2 + R1 + R2 and press ●, ●, ●, ●.

FIGHT NIGHT ROUND 3

ALL VENUES
Select Create Champ and change the first name to NEWVIEW.

FLATOUT 2

ALL CARS & 1,000,000 CREDITS
Select Enter Code from the Extras menu and enter GIEVEPIX.

1,000,000 CREDITS
Select Enter Code from the Extras menu and enter GIVECASH.

PIMPSTER CAR
Select Enter Code from the Extras menu and enter RUTTO.

FLATMOBILE CAR
Select Enter Code from the Extras menu and enter WOTKINS.

MOB CAR
Select Enter Code from the Extras menu and enter BIGTRUCK.

SCHOOL BUS
Select Enter Code from the Extras menu and enter GIEVCARPLZ.

ROCKET CAR
Select Enter Code from the Extras menu and enter KALJAKOPPA.

TRUCK
Select Enter Code from the Extras menu and enter ELPUEBLO.

FUNKMASTER FLEX'S DIGITAL HITZ FACTORY

EXTRA SKIN 1
At the main menu, press SELECT, Left, Right, Left, Right, Left, Right, Left, Right, Left, Right, Left, Right.

EXTRA SKIN 2
At the main menu, press SELECT, Left, Left, Right, Right, Left, Left, Right, Right, Left, Left, Right, Right.

EXTRA SKIN 3
At the main menu, press SELECT, Left, Left, Left, Right, Right, Right, Left, Left, Left, Right, Right, Right.

EXTRA SKIN 4
At the main menu, press SELECT, Left, Left, Left, Left, Right, Right, Right, Right, Left, Left, Left, Left.

EXTRA SONG – MUDDY BY MOTLEY
At the main menu, press SELECT, Up, Down, Left, Right, Up, Down, Left, Right, Up, Down, Left, Right.

GI JOE: THE RISE OF COBRA

CLASSIC DUKE
At the main menu, press Left, Up, X, Up, Right, ▲.

CLASSIC SCARLETT
At the main menu, press Right, Up, Down, Down, ▲.

THE GOLDEN COMPASS

The following codes are entered in the order of top/left, bottom/left, top/right. The Featurettes can then be accessed through the Extras menu.

VOICE SESSION 1 FETUREETE
In Extras, select Enter Code from the Game Secrets menu and enter Compass, Sun, Madonna.

 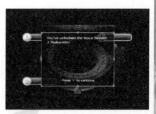

VOICE SESSION 2 FEATURETTE
In Extras, select Enter Code from the Game Secrets menu and enter Compass, Moon, Wild Man.

BEHIND THE SCENES FEATURETTE
In Extras, select Enter Code from the Game Secrets menu and enter Alpha/Omega, Alpha/Omega, Compass.

WILDLIFE WAYSTATION FEATURETTE
In Extras, select Enter Code from the Game Secrets menu and enter Griffin, Elephant, Owl.

POLAR BEARS IN MOTION FEATURETTE
In Extras, select Enter Code from the Game Secrets menu and enter Sun, Moon, Wild Man.

GRADIUS V

You can use one of these for each level completed.

DOUBLE SHOT POWER
After the first boss, pause the game and press Up, Up, Down, Down, Left, Right, Left, Right, L2, R2.

LASER POWER
After the first boss, pause the game and press Up, Up, Down, Down, Left, Right, Left, Right, L1, R1.

GRAND THEFT AUTO: SAN ANDREAS

During a game, enter the following cheats:

FULL HEALTH, FULL ARMOR & $250,000
Press R1, R2, L1, ✕, Left, Down, Right, Up, Left, Down, Right, Up.

INFINITE LUNG CAPACITY
Press Down, Left, L1, Down, Down, R2, Down, L2, Down.

0 FAT & 0 MUSCLE
Press ●, Up, Up, Left, Right, ●, ●, Right.

MAXIMUM MUSCLES
Press ●, Up, Up, Left, Right, ●, ●, Left.

MAXIMUM FAT
Press ●, Up, Up, Left, Right, ●, ●, Down.

BIG JUMPS
Press Up, Up, ●, ●, Up, Up, Left, Right, ●, R2, R2.

OVERLOAD

PLAYSTATION 2

BIG BUNNY HOPS ON BMX
Press △, □, ●, ●, ●, ●, ●, L1, L2, L2, R1, R2.

SUICIDE
Press Right, L2, Down, R1, Left, Left, R1, L1, L2, L1.

FASTER GAMEPLAY
Press △, Up, Right, Down, L2, L1, ●.

SLOWER GAMEPLAY
Press △, Up, Right, Down, ●, R2, R1.

FASTER TIME
Press ●, ●, L1, ●, L1, ●, ●, ●, L1, △, ●, △.

BLACK CARS
Press ●, L2, Up, R1, Left, ✕, R1, L1, Left, ●.

PINK CARS
Press ●, L1, Down, L2, Left, ✕, R1, L1, Right, ●.

FAST CARS
Press Up, L1, R1, Up, Right, Up, ✕, L2, ✕, L1.

TAXIS HAVE NITROUS & HOP WITH L3
Press Up, ✕, △, ✕, △, ✕, □, R2, Right.

INVISIBLE VEHICLES
Press △, L1, △, R2, ●, L1, L1.

INVINCIBLE VEHICLE
Press L1, L2, L2, Up, Down, Down, Up, R1, R2, R2.

DRIVE-BY WHILE DRIVING
Press Up, Up, □, L2, Right, ✕, R1, Down, R2, ●.

GREEN STOPLIGHTS
Press Right, R1, Up, L2, L2, Left, R1, L1, R1, R1.

AGGRESSIVE TRAFFIC
Press R2, ●, R1, L2, Left, R1, L1, R2, L2.

LESS TRAFFIC
Press ✕, Down, Up, R2, Down, △, L1, △, Left.

FASTER CARS
Press Right, R1, Up, L2, L2, Left, R1, L1, R1, R1.

BETTER CAR HANDLING
Press △, R1, R1, Left, R1, L1, R2, L1.

CARS FLOAT
Press Right, R2, ●, R1, L2, ●, R1, R2.

CARS FLY
Press Up, Down, L1, R1, L1, Right, Left, L1, Left.

ALL CARS EXPLODE
Press R2, L2, R1, L1, L2, R2, □, △, ●, △, L2, L1.

FLYING BOATS
Press R2, ●, Up, L1, Right, R1, Right, Up, □, △.

PEDESTRIANS ATTACK YOU
Press Down, Up, Up, Up, ✕, R2, R1, L2, L2.

PEDESTRIANS ATTACK EACH OTHER
Press Down, Left, Up, Left, ✕, R2, R1, L2, L1.

PEDESTRIANS CARRY WEAPONS
Press R2, R1, ✕, △, ✕, △, Up, Down.

ELVISES EVERYWHERE
Press L1, ●, △, L1, L1, □, L2, Up, Down, Left.

CJ IS A CLOWN, CIVILIANS IN FAST FOOD APPAREL & MORE!
Press △, △, L1, ●, ●, L2, ●, Down, ●.

PEOPLE IN SWIMSUITS
Press Up, Up, Down, Down, □, ●, L1, R1, △, Down.

GANGS
Press L2, Up, R1, R1, Left, R1, R1, R2, Right, Down.

REDUCE WANTED LEVEL
Press R1, R1, ●, R2, Up, Down, Up, Down, Up, Down.

RAISE WANTED LEVEL
Press R1, R1, ●, R2, Left, Right, Left, Right, Left, Right.

CLEAR WEATHER
Press R2, ✕, L1, L1, L2 (x3), △.

SUNNY WEATHER
Press R2, ✕, L1, L1, L2 (x3), Down.

FOGGY WEATHER
Press R2, ✕, L1, L1, L2 (x3), ✕.

CLOUDY WEATHER
Press R2, ✕, L1, L1, L2 (x3), □.

RAINY WEATHER
Press R2, ✕, L1, L1, L2 (x3), ●.

WEAPON SET 1
Press R1, R2, L1, R2, Left, Down, Right, Up, Left, Down, Right, Up.

WEAPON SET 2
Press R1, R2, L1, R2, Left, Down, Right, Up, Left, Down, Down, Left.

WEAPON SET 3
Press R1, R2, L1, R2, Left, Down, Right, Up, Left, Down, Down, Down.

PARACHUTE
Press Left, Right, L1, L2, R1, R2, R2, Up, Down, Right, L1.

JETPACK
Press L1, L2, R1, R2, Up, Down, Left, Right, L1, L2, R1, R2, Up, Down, Left, Right.

BLOODRING BANGER
Press Down, R1, ●, L2, L2, ✖, R1, L1, Left, Left.

CADDY
Press ●, L1, Up, R1, L2, ✖, R1, L1, ●, ✖.

DOZER
Press R2, L1, L1, Right, Right, Up, Up, ✖, L1, Left.

HOTRING RACER 1
Press R1, ●, R2, Right, L1, L2, ✖, ✖, ●, R1.

HOTRING RACER 2
Press R2, L1, ●, Right, L1, R1, Right, Up, ●, R2.

HYDRA
Press ▲, ▲, ●, ●, ✖, L1, L1, Down, Up.

GRAN TURISMO 4

EXTRA TRACKS FOR ARCADE MODE
Play through the indicated number of days to unlock the corresponding track in Arcade Mode.

DAYS	UNLOCKS
15	Deep Forest Raceway
29	Opera Paris
43	Fuji Speedway 80s
57	Special Stage Route 5
71	Suzuka Circuit
85	Twin Ring Motegi Road Course East Short
99	Grand Valley Speedway
113	Hong Kong
127	Suzuka Circuit West Course
141	Fuji Speedway 2005 GT
155	Ice Arena
169	Apricot Hill Raceway
183	Cote d Azur
197	Tahiti Maze

DAYS	UNLOCKS
211	Twin Ring Motegi Road Course
225	George V Paris
239	Cathedral Rocks Trail I
253	Costa di Amalfi
267	Circuit de la Sarthe 1
281	Autumn Ring
309	Chamonix
309	Infineon Raceway Stock Car Course
323	Fuji Speedway 2005 F
337	Tsukuba Circuit Wet
351	Circuit de la Sarthe 2 (not chicaned)

GUITAR HERO

UNLOCK ALL CHEATS
At the Main menu, press Yellow, Orange, Blue, Blue, Orange, Yellow, Yellow.

GUITAR HERO GUITAR CHEAT
At the Main menu, press Blue, Orange, Yellow, Blue, Blue.

CROWD METER CHEAT
At the Main menu, press Yellow, Blue, Orange, Orange, Blue, Blue, Yellow, Orange.

MONKEY HEAD CROWD
At the Main menu, press Blue, Orange, Yellow, Yellow, Yellow, Blue, Orange.

PLAYSTATION 2

SKULL HEAD CROWD
At the Main menu, press Orange, Yellow, Blue, Blue, Orange, Yellow, Blue, Blue.

AIR GUITAR CHEAT
At the Main menu, press Orange, Orange, Blue, Yellow, Orange.

NO VENUE CHEAT
At the Main menu, press Blue, Yellow, Orange, Blue, Yellow, Orange.

GUITAR HERO II

AIR GUITAR
At the Main menu, press Yellow, Yellow, Blue, Orange, Yellow, Blue.

EYEBALL HEAD CROWD
At the Main menu, press Blue, Orange, Yellow, Orange, Yellow, Orange, Blue.

MONKEY HEAD CROWD
At the Main menu, press Orange, Blue, Yellow, Yellow, Orange, Blue, Yellow, Yellow.

FLAMING HEAD
At the Main menu, press Orange, Yellow, Orange, Orange, Yellow, Orange, Yellow, Yellow.

HORSE HEAD
At the Main menu, press Blue, Orange, Orange, Blue, Orange, Orange, Blue, Orange, Orange, Blue.

HYPER SPEED DEACTIVATE
At the Main menu, press Orange, Blue, Orange, Yellow, Orange, Blue, Orange, Yellow.

PERFORMANCE MODE
At the Main menu, press Yellow, Yellow, Blue, Yellow, Yellow, Orange, Yellow, Yellow.

GUITAR HERO III: LEGENDS OF ROCK

To enter the following cheats, strum the guitar with the given buttons held. For example, if it says Yellow + Orange, hold Yellow and Orange as you strum. Some cheats can be toggled on and off from the Cheats menu. You can also change between five different levels of Hyperspeed at this menu.

UNLOCK EVERYTHING
Select Cheats from the Options. Choose Enter Cheat and enter Green + Red + Blue + Orange, Green + Red + Yellow + Blue, Green + Red + Yellow + Orange, Green + Yellow + Blue + Orange, Green + Red + Yellow + Blue, Red + Yellow + Blue + Orange, Green + Red + Yellow + Blue, Green + Yellow + Blue + Orange, Green + Red + Yellow + Blue, Green + Red + Yellow + Orange, Green + Red + Yellow + Orange, Green + Red + Yellow + Blue, Green + Red + Yellow + Orange. No sounds play while this code is entered.

An easier way to show this code is by representing Green as 1 down to Orange as 5. For example, if you have 1345, you would hold down Green + Yellow + Blue + Orange while strumming. 1245 + 1234 + 1235 + 1345 + 1234 + 2345 + 1234 + 1345 + 1234 + 1235 + 1235 + 1234 + 1235.

ALL SONGS
Select Cheats from the Options. Choose Enter Cheat and enter Yellow + Orange, Red + Blue, Red + Orange, Green + Blue, Red + Yellow, Yellow + Orange, Red + Yellow, Red + Blue, Green + Yellow, Green + Yellow, Yellow + Blue, Yellow + Blue, Yellow + Orange, Yellow + Orange, Yellow + Blue, Yellow, Red, Red + Yellow, Red, Yellow, Orange.

NO FAIL

Select Cheats from the Options. Choose Enter Cheat and enter Green + Red, Blue, Green + Red, Green + Yellow, Blue, Green + Yellow, Red + Yellow, Orange, Red + Yellow, Green + Yellow, Yellow, Green + Yellow, Green + Red.

AIR GUITAR

Select Cheats from the Options. Choose Enter Cheat and enter Blue + Yellow, Green + Yellow, Green + Yellow, Red + Blue, Red + Blue, Red + Yellow, Red + Yellow, Blue + Yellow, Green + Yellow, Green + Yellow, Red + Blue, Red + Blue, Red + Yellow, Red + Yellow, Green + Yellow, Green + Yellow, Red + Yellow, Red + Yellow.

HYPERSPEED

Select Cheats from the Options. Choose Enter Cheat and enter Orange, Blue, Orange, Yellow, Orange, Blue, Orange, Yellow.

PERFORMANCE MODE

Select Cheats from the Options. Choose Enter Cheat and enter Red + Yellow, Red + Blue, Red + Orange, Red + Blue, Red + Yellow, Green + Blue, Red + Yellow, Red + Blue.

EASY EXPERT

Select Cheats from the Options. Choose Enter Cheat and enter Green + Red, Green + Yellow, Yellow + Blue, Red + Blue, Blue + Orange, Yellow + Orange, Red + Yellow, Red + Blue.

PRECISION MODE

Select Cheats from the Options. Choose Enter Cheat and enter Green + Red, Green + Red, Green + Red, Red + Yellow, Red + Yellow, Red + Blue, Red + Blue, Yellow + Blue, Yellow + Orange, Yellow + Orange, Green + Red, Green + Red, Green + Red, Red + Yellow, Red + Yellow, Red + Blue, Red + Blue, Yellow + Blue, Yellow + Orange, Yellow + Orange.

LARGE GEMS

Select Cheats from the Options. Choose Enter Cheat and enter Green, Red, Green, Yellow, Green, Blue, Green, Orange, Green, Blue, Green, Yellow, Green, Red, Green, Green + Red, Red + Yellow, Green + Red, Yellow + Blue, Green + Red, Blue + Orange, Green + Red, Yellow + Blue, Green + Red, Red + Yellow, Green + Red, Green + Yellow.

GUITAR HERO 5

ALL HOPOS

Select Input Cheats from the Options menu and enter Green, Green, Blue, Green, Green, Green, Yellow, Green.

ALWAYS SLIDE

Select Input Cheats from the Options menu and enter Green, Green, Red, Red, Yellow, Red, Yellow, Blue.

AUTO KICK

Select Input Cheats from the Options menu and enter Yellow, Green, Red, Blue, Blue, Blue, Blue, Red.

FOCUS MODE

Select Input Cheats from the Options menu and enter Yellow, Green, Red, Green, Yellow, Blue, Green, Green.

HUD FREE MODE

Select Input Cheats from the Options menu and enter Green, Red, Green, Green, Yellow, Green, Green, Green.

HYPERSPEED

Select Input Cheats from the Options menu and enter Green, Blue, Red, Yellow, Yellow, Red, Green, Green.

PERFORMANCE MODE

Select Input Cheats from the Options menu and enter Yellow, Yellow, Blue, Red, Blue, Green, Red, Red.

FLAME COLOR

Select Input Cheats from the Options menu and enter Green, Red, Green, Blue, Red, Red, Yellow, Blue.

GEM COLORS

Select Input Cheats from the Options menu and enter Blue, Red, Red, Green, Red, Green, Red, Yellow.

STAR COLOR

Select Input Cheats from the Options menu and enter Red, Red, Yellow, Red, Blue, Red, Red, Blue.

VOCAL FIREBALL

Select Input Cheats from the Options menu and enter Red, Green, Green, Yellow, Blue, Green, Yellow, Green.

AIR INSTRUMENTS

Select Input Cheats from the Options menu and enter Red, Red, Blue, Yellow, Green, Green, Green, Yellow.

INVISIBLE ROCKER

Select Input Cheats from the Options menu and enter Green, Red, Yellow, Yellow, Yellow, Blue, Blue, Green.

GUITAR HERO: AEROSMITH

At the Main menu, select "Options", "Cheats", "Enter New Cheat", then enter one of the following codes to unlock the corresponding cheat option. Note: Each note or chord must be strummed. Press Green at the "Cheats" menu to turn off a particular cheat.

AIR GUITAR

Press Red + Yellow, Green + Red, [Red + Yellow] two times, [Red + Blue] five times, [Yellow + Blue] two times, Yellow + Orange.

HYPERSPEED

Yellow + Orange, Yellow + Orange, Yellow + Orange, Yellow + Orange, Yellow + Orange, Red + Yellow, Red + Yellow, Red + Yellow, Red + Yellow, Red + Blue, Red + Blue, Red + Blue, Red + Blue, Red + Blue, Yellow + Blue, Yellow + Orange, Yellow + Orange

NO FAIL

Press Green + Red, Blue, Green + Red, Green + Yellow, Blue, Green + Yellow, Red + Yellow, Orange, Red + Yellow, Green + Yellow, Yellow, Green + Yellow.

ALL SONGS

Press Red + Yellow, [Green + Red] two times, [Red + Yellow] two times, Green + Red, [Red + Yellow] two times, [Green + Red] two times, [Red + Yellow].

GUITAR HERO ENCORE: ROCKS THE 80S

UNLOCK EVERYTHING

At the Main menu, press Blue, Orange, Yellow, Red, Orange, Yellow, Blue, Yellow, Red, Yellow, Blue, Yellow, Red, Yellow, Blue, Yellow.

HYPERSPEED

At the Main menu, press Yellow, Blue, Orange, Orange, Blue, Yellow, Yellow, Orange.

PERFORMANCE MODE

At the Main menu, press Blue, Blue, Orange, Yellow, Yellow, Blue, Orange, Blue.

AIR GUITAR

At the Main menu, press Yellow, Blue, Yellow, Orange, Blue, Blue.

EYEBALL HEAD CROWD

At the Main menu, press Yellow, Blue, Orange, Orange, Orange, Blue, Yellow.

MONKEY HEAD CROWD

At the Main menu, press Blue, Blue, Orange, Yellow, Blue, Blue, Orange, Yellow.

FLAME HEAD

At the Main menu, press Yellow, Orange, Yellow, Orange, Yellow, Orange, Blue, Orange.

HORSE HEAD

At the Main menu, press Blue, Orange, Orange, Blue, Yellow, Blue, Orange, Orange, Blue, Yellow.

GUITAR HERO: METALLICA

METALLICA COSTUMES

Select Cheats from Settings and enter Green, Red, Yellow, Blue, Blue, Yellow, Red, Green.

HYPERSPEED

Select Cheats from Settings and enter Green, Blue, Red, Yellow, Yellow, Red, Green, Green.

PERFORMANCE MODE

Select Cheats from Settings and enter Yellow, Yellow, Blue, Red, Blue, Green, Red, Red.

INVISIBLE ROCKER

Select Cheats from Settings and enter Green, Red, Yellow (x3), Blue, Blue, Green.

AIR INSTRUMENTS
Select Cheats from Settings and enter Red, Red, Blue, Yellow, Green (x3), Yellow.

ALWAYS DRUM FILL
Select Cheats from Settings and enter Red (x3), Blue, Blue, Green, Green, Yellow.

AUTO KICK
Select Cheats from Settings and enter Yellow, Green, Red, Blue (x4), Red. With this cheat activated, the bass pedal is automatically hit.

ALWAYS SLIDE
Select Cheats from Settings and enter Green, Green, Red, Red, Yellow, Red, Yellow, Blue. All Guitar Notes Become Touch Pad Sliding Notes.

BLACK HIGHWAY
Select Cheats from Settings and enter Yellow, Red, Green, Red, Green, Red, Red, Blue.

FLAME COLOR
Select Cheats from Settings and enter Green, Red, Green, Blue, Red, Red, Yellow, Blue.

GEM COLOR
Select Cheats from Settings and enter Blue, Red, Red, Green, Red, Green, Red, Yellow.

STAR COLOR
Select Cheats from Settings and enter Press Red, Red, Yellow, Red, Blue, Red, Red, Blue.

ADDITIONAL LINE 6 TONES
Select Cheats from Settings and enter Green, Red, Yellow, Blue, Red, Yellow, Blue, Green.

VOCAL FIREBALL
Select Cheats from Settings and enter Red, Green, Green, Yellow, Blue, Green, Yellow, Green.

GUITAR HERO: SMASH HITS

ALWAYS DRUM FILL
Select Cheats from the Options menu and enter Green, Green, Red, Red, Blue, Blue, Yellow, Yellow.

ALWAYS SLIDE
Select Cheats from the Options menu and enter Blue, Yellow, Red, Green, Blue, Green, Green, Yellow.

AIR INSTRUMENTS
Select Cheats from the Options menu and enter Yellow, Red, Blue, Green, Yellow, Red, Red, Red.

INVISIBLE ROCKER
Select Cheats from the Options menu and enter Blue, Red, Red, Red, Red, Yellow, Blue, Green.

HYPERSPEED
Select Cheats from the Options menu and enter Red, Green, Blue, Yellow, Green, Yellow, Red, Red. This unlocks the HyperGuitar, HyperBass, and HyperDrums cheats.

GEM COLOR
Select Cheats from the Options menu and enter Red, Red, Red, Blue, Blue, Blue, Yellow, Green.

FLAME COLOR
Select Cheats from the Options menu and enter Yellow, Blue, Red, Green, Yellow, Red, Green, Blue.

STAR COLOR
Select Cheats from the Options menu and enter Green, Red, Green, Yellow, Green, Blue, Yellow, Red.

VOCAL FIREBALL
Select Cheats from the Options menu and enter Green, Blue, Red, Red, Yellow, Yellow, Blue, Blue.

GUITAR HERO: VAN HALEN

ALWAYS DRUM FILL
Select Input Cheats from the Options menu and enter Red, Red, Red, Blue, Blue, Green, Green, Yellow.

ALWAYS SLIDE
Select Input Cheats from the Options menu and enter Green, Green, Red, Red, Yellow, Red, Yellow, Blue.

AUTO KICK
Select Input Cheats from the Options menu and enter Yellow, Green, Red, Blue, Blue, Blue, Blue, Red.

HYPERSPEED (HYPERGUITAR, HYPERBASS, HYPERDRUMS)
Select Input Cheats from the Options menu and enter Green, Blue, Red, Yellow, Yellow, Red, Green, Green.

PERFORMANCE MODE

Select Input Cheats from the Options menu and enter Yellow, Yellow, Blue, Red, Blue, Green, Red, Red.

AIR INSTRUMENTS

Select Input Cheats from the Options menu and enter Red, Red, Blue, Yellow, Green, Green, Green, Yellow.

INVISIBLE ROCKER

Select Input Cheats from the Options menu and enter Green, Red, Yellow, Yellow, Yellow, Blue, Blue, Green.

BLACK HIGHWAY

Select Input Cheats from the Options menu and enter Yellow, Red, Green, Red, Green, Red, Red, Blue.

FLAME COLOR

Select Input Cheats from the Options menu and enter Green, Red, Green, Blue, Red, Red, Yellow, Blue.

GEM COLOR

Select Input Cheats from the Options menu and enter Blue, Red, Red, Green, Red, Green, Red, Yellow.

GUITAR HERO WORLD TOUR

ALL SONGS IN QUICK PLAY

At the Cheats menu, select Enter New Cheat and press Blue, Blue, Red, Green, Green, Blue, Blue, Yellow.

AIR INSTRUMENTS

At the Cheats menu, select Enter New Cheat and press Red, Red, Blue, Yellow, Green, Green, Green, Yellow.

ALWAYS SLIDE

At the Cheats menu, select Enter New Cheat and press Green, Green, Red, Red, Yellow, Red, Yellow, Blue.

AT&T BALL PARK

At the Cheats menu, select Enter New Cheat and press Yellow, Green, Red, Red, Green, Blue, Red, Yellow.

AUTO KICK

At the Cheats menu, select Enter New Cheat and press Yellow, Green, Red, Blue, Blue, Blue, Blue, Red.

EXTRA LINE 6 TONES

At the Cheats menu, select Enter New Cheat and press Green, Red, Yellow, Blue, Red, Yellow, Blue, Green.

FLAME COLORS

At the Cheats menu, select Enter New Cheat and press Green, Red, Green, Blue, Red, Red, Yellow, Blue.

GEM COLORS

At the Cheats menu, select Enter New Cheat and press Blue, Red, Red, Green, Red, Green, Red, Yellow.

HYPER SPEED

At the Cheats menu, select Enter New Cheat and press Green, Blue, Red, Yellow, Yellow, Red, Green, Green.

INVISIBLE ROCKER

At the Cheats menu, select Enter New Cheat and press Green, Red, Yellow, Yellow, Yellow, Blue, Blue, Green.

PERFORMANCE MODE

At the Cheats menu, select Enter New Cheat and press Yellow, Yellow, Blue, Red, Blue, Green, Red, Red.

STAR COLORS

At the Cheats menu, select Enter New Cheat and press Red, Red, Yellow, Red, Blue, Red, Red, Blue.

AARON STEELE

At the Cheats menu, select Enter New Cheat and press Blue, Red, Yellow, Yellow, Yellow, Yellow, Yellow, Green.

JOHNNY VIPER

At the Cheats menu, select Enter New Cheat and press Blue, Red, Blue, Blue, Yellow, Yellow, Yellow, Green.

NICK

At the Cheats menu, select Enter New Cheat and press Green, Red, Blue, Green, Red, Blue, Blue, Green.

RINA

At the Cheats menu, select Enter New Cheat and press Blue, Red, Green, Green, Yellow, Yellow, Yellow, Green.

VOCAL FIREBALL

At the Cheats menu, select Enter New Cheat and press Red, Green, Green, Yellow, Blue, Green, Yellow, Green.

BONUS TWO-PLAYER DUELING ARENA CASTLE GATES
At the Rewards menu, press Right, Right, Down, Down, Left, Right, Left, Right, Left, Right, Start.

HOT SHOTS GOLF FORE!

Select Password from the Options menu and enter the following codes to enable these cheats.

ALL CHARACTERS IN VS MODE
Enter REZTWS.

PRICE REDUCTION SALE IN SHOP
Enter MKJEFQ.

ALOHA BEACH RESORT COURSE IN SHOP
Enter XSREHD.

BAGPIPE CLASSIC COURSE IN SHOP
Enter CRCNHZ.

BLUE LAGOON C.C. COURSE IN SHOP
Enter WVRJQS.

DAY DREAM G.C. IN SHOP
Enter OQUTNA.

MINI-GOLF 2 G.C. IN SHOP
Enter RVMIRU.

SILKROAD CLASSIC COURSE IN SHOP
Enter ZKOGJM.

UNITED FOREST G.C. IN SHOP
Enter UIWHLZ.

WESTERN VALLEY COUNTRY CLUB COURSE IN SHOP
Enter LIBTFL.

WILD GREEN C.C. COURSE IN SHOP
Enter YZLOXE.

CAPSULE 01 IN SHOP
Enter WXAFSJ.

CAPSULE 2 IN SHOP
Enter OEINLK.

CAPSULE 3 IN SHOP
Enter WFKVTG.

CAPSULE 4 IN SHOP
Enter FCAVDO.

CAPSULE 5 IN SHOP
Enter YYPOKK.

CAPSULE 6 IN SHOP
Enter GDQDOF.

CAPSULE 7 IN SHOP
Enter HHXKPV.

CAPSULE 8 IN SHOP
Enter UOKXPS.

CAPSULE 9 IN SHOP
Enter LMIRYD.

CAPSULE 10 IN SHOP
Enter MJLJEQ.

CAPSULE 11 IN SHOP
Enter MHNCQI

LOWER TOURNEY STAGE
Enter XKWGFZ.

CADDIE CLANK IN SHOP
Enter XCQGWJ.

CADDIE DAXTER IN SHOP
Enter WSIKIN.

CADDIE KAYLA IN SHOP
Enter MZIMEL.

CADDIE KAZ IN SHOP
Enter LNNZJV.

CADDIE MOCHI IN SHOP
Enter MYPWPA.

CADDIE SIMON IN SHOP
Enter WRHZNB.

CADDIE SOPHIE IN SHOP
Enter UTWIVQ.

BEGINNER'S BALL IN SHOP
Enter YFQJJI.

BIR AIR BALL IN SHOP
Enter CRCGKR.

INFINITY BALL IN SHOP
Enter DJXBRG.

PIN HOLE BALL IN SHOP
Enter VZLSGP.

SIDESPIN BALL IN SHOP
Enter JAYQRK.

TURBO SPIN BALL IN SHOP
Enter XNETOK.

100T HAMMER CLUB (B-CLASS) IN SHOP
Enter NFSNHR.

UPGRADE 100T HAMMER CLUB (A-CLASS) IN SHOP
Enter BVLHSI.

PLAYSTATION 2

OVERLOAD

UPGRADE 100T HAMMER CLUB (S-CLASS) IN SHOP
Enter MCSRUK.

BIG AIR CLUB (B-CLASS) IN SHOP
Enter DLJMFZ.

UPGRADE BIG AIR CLUB (A-CLASS) IN SHOP
Enter TOSXUJ.

UPGRADE BIG AIR CLUB (S-CLASS) IN SHOP
Enter JIDTQI.

INFINITY CLUB IN SHOP
Enter RZTQGV.

UPGRADE INFINITY CLUB (A-CLASS) IN SHOP
Enter WTGFOR.

UPGRADE INFINITY CLUB (S-CLASS) IN SHOP
Enter EIPCUL.

PIN HOLE CLUB (B-CLASS) IN SHOP
Enter DGHFRP.

UPGRADE PIN HOLE CLUB (A-CLASS) IN SHOP
Enter TTIMHT.

UPGRADE PIN HOLE CLUB (S-CLASS) IN SHOP
Enter RBXVEL.

UPGRADE TURBO SPIN CLUB (A-CLASS) IN SHOP
Enter NIWKWP.

UPGRADE TURBO SPIN CLUB (S-CLASS) IN SHOP
Enter DTIZAB.

EXTRA POSE CAM IN SHOP
Enter UEROOK.

EXTRA SWING CAM IN SHOP
Enter RJIFQS.

EXTRA VIDEO IN SHOP
Enter DPYHIU.

HECKLETS IN SHOP
Enter DIXWFE.

HSG CD/VOICE IN SHOP
Enter UITUGF.

HSG CD/MUSIC IN SHOP
Enter PAJXLI.

HSG RULES IN SHOP
Enter FKDHDS.

LANDING GRID IN SHOP
Enter MQTIMV.

REPLAY CAM A IN SHOP
Enter PVJEMF.

REPLAY CAM B IN SHOP
Enter EKENCR.

REPLAY CAM C IN SHOP
Enter ZUHHAC.

MENU CHARACTER BRAD IN SHOP
Enter ZKJSIO.

MENU CHARACTER PHOEBE IN SHOP
Enter LWVLCB.

MENU CHARACTER RENEE IN SHOP
Enter AVIQXS.

WALLPAPER SET 2 IN SHOP
Enter RODDHQ.

MIKE'S COSTUME IN SHOP
Enter YKCFEZ.

LIN'S COSTUME IN SHOP
Enter BBLSKQ.

MEL'S COSTUME IN SHOP
Enter ARFLCR.

PHOEBE'S COSTUME IN SHOP
Enter GJBCHY.

IRON MAN

ARMOR SELECTION

Iron Man's different armor suits are unlocked by completing certain missions. Refer to the following tables for when each is unlocked. After selecting a mission to play, you get the opportunity to pick the armor you wish to use.

COMPLETE MISSION	SUIT UNLOCKED
1: Escape	Mark I
2: First Flight	Mark II
3: Fight Back	Mark III

COMPLETE MISSION	SUIT UNLOCKED
6: Flying Fortress	Comic Tin Can
9: Home Front	Classic
13: Showdown	Silver Centurion

CONCEPT ART

Concept Art is unlocked after finding certain numbers of Weapon Crates.

CONCEPT ART UNLOCKED	NUMBER OF WEAPON CRATES FOUND
Environments Set 1	6
Environments Set 2	12
Iron Man	18
Environments Set 3	24
Enemies	30

CONCEPT ART UNLOCKED	NUMBER OF WEAPON CRATES FOUND
Environments Set 4	36
Villains	42
Vehicles	48
Covers	50

ASCARI KZ1

Select Cheats and Codes from the DNA Lab menu and enter KNOX. Defeat the challenge to earn the car.

NISSAN SKYLINE R34 GT-R

Select Cheats and Codes from the DNA Lab menu and enter JWRS. Defeat the challenge to earn the car.

KATAMARI DAMACY

COMETS

Finish a "Make a Star" level under a certain time to earn a comet.

LEVEL	FINISH WITHIN	LEVEL	FINISH WITHIN
Make a Star 1	1 minute	Make a Star 6	8 minutes
Make a Star 2	3 minutes	Make a Star 7	8 minutes
Make a Star 3	4 minutes	Make a Star 8	12 minutes
Make a Star 4	6 minutes	Make a Star 9	15 minutes
Make a Star 5	8 minutes	Make the Moon	20 minutes

KUNG FU PANDA

INVULNERABILITY

Select Cheats from the Extras menu and enter Down, Down, Right, Up, Left.

INFINITE CHI

Select Cheats from the Extras menu and enter Down, Right, Left, Up, Down.

BIG HEAD MODE

Select Cheats from the Extras menu and enter Down, Up, Left, Right, Right.

ALL MULTIPLAYER CHARACTERS

Select Cheats from the Extras menu and enter Left, Down, Left, Right, Down.

DRAGON WARRIOR OUTFIT IN MULTIPLAYER

Select Cheats from the Extras menu and enter Left, Down, Right, Left, Up.

THE LEGEND OF SPYRO: DAWN OF THE DRAGON

INFINITE HEALTH

Pause the game, hold L1 and press Right, Right, Down, Down, Left with the Left Analog Stick.

INFINITE MANA

Pause the game, hold L1 and press Up, Right, Up, Left, Down with the Left Analog Stick.

MAX XP

Pause the game, hold L1 and press Up, Left, Left, Down, Up with the Left Analog Stick.

ALL ELEMENTAL UPGRADES

Pause the game, hold L1 and press Left, Up, Down, Up, Right with the Left Analog Stick.

LEGO BATMAN

BATCAVE CODES

Using the computer in the Batcave, select Enter Code and enter the following:

CHARACTERS

CHARACTER	CODE	CHARACTER	CODE
Alfred	ZAQ637	Joker Henchman	YUN924
Batgirl	JKR331	Mad Hatter	JCA283
Bruce Wayne	BDJ327	Man-Bat	NYU942
Catwoman (Classic)	M1AAWW	Military Policeman	MKL382
Clown Goon	HJK327	Nightwing	MVY759
Commissioner Gordon	DDP967	Penguin Goon	NKA238
Fishmonger	HGY748	Penguin Henchman	BJH782
Freeze Girl	XVK541	Penguin Minion	KJP748
Joker Goon	UTF782	Poison Ivy Goon	GTB899
		Police Marksman	HKG984

CHARACTER	CODE
Police Officer	JRY983
Riddler Goon	CRY928
Riddler Henchman	XEU824
S.W.A.T.	HTF114
Sailor	NAV592

CHARACTER	CODE
Scientist	JFL786
Security Guard	PLB946
The Joker (Tropical)	CCB199
Yeti	NJL412
Zoo Sweeper	DWR243

VEHICLES

VEHICLE	CODE
Bat-Tank	KNTT4B
Bruce Wayne's Private Jet	LEA664
Catwoman's Motorcycle	HPL826
Garbage Truck	DUS483
Goon Helicopter	GCH328
Harbor Helicopter	CHP735
Harley Quinn's Hammer Truck	RDT637
Mad Hatter's Glider	HS000W
Mad Hatter's Steamboat	M4DM4N
Mr. Freeze's Iceberg	ICYICE

VEHICLE	CODE
The Joker's Van	JUK657
Mr. Freeze's Kart	BCT229
Penguin Goon Submarine	BTN248
Police Bike	LJP234
Police Boat	PLC999
Police Car	KJL832
Police Helicopter	CWR732
Police Van	MAC788
Police Watercraft	VJD328
Riddler's Jet	HAHAHA
Robin's Submarine	TTF453
Two-Face's Armored Truck	EFE933

CHEATS

CHEAT	CODE
Always Score Multiply	9LRGNB
Fast Batarangs	JRBDCB
Fast Walk	ZOLM6N
Flame Batarang	D8NYWH
Freeze Batarang	XPN4NG
Extra Hearts	ML3KHP
Fast Build	EVG26J
Immune to Freeze	JXUDY6
Invincibility	WYD5CP
Minikit Detector	ZXGH9J

CHEAT	CODE
More Batarang Targets	XWP645
Piece Detector	KHJ554
Power Brick Detector	MMN786
Regenerate Hearts	HJH7HJ
Score x2	N4NR3E
Score x4	CX9MAT
Score x6	MLVNF2
Score x8	WCCDB9
Score x10	18HW07

LEGO STAR WARS II: THE ORIGINAL TRILOGY

EACH TROOPER
At Mos Eisley Canteena, select Enter Code and enter UCK868. You must still select Characters and purchase this character for 20,000 studs.

BEN KENOBI (GHOST)
At Mos Eisley Canteena, select Enter Code and enter BEN917. You must still select Characters and purchase this character for 1,100,000 studs.

BESPIN GUARD
At Mos Eisley Canteena, select Enter Code and enter VHY832. You must still select Characters and purchase this character for 15,000 studs.

BIB FORTUNA
At Mos Eisley Canteena, select Enter Code and enter WTY721. You must still select Characters and purchase this character for 16,000 studs.

BOBA FETT
At Mos Eisley Canteena, select Enter Code and enter HLP221. You must still select Characters and purchase this character for 175,000 studs.

DEATH STAR TROOPER
At Mos Eisley Canteena, select Enter Code and enter BNC332. You must still select Characters and purchase this character for 19,000 studs.

EWOK
At Mos Eisley Canteena, select Enter Code and enter TTT289. You must still select Characters and purchase this character for 34,000 studs.

GAMORREAN GUARD
At Mos Eisley Canteena, select Enter Code and enter YZF999. You must still select Characters and purchase this character for 40,000 studs.

GONK DROID

At Mos Eisley Canteena, select Enter Code and enter NFX582. You must still select Characters and purchase this character for 1,550 studs.

GRAND MOFF TARKIN

At Mos Eisley Canteena, select Enter Code and enter SMG219. You must still select Characters and purchase this character for 38,000 studs.

GREEDO

At Mos Eisley Canteena, select Enter Code and enter NAH118. You must still select Characters and purchase this character for 60,000 studs.

HAN SOLO (HOOD)

At Mos Eisley Canteena, select Enter Code and enter YWM840. You must still select Characters and purchase this character for 20,000 studs.

IG-88

At Mos Eisley Canteena, select Enter Code and enter NXL973. You must still select Characters and purchase this character for 30,000 studs.

IMPERIAL GUARD

At Mos Eisley Canteena, select Enter Code and enter MMM111. You must still select Characters and purchase this character for 45,000 studs.

IMPERIAL OFFICER

At Mos Eisley Canteena, select Enter Code and enter BBV889. You must still select Characters and purchase this character for 28,000 studs.

IMPERIAL SHUTTLE PILOT

At Mos Eisley Canteena, select Enter Code and enter VAP664. You must still select Characters and purchase this character for 29,000 studs.

IMPERIAL SPY

At Mos Eisley Canteena, select Enter Code and enter CVT125. You must still select Characters and purchase this character for 13,500 studs.

JAWA

At Mos Eisley Canteena, select Enter Code and enter JAW499. You must still select Characters and purchase this character for 24,000 studs.

LOBOT

At Mos Eisley Canteena, select Enter Code and enter UUB319. You must still select Characters and purchase this character for 11,000 studs.

PALACE GUARD

At Mos Eisley Canteena, select Enter Code and enter SGE549. You must still select Characters and purchase this character for 14,000 studs.

REBEL PILOT

At Mos Eisley Canteena, select Enter Code and enter CYG336. You must still select Characters and purchase this character for 15,000 studs.

REBEL TROOPER (HOTH)

At Mos Eisley Canteena, select Enter Code and enter EKU849. You must still select Characters and purchase this character for 16,000 studs.

SANDTROOPER

At Mos Eisley Canteena, select Enter Code and enter YDV451. You must still select Characters and purchase this character for 14,000 studs.

SKIFF GUARD

At Mos Eisley Canteena, select Enter Code and enter GBU888. You must still select Characters and purchase this character for 12,000 studs.

SNOWTROOPER

At Mos Eisley Canteena, select Enter Code and enter NYU989. You must still select Characters and purchase this character for 16,000 studs.

STORMTROOPER

At Mos Eisley Canteena, select Enter Code and enter PTR345. You must still select Characters and purchase this character for 10,000 studs.

THE EMPEROR

At Mos Eisley Canteena, select Enter Code and enter HHY382. You must still select Characters and purchase this character for 275,000 studs.

TIE FIGHTER

At Mos Eisley Canteena, select Enter Code and enter HDY739. You must still select Characters and purchase this item for 60,000 studs.

TIE FIGHTER PILOT

At Mos Eisley Canteena, select Enter Code and enter NNZ316. You must still select Characters and purchase this character for 21,000 studs.

TIE INTERCEPTOR

At Mos Eisley Canteena, select Enter Code and enter QYA828. You must still select Characters and purchase this item for 40,000 studs.

TUSKEN RAIDER

At Mos Eisley Canteena, select Enter Code and enter PEJ821. You must still select Characters and purchase this character for 23,000 studs.

UGNAUGHT

At Mos Eisley Canteena, select Enter Code and enter UGN694. You must still select Characters and purchase this character for 36,000 studs.

MAJOR LEAGUE BASEBALL 2K9

BIG HEADS

At the Cheats menu, enter Black Sox.

MANHUNT 2

EXTRA LEVEL AS LEO
Defeat the game.

RELIVE SCENE
Defeat the game. This allows you to replay any level.

MARVEL SUPER HERO SQUAD

IRON MAN & BONUS COSTUME
Select Enter Code from the Options menu and enter 111111. The bonus costume is "War Machine."

HULK & BONUS COSTUMES
Select Enter Code from the Options menu and enter 222222. The bonus costumes are "Grey Hulk" & "Red Hulk."

WOLVERINE & BONUS COSTUMES
Select Enter Code from the Options menu and enter 333333. The bonus costumes are "Wolverine" & "Feral Wolverine."

THOR & BONUS COSTUMES
Select Enter Code from the Options menu and enter 444444. The bonus costumes are "Thor (Chain Armor)" & "Loki-Thor."

SILVER SURFER & BONUS COSTUMES
Select Enter Code from the Options menu and enter 555555. The bonus costumes are "Anti-Surfer" & "Gold Surfer."

FALCON & BONUS COSTUME
Select Enter Code from the Options menu and enter 666666. The bonus costume is "Ultimate Falcon."

DOCTOR DOOM & BONUS COSTUMES
Select Enter Code from the Options menu and enter 999999. The bonus costumes are "Ultimate Doctor Doom" & "Professor Doom."

CAPTAIN AMERICA & BONUS COSTUME
Select Enter Code from the Options menu and enter 177674. The bonus costume is "Ultimate Captain America."

A.I.M. AGENT & BONUS COSTUME
Select Enter Code from the Options menu and enter 246246. The bonus costume is "Blue Suit A.I.M."

SUPER KNOCKBACK
Select Enter Code from the Options menu and enter 777777.

NO BLOCK MODE
Select Enter Code from the Options menu and enter 888888.

GROUNDED
Select Enter Code from the Options menu and enter 476863

ONE-HIT TAKEDOWN
Select Enter Code from the Options menu and enter 663448

INFINITE SHARD DURATION
Select Enter Code from the Options menu and enter 742737

THROWN OBJECT TAKEDOWN
Select Enter Code from the Options menu and enter 847936

MARVEL: ULTIMATE ALLIANCE 2

GOD MODE
At any point during a game, press Up, Up, Down, Down, Left, Right, Down.

GIVE MONEY
At the Team Select or Hero Details screen press Up, Up, Down, Down, Up, Up, Up, Down.

UNLOCK ALL POWERS
At the Team Select or Hero Details screen press Up, Up, Down, Down, Left, Right, Right, Left.

ADVANCE ALL CHARACTERS TO L99
At the Hero Details screen press Down, Up, Left, Up, Right, Up, Left, Down.

UNLOCK ALL BONUS MISSIONS
While using the Bonus Mission Simulator, press Up, Right, Down, Left, Left, Right, Up, Up.

ADD 1 CHARACTER LEVEL
During a game, press Down, Up, Right, Up, Right, Up, Right, Down.

ADD 10 CHARACTER LEVELS
During a game, press Down, Up, Left, Up, Left, Up, Left, Down.

MEDAL OF HONOR: VANGUARD

EXTRA ARMOR
Pause the game and press Up, Down, Up, Down to get the Enter Cheat Code message. Then, press Right, Left, Right, Down, Up, Right.

MERCENARIES 2: WORLD IN FLAMES

$1,000,000
At the Faction menu, press Right, Down, Left, Up, Up, Left, Down, Right.

INFINITE AMMO
At the Faction menu, press Right, Left, Right, Right, Left, Right, Left, Left.

INFINITE HEALTH
At the Faction menu, press Press Up, Down, Up, Down, Left, Right, Left, Right.

ALL FACTIONS TO NEUTRAL
At the Faction menu, press Up, Up, Up, Up, Down, Down, Right, Left.

MLB 08: THE SHOW

ALL CLASSIC STADIUMS
At the Main menu, press Down, Right, ●, ●, Left, ▲, Up, L1. The controller will vibrate if entered correctly.

ALL GOLDEN & SILVER ERA PLAYERS IN EXHIBITION
At the Main menu, press L1, L2, ●, ●, ▲, ●, Down. The controller will vibrate if entered correctly.

MX VS. ATV UNTAMED

EVERYTHING
Select Cheat Codes from the Options menu and enter YOUGOTIT.

1000000 STORE POINTS
Select Cheat Codes from the Options menu and enter MANYZEROS.

50CC BIKE CLASS
Select Cheat Codes from the Options menu and enter LITTLEGUY.

ALL BIKES
Select Cheat Codes from the Options menu and enter ONRAILS.

ALL CHALLENGES
Select Cheat Codes from the Options menu and enter MORESTUFF.

ALL FREESTYLE TRACKS
Select Cheat Codes from the Options menu and enter ALLSTYLE.

ALL GEAR
Select Cheat Codes from the Options menu and enter WELLDRESSED.

ALL MACHINES
Select Cheat Codes from the Options menu and enter MCREWHEELS.

ALL RIDERS
Select Cheat Codes from the Options menu and enter WHOSTHAT.

ALL TRACKS
Select Cheat Codes from the Options menu and enter FREETICKET.

MONSTER TRUCK
Select Cheat Codes from the Options menu and enter PWNAGE.

NARUTO: ULTIMATE NINJA 2

In Naruto's house, select Input Password. Here you are able to enter an element, then three signs. Enter the following here:

1,000 RYO
Water, Hare, Monkey, Monkey
Water, Ram, Horse, Dog
Water, Horse, Horse, Horse
Water, Rat, Rooster, Boar
Water, Rat, Monkey, Rooster
Fire, Rat, Dragon, Dog

5,000 RYO
Water, Tiger, Dragon, Tiger
Water, Snake, Rooster, Horse

10,000 RYO
Fire, Tiger, Tiger, Rooster
Fire, Tiger, Dragon, Hare

OVERLOAD

PLAYSTATION 2

NASCAR 09

WALMART TRACK AND THE WALMART CAR
In Chase for the Sprint Cup, enter the driver's name as WalMart EveryDay.

NBA 09 THE INSIDE

ALL-STAR 09 EAST
Select Trophy Room from the Options. Press L1, then ⊙, and enter SHPNV2K699.

ALL-STAR 09 WEST
Select Trophy Room from the Options. Press L1, then ⊙, and enter K8AV6YMLNF.

ALL TROPHIES
Select Trophy Room from the Options. Press L1, then ⊙, and enter K@ZZ@@M!.

LA LAKERS LATIN NIGHTS
Select Trophy Room from the Options. Press L1, then ⊙, and enter NMTWCTC84S.

MIAMI HEAT LATIN NIGHTS
Select Trophy Room from the Options. Press L1, then ⊙, and enter WCTGSA8SPD.

PHOENIX SUNS LATIN NIGHTS
Select Trophy Room from the Options. Press L1, then ⊙, and enter LKUTSENFJH.

SAN ANTONIO LATIN NIGHTS
Select Trophy Room from the Options. Press L1, then ⊙, and enter JFHSY73MYD.

NBA 2K10

ABA BALL
Select Codes from Options and enter payrespect.

NBA 2K TEAM
Select Codes from Options and enter nba2k.

2K SPORTS TEAM
Select Codes from Options and enter 2ksports.

VISUAL CONCEPTS TEAM
Select Codes from Options and enter vcteam.

NBA 2K11

2K CHINA TEAM
In Features, select Codes from the Extras menu. Choose Enter Code and input 2kchina.

2K SPORTS TEAM
In Features, select Codes from the Extras menu. Choose Enter Code and input 2Ksports.

NBA 2K TEAM
In Features, select Codes from the Extras menu. Choose Enter Code and input nba2k.

VC TEAM
In Features, select Codes from the Extras menu. Choose Enter Code and input vcteam.

ABA BALL
In Features, select Codes from the Extras menu. Choose Enter Code and input payrespect.

NEED FOR SPEED PROSTREET

$2,000
Select Career and then choose Code Entry. Enter 1MA9X99.

$4,000
Select Career and then choose Code Entry. Enter W2IOLL01.

$8,000
Select Career and then choose Code Entry. Enter L1IS97A1.

$10,000
Select Career and then choose Code Entry. Enter 1MI9K7E1.

$10,000
Select Career and then choose Code Entry. Enter CASHMONEY.

$10,000
Select Career and then choose Code Entry. Enter REGGAME.

AUDI TT
Select Career and then choose Code Entry. Enter ITSABOUTYOU.

CHEVELLE SS
Select Career and then choose Code Entry. Enter HORSEPOWER.

COKE ZERO GOLF GTI
Select Career and then choose Code Entry. Enter COKEZERO.

DODGE VIPER
Select Career and then choose Code Entry. Enter WORLDSLONGESTLASTING.

MITSUBISHI LANCER EVOLUTION
Select Career and then choose Code Entry. Enter MITSUBISHIGOFAR.

UNLOCK ALL BONUSES
Select Career and then choose Code Entry. Enter UNLOCKALLTHINGS.

5 REPAIR MARKERS
Select Career and then choose Code Entry. Enter SAFETYNET.

ENERGIZER VINYL
Select Career and then choose Code Entry. Enter ENERGIZERLITHIUM.

CASTROL SYNTEC VINYL
Select Career and then choose Code Entry. Enter CASTROLSYNTEC. This also gives you $10,000.

NHL 09

UNLOCK 3RD JERSEYS
At the Cheat menu, enter xe6377uyrwm48frf.

NICKTOONS: ATTACK OF THE TOYBOTS

DAMAGE BOOST
Select Cheats from the Extras menu. Choose Enter Cheat Code and enter 456645.

INVULNERABILITY
Select Cheats from the Extras menu. Choose Enter Cheat Code and enter 313456.

UNLOCK EXO-HUGGLES 9000
Select Cheats from the Extras menu. Choose Enter Cheat Code and enter 691427.

UNLOCK MR. HUGGLES
Select Cheats from the Extras menu. Choose Enter Cheat Code and enter 654168.

UNLIMITED LOBBER GOO
Select Cheats from the Extras menu. Choose Enter Cheat Code and enter 118147.

UNLIMITED SCATTER GOO
Select Cheats from the Extras menu. Choose Enter Cheat Code and enter 971238.

UNLIMITED SPLITTER GOO
Select Cheats from the Extras menu. Choose Enter Cheat Code and enter 854511.

OVER THE HEDGE

COMPLETE LEVELS
Pause the game, hold L1 + R1 and press ▲, ●, ▲, ●, ●, ■.

ALL MINI-GAMES
Pause the game, hold L1 + R1 and press ▲, ●, ▲, ▲, ●, ■.

MORE HP FROM FOOD
Pause the game, hold L1 + R1 and press ▲, ●, ▲, ●, ■, ▲.

ALWAYS POWER PROJECTILE
Pause the game, hold L1 + R1 and press ▲, ●, ▲, ●, ■, ●.

BONUS COMIC 14
Pause the game, hold L1 + R1 and press ▲, ●, ■, ●, ●, ▲.

BONUS COMIC 15
Pause the game, hold L1 + R1 and press ▲, ▲, ●, ●, ■, ●.

PRINCE OF PERSIA: THE TWO THRONES

BABY TOY HAMMER WEAPON
Pause the game and press Left, Left, Right, Right, ●, ■, ■, ●, Up, Down.

CHAINSAW WEAPON
Pause the game and press Up, Up, Down, Down, Left, Right, Left, Right, ●, ■, ●, ■.

SWORDFISH WEAPON
Pause the game and press Up, Down, Up, Down, Left, Right, Left, Right, ●, ■, ●, ■.

TELEPHONE OF SORROW WEAPON
Pause the game and press Left, Right, Left, Right, ●, ■, ●, ●, ■, ●.

RATCHET AND CLANK: UP YOUR ARSENAL

DUEL BLADE LASER SWORD
Pause the game and press ◉, ◉, ◉, ◉, Up, Down, Left, Left.

QWARK'S ALTERNATE COSTUME
Start a game of Qwark Vid-Comic and press Up, Up, Down, Down, Left, Right, ◉, ◉, ◉.

PIRATE VS NINJA MINI-GAME
At the Qwark Comics Issue select, press ◉ to bring up a password screen. Enter _MEGHAN_ as a password.

4-PLAYER BOMB MINI-GAME
At the Qwark Comics Issue select, press ◉ to bring up a password screen. Enter YING_TZU as a password. Press Start, Select to return to Starship Phoenix.

SLY 2: BAND OF THIEVES DEMO
At the Title screen, hold L1 + L2 + R1 + R2.

RESERVOIR DOGS

UNLIMITED AMMO
Select Cheats from the Extras menu and press R2, L2, ◉, L2, ✪, R2.

ALL LEVELS
Select Cheats from the Extras menu and press L2, R2, L2, R2, L1, R1.

ART GALLERY
Select Cheats from the Extras menu and press ◉, ✪, L2, R2, ◉, ✪.

MOVIE GALLERY
Select Cheats from the Extras menu and press L1, L1, ◉, ✪, L1, R1.

RESIDENT EVIL 4

ALTERNATE TITLE SCREEN
Complete the game.

MATILDA
Complete the game.

MERCENARIES
Complete the game.

PROFESSIONAL DIFFICULTY
Complete the game.

SEPERATE WAYS
Complete the game.

ASHLEY'S ARMOR OUTFIT
Defeat Separate Ways.

LEON'S GANGSTER OUTFIT
Defeat Separate Ways.

ROBOTS

BIG HEAD
Pause the game and press Up, Down, Down, Up, Right, Right, Left, Right.

UNLIMITED HEALTH
Pause the game and press Up, Right, Down, Up, Left, Down, Right, Left.

UNLIMITED SCRAP
Pause the game and press Down, Down, Left, Up, Up, Right, Up, Down.

ROCK BAND

ALL SONGS
At the Title screen, press Red, Yellow, Blue, Red, Red, Blue, Blue, Red, Yellow, Blue. Using this code disables the ability to save your game.

SAKURA WARS: SO LONG, MY LOVE

ALL EVENTS
In Free & Easy Day in N.Y., visit Romando and enter 111374572138 as a password.

ALL PHOTOS
In Free & Easy Day in N.Y., visit Romando and enter 966213278048 as a password.

ALL RINGTONES
In Free & Easy Day in N.Y., visit Romando and enter 113742917238 as a password.

PASSWORDS
In Free & Easy Day in N.Y., visit Romando and enter the following as passwords.

PASSWORD	UNLOCKS
114005404218	Photograph 1
172845219998	Photograph 2
196725818238	Photograph 3
153265510968	Photograph 4
135585779248	Photograph 5
187039076518	Photograph 6
161859270498	Photograph 7
160799895538	Photograph 8
122279596468	Photograph 9
146519751548	Photograph 10
103407055018	Photograph 11
715304330718	Photograph 12
779144989698	Photograph 13
791624186738	Photograph 14
790962480668	Photograph 15
752482665748	Photograph 16
736332366218	Photograph 17
788152921998	Photograph 18
765692125238	Photograph 19
729976422968	Photograph 20
741416641248	Photograph 21

PASSWORD	UNLOCKS
740506343518	Photograph 22
702046942498	Photograph 23
916826107538	Photograph 24
978768403468	Photograph 25
995288604548	Photograph 26
959538817018	Photograph 27
931058518398	Photograph 28
930898714038	Photograph 29
984773079368	Photograph 30
119880017018	Ringtone: Gemini
117301583548	Ringtone: Cheiron
111088841698	Ringtone: Rosita
111391416468	Ringtone: Diana
111379387198	Ringtone: Subaru
111374272018	Ringtone: Ratchet
111315063698	Special Event 1
111374210238	Special Event 2
111315455138	Special Event 3
111315453168	Unlock Shinjiro's Girl Costume

SAMURAI JACK: THE SHADOW OF AKU

MAXIMUM HEALTH
During a game, hold Left on the Left Analog Stick + Right on the Right Analog Stick and press ✕, ●, ▲, ■.

MAXIMUM ZEN
During a game, hold Left on the Left Analog Stick + Right on the Right Analog Stick and press ●, ✕, ■, ▲.

CRYSTAL SWORD
During a game, press Left on the Left Analog Stick Down + Up on the Right Analog Stick and press ✕, ●, ■, ▲.

FIRE SWORD
During a game, press Down on the Left Analog Stick + Up on the Right Analog Stick and press ●, ✕, ●, ▲.

LIGHTNING SWORD
During a game, press Down on the Left Analog Stick + Up on the Right Analog Stick and press ●, ✕, ▲, ■.

SCARFACE: THE WORLD IS YOURS

After entering the following Cheats, highlight the cheat and press A to "DO IT."

MAX AMMO
Pause the game, select Cheats and enter AMMO.

REFILL HEALTH
Pause the game, select Cheats and enter MEDIK.

FILL BALLS METER
Pause the game, select Cheats and enter FPATCH.

KILL TONY
Pause the game, select Cheats and enter KILTONY.

DECREASE COP HEAT
Pause the game, select Cheats and enter FLYSTRT.

INCREASE COP HEAT
Pause the game, select Cheats and enter DONUT.

DECREASE GANG HEAT
Pause the game, select Cheats and enter NOBALLS.

INCREASE GANG HEAT
Pause the game, select Cheats and enter GOBALLS.

REPAIR TONY'S VEHICLE
Pause the game, select Cheats and enter TBURGLR.

SPAWN ARIEL MK III
Pause the game, select Cheats and enter OLDFAST.

SPAWN BACINARI
Pause the game, select Cheats and enter 666999.

SPAWN BODOG STAMPEDE
Pause the game, select Cheats and enter BUMMER.

SPAWN BULLDOZER
Pause the game, select Cheats and enter DOZER.

SPAWN ODIN VH88
Pause the game, select Cheats and enter DUMPER.

BLACK SUIT TONY
Pause the game, select Cheats and enter BLACK.

BLUE PINSTRIPE SUIT TONY WITH SHADES
Pause the game, select Cheats and enter BLUESH.

GRAY SUIT TONY
Pause the game, select Cheats and enter GRAY.

GRAY SUIT TONY WITH SHADES
Pause the game, select Cheats and enter GRAYSH.

HAWAIIAN SHIRT TONY
Pause the game, select Cheats and enter HAWAII.

HAWAIIAN SHIRT TONY WITH SHADES
Pause the game, select Cheats and enter HAWAIIG.

SANDY SHIRT TONY
Pause the game, select Cheats and enter SANDY.

SANDY SHIRT TONY WITH SHADES
Pause the game, select Cheats and enter SANDYSH.

WHITE SUIT TONY
Pause the game, select Cheats and enter WHITE.

WHITE SUIT TONY WITH SHADES
Pause the game, select Cheats and enter WHITESH.

CHANGE TIME OF DAY
Pause the game, select Cheats and enter MARTHA.

TOGGLE LIGHTNING
Pause the game, select Cheats and enter SHAZAAM.

TOGGLE RAIN
Pause the game, select Cheats and enter RAINY.

BREAL "THE WORLD IS YOURS" MUSIC TRACK
Pause the game, select Cheats and enter TUNEME.

SCOOBY-DOO! FIRST FRIGHTS

DAPHNE'S SECRET COSTUME
Select Codes from the Extras menu and enter 2839.

FRED'S SECRET COSTUME
Select Codes from the Extras menu and enter 4826.

SCOOBY DOO'S SECRET COSTUME
Select Codes from the Extras menu and enter 1585.

SHAGGY'S SECRET COSTUME
Select Codes from the Extras menu and enter 3726.

VELMA'S SECRET COSTUME
Select Codes from the Extras menu and enter 6588.

THE SECRET SATURDAYS: BEASTS OF THE 5TH SUN

ALL LEVELS
Select Enter Secret Code from the Secrets menu and input Zon, Zon, Zon, Zon.

UNLOCK AMAROK TO BE SCANNED IN LEVEL 2
Select Enter Secret Code from the Secrets menu and input Fiskerton, Zak, Zon, Komodo.

UNLOCK BISHOPVILLE LIZARDMAN TO BE SCANNED IN LEVEL 3
Select Enter Secret Code from the Secrets menu and input Komodo, Zon, Zak, Komodo.

UNLOCK NAGA TO BE SCANNED IN LEVEL 7
Select Enter Secret Code from the Secrets menu and input Zak, Zak, Zon, Fiskerton.

UNLOCK RAKSHASA TO BE SCANNED IN LEVEL 8
Select Enter Secret Code from the Secrets menu and input Zak, Komodo, Fiskerton, Fiskerton.

UNLOCK BILOKO TO BE SCANNED IN LEVEL 9
Select Enter Secret Code from the Secrets menu and input Zon, Zak, Zon, Fiskerton.

Before using the following cheats, select the ABC Control option. This sets the controller to the following: ● is A, ✪ is B, ● is C.

ALTERED BEAST

OPTIONS MENU
At the title screen, hold B and press Start.

LEVEL SELECT
After enabling the Options menu, select a level from the menu. At the title screen, hold A and press Start.

BEAST SELECT
At the title screen, hold A + B + C + Down/Left and then press Start

SOUND TEST
At the title screen, hold A + C + Up/Right and press Start.

COMIX ZONE

INVINCIBILITY
At the jukebox screen, press C on the following sounds:
3, 12, 17, 2, 2, 10, 2, 7, 7, 11

LEVEL SELECT
At the jukebox screen, press C on the following sounds:
14, 15, 18, 5, 13, 1, 3, 18, 15, 6
Press C on the desired level.

ECCO THE DOLPHIN

INVINCIBILITY
When the level name appears, hold A + Start until the level begins.

DEBUG MENU
Pause the game with Ecco facing the screen and press Right, B, C, B, C, Down, C, Up.

INFINITE AIR
Enter LIFEFISH as a password.

PASSWORDS

LEVEL	PASSWORD	LEVEL	PASSWORD
The Undercaves	WEFIDNMP	Deep City	DDXPQQLJ
The Vents	BQDPXJDS	City of Forever	MSDBRQLA
The Lagoon	JNSBRIKY	Jurassic Beach	IYCBUNLB
Ridge Water	NTSBZTKB	Pteranodon Pond	DMXEUNLI
Open Ocean	YWGTTJNI	Origin Beach	EGRIUNLB
Ice Zone	HZIFZBMF	Trilobite Circle	IELMUNLB
Hard Water	LRFJRQLI	Dark Water	RKEQUNLN
Cold Water	UYNFRQLC	City of Forever 2	HPQIGPLA
Island Zone	LYTIOQLZ	The Tube	JUMFKMLB
Deep Water	MNOPOQLR	The Machine	GXUBKMLF
The Marble	RJNTQQLZ	The Last Fight	TSONLMLU
The Library	RTGXQQLE		

FLICKY

ROUND SELECT
Begin a new game. Before the first round appears, hold A + C + Up + Start. Press Up or Down to select a Round.

GAIN GROUND

LEVEL SELECT
At the Options screen, press A, C, B, C.

GOLDEN AXE

LEVEL SELECT
Select Arcade Mode. At the character select, hold Down/Left + B and press Start. Press Up or Down to select a level.

RISTAR

Select Passwords from the Options menu and enter the following:

LEVEL SELECT
ILOVEU

BOSS RUSH MODE
MUSEUM

TIME ATTACK MODE
DOFEEL

TOUGHER DIFFICULTY
SUPER

ONCHI MUSIC
MAGURO. Activate this from the Sound Test.

CLEARS PASSWORD
XXXXXX

GAME COPYRIGHT INFO
AGES

SONIC THE HEDGEHOG

LEVEL SELECT
At the title screen, press Up, Down, Left, Right. Hold A and press Start.

SONIC THE HEDGEHOG 2

LEVEL SELECT
Select Sound Test from the options. Press C on the following sounds in order: 19, 65, 09, 17. At the title screen, hold A and press Start.

VECTORMAN

DEBUG MODE
At the options screen, press A, B, B, A, Down, A, B, B, A.

REFILL LIFE
Pause the game and press A, B, Right, A, C, A, Down, A, B, Right, A.

VECTORMAN 2

LEVEL SELECT
Pause the game and press Up, Right, A, B, A, Down, Left, A, Down.

EXTRA LIFE
Pause the game and press Right, Up, B, A, Down, Up, B, Down, Up, B. Repeat for more lives.

FULL ENERGY
Pause the game and press B, A, B, A, Left, Up, Up.

NEW WEAPON
Pause the game and press C, A, Left, Left, Down, A, Down. Repeat for more weapons.

SEGA SUPERSTARS TENNIS

UNLOCK CHARACTERS
Complete the following missions to unlock the corresponding character.

CHARACTER	COMPLETE THIS MISSION
Alex Kidd	Mission 1 of Alex Kidd's World
Amy Rose	Mission 2 of Sonic the Hedgehog's World
Gilius	Mission 1 of Golden Axe's World
Gum	Mission 12 of Jet Grind Radio's World
Meemee	Mission 8 of Super Monkey Ball's World
Pudding	Mission 1 of Space Channel 5's World
Reala	Mission 2 of NiGHTs' World
Shadow The Hedgehog	Mission 14 of Sonic the Hedgehog's World

SHAMAN KING: POWER OF SPIRIT

VERSUS MODE
Complete all 20 episodes in Story Mode.

MASKED MERIL IN VERSUS MODE
Press Select on Meril.

MATILDA IN VERSUS MODE
Press Select on Kanna.

MARION FAUNA IN VERSUS MODE
Press Select on Matilda.

ZEKE ASAKURA IN VERSUS MODE
Press Select on Yoh Asakura.

SHREK THE THIRD

10,000 GOLD COINS
At the gift shop, press Up, Up, Down, Up, Right, Left.

SILENT HILL: ORIGINS

CODEBREAKER SUIT
During a game, press Up, Up, Down, Down, Left, Right, Left, Right, ✕, ◉.
You must first finish the game to get this suit.

THE SIMPSONS GAME

UNLIMITED POWER FOR ALL CHARACTERS
At the Extras menu, press ◉, Left, Right, ◉, ◉, L1.

ALL CLICHÉS.
At the Extras menu, press Left, ◉, Right, ◉, Right, L1.

ALL MOVIES
At the Extras menu, press ◉, Left, ◉, Right, ◉, R1.

THE SIMS 2: CASTAWAY

CHEAT GNOME
During a game, press R1, L1, Down, ◉, R2. You can now use this Gnome to get the following:

EXCLUSIVE VEST AND TANKTOP
Pause the game and go to Fashion and Grooming. Press ◉, R2, R2, ◉, Down.

MAX ALL MOTIVES
During a game, press R2, Up, X, ◉, L1.

MAX CURRENT INVENTORY
During a game, press Left, Right, ◉, R2, ◉.

MAX RELATIONSHIPS
During a game, press L1, Up, R2, Left, ◉.

ALL RESOURCES
During a game, press ◉, ◉, Down, X, Left.

ALL CRAFTING PLANS
During a game, press X, ◉, L2, ◉, R1.

ADD 1 TO SKILL
During a game, press ◉, L1, L1, Left, ◉.

THE SIMS 2: PETS

CHEAT GNOME
During a game, press L1, L1, R1, ✕, ✕, Up.

GIVE SIM PET POINTS
After activating the Cheat Gnome, press ◉, ◉, ✕, ◉, L1, R1 during a game. Select the Gnome to access the cheat.

ADVANCE 6 HOURS
After activating the Cheat Gnome, press Up, Left, Down, Right, R1 during a game. Select the Gnome to access the cheat.

GIVE SIM SIMOLEONS
After activating the Cheat Gnome, enter the Advance 6 Hours cheat. Access the Gnome and exit. Enter the cheat again. Now, Give Sim Simoleons should be available from the Gnome.

CAT AND DOG CODES
When creating a family, press ◉ to Enter Unlock Code. Enter the following for new fur patterns.

FUR PATTERN/CAT OR DOG	UNLOCK CODE
Bandit Mask Cats	EEGJ2YRQZZAIZ9QHA64
Bandit Mask Dogs	EEGJ2YRQZQARQ9QHA64
Black Dot Cats	EEGJ2YRZQQ1IQ9QHA64
Black Dot Dogs	EEGJ2YRQZZ1IQ9QHA64
Black Smiley Cats	EEGJ2YRQQZ1RQ9QHA64
Black Smiley Dogs	EEGJ2YRZQQARQ9QHA64
Blue Bones Cats	EEGJ2YRQZZARQ9QHA64
Blue Bones Dogs	EEGJ2YRZZZ1IZ9QHA64
Blue Camouflage Cats	EEGJ2YRZZQ1IQ9QHA64
Blue Camouflage Dogs	EEGJ2YRZZZ1RQ9QHA64

FUR PATTERN/CAT OR DOG	UNLOCK CODE
Blue Cats	EEGJ2YRQZZAIQ9QHA64
Blue Dogs	EEGJ2YRQQQ1IZ9QHA64
Blue Star Cats	EEGJ2YRQQZ1IZ9QHA64
Blue Star Dogs	EEGJ2YRQZQ1IQ9QHA64
Deep Red Cats	EEGJ2YRQQQAIQ9QHA64
Deep Red Dogs	EEGJ2YRQQQ1RQ9QHA64
Goofy Cats	EEGJ2YRQZQ1IZ9QHA64
Goofy Dogs	EEGJ2YRZZZARQ9QHA64
Green Cats	EEGJ2YRZQQAIZ9QHA64
Green Dogs	EEGJ2YRQZQAIQ9QHA64
Green Flower Cats	EEGJ2YRZQZAIQ9QHA64
Green Flower Dogs	EEGJ2YRZQQ1RQ9QHA64
Light Green Cats	EEGJ2YRZZZ1RQ9QHA64
Light Green Dogs	EEGJ2YRZQQ1RQ9QHA64
Navy Hearts Cats	EEGJ2YRQZQZ1IQ9QHA64
Navy Hearts Dogs	EEGJ2YRQQZ1IQ9QHA64
Neon Green Cats	EEGJ2YRZZQAIQ9QHA64
Neon Green Dogs	EEGJ2YRZQQAIQ9QHA64
Neon Yellow Cats	EEGJ2YRZZQARQ9QHA64
Neon Yellow Dogs	EEGJ2YRQQQAIZ9QHA64
Orange Diagonal Cats	EEGJ2YRQQZAIQ9QHA64
Orange Diagonal Dogs	EEGJ2YRZQZ1IZ9QHA64
Panda Cats	EEGJ2YRQZQAIZ9QHA64
Pink Cats	EEGJ2YRQZZ1IZ9QHA64
Pink Dogs	EEGJ2YRZQZ1RQ9QHA64
Pink Vertical Strip Cats	EEGJ2YRQQQARQ9QHA64
Pink Vertical Strip Dogs	EEGJ2YRZZZAIQ9QHA64
Purple Cats	EEGJ2YRQQZARQ9QHA64
Purple Dogs	EEGJ2YRQQZAIZ9QHA64
Star Cats	EEGJ2YRQZQARQ9QHA64
Star Dogs	EEGJ2YRZQZAIZ9QHA64
White Paws Cats	EEGJ2YRQQQ1RQ9QHA64
White Paws Dogs	EEGJ2YRZQZQ1RQ9QHA64
White Zebra Stripe Cats	EEGJ2YRZZQ1IZ9QHA64
White Zebra Stripe Dogs	EEGJ2YRZZZ1IQ9QHA64
Zebra Stripes Dogs	EEGJ2YRZZQAIZ9QHA64

SLY 3: HONOR AMONG THIEVES

TOONAMI PLANE
While flying the regular plane, pause the game and press R1, R1, Right, Down, Down, Right.

RESTART EPISODES
Pause the game during the Episode and enter the following codes to restart that Episode. You must first complete that part of the Episode to use the code.

EPISODE	CODE
Episode 1, Day 1	Left, R2, Right, L1, R2, L1
Episode 1, Day 2	Down, L2, Up, Left, R2, L2
Episode 2, Day 1	Right, L2, Left, Up, Right, Down
Episode 2, Day 2	Down, Up, R1, Up, R2, L2
Episode 3, Day 1	R2, R1, L1, Left, L1, Down
Episode 3, Day 2	L2, R1, R2, L2, L1, Up
Episode 4, Day 1	Left, Right, L1, R2, Right, R2
Episode 4, Day 2	L1, Left, L2, Left, Up, L1
Episode 5, Day 1	Left, R2, Right, Up, L1, R2
Episode 5, Day 2	R2, R1, L1, R1, R2, R1
Operation Laptop Retrieval	L2, Left, R1, L2, L1, Down
Operation Moon Crash	L2, Up, Left, L1, L2, L1
Operation Reverse Double Cross	Right, Left, Up, Left, R2, Left
Operation Tar Be-Gone	Down, L2, R1, L2, R1, Right
Operation Turbo Dominant Eagle	Down, Right, Left, L2, R1, Right
Operation Wedding Crasher	L2, R2, Right, Down, L1, R2

SOCOM 3: U.S. NAVY SEALS

DISPLAY COORDINATES
Pause the game and press ●, ▲, ◉, ◉, L1, ▲, ◉, ◉, ▲, ⬤.

SOCOM U.S. NAVY SEALS: COMBINED ASSAULT

SHOW COORDINATES
Pause the game and press ●, ▲, ◉, ◉, L1, ▲, ◉, ◉, ▲, ⬤.

THE SOPRANOS: ROAD TO RESPECT

INFINITE AMMO
During a game, hold L2 + R2 and press ◉, ●, ✖, ●, ▲, ▲.

INFINITE RESPECT
During a game, hold L2 + R2 and press ✖, ●, ✖, ●, ▲, ▲.

SPIDER-MAN: FRIEND OR FOE

NEW GREEN GOBLIN AS A SIDEKICK
While standing in the Helicarrier between levels, press Left, Down, Right, Right, Down, Left.

VENOM AS A SIDEKICK
While standing in the Helicarrier between levels, press Left, Left, Right, Up, Down, Down.

SANDMAN AS A SIDEKICK
While standing in the Helicarrier between levels, press Right, Right, Right, Up, Down, Left.

5000 TECH TOKENS
While standing in the Helicarrier between levels, press Up, Up, Down, Down, Left, Right.

THE SPIDERWICK CHRONICLES

INVULNERABILITY
During the game, hold L1 + R1 and press ▲, ◉, ▲, ▲, ✖, ✖, ▲, ▲.

HEAL
During the game, hold L1 + R1 and press ▲, ●, ✖, ◉, ▲, ●, ✖, ●.

COMBAT LOADOUT
During the game, hold L1 + R1 and press ▲, ◉, ✖, ✖, ●, ◉, ●, ◉.

INFINITE AMMO
During the game, hold L1 + R1 and press ●, ◉, ●, ◉, ✖, ✖, ✖, ▲.

FIELD GUIDE UNLOCKED
During the game, hold L1 + R1 and press ◉, ◉, ◉, ●, ▲, ▲, ▲, ✖.

SPRITE A
During the game, hold L2 + R2 and press ▲, ✖, ◉, ●, ✖, ▲, ●, ◉.

SPRITE B
During the game, hold L2 + R2 and press ✖, ✖, ▲, ●, ●, ◉, ▲, ✖.

SPRITE C
During the game, hold L2 + R2 and press ◉, ▲, ●, ✖, ◉, ▲, ●, ✖.

SPONGEBOB SQUAREPANTS: CREATURE FROM THE KRUSTY KRAB

30,000 EXTRA Z'S
Select Cheat Codes from the Extras menu and enter ROCFISH.

PUNK SPONGEBOB IN DIESEL DREAMING
Select Cheat Codes from the Extras menu and enter SPONGE. Select Activate Bonus Items to enable this bonus item.

HOT ROD SKIN IN DIESEL DREAMING
Select Cheat Codes from the Extras menu and enter HOTROD. Select Activate Bonus Items to enable this bonus item.

PATRICK TUX IN STARFISHMAN TO THE RESCUE
Select Cheat Codes from the Extras menu and enter PATRICK. Select Activate Bonus Items to enable this bonus item.

SPONGEBOB PLANKTON IN SUPER-SIZED PATTY
Select Cheat Codes from the Extras menu and enter PANTS. Select Activate Bonus Items to enable this bonus item.

PATRICK LASER COLOR IN ROCKET RODEO
Select Cheat Codes from the Extras menu and enter ROCKET. Select Activate Bonus Items to enable this bonus item.

PATRICK ROCKET SKIN COLOR IN ROCKET RODEO
Select Cheat Codes from the Extras menu and enter SPACE. Select Activate Bonus Items to enable this bonus item.

PLANKTON EYE LASER COLOR IN REVENGE OF THE GIANT PLANKTON MONSTER
Select Cheat Codes from the Extras menu and enter LASER. Select Activate Bonus Items to enable this bonus item.

PIRATE PATRICK IN ROOFTOP RUMBLE
Select Cheat Codes from the Extras menu and enter PIRATE. Select Activate Bonus Items to enable this bonus item.

HOVERCRAFT VEHICLE SKIN IN HYPNOTIC HIGHWAY—PLANKTON
Select Cheat Codes from the Extras menu and enter HOVER. Select Activate Bonus Items to enable this bonus item.

SPONGEBOB SQUAREPANTS FEATURING NICKTOONS: GLOBS OF DOOM

When entering the following codes, the order of the characters going down is: SpongeBob SquarePants, Nicolai Technus, Danny Phantom, Dib, Zim, Tlaloc, Tak, Beautiful Gorgeous, Jimmy Neutron, Plankton. These names are shortened to the first name in the following.

ATTRACT COINS
Using the Upgrade Machine on the bottom level of the lair, select "Input cheat codes here". Enter Tlaloc, Plankton, Danny, Plankton, Tak. Coins are attracted to you making them much easier to collect.

DON'T LOSE COINS
Using the Upgrade Machine on the bottom level of the lair, select "Input cheat codes here". Enter Plankton, Jimmy, Beautiful, Jimmy, Plankton. You don't lose coins when you get knocked out.

GOO HAS NO EFFECT
Using the Upgrade Machine on the bottom level of the lair, select "Input cheat codes here". Enter Danny, Danny, Danny, Nicolai, Nicolai. Goo does not slow you down.

MORE GADGET COMBO TIME
Using the Upgrade Machine on the bottom level of the lair, select "Input cheat codes here". Enter SpongeBob, Beautiful, Danny, Plankton, Nicolai. You have more time to perform gadget combos.

SPY HUNTER: NOWHERE TO RUN

SPY HUNTER ARCADE
You must activate the machine when you come across it in the safe house on Level 7 (Cleaning Up).

SSX ON TOUR

NEW THREADS
Select Cheats from the Extras menu and enter FLYTHREADS.

THE WORLD IS YOURS
Select Cheats from the Extras menu and enter BACKSTAGEPASS.

SHOW TIME (ALL MOVIES)
Select Cheats from the Extras menu and enter THEBIGPICTURE.

BLING BLING (INFINITE CASH)
Select Cheats from the Extras menu and enter LOOTSNOOT.

FULL BOOST, FULL TIME
Select Cheats from the Extras menu and enter ZOOMJUICE.

MONSTERS ARE LOOSE (MONSTER TRICKS)
Select Cheats from the Extras menu and enter JACKALOPESTYLE.

SNOWBALL FIGHT
Select Cheats from the Extras menu and enter LETSPARTY.

FEEL THE POWER (STAT BOOST)
Select Cheats from the Extras menu and enter POWERPLAY.

CHARACTERS ARE LOOSE
Select Cheats from the Extras menu and enter ROADIEROUNDUp.

UNLOCK CONRAD
Select Cheats from the Extras menu and enter BIGPARTYTIME.

UNLOCK MITCH KOOBSKI
Select Cheats from the Extras menu and enter MOREFUNTHANONE.

UNLOCK NIGEL
Select Cheats from the Extras menu and enter THREEISACROWD.

UNLOCK SKI PATROL
Select Cheats from the Extras menu and enter FOURSOME.

STAR TREK: ENCOUNTERS

ALL LEVELS AND SHIPS
Get a high score in Onslaught Mode and enter your name as 4jstudios.

ALL CREW CARDS
Get a high score in Onslaught Mode and enter your name as Bethesda.

STAR WARS: BATTLEFRONT II

INFINITE AMMO
Pause the game, hold L2 + R2 and press Up, Down, Left, Down, Down, Left, Down, Down, Left, Down, Down, Down, Left, Right.

INVINCIBILITY
Pause the game, hold L2 + R2 and press Up, Up, Up, Left, Down, Down, Down, Left, Up, Up, Up, Left, Right.

NO HUD
Pause the game, hold L2 + R2 and press Up, Up, Up, Up, Left, Up, Up, Down, Left, Down, Up, Up, Left, Right. Re-enter the code to enable the HUD again.

ALTERNATE SOLDIERS
Pause the game, hold L2 + R2 and press Down, Down, Down, Up, Up, Left, Down, Down, Down, Down, Down, Left, Up, Up, Up, Left.

ALTERNATE SOUNDS
Pause the game, hold L2 + R2 and press Up, Up, Up, Left, Up, Down, Up, Up, Left, Down, Down, Down, Left, Up, Down, Down, Left, Right.

FUNNY MESSAGES WHEN REBELS DEFEATED
Pause the game, hold L2 + R2 and press Up, Down, Left, Down, Left, Right.

STAR WARS THE CLONE WARS: REPUBLIC HEROES

BIG HEAD MODE
Pause the game, select Shop, and enter the following in Cheats: Up, Down, Left, Right, Left, Right, Down, Up.

MINI-GUN
Pause the game, select Shop, and enter the following in Cheats: Down, Left, Right, Up, Right, Up, Left, Down.

ULTIMATE LIGHTSABER
Pause the game, select Shop, and enter the following in Cheats: Right, Down, Down, Up, Left, Up, Up, Down.

LIGHTSABER THROW UPGRADE
Pause the game, select Shop, and enter the following in Combat Upgrades: Left, Left, Right, Right, Up, Down, Down, Up.

SPIDER DROID UPGRADE
Pause the game, select Shop, and enter the following in Droid-Jak Upgrades: Up, Left, Down, Left, Right, Left, Left, Left.

STAR WARS EPISODE III: REVENGE OF THE SITH

INFINITE FORCE
Select Codes from the Settings menu and enter KAIBURR.

INFINITE HEALTH
Select Codes from the Settings menu and enter XUCPHRA.

QUICK HEALTH & FORCE RESTORATION
Select Codes from the Settings menu and enter BELSAVIS.

ALL STORY, BONUS & CO-OP MISSIONS AND DUELISTS
Select Codes from the Settings menu and enter 021282.

ALL STORY MISSIONS
Select Codes from the Settings menu and enter KORRIBAN.

ALL BONUS MISSIONS
Select Codes from the Settings menu and enter NARSHADDAA.

ALL DUEL ARENAS
Select Codes from the Settings menu and enter TANTIVIEV.

ALL DUELISTS
Select Codes from the Settings menu and enter ZABRAK.

ALL POWERS & MOVES
Select Codes from the Settings menu and enter JAINA.

SUPER LIGHTSABER MODE
Select Codes from the Settings menu and enter SUPERSABERS.

TINY DROID MODE
Select Codes from the Settings menu and enter 071779.

ALL REPLAY MOVIES
Select Codes from the Settings menu and enter COMLINK.

ALL CONCEPT ART
Select Codes from the Settings menu and enter AAYLASECURA.

STAR WARS: THE FORCE UNLEASHED

CHEATS
Once you have accessed the Rogue Shadow, select Enter Code from the Extras menu. Now you can enter the following:

CHEAT	CODE
Invincibility	CORTOSIS
Unlimited Force	VERGENCE
1,000,000 Force Points	SPEEDER
All Force Powers	TYRANUS

CHEAT	CODE
Max Force Power Level	KATARN
Max Combo Level	COUNTDOOKU
Stronger Lightsaber	LIGHTSABER

COSTUMES
Once you have accessed the Rogue Shadow, select Enter Code from the Extras menu. Now you can enter the following codes:

COSTUME	CODE
All Costumes	GRANDMOFF
501st Legion	LEGION
Aayla Secura	AAYLA
Admiral Ackbar	ITSATWAP
Anakin Skywalker	CHOSENONE
Asajj Ventress	ACOLYTE
Ceremonial Jedi Robes	DANTOOINE
Chop'aa Notimo	NOTIMO
Classic stormtrooper	TK421
Count Dooku	SERENNO

COSTUME	CODE
Darth Desolous	PAUAN
Darth Maul	ZABRAK
Darth Phobos	HIDDENFEAR
Darth Vader	SITHLORD
Drexl Roosh	DREXLROOSH
Emperor Palpatine	PALPATINE
General Rahm Kota	MANDALORE
Han Solo	NERFHERDER
Heavy trooper	SHOCKTROOP
Juno Eclipse	ECLIPSE
Kento's Robe	WOOKIEE
Kleef	KLEEF

COSTUME	CODE
Lando Calrissian	SCOUNDREL
Luke Skywalker	T16WOMPRAT
Luke Skywalker (Yavin)	YELLOWJCKT
Mace Windu	JEDIMASTER
Mara Jade	MARAJADE
Maris Brook	MARISBROOD
Navy commando	STORMTROOP

COSTUME	CODE
Obi Wan Kenobi	BENKENOBI
Proxy	HOLOGRAM
Qui Gon Jinn	MAVERICK
Shaak Ti	TOGRUTA
Shadow trooper	INTHEDARK
Sith Robes	HOLOCRON
Sith Stalker Armor	KORRIBAN
Twi'lek	SECURA

STREET FIGHTER ALPHA ANTHOLOGY

STREET FIGHTER ALPHA

PLAY AS DAN

At the character select screen in Arcade Mode, hold the Start button and place the cursor on the Random Select space then input one of the following commands within 1 second:

LP LK MK HK HP MP
HP HK MK LK LP MP
LK LP MP HP HK MK
HK HP MP LP LK HK

PLAY AS M.BISON

At the character select screen, hold the Start button, place the cursor on the random select box, and input:

1P side: Down, Down, Back, Back, Down, Back, Back + LP + HP
2P side: Down, Down, Forward, Forward, Down, Forward, Forward + LP + HP

PLAY AS AKUMA

At the character select screen, hold the Start button, place the cursor on the random select box, and input:

1P side: Down, Down, Down, Back, Back, Back + LP + HP
2P side: Down, Down, Down, Forward, Forward, Forward + LP + HP

AKUMA MODE

Select your character in Arcade mode, then press and hold Start + MP + MK as the character selection screen ends.

RYU AND KEN VS. M.BISON

On both the 1p and 2p side in Arcade mode, press and hold Start, then:

1P side: place the cursor on Ryu and input Up, Up, release Start, Up, Up + LP
2P side: place the cursor on Ken and input Up, Up, release Start, Up, Up + HP

LAST BOSS MODE

Select Arcade mode while holding ●, ⊗, and R1.

DRAMATIC BATTLE MODE

Select Dramatic Battle mode while holding ●, ⊗, and R2.

RANDOM BATTLE MODE

Select Versus mode while holding ●, ⊗, and R2.

STREET FIGHTER ALPHA 2

PLAY AS ORIGINAL CHUN-LI

Highlight Chun-Li on the character select screen, hold the Start button for 3 seconds, then select Chun-Li normally.

PLAY AS SHIN AKUMA

Highlight Akuma on the character select screen, hold the Start button for 3 seconds, then select Akuma normally.

PLAY AS EVIL RYU

Highlight Ryu on the character select screen, hold the Start button, input Forward, Up, Down, Back, then select Ryu normally.

PLAY AS EX DHALSIM

Highlight Dhalsim on the character select screen, hold the Start button, input Back, Down, Forward, Up, then select Dhalsim normally.

PLAY AS EX ZANGIEF

Highlight Zangief on the character select screen, hold the Start button, input Down, Back, Back, Back, Back, Up, Up, Forward, Forward, Forward, Forward, Down, then select Zangief normally.

LAST BOSS MODE

Select Arcade mode while holding the ●, ◉, and R1 buttons.

DRAMATIC BATTLE MODE

Select Dramatic Battle mode while holding the ● + ⊗ + R2.

SELECT SPECIAL ROUTE IN SURVIVAL MODE

Select Survival Battle while holding the R1 or R2.

RANDOM BATTLE MODE

Select Versus mode while holding the ● + ⊗ + R2.

STREET FIGHTER ALPHA 2 GOLD

PLAY AS EX RYU

Highlight Ryu and press the Start button once before selecting normally.

PLAY AS EVIL RYU
Highlight Ryu and press the Start button twice before selecting normally.

PLAY AS ORIGINAL CHUN-LI
Highlight Chun-Li and press the Start button once before selecting normally.

PLAY AS EX CHUN-LI
Highlight Chun-Li and press the Start button twice before selecting normally.

PLAY AS EX KEN
Highlight Ken and press the Start button once before selecting normally.

PLAY AS EX DHALSIM
Highlight Dhalsim and press the Start button once before selecting normally.

PLAY AS EX ZANGIEF
Highlight Zangief and press the Start button once before selecting normally.

PLAY AS EX SAGAT
Highlight Sagat and press the Start button once before selecting normally.

PLAY AS EX M.BISON
Highlight M.Bison and press the Start button once before selecting normally.

PLAY USING SAKURA'S ALTERNATE COLORS
Highlight Sakura and press the Start button five times before selecting normally.

PLAY AS SHIN AKUMA
Highlight Akuma and press the Start button five times before selecting normally.

PLAY AS CAMMY
Highlight M.Bison and press the Start button twice before selecting normally.

HIDDEN MODES

LAST BOSS MODE
Select Arcade mode while holding ● + ● + R1.

SELECT SPECIAL ROUTE IN SURVIVAL MODE
Select Survival Battle while holding the R1 or R2.

DRAMATIC BATTLE MODE
Select Dramatic Battle mode while holding ● + ❷ + R2.

RANDOM BATTLE MODE
Select Versus mode while holding ● + ❷ + R2.

STREET FIGHTER ALPHA 3

PLAY AS BALROG
Highlight Karin for one second, then move the cursor to the random select box and hold Start before selecting normally.

PLAY AS JULI
Highlight Karin for one second, then move the cursor to the random select box and press Up, or Down, while selecting normally.

PLAY AS JUNI
Highlight Karin for one second, then move the cursor to the random select box and press Back, or Forward, while selecting normally.

CLASSICAL MODE
Press and hold HP + HK while starting game.

SPIRITED MODE
Press and hold MP + MK while starting game.

SAIKYO MODE
Press and hold LP + LK while starting game.

SHADALOO MODE
Press and hold LK + MK + HK while starting game.

SELECT SPECIAL ROUTE IN SURVIVAL MODE
Select Survival mode while holding R1 or R2.

DRAMATIC BATTLE MODE
Select Dramatic Battle mode while holding ● + ❷ + R2.

RANDOM BATTLE MODE
Select Versus mode while holding ● + ❷ + R2.

STUNTMAN IGNITION

3 PROPS IN STUNT CREATOR MODE
Select Cheats from Extras and enter COOLPROP.

ALL ITEMS UNLOCKED FOR CONSTRUCTION MODE
Select Cheats from Extras and enter NOBLEMAN.

MVX SPARTAN
Select Cheats from Extras and enter fastride.

ALL CHEATS
Select Cheats from Extras and enter Wearefrozen. This unlocks the following cheats: Slo-mo Cool, Thrill Cam, Vision Switcher, Nitro Addiction, Freaky Fast, and Ice Wheels.

ALL CHEATS
Select Cheats from Extras and enter Kungfoopete.

ICE WHEELS CHEAT
Select Cheats from Extras and enter IceAge.

NITRO ADDICTION CHEAT
Select Cheats from Extras and enter TheDuke.

VISION SWITCHER CHEAT
Select Cheats from Extras and enter GFXMODES.

THE SUFFERING: TIES THAT BIND

SUICIDE
During gameplay, hold L1 + R1 + ✖ and press Down, Down, Down, Down.

SHOTGUN & AMMO
During gameplay, hold L1 + R1 + ✖ and press Left, Left, Left, Down, Down, Down.

MOLOTOV COCKTAILS
During gameplay, hold L1 + R1 + ✖ and press Down, Down, Down, Up, Up, Up.

FULL FLASHLIGHT
During gameplay, hold L1 + R1 + ✖ and press Up, Left, Down, Right, Up, Right, Down, Left, R2.

FULL AMMO CURRENT WEAPON
During gameplay, hold L1 + R1 + ✖ and press Right, Right, Down, Up, Left, Right, Left, Left, R2.

FULL AMMO CURRENT THROWN
During gameplay, hold L1 + R1 + ✖ and press Left, Left, Up, Down, Right, Left, Right, Right, R2.

FULL INSANITY
During gameplay, hold L1 + R1 + ✖ and press Right, Right, Right, R2, Left, Left, Right, Left, R2.

FULL HEALTH
During gameplay, hold L1 + R1 + ✖ and press Down, Down, Down, R2, Up, Up, Down, Up, R2.

ARSENAL
During gameplay, hold L1 + R1 + ✖ and press Down, Right, Up, Left, Down, R2, Left, Left, Right, Right, R2, Down, Up, Left, Right, R2.

INVINCIBILITY
During gameplay, hold L1 + R1 + ✖ and press Down, Up, Down, Up.

MINUS 50 REP
During gameplay, hold L1 + R1 + ✖ and press Left, Left, Down, Up.

PLUS 50 REP
During gameplay, hold L1 + R1 + ✖ and press Up, Up, Right, Up.

FULL BLOOD
During gameplay, hold L1 + R1 + ✖ and press Up, Down, Left, Right.

ZERO BLOOD
During gameplay, hold L1 + R1 + ✖ and press Down, Up, Right, Left.

SHRAPNEL
During gameplay, hold L1 + R1 + ✖ and press Right, Right, Right, Left, Left, Left.

MAX EVIL REP
During gameplay, hold L1 + R1 + ✖ and press Left, Down, Left, Down, Left, Down, R2.

MAX GOOD REP
During gameplay, hold L1 + R1 + ✖ and press Up, Right, Up, Right, Up, Right, R2.

FULL BOTTLES
During gameplay, hold L1 + R1 + ✖ and press Right, Right, Up, Up, R2, Left, Right, R2, Right, Up, Right, R2.

SUPER BAD DUDE
During gameplay, hold L1 + R1 + ✖ and press Down, Up, Down, Left, Right, Left, R2, Up, Left, Down, Right, Up, Right, Down, Left, R2, Down, Down, Down, R2, R2.

PROJECTOR STATE
During gameplay, hold L1 + R1 + ✖ and press Up, R2, Left, R2, Down, R2, Right, R2.

DREAM STATE
During gameplay, hold L1 + R1 + ✖ and press Left, Left, R2, Right, Right, R2, Up, Up, R2, Down, Down, R2.

ALL NOTES
During gameplay, hold L1 + R1 + ✖ and press Right, Left, Up, Left, R2, Right, Down, Right.

ALL MAPS
During gameplay, hold L1 + R1 + ✖ and press Left, Right, Down, Right, R2, Left, Up, Left.

SUPERMAN RETURNS

GOD MODE
Pause the game, select Options and press Up, Up, Down, Down, Left, Right, Left, Right, ●, ●.

INFINITE CITY HEALTH
Pause the game, select Options and press ●, Right, ●, Right, Up, Left, Right, ●.

OVERLOAD

PLAYSTATION 2

ALL POWER-UPS

Pause the game, select Options and press Left, ●, Right, ●, Down, ●, Up, Down, ●, ●, ●.

ALL UNLOCKABLES

Pause the game, select Options and press Left, Up, Right, Down, ●, ●, ●, Up, Right, ●.

FREE ROAM AS BIZARRO

Pause the game, select Options and press Up, Right, Down, Right, Up, Left, Down, Right, Up.

SUZUKI TT SUPERBIKES

CHEAT SCREEN

At the Main menu, press R1, R2, L1, L2, R1, R2, L1, L2. Now you can enter the following:

ALL EVENTS

Enter BORN FREE.

RED BULL MAD SUNDAY EVENTS

Enter SUNDAYSUNDAY.

ALL HELMETS

Enter SKID LIDS.

ALL LEATHERS

Enter COLORED HIDE.

ALL BIKES

Enter ROCKETS.

ALL WHEELS

Enter TIRE CITY.

ALL COLLECTION BOOK

Enter COUCH POTATO.

TAITO LEGENDS

EXTRA GAMES

At the Title screen, press L1, R1, R2, L2, Select, Start.

TAK AND THE GUARDIANS OF GROSS

INVULNERABILITY

Select Cheat Codes from the Extras menu and enter KRUNKIN.

INFINITE NOVA

Select Cheat Codes from the Extras menu and enter CAKEDAY.

WEAK ENEMIES

Select Cheat Codes from the Extras menu and enter CODMODE.

ALL LEVELS

Select Cheat Codes from the Extras menu and enter GUDGEON.

ALL MINIGAMES

Select Cheat Codes from the Extras menu and enter CURLING.

ALL AWARDS

Select Cheat Codes from the Extras menu and enter SNEAKER.

ALL CONCEPT ART

Select Cheat Codes from the Extras menu and enter FRIVERS.

RAINBOW TRAIL

Select Cheat Codes from the Extras menu and enter UNICORN.

TAK: THE GREAT JUJU CHALLENGE

BONUS SOUND EFFECTS

In Juju's Potions, select Universal Card and enter the following for Bugs, Crystals and Fruits respectively: 20, 17, 5.

BONUS SOUND EFFECTS 2

In Juju's Potions, select Universal Card and enter the following for Bugs, Crystals and Fruits respectively: 50, 84, 92.

BONUS MUSIC TRACK 1

In Juju's Potions, select Universal Card and enter the following for Bugs, Crystals and Fruits respectively: 67, 8, 20.

BONUS MUSIC TRACK 2

In Juju's Potions, select Universal Card and enter the following for Bugs, Crystals and Fruits respectively: 6, 18, 3.

MAGIC PARTICLES

In Juju's Potions, select Universal Card and enter the following for Bugs, Crystals and Fruits respectively: 24, 40, 11.

MORE MAGIC PARTICLES

In Juju's Potions, select Universal Card and enter the following for Bugs, Crystals and Fruits respectively: 48, 57, 57.

VIEW JUJU CONCEPT ART
In Juju's Potions, select Universal Card and enter the following for Bugs, Crystals and Fruits respectively: 33, 22, 28.

VIEW VEHICLE ART
In Juju's Potions, select Universal Card and enter the following for Bugs, Crystals and Fruits respectively: 11, 55, 44.

VIEW WORLD ART
In Juju's Potions, select Universal Card and enter the following for Bugs, Crystals and Fruits respectively: 83, 49, 34.

TEENAGE MUTANT NINJA TURTLES 3: MUTANT NIGHTMARE

INVINCIBILITY
Select Passwords from the Options menu and enter MDLDSSLR.

HEALTH POWER-UPS BECOME SUSHI
Select Passwords from the Options menu and enter SLLMRSLD.

NO HEALTH POWER-UPS
Select Passwords from the Options menu and enter DMLDMRLD.

ONE HIT DEFEATS TURTLE
Select Passwords from the Options menu and enter LDMSLRDD.

MAX OUGI
Select Passwords from the Options menu and enter RRDMLSDL.

UNLIMITED SHURIKEN
Select Passwords from the Options menu and enter LMDRRMSR.

NO SHURIKEN
Select Passwords from the Options menu and enter LLMSRDMS.

DOUBLE ENEMY ATTACK
Select Passwords from the Options menu and enter MSRLSMML.

DOUBLE ENEMY DEFENSE
Select Passwords from the Options menu and enter SLRMLSSM.

TEENAGE MUTANT NINJA TURTLES: SMASH-UP

CYBER SHREDDER
At the Bonus Content menu, press Up, Down, Right, Up, Down, Right, Left, Up, Right, Down.

4 NINJA TURTLES' ALTERNATE COSTUMES
At the Bonus Content menu, press Up, Left, Down, Right, Up, Down, Left, Up, Left, Left.

TEST DRIVE UNLIMITED

ALL CARS AND MONEY
At the Main menu, press ▲, ●, L1, R1, ▲.

THRILLVILLE: OFF THE RAILS

ALL PARKS
While in a park, press ●, ●, ▲, ●, ●, ▲, ●.

ALL RIDES IN PARK
While in a park, press ●, ●, ▲, ●, ●, ▲, ▲.

$50,000
While in a park, press ●, ●, ▲, ●, ●, ▲, ✕.

MISSION COMPLETE
While in a park, press ●, ●, ▲, ●, ●, ▲, ●.

TIGER WOODS PGA TOUR 09

$1,000,000
Select Passwords from the Extras menu and enter JACKPOT.

MAX SKILL POINTS
Select Passwords from the Extras menu and enter IAMRUBBISH.

PLAYSTATION 2

ALL CLOTHING & EQUIPMENT
Select Passwords from the Extras menu and enter SHOP2DROP.

ALL PGA TOUR EVENTS
Select Passwords from the Extras menu and enter BEATIT.

ALL COVER STORIES
Select Passwords from the Extras menu and enter HEADLINER.

TIM BURTON'S THE NIGHTMARE BEFORE CHRISTMAS: OOGIE'S REVENGE

ALL LEVELS
At the Title screen, press L1, L2, L1, L2, L3, R1, R2, R1, R2, R3.

INVINCIBILITY
During a game, press Right, Left, L3, R3, Left, Right, R3, L3.

UPGRADE SOUL ROBBER
During a game, press Up, Right, Left, Down, R3, L3.

UNLIMITED POWER FOR PUMPKIN KING
During a game, press Left, Down, Right, Up, Right, Down, Left, Up.

UNLIMITED SANTA JACK PRESENTS
During a game, press Down, Left, Right, Up, L3, R3.

ONE BUTTON MUSICAL BATTLES
During a boss fight, press Left, Up, Right, Down, Left, R3, L3.

PUMPKIN JACK AND SANTA JACK COSTUMES
During a game, press Down, Up, Right, Left, L3, R3.

UNLOCK DANCING JACK, PHANTOM JACK, PJ JACK, AND THESPIAN JACK
At Jack's house, press Up, Down, Left, Right, R3, L3.

UNLOCK STATUE COLLECTION
At Jack's house, press Up, Up, R3, Up.

TMNT

DON'S BIG HEAD GOODIE
At the Main menu, hold L1 and press ○, △, ×, □.

CHALLENGE MAP 2
At the Main menu, hold L1 and press ×, ×, ○, ×.

TOMB RAIDER: LEGEND

You must unlock the following codes in the game before using them.

BULLETPROOF
During gameplay, hold L1 and press ×, R1, △, R1, □, L2.

DRAIN ENEMY HEALTH
During gameplay, hold L1 and press □, ○, ×, L2, R1, △.

INFINITE ASSAULT RIFLE AMMO
During gameplay, hold L2 and press ×, ○, ×, L1, □, △.

INFINITE GRENADE LAUNCHER AMMO
During gameplay, hold L2 and press L1, △, R1, ○, L1, □.

INFINITE SHOTGUN AMMO
During gameplay, hold L2 and press R1, ○, □, L1, □, ×.

INFINITE SMG AMMO
During gameplay, hold L2 and press ○, △, L1, R1, ×, ○.

EXCALIBUR
During gameplay, hold L2 and press △, ×, ○, R1, △, L1.

ONE-SHOT KILL
During gameplay, hold L1 and press △, ×, △, □, L2, ○.

NO TEXTURE MODE
During gameplay, hold L1 and press L2, ×, ○, ×, △, R1.

TOMB RAIDER: UNDERWORLD

BULLETPROOF LARA
During a game, hold L2 and press ×, R2, △, R2, □, L1.

ONE-SHOT KILL
During a game, hold L2 and press △, ×, △, □, L1, ○.

SHOW ENEMY HEALTH
During a game, hold L2 and press □, ○, ×, L1, R2, △.

ALL SOLO LEVELS
At the Solo menu, hold L1 + L2 +
R1 + R2 and press ● (x5), ● (x5).

ALL COOP LEVELS
At the Coop menu, hold L1 + L2 +
R1 + R2 and press ● (x5), ● (x5).

TEAM PICTURE
At the Main menu, press R2, ●
(x5), ●.

TONY HAWK'S DOWNHILL JAM

CHEAT CODES

Select Cheat Codes from the Options menu and enter the following cheats.
Select Toggle Cheats to enable/disable them.

FREE BOOST
Enter OOTBAGHFOREVER.

ALWAYS SPECIAL
Enter POINTHOGGER.

UNLOCK MANUALS
Enter IMISSMANUALS.

PERFECT RAIL
Enter LIKETILTINGAPLATE.

PERFECT MANUAL
Enter TIGHTROPEWALKER.

PERFECT STATS
Enter IAMBOB.

FIRST-PERSON SKATER
Enter FIRSTPERSONJAM.

SHADOW SKATER
Enter CHIMNEYSWEEP.

DEMON SKATER
Enter EVILCHIMNEYSWEEP.

MINI SKATER
Enter DOWNTHERABBITHOLE.

GIGANTO-SKATER
Enter IWANNABETALLTALL.

INVISIBLE SKATER
Enter NOWYOUSEEME.

FREE BOOST
Enter OOTBAGHFOREVER.

ALWAYS SPECIAL
Enter POINTHOGGER.

UNLOCK MANUALS
Enter IMISSMANUALS.

PERFECT RAIL
Enter LIKETILTINGAPLATE.

PERFECT MANUAL
Enter TIGHTROPEWALKER.

PERFECT STATS
Enter IAMBOB.

FIRST-PERSON SKATER
Enter FIRSTPERSONJAM.

SHADOW SKATER
Enter CHIMNEYSWEEP.

DEMON SKATER
Enter EVILCHIMNEYSWEEP.

MINI SKATER
Enter DOWNTHERABBITHOLE.

GIGANTO-SKATER
Enter IWANNABETALLTALL.

INVISIBLE SKATER
Enter NOWYOUSEEME.

SKATE AS A WORK OF ART
Enter FOURLIGHTS.

DISPLAY COORDINATES
Enter DISPLAYCOORDINATES.

LARGE BIRDS
Enter BIRDBIRDBIRDBIRD.

ESPECIALLY LARGE BIRDS
Enter BIRDBIRDBIRDBIRDBIRD.

TINY PEOPLE
Enter SHRINKTHEPEOPLE.
*There is no need to toggle on the
following cheats. They take effect
after entering them.

ALL EVENTS
Enter ADVENTURESOFKWANG.

ALL SKATERS
Enter IMINTERFACING.

ALL BOARDS/OUTFITS
Enter RAIDTHEWOODSHED.

ALL MOVIES
Enter FREEBOZZLER.

TONY HAWK'S PROVING GROUND

CHEAT CODES

Select Cheat Codes from the Options and enter the following cheats. Some codes need to be enabled by selecting Cheats from the Options during a game.

UNLOCK	CHEAT
Unlocks Bosco	MOREMILK
Unlocks Cam	NOTACAMERA
Unlocks Cooper	THECOOP
Unlocks Eddie X	SKETCHY
Unlocks El Patinador	PILEDRIVER
Unlocks Eric	FLYAWAY
Unlocks Judy Nails	LOVEROCKNROLL
Unlocks Mad Dog	RABBIES
Unlocks MCA	INTERGALACTIC
Unlocks Mel	NOTADUDE
Unlocks Rube	LOOKSSMELLY
Unlocks Spence	DAPPER
Unlocks Shayne	MOVERS
Unlocks TV Producer	SHAKER
Unlock FDR	THEPREZPARK
Unlock Lansdowne	THELOCALPARK

UNLOCK	CHEAT
Unlock Air & Space Museum	THEINDOORPARK
Unlocks all Fun Items	OVERTHETOP
Unlock all Game Movies	WATCHTHIS
Unlock all Rigger Pieces	IMGONNABUILD
All specials unlocked and in player's special list	LOTSOFTRICKS
Full Stats	BEEFEDUP
Give player +50 skill points	NEEDSHELP
Unlocks Perfect Manual	STILLAINTFALLIN
Unlocks Perfect Rail	AINTFALLIN
Unlocks Unlimited Focus	MYOPIC
Invisible Man	THEMISSING
Mini Skater	TINYTATER

TOTAL OVERDOSE: A GUNSLINGER'S TALE IN MEXICO

CHEAT MODE
Hold L1 + R1 + L2 + R2 + L3 + R3 for a few seconds, then you can enter the following codes.

RESTORE HEALTH
Press ✕, ●, ◉, ▲.

ALL LOCO MOVES
During a game, hold L1 + L2 + L3 + R1 + R2 + R3 for three seconds. Then press ●, ●, L2, R2.

MAXIMUM HEALTH
During a game, hold L1 + L2 + L3 + R1 + R2 + R3 for three seconds. Then press ✕, ●, ●, ▲.

MAXIMUM REWINDINGS
During a game, hold L1 + L2 + L3 + R1 + R2 + R3 for three seconds. Then press R1, R2, L2, ✕.

FREE ALL WEAPONS
During a game, hold L1 + L2 + L3 + R1 + R2 + R3 for three seconds. Then press ▲, L1, R2, ●.

TRANSFORMERS: THE GAME

INFINITE HEALTH
At the Main menu, press Left, Left, Up, Left, Right, Down, Right.

INFINITE AMMO
At the Main menu, press Up, Down, Left, Right, Up, Up, Down.

NO MILITARY OR POLICE
At the Main menu, press Right, Left, Right, Left, Right, Left, Right.

ALL MISSIONS
At the Main menu, press Down, Up, Left, Right, Right, Right, Up, Down.

BONUS CYBERTRON MISSIONS
At the Main menu, press Right, Up, Up, Down, Right, Left, Left.

GENERATION 1 SKIN: JAZZ
At the Main menu, press Left, Up, Down, Down, Left, Up, Right.

GENERATION 1 SKIN: MEGATRON
At the Main menu, press Down, Left, Left, Down, Right, Right, Up.

GENERATION 1 SKIN: OPTIMUS PRIME
At the Main menu, press Down, Right, Left, Up, Down, Down, Left.

GENERATION 1 SKIN: ROBOVISION OPTIMUS PRIME
At the Main menu, press Down, Down, Up, Up, Right, Right, Right.

GENERATION 1 SKIN: STARSCREAM
At the Main menu, press Right, Down, Left, Left, Down, Up, Up.

TWISTED METAL: HEAD ON - EXTRA TWISTED EDITION

Hold L1 + R1 + L2 + R2 during gameplay, then press the button combination. Do the same thing to turn it off.

INVULNERABILITY
During a game, hold L1 + R1 + L2 + R2 and press Up, Down, Left, Right, Right, Left, Down, Up.

TRADE WEAPONS FOR HEALTH
During a game, hold L1 + R1 + L2 + R2 and press ●, ⊗, ●, ●.

INFINITE WEAPONS
During a game, hold L1 + R1 + L2 + R2 and press ●, ●, Down, Down.

KILLER WEAPONS
During a game, hold L1 + R1 + L2 + R2 and press ⊗, ⊗, Up, Up.

MEGA GUNS
During a game, hold L1 + R1 + L2 + R2 and press ⊗, ●, ⊗, ●.

RADIAL BLAST
During a game, hold L1 + R1 + L2 + R2 and press Left, Left, Up, Down, Left, Right.

ULTIMATE SPIDER-MAN

ALL CHARACTERS
Pause the game and select Controller Setup from the Options menu. Press Right, Down, Right, Down, Left, Up, Left, Right.

ALL COVERS
Pause the game and select Controller Setup from the Options menu. Press Left, Left, Right, Left, Up, Left, Left, Down.

ALL CONCEPT ART
Pause the game and select Controller Setup from the Options menu. Press Down, Down, Down, Up, Down, Up, Left, Left.

ALL LANDMARKS
Pause the game and select Controller Setup from the Options menu. Press Up, Right, Down, Left, Down, Up, Right, Left.

UP

RUSSELL ATTRACTS ALL BUTTERFLIES
Select Cheats from the Bonuses menu and enter BUTTERFLY. Activate the cheat at the Pause menu after entering it.

MUNTZ'S AVIATOR GOGGLES FOR CARL
Select Cheats from the Bonuses menu and enter AVIATORGOGGLES. Activate the cheat at the Pause menu after entering it.

CARL JUMPS FROM TEETER TOTTER TO LIFT RUSSEL
Select Cheats from the Bonuses menu and enter CARLHEAVYWEIGHT. Activate the cheat at the Pause menu after entering it.

BALLOONS WHEN CARL JUMPS
Select Cheats from the Bonuses menu and enter BALLOONPARTY. Activate the cheat at the Pause menu after entering it.

WAY OF THE SAMURAI 2

MORE CHARACTER MODELS
At the Character Customization screen, highlight Name and press L1, R2, R1, L2, L1, R2, R1, L2, ●. Press Right or Left to change character models.

WWE SMACKDOWN VS. RAW 2009

BOOGEYMAN
Select Cheat Codes from My WWE and enter BoogeymanEatsWorms!!.

GENE SNITSKY
Select Cheat Codes from My WWE and enter UnlockSnitskySvR2009.

HAWKINS & RYDER
Select Cheat Codes from My WWE and enter Ryder&HawkinsTagTeam.

JILLIAN HALL
Select Cheat Codes from My WWE and enter PlayAsJillianHallSvR.

LAYLA
Select Cheat Codes from My WWE and enter UnlockECWDivaLayla09.

RIC FLAIR
Select Cheat Codes from My WWE and enter FlairWoooooooooooooo.

TAZZ
Select Cheat Codes from My WWE and enter UnlockECWTazzSvR2009.

VINCENT MCMAHON
Select Cheat Codes from My WWE and enter VinceMcMahonNoChance.

HORNSWOGGLE AS MANAGER
Select Cheat Codes from My WWE and enter HornswoggleAsManager.

CHRIS JERICHO COSTUME B
Select Cheat Codes from My WWE and enter AltJerichoModelSvR09.

CM PUNK COSTUME B
Select Cheat Codes from My WWE and enter CMPunkAltCostumeSvR!.

REY MYSTERIO COSTUME B
Select Cheat Codes from My WWE and enter BooyakaBooyaka619SvR.

SATURDAY NIGHT'S MAIN EVENT ARENA
Select Cheat Codes from My WWE and enter SatNightMainEventSvR.

WWE SMACKDOWN VS. RAW 2010

THE ROCK
Select Cheat Codes from the Options and enter The Great One.

VINCE'S OFFICE AND DIRT SHEET FOR BACKSTAGE BRAWL
Select Cheat Codes from the Options menu and enter BonusBrawl.

SHAWN MICHAELS' NEW COSTUME
Select Cheat Codes from the Options menu and enter Bow Down.

RANDY ORTON'S NEW COSTUME
Select Cheat Codes from the Options menu and enter ViperRKO.

TRIPLE H'S NEW COSTUME
Select Cheat Codes from the Options menu and enter Suck IT!.

WWE SMACKDOWN VS. RAW 2011

JOHN CENA (ENTRANCE/CIVILIAN)
In My WWE, select Cheat Codes from the Options menu and enter SLURPEE.

RANDY ORTON'S COSTUMES
In My WWE, select Cheat Codes from the Options menu and enter apexpredator.

TRIBUTE TO THE TROOPS ARENA
In My WWE, select Cheat Codes from the Options menu and enter 8thannualtribute.

X-MEN: THE OFFICIAL GAME

DANGER ROOM ICEMAN
At the Cerebro Files menu, press Right, Right, Left, Left, Down, Up, Down, Up, Start.

DANGER ROOM NIGHTCRAWLER
At the Cerebro Files menu, press Up, Up, Down, Down, Left, Right, Left, Right, Start.

DANGER ROOM WOLVERINE
At the Cerebro Files menu, press Down, Down, Up, Up, Right, Left, Right, Left, Start.

GAMES

ADVANCE WARS: DAYS OF RUIN

UNLOCK COS

Complete the following missions to unlock the corresponding CO.

COMPLETE MISSION	CO UNLOCKED	COMPLETE MISSION	CO UNLOCKED
12	Tasha	21	Greyfield
13	Gage	24	Penny
14	Forthsythe	25	Tabitha
20	Waylon	26	Caulder

ADVANCE WARS: DUAL STRIKE

ADVANCE WARS MAP

Select Map from the Design Room menu and immediately press and hold L + R. This reveals a map that spells out Advance Wars.

ADVANCE WARPAPER

Insert Advance Wars into the GBA slot of your Nintendo DS. Start Advance Wars: Dual Strike. Select Battle maps and purchase Advance Warpaper. Select Display from the Design Room and choose Classic 1.

HACHI'S LAND

Insert Advance Wars into the GBA slot of your Nintendo DS. Start Advance Wars: Dual Strike. Select Battle Maps and purchase Hachi's Land for 1.

NELL'S LAND

Insert Advance Wars into the GBA slot of your Nintendo DS. Start Advance Wars: Dual Strike. Select Battle Maps and purchase Nell's Land for 1.

ADVANCE WARPAPER 2

Insert Advance Wars 2: Black Hole Rising into the GBA slot of your
Nintendo DS. Start Advance Wars: Dual Strike. Select Battle maps and
purchase Advance Warpaper 2. Select Display from the Design Room and
choose Classic 2.

LASH'S LAND

Insert Advance Wars 2: Black Hole Rising into the GBA slot of your
Nintendo DS. Start Advance Wars: Dual Strike. Select Battle Maps and
purchase Lash's Land for 1.

STRUM'S LAND

Insert Advance Wars 2: Black Hole Rising into the GBA slot of your
Nintendo DS. Start Advance Wars: Dual Strike. Select Battle Maps and
purchase Strum's Land for 1.

ALICE IN WONDERLAND

DORMOUSE COAT
Enter 3676 as a cheat code.

RED GUARD SHIELD
Enter 7453 as a cheat code.

RED QUEEN MASK
Enter 7675 as a cheat code.

TAN ALICE BOOK
Enter 2625 as a cheat code.

TWEEDLE OUTFIT
Enter 8946 as a cheat code.

ANIMANIACS: LIGHTS, CAMERA, ACTION!

SKIP LEVEL
Pause the game and press L, L, R,
R, Down, Down.

DISABLE TIME
Pause the game and press L, R,
Left, Left, Up, Up.

KINGSIZE PICK-UPS
Pause the game and press Right,
Right, Right, Left, Left, Left, R, L.

PASSWORDS

LEVEL	PASSWORD
1	Wakko, Wakko, Wakko, Wakko, Wakko
2	Dot, Yakko, Brain, Wakko, Pinky
3	Yakko, Dot, Wakko, Wakko, Brain
4	Pinky, Yakko, Yakko, Dot, Brain
5	Pinky, Pinky, Yakko, Wakko, Wakko
6	Brain, Dot, Brain, Pinky, Yakko
7	Brain, Pinky, Wakko, Pinky, Brain
8	Brain Pinky, Pinky, Wakko, Wakko
9	Dot, Dot, Yakko, Pinky, Wakko
10	Brain, Dot, Brain, Yakko, Wakko
11	Akko, Yakko, Pinky, Dot, Dot
12	Pinky, Pinky, Brain, Dot, Wakko
13	Yakko, Wakko, Pinky, Wakko, Brain
14	Pinky, Wakko, Brain, Wakko, Yakko
15	Dot, Pinky, Wakko, Wakko, Yakko

BAKUGAN BATTLE BRAWLERS

1000 BP
Start a new game and enter the
name as 180978772269.

5000 BP
Start a new game and enter the
name as 332044292925.

10,000 BP
Start a new game and enter the
name as 423482942968.

BRONZE WARIUS
Start a new game and enter the
name as 449824934071.

BATMAN: THE BRAVE AND THE BOLD— THE VIDEOGAME

BATMAN COSTUME: MEDIEVAL SUIT
In the Batcave, use the left terminal to enter 5644863.

PROTO SPARRING CHALLENGE
In the Batcave, use the left terminal to enter 6677686.

WEAPON: BARRIER
In the Batcave, use the left terminal to enter 2525655.

WEAPON: BELT SWORD
In the Batcave, use the left terminal to enter 2587973.

WEAPON: FLASHBANGS
In the Batcave, use the left terminal to enter 3527463.

WEAPON: SMOKE PELLETS
In the Batcave, use the left terminal to enter 7665336.

BATTLE OF GIANTS: DRAGONS

Select Unlock Gold Gems from the Extras Menu and enter the following passwords:

BREATH ATTACK GOLD GEMS

LEVEL	ATTACK	PASSWORD
1	NAMGILIMA	ISAM SKNF DKTD
2	NIGHHALAMA	ZNBN QOKS THGO
3	KUGDIM	AWBF CRSL HGAT
4	KUZEN	ACLC SCRS VOSK
5	SUGZAG	XSPC LLSL KJLP

CLAW ATTACK GOLD GEMS

LEVEL	ATTACK	PASSWORD
1	USUD	NAKF HLAP SDSP
2	ULUH	SAPO RLNM VUSD
3	NIGHZU	POZX MJDR GJSA
4	GHIDRU	GPGE SMEC TDTB
5	MUDRU	ABLP CGPG SGAM

HEAD ATTACK GOLD GEMS

LEVEL	ATTACK	PASSWORD
1	MEN	PQTM AONV UTNA
2	SAGHMEN	TNAP CTJS LDUF
3	KINGAL	FHSK EUFV KALP
4	DALLA	EPWB MPOR TRTA
5	AGA	GPKT BBWT SGNR

TAIL ATTACK GOLD GEMS

LEVEL	ATTACK	PASSWORD
1	A'ASH	LSSN GOAJ READ
2	ASH	FUTY HVNS LNVS
3	ASH SAR	LPAQ KOYH TGDS
4	AHS BALA	VLQL QELB IYDS
5	NAMTAGTAG	VLDB DDSL NCJA

WING ATTACK GOLD GEMS

LEVEL	ATTACK	PASSWORD
1	NIM	SGHJ VLPO QEIK
2	NIMSAHARA	QPLA OKFC NBUS
3	BARASH	IQUW ENPC SRGA
4	A'SHUM	LRYV LCJC MEBT
5	ATUKU	ALVN HRSF MSEP

BATTLE OF GIANTS: MUTANT INSECTS

ELECTICITY UPGRADE
Select Unlock Rewards from Options and enter WLUA DZCN ZNKE.

ICE UPGRADE
Select Unlock Rewards from Options and enter PLAL TALG JPZV.

BEN 10: PROTECTOR OF EARTH

GALACTIC ENFORCER SKINS
At the level select, press A, B, X, Y, L, R, SELECT.

GWEN 10 SKINS
At the level select, press Left, Right, Left, Right, L, R, SELECT.

ULTRA BEN SKINS
At the level select, press Up, Right, Down, Left, A, B, SELECT.

UPCHUCK
At the level select, press A, Left, Y, Right, X, Up, B, Down, SELECT.

BONUS MISSION
At the level select, press Left, L, Right, R, Up, Down, SELECT.

BRAIN AGE: TRAIN YOUR BRAIN IN MINUTES A DAY

BRAIN AGE CHECK SELECTION MENU
At the Daily Training Menu, hold Select while choosing Brain Age Check.

TOP 3 LISTS
At the Daily Training Menu, hold Select while choosing Graph.

BRAIN AGE EXPRESS: ARTS & LETTERS

ELIMINATE ENEMIES IN WORD ATTACK
In Word Attack, during the Space mode, press A, Y, X, B. You can use this once each training session.

BRAIN VOYAGE

ALL GOLD MEDALS
At the World Map, press A, B, Up, L, L, Y.

INFINITE COINS
At the World Tour Mode, press L, Up, X, Up, R, Y.

BUBBLE BOBBLE REVOLUTION

BONUS LEVELS IN CLASSIC MODE
At the Classic Mode title screen, press L, R, L, R, L, R, Right, Select. Touch the door at Level 20.

POWER UP! MODE IN CLASSIC VERSION
At the Classic Mode title screen, press Select, R, L, Left, Right, R, Select, Right.

SUPER BUBBLE BOBBLE IN CLASSIC VERSION
You must first defeat the boss with two players. Then at the Classic Mode title screen, press Left, R, Left, Select, Left, L, Left, Select.

BUST-A-MOVE DS

DARK WORLD
Complete the game then press A, Left, Right, A at the Title screen.

SOUND TEST
At the Main menu, press Select, A, B, Left, Right, A, Select, Right.

CALL OF DUTY: MODERN WARFARE: MOBILIZED

SURVIVAL MODE
Select Options from the War Room and press SELECT, L, R, SELECT, Y, Y, X, R, L, X, R, Y

CALL OF DUTY: WORLD AT WAR

ALL CAMPAIGN AND CHALLENGE MISSIONS
At the War Room Options screen, press Y, X, Y, Y, Y, X, Y, X, X, Y.

NINTENDO DS

CARS

SECRET MUSIC TRACK FOR RAMONE'S STYLE
At the Title screen, press Up, Down, Up, Down, A, B, X, Y.

EVERYTHING EXCEPT HIDDEN MUSIC
At the Title screen, press Up, Up, Down, Down, Left, Right, Left, Right, B, A, B.

CARTOON NETWORK RACING

The following codes will disable the ability to save:

UNLOCK EVERYTHING
Select Nickname from the Options and enter GIMMIE.

ENABLES ALL HAZARDS AND PICKUPS IN TIME TRIAL
Select Nickname from the Options and enter AAARGH.

ROCKETS TURN NON-INVULNERABLE OPPONENTS INTO STONE
Select Nickname from the Options and enter STONEME.

UNLIMITED DUMB ROCKETS
Select Nickname from the Options and enter ROCKETMAN.

UNLIMITED SUPERPOWER ENERGY
Select Nickname from the Options and enter SPINACH.

TOP-DOWN VIEW
Select Nickname from the Options and enter IMACOPTER.

CASTLEVANIA: DAWN OF SORROW

POTION
Complete Boss Rush Mode.

RPG
Complete Boss Rush Mode in less than 5 minutes.

DEATH'S ROBE
Complete Boss Rush Mode in less than 6 minutes.

TERROR BEAR
Complete Boss Rush Mode in less than 7 minutes.

NUNCHAKUS
Complete Boss Rush Mode in less than 8 minutes.

CASTLEVANIA: PORTRAIT OF RUIN

JAPANESE VOICEOVERS
At the Main menu, hold L and press A.

THE CHRONICLES OF NARNIA: THE LION, THE WITCH AND THE WARDROBE

RESTORE HEALTH
At the Main menu, press Left, Right, Up, Down, A (x4).

INVINCIBILITY
At the Main menu, press A, Y, X, B, Up, Up, Down, Down.

ARMOR
At the Main menu, press A, X, Y, B, Up, Up, Up, Down.

EXTRA MONEY
At the Main menu, press Up, X, Up, X, Down, B, Down, B.

ALL BLESSINGS
At the Main menu, press Left, Up, A, B, Right, Down, X, Y.

MAXIMUM ATTRIBUTES
At the Main menu, press Left, B, Up, Y, Down, X, Right, A.

MAX SKILLS
At the Main menu, press A, Left, Right, B, Down, Up, X, X.

STRONGER ATTACKS
At the Main menu, press A, Up, B, Down, X, X, Y, Y.

CITY LIFE DS

1,000,000
Pause the game and press A, B, Y, L, R.

ALL BUILDINGS
Pause the game and hold B + Y + X + R for 2 seconds.

CLUB PENGUIN: ELITE PENGUIN FORCE

FLOWER HUNT MISSION
Change your system's date to April 1st.

APRIL ITEMS IN CATALOG
Change your system's date to April 1st.

SUMMER PARTY MISSION
Change your system's date to June 21st.

FIESTA HAT ON FROZEN POND
Change your system's date to June 21st.

JUNE ITEMS IN CATALOG
Change your system's date to June 21st.

HALLOWEEN PARTY MISSION
Change your system's date to October 31st.

FISH COSTUME IN LODGE ATTIC
Change your system's date to October 31st.

DELIVER THE PRESENTS MISSION
Change your system's date to December 25th.

ICE SKATES ON THE ICEBERG
Change your system's date to December 25th.

CODE LYOKO

CODELYOKO.COM SECRET FILES
Enter the following as Secret Codes on the My Secret Album page of www.codelyoko.com:

SECRET FILE	CODE	SECRET FILE	CODE
Dark Enemies Wallpaper	9L8Q	Overboard	8P3M
Desert Sketch	6G7T	Overwing	8N2N
Fight Video	4M9P	Scorpion Video	9H8S
FMV Ending	5R5K	Scorpion Wallpaper	3D4W
Forest Sketch	8C3X	Sector 5 Sketch	5J9R
Ice Sketch	2F6U	Ulrich	9A9Z
Mountain Sketch	7E5V	Yumi	4B2Y
Overbike	3Q4L		

CONTRA 4

SUPER C

10 LIVES
At the title screen, press Right, Left, Down, Up, B, Y.

SOUND TEST
As the logo fades in to the title screen, hold Y + B and press Start

CONTRA

30 LIVES
At the title screen, press Up, Up, Down, Down, Left, Right Left, Right, Y, B.

UPGRADE WEAPONS
Pause the game and press Up, Up, Down, Down, Left, Right Left, Right, B, A, Start. This code can be used once per life. If you enter it a second time, you will die.

DINOSAUR KING

STONE CIRCLE PASSWORDS
Defeat the game to unlock the Stone Circle in South Euro. Now you can enter the following passwords to unlock dinosaurs. Find the level 1 dinosaur in a chest at the shrine.

009 DASPLETEOSARUS
Enter Grass, Water, Lightning, Lightning, Earth, Earth, Water, Wind.

012 SIAMOTYRRANUS
Enter Fire, Wind, Fire, Water, Wind, Grass, Fire, Water.

025 JOBARIA
Enter Water, Lightning, Lightning, Earth, Fire, Earth, Fire, Wind.

029 TRICERATOPS
Enter Lightning, Fire, Lightning, Fire, Water, Lightning, Grass, Earth.

038 MONOCLONIUS
Enter Lightning, Earth, Water,

Water, Grass, Fire, Earth, Wind.

046 EUOPLOCEPHALUS
Enter Earth, Earth, Grass, Water, Wind, Earth, Wind, Fire.

058 ALTIRHINUS
Enter Wind, Fire, Fire, Fire, Lightning, Earth, Water, Grass.

061 CARNOTAURUS
Enter Earth, Wind, Water, Lightning, Fire, Wind, Wind, Water.

EX ACE/EX CHOMP
Enter Lightning, Grass, Fire, Earth, Water, Water, Lightning, Fire. This gives you Ace if you are playing as Rex and Chomp as Max.

EX MINI-KING
Enter Lightning, Wind, Earth, Lightning, Grass, Wind, Fire, Water.

EX PARIS
Enter Grass, Water, Water, Earth, Wind, Grass, Lightning, Lightning.

EX SAUROPHAGANAX
Enter Fire, Water, Earth, Grass, Wind, Lightning, Fire, Water.

EX SPINY
Enter Water, Earth, Fire, Water, Fire, Grass, Wind, Earth.

EX TANK
Enter Earth, Grass, Earth, Water, Wind, Water, Grass, Fire.

EX TERRY
Enter Fire, Lightning, Wind, Wind, Water, Fire, Fire, Earth.

DISGAEA DS

ETNA MODE
At the Main menu, highlight New Game and press X, Y, B, X, Y, B, A.

DISNEY FAIRIES: TINKER BELL

TINKERBELL MAGIC BOOK CODES
Talk to Queen Clarion about the Magic Book to enter the following codes.

UNLOCK	CODE	UNLOCK	CODE
Augustus	5318 3479 7972	One Fairy Medal	1111 1111 1111
Baden	1199 2780 8802	One Green Leaf	4444 4444 4444
Blair	6899 6003 4480	One Pink Petal	2222 2222 2222
Cera	1297 0195 5747	One Red Leaf	5555 5555 5555
Chipper	7980 9298 9818	One Snow Grain	7777 7777 7777
Dewberry	0241 4491 0630		
Elwood	3527 5660 3684	One Weak Thread	9999 9999 9999
Fawn	9556 0047 1043		
Idalia	2998 8832 2673	One White Feather	8888 8888 8888
Iridessa	0724 0213 6136		
Luminaria	8046 5868 5678	One Yellow Leaf	6666 6666 6666
Magnolia	1697 4780 6430	One Yellow Petal	3333 3333 3333
Mariana	5138 8216 9240		
Minister Autumn	2294 0281 6332	Party Shoes	1390 5107 4096
Minister Spring	2492 1155 4907	Party Skirt	6572 4809 6680
Minister Summer	2582 7972 6926	Party Tiara	8469 7886 7938
		Party Top	0977 4584 3869
Minister Winter	2618 8587 2083	Queen Clarion	1486 4214 8147
Nollie	5905 2346 9329	Rosetta	8610 2523 6122
Olwen	7629 0545 7105	Rune	3020 5768 5351
One Black Shell	1234 5678 9012	Silvermist	0513 4563 6800
One Blue Dewdrop	0987 6543 2109	Terence	8606 6039 6383
		Tinkerbell	2495 7761 9313
		Vidia	3294 3220 0349

DRAGLADE

CHARACTERS

CHARACTER	TO UNLOCK	CHARACTER	TO UNLOCK
Asuka	Defeat Daichi's story	Koki	Defeat Hibito's story
Gyamon	Defeat Guy's story	Shura	Defeat Kairu's story

HIDDEN QUEST: SHADOW OF DARKNESS
Defeat Story Mode with all of the main characters. This unlocks this hidden quest in Synethesia.

ZEKE
Complete all of the quests including Shadow of Darkness to unlock Zeke in wireless battle.

DRAGON QUEST IX: SENTINELS OF THE STARRY SKIES

MINI MEDAL REWARDS
Trade your mini medals with Cap'N Max Meddlin in Dourbridge. The effects are cumulative, so giving him 80 medals unlocks all of the rewards.

# MINI MEDALS	REWARD	# MINI MEDALS	REWARD
4	Thief's Key	32	Miracle Sword
8	Mercury Bandanna	40	Sacred Armor
13	Bunny Suit	50	Meteorite Bracer
18	Jolly Roger Jumper	62	Rusty Helmet
25	Transparent Tights	80	Dragon Robe

After giving him 80 mini medals, he will sell the following items for mini medals.

# MINI MEDALS	ITEM	# MINI MEDALS	ITEM
3	Prayer Ring	10	Reset Stone
5	Elfin Elixir	15	Orichalcum
8	Saint's Ashes	20	Pixie Boots

DOURBRIDGE SECRET SHOP
In Dourbridge, there is a secret shop behind the Dourbridge Item Shop. You need the Ultimate Key to access the shop.

DRAGON QUEST HEROES: ROCKET SLIME

KNIGHTRO TANK IN MULTIPLAYER
While inside the church, press Y, L, L, Y, R, R, Y, Up, Down, Select.

THE NEMESIS TANK IN MULTIPLAYER
While inside the church, press Y, R, R, Up, L, L, Y, Down, Down, Down, Y, Select.

DRAGON QUEST MONSTERS: JOKER

CAPTAIN CROW
As you travel between the islands on the sea scooters, you are occasionally attacked by pirates. Find out which route the pirates are located on the bulletin board in any scoutpost den. When you face them between Infant Isle and Celeste Isle, Captain Crow makes an appearance. Defeat him and he forces himself into your team.

SOLITAIRE'S CHALLENGE
After completing the main game, load your game back up for a new endeavor. The hero is in Solitaire's office where she proposes a new non-stop challenge known as Solitaire's Challenge.

METAL KING SLIME
Acquire 100 different skills for your library and talk to the woman in Solitaire's office.

METAL KAISER SLIME
Acquire 150 different skills for your library and talk to the woman in Solitaire's office.

LEOPOLD
Acquire all of the skills for your library and talk to the woman in Solitaire's office.

LIQUID METAL SLIME
Collect 100 monsters in your library and talk to the man in Solitaire's office.

GRANDPA SLIME
Collect 200 monsters in your library and talk to the man in Solitaire's office.

EMPYREA
Collect all of the monsters in your library and talk to the man in Solitaire's office.

TRODE AND ROBBIN' HOOD
Complete both the skills and monster libraries and talk to both the man and woman in Solitaire's office.

DRAWN TO LIFE

HEAL ALL DAMAGE
During a game, press Start, hold L and press Y, X, Y, X, Y, X, A.

INVINCIBLITY
During a game, press Start, hold L and press A, X, B, B, Y.

ALIEN TEMPLATES
During a game, press Start, hold L and press X, Y, B, A, A.

ANIMAL TEMPLATES
During a game, press Start, hold L and press B, B, A, A, X.

ROBOT TEMPLATES
During a game, press Start, hold L and press Y, X, Y, X, A.

SPORTS TEMPLATES
During a game, press Start, hold L and press Y, A, B, A, X.

DRAWN TO LIFE: THE NEXT CHAPTER

TEMPLATES
At the Creation Hall, hold L and press X, Y, B, A, A to unlock the following Templates.

Astronaut Template
Knight Template
Ninja Girl Template
Spartan Template
Super Girl Template

DRAWN TO LIFE: SPONGEBOB SQUAREPANTS EDITION

EXTRA REWARD COINS
Select Cheat Entry and enter Down, Down, B, B, Down, Left, Up, Right, A.

ED, EDD N EDDY: SCAM OF THE CENTURY

INVINCIBILITY
During a game, press Select + A, Up, Select + R, Down, Up.

RESTORE HALF HEALTH
During a game, press A, A, Select + A, Down, Down, Down.

RESTORE HEALTH
During a game, press B, B, Select + X, A + R, Select.

HALF SPECIAL ATTACK GAUGE
During a game, press Down, Down, Left, Right, Select + X.

CAMERA
During a game, press Down, Up, Right, Right, Select + B.

MARSHMALLOW
During a game, press Down, Down, Left, Left, Select + A.

ELEBITS: THE ADVENTURES OF KAI & ZERO

BIG RED BONUS OMEGA
Select Download Additional Omegas from the Extra menu. Choose Download Data and press B, Y, Up, L, Right, R, Down, Left, X, A.

FINAL FANTASY FABLES: CHOCOBO TALES

OMEGA – WAVE CANNON CARD
Select Send from the Main Menu and then choose Download Pop-Up Card. Press L, L, Up, B, B, Left.

GODZILLA UNLEASHED: DOUBLE SMASH

ANGUIRUS
Defeat Hedorah Terrorizes San Francisco.

DESTOROYAH
Defeat Monster Island, The Final Battle.

FIRE RODAN
Defeat Biollante Attacks Paris.

KING GHIDORAH
Defeat Mecha King Ghidorah Ravages Bangkok.

GRAND THEFT AUTO: CHINATOWN WARS

FULL HEALTH AND ARMOR
During a game, press L, L, R, A, A, B, B, R.

FULL ARMOR
During a game, press L, L, R, B, B, A, A, R.

INCREASE WANTED LEVEL
During a game, press L, L, R, Y, Y, X, X, R.

DECREASE WANTED LEVEL
During a game, press R, X, X, Y, Y, R, L, L.

EXPLOSIVE PISTOL ROUND
During a game, press L, R, X, Y, A, B, Up, Down.

WEAPONS SET 1
During a game, press R, Up, B, Down, Left, R, B, Right. This gives you the Pistol, Nightstick, Minigun, Assault Rifle, Micro SMG, Stubby Shotgun, and Grenades with max ammo.

WEAPONS SET 2
During a game, press R, Up, A, Down, Left, R, A, Right. This gives you the Twin Pistol, Teaser, Flame Thrower, Carbine Rifle, SMG, Double Barreled Shotgun, and Molotovs with max ammo.

WEAPONS SET 3
During a game, press R, Up, Y, Down, Left, R, Y, Right. This gives you the Revolver, Chainsaw, Flame Thrower, Carbine Rifle, SMG, Double Barreled Shotgun, and Proximity Mines with max ammo.

WEAPONS SET 4
During a game, press R, Up, X, Down, Left, R, X, Right. This gives you the Pistol, Baseball Bat, Carbine Rifle, RPG, Micro SMG, Shotgun, and Flashbangs with max ammo.

WEATHER: SUNNY
During a game, press Up, Down, Left, Right, A, B, L, R.

WEATHER: CLOUDY
During a game, press Up, Down, Left, Right, X, Y, L, R.

WEATHER: RAIN
During a game, press Up, Down, Left, Right, Y, A, L, R.

WEATHER: HEAVY RAIN
During a game, press Up, Down, Left, Right, A, X, R, L.

WEATHER: THUNDERSTORMS
During a game, press Up, Down, Left, Right, B, Y, R, L.

GRID

UNLOCK ALL
Select Cheat Codes from the Options and enter 233558.

INVULNERABILITY
Select Cheat Codes from the Options and enter 161650.

DRIFT MASTER
Select Cheat Codes from the Options and enter 789520.

PERFECT GRIP
Select Cheat Codes from the Options and enter 831782.

HIGH ROLLER
Select Cheat Codes from the Options and enter 401134.

GHOST CAR
Select Cheat Codes from the Options and enter 657346.

TOY CARS
Select Cheat Codes from the Options and enter 592014.

MM MODE
Select Cheat Codes from the Options and enter 800813.

INFINITE SPACE

NEW GAME+ & EXTRA MODE
Complete the game. New Game+ unlocks additional blue prints, while Extra Mode is another game mode with limited resources.

IZUNA: LEGEND OF THE UNEMPLOYED NINJA

PATH OF TRAILS BONUS DUNGEON
After completing the game, touch the crystal from the beginning.

JACKASS THE GAME

CHANGE MUSIC
Press A + Y + Up.

JAKE HUNTER: DETECTIVE CHRONICLES

PASSWORDS
Select Password from the Main menu and enter the following:

UNLOCKABLE	PASSWORD
1 Password Info	AAAA
2 Visuals	LEET
3 Visuals	GONG
4 Visuals	CARS

UNLOCKABLE	PASSWORD
5 Movies	ROSE
6 Jukebox	BIKE
7 Hints	HINT

JAKE HUNTER DETECTIVE STORY: MEMORIES OF THE PAST

JAKE HUNTER QUIZ
Select Password and enter NEET.

JAKE HUNTER SERIES
Select Password and enter MISS.

JAKE HUNTER UNLEASHED 01 BONUS
Select Password and enter NONE.

JAKE HUNTER UNLEASHED 02 BONUS
Select Password and enter ANGL.

JAKE HUNTER UNLEASHED 03 BONUS
Select Password and enter SNAP.

JAKE HUNTER UNLEASHED 04 BONUS
Select Password and enter DOOR.

JAKE HUNTER UNLEASHED 05 BONUS
Select Password and enter STOP.

JAKE HUNTER UNLEASHED DS1 BONUS
Select Password and enter KING.

JAKE HUNTER VISUALS 1
Select Password and enter LEET.

JAKE HUNTER VISUALS 2
Select Password and enter GONG.

JAKE HUNTER VISUALS 3
Select Password and enter CARS.

JAKE HUNTER VISUALS 4
Select Password and enter TREE.

JAKE HUNTER VISUALS 5
Select Password and enter PAPA.

JUKEBOX
Select Password and enter BIKE.

MOVIE GALLERY
Select Password and enter ROSE.

PASSWORD HINTS
Select Password and enter HINT.

SIDE CHARACTER'S BONUS STORY
Select Password and enter MINU.

STAFF COMMENTS 1
Select Password and enter AQUA.

STAFF COMMENTS 2
Select Password and enter MOTO.

WHAT IS A PASSWORD?
Select Password and enter AAAA.

JAM SESSIONS

BONUS SONGS
At the Free Play menu, press Up, Up, Down, Down, Left, Right, Left, Right. This unlocks I'm Gonna Miss Her by Brad Paisley, Needles and Pins by Tom Petty, and Wild Thing by Jimi Hendrix.

JUICED 2: HOT IMPORT NIGHTS

$5000
At the Cheat menu, enter HSAC.

ALL CARS
At the Cheat menu, enter SRAC.

ALL RACES
At the Cheat menu, enter EDOM.

ALL TRACKS
At the Cheat menu, enter KART.

JUMBLE MADNESS

FEBRUARY 31 PUZZLE
For Daily Jumble and Jumble Crosswords, select the square under February 28, 2009.

KIRBY: CANVAS CURSE

JUMP GAME
Defeat the game with all five characters, then select the game file to get Jump Game next to the Options on the Main menu.

THE LAST AIRBENDER

FOCUS UPGRADE
Select Cheats from the Options menu and enter Earth, Earth, Water, Earth.

HEALTH UPGRADE
Select Cheats from the Options menu and enter Air, Water, Fire, Fire.

HEAVY HITTER
Select Cheats from the Options menu and enter Water, Earth, Fire, Fire.

LEGO BATMAN

ALFRED PENNYWORTH
Use the computer in the Batcave, select Enter Code and enter ZAQ637.

BATGIRL
Use the computer in the Batcave, select Enter Code and enter JKR331.

BRUCE WAYNE
Use the computer in the Batcave, select Enter Code and enter BDJ327.

CLASSIC CATWOMAN
Use the computer in the Batcave, select Enter Code and enter M1AAWW.

NINTENDO DS

CLOWN GOON
Use the computer in the Batcave, select Enter Code and enter HJK327.

COMMISSIONER GORDON
Use the computer in the Batcave, select Enter Code and enter DDP967.

FISHMONGER
Use the computer in the Batcave, select Enter Code and enter HGY748.

FREEZE GIRL
Use the computer in the Batcave, select Enter Code and enter XVK541.

FREEZE HENCHMAN
Use the computer in the Batcave, select Enter Code and enter NJL412.

JOKER GOON
Use the computer in the Batcave, select Enter Code and enter UTF782.

JOKER HENCHMAN
Use the computer in the Batcave, select Enter Code and enter YUN924.

NIGHTWING
Use the computer in the Batcave, select Enter Code and enter MVY759.

TROPICAL JOKER
Use the computer in the Batcave, select Enter Code and enter CCB199.

1 MILLION STUDS
At the Main menu, press X, Y, B, B, Y, X, L, L, R, R, Up, Down, Left, Right, Start, Select.

3 MILLION STUDS
At the Main menu, press Up, Up, B, Down, Down, X, Left, Left, Y, L, R, L, R, B, Y, X, Start, Select.

ALL CHARACTERS
At the Main menu, press X, Up, B, Down, Y, Left, Start, Right, R, R, L, R, R, Down, Down, Up, Y, Y, Y, Start, Select.

ALL EPISODES AND FREE PLAY MODE
At the Main menu, press Right, Up, R, L, X, Y, Right, Left, B, L, R, L, Down, Down, Up, Y, Y, X, X, B, B, Up, Up, L, R, Start, Select.

ALL EXTRAS
At the Main menu, press Up, Down, L, R, L, R, L, Left, Right, X, X, Y, Y, B, B, L, Up, Down, L, R, L, R, Up, Up, Down, Start, Select.

LEGO BATTLES

To activate the following cheats, pause the game and tap the red brick.

INVINCIBLE HERO
At the LEGO Store, tap the Red Brick and enter HJCRAWK.

REGENERATING HEALTH
At the LEGO Store, tap the Red Brick and enter ABABLRX.

ONE-HIT KILL (HEROES)
At the LEGO Store, tap the Red Brick and enter AVMPWHK.

LONG-RANGE MAGIC
At the LEGO Store, tap the Red Brick and enter ZPWJFUQ.

SUPER MAGIC
At the LEGO Store, tap the Red Brick and enter DWFTBNS.

DOUBLE LEGO BRICKS
At the LEGO Store, tap the Red Brick and enter BGQOYRT.

FAST BUILDING
At the LEGO Store, tap the Red Brick and enter QMSLPOE.

FAST HARVESTING
At the LEGO Store, tap the Red Brick and enter PQZLJOB.

FAST MAGIC
At the LEGO Store, tap the Red Brick and enter JRTPASX.

FAST MINING
At the LEGO Store, tap the Red Brick and enter KVBPQRJ.

FULL UNIT CAP
At the LEGO Store, tap the Red Brick and enter UMSXIRQ.

SUPER EXPLOSIONS
At the LEGO Store, tap the Red Brick and enter THNBGRE.

UPGRADED TOWERS
At the LEGO Store, tap the Red Brick and enter EDRFTGY.

SHOW ENEMIES
At the LEGO Store, tap the Red Brick and enter IBGOFWX.

SHOW LEGO STUDS
At the LEGO Store, tap the Red Brick and enter CPLYREK.

SHOW MINIKIT
At the LEGO Store, tap the Red Brick and enter LJYQRAC.

SHOW RED BRICKS
At the LEGO Store, tap the Red Brick and enter RTGYPKC.

REVEAL MAP
At the LEGO Store, tap the Red Brick and enter SKQMXPL.

UNLOCK ISLANDER
At the LEGO Store, tap the Red Brick and enter UGDRSQP.

UNLOCK NINJA MASTER
At the LEGO Store, tap the Red Brick and enter SHWSDGU.

UNLOCK SPACE CRIMINAL LEADER
At the LEGO Store, tap the Red Brick and enter ZVDNJSU.

UNLOCK TROLL KING
At the LEGO Store, tap the Red Brick and enter XRCTVYB.

LEGO INDIANA JONES: THE ORIGINAL ADVENTURES

You should hear a confirmation sound after the following codes are entered.

ALL CHARACTERS
At the Title screen, press X, Up, B, Down, Y, Left, Start, Right, R, R, L, R, R, Down, Down, Up, Y, Y, Y, Start, Select.

ALL EPISODES AND FREE PLAY MODE
Right, Up, R, L, X, Y, Right, Left, B, L, R, L, Down, Down, Up, Y, Y, X, X, B, B, Up, Up, L, R, Start, Select.

ALL EXTRAS
Up, Down, L, R, L, R, L, Left, Right, X, X, Y, Y, B, B, L, Up, Down, L, R, L, R, Up, Up, Down, Start, Select.

1,000,000 STUDS
At the Title screen, press X, Y, B, B, Y, X, L, L, R, R, Up, Down, Left, Right, Start, Select.

3,000,000 STUDS
At the Title screen, press Up, Up, B, Down, Down, X, Left, Left, Y, L, R, L, R, B, Y, X, Start, Select.

LEGO ROCK BAND

BLUR
In Tour Mode, complete Song 2.

DAVID BOWIE
In Tour Mode, complete Let's Dance.

IGGY POP
In Tour Mode, complete The Passenger.

QUEEN
In Tour Mode, complete We Are the Champions.

LEGO STAR WARS: THE COMPLETE SAGA

3,000,000 STUDS
At the main menu, press START, START, Down, Down, Left, Left, Up, Up, SELECT. This cheat can only be used once.

DEBUG MENUS
At the main menu, press Up, Left, Down, Right, Up, Left, Down, Right, Up, Left, Down, Right, R, L, START, SELECT.

BONUS TOUCH GAME 1
At the main menu, press Up, Up, Down, L, L, R, R.

LEGO STAR WARS II: THE ORIGINAL TRILOGY

10 STUDS
At the Mos Eisley cantina, enter 4PR28U.

OBI WAN GHOST
At the Mos Eisley cantina, enter BEN917.

LITTLEST PET SHOP: GARDEN

GIRAFFE PET
Select Passwords from the Options and enter LPSTRU. It is available in the Meow Market.

LITTLEST PET SHOP: JUNGLE

GIRAFFE PET
Select Passwords from the Options and enter LPSTRU. It is available in the Meow Market.

LOCK'S QUEST

REPLACE CLOCKWORKS WITH KINGDOM FORCE
After completing the game, hold R and select your profile.

ENDING STORY
After completing the game, hold L and select your profile.

LUNAR KNIGHTS

SOUND DATA (BOKTAI)
With Boktai in the GBA slot, purchase this from the General Store in Acuna.

SOUND DATA (BOKTAI 2)
With Boktai 2 in the GBA slot, purchase this from the General Store in Acuna.

MARIO & LUIGI: BOWSER'S INSIDE STORY

LUMBAR NOOK ALARM
In the Lumbar Nook, when you dig into the bone, press A, B, X, Y, L, R, Y, X, B, A to set off the alarm. Otherwise, you have to wait awhile for it.

MARIO PARTY DS

BOSS BASH
Complete Story Mode.

EXPERT CPU DIFFICULTY LEVEL
Complete Story Mode.

MUSIC AND VOICE ROOM
Complete Story Mode.

SCORE SCUFFLE
Complete Story Mode.

TRIANGLE TWISTER PUZZLE MODE
Complete Story Mode.

MARVEL SUPER HERO SQUAD

APOCALYPSE MODE
Select Cheats from the Settings and enter Wolverine, Wolverine, Dr Doom, Abomination, Wolverine. This gives everyone one hit kills.

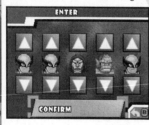

MEGAMAN BATTLE NETWORK 5: DOUBLE TEAM

NUMBERMAN CODES

When the Numberman machine is available in Higsby's Shop, enter the following codes.

CODE	ENTER
Area Steal *	99428938
Dark Recovery *	91182599
DoroTsunamiBall *	78234329
Leaders Raid L	01285874
Lord of Chaos X	39285712
MagmaSeed *	29387483
NumberBall *	64836563
P. Battle Pack 1	22323856
P. Battle Pack 2	66426428
P.Attack+3	76820385
P.Chip+50	48582829
P.HP+100	28475692
P.HP+50	53891756
Super Kitakaze *	29486933
Sword *	12495783
TP Chip	85375720
Tsunami Hole *	19283746
Unlocker	15733751

NUMBERMAN NAVI CUSTOMIZER PROGRAM

Enter the following codes in the Numberman Lotto Number.

CODE	ENTER
Attack Max Yellow	63231870
Beat Blue	79877132
BodyPack Green	30112002
BustPack Blue	80246758
Charge Max White	87412146
HP+200 Pink	90630807
HP+300 Pink	48785625
HP+300 White	13926561
HP+400 Pink	03419893
HP+400 Yellow	45654128
HP+500 Pink	50906652
HP+500 White	72846472
Mega Folder 2 Green	97513648
Rush Yellow	09609807
SoulT+1 Yellow	28256341
Speed Max Pink	36695497
Spin Blue	12541883
Spin Green	78987728
Spin Red	30356451
Tango Green	54288793

MEGA MAN STAR FORCE 3: BLACK ACE

STARS ON NEW GAME/CONTINUE SCREEN

Do the following to earn each star on the New Game/Continue screen.

NAME	HOW TO EARN
Black Ace	Defeat the game
G Comp	Collect all Giga cards
M Comp	Collect all Mega cards
S Comp	Collect all Standard cards
SS	Defeat Sirius

RANDOM SIGMA BOSSES

At the New Game/Continue screen, hold L and tap S Comp Star, G Comp Star, S Comp Star, M Comp Star, SS Star, SS Star, Black Ace Star.

FIGHT ROGUEZZ

At the New Game/Continue screen, hold L and tap G Comp Star, M Comp Star, M Comp Star, SS Star, G Comp Star, S Comp Star, Black Ace Star. RogueZZ appears in Meteor G Control CC.

MEGA MAN STAR FORCE 3: RED JOKER

STARS ON NEW GAME/CONTINUE SCREEN

Do the following to earn each star on the New Game/Continue screen.

NAME	HOW TO EARN
Red Joker	Defeat the game
G Comp	Collect all Giga cards
M Comp	Collect all Mega cards
S Comp	Collect all Standard cards
SS	Defeat Sirius

RANDOM SIGMA BOSSES
At the New Game/Continue screen, hold L and tap S Comp Star, G Comp Star, S Comp Star, M Comp Star, SS Star, SS Star, Red Joker Star.

FIGHT ROGUEZZ
At the New Game/Continue screen, hold L and tap G Comp Star, M Comp Star, M Comp Star, SS Star, G Comp Star, S Comp Star, Red Joker Star. RogueZZ appears in Meteor G Control CC.

METROID PRIME PINBALL

PHAZON MINES
Complete Omega Pirate in Multi Mission Mode.

PHENDRANA DRIFTS
Complete Thardus in Multi Mission Mode.

MIGHT & MAGIC: CLASH OF HEROES

UNLOCK CHARACTERS IN QUICK BATTLE AND MULTIPLAYER
Unlock new characters in Quick Battle and Multiplayer modes as you complete the chapters.

CHARACTER UNLOCKED	CHAPTER COMPLETED
Findan	1 - Anwen
Varkas	2 - Godric
Markal	3 - Fiona
Jezebeth	4 - Aidan
Cyrus	5 – Nadia

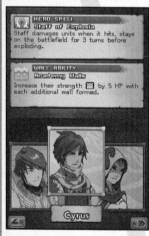

MIMANA IYAR CHRONICLE

ARCANUM OF LIFE
At the Lucky Cat Bakery when the owner asks for a password, enter LITTLE DEVIL.

FOOD KIT
At the Lucky Cat Bakery when the owner asks for a password, enter AKSYS GAMES.

SEXY SWIMSUIT
At the Lucky Cat Bakery when the owner asks for a password, enter LITTLE ANGEL.

MY JAPANESE COACH

UNLOCK LESSONS
Look up the word cheat in the dictionary. Touch the V next to the verb to open the conjugation chart. Hold L + R for a few seconds. You should hear the word cheat in Japanese. Return to the Main menu, go to Options, then Sound. Pressing R will advance you one lesson, and pressing L will advance you to the beginning of the next lesson group.

MYSIMS KINGDOM

COW COSTUME
Pause the game and press R, X, L, Y, Up, Right, Left, Down.

COW HEADGEAR
Pause the game and press L, R, Y, X, Left, Down, Left, Right.

PATCHWORK CLOTHES
Pause the game and press Right, Down, Left, Up, L, R, L, R.

PATCHWORK PANTS
Pause the game and press Down, L, Left, R, Up, Y, Right, X.

PUNK BOTTOM
Pause the game and press Left, R, L, Right, Y, Y, X, X.

PUNK TOP
Pause the game and press Up, X, Down, Y, Left, L, Right, R.

SAMURAI ARMOR
Pause the game and press Y, X, Right, Left, L, R, Down, Up.

SAMURAI HELMET
Pause the game and press X, Y, R, L, X, Y, R, L.

MY WORD COACH

WORD POPPERS MINIGAME
After reaching 200 word successes, press A, B, X, Y, A, B at the Options menu.

N+

ATARI BONUS LEVELS
Select Unlockables from the Main menu, hold L + R and press A, B, A, B, A, A, B.

NARUTO: PATH OF THE NINJA

After defeating the game, talk to Knohamaru on the roof of the Ninja Academy. He allows you go get certain cheats by tapping four successive spots on the touch screen in order. There are 12 different spots on the screen, we have numbered them from left to right, top to bottom as follows:

1	2	3	4
5	6	7	8
9	10	11	12

Now enter the following by touching the four spots in the order given.

UNLOCK	CODE
4th Hokage's Sword	4, 7, 11, 5
Fuji Fan	8, 11, 2, 5
Jiraiya	11, 3, 1, 6
Rajin's Sword	7, 6, 5, 11
Rasengan	9, 2, 12, 7

NARUTO: PATH OF THE NINJA 2

CHARACTER PASSWORDS

Talk to Konohamaru at the school to enter the following passwords. You must first complete the game for the passwords to work.

CHARACTER	PASSWORD
Gaara	D K F I A B J L
Gai	I K A G D E F L
Iruka	J G D L K A I B
Itachi Uchiha	G B E I D A L F
Jiraiya	E B J D A G F L
Kankuro	A L J K B E D G
Kyuubi Naruto	G J H L B F D E
Orochimaru	A H F B L E J G

NEW SUPER MARIO BROS.

PLAY AS LUIGI IN SINGLE-PLAYER MODE

At the Select a File screen, press and hold L + R while selecting a saved game.

SECRET CHALLENGE MODE

While on the map, pause the game and press L, R, L, R, X, X, Y, Y.

THE NEW YORK TIMES CROSSWORDS

BLACK & WHITE

At the Main menu, press Up, Up, Down, Down, B, B, Y, Y.

NICKTOONS: ATTACK OF THE TOYBOTS

DANNY PHANTOM 2

Select Unlock Code from the Options and enter Tak, Jimmy, Zim, El Tigre.

SPONGEBOB 2

Select Unlock Code from the Options and enter Patrick, Jenny, Timmy, Tak.

NIGHT AT THE MUSEUM: BATTLE OF THE SMITHSONIAN

SUPER LARRY

During a game, hold L + R, and press Left, A, Right, Right, Y.

PEGGLE: DUAL SHOT

Q LEVEL 10

Send the trial game to another DS.

PHANTASY STAR ZERO

PASSWORD MACHINE

Check out the vending machine on the far right side of the sewers. Type in special passwords here to find free items.

ITEM	PASSWORD	ITEM	PASSWORD
Selvaria's Spear	5703-8252	INGame: Greg&Kiri (Nintendo Dream)	5531-0215
Selvaria's Shield	4294-2273	Nintendo Power (Dengeki DS)	3171-0109
Blade Cannon	7839-3594		
Caduceus's Rod	5139-6877	Puyo Soul	3470-1424
Game Master (Ge-maga)	7162-5792	Taupy Soul	9475-6843
CONSOLES+ (Famitsu)	9185-6189	Lassie Soul	4775-7197

PHINEAS AND FERB

STOP CANDACE
At the Title screen, press X, Y, L, R, Select.

DOUBLE SPEED
At the Title screen, press A, B, L, R, Select.

PHOTO DOJO

FAST FIGHTERS
At the Title screen, hold Select and choose Head into Battle. Continue to hold Select and choose Vs. Mode.

PIRATES OF THE CARIBBEAN: DEAD MAN'S CHEST

10 GOLD
During a game, press Right, X, X, Right, Left.

INVINCIBILITY
During a game, press Up, Down, Left, Right (x5), Left, Right, Up, Down, Left, Right, Up (x5), Left.

UNLIMITED POWER
During a game, press Up, Up, Down, Down, Left, Right, Left, Right, L, R.

RESTORE HEALTH
During a game, press Y, Y, Select, Left, Right, Left, Right, Left.

RESTORE SAVVY
During a game, press X, X, Select, Up, Down, Up, Down, Up.

GHOST FORM MODE
During a game, press Y, X, Y, X, Y, X.

SEASICKNESS MODE
During a game, press X, X, Y, X, X, Y.

SILLY WEAPONS
During a game, press Y, Y, X, Y (x3).

AXE
During a game, press Left, L, L, Down, Down, Left, Up, Up, Down, Down.

BLUNDERBUSS
During a game, press Down, L, L, Down (x3).

CHICKEN
During a game, press Right, L, L, Up, Down, Down.

EXECUTIONER AXE
During a game, press Right, L, L, Up, Down, Up, Right, Right, Left (x2).

PIG
During a game, press Right, R, R, Down, Up, Up.

PISTOL
During a game, press Down, L, L, Down, Down, Right.

RIFLE
During a game, press Left, L, L, Up (x3).

FAST MUSIC
During a game, press Y, Select, Y (x4).

SLOW MUSIC
During a game, press Y, Select, X (x4).

DISABLE CHEATS
During a game, press X (x6).

POKEMON MYSTERY DUNGEON: EXPLORERS OF DARKNESS/TIME

Select Wonder Mail before starting your game, and then enter the following passwords to add a mission to your Job List. These are listed by the reward you receive for completing the mission.

Each password can only be used once. There are many possible passwords, here we list some examples. These passwords work on Explorers of Darkness and Explorers of Time.

ACCESSORY

ACCESSORY	PASSWORD
Gold Ribbon	5+KPKXT9RYP754&M2-58&&1-
Golden Mask	@QYPSJ@-N-J%TH6=4-SK32CR
Joy Ribbon	597C6#873795@Q6=F+TSQ68J
Mobile Scarf	R2MQ0X0&&-RN+64#4S0R+&-1
Miracle Chest	FX199P@CW@-XK54Q%4628XT#
No-Stick Cap	1@484PJ7NJW@XCHC2&-+H=@P
Pecha Scarf	8%2R-T&T1F-KR5#08P#&T=@=
Persim Band	TCX#TJQ0%#46Q6MJYMH2S#C9

ACCESSORY	PASSWORD
Power Band	FHSM5950-2QNFTH9S-JM3Q9F
Racket Band	-F773&1XM0FRJT7Y@PJ%9C40
Special Band	752PY8M-Q1NHY#QX92836MHT
Stamina Band	F9RM4Y6W1&2T7@%SWF=R0NK&
X-Ray Specs	C#7H-#P2J9QPHCFPM5F674H=
Wonder Chest	0@R#3-+&7SC2K3@4NQ0-JQX9
Zinc Band	@WWHK8X18@C+C8KTN51H#213

ITEM

ITEM	PASSWORD
Beauty Scarf	@+CWF98#5CPYR13RJ#3YWKS5
Calcium	Y=59NRNS-#M2%C25725NJMQQ
Coronet Rock	S%9@47NTYP#Y105SR#%QH9MX
Dawn Stone	N54=MK=FSH1FCR8=R@HN14#Y
Deepseascale	WT192-H2=K@-WTJ3=JJ64C16
Deepseatooth	WQCM0-H=QH&-W+JP7FKT4CP+
Dusk Stone	X0=-JQ&X1X4KRY=8Y=23M=FH
Electrilizer	4SJYCFNX0-N@JN%NQ#+7-Q7#
Frozen Rock	YT&8WY&+278+2QJT@53TM3M8
Heal Seed	TWTN%RFRK+39-P#M2X+CXQS#
Joy Seed	PQS39&-7WC+R&QJQM2Y@@1KN
Leaf Stone	NP96N4K0HW3CJX8#FNK%=F&+
Link Box	&%8FXT9C76F4Q4SP5F8X3RW%
Lost Loot	J%0+F18XW5%P-9@&17+F8P9M
Lunar Ribbon	%-94RKFY%505XXMMC=FYK45N
Magmarizer	=TK+0KH72MNJNRW5P@RS&Y6=
Max Elixir	4Q9F-K6X66YW5TJY6MXK+RX7
Metal Coat	NP3SMTH-T&TMQFY@N1Q&SFNK
Mossy Rock	@JH#ST1&S14W3T2XJ8=7KR+7
Mystery Part	PXJ634F44Q3FQW&KYRX538+=
Oval Stone	@&FYQ977C#0YN-77TM&=X&+Q
Razor Claw	6JK2T26&MPC7&%-HWRXK2&-W
Reviver Seed	W+P0MYKJFNN3&Q%&-J12J2QH
Secret Slab	K=&4Q=@908N7=X&XHQ+Q1-CS
Shiny Stone	69-HHQX%K@#%7+5SMSPSQP#2
Sun Ribbon	7C8W308RYJ2XM@&QTYSJ%3=9
Thunderstone	+4QQK3PY84Y39P&=KN3=@XYR
Vile Seed	8#8%4496C#=JKRX9M&RKQW4%
Zinc	X=S#N&RNYSP9R2S01HT4MP8&

TM

TM	PASSWORD
Attract	Y@=JC48#K4SQ0NS9#S7@/32%3
Blizzard	Y#ST42FMC4H+NM@M=T999#PR
Brick Break	@MF=%8400Y8X#T8FCTQC5XTS
Brine	9C04WP5XXN@=4NPFR08SS&03
Calm Mind	SH&YH&96C%&JK9Y0H99%3WM9
Dig	SQ96Y08RXJJXMJJ7=SSQK3K3
Embargo	1PQ7K%JX#4=HFHXPPK%7K04H
Energy Ball	5016-@1X8@&5H46@51M&+-XC
Fire Blast	W0T+NF98J13+F&NN=XNR&J-7
Flamethrower	JQ78%-CK%1PTP-77M740=F98
Flash	FS272Y61F1@MNN8FCSSTJ6TP
Gyro Ball	C#S@Y4%9YFQ+SQ6WRK36@1N0
Iron Tail	8+R006Y-&X57XX#&N-PT@R&6
Overheat	F=X5&K=FYJ3FC-N-@QXK34QJ
Payback	K3%0=W61FQCMN-FPHP=J5&W3
Poison Jab	S==YMX%92R54TSK6=F8%-%MN
Protect	Q@#6762JK@967H#CMX#RQ3&M3
Psych Up	6=49WKH72&-JN%14SKNF&40N

TM	PASSWORD
Recycle	M@56C+=@H%K13WF4Q%RJ2JP9
Reflect	F=YTCK297HC02MT+MF13SQ4W
Rest	KR=WT#JC#@+HFS5K0JJM-0-2
Roar	C&0FWPTCRMKT&7NQ@N0&RQS+
Rock Slide	CN%+TMSHM0&3#&5YC4M1#C@2
Skill Swap	-H4TNNKY&1-P%4HSJY&XHW%Q
Sleep Talk	1M5972RY8X6NCC3CPPRS0K8J
Swords Dance	=633=JSY147RT=&0R9PJJ1FM
Thunder	WKY&7==@HR2%32YX6755JQ85
Vacuum-Cut	7PS2#26WN7HNX83M23J6F@C5
X-Scissor	S6P&198+-5QYR&22FJMKW1XF

POP CUTIE! STREET FASHION SIMULATION

LAYERED DRESS
At a phone, enter 7247.

POODLE OUTFIT
At a phone, enter 3107.

HOTEL PATAGONIA/EDDIE RETURNS
At a phone, enter 9901.

CALL GIBSONS
At a phone, enter 9801.

FASHION HOTLINE
At a phone enter 0000, 1111, 2222, 3333, 4444, 5555, 6666.

PRINCESS NATASHA

ALL GADGETS
Select Codes from the Extras menu and enter OLEGSGIZMO.

EXTRA LEVELS
Select Codes from the Extras menu and enter SMASHROBOT.

INFINITE LIVES
Select Codes from the Extras menu and enter CRUSHLUBEK.

RACE DRIVER: CREATE & RACE

ALL CHALLENGES
Select Cheat Codes from Extras and enter 942785.

ALL CHAMPIONSHIPS
Select Cheat Codes from Extras and enter 761492.

ALL REWARDS
Select Cheat Codes from Extras and enter 112337.

FREE DRIVE
Select Cheat Codes from Extras and enter 171923.

NO DAMAGE
Select Cheat Codes from Extras and enter 505303.

EASY STEERING
Select Cheat Codes from Extras and enter 611334.

MINIATURE CARS
Select Cheat Codes from Extras and enter 374288.

MM VIEW
Select Cheat Codes from Extras and enter 467348.

RETRO GAME CHALLENGE

COSMIC GATE

HARD MODE
At the Title screen, press Down, Down, B, B, A, A, Start.

POWERED-UP INFINITY
Pause the game and press Up, Up, A, B. This cheat can only be used once per game.

SHIP POWER-UP
Pause the game and press Up, Up, A, A, B, B.

CONTINUE GAME
At the Game Over screen, press Left + Start. You will continue the game with a score of 000.

HAGGLE MAN

FULL HEALTH
Pause the game and press Down, Right, Up, Left, B, B, B, B, A, A, A, A.

SCROLLS APPEAR
Pause the game and press Up, Right, Down, Left, A, A, A, A, B, B, B, B.

INFINITE TIME
Before a level, hold Up/Left and press A + B.

HAGGLE MAN 2

STAGE SELECT
At the Title screen, hold A and press Up, Up, Right, Right, Right, Down, Down, Left, Left, Left.

FULL POWER
Pause the game and press Up, Down, Up, Down, B, B, A, A.

SCROLLS APPEAR
Pause the game and press Down, Up, Down, Up, A, A, B, B.

CONTINUE
At the Game Over screen, hold Left and press Start.

HAGGLE MAN 3

99 LIVES
Pause the game and press A, B, A, B, Left, Right, Left, Right.

9999 GEARS
Pause the game and press B, A, B, A, Right, Left, Right, Left.

WARP TO BOSS
Pause the game and press B, B, A, A, Left, Left, Right, Right.

RALLY KING

INVINCIBILITY
At the Title screen, press Select + Left.

CARS DISAPPEAR
At the Title screen, hold Select and press Down/Right.

START AT COURSE 2
At the Title screen, press A, B, A, B, Up + Select.

START AT COURSE 3
At the Title screen, press A, B, A, B, Left + Select.

START AT COURSE 4
At the Title screen, press A, B, A, B, Down + Select.

STAR PRINCE

INVINCIBILITY
At the Title screen, hold Up and press A, A, A. Then hold Down and press B, B, B.

CONTINUE
At the Game Over screen, hold Left and press Start.

RHYTHM HEAVEN

RHYTHM TOYS — TELEPHONE NUMBERS
Enter the following numbers into the telephone in Rhythm Toys to unlock sounds from Rhythm Tengoku:
5553282338
5557325937
5557268724
5557625688

RIDGE RACER DS

00-AGENT CAR
Finish more than 10 races in Multiplayer.

CADDY CAR
Finish more than 10 races in Multiplayer.

GALAGA '88 CAR
Finish more than 10 races in Multiplayer.

MARIO RACING CAR
Finish more than 10 races in Multiplayer.

POOKA CAR
Finish more than 10 races in Multiplayer.

RED SHIRT RAGE CAR
Finish more than 10 races in Multiplayer.

SHY GUY CAR
Finish more than 10 races in Multiplayer.

GALAGA PAC JAM SONG
Unlock the Pooka car.

MUSHROOM KINGDOM II SONG
Unlock the DK Team Racing car.

RUBIK'S PUZZLE WORLD

ALL LEVELS AND CUBIES
At the Main menu, press X, Y, Y, X, X.

SCOOBY-DOO! FIRST FRIGHTS

DAPHNE'S SECRET COSTUME
Select Codes from the Extras menu and enter 2839.

FRED'S SECRET COSTUME
Select Codes from the Extras menu and enter 4826.

SCOOBY DOO'S SECRET COSTUME
Select Codes from the Extras menu and enter 1585.

SHAGGY'S SECRET COSTUME
Select Codes from the Extras menu and enter 3726.

VELMA'S SECRET COSTUME
Select Codes from the Extras menu and enter 6588.

SHIN MEGAMI TENSEI: STRANGE JOURNEY

Enter the following passwords to unlock the Demons.

HATHOR
Nymph and Angel harem

ISHTAR
ISHTAR FIGHTS
TAMMUZ ANGELS

JUEYUAN
Beast and Snake tangle

KOPPA TENGU
Left hand freeze
Right hand shock

MOTHMAN
Prophecy of wind

ONI
Thick red skin

SILKY
Soothing ice

SHREK SUPERSLAM

ALTERNATE OUTFIT FOR SHREK
Start the game with the GBA version of Shrek SuperSlam in the GBA slot.

SIMCITY CREATOR

99999999 MONEY
Enter MONEYBAGS as a password.

AMERICAN PROSPERITY AGE MAP
Enter NEWWORLD as a password.

ASIA AGE MAP
Enter SAMURAI as a password.

ASIA AGE BONUS MAP
Enter FEUDAL as a password.

DAWN OF CIVILIZATION MAP
Enter ANCIENT as a password.

GLOBAL WARMING MAP
Enter MODERN as a password.

GLOBAL WARMING BONUS MAP
Enter BEYOND as a password.

RENAISSANCE BONUS MAP
Enter HEREANDNOW as a password.

SIMCITY DS

LANDMARK BUILDINGS
Select Landmark Collection from the Museum menu. Choose Password and enter the following:

BUILDING	PASSWORD
Anglican Cathedral (UK)	kipling
Arc de Triomphe (France)	gaugin
Atomic Dome (Japan)	kawabata
Big Ben (UK)	orwell
Bowser Castle (Nintendo)	hanafuda
Brandenburg Gate (Germany)	gropius
Coit Tower	kerouac
Conciergerie (France)	rodin
Daibutsu (Japan)	mishima
Edo Castle (Japan)	shonagon
Eiffel Tower (France)	camus
Gateway Arch (USA)	twain
Grand Central Station (USA)	f.scott
Great Pyramids (Egypt)	mahfouz
Hagia Sofia (Turkey)	ataturk
Helsinki Cathedral (Finland)	kivi
Himeji Castle (Japan)	hokusai
Holstentor (Germany)	durer

OVERLOAD

NINTENDO DS

BUILDING	PASSWORD
Independence Hall (USA)	mlkingjr
Jefferson Memorial (USA)	thompson
Kokkai (Japan)	soseki
LA Landmark (USA)	hemingway
Lincoln Memorial (USA)	melville
Liver Building (UK)	dickens
Melbourne Cricket Ground (Australia)	damemelba
Metropolitan Cath. (UK)	austen
Moai (Chile)	allende
Mt. Fuji (Japan)	hiroshige
National Museum (Taiwan)	yuanlee
Neuschwanstein Castle (Germany)	beethoven
Notre Dame (France)	hugo
Palace of Fine Arts (USA)	bunche
Palacio Real (Spain)	cervantes
Paris Opera (France)	daumier
Parthenon (Greece)	callas
Pharos of Alexandria (Egypt)	zewail
Rama IX Royal Park (Thailand)	phu
Reichstag (Germany)	goethe
Sagrada Familia (Spain)	dali
Shuri Castle (Japan)	basho
Smithsonian Castle (USA)	pauling
Sphinx (Egypt)	haykal
St Paul's Cathedral (UK)	defoe
St. Basil's Cathedral (Russia)	tolstoy
St. Stephen's Cathedral (Austria)	mozart
Statue of Liberty (USA)	pollack
Stockholm Palace (Sweden)	bergman
Taj Mahal (India)	tagore
Tower of London (UK)	maugham
Trafalgar Square (UK)	joyce
United Nations (UN)	amnesty
United States Capitol (USA)	poe
Washington Monument	capote
Westminster Abbey (UK)	greene
White House (USA)	Steinbeck

THE SIMS 2

MONGOO MONKEY FOR THE CASINO
Start the game with Sims 2 in the GBA slot of your Nintendo DS.

THE SIMS 2 APARTMENT PETS

$10,000
From the PDA screen, select the disk icon. Then choose Unlockable from the Options and enter Cash.

SKATE IT

EMO CRYS
At the Credits screen, press Up, Up, Left, Left, Down, Down, Right, Right.

JACK KNIFE
At the Credits screen, press X, A, X, Y, Up, Left, Down, Right.

JAY JAY
At the Credits screen, press L, R, A, Left, Right, Y, R, L.

LIL' ROB
At the Credits screen, press L, Left, Y, R, Right, A, Up, X.

SPITBALL
At the Credits screen, press Up, Up, Down, Down, L, R, L, R.

SONIC CLASSIC COLLECTION

SONIC THE HEDGEHOG

DEBUG MODE
At the title screen, press A, A, Up, Down, Left, Right, hold Y and press START.

LEVEL SELECT
At the title screen press Up, Down, Left, Right, hold Y and press START.

SONIC THE HEDGEHOG 2

LEVEL SELECT
At the title screen, press Up, Up, Up, Down, Down, Down, Left, Right, Left, Right, hold Y and press START.

SONIC THE HEDGEHOG 3

LEVEL SELECT
As the SEGA logo fades, quickly press Up, Up, Down, Down, Up, Up, Up, Up. Highlight Sound Test and press START.

SONIC KNUCKLES

LEVEL SELECT WITH SONIC THE HEDGEHOG 2
At the title screen, press Up, Up, Up, Down, Down, Down, Left, Right, Left, Right, hold A and press START.

SOUL BUBBLES

REVEAL ALL CALABASH LOCATIONS
Pause the game and press A, L, L, R, A, Down, A, R.

ALL LEVELS
At the World Select, press L, Up, X, Up, R, Y.

ALL GALLERY ITEMS
At the Gallery, press B, Up, B, B, L, Y.

SPECTROBES

CARD INPUT SYSTEM
When the Upsilon Cube is unearthed and shown to Aldous, the Card Input System feature becomes available. This will allow you to input data from Spectrobe Cards. These give you new Spectrobes and Custom Parts.

If you get your hands on a Spectrobe Card and the system is unlocked, investigate the card input system in the spaceship's lower deck. Follow the instructions on the upper screen to match the four corner points of the card to the corners of the touch screen. Touch the screen through the seven holes in the card in the order indicated on the card. If the code you input is

correct, you receive Spectrobes, custom Parts, minerals or Cubes.

You can input the same card a maximum of four times. This means that you can only obtain four of the same Spectrobes from a single card. Some cards are only able to be inputted once. And some cards cannot be input until you have reached a certain point in the game.

Here we give you the codes without needing the actual cards. There are 16 different spots that are used for these codes. These spots are labeled on the following image as A through P.

The following table gives you a seven character code which refers to the spots you touch in order. The first four characters have you touching the four corners and the final three are spots among the 12 in the middle. To get Cyclone Geo, Hammer Geo, Ice Geo, Plasma Geo, or Thunder Geo; you must first beat the game.

EFFECT	CODE	EFFECT	CODE
Aobasat Apex	BACD HEP	Grildragos Drafly	CDAB MHK
Cyclone Geo	CDAB LGM	Gristar	BACD EJN
Danaphant Tuska	ABDC ELI	Effect	Code
Danilob	DABC GLO	Hammer Geo	ABDC ELH
Emerald Mineral	BACD FKN	Harumitey Lazos	DABC ILM
Grilden Biblad	ABDC FIH	Ice Geo	CDAB HEK

EFFECT	CODE
Inataflare Auger	ABDC IGH
Inkalade	ABDC GLP
Iota Cube	ABDC OHE
Komainu	CDAB HMJ
Kugaster Sonara	DABC LOE
Mossax Jetspa (Custom Color 1)	BACD JML
Naglub	ABDC EJM
Plasma Geo	BACD KLE
Rho Cube	BACD PNI
Ruby Mineral	CDAB FKO
Samukabu	ABDC OIL
Samurite Voltar	BACD LHM
Sapphire Mineral	ABDC FJO
Segulos Propos	CDAB KIH
Seguslice	CDAB GKP
Shakor Bristle	DABC MLK
Sigma Cube	CDAB PML
Tau Cube	DABC LIF
Thunder Geo	DABC MEL
Vilagrisp (Custom Part)	DABC EIN

EFFECT	CODE
Vilakroma	BACD NLM
Vilakroma (Custom Color 1)	CDAB LJI
Vilakroma (Custom Color 2)	DABC EGP
Windora	ABDC MGP
Windora (Custom Color 1)	DABC EHG
Windora (Custom Color 2)	CDAB JPM
Windora Ortex	BACD IPG
Windora Ortex (Custom Color 1)	ABDC MPH
Windora Ortex (Custom Color 2)	DABC MGH
Windora Sordina	CDAB PEO
Windora Sordina (Custom Color 1)	BACD MOH
Windora Sordina (Custom Color 2)	ABDC LEN
Wing Geo (must beat game	DABC MNP

SPONGEBOB SQUAREPANTS FEATURING NICKTOONS: GLOBS OF DOOM

INFINITE HEALTH
Select Unlock Codes from the Options and enter Tak, Tlaloc, Jimmy Neutron, Beautiful Gorgeous.

INSTANT KO
Select Unlock Codes from the Options and enter Dib, Tak, Beautiful Gorgeous, Plankton.

EXTRA ATTACK
Select Unlock Codes from the Options and enter Dib, Plankton, Technus, Jimmy Neutron.

EXTRA DEFENSE
Select Unlock Codes from the Options and enter Zim, Danny Phantom, Plankton, Beautiful Gorgeous.

MAX DEFENSE
Select Unlock Codes from the Options and enter Plankton, Dib, Beautiful Gorgeous, Plankton.

ITEMS +
Select Unlock Codes from the Options and enter Danny Phantom, Beautiful Gorgeous, Jimmy Neutron, Technus.

ITEMS + +
Select Unlock Codes from the Options and enter SpongeBob, Tlaloc, SpongeBob, Danny Phantom.

NO HEALTH ITEMS
Select Unlock Codes from the Options and enter Tak, SpongeBob, Technus, Danny Phantom.

LOWER PRICES
Select Unlock Codes from the Options and enter Tlaloc, Zim, Beautiful Gorgeous, SpongeBob.

SUPER BEAUTIFUL GORGEOUS
Select Unlock Codes from the Options and enter Beautiful Gorgeous, Technus, Jimmy Neutron, Beautiful Gorgeous.

SUPER DANNY PHANTOM
Select Unlock Codes from the Options and enter Danny Phantom, Zim, Danny Phantom, Beautiful Gorgeous.

SUPER DIB
Select Unlock Codes from the Options and enter Zim, Plankton, Dib, Plankton.

SUPER JIMMY
Select Unlock Codes from the Options and enter Technus, Danny Phantom, Jimmy Neutron, Technus.

SUPER PLANKTON
Select Unlock Codes from the Options and enter Tak, Plankton, Dib, Technus.

SUPER SPONGEBOB
Select Unlock Codes from the Options and enter Technus, SpongeBob, Technus, Tlaloc.

SUPER TAK
Select Unlock Codes from the Options and enter Danny Phantom, Jimmy Neutron, Tak, Tlaloc.

SUPER TECHNUS
Select Unlock Codes from the Options and enter Danny Phantom, Technus, Tak, Technus.

SUPER TLALOC
Select Unlock Codes from the Options and enter Tlaloc, Beautiful Gorgeous, Dib, SpongeBob.

SUPER ZIM
Select Unlock Codes from the Options and enter Plankton, Zim, Technus, SpongeBob.

SUPER JETPACK
Select Unlock Codes from the Options and enter Beautiful Gorgeous, Tlaloc, Jimmy Neutron, Jimmy Neutron.

COLORLESS ENEMIES
Select Unlock Codes from the Options and enter Technus, Jimmy Neutron, Tlaloc, Plankton.

BLUE ENEMIES
Select Unlock Codes from the Options and enter Beautiful Gorgeous, Zim, Plankton, Technus.

RED ENEMIES
Select Unlock Codes from the Options and enter SpongeBob, Tak, Jimmy Neutron, Danny Phantom.

DIFFICULT ENEMIES
Select Unlock Codes from the Options and enter SpongeBob, Dib, Dib, Technus.

DIFFICULT BOSSES
Select Unlock Codes from the Options and enter Plankton, Beautiful Gorgeous, Technus, Tlaloc.

INVINCIBLE PARTNER
Select Unlock Codes from the Options and enter Plankton, Tak, Beautiful Gorgeous, SpongeBob.

STAR WARS: THE FORCE UNLEASHED

INCREASED HEALTH
Select Unleashed Codes from the Extras menu and enter QSSPVENXO.

MAX OUT FORCE POWERS
Select Unleashed Codes from the Extras menu and enter CPLOOLKBF.

UNLIMITED FORCE ENERGY
Select Unleashed Codes from the Extras menu and enter TVENCVMJZ.

MORE POWERFUL LIGHTSABER
Select Unleashed Codes from the Extras menu and enter lightsaber.

UBER LIGHTSABER
Select Unleashed Codes from the Extras menu and enter MOMIROXIW.

ROM KOTA
Select Unleashed Codes from the Extras menu and enter mandalore.

CEREMONIAL JEDI ROBES
Select Unleashed Codes from the Extras menu and enter CURSEZRUX.

DAD'S ROBES
Select Unleashed Codes from the Extras menu and enter wookiee.

DARTH VADER'S COSTUME
Select Unleashed Codes from the Extras menu and enter HRMXRKVEN.

KENTO'S ROBE
Select Unleashed Codes from the Extras menu and enter KBVMSEVNM.

KOTA'S OUTFIT
Select Unleashed Codes from the Extras menu and enter EEDOPVENG.

SITH ROBE
Select Unleashed Codes from the Extras menu and enter ZWSFVENXA.

SITH ROBES
Select Unleashed Codes from the Extras menu and enter holocron.

SITH STALKER ARMOR
Select Unleashed Codes from the Extras menu and enter CPLZKMZTD.

SUPER PRINCESS PEACH

MINI-GAME
At the Title screen, hold R and press Start.

SUPER ROBOT TAISEN OG SAGA: ENDLESS FRONTIER

NEW GAME +
After you have finished the game and saved, load your save to start again with your items and money.

OG1 CHOKER
Start a new game or load a saved file with the GBA game Super Robot Taisen: Original Generation in the GBA slot. This item boosts your SP by 100.

OG2 PENDANT
Start a new game or load a saved file with the GBA game Super Robot Taisen 2: Original Generation in the GBA slot. This item boosts your HP by 250.

SUPER SPEED MACHINES

UNLOCK VEHICLES

WIN GP	VEHICLE UNLOCKED
1	Haima (Rally)
2	Sandstrom (4x4)
3	Striker (Sports)

WIN GP	VEHICLE UNLOCKED
4	Copperhead (Muscle)
6	Gold Digger (Custom)
7	Blue Flame (Classic)

TAMAGOTCHI CONNECTION: CORNER SHOP 3

DOUBLE LAYERED CAKE
Select Enter Code from the Special menu and enter R6194BJD6F.

TAO'S ADVENTURE: CURSE OF THE DEMON SEAL

DEBUG MODE
During a game, press Up, Up, Down, Down, Left, Left, Right, Right, Select, Select, Start, Start, L, R, L, R, A, A, A, A, A, A, A, A, A, A, B.

TOM CLANCY'S SPLINTER CELL CHAOS THEORY

UNLIMITED AMMO/GADGETS
Defeat the game.

CHARACTER SKINS
Defeat the game.

TONY HAWK'S DOWNHILL JAM

ALWAYS SNOWSKATE
Select Buy Stuff from the Skateshop. Choose Enter Code and enter SNOWSK8T.

MIRRORED MAPS
Select Buy Stuff from the Skateshop. Choose Enter Code and enter MIRRORBALL.

ABOMINABLE SNOWMAN OUTFIT
Select Buy Stuff from the Skateshop. Choose Enter Code and enter BIGSNOWMAN.

ZOMBIE SKATER OUTFIT
Select Buy Stuff from the Skateshop. Choose Enter Code and enter ZOMBIEALIVE.

TRANSFORMERS: WAR FOR CYBERTRON—AUTOBOTS

AUTOBOT SILVERBOLT (STORY & ARENA)
Select Cheats from the Main menu and enter 10141.

DECEPTICON RAMJET (IN ARENA)
Select Cheats from the Main menu and enter 99871.

TRANSFORMERS: WAR FOR CYBERTRON—DECEPTICONS

DECEPTICON RAMJET (STORY & ARENA)
Select Cheats from the Main menu and enter 99871.

AUTOBOT SILVERBOLT (ARENA)
Select Cheats from the Main menu and enter 10141.

X1: KYRIAKI MISSION
Defeat the game. Find the X Missions under Challenge Mode.

X2: DEFTERA MISSION
Defeat X1: Kyriaki Mission. Find the X Missions under Challenge Mode.

X3: TRITI MISSION
Defeat X2: Deftera Mission. Find the X Missions under Challenge Mode.

X4: TETARTI MISSION
Defeat X3: Triti Mission. Find the X Missions under Challenge Mode.

X5: PEMPTI MISSION
Defeat X4: Tetarti Mission. Find the X Missions under Challenge Mode.

X6: PARAKEVI MISSION
Defeat X5: Pempti Mission. Find the X Missions under Challenge Mode.

X7: SAVATO MISSION
Defeat X6: Parakevi Mission. Find the X Missions under Challenge Mode.

ULTIMATE MORTAL KOMBAT

VS CODES

At the VS screen, each player must use LP, BLK, and LK to enter the following codes:

EFFECT	PLAYER 1	PLAYER 2
You are now entering the realm	642	468
Blocking Disabled	020	020
Dark Kombat	448	844
Infinite Run	466	466
Play in Kahn's Kave	004	700
Play in the Kombat Temple	600	N/A
Play in the Soul Chamber	123	901
Play on Jade's Deset	330	033
Play on Kahn's Tower	880	220
Play on Noob Saibot Dorfen	050	050
Play on Rooftops	343	343
Play on Scislac Busorez	933	933
Play on Subway	880	088
Play on the Belltower	091	190
Play on the Bridge	077	022
Play on the Graveyard	666	333
Play on the Pit 3	820	028
Play on the Street	079	035
Play on the Waterfront	002	003
Play Scorpions Lair	666	444
Player 1 Half Power	033	N/A
Player 1 Quarter Power	707	N/A
Player 2 Half Power	N/A	033
Player 2 Quarter Power	N/A	707
Power Bars Disabled	987	123
Random Kombat	444	444
Revision 1.2	999	999
Sans Power	044	440
Silent Kombat	300	300
Throwing Disabled	100	100
Throwing Encouraged	010	010
Winner of round fights Motaro	969	141
Winner of round fights Noob Saibot	769	342
Winner of round fights Shao Kahn	033	564
Winner of round fights Smoke	205	205

UNLOCK ERMAC, MILEENA, CLASSIC SUB-ZERO

At the Ultimate Kombat Kode screen input the following codes:
(Note: To easily access the Ultimate Kombat Kode screen just get defeated and don't continue.)

NINTENDO DS

CLASSIC SUB-ZERO

At the Ultimate Kombat Kode screen, enter 81835. You can reach this screen by losing and not continuing.

ERMAC

At the Ultimate Kombat Kode screen, enter 12344. You can reach this screen by losing and not continuing.

MILEENA

At the Ultimate Kombat Kode screen, enter 22264. You can reach this screen by losing and not continuing.

HUMAN SMOKE

Select ROBO Smoke. Hold Block + Run + High Punch + High Kick + Back before the fight begins.

UP

INVINCIBILITY

After completing the game, enter B, Y, B, Y, X, Y, X, Y, B, A at the title screen. This cheat disables saving.

WORLD CHAMPIONSHIP POKER

UNLOCK CASINOS

At the Title screen, press Y, X, Y, B, L, R. Then press the following direction:

DIRECTION	CASINO
Left	Amazon
Right	Nebula
Down	Renaissance

YU-GI-OH! NIGHTMARE TROUBADOUR

CREDITS

Unlock the Password Machine by defeating the Expert Cup. Enter the Duel Shop and select the Slot Machine, then enter 00000375.

SOUND TEST

Unlock the Password Machine by defeating the Expert Cup. Enter the Duel Shop and select the Slot Machine, then enter 57300000.

YU-GI-OH! WORLD CHAMPIONSHIP 2008

CARD PASSWORDS

Enter the following in the password machine to receive the corresponding card. You need to have the card already to use the password.

CARD	PASSWORD
7	67048711
7 Colored Fish	23771716
7 Completed	86198326
A Feint Plan	68170903
A Hero Emerges	21597117
Abyss Soldier	18318842
Acid Rain	21323861
Acid Trap Hole	41356845
Adhesive Explosive	53828196
Agido	16135253
Airknight Parshath	18036057
Aitsu	48202661
Alkana Knight Joker	06150044
Alligator's Sword	64428736
Alligator's Sword Dragon	03366982
Alpha the Magnet Warrior	99785935
Altar for Tribute	21070956

CARD	PASSWORD
Amazon Archer	91869203
Amazoness Archers	67987611
Amazoness Blowpiper	73574678
Amazoness Chain Master	29654737
Amazoness Fighter	55821894
Amazoness Paladin	47480070
Amazoness Spellcaster	81325903
Amazoness Swords Woman	94004268
Amazoness Tiger	10979723
Amphibian Beast	67371383
Amplifier	00303660
Anti-Spell	53112492
Aqua Madoor	85639257
Aqua Spirit	40916023
Archfiend of Gilfer	50287060
Armed Changer	90374791
Armed Ninja	09076207
Armored Glass	21070956
Armored Zombie	20277860
Array of Revealing Light	69296555
Arsenal Bug	42364374
Arsenal Robber	55348096
Assault on GHQ	62633180
Asura Priest	02134346
Attack and Receive	63689843
Autonomous Action Unit	71453557
Axe of Despair	40619825
Axe Raider	48305365
B. Skull Dragon	11901678
Baby Dragon	88819587
Back to Square One	47453433
Backfire	82705573
Bad Reaction to Simochi	40633297
Bait Doll	07165085
Ballista of Rampart Smashing	00242146
Banisher of the Light	61528025
Banner of Courage	10012614
Bark of The Dark Ruler	41925941
Baron of the Fiend Sword	86325596
Barrel Behind the Door	78783370
Barrel Dragon	81480460
Battery Charger	61181383
Batteryman AA	63142001
Batteryman C	19733961
Batteryman D	55401221
Battle Ox	05053103
Battle Warrior	55550921
Beast Fangs	46009906
Beast Soul Swap	35149085
Beastking of the Swamps	99426834
Beautiful Headhuntress	16899564
Beckoning Light	16255442
Berfomet	77207191
Berserk Gorilla	39168895
Beta the Magnet Warrior	39256679
Bickuribox	25655502
Big Bang Shot	61127349
Big Eye	16768387
Big Shield Gardna	65240384
Birdface	45547649

CARD	PASSWORD
Black Illusion Ritual	41426869
Black Luster Ritual	55761792
Black Luster Soldier	72989439
Black Magic Ritual	76792184
Black Pendant	65169794
Bladefly	28470714
Blast Held by a Tribute	89041555
Blast Magician	21051146
Blast Sphere	26302522
Blast with Chain	98239899
Blasting the Ruins	21466326
Blessings of the Nile	30653173
Blowback Dragon	25551951
Blue Medicine	20871001
Blue-Eyes Toon Dragon	53183600
Blue-Eyes Ultimate Dragon	23995346
Blue-Eyes White Dragon	80906030
Blue-Eyes White Dragon	80906030
Book of Taiyou	38699854
Bottomless Trap Hole	29401950
Bowganian	52090844
Bracchio-Raidus	16507828
Brain Control	87910978
Breaker the Magical Warrior	71413901
Breath of Light	20101223
Bright Castle	82878489
Burning Land	24294108
Burning Spear	18937875
Burst Return	27191436
Burst Stream of Destruction	17655904
Buster Rancher	84740193
Cannon Soldier	11384280
Cannonball Spear Shellfish	95614612
Card Destruction	72892473
Card of Sanctity	04266498
Card Shuffle	12183332
Castle of Dark Illusions	00062121
Castle Walls	44209392
Catapult Turtle	95727991
Ceasefire	36468556
Celtic Guardian	91152256
Cemetery Bomb	51394546
Centrifugal Field	01801154
Cestus of Dagla	28106077
Chain Destruction	01248895
Chain Disappearance	57139487
Chain Energy	79323590
Chaos Command Magician	72630549
Chaos End	61044390
Chaos Greed	97439308
Chimera the Flying Mythical Beast	04796100
Chiron the Mage	16956455
Chorus of Sanctuary	81380218
Chthonian Alliance	46910446
Chthonian Blast	18271561
Chthonian Polymer	72287557
Clay Charge	22479888
Cocoon of Evolution	40240595
Coffin Seller	65830223
Cold Wave	60682203

CARD	PASSWORD
Command Knight	10375182
Conscription	31000575
Continuous Destruction Punch	68057622
Contract with Exodia	33244944
Contract with the Dark Master	96420087
Convulsion of Nature	62966332
Copycat	26376390
Cosmo Queen	38999506
Covering Fire	74458486
Crass Clown	93889755
Crawling Dragon #2	38289717
Crimson Sunbird	46696593
Crush Card Virus	57728570
Curse of Anubis	66742250
Curse of Darkness	84970821
Curse of Dragon	28279543
Curse of the Masked Beast	94377247
Cursed Seal of the Forbidden Spell	58851034
Cyber Raider	39978267
Cyber Shield	63224564
Cyber-Tech Alligator	48766543
D.D. Borderline	60912752
D.D. Designator	33423043
D.D. Assailant	70074904
D.D. Dynamite	08628798
D.D. Trap Hole	05606466
D.D. Warrior	37043180
D.D. Warrior Lady	07572887
D. Tribe	02833249
Dark Artist	72520073
Dark Deal	65824822
Dark Dust Spirit	89111398
Dark Elf	21417692
Dark Energy	04614116
Dark Factory of Mass Production	90928333
Dark Jeroid	90980792
Dark Magic Attack	02314238
Dark Magic Curtain	99789342
Dark Magician	46986414
Dark Magician Girl	38033121
Dark Magician of Chaos	40737112
Dark Master - Zorc	97642679
Dark Mimic LV1	74713516
Dark Mimic LV3	01102515
Dark Mirror Force	20522190
Dark Necrofear	31829185
Dark Paladin	98502113
Dark Rabbit	99261403
Dark Room of Nightmare	85562745
Dark Sage	92377303
Dark Snake Syndrome	47233801
Dark Spirit of the Silent	93599951
Dark World Lightning	93554166
Darkness Approaches	80168720
Dark-Piercing Light	45895206
Deck Devastation Virus	35027493
Decoy Dragon	02732323
Dedication through Light and Darkness	69542930
De-Fusion	95286165
Delta Attacker	39719977

CARD	PASSWORD
Despair from the Dark	71200730
De-Spell	19159413
Destiny Board	94212438
Destruction Ring	21219755
Dian Keto the Cure Master	84257639
Dice Re-Roll	83241722
Different Dimension Capsule	11961740
Different Dimension Dragon	50939127
Different Dimension Gate	56460688
Diffusion Wave-Motion	87880531
Dimension Fusion	23557835
Dimension Wall	67095270
Dimensional Prison	70342110
Dimensionhole	22959079
Disappear	24623598
Disarmament	20727787
Divine Sword - Phoenix Blade	31423101
Divine Wrath	49010598
DNA Surgery	74701381
Doomcaliber Knight	78700060
Double Coston	44436472
Double Snare	03682106
Double Spell	24096228
Dragged Down into the Grave	16435235
Dragon Capture Jar	50045299
Dragon Seeker	28563545
Dragon Treasure	01435851
Dragonic Attack	32437102
Dragon's Mirror	71490127
Draining Shield	43250041
Dramatic Rescue	80193355
Dream Clown	13215230
Drill Bug	88733579
Driving Snow	00473469
Drop Off	55773067
Dunames Dark Witch	12493482
Dust Barrier	31476755
Dust Tornado	60082867
Earth Chant	59820352
Earthbound Spirit's Invitation	65743242
Earthquake	82828051
Eatgaboon	42578427
Ectoplasmer	97342942
Ekibyo Drakmord	69954399
Electro-Whip	37820550
Elegant Egotist	90219263
Elemental Hero Avian	21844576
Elemental Hero Burstinatrix	58932615
Elemental Hero Clayman	84327329
Elemental Hero Flame Wingman	35809262
Elemental Hero Rampart Blaster	47737087
Elemental Hero Sparkman	20721928
Elemental Hero Thunder Giant	61204971
Embodiment of Apophis	28649820
Emergency Provisions	53046408
Enchanted Arrow	93260132
Enchanting Fitting Room	30531525
Enemy Controller	98045062
Energy Drain	56916805
Enervating Mist	26022485

CARD	PASSWORD
Enraged Battle Ox	76909279
Eradicating Aerosol	94716515
Eternal Drought	56606928
Eternal Rest	95051344
Exarion Universe	63749102
Exchange	05556668
Exhausting Spell	95451366
Exodia Necross	12600382
Exodia the Forbidden One	33396948
Fairy Box	21598948
Fairy King Truesdale	45425051
Fairy Meteor Crush	97687912
Fairy's Hand Mirror	17653779
Fake Trap	03027001
Feather Shot	19394153
Feather Wind	71060915
Fengsheng Mirror	37406863
Feral Imp	41392891
Fiend Comedian	81172176
Fiend Skull Dragon	66235877
Fiend's Hand Mirror	58607704
Fiend's Sanctuary	24874630
Final Countdown	95308449
Final Destiny	18591904
Firewing Pegasus	27054370
Fissure	66788016
Flame Cerebrus	60862676
Flame Manipulator	34460851
Flame Swordsman	40502030
Flying Kamakiri #1	84834865
Foolish Burial	81439173
Forced Ceasefire	97806240
Forest	87430998
Fortress Whale	62337487
Fortress Whale's Oath	77454922
Frozen Soul	57069605
Fulfillment of the Contract	48206762
Full Salvo	70865988
Fusilier Dragon, the Duel-Mode Beast	51632798
Fusion Gate	24094653
Fusion Sage	26902560
Fusion Sword Murasame Blade	37684215
Gaia Power	56594520
Gaia the Dragon Champion	66889139
Gaia the Fierce Knight	06368038
Gamma the Magnet Warrior	11549357
Garoozis	14977074
Garuda the Wind Spirit	12800777
Gazelle the King of Mythical Beasts	05818798
Gear Golem the Moving Fortress	30190809
Gearfried the Iron Knight	00423705
Gearfried the Swordmaster	57046845
Gemini Elf	69140098
Generation Shift	34460239
Germ Infection	24668830
Getsu Fuhma	21887179
Giant Flea	41762634
Giant Germ	95178994
Giant Rat	97017120
Giant Red Seasnake	58831685

CARD	PASSWORD
Giant Soldier of Stone	13039848
Giant Trunade	42703248
Gigantes	47606319
Gilasaurus	45894482
Gilford the Legend	69933858
Gilford the Lightning	36354007
Gil Garth	38445524
Goblin Attack Force	78658564
Goblin Fan	04149689
Goblin King	18590133
Goblin Thief	45311864
Goblin's Secret Remedy	11868825
Goddess of Whim	67959180
Goddess with the Third Eye	53493204
Gokibore	15367030
Gorgon's Eye	52648457
Graceful Dice	74137509
Gradius' Option	14291024
Granadora	13944422
Grand Tiki Elder	13676474
Gravedigger Ghoul	82542267
Gravekeeper's Assailant	25262697
Gravekeeper's Cannonholder	99877698
Gravekeeper's Chief	62473983
Gravekeeper's Commandant	17393207
Gravekeeper's Curse	50712728
Gravekeeper's Guard	37101832
Gravekeeper's Servant	16762927
Gravekeeper's Spear Soldier	63695531
Gravekeeper's Spy	24317029
Gravekeeper's Vassal	99690140
Gravekeeper's Watcher	26084285
Gravity Axe - Grarl	32022366
Gravity Bind	85742772
Great Moth	14141448
Greed	89405199
Green Baboon, Defender of the Forest	46668237
Greenkappa	61831093
Ground Collapse	90502999
Gust	73079365
Gust Fan	55321970
Gyaku-Gire Panda	09817927
Hammer Shot	26412047
Hand Collapse	74519184
Hannibal Necromancer	05640330
Harpie Lady	76812113
Harpie Lady 1	91932350
Harpie Lady 2	27927359
Harpie Lady 3	54415063
Harpie Lady Sisters	12206212
Harpies' Hunting Ground	75782277
Harpie's Pet Dragon	52040216
Headless Knight	5434080
Heart of Clear Water	64801562
Heart of the Underdog	35762283
Heavy Mech Support Platform	23265594
Heavy Slump	52417194
Heavy Storm	19613556
Helpoemer	76052811
Hercules Beetle	52584282

CARD	PASSWORD
Hero Kid	32679370
Hero Signal	22020907
Hidden Book of Spell	21840375
Hieroglyph Lithograph	10248192
Hinotama	46130346
Hiro's Shadow Scout	81863068
Hitotsu-Me Giant	76184692
Horn Imp	69669405
Horn of Light	38552107
Horn of the Unicorn	64047146
Hoshiningen	67629977
House of Adhesive Tape	15083728
Human-Wave Tactics	30353551
Illusionist Faceless Mage	28546905
Impenetrable Formation	96631852
Inferno	74823665
Inferno Fire Blast	52684508
Infinite Cards	94163677
Infinite Dismissal	54109233
Injection Fairy Lily	79575620
Insect Armor with Laser Cannon	03492538
Insect Barrier	23615409
Insect Imitation	96965364
Insect Queen	91512835
Inspection	16227556
Interdimensional Matter Transporter	36261276
Invigoration	98374133
Jack's Knight	90876561
Jade Insect Whistle	95214051
Jam Breeding Machine	21770260
Jam Defender	21558682
Jar of Greed	83968380
Jigen Bakudan	90020065
Jinzo	77585513
Jinzo #7	77585513
Jowgen the Spiritualist	41855169
Jowls of Dark Demise	05257687
Judge Man	30113682
Judgment of the Pharaoh	55948544
Just Desserts	24068492
Kabazauls	51934376
Kabazauls	51934376
Kanan the Swordsmistress	12829151
Killer Needle	88979991
Kinetic Soldier	79853073
King of the Skull Servants	36021814
King of the Swamp	79109599
King Tiger Wanghu	83986578
King's Knight	64788463
Koitsu	69456283
Krokodilus	76512652
Kryuel	82642348
Kunai with Chain	37390589
Kuriboh	40640057
Kycoo the Ghost Destroyer	88240808
Labyrinth of Nightmare	66526672
Labyrinth Tank	99551425
Larvae Moth	87756343
Laser Cannon Armor	77007920
Last Day of the Witch	90330453

CARD	PASSWORD
Launcher Spider	87322377
Lava Battleguard	20394040
Lava Golem	00102380
Left Arm of the Forbidden One	07902349
Left Leg of the Forbidden One	44519536
Legacy of Yata-Garasu	30461781
Legendary Sword	61854111
Level Conversion Lab	84397023
Level Limit - Area A	54976796
Level Limit - Area B	03136426
Level Modulation	61850482
Level Up!	25290459
Light of Judgment	44595286
Lighten the Load	37231841
Lightforce Sword	49587034
Lightning Vortex	69162969
Little Chimera	68658728
Luminous Soldier	57482479
Luminous Spark	81777047
Luster Dragon	11091375
Machine Duplication	63995093
Machine King	46700124
Mad Sword Beast	79870141
Mage Power	83746708
Magic Cylinder	62279055
Magic Drain	59344077
Magic Formula	67227834
Magic Jammer	77414722
Magical Arm Shield	96008713
Magical Dimension	28553439
Magical Explosion	32723153
Magical Hats	81210420
Magical Stone Excavation	98494543
Magical Thorn	53119267
Magician of Black Chaos	30208479
Magician of Faith	31560081
Magician's Circle	00050755
Magician's Unite	36045450
Magician's Valkyria	80304126
Maha Vailo	93013676
Maharaghi	40695128
Maiden of the Aqua	17214465
Major Riot	09074847
Malevolent Catastrophe	01224927
Malevolent Nuzzler	99597615
Malfunction	06137091
Malice Dispersion	13626450
Man-Eater Bug	54652250
Man-Eating Treasure Chest	13723605
Manga Ryu-Ran	38369349
Marauding Captain	02460565
Marie the Fallen One	57579381
Marshmallon	31305911
Marshmallon Glasses	66865880
Mask of Brutality	82432018
Mask of Darkness	28933734
Mask of Dispel	20765952
Mask of Restrict	29549364
Mask of the Accursed	56948373
Mask of Weakness	57882509

CARD	PASSWORD
Masked Sorcerer	10189126
Mass Driver	34906152
Master Kyonshee	24530661
Mataza the Zapper	22609617
Mausoleum of the Emperor	80921533
Mechanicalchaser	07359741
Mega Ton Magical Cannon	32062913
Megamorph	22046459
Melchid the Four-Faced Beast	86569121
Meltiel, Sage of the Sky	49905576
Mesmeric Control	48642904
Messenger of Peace	44656491
Metal Detector	75646520
Metal Reflect Slime	26905245
Metalmorph	68540058
Metalzoa	50705071
Meteor Black Dragon	90660762
Meteor Dragon	64271667
Michizure	37580756
Micro Ray	18190572
Millennium Shield	32012841
Milus Radiant	07489323
Mind Control	37520316
Mind Crush	15800838
Miracle Dig	63434080
Miracle Kids	55985014
Miracle Restoring	68334074
Mirror Force	44095762
Mispolymerization	58392024
Mist body	47529357
Moisture Creature	75285069
Mokey Mokey	27288416
Mokey Mokey King	13803864
Mokey Mokey Smackdown	01965724
Molten Destruction	19384334
Monster Gate	43040603
Monster Recovery	93108433
Monster Reincarnation	74848038
Mooyan Curry	58074572
Morphing Jar	33508719
Morphing Jar #2	79106360
Mother Grizzly	57839750
Mountain	50913601
Muka Muka	46657337
Multiplication of Ants	22493811
Multiply	40703222
Mushroom Man	14181608
My Body as a Shield	69279219
Mysterious Puppeteer	54098121
Mystic Box	25774450
Mystic Horseman	68516705
Mystic Probe	49251811
Mystic Swordsman LV2	47507260
Mystic Swordsman LV4	74591968
Mystic Swordsman LV6	60482781
Mystic Tomato	83011277
Mystical Elf	15025844
Mystical Moon	36607978
Mystical Refpanel	35563539
Mystical Sheep #1	30451366

CARD	PASSWORD
Mystical Space Typhoon	05318639
Narrow Pass	40172183
Necrovalley	47355498
Needle Wall	38299233
Needle Worm	81843628
Negate Attack	14315573
Neo the Magic Swordsman	50930991
Newdoria	04335645
Next to be Lost	07076131
Nightmare Wheel	54704216
Nimble Momonga	22567609
Nitro Unit	23842445
Non Aggression Area	76848240
Non-Fusion Area	27581098
Non-Spellcasting Area	20065549
Numinous Healer	02130625
Nuvia the Wicked	12953226
Obnoxious Celtic Guard	52077741
Ojama Black	79335209
Ojama Delta Hurricane!!	08251996
Ojama Green	12482652
Ojama King	90140980
Ojama Trio	29843091
Ojama Yellow	42941100
Ojamagic	24643836
Ojamuscle	98259197
Ominous Fortunetelling	56995655
Ookazi	19523799
Opti-Camouflage Armor	44762290
Order to Charge	78986941
Order to Smash	39019325
Otohime	39751093
Overpowering Eye	60577362
Panther Warrior	42035044
Paralyzing Potion	50152549
Parasite Paracide	27911549
Parrot Dragon	62762898
Patrician of Darkness	19153634
Pendulum Machine	24433920
Penguin Knight	36039163
Penguin Soldier	93920745
Perfectly Ultimate Great Moth	48579379
Petit Moth	58192742
Pharaoh's Treasure	63571750
Pigeonholing Books of Spell	96677818
Pikeru's Second Sight	58015506
Pinch Hopper	26185991
Pitch-Black Power Stone	34029630
Poison Fangs	76539047
Poison of the Old Man	08842266
Polymerization	35550694
Pot of Avarice	67169062
Premature Burial	70828912
Prepare to Strike Back	04483989
Prevent Rat	00549481
Princess of Tsurugi	51371017
Prohibition	43711255
Protector of the Sanctuary	24221739
Pumpking the King of Ghosts	29155212
Queen's Knight	25652259

CARD	PASSWORD
Rabid Horseman	94905343
Radiant Jeral	84177693
Radiant Mirror Force	21481146
Raigeki Break	04178474
Rapid-Fire Magician	06337436
Ray of Hope	82529174
Ready for Intercepting	31785398
Really Eternal Rest	28121403
Reaper of the Cards	33066139
Reckless Greed	37576645
Recycle	96316857
Red Archery Girl	65570596
Red Medicine	38199696
Red-Eyes B. Chick	36262024
Red-Eyes Black Dragon	74677422
Red-Eyes Black Metal Dragon	64335804
Reflect Bounder	02851070
Reinforcement of the Army	32807846
Reinforcements	17814387
Release Restraint	75417459
Relieve Monster	37507488
Relinquished	64631466
Remove Trap	51482758
Respect Play	08951260
Restructer Revolution	99518961
Reversal Quiz	05990062
Reverse Trap	77622396
Revival Jam	31709826
Right Arm of the Forbidden One	70903634
Right Leg of the Forbidden One	08124921
Rigorous Reaver	39180960
Ring of Magnetism	20436034
Riryoku Field	70344351
Rising Energy	78211862
Rite of Spirit	30450531
Ritual Weapon	54351224
Robbin' Goblin	88279736
Robbin' Zombie	83258273
Robotic Knight	44203504
Rock Bombardment	20781762
Rocket Warrior	30860696
Rod of Silence - Kay'est	95515060
Rogue Doll	91939608
Roll Out!	91597389
Royal Command	33950246
Royal Decree	51452091
Royal Magical Library	70791313
Royal Oppression	93016201
Royal Surrender	56058888
Royal Tribute	72405967
Rude Kaiser	26378150
Rush Recklessly	70046172
Ryu Kokki	57281778
Ryu-Kishin	15303296
Ryu-Ran	02964201
Sage's Stone	13604200
Saggi the Dark Clown	66602787
Sakuretsu Armor	56120475
Salamandra	32268901
Salvage	96947648

CARD	PASSWORD
Sangan	26202165
Sasuke Samurai #3	77379481
Sasuke Samurai #4	64538655
Satellite Cannon	50400231
Second Coin Toss	36562627
Sengenjin	76232340
Serial Spell	49398568
Serpentine Princess	71829750
Seven Tools of the Bandit	03819470
Shadow Ghoul	30778711
Shadow of Eyes	58621589
Share the Pain	56830749
Shield & Sword	52097679
Shield Crush	30683373
Shift	59560625
Shifting Shadows	59237154
Shinato, King of a Higher Plane	86327225
Shinato's Ark	60365591
Shining Abyss	87303357
Shining Angel	95956346
Shooting Star Bow - Ceal	95638658
Shrink	55713623
Silver Bow and Arrow	01557499
Simultaneous Loss	92219931
Skilled Dark Magician	73752131
Skilled White Magician	46363422
Skull Dice	00126218
Skull Servant	32274490
Skull-Mark Ladybug	64306248
Skyscraper	63035430
Slate Warrior	78636495
Slot Machine	03797883
Smashing Ground	97169186
Smoke Grenade of the Thief	63789924
Snake Fang	00596051
Sogen	86318356
Solar Ray	44472639
Solemn Judgment	41420027
Solemn Wishes	35346968
Sorcerer of the Doomed	49218300
Soul Absorption	68073522
Soul Demolition	76297408
Soul Exchange	68005187
Soul of Purity and Light	77527210
Soul of the Pure	47852924
Soul Release	05758500
Soul Resurrection	92924317
Soul Reversal	78864369
Soul Taker	81510157
Spark Blaster	97362768
Spatial Collapse	20644748
Special Hurricane	42598242
Spell Absorption	51481927
Spell Reproduction	29228529
Spell Vanishing	29735721
Spellbinding Circle	18807108
Spell-stopping Statute	10069180
Spiral Spear Strike	49328340
Spirit Message "A"	94772232
Spirit Message "I"	31893528

CARD	PASSWORD
Spirit Message "L"	30170981
Spirit Message "N"	67287533
Spirit of Flames	13522325
Spirit of the Pharaoh	25343280
Spirit's Invitation	92394653
Spiritual Earth Art - Kurogane	70156997
Spiritual Energy Settle Machine	99173029
Spiritual Fire Art - Kurenai	42945701
Spiritual Water Art - Aoi	06540606
Spiritual Wind Art - Miyabi	79333300
Spiritualism	15866454
St. Joan	21175632
Staunch Defender	92854392
Steel Ogre Grotto #2	90908427
Steel Scorpion	13599884
Stim-Pack	83225447
Stone Statue of the Aztecs	31812496
Stop Defense	63102017
Stray Lambs	60764581
Stumbling	34646691
Swamp Battleguard	40453765
Swift Gaia the Fierce Knight	16589042
Sword of Deep-Seated	98495314
Sword of the Soul-Eater	05371656
Swords of Concealing Light	12923641
Swords of Revealing Light	72302403
Swordsman of Landstar	03573512
System Down	07672244
Tailor of the Fickle	43641473
Terraforming	73628505
The A. Forces	00403847
The Agent of Force - Mars	91123920
The Agent of Judgement - Saturn	91345518
The Big March of Animals	01689516
The Bistro Butcher	71107816
The Cheerful Coffin	41142615
The Creator	61505339
The Creator Incarnate	97093037
The Dark Door	30606547
The Earl of Demise	66989694
The Fiend Megacyber	66362965
The First Sarcophagus	31076103
The Flute of Summoning Kuriboh	20065322
The Forgiving Maiden	84080938
The Gross Ghost of Fled Dreams	68049471
The Illusory Gentleman	83764996
The Inexperienced Spy	81820689
The Last Warrior from Another Planet	86099788
The Law of the Normal	66926224
The League of Uniform Nomenclature	55008284
The Little Swordsman of Aile	25109950
The Masked Beast	49064413
The Portrait's Secret	32541773
The Regulation of Tribe	00296499
The Reliable Guardian	16430187
The Rock Spirit	76305638
The Sanctuary in the Sky	56433456
The Second Sarcophagus	04081094
The Secret of the Bandit	99351431
The Shallow Grave	43434803

CARD	PASSWORD
The Snake Hair	29491031
The Spell Absorbing Life	99517131
The Statue of Easter Island	10261698
The Third Sarcophagus	78697395
The Unhappy Girl	27618634
The Unhappy Maiden	51275027
The Warrior Returning Alive	95281259
The Wicked Worm Beast	06285791
Thestalos the Firestorm Monarch	26205777
Thousand Dragon	41462083
Thousand Energy	05703682
Thousand Knives	63391643
Thousand-Eyes Idol	27125110
Threatening Roar	36361633
Three-Headed Geedo	78423643
Thunder Crash	69196160
Thunder Dragon	31786629
Thunder Nyan Nyan	70797118
Time Machine	80987696
Time Wizard	06285791
Token Feastevil	83675475
Toon Alligator	59383041
Toon Cannon Soldier	79875176
Toon Dark Magician Girl	90960358
Toon Defense	43509019
Toon Gemini Elf	42386471
Toon Goblin Attack Force	15270885
Toon Masked Sorcerer	16392422
Toon Mermaid	65458948
Toon Summoned Skull	91842653
Toon Table of Contents	89997728
Toon World	15259703
Tornado	61068510
Tornado Wall	18605135
Torpedo Fish	90337190
Tower of Babel	94256039
Tragedy	35686187
Transcendent Wings	25573054
Trap Hole	04206964
Trap Jammer	19252988
Trap Master	46461247
Tremendous Fire	46918794
Triage	30888983
Triangle Ecstasy Spark	12181376
Triangle Power	32298781
Tribute Doll	02903036
Tribute to the Doomed	79759861
Tri-Horned Dragon	39111158
Twin Swords of Flashing Light - Tryce	21900719
Twin-Headed Behemoth	43586926
Twin-Headed Thunder Dragon	54752875
Two-Headed King Rex	94119974
Two-Pronged Attack	83887306
Tyhone	72842870
Type Zero Magic Crusher	35346968
UFO Turtle	60806437
Ultimate Offering	80604091
Ultra Evolution Pill	22431243
Umiiruka	82999629
Union Attack	60399954

CARD	PASSWORD
United We Stand	56747793
Unity	14731897
Upstart Goblin	70368879
Uraby	01784619
Valkyrion the Magna Warrior	75347539
Versago the Destroyer	50259460
Vile Germs	39774685
Vorse Raider	14898066
Waboku	12607053
Wall of Illusion	13945283
Wall of Revealing Light	17078030
Wall Shadow	63162310
Warrior Elimination	90873992
Warrior Lady of the Wasteland	05438492
Wasteland	98239899
Weapon Change	10035717
Weather Report	72053645
Weed Out	28604635
White Magical Hat	15150365
White-Horned Dragon	73891874
Wicked-Breaking Flamberge - Baou	68427465
Widespread Ruin	77754944
Wild Nature's Release	61166988
Winged Dragon, Guardian of the Fortress #1	87796900
Winged Kuriboh	57116033
Winged Kuriboh LV10	98585345
Witch's Apprentice	80741828
Wolf	49417509
Wolf Axwielder	56369281
Woodland Sprite	06979239
World Suppression	12253117
Xing Zhen Hu	76515293
Yamata Dragon	76862289
Yami	59197169
Yellow Luster Shield	04542651
Yu-Jo Friendship	81332143
Zaborg the Thunder Monarch	51945556
Zero Gravity	83133491
Zoa	24311372
Zolga	16268841
Zombie Warrior	31339260

300: MARCH TO GLORY

25,000 KLEOS
Pause the game and press Down, Left, Down, Left, Up, Left. You can only use this code once.

ASTRO BOY: THE VIDEO GAME

INVULNERABLE
Pause the game and press Up, Down, Down, Up, L1, R.

MAX STATS
Pause the game and press Left, Left, R, Down, Down, L1.

INFINITE SUPERS
Pause the game and press Left, L1, Right, L1, Up, Down.

INFINITE DASHES
Pause the game and press R, R, L1, R, Left, Up.

DISABLE SUPERS
Pause the game and press L1, L1, R, R, L1, Left.

COSTUME SWAP (ARENA AND CLASSIC COSTUMES)
Pause the game and press R, Up, L1, Up, Down, R.

UNLOCK LEVELS
Pause the game and press Up, L1, Right, L1, Down, L1. This allows you to travel to any level from the Story menu.

ATV OFFROAD FURY: BLAZIN' TRAILS

UNLOCK EVERYTHING EXCEPT THE FURY BIKE
Select Player Profile from the Options menu. Choose Enter Cheat and enter All Access.

1500 CREDITS
Select Player Profile from the Options menu. Choose Enter Cheat and enter $moneybags$.

ALL RIDER GEAR
Select Player Profile from the Options menu. Choose Enter Cheat and enter Duds.

TIRES
Select Player Profile from the Options menu. Choose Enter Cheat and enter Dubs.

MUSIC VIDEOS
Select Player Profile from the Options menu. Choose Enter Cheat and enter Billboards.

BEN 10: ALIEN FORCE: THE GAME

LEVEL LORD
Enter Gwen, Kevin, Big Chill, Gwen as a code.

INVINCIBILITY
Enter Kevin, Big Chill, Swampfire, Kevin as a code.

ALL COMBOS
Enter Swampfire, Gwen, Kevin, Ben as a code.

INFINITE ALIENS
Enter Ben, Swampfire, Gwen, Big Chill as a code.

BEN 10: ALIEN FORCE VILGAX ATTACKS

LEVEL SKIP
Pause the game and enter Portal in the Cheats menu.

UNLOCK ALL SPECIAL ATTACKS (ALL FORMS)
Pause the game and enter Everythingproof in the Cheats menu.

UNLOCK ALL ALIEN FORMS
Pause the game and enter Primus in the Cheats menu.

TOGGLE INVULNERABILITY ON AND OFF
Pause the game and enter XImrsmoothy in the Cheats menu.

FULL HEALTH
Pause the game and enter Herotime in the Cheats menu.

QUICK ENERGY REGENERATION
Pause the game and enter Generator in the Cheats menu.

BEN 10: PROTECTOR OF EARTH

INVINCIBILITY
Select a game from the Continue option. Go to the Map Selection screen, press Start and choose Extras. Select Enter Secret Code and enter XLR8, Heatblast, Wildvine, Fourarms.

ALL COMBOS
Select a game from the Continue option. Go to the Map Selection screen, press Start and choose Extras. Select Enter Secret Code and enter Cannonblot, Heatblast, Fourarms, Heatblast.

ALL LOCATIONS
Select a game from the Continue option. Go to the Map Selection screen, press Start and choose Extras. Select Enter Secret Code and enter Heatblast, XLR8, XLR8, Cannonblot.

DNA FORCE SKINS
Select a game from the Continue option. Go to the Map Selection screen, press Start and choose Extras. Select Enter Secret Code and enter Wildvine, Fourarms, Heatblast, Cannonbolt.

DARK HEROES SKINS
Select a game from the Continue option. Go to the Map Selection screen, press Start and choose Extras. Select Enter Secret Code and enter Cannonbolt, Cannonbolt, Fourarms, Heatblast.

ALL ALIEN FORMS
Select a game from the Continue option. Go to the Map Selection screen, press Start and choose Extras. Select Enter Secret Code and enter Wildvine, Fourarms, Heatblast, Wildvine.

MASTER CONTROL
Select a game from the Continue option. Go to the Map Selection screen, press Start and choose Extras. Select Enter Secret Code and enter Cannonbolt, Heatblast, Wildvine, Fourarms.

To remove these cheats, you must start a new game.

1,000,000 DNA
Pause the game, select Cheats, and enter Cash.

REGENERATE HEALTH
Pause the game, select Cheats, and enter Health.

REGENERATE ENERGY
Pause the game, select Cheats, and enter Energy.

UPGRADE EVERYTHING
Pause the game, select Cheats, and enter Upgrade.

ALL LEVELS
Pause the game, select Cheats, and enter Levels.

DAMAGE
Pause the game, select Cheats, and enter Hard. Enemies cause double the damage, while you inflict half damage.

BLITZ: OVERTIME

The following codes only work for Quick Play mode.

BALL TRAILS ALWAYS ON
Select Extras from the Main menu and enter ONFIRE.

BEACH BALL
Select Extras from the Main menu and enter BOUNCY.

DOUBLE UNLEASH ICONS
Select Extras from the Main menu and enter PIPPED.

STAMINA DISABLED
Select Extras from the Main menu and enter NOTTIRED.

SUPER CLASH MODE
Select Extras from the Main menu and enter CLASHY.

SUPER UNLEASH CLASH MODE
Select Extras from the Main menu and enter BIGDOGS.

INSTANT WIN IN CAMPAIGN MODE
Select Extras from the Main menu and enter CHAMPS. In Campaign mode, highlight a team and press ●, ●, ▲ to win against that team.

TWO PLAYER CO-OP MODE
Select Extras from the Main menu and enter CHUWAY.

BROTHERS IN ARMS D-DAY

LEVEL SELECT
Enter JUNESIX as your profile name.

BURNOUT LEGENDS

COP RACER
Earn a Gold in all Pursuit events.

FIRE TRUCK
Earn a Gold in all Crash Events.

GANGSTER BOSS
Earn Gold in all Race events.

CAPCOM CLASSICS COLLECTION REMIXED

UNLOCK EVERYTHING
At the title screen, press Left on D-pad, Right on D-pad, Left on Analog stick, Right on Analog stick, ●, ●, Up on D-pad, Down on D-pad.

CAPCOM PUZZLE WORLD

SUPER BUSTER BROS.

LEVEL SELECT IN TOUR MODE
At the Main menu, highlight Tour Mode, hold Down and press ✖.

SUPER PUZZLE FIGHTER

PLAY AS AKUMA
At the character select, highlight Hsien-Ko and press Down.

PLAY AS DAN
At the character select, highlight Donovan and press Down.

PLAY AS DEVILOT
At the character select, highlight Morrigan and press Down.

PLAY AS ANITA
At the character select, hold L + R and choose Donovan.

PLAY AS HSIEN-KO'S TALISMAN
At the character select, hold L + R and choose Hsien-Ko.

PLAY AS MORRIGAN AS A BAT
At the character select, hold L + R and choose Morrigan.

CARS

BONUS SPEEDWAY (REVERSED) IN CUSTOM RACE
At the Main menu, hold L and press ✕, ■, ▲, ✕, ■, ▲.

ALL CARS, PAINTJOBS, TRACKS, MOVIE CLIPS AND MODES
At the Main menu, hold L and press ▲, ■, ✕, ■, ▲, ✕, ■, ▲, ■, ✕.

UNLIMITED NITROUS
At the Main menu, hold L and ✕, ■, ■, ■, ■, ▲, ■, ✕.

CASTLEVANIA: THE DRACULA X CHRONICLES

ORIGINAL RONDO OF BLOOD

LEVEL SELECT
Enter X-X!V"Q as your player name

SYMPHONY OF THE NIGHT

PLAY AS ALUCARD WITH 99 LUCK AND LAPIS LAZULI
Start a new game with the name X-X!V"Q.

PLAY AS ALUCARD WITH AXE LORD ARMOR
After clearing the game once, start a new game with the name AXEARMOR.

PLAY AS MARIA RENARD
After clearing the game once, start a new game with the name MARIA.

PLAY AS RICHTER BELMONT
After clearing the game once, start a new game with the name RICHTER.

CRASH: MIND OVER MUTANT

A cheat can be deactivated by re-entering the code.

FREEZE ENEMIES WITH TOUCH
Pause the game, hold R and press Down, Down, Down, Up.

ENEMIES DROP X4 DAMAGE
Pause the game, hold R and press Up, Up, Up, Left.

ENEMIES DROP PURPLE FRUIT
Pause the game, hold R and press Up, Down, Down, Up.

ENEMIES DROP SUPER KICK
Pause the game, hold R and press Up, Right, Down, Left.

ENIMIES DROP WUMPA FRUIT
Pause the game, hold R and press Right, Right, Right, Up.

SHADOW CRASH
Pause the game, hold R and press Left, Right, Left, Right.

DEFORMED CRASH
Pause the game, hold R and press Left, Left, Left, Down.

CRASH TAG TEAM RACING

FASTER VEHICLES
At the Main menu, hold L + R and press ●, ●, ▲, ▲.

1-HIT KO
At the Main menu, hold L + R and press ✕, ●, ●, ✕.

DISABLE HUD
At the Main menu, hold L + R and press ✕, ■, ▲, ●.

CHICKEN HEADS
At the Main menu, hold L + R and press ✕, ●, ●, ■.

JAPANESE CRASH
At the Main menu, hold L + R and press ■, ●, ■, ●.

DRIVE A BLOCK VEHICLE
At the Main menu, hold L + R and press ●, ●, ▲, ●.

NEW GAME+

After completing the game, you'll be prompted to make a new save. Loading a game from this new save will begin a New Game+, starting the game over while allowing Zack to retain almost everything he's earned.

The following items transfer to a New Game+: Level, Experience, SP, Gil, Playtime, Non-Key Items, Materia, and DMW Completion Rate

The following items do not transfer: Key Items, Materia/Accessory Slot Expansion, Ability to SP Convert, DMW Images, Mission Progress, Mail, and Unlocked Shops

DANTE'S INFERNO

UNLOCK EARTHLY REWARDS FOR YOUR COMPUTER

Go to www.hellisnigh.com and enter the following passwords:

Password #1: excommunicate
Password #2: scythe
Password #3: grafter
Password #4: styx
Password #5: unbaptized
Password #6: alighieri

DARKSTALKERS CHRONICLE:THE CHAOS TOWER

EX OPTIONS

At the Main menu, hold L and select Options.

MARIONETTE IN ARCADE MODE

At the Character Select screen, highlight ? and press START (x7), then press P or K.

OBORO BISHAMON IN ALL MODES

At the Character Select screen, highlight Bishamon, hold START, and press P or K.

SHADOW IN ARCADE MODE

At the Character Select screen, highlight ? and press START (x5), then press P or K.

DAXTER

THE MATRIX DREAM SEQUENCE
Collect 1 Precursor Orb.

BRAVEHEART DREAM SEQUENCE
Collect 100 Precursor Orbs.

THE LORD OF THE RINGS DREAM SEQUENCE
Collect 200 Precursor Orbs.

INDIANA JONES DREAM SEQUENCE
Collect 300 Precursor Orbs.

THE MATRIX DREAM SEQUENCE 2
Collect 400 Precursor Orbs.

THE LORD OF THE RINGS DREAM SEQUENCE 2
Collect 500 Precursor Orbs.

E3 2005 TRAILER
Collect 600 Precursor Orbs, then pause the game and select Extras from the Secrets menu.

CONCEPT ART
Collect 700 Precursor Orbs, then pause the game and select Extras from the Secrets menu.

INTRO ANIMATIC
Collect 800 Precursor Orbs, then pause the game and select Extras from the Secrets menu.

GAME UNDER CONSTRUCTION
Collect 900 Precursor Orbs, then pause the game and select Extras from the Secrets menu.

BEHIND THE SCENES

Collect 1000 Precursor Orbs, then pause the game and select Extras from the Secrets menu.

PANTS

Earn Gold on The Lord of the Rings Dream Sequence 2, then pause the game and select Cheats from the Secrets menu.

HAT

Earn Gold on the Indiana Jones Dream Sequence, then pause the game and select Cheats from the Secrets menu.

DEATH JR.

CAN'T TOUCH THIS (INVINCIBILITY)

Pause the game, hold L + R and press Up, Up, Down, Down, Left, Left, Right, Right, ●, ▲.

INCREASED HEALTH

Pause the game, hold L + R and press Up, Up, Down, Down, ✕, ●, ▲, ●, ✕, ✕.

WEAPONS UPGRADED (GIVES ALL WEAPONS)

Pause the game, hold L + R and press Up, Up, Down, Down, Left, Right, Left, Right, ✕, ●.

AMMO REFILLED

Pause the game, hold L + R and press ▲, ▲, ✕, ✕, ●, ●, ●, ●, Down, Right.

UNLIMITED AMMO

Pause the game, hold L + R and press ▲, ▲, ✕, ✕, ●, ●, ●, ●, Right, Down.

MY HEAD FEELS FUNNY (BIG HEAD)

Pause the game, hold L + R and press ▲, ●, ✕, ●, ▲, Up, Right, Down, Left, Up. Re-enter the code for normal head size.

GIANT BLADE (BIG SCYTHE)

Pause the game, hold L + R and press ▲, ●, ✕, ●, ▲, Up, Left, Down, Right, Up.

FREE SEEP

Pause the game, hold L + R and press Left, Left, Right, Right, Left, Right, Left, Right, ✕, ●.

A LITTLE MORE HELP (ASSIST EXTENDER)

Pause the game, hold L + R and press Up, Up, Down, Down, ▲, ▲, ✕, ✕, ▲, ▲.

FREE WIDGET

Pause the game, hold L + R and press Right, Up, Down, Up, ▲, Up, Left, ●, ▲, Right.

ALL LEVELS & FREE ALL CHARACTERS

Pause the game, hold L + R and press Up (x4), Down (x4), ✕, ✕. Enter a stage and exit back to the museum for the code to take effect.

I'D BUY THAT FOR A DOLLAR (FILL PANDORA ASSIST METER)

Pause the game, hold L + R and press Up, Up, Down, Down, Up, Right, Down, Left, ✕, ✕.

THIS WAS JED'S IDEA (ATTACKS HAVE DIFFERENT NAMES)

Pause the game, hold L + R and press Up, Up, Down, Left, ▲, ▲, ●, ✕, ●, ●.

WEAPON NAMES = NORMAL (WEAPONS HAVE DIFFERENT NAMES)

Pause the game, hold L + R and press Down, Down, Up, Up, Left, Right, Left, Right, ●, ▲.

EYEDOOR SOLIDITY QUESTIONABLE (NO LONGER REQUIRE SOULS)

Pause the game, hold L + R and press Up, Left, Down, Right, Left, ▲, ●, ✕, ●, ●.

BUDDY DECALS (BULLET HOLES BECOME PICTURES)

Pause the game, hold L + R and press Up, Right, Down, Left, Up, ▲, ●, ✕, ●, ▲.

STAGE WARP

Pause the game, hold L + R and enter the following codes to warp to that stage.

STAGE	CODE
Advanced Training	Down, ✕, Down, ✕, Down, ✕, Down, ✕, Down, ●
The Basement	Down, ✕, Down, ✕, Down, ✕, Down, ✕, Up, ●
Basic Training	Up, ●, Up, ✕, Down, ✕, Down, ✕, Down, ✕
Big Trouble in Little Downtown	Up, ●, Down, ✕, Down, ✕, Down, ✕, Down, ✕

STAGE	CODE
Bottom of the Bell Curve	Down, ✕, Down, ✕, Down, ✕, Down, ✕, Down, ●
The Burger Tram	Down, ✕, Down, ✕, Down, ✕, Up, ✕, Down, ✕
Burn It Down	Down, ✕, Up, ●, Down, ✕, Down, ✕, Down, ✕
The Corner Store	Down, ✕, Up, ●, Down, ✕, Down, ✕, Down, ✕
Final Battle	Down, ✕, Down, ✕, Down, ✕, Down, ●, Up, ✕
Growth Spurt	Down, ✕, Down, ✕, Down, ✕, Down, ✕, Up, ✕
Happy Trails Insanitarium	Down, ✕, Down, ●, Up, ✕, Down, ✕, Down, ✕
Higher Learning	Down, ✕, Down, ✕, Down, ✕, Down, ●, Down, ✕
How a Cow Becomes a Steak	Down, ✕, Down, ✕, Down, ●, Down, ✕, Down, ✕
Inner Madness	Down, ✕, Down, ✕, Up, ●, Down, ✕, Down, ✕
Into the Box	Down, ✕, Down, ✕, Down, ✕, Up, ●, Down, ✕
Moving on Up	Down, ●, Up, ✕, Down, ✕, Down, ✕, Down, ✕
The Museum	Up, ✕, Down ✕, Down, ✕, Down, ✕, Down, ✕
My House	Down, ✕, Down, ●, Down, ✕, Down, ✕, Down, ✕
Seep's Hood	Down, ●, Down, ✕, Down, ✕, Down, ✕, Down, ✕
Shock Treatment	Down, ✕, Down, ✕, Down, ●, Up, ✕, Down, ✕
Udder Madness	Down, ✕, Down, ✕, Up, ✕, Down, ✕, Down, ✕

DESPICABLE ME: THE GAME

MINIONETTES COSTUME SET
In Gru's Lab, select Cheats from the Bonus menu and enter ●, ●, ■, ▲, ✕.

TAFFY WEB GUN
In Gru's Lab, select Cheats from the Bonus menu and enter ✕, ●, ■, ✕, ▲.

VILLAGE FOLK COSTUME SET
In Gru's Lab, select Cheats from the Bonus menu and enter ▲, ✕, ✕, ●, ✕.

DISGAEA: AFTERNOON OF DARKNESS

ETNA MODE
At the Main menu, highlight New Game and press ▲, ■, ●, ▲, ■, ●, ✕.

DISGAEA 2: DARK HERO DAYS

AXEL MODE
Highlight New Game and press ▲, ■, ●, ▲, ■, ●, ✕.

DISSIDIA: FINAL FANTASY

SECRET PASSWORDS
The following passwords can be entered into the personal message section of your Friend Card to make the following items appear in the shop. Use the NA Version passwords for the North American version of the game and use the EU Ver. Passwords for the European version of the game.

REWARDS	NA VER.	EU VER.		
Player Icon: Chocobo (FF5)	58205	2436	62942	36172
Player Icon: Moogle (FF5)	13410	3103	84626	93120
Capricorn Recipe	87032	2642	6199	27495
Aquarius Recipe	39275	40667	3894	27509
Pisces Recipe	5310	62973	15812	2748
Friend Card: Matoya	39392	58263	1849	16360
Friend Card: Ninja	27481	73856	46490	11483
Friend Card: Fusoya	2943	2971	2971	2943
Friend Card: Siegfried	2015	1231	25496	12772
Friend Card: Vivi	37842	27940	70271	8560
Friend Card: Auron	12982	28499	33705	59603

DRAGON BALL Z: SHIN BUDOKAI

MINI-GAME

At the Main menu, press L and then press R to begin the mini-game.

DUNGEON SIEGE: THRONE OF AGONY

ITEM CODES

Talk to Feydwer and Klaars in Seahaven and enter the following codes.
Enter the Master Code and one of the item codes.

ITEM	CODE
Master Code	MPJNKBHAKANLPGHD
Bloodstained Warboots	MHFMCJIFNDHOKLPM
Bolt Flingers	OBMIDNBJNPFKADCL
Enkindled Cleaver	MJPOBGFNLKELLLLP
Malignant Force	JDGJHKPOLNMCGHNC
Polychromatic Shiv	PJJEPCFHEIHAJEEE
Teasha's Ire	GDIMBNLEIGNNLOEG
Traveler's Handbook	PIJNPEGFJJPFALNO

ELITE MODE

Defeat the game to unlock this mode.

EA REPLAY

B.O.B.

PASSWORDS

LEVEL	PASSWORD
Anciena 1	672451
Anciena 2	272578
Anciena 3	652074
Anciena 4	265648
Anciena 5	462893
Anciena 6	583172
Goth 2	171058

LEVEL	PASSWORD
Goth 3	950745
Goth 4	472149
Ultraworld 1	743690
Ultraworld 2	103928
Ultraworld 3	144895
Ultraworld 4	775092
Ultraworld 5	481376

DESERT STRIKE

10 LIVES

At the Desert Strike menu, press ● to bring up the Password screen. Enter BQQQAEZ.

JUNGLE STRIKE

PASSWORDS

Press ● at the Jungle Strike menu to bring up the Password screen. Enter the following:

LEVEL	PASSWORD
Mountains	7LSPFBVWTWP
Night Strike	X4MFB4MHPH4
Puloso City	V6HGY39XVXL
Return Home	N4MK9N6MHM7
River Raid	TGB76MGCZCC
Training Ground	9NHDXMGCZCG
Washington D.C	BXYTNMGCYDB

WING COMMANDER

INVINCIBILITY AND STAGE SELECT

At the Wing Commander menu, press ✕, ●, ✕, ●, ✕, ●, L, ●, R, ●, Start.

ROAD RASH 2

WILD THING MOTORCYCLE

At the title screen, hold Up + ● + ● and press Start.

FAMILY GUY

ALL STAGES

At the Main menu, press Up, Left, Up, Left, Down, Right, Start.

MUSIC TEST MODE
Enter the main character's name as PolkaPolka at the name entry screen.

FLATOUT: HEAD ON

1 MILLION CREDITS
Select Enter Code from the Extras menu and enter GIVECASH.

ALL CARS AND 1 MILLION CREDITS
Select Enter Code from the Extras menu and enter GIEVEPIX.

BIG RIG
Select Enter Code from the Extras menu and enter ELPUEBLO.

BIG RIG TRUCK
Select Enter Code from the Extras menu and enter RAIDERS.

FLATMOBILE CAR
Select Enter Code from the Extras menu and enter WOTKINS.

MOB CAR
Select Enter Code from the Extras menu and enter BIGTRUCK.

PIMPSTER CAR
Select Enter Code from the Extras menu and enter RUTTO.

ROCKET CAR
Select Enter Code from the Extras menu and enter KALJAKOPPA.

SCHOOL BUS
Select Enter Code from the Extras menu and enter GIEVCARPLZ.

FULL AUTO 2: BATTLELINES

ALL CARS
Select Cheats from the Options and press Up, Up, Up, Up, Left, Down, Up, Right, Down, Down, Down, Down.

ALL EVENTS
Select Cheats from the Options and press Start, Left, Select, Right, Right, ⬤, ⓧ, ⬤, Start, R, Down, Select.

G.I. JOE: THE RISE OF COBRA

CLASSIC DUKE
At the Main menu, press Left, Up, ⬤, Up, Right, ⬤.

CLASSIC SCARLET
At the Main menu, press Right, Up, Down, Down, ⬤.

THE GODFATHER: MOB WARS

Each of the following codes will work once every five minutes.

$1000
Pause the game and press ⬤, ⬤, ⬤, ⬤, ⬤, L.

FULL AMMO
Pause the game and press ⬤, Left, ⬤, Right ⬤, R.

FULL HEALTH
Pause the game and press Left, ⬤, Right, ⬤, Right, L.

GRADIUS COLLECTION

AALL WEAPONS & POWER-UPS
Pause the game and press Up, Up, Down, Down, Left, Right, Left, Right, L, R. This code can be used once per level.

GRAND THEFT AUTO: CHINATOWN WARS

The following cheats will disable saving:

FULL HEALTH
During a game, press L, L, R, ●, ●, ⊗, ⊗, R.

FULL ARMOR
During a game, press L, L, R, ⊗, ⊗, ●, ●, R.

INCREASE WANTED LEVEL
During a game, press L, L, R, ●, ●, ▲, ▲, R.

DECREASE WANTED LEVEL
During a game, press R, ▲, ▲, ●, ●, R, L, L.

EXPLOSIVE PISTOL ROUND
During a game, press L, R, ▲, ●, ●, ⊗, Up, Down.

WEAPONS SET 1
During a game, press R, Up, ⊗, Down, Left, R, ⊗, Right. This gives you the Pistol, Nightstick, Minigun, Assault Rifle, Micro SMG, Stubby Shotgun, and Grenades with max ammo.

WEAPONS SET 2
During a game, press R, Up, ●, Down, Left, R, ●, Right. This gives you the Twin Pistol, Teaser, Flame Thrower, Carbine Rifle, SMG, Double Barreled Shotgun, and Molotovs with max ammo.

WEAPONS SET 3
During a game, press R, Up, ●, Down, Left, R, ●, Right. This gives you the Revolver, Chainsaw, Flame Thrower, Carbine Rifle, SMG, Double Barreled Shotgun, and Proximity Mines with max ammo.

WEAPONS SET 4
During a game, press R, Up, ▲, Down, Left, R, ▲, Right. This gives you the Pistol, Baseball Bat, Carbine Rifle, RPG, Micro SMG, Shotgun, and Flashbangs with max ammo.

WEATHER: SUNNY
During a game, press Up, Down, Left, Right, ●, ⊗, L, R.

WEATHER: EXTRA SUNNY
During a game, press Up, Down, Left, Right, ⊗, ▲, L, R.

WEATHER: CLOUDY
During a game, press Up, Down, Left, Right, ▲, ●, L, R.

WEATHER: RAIN
During a game, press Up, Down, Left, Right, ●, ●, L, R.

WEATHER: HEAVY RAIN
During a game, press Up, Down, Left, Right, ●, ▲, R, L.

WEATHER: THUNDERSTORMS
During a game, press Up, Down, Left, Right, ⊗, ●, R, L.

WEATHER: FOG
During a game, press Down, Left, Right, ●, ⊗, R, L.

GRAND THEFT AUTO: LIBERTY CITY STORIES

$250,000
During a game, press L, R, ▲, L, R, ●, L, R.

FULL HEALTH
During a game, press L, R, ⊗, L, R, ●, L, R.

FULL ARMOR
During a game, press L, R, ●, L, R, ⊗, L, R.

WEAPON SET 1
During a game, press Up, ●, ●, Down, L, ●, ●, R.

WEAPON SET 2
During a game, press Up, ●, ●, Down, Left, ●, ●, R.

WEAPON SET 3
During a game, press Up, ⊗, ⊗, Down, L, ⊗, ⊗, R.

CHROME PLATED CARS
During a game, press ▲, R, L, Down, Down, R, R, ▲.

BLACK CARS
During a game, press ●, ●, R, ▲, ▲, L, ●, ●.

WHITE CARS
During a game, press ⊗, ⊗, R, ●, ●, L, ▲, ▲.

CARS DRIVE ON WATER
During a game, press ●, ⊗, Down, ●, ⊗, Up, L, L.

PERFECT TRACTION
During a game, press L, Up, L, R, ▲, ●, Down, ⊗.

CHANGE BICYCLE TIRE SIZE
During a game, press ●, Right, ⊗, Up, R, ⊗, L, ●.

AGGRESSIVE DRIVERS
During a game, press ●, ●, R, ✕, ✕, L, ●, ●.

ALL GREEN LIGHTS
During a game, press ▲, ▲, R, ●, ●, L, ✕, ✕.

DESTROY ALL CARS
During a game, press L, L, Left, L, L, R, ✕, ●.

RAISE MEDIA ATTENTION
During a game, press L, Up, R, R, ▲, ●, Down, ✕.

RAISE WANTED LEVEL
During a game, press L, R, ●, L, R, ▲, L, R.

NEVER WANTED
During a game, press L, L, ▲, R, R, ✕, ●, ●.

CHANGE OUTFIT
During a game, press L, L, L, L, L, Right, ●, ▲.

BOBBLE HEAD WORLD
During a game, press Down, Down, Down, ●, ●, ✕, L, R.

PEOPLE ATTACK YOU
During a game, press L, L, R, L, L, R, Up, ▲.

PEOPLE FOLLOW YOU
During a game, press Down, Down, ▲, ●, ●, L, R.

PEOPLE HAVE WEAPONS
During a game, press R, R, L, R, R, L, R, ●.

PEOPLE RIOT
During a game, press L, L, R, L, L, R, L, ●.

SPAWN RHINO
During a game, press L, L, L, L, L, R, ▲, ●.

SPAWN TRASHMASTER
During a game, press ▲, ●, Down, ▲, ●, Up, L, L.

FASTER CLOCK
During a game, press L, L, L, L, L, R, ●, ✕.

FASTER GAMEPLAY
During a game, press R, R, L, R, R, L, Down, ✕.

SLOWER GAMEPLAY
During a game, press R, ▲, ✕, R, ●, ●, L, R.

ALL CHARACTERS, CARS, & ENTIRE CITY (MULTIPLAYER)
During a game, press Up (x3), ▲, ▲, ●, L, R.

43 CHARACTERS & 7 GANGS (MULTIPLAYER)
During a game, press Up (x3), ✕, ✕, ●, R, L.

28 CHARACTERS & 4 GANGS (MULTIPLAYER)
During a game, press Up (x3), ●, ●, ✕, L, R.

14 CHARACTERS & 2 GANGS (MULTIPLAYER)
During a game, press Up (x3), ●, ●, ▲, R, L.

CLEAR WEATHER
During a game, press Up, Down, ●, Up, Down, ●, L, R.

FOGGY WEATHER
During a game, press Up, Down, ▲, Up, Down, ✕, L, R.

OVERCAST WEATHER
During a game, press Up, Down, ✕, Up, Down, ▲, L, R.

RAINY WEATHER
During a game, press Up, Down, ●, Up, Down, ●, L, R.

SUNNY WEATHER
During a game, press L, L, ●, R, R, ●, ▲, ✕

UPSIDE DOWN
During a game, press Down, Down, Down, ✕, ✕, ●, R, L.

UPSIDE UP
During a game, press ✕, ✕, ✕, Down, Down, Right, L, R.

RIGHT SIDE UP
During a game, press ▲, ▲, ▲, Up, Up, Right, L, R.

COMMIT SUICIDE
During a game, press L, Down, Left, R, ✕, ●, Up, ▲.

GAME CREDITS
During a game, press L, R, L, R, Up, Down, L, R.

SUNNY WEATHER
During a game, press L, L, ●, R, R, ●, ▲, ✕

UPSIDE DOWN
During a game, press Down, Down, Down, ✕, ✕, ●, R, L.

UPSIDE UP
During a game, press ✕, ✕, ✕, Down, Down, Right, L, R.

RIGHT SIDE UP
During a game, press ▲, ▲, ▲, Up, Up, Right, L, R.

COMMIT SUICIDE
During a game, press L, Down, Left, R, ✕, ●, Up, ▲.

GAME CREDITS
During a game, press L, R, L, R, Up, Down, L, R.

GRAND THEFT AUTO: VICE CITY STORIES

Enter the following cheats during a game.

$250000
Press Up, Down, L, R, ✖, ✖, L, R.

ARMOR
Press Up, Down, L, R, ●, ●, L, R.

HEALTH
Press Up, Down, L, R, ●, ●, L, R.

NEVER WANTED
Press Up, R, ▲, ▲, Down, L, ●, ●.

LOWER WANTED LEVEL
Press Up, R, ▲, ▲, Down, L, ✖, ✖.

RAISE WANTED LEVEL
Press Up, R, ●, ●, Down, L, ●, ●.

WEAPON SET 1
Press L, R, ✖, Up, Down, ●, L, R.

WEAPON SET 2
Press L, R, ●, Up, Down, ●, L, R.

WEAPON SET 3
Press L, R, ▲, Up, Down, ●, L, R.

SPAWN RHINO
Press Up, L, Down, R, L, L, R, R.

SPAWN TRASHMASTER
Press Down, Up, R, ▲, L, ▲, L, ▲.

BLACK CARS
Press L, R, L, R, L, ●, Up, ✖.

CHROME CARS
Press R, Up, L, Down, ▲, ▲, L, R.

CARS AVOID YOU
Press Up, Up, R, L, ▲, ●, ●, ●.

DESTROY ALL CARS
Press L, R, R, L, R, ●, Down, R.

GUYS FOLLOW YOU
Press R, L, Down, L, ●, Up, L, ●.

PERFECT TRACTION
Press Down, Left, Up, L, R, ▲, ●, ✖.
Press Down to jump into a car.

PEDESTRIAN GETS INTO YOUR VEHICLE
Press Down, Up, R, L, L, ●, Up, L.

PEDESTRIANS ATTACK YOU
Press Down, ▲, Up, ✖, L, R, L, R.

PEDESTRIANS HAVE WEAPONS
Press Up, L, Down, R, L, ●, R, ▲.

PEDESTRIANS RIOT
Press R, L, L, Down, L, ●, Down, L.

SUICIDE
Press R, R, ●, ●, L, R, Down, ✖.

UPSIDE DOWN 1
Press ●, ●, ●, L, L, R, L, R.

UPSIDE DOWN 2
Press L, L, L, R, R, L, R, L.

FASTER CLOCK
Press R, L, L, Down, Up, ✖, Down, L.

FASTER GAMEPLAY
Press L, L, R, R, Up, ▲, Down, ✖.

SLOWER GAMEPLAY
Press L, L, ●, ●, Down, Up, ▲, ✖.

CLEAR WEATHER
Press L, Down, R, L, R, Up, L, ✖.

FOGGY WEATHER
Press L, Down, ▲, ✖, R, Up, L, L.

OVERCAST WEATHER
Press L, Down, L, R, R, Up, L, ●.

RAINY WEATHER
Press L, Down, L, R, R, Up, Left, ▲.

SUNNY WEATHER
Press L, Down, R, L, R, Up, L, ●.

GUILTY GEAR ×× ACCENT CORE PLUS

FIGHT EX CHARACTERS
Highlight Arcade or M.O.M. and hold R while starting the game.

FIGHT GOLD CHARACTERS
Highlight Arcade or M.O.M. and hold L while starting the game.

FIGHT GOLD/EX CHARACTERS
Highlight Arcade or M.O.M. and hold L + R while starting the game.

GUN SHOWDOWN

ALL CHAPTERS IN QUICK PLAY
Enter hunter as a profile name.

PLAY AS JENNY
Enter allies as a profile name.

UNLOCKS ALL WEAPONS IN STORY MODE
Enter nedwhite as a profile name. This does not unlock the final weapon.

FASTER GUN FIRING
Enter quivira as a profile name.

INCREASE AMMUNTION CAPACITY
Enter campbell as a profile name.

INFINITE AMMUNITION IN STORY MODE
Enter barton as a profile name.

NEW MULTIPLAYER MAP
Enter badlands as a profile name.

REFILL HEALTH
During a game, press Right, Down, Left, ⬤.

REFILL AMMO
During a game, press Left, Down, Right, ⬤.

REFILL RAGE
During a game, press Left, Down, Right, ⬤.

HOT BRAIN

119.99 TEMPERATURE IN ALL 5 CATEGORIES
Select New Game and enter Cheat.

HOT SHOTS GOLF 2

UNLOCK EVERYTHING
Enter 2gsh as your name.

INVIZIMALS

SPECIAL INVIZIMAL
At the World Map, press and hold Select and then press Up, Right, Down, Left. At the Big Secret, choose Capture Invizimals.

IRON MAN

ARMOR SUITS
Iron Man's different armor suits are unlocked by completing certain missions.

COMPLETE MISSION	SUIT UNLOCKED
1, Escape	Mark I
2, First Flight	Mark II
3, Fight Back	Mark III
5, Maggia Compound	Gold Tin Can
8, Frozen Ship	Classic
11, Island Meltdown	Stealth
13, Showdown	Titanium Man

PSP MINI-GAMES
Minigames can be unlocked by completing the following missions. Access the minigames through the Bonus menu.

COMPLETE MISSION	PSP MINI-GAME UNLOCKED
1, Escape	Tin Can Challenge 1 + 2
2, First Flight	DEATH RACE: STARK INDUSTRY
3, Fight Back	BOSS FIGHT: DREADNOUGHT
4, Weapons Transport	DEATH RACE: AFGHAN DESERT BOSS FIGHT: WHIPLASH
5, Maggia Compound	DEATH RACE: MAGGIA MANSION
6, Flying Fortress	SPEED KILL: FLYING FORTRESS SURVIVAL: FLYING FORTRESS
7, Nuclear Winter	DEATH RACE: ARTIC CIRCLE
8, Frozen Ship	SPEED KILL: FROZEN SHIP SURVIVAL: FROZEN SHIP
9, Home Front	BOSS FIGHT: TITANIUM MAN
10, Save Pepper	DEATH RACE: DAM BASSIN
11, Island Meltdown	SPEED KILL: GREEK ISLANDS SURVIVAL: GREEK ISLANDS
12, Battlesuit Factory	SPEED KILL: TINMEN FACTORY SURVIVAL: TINMEN FACTORY
13, Showdown	BOSS FIGHT: IRON MONGER

CONCEPT ART

As you progress through the game and destroy the Weapon Crates, bonuses are unlocked. You can find all of these in the Bonus menu once unlocked.

CONCEPT ART UNLOCKED	NUMBER OF WEAPON CRATES FOUND
Environments Set 1	6
Environments Set 2	12
Iron Man	18
Environments Set 3	24
Enemies	30
Environments Set 4	36
Villains	42
Vehicles	48
Covers	50

JUICED 2: HOT IMPORT NIGHTS

LAST MAN STANDING CHALLENGE AND AN ASCARI KZ1

Select Cheats and Challenges from the DNA Lab menu and enter KNOX. Defeat the challenge to earn the Ascari KZ1.

SPECIAL CHALLENGE AND AN AUDI TT 1.8 QUATTRO

Select Cheats and Challenges from the DNA Lab menu and enter YTHZ. Defeat the challenge to earn the Audi TT 1.8 Quattro.

SPECIAL CHALLENGE AND A BMW Z4

Select Cheats and Challenges from the DNA Lab menu and enter GVDL. Defeat the challenge to earn the BMW Z4.

SPECIAL CHALLENGE AND A HOLDEN MONARO

Select Cheats and Challenges from the DNA Lab menu and enter RBSG. Defeat the challenge to earn the Holden Monaro.

SPECIAL CHALLENGE AND A HYUNDAI COUPE 2.7 V6

Select Cheats and Challenges from the DNA Lab menu and enter BSLU. Defeat the challenge to earn the Hyundai Coupe 2.7 V6.

SPECIAL CHALLENGE AND AN INFINITY G35

Select Cheats and Challenges from the DNA Lab menu and enter MRHC. Defeat the challenge to earn the Infinity G35.

SPECIAL CHALLENGE AND AN INFINITY RED G35

Select Cheats and Challenges from the DNA Lab menu and enter MNCH. Defeat the challenge to earn the Infinity G35.

SPECIAL CHALLENGE AND A KOENIGSEGG CCX

Select Cheats and Challenges from the DNA Lab menu and enter KDTR. Defeat the challenge to earn the Koenigsegg CCX.

SPECIAL CHALLENGE AND A MITSUBISHI PROTOTYPE X

Select Cheats and Challenges from the DNA Lab menu and enter DOPX. Defeat the challenge to earn the Mitsubishi Prototype X.

SPECIAL CHALLENGE AND A NISSAN 350Z

Select Cheats and Challenges from the DNA Lab menu and enter PRGN. Defeat the challenge to earn the Nissan 350Z.

SPECIAL CHALLENGE AND A NISSAN SKYLINE R34 GT-R

Select Cheats and Challenges from the DNA Lab menu and enter JWRS. Defeat the challenge to earn the Nissan Skyline R34 GT-R.

SPECIAL CHALLENGE AND A SALEEN S7

Select Cheats and Challenges from the DNA Lab menu and enter WIKF. Defeat the challenge to earn the Saleen S7.

SPECIAL CHALLENGE AND A SEAT LEON CUPRA R

Select Cheats and Challenges from the DNA Lab menu and enter FAMQ. Defeat the challenge to earn the Seat Leon Cupra R.

JUSTICE LEAGUE HEROES

UNLOCK EVERYTHING

Pause the game, hold L + R and press Down, Left, Up, Right.

INVINCIBLE

Pause the game, hold L + R and press Left, Down, Right, Up, Left, Down, Right, Up.

UNLIMITED ENERGY
Pause the game, hold L + R and press Down, Down, Right, Right, Up, Up, Left, Left.

MAX ABILITIES
Pause the game, hold L + R and press Right, Down, Right, Down.

20 FREE SHIELDS
Pause the game, hold L + R and press Up, Up, Down, Down.

25 BOOSTS
Pause the game, hold L + R and press Left, Right, Left, Right.

KINGDOM HEARTS: BIRTH BY SLEEP

FINAL EPISODE
Find all of the Xehanort Reports and complete all three stories.

TRINITY ARCHIVES
Complete the story using any character.

TROPHY	UNLOCKED BY…
Power Walker	Taking 99,999 steps.
Keyslinger	Defeating 9999 Unversed.
Clockworks	Accumulating 80 hours or more of gameplay.
Arena Sweeper	Completing all arena matches.
Dairy Devotee	Activating Frozen Fortune 30 times.
In the Munny	Earning 33,333 munny.
One Down	Completing the story using any character.
Trinity	Completing all stories in at least Proud Mode.

LEGO BATMAN

BATCAVE CODES
Using the computer in the Batcave, select Enter Code and enter the following:

CHARACTERS

CHARACTER	CODE
Alfred	ZAQ637
Batgirl	JKR331
Bruce Wayne	BDJ327
Catwoman (Classic)	M1AAWW
Clown Goon	HJK327
Commissioner Gordon	DDP967
Fishmonger	HGY748
Freeze Girl	XVK541
Joker Goon	UTF782
Joker Henchman	YUN924
Mad Hatter	JCA283
Man-Bat	NYU942
Military Policeman	MKL382
Nightwing	MVY759
Penguin Goon	NKA238

CHARACTER	CODE
Penguin Henchman	BJH782
Penguin Minion	KJP748
Poison Ivy Goon	GTB899
Police Marksman	HKG984
Police Officer	JRY983
Riddler Goon	CRY928
Riddler Henchman	XEU824
S.W.A.T.	HTF114
Sailor	NAV592
Scientist	JFL786
Security Guard	PLB946
The Joker (Tropical)	CCB199
Yeti	NJL412
Zoo Sweeper	DWR243

VEHICLES

VEHICLE	CODE
Bat-Tank	KNTT4B
Bruce Wayne's Private Jet	LEA664
Catwoman's Motorcycle	HPL826
Garbage Truck	DUS483
Goon Helicopter	GCH328
Harbor Helicopter	CHP735
Harley Quinn's Hammer Truck	RDT637
Mad Hatter's Glider	HS000W
Mad Hatter's Steamboat	M4DM4N
Mr. Freeze's Iceberg	ICYICE
The Joker's Van	JUK657

VEHICLE	CODE
Mr. Freeze's Kart	BCT229
Penguin Goon Submarine	BTN248
Police Bike	LJP234
Police Boat	PLC999
Police Car	KJL832
Police Helicopter	CWR732
Police Van	MAC788
Police Watercraft	VJD328
Riddler's Jet	HAHAHA
Robin's Submarine	TTF453
Two-Face's Armored Truck	EFE933

CHEATS

CHEAT	CODE
Always Score Multiply	9LRGNB
Fast Batarangs	JRBDCB
Fast Walk	ZOLM6N
Flame Batarang	D8NYWH
Freeze Batarang	XPN4NG
Extra Hearts	ML3KHP
Fast Build	EVG26J
Immune to Freeze	JXUDY6
Invincibility	WYD5CP
Minikit Detector	ZXGH9J

CHEAT	CODE
More Batarang Targets	XWP645
Piece Detector	KHJ554
Power Brick Detector	MMN786
Regenerate Hearts	HJH7HJ
Score x2	N4NR3E
Score x4	CX9MAT
Score x6	MLVNF2
Score x8	WCCDB9
Score x10	18HW07

LEGO INDIANA JONES: THE ORIGINAL ADVENTURES

CHARACTERS

Approach the blackboard in the Classroom and enter the following codes.

CHARACTER	CODE
Bandit	12N68W
Bandit Swordsman	1MK4RT
Barranca	04EM94
Bazooka Trooper (Crusade)	MK83R7
Bazooka Trooper (Raiders)	S93Y5R
Belloq	CHN3YU
Belloq (Jungle)	TDR197
Belloq (Robes)	VEO29L
British Commander	B73EUA
British Officer	VJ5TI9
British Soldier	DJ5I2W
Captain Katanga	VJ3TT3
Chatter Lal	ENW936
Chatter Lal (Thuggee)	CNH4RY
Chen	3NK48T
Colonel Dietrich	2K9RKS
Colonel Vogel	8EAL4H
Dancing Girl	C7EJ21
Donovan	3NFTU8
Elsa (Desert)	JSNRT9
Elsa (Officer)	VMJ5US
Enemy Boxer	8246RB
Enemy Butler	VJ48W3
Enemy Guard	VJ7R51
Enemy Guard (Mountains)	YR47WM
Enemy Officer	572E61
Enemy Officer (Desert	2MK45O
Enemy Pilot	B84ELP
Enemy Radio Operator	1MF94R

CHARACTER	CODE
Enemy Soldier (Desert)	4NSU7Q
Fedora	V75YSP
First Mate	0GIN24
Grail Knight	NE6THI
Hovitos Tribesman	H0V1SS
Indiana Jones (Desert Disguise)	4J8S4M
Indiana Jones (Officer)	VJ85OS
Jungle Guide	24PF34
Kao Kan	WMO46L
Kazim	NRH23J
Kazim (Desert)	3M29TJ
Lao Che	2NK479
Maharajah	NFK5N2
Major Toht	13NS01
Masked Bandit	N48SF0
Mola Ram	FJUR31
Monkey Man	3RF6YJ
Pankot Assassin	2NKT72
Pankot Guard	VN28RH
Sherpa Brawler	VJ37WJ
Sherpa Gunner	ND762W
Slave Child	0E3ENW
Thuggee	VM683E
Thuggee Acolyte	T2R3F9
Thuggee Slave Driver	VBS7GW
Village Dignitary	KD48TN
Village Elder	4682E1
Willie (Dinner Suit)	VK93R7
Willie (Pajamas)	MEN4IP
Wu Han	3NSLT8

EXTRAS

Approach the blackboard in the Classroom and enter the following codes. Some cheats need to be enabled by selecting Extras from the pause menu.

CHEAT	CODE
Artifact Detector	VIKED7
Beep Beep	VNF59Q
Character Treasure	VIES2R
Disarm Enemies	VKRNS9

CHEAT	CODE
Disguises	4ID1N6
Fast Build	V83SLO
Fast Dig	378RS6
Fast Fix	FJ59WS

CHEAT	CODE
Fertilizer	B1GW1F
Ice Rink	33GM7J
Parcel Detector	VUT673
Poo Treasure	WWQ1SA
Regenerate Hearts	MDLP69
Secret Characters	3X44AA
Silhouettes	3HE85H
Super Scream	VN3R7S

CHEAT	CODE
Super Slap	0P1TA5
Treasure Magnet	H86LA2
Treasure x10	VI3PS8
Treasure x2	VM4TS9
Treasure x4	VLWEN3
Treasure x6	V84RYS
Treasure x8	A72E1M

LEGO STAR WARS II: THE ORIGINAL TRILOGY

BEACH TROOPER
At Mos Eisley Canteena, select Enter Code and enter UCK868. You still need to select Characters and purchase this character for 20,000 studs.

BEN KENOBI (GHOST)
At Mos Eisley Canteena, select Enter Code and enter BEN917. You still need to select Characters and purchase this character for 1,100,000 studs.

BESPIN GUARD
At Mos Eisley Canteena, select Enter Code and enter VHY832. You still need to select Characters and purchase this character for 15,000 studs.

BIB FORTUNA
At Mos Eisley Canteena, select Enter Code and enter WTY721. You still need to select Characters and purchase this character for 16,000 studs.

BOBA FETT
At Mos Eisley Canteena, select Enter Code and enter HLP221. You still need to select Characters and purchase this character for 175,000 studs.

DEATH STAR TROOPER
At Mos Eisley Canteena, select Enter Code and enter BNC332. You still need to select Characters and purchase this character for 19,000 studs.

EWOK
At Mos Eisley Canteena, select Enter Code and enter TTT289. You still need to select Characters and purchase this character for 34,000 studs.

GAMORREAN GUARD
At Mos Eisley Canteena, select Enter Code and enter YZF999. You still need to select Characters and purchase this character for 40,000 studs.

GONK DROID
At Mos Eisley Canteena, select Enter Code and enter NFX582. You still need to select Characters and purchase this character for 1,550 studs.

GRAND MOFF TARKIN
At Mos Eisley Canteena, select Enter Code and enter SMG219. You still need to select Characters and purchase this character for 38,000 studs.

GREEDO
At Mos Eisley Canteena, select Enter Code and enter NAH118. You still need to select Characters and purchase this character for 60,000 studs.

HAN SOLO (HOOD)
At Mos Eisley Canteena, select Enter Code and enter YWM840. You still need to select Characters and purchase this character for 20,000 studs.

IG-88
At Mos Eisley Canteena, select Enter Code and enter NXL973. You still need to select Characters and purchase this character for 30,000 studs.

IMPERIAL GUARD
At Mos Eisley Canteena, select Enter Code and enter MMM111. You still need to select Characters and purchase this character for 45,000 studs.

IMPERIAL OFFICER
At Mos Eisley Canteena, select Enter Code and enter BBV889. You still need to select Characters and purchase this character for 28,000 studs.

IMPERIAL SHUTTLE PILOT
At Mos Eisley Canteena, select Enter Code and enter VAP664. You still need to select Characters and purchase this character for 29,000 studs.

IMPERIAL SPY
At Mos Eisley Canteena, select Enter Code and enter CVT125. You still need to select Characters and purchase this character for 13,500 studs.

JAWA
At Mos Eisley Canteena, select Enter Code and enter JAW499. You still need to select Characters and purchase this character for 24,000 studs.

LOBOT
At Mos Eisley Canteena, select Enter Code and enter UUB319. You still need to select Characters and purchase this character for 11,000 studs.

PALACE GUARD
At Mos Eisley Canteena, select Enter Code and enter SGE549. You still need to select Characters and purchase this character for 14,000 studs.

REBEL PILOT
At Mos Eisley Canteena, select Enter Code and enter CYG336. You still need to select Characters and purchase this character for 15,000 studs.

REBEL TROOPER (HOTH)
At Mos Eisley Canteena, select Enter Code and enter EKU849. You still need to select Characters and purchase this character for 16,000 studs.

SANDTROOPER
At Mos Eisley Canteena, select Enter Code and enter YDV451. You still need to select Characters and purchase this character for 14,000 studs.

SKIFF GUARD
At Mos Eisley Canteena, select Enter Code and enter GBU888. You still need to select Characters and purchase this character for 12,000 studs.

SNOWTROOPER
At Mos Eisley Canteena, select Enter Code and enter NYU989. You still need to select Characters and purchase this character for 16,000 studs.

STORMTROOPER
At Mos Eisley Canteena, select Enter Code and enter PTR345. You still need to select Characters and purchase this character for 10,000 studs.

THE EMPEROR
At Mos Eisley Canteena, select Enter Code and enter HHY382. You still need to select Characters and purchase this character for 275,000 studs.

TIE FIGHTER
At Mos Eisley Canteena, select Enter Code and enter HDY739. You still need to select Characters and purchase this item for 60,000 studs.

TIE FIGHTER PILOT
At Mos Eisley Canteena, select Enter Code and enter NNZ316. You still need to select Characters and purchase this character for 21,000 studs.

TIE INTERCEPTOR
At Mos Eisley Canteena, select Enter Code and enter QYA828. You still need to select Characters and purchase this item for 40,000 studs.

TUSKEN RAIDER
At Mos Eisley Canteena, select Enter Code and enter PEJ821. You still need to select Characters and purchase this character for 23,000 studs.

UGNAUGHT
At Mos Eisley Canteena, select Enter Code and enter UGN694. You still need to select Characters and purchase this character for 36,000 studs.

MANHUNT 2

EXTRA LEVEL AS LEO
Defeat the game.

RELIVE SCENE
Defeat the game. This allows you to replay any level.

MARVEL SUPER HERO SQUAD

IRON MAN BONUS COSTUME
Select Enter Code from the Options menu and enter 111111. This unlocks the bonus costume "War Machine."

HULK BONUS COSTUMES
Select Enter Code from the Options menu and enter 222222. This unlocks the bonus costumes "Grey Hulk" and "Red Hulk."

WOLVERINE BONUS COSTUMES
Select Enter Code from the Options menu and enter 333333. This unlocks the bonus costumes "Wolverine (Brown Costume)" and "Feral Wolverine."

THOR BONUS COSTUMES
Select Enter Code from the Options menu and enter 444444. This unlocks the bonus costumes "Thor (Chain Armor)" and "Loki-Thor."

SILVER SURFER BONUS COSTUMES

Select Enter Code from the Options menu and enter 555555. This unlocks the bonus costumes "Anti-Surfer" and "Gold Surfer."

FALCON BONUS COSTUME

Select Enter Code from the Options menu and enter 666666. This unlocks the bonus costume "Ultimates Falcon."

DOCTOR DOOM BONUS COSTUMES

Select Enter Code from the Options menu and enter 999999. This unlocks the bonus costumes "Ultimates Doctor Doom" and "Professor Doom."

CAPTAIN AMERICA BONUS COSTUME

Select Enter Code from the Options menu and enter 177674. This unlocks the bonus costume "Ultimate Captain America Costume."

A.I.M. AGENT BONUS COSTUME

Select Enter Code from the Options menu and enter 246246. This unlocks the bonus costume "Blue Suit A.I.M."

SUPER KNOCKBACK

Select Enter Code from the Options menu and enter 777777.

NO BLOCK MODE

Select Enter Code from the Options menu and enter 888888.

GROUNDED

Select Enter Code from the Options menu and enter 476863.

ONE-HIT TAKEDOWN

Select Enter Code from the Options menu and enter 663448.

INFINITE SHARD DURATION

Select Enter Code from the Options menu and enter 742737.

THROWN OBJECT TAKEDOWN

Select Enter Code from the Options menu and enter 847936.

MARVEL TRADING CARD GAME

COMPLETE CARD LIBRARY

At the Deck menu, select new deck and name it BLVRTRSK.

ALL PUZZLES

At the Deck menu, select new deck and name it WHOWANTSPIE.

MARVEL ULTIMATE ALLIANCE

UNLOCK ALL SKINS

At the Team menu, press Up, Down, Left, Right, Left, Right, Start.

UNLOCK ALL HERO POWERS

At the Team menu, press Left, Right, Up, Down, Up, Down, Start.

ALL HEROES TO LEVEL 99

At the Team menu, press Up, Left, Up, Left, Down, Right, Down, Right, Start.

UNLOCK ALL HEROES

At the Team menu, press Up, Up, Down, Down, Left, Left, Left, Start

UNLOCK DAREDEVIL

At the Team Menu, press Left, Left, Right, Right, Up, Down, Up, Down, Start.

UNLOCK SILVER SURFER

At the Team menu, press Down, Left, Left, Up, Right, Up, Down, Left, Start.

GOD MODE

During gameplay, press Up, Down, Up, Down, Up, Left, Down, Right, Start.

TOUCH OF DEATH

During gameplay, press Left, Right, Down, Down, Right, Left, Start.

SUPER SPEED

During gameplay, press Up, Left, Up, Right, Down, Right, Start.

FILL MOMENTUM

During gameplay, press Left, Right, Right, Left, Up, Down, Down, Up, Start.

UNLOCK ALL COMICS

At the Review menu, press Left, Right, Left, Left, Up, Up, Right, Start.

UNLOCK ALL CONCEPT ART

At the Review menu, press Down, Down, Down, Right, Right, Left, Down, Start.

MARVEL ULTIMATE ALLIANCE 2

GOD MODE

At any point during a game, press Up, Up, Down, Down, Left, Right, Down.

GIVE MONEY

At the Team Select or Hero Details screen press Up, Up, Down, Down, Up, Up, Up, Down.

UNLOCK ALL POWERS
At the Team Select or Hero Details screen press Up, Up, Down, Down, Left, Right, Right, Left.

ADVANCE ALL CHARACTERS TO L99
At the Hero Details screen press Down, Up, Left, Up, Right, Up, Left, Down.

UNLOCK ALL BONUS MISSIONS
While using the Bonus Mission Simulator, press Up, Right, Down, Left, Left, Right, Up, Up.

ADD 1 CHARACTER LEVEL
During a game, press Down, Up, Right, Up, Right, Up, Right, Down.

ADD 10 CHARACTER LEVELS
During a game, press Down, Up, Left, Up, Left, Up, Left, Down.

MEDIEVIL: RESURRECTION

INVINCIBILITY & ALL WEAPONS
Pause the game, hold R and press Down, Up, ●, ▲, ▲, ●, Down, Up, ●, ▲. Pause the game to access the Cheat menu.

CHEAT MENU
Pause the game, hold R and press Down, Up, ●, ▲, ▲, ●, Down, Up, ●+▲. This gives you invincibility and all weapons.

ALL ARTIFACTS AND KEYS
Pause the game and press L + R, ✕, ✕, ●, ●, ▲, ✕.

METAL GEAR ACID 2

CARD NO. 046—STRAND
Enter nojiri as a password.

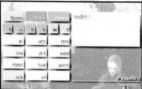

Unlocked
STRAND

CARD NO. 099—GIJIN-SAN
Enter shinta as a password.

CARD NO. 119—REACTION BLOCK
Enter konami as a password.

CARD NO. 161—VIPER
Enter viper as a password.

CARD NO. 166—MIKA SLAYTON
Enter mika as a password.

CARD NO. 170—KAREN HOJO
Enter karen as a password.

CARD NO. 172—JEHUTY
Enter jehuty as a password.

CARD NO. 187—XM8
Enter xmeight as a password.

CARD NO. 188—MR. SIGINT
Enter signt as a password.

CARD NO. 197—SEA HARRIER
Enter shrrr as a password.

CARD NO. 203—DECOY OCTOPUS
Enter dcy as a password.

CARD NO. 212—ROGER MCCOY
Enter mccy as a password.

CARD NO. 281—REIKO HINOMOTO
Enter hnmt as a password.

CARD NO. 285—AYUMI KINOSHITA
Enter aym as a password.

CARD NO. 286—MEGURU ISHII
Enter mgr as a password.

CARD NO. 287—NATSUME SANO
Enter ntm as a password.

CARD NO. 288—MGS4
Enter nextgen as a password.

CARD NO. 289—EMMA'S PARROT
Enter ginormousj as a password.

CARD NO. 290—BANANA SKIN
Enter ronaldsiu as a password.

CARD NO. 292—POSSESSED ARM
Enter thespaniard as a password.

CARD NO. 293—SOLID EYE
Enter tobidacid as a password.

CARD NO. 294—SOLID SNAKE (MGS4)
Enter snake as a password.

CARD NO. 295—OTACON (MGS4)
Enter otacon as a password.

CARD NO. 296—GEKKO
Enter gekko as a password.

CARD NO. 297—METAL GEAR MK. II (MGS4)
Enter mk2 as a password.

CARD NO. 298—NO SMOKING
Enter smoking as a password.

T-SHIRTS

From the Extras menu, select Network and then Enter Passcode. Now you can enter the following. Note that you need a PSN account and each passcode can only be used once per PSN account.

T-SHIRT	PASSCODE
Black with "Big Boss"	2000016032758
Black with "Peace Walker"	2000016032390
Black with Peace Walker Logo	2000016038415
Gray with Coffee Cup	2000016036022
Gray with MSF	2000016032567
Gray with MSF	2000016032574
Gray with Snake	2000016032338

T-SHIRT	PASSCODE
Navy Blue with MSF	2000016032635
Olive with Snake	2000016035902
Red with Big Boss	2000016537833
Tan	2000016038576
White with Big Boss	2000016756791
White with "Big Boss"	2000016032680
White with Coffee Cup	2000016032964

METAL GEAR SOLID: PORTABLE OPS

CUNNINGHAM
Enter JUNKER as a password.

ELISA
Enter THE-L as a password.

EVA
Enter E.APPLE as a password.

GA KO
Enter !TRAUMER as a password.

GENE
Enter ERBE as a password.

NULL
Enter Hunter-n as a password.

OCELOT
Enter R.R.R. as a password.

PARAMEDIC
Enter PM-EMS as a password.

PYTHON
Enter LQ.N2 as a password.

RAIKOV
Enter IVN =RV as a password.

SIGINT
Enter DARPA-1 as a password.

SOKOLOV
Enter SATURNV as a password.

TELIKO
Enter T.F-ACID as a password.

URSULA
Enter PK +ESP as a password.

VENUS
Enter MGA2VE as a password.

ZERO
Enter 1+2-3 as a password.

METAL GEAR SOLID: PORTABLE OPS PLUS

SOLDIER PASSWORDS

Enter the following as a password.

SOLDIER	PASSWORD
Alabama	BB6K768KM9
Alaska	XL5SW5NH9S
Arizona	ZHEFPVV947
Arkansas	VNRE7JNQ8WE
Black Genome	WYNGG3JBP3YS
Blue Genome	9GNPHGFFLH
California	6MSJQYWNCJ8
Colorado	W6TAH498DJ
Connecticut	2N2AB3JV2WA
Delaware	AJRL6E7TT9
Female Scientist 1	3W8WVVRGB2LNN
Female Scientist 2	FUC72C463KZ
Female Scientist 3	UCAWYTMXB5V
Female Soldier 1	UZZQYRPXM86

SOLDIER	PASSWORD
Female Soldier 2	QRQQ7GWKHJ
Female Soldier 3	MVNDAZAP8DWE
Florida	A44STZ3BHY5
Fox Soldier 1	FMXT79TPV4U8
Fox Soldier 2	HGMK3WCYURM
Fox Soldier 3	6ZY5NYW4TGK
Georgia	VD5H53JJCRH
Green Genome	TGQ6F5TUHD
GRU Soldier	9V8S7DVYFTR
Gurlukovich's Soldier	6VWM6A22FSS8
Hawaii	TW7ZMZHCBL
Hideochan Soldier	RU8XRCLPUUT
High Official	ADPS2SE5UC8

SOLDIER	PASSWORD
High Rank Officer 1	DVB2UDTQ5Z
High Rank Officer 2	84ZEC4X5PJ6
High Ranking Officer 3	DTAZ3QRQQDU
High-Tech Soldier	M4MSJ6R87XPP
Idaho	XAFGETZGXHGA
Illinois	QYUVCNDFUPZJ
Indiana	L68JVXVBL8RN
Iowa	B8MW36ZU56S
Kansas	TYPEVDEE24YT
Kentucky	LCD7WGS5X5
KGB Soldier	MNBVYRZP4QH
Louisiana	EHR5VVMHUSG
Maine	T5GYHQABGAC3
KGB Soldier	MNBVYRZP4QH
Louisiana	EHR5VVMHUSG
Maine	T5GYHQABGAC3
Maintenance Crew Member 1	T8EBSRK6F38
Maintenance Crew Member 2	YHQU74J6LLQ
Maintenance Crew Member 3	MFAJMUXZHHKJ
Male Scientist 1	ZFKHJKDEA2
Male Scientist 2	QQ4N3TPCL8PF
Male Scientist 3	CXFCXF4FP9R6
Maryland	L2W9G5N76MH7
Massachusetts	ZLU2S3ULDEVF
Michigan	HGDRBUB5P3SA
Minnesota	EEBBM888ZRA
Mississippi	TBF7H9G6TJH7
Missouri	WJND6M9N738
Montana	9FYUFV29B2Y
Nebraska	MCNB5S5K47H
Nevada	Z9D4UGG8T4U6
New Hampshire	7NQYDQ9Y4KMP
New Jersey	LGHTBU9ZTGR
New Mexico	RGJCMHNLSX
New York	6PV39FKG6X
Normal Soldier Long Sleeve	QK3CMV373Y
Normal Soldier Long Sleeve Magazine Vest	D8RV32E9774

SOLDIER	PASSWORD
Normal Soldier Short Sleeve	N524ZHU9N4Z
Normal Soldier Short Sleeve Magazine Vest	6WXZA7PTT9Z
North Carolina	JGVT2XV47UZ
North Dakota	T5LSAVMPWZCY
Ocelot Female A	9FS7QYSHZ56N
Ocelot Female B	F94XDZSQSGJ8
Ocelot Female C	CRF8PZGXR28
Ocelot Unit	GE6MU3DXL3X
Ohio	AUWGAXWCA3D
Oklahoma	ZQT75NUJH8A3
Oregon	HKSD3PJ5E5
Pennsylvania	PL8GVVUM4HD
Pink Genome	7WRG3N2MRY2
Red Genome	9CM4SY23C7X8
Rhode Island	MMYC99T3QG
Seal	X56YCKZP2V
South Carolina	ZR4465MD8LK
South Dakota	RY3NUDDPMU3
Tengu Soldier	PHHB4TY4J2D
Tennessee	TD2732GCX43U
Texas	QM84UPP6F3
Tsuhan soldier	A9KK7WYWVCV
USSR Female Soldier A	2VXUZQVH9R
USSR Female Soldier B	HPMRFSBXDJ3Y
USSR Female Soldier C	QXQVW9R3PZ
USSR Female Soldier D	GMC3M3LTPVW7
USSR Female Soldier E	5MXVX6UFPMZ5
USSR Female Soldier F	76AWS7WDAV
Utah	V7VRAYZ78GW
Vermont	L7T66LFZ63C8
Virginia	DRTCS77F5N
Washington	G3S4N42WWKTV
Washington DC	Y5YCFYHVZZW
West Virginia	72M8XR99B6
White Genome	QJ4ZTQSLUT8
Wisconsin	K9BUN2BGLMT3
Wyoming	C3THQ749RA
Yellow Genome	CE5HHYGTSSB

MLB 08: THE SHOW

CLASSIC FREE AGENTS AT THE PLAYER MOVEMENT MENU

At the Main menu, press Left, Right, Up, Left, Right, Up, Right, Down.

SILVER ERA AND GOLDEN ERA TEAMS

At the Main menu, press Right, Up, Right, Down, Down, Left, Up, Down.

BIG BALL

Pause the game and press Right, Down, Up, Left, Right, Left, Down, Up.

BIG HEAD MODE

Pause the game and press Right, Left, Down, Up, Left, Up, Down, Left.

SMALL HEAD MODE

Pause the game and press Left, Right, Down, Up, Right, Left, Down, Left.

MTX MOTOTRAX

ALL TRACKS
Enter BA7H as a password.

ALL BONUSES
Enter 2468GOA7 as a password.

SUPER SPEED
Enter JIH345 as a password.

MAXIMUM AIR
Enter BFB0020 as a password.

BUTTERFINGER GEAR
Enter B77393 as a password.

LEFT FIELD GEAR
Enter 12345 as a password.

SOBE GEAR
Enter 50BE as a password.

MVP BASEBALL

ALL REWARDS
Select My MVP and create a player with
the name Dan Carter.

MX VS. ATV UNLEASHED: ON THE EDGE

UNLOCK EVERYTHING
Select Cheat Codes from the Options screen and enter TOOLAZY.

1,000,000 POINTS
Select Cheat Codes from the Options screen and enter BROKEASAJOKE.

PRO PHYSICS
Select Cheat Codes from the
Options screen and enter
IAMTOOGOOD.

ALL GEAR
Select Cheat Codes from the
Options screen and enter
WARDROBE.

ALL BIKES
Select Cheat Codes from the
Options screen and enter BRAPP.

50CC BIKE CLASS
Select Cheat Codes from the
Options screen and enter
MINIMOTO.

500CC BIKE CLASS
Select Cheat Codes from the
Options screen and enter
BIGBORE.

ALL ATVS
Select Cheat Codes from the
Options screen and enter
COUCHES.

ALL MACHINES
Select Cheat Codes from the
Options screen and enter
LEADFOOT.

ALL FREESTYLE TRACKS
Select Cheat Codes from the
Options screen and enter HUCKIT.

ALL NATIONAL TRACKS
Select Cheat Codes from the Options screen and enter GOOUTSIDE.

ALL SUPERCROSS TRACKS
Select Cheat Codes from the Options screen and enter GOINSIDE.

ALL OPEN CLASS TRACKS
Select Cheat Codes from the Options screen and enter NOTMOTO.

ALL TRACKS
Select Cheat Codes from the Options screen and enter PITPASS.

N+

25 EXTRA LEVELS
At the Main menu, hold L + R and press ✖, ⬤, ✖, ⬤, ✖, ✖, ⬤.

NARUTO SHIPPUDEN: ULTIMATE NINJA HEROES 3

FIGURES
At the Tree of Mettle, select Enter Password and input the following passwords:

FIGURE	PASSWORD
Gods and Angels	Fire, Sheep, Ox, Tiger
Inheritor of the Will	Water, Dog, Snake, Ox
One Who Lurks in Darkness	Thunder, Dog, Tiger, Boar
Rivals	Earth, Sheep, Boar, Dog
Team Asuma	Fire, Dog, Rabbit, Tiger
Team Guy	Water, Dog, Rat, Rooster
Team Kurenai	Thunder, Snake, Dragon, Monkey
The Hokage's Office	Wind, Rabbit, Dragon, Ox
The Innocent Maiden	Water, Snake, Dragon, Ox
The Three Sand Siblings	Earth, Rooster, Ox, Snake

JUTSUS
At the Tree of Mettle, select Enter Password and input the following passwords:

NINJUTSU	PASSWORD
100m Punch	Thunder, Rat, Snake, Horse
Assault Blade	Wind, Rat, Rabbit, Ox
Bring Down the House Jutsu	Thunder, Sheep, Ox, Rooster
Cherry Blossom Clash	Fire, Monkey, Boar, Rabbit
Dead Soul Jutsu	Thunder, Monkey, Dog, Ox
Detonation Dispersion	Wind, Dragon, Horse, Rat
Dynamic Entry	Fire, Rooster, Rabbit, Boar
Feather Illusion Jutsu	Water, Dragon, Boar, Dog
Fire Style: Burning Ash	Fire, Rat, Rabbit, Monkey
Fire Style: Dragon Flame Bomb	Fire, Snake, Dragon, Rabbit
Fire Style: Fire Ball Jutsu	Fire, Dragon, Rat, Monkey
Fire Style: Yoruho'o	Fire, Horse, Rabbit, Sheep
Genjutsu: Haze	Wind, Dragon, Sheep, Rooster
Genjutsu: Madder Mist	Thunder, Rooster, Boar, Dog
Heaven Defending Kick	Earth, Rat, Boar, Monkey
Intensive Healing	Water, Rat, Tiger, Rat
Leaf Repeating Wind	Wind, Rooster, Ox, Tiger
Lightning Blade	Thunder, Monkey, Rooster, Snake
Lightning Style: Thunderbolt Flash	Thunder, Sheep, Ox, Dog
Slithering Snakes	Thunder, Tiger, Rooster, Dog
Summoning: Rashomon	Earth, Monkey, Boar, Rooster
Tunneling Fang	Wind, Dog, Boar, Horse
Water Style: Ripping Torrent	Water, Ox, Dog, Sheep
Water Style: Water Fang Bomb	Water, Horse, Rat, Ox
Weapon: Flash Kunai Ball	Fire, Sheep, Boar, Ox
Wind Style: Air Bullets	Wind, Ox, Boar, Rabbit

HOKAGE NARUTO WALLPAPER
At the Tree of Mettle, select Enter Password and enter Fire, Ox, Rabbit, Horse.

ALL CHASE PLATES
Go to Fight to the Top mode. Next, edit the driver's first and last name so that it says ItsAll ForMe. Note that the code is case-sensitive.

$10,000,000
In Fight to the Top mode, enter your driver's name as GiveMe More.

10,000,000 FANS
In Fight to the Top mode, enter your driver's name as AllBow ToMe.

ALL CHASE PLATES
In Fight to the Top mode, enter your driver's name as ItsAll ForMe.

OLD SPICE TRACKS AND CARS
In Fight to the Top mode, enter your driver's name as KeepCool SmellGreat.

NBA 2K10

ABA BALL
Select Codes from the Options menu. Then select Enter Code and enter payrespect.

2K CHINA TEAM
Select Codes from the Options menu. Then select Enter Code and enter 2kchina.

NBA 2K TEAM
Select Codes from the Options menu. Then select Enter Code and enter nba2k.

2K SPORTS TEAM
Select Codes from the Options menu. Then select Enter Code and enter 2ksports.

VISUAL CONCEPTS TEAM
Select Codes from the Options menu. Then select Enter Code and enter vcteam.

2010 ALL-STAR UNIFORMS
Select Codes from the Options menu. Then select Enter Code and enter otnresla.

HARDWOOD CLASSIC UNIFORMS
Select Codes from the Options menu. Then select Enter Code and enter wasshcicsl. This code gives Hardwood Classic Uniforms for the Cavaliers, Jazz, Magic, Raptors, timberwolves, Trail Blazers, and Warriors.

LATIN NIGHTS UNIFORMS
Select Codes from the Options menu. Then select Enter Code and enter aihinntslgt. This code gives Latin Nights jerseys for Bulls, Heat, Knicks, Lakers, Mavericks, Rockets, Spurs, and Suns.

NBA GREEN UNIFORMS
Select Codes from the Options menu. Then select Enter Code and enter nreogge. This code gives green uniforms for the Bobcats, Bulls, and Nuggets.

SECONDARY ROAD UNIFORMS
Select Codes from the Options menu. Then select Enter Code and enter eydonscar. This code gives Second Road Uniforms for the Grizzlies, Hawks, Mavericks, and Rockets.

ST. PATRICK'S DAY UNIFORMS
Select Codes from the Options menu. Then select Enter Code and enter riiasgerh. This code gives St. Patrick's Day jerseys for the Bulls, Celtics, Knicks, and Raptors.

BOBCATS RACING UNIFORM
Select Codes from the Options menu. Then select Enter Code and enter agsntrccai.

CAVALIERS CAVFANATICS UNIFORM
Select Codes from the Options menu. Then select Enter Code and enter aifnaatccv.

HORNETS MARDI GRAS UNIFORM
Select Codes from the Options menu. Then select Enter Code and enter asrdirmga.

TRAIL BLAZERS RIP CITY UNIFORM
Select Codes from the Options menu. Then select Enter Code and enter ycprtii.

NBA 2K11

2K CHINA TEAM
In Features, select Codes from the Extras menu. Choose Enter Code and key in 2kchina.

2K SPORTS TEAM
In Features, select Codes from the Extras menu. Choose Enter Code and key in 2Ksports.

NBA 2K TEAM
In Features, select Codes from the Extras menu. Choose Enter Code and key in nba2k.

VC TEAM
In Features, select Codes from the Extras menu. Choose Enter Code and key in vcteam.

ABA BALL
In Features, select Codes from the Extras menu. Choose Enter Code and key in payrespect.

NBA BALLERS: REBOUND

VERSUS SCREEN CHEATS
You must enter the following codes at the Vs screen. The ● button corresponds to the first number in the code, the ▲ is the second number, and the ● button corresponds to the last number. Press the D-pad in any direction to enter the code. The name of the code will appear when entered correctly. Some of the codes will give you the wrong code name when entered.

EFFECT	CODE
Big Head	1 3 4
Pygmy	4 2 5
Alternate Gear	1 2 3
Show Shot Percentage	0 1 2
Expanded Move Set	5 1 2
Super Push	3 1 5
Super Block Ability	1 2 4
Great Handles	3 3 2
Unlimited Juice	7 6 3
Super Steals	2 1 5
Perfect Free Throws	3 2 7
Better Free Throws	3 1 7
Speedy Players	2 1 3
Alley-Oop Ability	7 2 5
Back-In Ability	1 2 2
Hotspot Ability	6 2 7

EFFECT	CODE
Pass 2 Friend Ability	5 3 6
Put Back Ability	3 1 3
Stunt Ability	3 7 4
2x Juice Replenish	4 3 1
Legal Goal Tending	7 5 6
Play As Afro Man	5 1 7
Play As Agent	5 5 7
Play As Business-A	5 3 7
Play As Business-B	5 2 7
Play As Coach	5 6 7
Play As Secretary	5 4 7
Super Back-Ins	2 3 5
Half House	3 6 7
Random Moves	3 0 0
Tournament Mode	0 1 1

PHRASE-OLOGY CODES
Select Phrase-ology from the Inside Stuff option and enter the following to unlock that bonus.

BONUS	PHRASE
All Players and Cinemas	NBA BALLERS TRUE PLAYA
Special Shoe #2	COLD STREAK
Special Shoe #3	LOST YA SHOES

CRIBS
Select Phrase-ology from the Inside Stuff option and enter the following to unlock player cribs.

CRIB	PHRASE
Allen Iverson's Recording Studio	THE ANSWER
Karl Malone's Devonshire Estate	ICE HOUSE
Kobe Bryant's Italian Estate	EURO CRIB
Ben Gordon's Yacht	NICE YACHT
Yao Ming's Childhood Grade School	PREP SCHOOL

NBA LIVE 10

CHARLOTTE BOBCATS' 2009/2010 RACE DAY ALTERNATE JERSEYS
Select Options from My NBA Live and go to Select Codes. Enter ceobdabacarstcy.

NEW ORLEANS HORNETS' 2009/2010 MARDI GRAS ALTERNATE JERSEYS
Select Options from My NBA Live and go to Select Codes. Enter nishrag1rosmad0.

ALTERNATE JERSEYS
Select Options from My NBA Live and go to Select Codes. Enter ndnba1rooaesdc0. This unlocks alternate jerseys for Atlanta Hawks, Dallas Mavericks, Houston Rockets, and Memphis Grizzlies.

MORE HARDWOOD CLASSICS NIGHTS JERSEYS
Select Options from My NBA Live and go to Select Codes. Enter hdogdrawhoticns. This unlocks Hardwood Classics Nights jerseys for Cleveland Cavaliers, Golden State Warriors, Minnesota Timberwolves, Orlando Magic, Philadelphia 76ers.

ADIDAS EQUATIONS
Select Options from My NBA Live and go to Select Codes. Enter adaodqauieints1.

ADIDAS TS CREATORS WITH ANKLE BRACES
Select Options from My NBA Live and go to Select Codes. Enter atciadsstsdhecf.

ADIDAS TS SUPERNATURAL COMMANDERS
Select Options from My NBA Live and go to Select Codes. Enter andsicdsmatdnsr.

ADIDAS TS SUPERNATURAL CREATORS
Select Options from My NBA Live and go to Select Codes. Enter ard8siscdnatstr.

AIR MAX LEBRON VII
Select Options from My NBA Live and go to Select Codes. Enter ere1nbvlaoeknii, 2ovnaebnkrielei, 3rioabeneikenvl, ri4boenanekilve, ivl5brieekaeonn, or n6ieirvalkeeobn.

KOBE V
Select Options from My NBA Live and go to Select Codes. Enter ovze1bimenkoko0, m0kveokoiebozn2, eev0nbimokk3ozo, or bmo4inozeeo0kvk.

JORDAN CP3 IIIS
Select Options from My NBA Live and go to Select Codes. Enter iaporcdian3ejis.

JORDAN MELO M6S
Select Options from My NBA Live and go to Select Codes. Enter emlarmeoo6ajdsn.

JORDAN SIXTY PLUSES
Select Options from My NBA Live and go to Select Codes. Enter aondsuilyjrspxt.

NIKE HUARACHE LEGIONS
Select Options from My NBA Live and go to Select Codes. Enter aoieuchrahelgn.

NIKE KD 2S
Select Options from My NBA Live and go to Select Codes. Enter kk2tesaosepinrd.

NIKE ZOOM FLIP'NS
Select Options from My NBA Live and go to Select Codes. Enter epfnozaeminolki.

NEED FOR SPEED CARBON: OWN THE CITY

UNLOCK EVERYTHING
At the Start menu, press X, X, Right, Left, ●, Up, Down.

JET CAR
At the Start menu, press Up, Down, Left, R1, L1, ●, ▲.

LAMBORGINI MERCIALAGO
At the Start menu, press X, X, Up, Down, Left, Right, ●, ●.

TRANSFORMERS CAR
At the Start menu, press X, X, X, ●, ▲, ▲, Up, Down.

NEOPETS PETPET ADVENTURE: THE WAND OF WISHING

START GAME WITH 5 CHOCOLATE TREATS
Enter treat4u as your Petpet's name. You can then rename your character. The chocolate treats are shaped according to the character you chose.

PAC-MAN WORLD 3

ALL LEVELS AND MAZES
At the Main menu, press Left, Right, Left, Right, ●, Up.

PHANTASY STAR PORTABLE 2

VISION PHONE
Use the Vision Phone to enter the following passwords:

NAME	PASSWORD	NAME	PASSWORD
Akahara Reisou	24932278	Miku's T. Leek Sabers	39395344
Akahara Reisou	24932279	Mr. Ekoeko Stick	55687362
Akahara Reisou	24932280	Ogi's Head	74612418
Alis Landale Poster	41325468	Pizza Shack D Box	89747981
Angry Marshmellow	32549410	Platinum Tiger	32549412
Art Javelin	72401990	Platinum Tiger	32549414
Blank Epoch	48168861	Platinum Tiger	32549411
Blank Epoch	48168862	Platinum Tiger	32549413
Bullet Lancer	32091120	Plug Suit Asuka	34336181
Clarita Visas	29888026	Plug Suit Asuka	34336182
Crutches	98443460	Plug Suit Rei	46211351
Edelweiss Figurine	54333358	Plug Suit Rei	46211352
Hanhei Tsunagin	41761771	Plug Suit Shinji	15644322
Hanhei Tsunagin	41761772	Puyo Pop Fever Gun	54186516
Hatsune Miku's Leek Wand	12344321	Puyo Pop Fists	11293398
Kansho Bayuka	46815464	Scouring Bubble	33286491
Longinus Lance	32143166	Sonic Knuckles	34819852
Lovely Feathers	72401991	Special Pizza Cutter	34162313
Lovely Feathers	72401992	Telltale Hearts	48168860
Magical Princess	55687361	The Rappy of Hope	54684698
Magical Princess	55687362	Toop Nasur	30495153
Maverick Rifle	53962481	Trauma Bandages	98443462
Miku Hatsune Dress	39395341	Trauma Bandages	98443464
Miku Hatsune Dress	39395342	Trauma Bandages	98443461
Miku's Leek Rifle	39395345	Trauma Bandages	98443463
Miku's Leek Saber	39395343	True Hash	41761770

PINBALL HALL OF FAME

CUSTOM BALLS OPTION
Enter CKF as a code.

TILT OPTION
Enter BZZ as a code.

PAYOUT MODE
Enter WGR as a code.

ACES HIGH IN FREEPLAY
Enter UNO as a code.

CENTRAL PARK IN FREEPLAY
Enter NYC as a code.

LOVE MACHINE IN FREEPLAY
Enter HOT as a code.

PLAYBOY TABLE IN FREEPLAY
Enter HEF as a code.

STRIKES 'N SPARES IN FREEPLAY
Enter PBA as a code.

TEE'D OFF IN FREEPLAY
Enter PGA as a code.

XOLTEN IN FREEPLAY
Enter BIG as a code.

POCKET POOL

ALL PICTURES AND VIDEOS
At the Title screen, press L, R, L, L, R, R, L (x3), R (x3), L (x4), R (x4).

PRINNY: CAN I REALLY BE THE HERO?

START A NEW GAME WITH THE ALTERNATE STORYLINE
At the Main menu, highlight New Game and press ▲, ●, ●, ●, ▲, ●, ●, ✕.

ROCKET RACING

TRIGGER MODE
At the main menu or during a game, hold L and press Up, Down, Left, Right, ▲, release L.

TRIGGER MODE (REVERSED)
At the main menu or during a game, hold L and press Up, Down, Left, Right, ●, release L.

STICK MODE (DEFAULT)
At the main menu or during a game, hold L and press Up, Down, Left, Right, R, release L

SECRET AGENT CLANK

ACTIVATE CHALICE OF POWER
Press Up, Up, Down, Down, Left, Right, Left, Right to regain health once per level.

THE SECRET SATURDAYS: BEASTS OF THE 5TH SUN

ALL LEVELS
Select Enter Secret Code from the Secrets menu and input Zon, Zon, Zon, Zon.

UNLOCK AMAROK TO BE SCANNED IN LEVEL 2
Select Enter Secret Code from the Secrets menu and input Fiskerton, Zak, Zon, Komodo.

UNLOCK BISHOPVILLE LIZARDMAN TO BE SCANNED IN LEVEL 3
Select Enter Secret Code from the Secrets menu and input Komodo, Zon, Zak, Komodo.

UNLOCK NAGA TO BE SCANNED IN LEVEL 7
Select Enter Secret Code from the Secrets menu and input Zak, Zak, Zon, Fiskerton.

UNLOCK RAKSHASA TO BE SCANNED IN LEVEL 8
Select Enter Secret Code from the Secrets menu and input Zak, Komodo, Fiskerton, Fiskerton.

UNLOCK BILOKO TO BE SCANNED IN LEVEL 9
Select Enter Secret Code from the Secrets menu and input Zon, Zak, Zon, Fiskerton.

SEGA GENESIS COLLECTION

Before using the following cheats, select the ABC Control option. This sets the controller to the following: ● is A, ✕ is B, ● is C.

ALTERED BEAST

OPTIONS MENU
At the Title screen, hold B and press Start.

LEVEL SELECT
After enabling the Options menu, select a level from the menu. At the Title screen, hold A and press Start.

BEAST SELECT
At the Title screen, hold A + B + C + Down/Left and then press Start.

SOUND TEST
At the Title screen, hold A + C + Up/Right and press Start.

COMIX ZONE

INVINCIBILITY
At the Jukebox screen, press C on the following sounds:
3, 12, 17, 2, 2, 10, 2, 7, 7, 11

LEVEL SELECT
At the Jukebox screen, press C on the following sounds:
14, 15, 18, 5, 13, 1, 3, 18, 15, 6
Press C on the desired level.

ECCO THE DOLPHIN

INVINCIBILITY
When the level name appears, hold A + Start until the level begins.

DEBUG MENU

Pause the game with Ecco facing the screen and press Right, B, C, B, C, Down, C, Up.

PASSWORDS

INFINITE AIR

Enter LIFEFISH as a password.

LEVEL	PASSWORD	LEVEL	PASSWORD
The Undercaves	WEFIDNMP	Deep City	DDXPQQLJ
The Vents	BQDPXJDS	City of Forever	MSDBRQLA
The Lagoon	JNSBRIKY	Jurassic Beach	IYCBUNLB
Ridge Water	NTSBZTKB	Pteranodon Pond	DMXEUNLI
Open Ocean	YWGTTJNI	Origin Beach	EGRIUNLB
Ice Zone	HZIFZBMF	Trilobite Circle	IELMUNLB
Hard Water	LRFJRQLI	Dark Water	RKEQUNLN
Cold Water	UYNFRQLC	City of Forever 2	HPQIGPLA
Island Zone	LYTIOQLZ	The Tube	JUMFKMLB
Deep Water	MNOPOQLR	The Machine	GXUBKMLF
The Marble	RJNTQQLZ	The Last Fight	TSONLMLU
The Library	RTGXQQLE		

FLICKY

ROUND SELECT

Begin a new game. Before the first round appears, hold A + C + Up + Start. Press Up or Down to select a Round.

GAIN GROUND

LEVEL SELECT

At the Options screen, press A, C, B, C.

GOLDEN AXE

LEVEL SELECT

Select Arcade Mode. At the character select, hold Down/Left + B and press Start. Press Up or Down to select a level.

RISTAR

Select Passwords from the Options menu and enter the following:

LEVEL SELECT
ILOVEU

BOSS RUSH MODE
MUSEUM

TIME ATTACK MODE
DOFEEL

TOUGHER DIFFICULTY
SUPER

ONCHI MUSIC
MAGURO. Activate this from the Sound Test.

CLEARS PASSWORD
XXXXXX

GAME COPYRIGHT INFO
AGES

SONIC THE HEDGEHOG

LEVEL SELECT

At the title screen, press Up, Down, Left, Right. Hold A and press Start.

SONIC THE HEDGEHOG 2

LEVEL SELECT

Select Sound Test from the options. Press C on the following sounds in order: 19, 65, 09, 17. At the title screen, hold A and press Start.

VECTORMAN

DEBUG MODE

At the options screen, press A, B, B, A, Down, A, B, B, A.

REFILL LIFE

Pause the game and press A, B, Right, A, C, A , Down, A, B, Right, A.

VECTORMAN 2

LEVEL SELECT

Pause the game and press Up, Right, A, B, A, Down, Left, A, Down.

EXTRA LIFE

Pause the game and press Right, Up, B, A, Down, Up, B, Down, Up, B. Repeat for more lives.

FULL ENERGY

Pause the game and press B, A, B, A, Left, Up, Up.

NEW WEAPON

Pause the game and press C, A, Left, Left, Down, A, Down. Repeat for more weapons.

SHREK THE THIRD

10,000 BONUS COINS

Press Up, Up, Down, Up, Right, Left at the Gift Shop.

SILENT HILL: ORIGINS

CODEBREAKER SUIT
During a game, press Up, Up, Down, Down, Left, Right, Left, Right, ✕, ⬤.
You must first finish the game to get this suit.

THE SIMPSONS GAME

UNLIMITED POWER FOR ALL CHARACTERS
At the Extras menu, press ▲, Left, Right, ▲, ⬤, L.

ALL MOVIES
At the Extras menu, press ⬤, Left, ⬤, Right, ▲, R.

ALL CLICHÉS
At the Extras menu, press Left, ⬤, Right, ▲, Right, L.

THE SIMS 2

PERK CHEAT
At the Buy Perks screen, hold L + R + ⬤. Buy the Cheat Perk to get some money, skills, and more.

THE SIMS 2: CASTAWAY

CHEAT GNOME
During a game, press L, R, Up, ✕, R. You can now use this Gnome to get the following during Live mode:

ALL PLANS
During a game, press ✕, R, ✕, R, ✕.

ALL CRAFT AND RESOURCES
During a game, press ⬤, ▲, R, Down, Down, Up.

MAX FOOD AND RESOURCES
During a game, press ⬤(x4), L.

THE SIMS 2: PETS

CHEAT GNOME
During a game, press L, L, R, ✕, ✕, Up. Now you can enter the following cheats:

ADVANCE TIME 6 HOURS
During a game, press Up, L, Down, R, R.

GIVE SIM PET POINTS
During a game, press ▲, ⬤, ✕, ⬤, L, R.

$10,000
During a game, press ▲, Up, Left, Down, R.

SPIDER-MAN: FRIEND OR FOE

NEW GREEN GOBLIN AS A SIDEKICK
While standing in the Helicarrier between levels, press Left, Down, Right, Right, Down, Left.

SANDMAN AS A SIDEKICK
While standing in the Helicarrier between levels, press Right, Right, Right, Up, Down, Left.

VENOM AS A SIDEKICK
While standing in the Helicarrier between levels, press Left, Left, Right, Up, Down, Down.

5000 TECH TOKENS
While standing in the Helicarrier between levels, press Up, Up, Down, Down, Left, Right.

NEW GOBLIN
At the stage complete screen, hold L + R and press ⬤, Down, ✕, Right, ⬤, Up, ▲, Left.

STAR WARS: THE FORCE UNLEASHED

CHEATS

Once you have accessed the Rogue Shadow, select Enter Code from the Extras menu. Now you can enter the following:

CHEAT	CODE
Invincibility	CORTOSIS
Unlimited Force	VERGENCE
1,000,000 Force Points	SPEEDER
All Force Powers	TYRANUS
Max Force Power Level	KATARN
Max Combo Level	COUNTDOOKU
Amplified Lightsaber Damage	LIGHTSABER

COSTUMES

Once you have accessed the Rogue Shadow, select Enter Code from the Extras menu. Now you can enter the following:

COSTUME	CODE
All Costumes	GRANDMOFF
501st Legion	LEGION
Aayla Secura	AAYLA
Admiral Ackbar	ITSATWAP
Anakin Skywalker	CHOSENONE
Asajj Ventress	ACOLYTE
Ceremonial Jedi Robes	DANTOOINE
Chop'aa Notimo	NOTIMO
Classic stormtrooper	TK421
Count Dooku	SERENNO
Darth Desolous	PAUAN
Darth Maul	ZABRAK
Darth Phobos	HIDDENFEAR
Darth Vader	SITHLORD
Drexl Roosh	DREXLROOSH
Emperor Palpatine	PALPATINE
General Rahm Kota	MANDALORE
Han Solo	NERFHERDER
Heavy trooper	SHOCKTROOP
Juno Eclipse	ECLIPSE
Kento's Robe	WOOKIEE
Kleef	KLEEF
Lando Calrissian	SCOUNDREL
Luke Skywalker	T16WOMPRAT
Luke Skywalker (Yavin)	YELLOWJCKT
Mace Windu	JEDIMASTER
Mara Jade	MARAJADE
Maris Brook	MARISBROOD
Navy commando	STORMTROOP
Obi Wan Kenobi	BENKENOBI
Proxy	HOLOGRAM
Qui Gon Jinn	MAVERICK
Shaak Ti	TOGRUTA
Shadow trooper	INTHEDARK
Sith Robes	HOLOCRON
Sith Stalker Armor	KORRIBAN
Twi'lek	SECURA

STAR WARS: LETHAL ALLIANCE

ALL LEVELS

Select Create Profile from the Profiles menu and enter HANS0L0.

ALL LEVELS AND REFILL HEALTH WHEN DEPLETED
Select Create Profile from the Profiles menu and enter JD1MSTR.

REFILL HEALTH WHEN DEPLETED
Select Create Profile from the Profiles menu and enter B0BAF3T.

STRIKERS 1945 PLUS PORTABLE

XP-55 ASCENDER
At the Random Select screen, press Down, Up, Down, Up, Down, Down, Down, Down, Up.

SUPER MONKEY BALL ADVENTURE

ALL CARDS
At the mode select, press ●, ▲, ●, ●, ▲, ●, ●, ▲, ●, ●, ▲, ●.

THRILLVILLE: OFF THE RAILS

$50,000
During a game, press ●, ●, ▲, ●, ●, ▲, ✖. Repeat this code as much as desired.

ALL PARKS
During a game, press ●, ●, ▲, ●, ●, ▲, ●.

ALL RIDES
During a game, press ●, ●, ▲, ● ●, ▲, ▲. Some rides still need to be researched.

COMPLETE MISSIONS
During a game, press ●, ●, ▲, ●, ●, ▲, ●. Then, at the Missions menu, highlight a mission and press ● to complete that mission. Some missions have Bronze, Silver, and Gold objectives. For these missions the first press of ● earns the Bronze, the second earns the Silver, and the third earns the Gold.

TIGER WOODS PGA TOUR 09

UNLOCK PGA TOUR EVENTS
Enter BEATIT as a password.

$1,000,000
Enter JACKPOT as a password.

UNLOCK ALL CLOTHING AND EQUIPMENT
Enter SHOP2DROP as a password.

MAX SKILL POINTS AND ALL CLOTHING AND EQUIPMENT
Enter IAMRUBBISH as a password.

UNLOCK ALL COVER STORIES
Enter HEADLINER as a password.

TOMB RAIDER: LEGEND

You must unlock the following cheats before you can use them.

BULLETPROOF
During a game, hold L and press ✖, R, ▲, R, ●, R.

DRAW ENEMY HEALTH
During a game, hold L and press ●, ●, ✖, R, R, ▲.

INFINITE ASSAULT RIFLE AMMO
During a game, hold L and press ✖, ●, ✖, R, ●, ▲.

INFINITE GRENADE LAUNCHER
During a game, hold L and press R, ▲, R, ●, R, ●.

INFINITE SHOTGUN AMMO
During a game, hold L and press R, ●, ●, R, ●, ✖.

INFINITE SMG AMMO
During a game, hold L and press ●, ▲, R, R, ✖, ●.

1-SHOT KILL
During a game, hold L and press ▲, ✖, ▲, ●, R, ●.

TEXTURELESS MODE
Hold L and press R, ✖, ●, ✖, ▲, R.

WIELD EXCALIBUR
During a game, hold L and press ▲, ✖, ●, R, ▲, R.

PSP

TOY STORY 3

For the following Toy Story 3 codes, you must activate the cheat from the Pause menu after entering it.

BUZZ USES LASER (ALL STORY LEVELS)
Select Cheat Codes from the Bonus menu and enter BLASER.

WOODY'S BANDIT OUTFIT
Select Cheat Codes from the Bonus menu and enter BANDIT.

TOY ALIENS WITH 3D GLASSES
Select Cheat Codes from the Bonus menu and enter 3DGLAS.

OLD MOVIE EFFECT
Select Cheat Codes from the Bonus menu and enter OLDMOV.

TWISTED METAL: HEAD-ON

Note that the following codes will not work for Multiplayer or Online modes.

HEALTH RECHARGED
Hold L + R and press ▲, ✕, ●, ●.

INFINITE AMMO
Hold L + R and press ●, ▲, Down, Down, Left.

INVULNERABLE
Hold L + R and press Right, Left, Down, Up.

INFINITE WEAPONS
Hold L + R and press ▲, ▲, Down, Down.

KILLER WEAPONS
Hold L + R and press ✕, ✕, Up, Up.

MEGA GUNS
Hold L + R and press ✕, ▲, ✕, ▲

VALKYRIA CHRONICLES II

TANK STICKERS

Enter the following codes in Extra Mode for the desired effect.

STICKER	ENTER
Alicia Gunther	K1C7XKLJMXUHRD8S
Blitz Logo	VWUYNJQ8HGSVXR7J
Edy Nelson	R5PT1MXEY3BW8VBE
Edy's Squad	CR6BG1A9LYQKB6WJ
SEGA Logo	6RK45S59F7U2JLTD
Skies of Arcadia	WVZLPTYXURS1Q8TV
Crazy Taxi	38WV17PK45TYAF8V
Faldio	GWNU95RSETW1VGNQ
Gallian Military	TXU14EUV74PCR3TE
Isara Gunther and Isara's Dream	37LRK5D214VQVFYH
Prince Maximilian and Imperial Flag	H73G4L9GLJR1CHJP
Selvaria	53K8FKGP1GHQ4SBN
Sonic the Hedgehog	CUP34ASEZ9WDKBYV
Super Monkey Ball	7JMNHZ83TGH7XFKT
Yakuza	QAKVXZTALF4TU7SK
Vanquish Tank	BUNLT4EXDS74QRCR

CHARACTERS

Enter the following codes in Extra Mode for the desired effect.

CHARACTER	ENTER
Alicia Gunther	KBAFLFHICAJTKMIY
Edy's Detachment	TKBHCNBERHRKJNFG
Julius Kroze	AMNKZKYTKNBNKYMT
Lamar/Ramal	LITSGAAMEORFRCRQ
Landzaat Farudio	KNWRJRGSMLASTNSQ
Maximillian	KBFHZRJTKMKSKNKP
Mintz	CKRJWNSXTYMNGZRT
Selvaria	KSNEGA56LPY7CTQ9
Support-Class Aliasse, Lancer-Class Cosette and Armor-Type Zeri	PZRJQM7SK4HPXTYM

VIRTUA TENNIS 3

ALL COURTS
At the Game Mode screen, press Up, Up, Down, Down, Left, Right, Left, Right.

ALL GEAR
At the Game Mode screen, press Left, Right, ●, Left, Right, ●, Up, Down.

KING & DUKE
At the Game Mode screen, press Up, Up, Down, Down, Left, Right, L, R.

WALL-E

KILL ALL
Select Cheats and then Secret Codes. Enter BOTOFWAR.

UNDETECTED BY ENEMIES
Select Cheats and then Secret Codes. Enter STEALTHARMOR.

LASERS CHANGE COLORS
Select Cheats and then Secret Codes. Enter RAINBOWLAZER.

CUBES ARE EXPLOSIVE
Select Cheats and then Secret Codes. Enter EXPLOSIVEWORLD.

LIGHTEN DARK AREAS
Select Cheats and then Secret Codes. Enter GLOWINTHEDARK.

GOGGLES
Select Cheats and then Secret Codes. Enter BOTOFMYSTERY.

GOLD TRACKS
Select Cheats and then Secret Codes. Enter GOLDENTRACKS.

THE WARRIORS

100% COMPLETION IN STORY MODE
During a game, press L, Select, ●, Down, L, Right.

COMPLETE CURRENT MISSION
During a game, press Down, ●, ⊗, Select, R, Left.

UNLIMITED HEALTH
During a game, press Up, ●, R, Select, ⊗, L.

UPGRADES STAMINA
During a game, press ⊗, L, Down, ●, Up, ⊗.

UNLIMITED RAGE
During a game, press ●, ●, ▲, Select, ⊗, Left.

BRASS KNUCKLES
During a game, press ●, ●, ●, L, Select, ●.

HANDCUFFS
During a game, press ⊗, Up, Select, L, L.

HAND CUFF KEYS
During a game, press Left, ⊗, ⊗, R, L, Down.

KNIFE
During a game, press Down, Down, Select, Up, Up, L.

MACHETE
During a game, press L, ⊗, R(x2), Select, R.

UNBREAKABLE BAT
During a game, press L, L, ●, Up, ●, Select.

ALL DEALERS
During a game, press right, R, ●, ⊗, Select, ●.

UPGRADE FLASH CAPACITY
During a game, press L, ⊗, R, L, L, ●.

99 CREDITS IN ARMIES OF THE NIGHT
During a game of Armie of the Night, press Up, Up, Down, Down, Left, Right.

WHAT DID I DO TO DESERVE THIS, MY LORD!? 2

WHAT DID I DO TO DESERVE THIS, MY LORD!?
At the Title screen, press L, R, L, R, L, R, L, R, L, R to play the first What Did I Do to Deserve This, My Lord!?

WHAT DID I NOT DO TO DESERVE THIS, MY LORD!?
After entering the previous code and the game loads, enter the same code again at the Title screen. This unlocks the Hard Mode of What Did I Do to Deserve This, My Lord!?.

PSP

WRC: FIA WORLD RALLY CHAMPIONSHIP

UNLOCK EVERYTHING
Create a new profile with the name PADLOCK.

EXTRA AVATARS
Create a new profile with the name UGLYMUGS.

GHOST CAR
Create a new profile with the name SPOOKY.

SUPERCHARGER
Create a new profile with the name MAXPOWER.

TIME TRIAL GHOST CARS
Create a new profile with the name AITRIAL.

BIRD CAMERA
Create a new profile with the name dovecam.

REVERSES CONTROLS
Create a new profile with the name REVERSE.

WWE SMACKDOWN VS. RAW 2010

THE ROCK
Select Cheat Codes from the Options and enter The Great One.

VINCE'S OFFICE AND DIRT SHEET FOR BACKSTAGE BRAWL
Select Cheat Codes from the Options menu and enter BonusBrawl.

HBK/SHAWN MICHAEL'S ALTERNATE COSTUME
Select Cheat Codes from the Options menu and enter Bow Down.

JOHN CENA'S ALTERNATE COSTUME
Select Cheat Codes from the Options menu and enter CENATION.

RANDY ORTON'S ALTERNATE COSTUME
Select Cheat Codes from the Options menu and enter ViperRKO.

SANTINO MARELLA'S ALTERNATE COSTUME
Select Cheat Codes from the Options menu and enter Milan Miracle.

TRIPLE H'S ALTERNATE COSTUME
Select Cheat Codes from the Options menu and enter Suck IT!.

WWE SMACKDOWN VS. RAW 2011

JOHN CENA (ENTRANCE/CIVILIAN)
In My WWE, select Cheat Codes from the Options menu and enter SLURPEE.

RANDY ORTON'S COSTUMES
In My WWE, select Cheat Codes from the Options menu and enter apexpredator.

TRIBUTE TO THE TROOPS ARENA
In My WWE, select Cheat Codes from the Options menu and enter 8thannualtribute.

X-MEN LEGENDS II: RISE OF APOCALYPSE

ALL CHARACTERS
At the Team Management screen, press Right, Left, Left, Right, Up, Up, Up, Start.

LEVEL 99 CHARACTERS
At the Team Management screen, press Up, Down, Up, Down, Left, Up, Left, Right, Start.

ALL SKILLS
At the Team Management screen, press Left, Right, Left, Right, Down, Up, Start.

392

SUPER SPEED
Pause the game and press Up, Up, Up, Down, Up, Down, Start.

UNLIMITED XTREME POWER
Pause the game and press Left, Down, Right, Down, Up, Up, Down, Up Start.

100,000 TECHBITS
At Forge or Beast's equipment screen, press Up, Up, Up, Down, Right, Right, Start.

ALL CINEMATICS
At the Review menu, press Left, Right, Right, Left, Down, Down, Left, Start.

ALL COMIC BOOKS
At the Review menu, press Right, Left, Left, Right, Up, Up, Right, Start.

YU-GI-OH! GX TAG FORCE 2

MIDDDAY CONSTELLATION BOOSTER PACK
When buying booster packs, press Up, Up, Down, Down, Left, Right, Left, Right, ✪, ◉.

CARD PASSWORDS

CARD	PASSWORD	CARD	PASSWORD
4-Starred Ladybug of Doom	83994646	Amphibian Beast	67371383
7 Colored Fish	23771716	Amphibious Bugroth MK-3	64342551
A Cat of Ill Omen	24140059	Amplifier	00303660
A Deal With Dark Ruler	06850209	An Owl of Luck	23927567
A Feather of the Phoenix	49140998	Ancient Elf	93221206
A Feint Plan	68170903	Ancient Gear	31557782
A Hero Emerges	21597117	Ancient Gear Beast	10509340
A Legendary Ocean	00295517	Ancient Gear Cannon	80045583
A Man With Wdjat	51351302	Ancient Gear Castle	92001300
A Rival Appears!	05728014	Ancient Gear Drill	67829249
A Wingbeat of Giant Dragon	28596933	Ancient Gear Golem	83104731
A-Team: Trap Disposal Unit	13026402	Ancient Gear Soldier	56094445
Abare Ushioni	89718302	Ancient Lamp	54912977
Absolute End	27744077	Ancient Lizard Warrior	43230671
Absorbing Kid From the Sky	49771608	Andro Sphinx	15013468
Abyss Soldier	18318842	Anteatereatingant	13250922
Abyssal Designator	89801755	Anti-Aircraft Flower	65064143
Acid Trap Hole	41356845	Anti-Spell	53112492
Acrobat Monkey	47372349	Apprentice Magician	09156135
Adhesion Trap Hole	62325062	Appropriate	48539234
Adhesive Explosive	53828396	Aqua Madoor	85639257
After the Struggle	25345186	Aqua Spirit	40916023
Agido	16135253	Arcane Archer of the Forest	55001420
Airknight Parshath	18036057	Archfiend of Gilfer	50287060
Aitsu	48202661	Archfiend Soldier	49881766
Alkana Knight Joker	06150044	Archlord Zerato	18378582
Alpha the Magnet Warrior	99785935	Armaill	53153481
Altar for Tribute	21070956	Armed Changer	90374791
Amazon Archer	91869203	Armed Dragon LV 3	00980973
Amazoness Archers	67987611	Armed Dragon LV 5	46384672
Amazoness Blowpiper	73574678	Armed Dragon LV 7	73879377
Amazoness Chain Master	29654737	Armed Dragon LV10	59464593
Amazoness Paladin	47480070	Armed Ninja	09076207
Amazoness Swords Woman	94004268	Armed Samurai - Ben Kei	84430950
Amazoness Tiger	10979723	Armor Axe	07180418
Ambulance Rescueroid	98927491	Armor Break	79649195
Ambulanceroid	36378213	Armored Lizard	15480588
Ameba	95174353	Armored Starfish	17535588
		Armored Zombie	20277860
		Array of Revealing Light	69296555
		Arsenal Bug	42364374

PSP

CARD	PASSWORD
Arsenal Robber	55348096
Arsenal Summoner	85489096
Assault on GHQ	62633180
Astral Barrier	37053871
Asura Priest	02134346
Aswan Apparition	88236094
Atomic Firefly	87340664
Attack and Receive	63689843
Attack Reflector Unit	91989718
Aussa the Earth Charmer	37970940
Autonomous Action Unit	71453557
Avatar of the Pot	99284890
Axe Dragonute	84914462
Axe of Despair	40619825
B. Skull Dragon	11901678
B.E.S. Covered Core	15317640
B.E.S. Crystal Core	22790789
B.E.S. Tetran	44954628
Baby Dragon	88819587
Back to Square One	47453433
Backfire	82705573
Backup Soldier	36280194
Bad Reaction to Simochi	40633297
Bait Doll	07165085
Ballista of Rampart Smashing	00242146
Banisher of the Light	61528025
Bark of Dark Ruler	41925941
Barrel Dragon	81480460
Basic Insect	89091579
Battery Charger	61181383
Batteryman AA	63142001
Batteryman C	19733961
Batteryman D	55401221
Battle Footballer	48094997
Battle Ox	05053103
Battle-Scarred	94463200
Bazoo The Soul-Eater	40133511
Beast Soul Swap	35149085
Beaver Warrior	32452818
Beckoning Light	16255442
Beelze Frog	49522489
Begone, Knave	20374520
Behemoth the King of All Animals	22996376
Beiige, Vanguard of Dark World	33731070
Berserk Dragon	85605684
Berserk Gorilla	39168895
Beta the Magnet Warrior	39256679
Bickuribox	25655502
Big Bang Shot	61127349
Big Burn	95472621
Big Core	14148099
Big Koala	42129512
Big Shield Gardna	65240384
Big Wave Small Wave	51562916
Big-Tusked Mammoth	59380081
Bio-Mage	58696829
Birdface	45547649
Black Illusion Ritual	41426869
Black Luster Soldier - Envoy of the Beginning	72989439

CARD	PASSWORD
Black Pendant	65169794
Black Tyranno	38670435
Blackland Fire Dragon	87564352
Blade Knight	39507162
Blade Rabbit	58268433
Blade Skater	97023549
Bladefly	28470714
Blast Held By a Tribute	89041555
Blast Magician	21051146
Blast with Chain	98239899
Blasting the Ruins	21466326
Blazing Inpachi	05464695
Blind Destruction	32015116
Blindly Loyal Goblin	35215622
Block Attack	25880422
Blockman	48115277
Blowback Dragon	25551951
Blue-Eyes Shining Dragon	53347303
Blue-Eyes Toon Dragon	53183600
Blue-Eyes Ultimate Dragon	23995346
Blue-Eyes White Dragon	89631139
Blue-Winged Crown	41396436
Bokoichi the Freightening Car	08715625
Bombardment Beetle	57409948
Bonding - H2O	45898858
Boneheimer	98456117
Book of Life	02204140
Book of Moon	14087893
Book of Taiyou	38699854
Boss Rush	66947414
Bottom Dweller	81386177
Bottomless Shifting Sand	76532077
Bottomless Trap Hole	29401950
Bountiful Artemis	32296881
Bowganian	52090844
Bracchio-Raidus	16507828
Brain Control	87910978
Brain Jacker	40267580
Branch!	30548775
Breaker the Magical Warrior	71413901
Broww, Huntsman of Dark World	79126789
Brron, Mad King of Dark World	06214884
Bubble Blaster	53586134
Bubble Illusion	80075749
Bubble Shuffle	61968753
Bubonic Vermin	06104968
Burning Algae	41859700
Burning Beast	59364406
Burning Land	24294108
Burst Breath	80163754
Burst Return	27191436
Burst Stream of Destruction	17655904
Buster Blader	78193831
Buster Rancher	84740193
Butterfly Dagger - Elma	69243953
Byser Shock	17597059

CARD	PASSWORD
Call of The Haunted	97077563
Call of the Mummy	04861205
Cannon Soldier	11384280
Cannonball Spear Shellfish	95614612
Card of Safe Return	57953380
Card Shuffle	12183332
Castle of Dark Illusions	00062121
Cat's Ear Tribe	95841282
Catapult Turtle	95727991
Cathedral of Nobles	29762407
Catnipped Kitty	96501677
Cave Dragon	93220472
Ceasefire	36468556
Celtic Guardian	91152256
Cemetery Bomb	51394546
Centrifugal	01801154
Ceremonial Bell	20228463
Cetus of Dagala	28106077
Chain Burst	48276469
Chain Destruction	01248895
Chain Disappearance	57139487
Chain Energy	79323590
Chain Thrasher	88190453
Chainsaw Insect	77252217
Change of Heart	04031928
Chaos Command Magician	72630549
Chaos Emperor Dragon - Envoy of the End	82301904
Chaos End	61044390
Chaos Greed	97439308
Chaos Necromancer	01434352
Chaos Sorcerer	09596126
Chaosrider Gutaph	47829960
Charcoal Inpachi	13179332
Charm of Shabti	50412166
Charubin the Fire Knight	37421579
Chiron the Mage	16956455
Chopman the Desperate Outlaw	40884383
Chorus of Sanctuary	81380218
Chthonian Alliance	46910446
Chthonian Blast	18271561
Chthonian Polymer	72287557
Chu-Ske the Mouse Fighter	08508055
Clay Charge	22479888
Cliff the Trap Remover	06967870
Cobra Jar	86801871
Cobraman Sakuzy	75109441
Cold Wave	60682203
Collected Power	07565547
Combination Attack	08964854
Command Knight	10375182
Commander Covington	22666164
Commencement Dance	43417563
Compulsory Evacuation Device	94192409
Confiscation	17375316
Conscription	31000575
Continuous Destruction Punch	68057622
Contract With Exodia	33244944

CARD	PASSWORD
Contract With the Abyss	69035382
Contract with the Dark Master	96420087
Convulsion of Nature	62966332
Cost Down	23265313
Covering Fire	74458486
Crab Turtle	91782219
Crass Clown	93889755
Creature Swap	31036355
Creeping Doom Manta	52571838
Crimson Ninja	14618326
Criosphinx	18654201
Cross Counter	37083210
Crush D. Gandra	64681432
Cure Mermaid	85802526
Curse of Aging	41398771
Curse of Anubis	66742250
Curse of Darkness	84970821
Curse of Dragon	28279543
Curse of the Masked Beast	94377247
Curse of Vampire	34294855
Cyber Dragon	70095154
Cyber End Dragon	01546123
Cyber Twin Dragon	74157028
Cyber-Dark Edge	77625948
Cyber-Stein	69015963
Cyberdark Dragon	40418351
Cyberdark Horn	41230939
Cyberdark Keel	03019642
D - Shield	62868900
D - Time	99075257
D. D. Assailant	70074904
D. D. Borderline	60912752
D. D. Crazy Beast	48148828
D. D. Dynamite	08628798
D. D. M. - Different Dimension Master	82112775
D. D. Trainer	86498013
D. D. Trap Hole	05606466
D. D. Warrior Lady	07572887
Dancing Fairy	90925163
Dangerous Machine TYPE-6	76895648
Dark Artist	72520073
Dark Bat	67049542
Dark Blade	11321183
Dark Blade the Dragon Knight	86805855
Dark Driceratops	65287621
Dark Dust Spirit	89111398
Dark Elf	21417692
Dark Energy	04614116
Dark Factory of Mass Production	90928333
Dark Flare Knight	13722870
Dark Hole	53129443
Dark Magic Attack	02314238
Dark Magic Ritual	76792184
Dark Magician	46986414
Dark Magician Girl	38033121
Dark Magician of Chaos	40737112
Dark Magician's Tome of Black Magic	67227834

CARD	PASSWORD	CARD	PASSWORD
Dark Master - Zorc	97642679	Doriado's Blessing	23965037
Dark Mirror Force	20522190	Dragon Seeker	28563545
Dark Paladin	98502113	Dragon Treasure	01435851
Dark Room of Nightmare	85562745	Dragon Zombie	66672569
Dark Sage	92377303	Dragon's Mirror	71490127
Dark Snake Syndrome	47233801	Dragon's Rage	54178050
Dark-Piercing Light	45895206	Dragoness the Wicked Knight	70681994
Darkfire Dragon	17881964	Draining Shield	43250041
Darkfire Soldier #1	05388481	Dream Clown	13215230
Darkfire Soldier #2	78861134	Drillago	99050989
Darkworld Thorns	43500484	Drillroid	71218746
De-Spell	19159413	Dunames Dark Witch	12493482
Deal of Phantom	69122763	Dust Tornado	60082867
Decayed Commander	10209545	Earth Chant	59820352
Dedication Through Light And Darkness	69542930	Earthbound Spirit	67105242
Deepsea Shark	28593363	Earthquake	82828051
Dekoichi the Battlechanted Locomotive	87621407	Eatgaboon	42578427
		Ebon Magician Curran	46128076
Delinquent Duo	44763025	Electro-Whip	37820550
Demotion	72575145	Elegant Egotist	90219263
Des Counterblow	39131963	Element Dragon	30314994
Des Croaking	44883830	Elemental Burst	61411502
Des Dendle	12965761	Elemental Hero Avian	21844576
Des Feral Imp	81985784	Elemental Hero Bladedge	59793705
Des Frog	84451804	Elemental Hero Bubbleman	79979666
Des Kangaroo	78613627		
Des Koala	69579761	Elemental Hero Burstinatrix	58932615
Des Lacooda	02326738		
Des Wombat	09637706	Elemental Hero Clayman	84327329
Desert Sunlight	93747864	Elemental Hero Electrum/Erekshieler	29343734
Destertapir	13409151		
Destiny Board	94212438	Elemental Hero Flame Wingman	35809262
Destiny Hero - Captain Tenacious	77608643	Elemental Hero Mariner	14225239
Destiny Hero - Diamond Dude	13093792	Elemental Hero Necroid Shaman	81003500
Destiny Hero - Doom Lord	41613948	Elemental Hero Neos	89943723
		Elemental Hero Phoenix Enforcer	41436536
Destiny Hero - Dreadmaster	40591390	Elemental Hero Shining Flare Wingman	25366484
Destiny Signal	35464895		
Destroyer Golem	73481154	Elemental Hero Shining Phoenix Enforcer	88820235
Destruction Ring	21219755		
Dian Keto the Cure Master	84257639	Elemental Hero Sparkman	20721928
Dice Jar	03549275	Elemental Hero Thunder Giant	61204971
Dimension Distortion	95194279		
Dimensional Warrior	37043180	Elemental Mistress Doriado	99414158
Disappear	24623598		
Disarmament	20727787	Elemental Recharge	36586443
Disc Fighter	19612721	Elf's Light	39897277
Dissolverock	40826495	Emblem of Dragon Destroyer	06390406
Divine Dragon Ragnarok	62113340		
Divine Wrath	49010598	Embodiment of Apophis	28649820
DNA Surgery	74701381	Emergency Provisions	53046408
DNA Transplant	56769674	Emes the Infinity	43580269
Doitsu	57062206	Empress Judge	15237615
Dokurorider	99721536	Empress Mantis	58818411
Dokuroyaiba	30325729	Enchanted Javelin	96355986
Don Turtle	03493978	Enchanting Mermaid	75376965
Don Zaloog	76922029	Enemy Controller	98045062
Doriado	84916669	Enraged Battle Ox	76909279
		Enraged Muka Muka	91862578

CARD	PASSWORD	CARD	PASSWORD
Eradicating Aerosol	94716515	Fushi No Tori	38538445
Eternal Draught	56606928	Fusion Gate	33550694
Eternal Rest	95051344	Fusion Recovery	18511384
Exhausting Spell	95451366	Fusion Sage	26902560
Exile of the Wicked	26725158	Fusion Weapon	27967615
Exiled Force	74131780	Fusionist	01641883
Exodia Necross	12600382	Gadget Soldier	86281779
Exodia the Forbidden One	33396948	Gagagigo	49003308
		Gaia Power	56594520
Fairy Box	21598948	Gaia the Dragon Champion	66889139
Fairy Dragon	20315854		
Fairy King Truesdale	45425051	Gaia the Fierce Knight	06368038
Fairy Meteor Crush	97687912	Gale Dogra	16229315
Faith Bird	75582395	Gale Lizard	77491079
Fatal Abacus	77910045	Gamble	37313786
Fenrir	00218704	Gamma the Magnet Warrior	11549357
Feral Imp	41392891		
Fiber Jar	78706415	Garma Sword	90844184
Fiend Comedian	81172176	Garma Sword Oath	78577570
Fiend Scorpion	26566878	Garoozis	14977074
Fiend's Hand	52800428	Garuda the Wind Spirit	12800777
Fiend's Mirror	31890399	Gatling Dragon	87751584
Final Countdown	95308449	Gazelle the King of Mythical Beasts	05818798
Final Destiny	18591904		
Final Flame	73134081	Gear Golem the Moving Fortress	30190809
Final Ritual of the Ancients	60369732		
		Gearfried the Iron Knight	00423705
Fire Darts	43061293	Gearfried the Swordmaster	57046845
Fire Eye	88435542		
Fire Kraken	46534755	Gemini Elf	69140098
Fire Princess	64752646	Getsu Fuhma	21887179
Fire Reaper	53581214	Giant Axe Mummy	78266168
Fire Sorcerer	27132350	Giant Germ	95178994
Firegrass	53293545	Giant Kozaky	58185394
Firewing Pegasus	27054370	Giant Orc	73698349
Fireyarou	71407486	Giant Rat	97017120
Fissure	66788016	Giant Red Seasnake	58831685
Five God Dragon (Five Headed Dragon)	99267150	Giant Soldier of Stone	13039848
		Giant Trunade	42703248
Flame Cerebrus	60862676	Gift of the Mystical Elf	98299011
Flame Champion	42599677	Giga Gagagigo	43793530
Flame Dancer	12883044	Giga-Tech Wolf	08471389
Flame Ghost	58528964	Gigantes	47606319
Flame Manipulator	34460851	Gigobyte	53776525
Flame Swordsman	45231177	Gil Garth	38445524
Flame Viper	02830619	Gilasaurus	45894482
Flash Assailant	96890582	Giltia the D. Knight	51828629
Flower Wolf	95952802	Girochin Kuwagata	84620194
Flying Fish	31987274	Goblin Attack Force	78658564
Flying Kamakiri #1	84834865	Goblin Calligrapher	12057781
Flying Kamakiri #2	03134241	Goblin Elite Attack Force	85306040
Follow Wind	98252586	Goblin Thief	45311864
Foolish Burial	81439173	Goblin's Secret Remedy	11868825
Forest	87430998	Gogiga Gagagigo	39674352
Fortress Whale	62337487	Golem Sentry	82323207
Fortress Whale's Oath	77454922	Good Goblin Housekeeping	09744376
Frenzied Panda	98818516		
Frozen Soul	57069605	Gora Turtle	80233946
Fruits of Kozaky's Studies	49998907	Graceful Charity	79571449
		Graceful Dice	74137509
Fuh-Rin-Ka-Zan	01781310	Gradius	10992251
Fuhma Shuriken	09373534	Gradius' Option	14291024
Fulfillment of the Contract	48206762	Granadora	13944422
		Grand Tiki Elder	13676474

CARD	PASSWORD	CARD	PASSWORD
Granmarg the Rock Monarch	60229110	Helping Robo for Combat	47025270
Gravedigger Ghoul	82542267	Hero Barrier	44676200
Gravekeeper's Cannonholder	99877698	HERO Flash!!	00191749
Gravekeeper's Curse	50712728	Hero Heart	67951831
Gravekeeper's Guard	37101832	Hero Kid	32679370
Gravekeeper's Servant	16762927	Hero Ring	26647858
Gravekeeper's Spear Soldier	63695531	Hero Signal	22020907
Gravekeeper's Spy	24317029	Hidden Book of Spell	21840375
Gravekeeper's Vassal	99690140	Hidden Soldier	02047519
Graverobber's Retribution	33737664	Hieracosphinx	82260502
Gravity Bind	85742772	Hieroglyph Lithograph	10248192
Gray Wing	29618570	High Tide Gyojin	54579801
Great Angus	11813953	Hiita the Fire Charmer	00759393
Great Long Nose	02356994	Hino-Kagu-Tsuchi	75745607
Great Mammoth of Goldfine	54622031	Hinotama Soul	96851799
Green Gadget	41172955	Hiro's Shadow Scout	81863068
Gren Maju Da Eiza	36584821	Hitotsu-Me Giant	76184692
Ground Attacker Bugroth	58314394	Holy Knight Ishzark	57902462
Ground Collapse	90502999	Homunculus the Alchemic Being	40410110
Gruesome Goo	65623423	Horn of Heaven	98069388
Gryphon Wing	55608151	Horn of Light	38552107
Gryphon's Feather Duster	34370473	Horn of the Unicorn	64047146
Guardian Angel Joan	68007326	Horus The Black Flame Dragon LV4	75830094
Guardian of the Labyrinth	89272878	Horus The Black Flame Dragon LV6	11224103
Guardian of the Sea	85448931	Horus The Black Flame Dragon LV8	48229808
Guardian Sphinx	40659562	Hoshiningen	67629977
Guardian Statue	75209824	House of Adhesive Tape	15083728
Gust Fan	55321970	Howling Insect	93107608
Gyaku-Gire Panda	09817927	Huge Revolution	65396880
Gyroid	18325492	Human-Wave Tactics	30353551
Hade-Hane	28357177	Humanoid Slime	46821314
Hamburger Recipe	80811661	Humanoid Worm Drake	05600127
Hammer Shot	26412047	Hungry Burger	30243636
Hamon	32491822	Hydrogeddon	22587018
Hand of Nephthys	98446407	Hyena	22873798
Hane-Hane	07089711	Hyozanryu	62397231
Hannibal Necromancer	05640330	Hyper Hammerhead	02671330
Hard Armor	20060230	Hysteric Fairy	21297224
Harpie Girl	34100324	Icarus Attack	53567095
Harpie Lady 1	91932350	Illusionist Faceless Mage	28546905
Harpie Lady 2	27927359	Impenetrable Formation	96631852
Harpie Lady 3	54415063	Imperial Order	61740673
Harpie Lady Sisters	12206212	Inaba White Rabbit	77084837
Harpie's Brother	30532390	Incandescent Ordeal	33031674
Harpies' Hunting Ground	75782277	Indomitable Fighter Lei Lei	84173492
Hayabusa Knight	21015833	Infernal Flame Emperor	19847532
Headless Knight	05434080	Infernal Queen Archfiend	08581705
Heart of Clear Water	64801562	Inferno	74823665
Heart of the Underdog	35762283	Inferno Fire Blast	52684508
Heavy Mech Support Platform	23265594	Inferno Hammer	17185260
Heavy Storm	19613556	Inferno Reckless Summon	12247206
Helios - The Primordial Sun	54493213	Inferno Tempest	14391920
Helios Duo Megistus	80887952	Infinite Cards	94163677
Helios Tris Megiste	17286057	Infinite Dismissal	54109233
		Injection Fairy Lily	79575620
		Inpachi	97923414

CARD	PASSWORD
Insect Armor with Laser Cannon	03492538
Insect Barrier	23615409
Insect Imitation	96965364
Insect Knight	35052053
Insect Princess	37957847
Insect Queen	91512835
Insect Soldiers of the Sky	07019529
Inspection	16227556
Interdimensional Matter Transporter	36261276
Invader From Another Dimension	28450915
Invader of Darkness	56647086
Invader of the Throne	03056267
Invasion of Flames	26082229
Invigoration	98374133
Iron Blacksmith Kotetsu	73431236
Island Turtle	04042268
Jack's Knight	90876561
Jade Insect Whistle	95214051
Jam Breeding Machine	21770260
Jam Defender	21558682
Jar of Greed	83968380
Jar Robber	33784505
Javelin Beetle	26932788
Javelin Beetle Pact	41182875
Jellyfish	14851496
Jerry Beans Man	23635815
Jetroid	43697559
Jinzo	77585513
Jinzo #7	32809211
Jirai Gumo	94773007
Jowgen the Spiritualist	41855169
Jowls of Dark Demise	05257687
Judge Man	30113682
Judgment of Anubis	55256016
Just Desserts	24068492
KA-2 Des Scissors	52768103
Kabazauls	51934376
Kagemusha of the Blue Flame	15401633
Kaibaman	34627841
Kaiser Dragon	94566432
Kaiser Glider	52824910
Kaiser Sea Horse	17444133
Kaminari Attack	09653271
Kaminote Blow	97570038
Kamionwizard	41544074
Kangaroo Champ	95789089
Karate Man	23289281
Karbonala Warrior	54541900
Karma Cut	71587526
Kelbek	54878498
Keldo	80441106
Killer Needle	88979991
Kinetic Soldier	79853073
King Dragun	13756293
King Fog	84686841
King of the Skull Servants	36021814
King of the Swamp	79109599
King of Yamimakai	69455834

CARD	PASSWORD
King Tiger Wanghu	83986578
King's Knight	64788463
Kiryu	84814897
Kiseitai	04266839
Kishido Spirit	60519422
Knight's Title	87210505
Koitsu	69456283
Kojikocy	01184620
Kotodama	19406822
Kozaky	99171160
Kozaky's Self-Destruct Button	21908319
Kryuel	82642348
Kumootoko	56283725
Kurama	85705804
Kuriboh	40640057
Kuwagata Alpha	60802233
Kwagar Hercules	95144193
Kycoo The Ghost Destroyer	88240808
La Jinn The Mystical Genie of The Lamp	97590747
Labyrinth of Nightmare	66526672
Labyrinth Tank	99551425
Lady Assailant of Flames	90147755
Lady Ninja Yae	82005435
Lady of Faith	17358176
Larvas	94675535
Laser Cannon Armor	77007920
Last Day of Witch	90330453
Last Turn	28566710
Launcher Spider	87322377
Lava Battleguard	20394040
Lava Golem	00102380
Layard the Liberator	67468948
Left Arm of the Forbidden One	07902349
Left Leg of the Forbidden One	44519536
Legendary Black Belt	96438440
Legendary Flame Lord	60258960
Legendary Jujitsu Master	25773409
Legendary Sword	61854111
Leghul	12472242
Lekunga	62543393
Lesser Dragon	55444629
Lesser Fiend	16475472
Level Conversion Lab	84397023
Level Limit - Area A	54976796
Level Limit - Area B	03136426
Level Modulation	61850482
Level Up!	25290459
Levia-Dragon	37721209
Light of Intervention	62867251
Light of Judgment	44595286
Lighten the Load	37231841
Lightforce Sword	49587034
Lightning Blade	55226821
Lightning Conger	27671321
Lightning Vortex	69162969
Limiter Removal	23171610
Liquid Beast	93108297
Little Chimera	68658728

CARD	PASSWORD
Little-Winguard	90790253
Lizard Soldier	20831168
Lord of D.	17985575
Lord of the Lamp	99510761
Lost Guardian	45871897
Luminous Soldier	57282479
Luminous Spark	81777047
Luster Dragon	11091375
Luster Dragon #2	17658803
M-Warrior #1	56342351
M-Warrior #2	92731455
Machine Conversion Factory	25769732
Machine Duplication	63995093
Machine King	46700124
Machine King Prototype	89222931
Machiners Defender	96384007
Machiners Force	58054262
Machiners Sniper	23782705
Machiners Soldier	60999392
Mad Dog of Darkness	79182538
Mad Lobster	97240270
Mad Sword Beast	79870141
Mage Power	83746708
Magic Drain	59344077
Magic Jammer	77414722
Magical Cylinder	62279055
Magical Dimension	28553439
Magical Explosion	32723153
Magical Hats	81210420
Magical Labyrinth	64389297
Magical Marionette	08034697
Magical Merchant	32362575
Magical Plant Mandragola	07802006
Magical Scientist	34206604
Magical Thorn	53119267
Magician of Black Chaos	30208479
Magician of Faith	31560081
Magician's Circle	00050755
Magician's Unite	36045450
Magician's Valkyria	80304126
Magnet Circle	94940436
Maha Vailo	93013676
Maharaghi	40695128
Maiden of the Aqua	17214465
Maji-Gire Panda	60102563
Maju Garzett	08794435
Makiu	27827272
Makyura the Destructor	21593977
Malevolent Nuzzler	99597615
Malfunction	06137095
Malice Ascendant	14255590
Malice Dispersion	13626450
Mammoth Graveyard	40374923
Man Eater	93553943
Man-Eater Bug	54652250
Man-Eating Black Shark	80727036
Man-Eating Treasure Chest	13723605
Man-Thro' Tro'	43714890
Manga Ryu-Ran	38369349
Manju of the Ten Thousand Hands	95492061

CARD	PASSWORD
Manticore of Darkness	77121851
Marauding Captain	02460565
Marie the Fallen One	57579381
Marine Beast	29929832
Marshmallon	31305911
Marshmallon Glasses	66865880
Maryokutai	71466592
Masaki the Legendary Swordsman	44287299
Mask of Brutality	82432018
Mask of Darkness	28933734
Mask of Restrict	29549364
Mask of Weakness	57882509
Masked Dragon	39191307
Masked of the Accursed	56948373
Masked Sorcerer	10189126
Mass Driver	34906152
Master Kyonshee	24530661
Master Monk	49814180
Master of Dragon Knight	62873545
Master of Oz	27134689
Mataza the Zapper	22609617
Mavelus	59036972
Maximum Six	30707994
Mazera DeVille	06133894
Mech Mole Zombie	63545455
Mecha-Dog Marron	94667532
Mechanical Hound	22512237
Mechanical Snail	34442949
Mechanical Spider	45688586
Mechanicalchaser	07359741
Meda Bat	76211194
Medusa Worm	02694423
Mefist the Infernal General	46820049
Mega Thunderball	21817254
Mega Ton Magical Cannon	32062913
Megamorph	22046459
Megarock Dragon	71544954
Melchid the Four-Face Beast	86569121
Memory Crusher	48700891
Mermaid Knight	24435369
Messenger of Peace	44656491
Metal Armored Bug	65957473
Metal Dragon	09293977
Metallizing Parasite	07369217
Metalmorph	68540058
Metalzoa	50705071
Metamorphosis	46411259
Meteor B. Dragon	90660762
Meteor Dragon	64271667
Meteor of Destruction	33767325
Meteorain	64274292
Michizure	37580756
Micro-Ray	18190572
Mid Shield Gardna	75487237
Mighty Guard	62327910
Mikazukinoyaiba	38277918
Millennium Golem	47986555
Millennium Scorpion	82482194
Millennium Shield	32012841
Milus Radiant	07489323

CARD	PASSWORD	CARD	PASSWORD
Minar	32539892	Mystical Knight of Jackal	98745000
Mind Control	37520316	Mystical Moon	36607978
Mind Haxorz	75392615	Mystical Sand	32751480
Mind on Air	66690411	Mystical Sheep #2	30451366
Mind Wipe	52718046	Mystical Shine Ball	39552864
Mine Golem	76321376	Mystical Space Typhoon	05318639
Minefield Eruption	85519211	Mystik Wok	80161395
Minor Goblin Official	01918087	Mythical Beast Cerberus	55424270
Miracle Dig	06343408	Nanobreaker	70948327
Miracle Fusion	45906428	Necklace of Command	48576971
Miracle Kid	55985014	Necrovalley	47355498
Miracle Restoring	68334074	Needle Ball	94230224
Mirage Dragon	15960641	Needle Burrower	98162242
Mirage Knight	49217579	Needle Ceiling	38411870
Mirage of Nightmare	41482598	Needle Wall	38299233
Mirror Force	44095762	Needle Worm	81843628
Mirror Wall	22359980	Negate Attack	14315573
Misfortune	01036974	Nemuriko	90963488
Mispolymerization	58392024	Neo Aqua Madoor	49563947
Mistobody	47529357	Neo Bug	16587243
Moai Interceptor Cannons	45159319	Neo the Magic Swordsman	50930991
Mobius the Frost Monarch	04929256	Neo-Space	40215635
Moisture Creature	75285069	Neo-Spacian Aqua Dolphin	17955766
Mokey Mokey	27288416	Newdoria	04335645
Mokey Mokey King	13803864	Next to be Lost	07076131
Mokey Mokey Smackdown	01965724	Night Assailant	16226786
Molten Behemoth	17192817	Nightmare Horse	59290628
Molten Destruction	19384334	Nightmare Penguin	81306586
Molten Zombie	04732017	Nightmare Wheel	54704216
Monk Fighter	03810071	Nightmare's Steelcage	58775978
Monster Egg	36121917	Nimble Momonga	22567609
Monster Eye	84133008	Nin-Ken Dog	11987744
Monster Gate	43040603	Ninja Grandmaster Sasuke	04041838
Monster Reborn	83764718	Ninjitsu Art of Decoy	89628781
Monster Recovery	93108433	Ninjitsu Art of Transformation	70861343
Monster Reincarnation	74848038	Nitro Unit	23842445
Mooyan Curry	58074572	Niwatori	07805359
Morale Boost	93671934	Nobleman of Crossout	71044499
Morphing Jar	33508719	Nobleman of Extermination	17449108
Morphing Jar #2	79106360	Nobleman-Eater Bug	65878864
Mother Grizzly	57839750	Non Aggression Area	76848240
Mountain	50913601	Non-Fusion Area	27581098
Mr. Volcano	31477025	Non-Spellcasting Area	20065549
Mudora	82108372	Novox's Prayer	43694075
Muka Muka	46657337	Nubian Guard	51616747
Multiplication of Ants	22493811	Numinous Healer	02130625
Multiply	40703222	Nutrient Z	29389368
Musician King	56907389	Nuvia the Wicked	12953226
Mustering of the Dark Scorpions	68191243	O - Oversoul	63703130
Mysterious Puppeteer	54098121	Obnoxious Celtic Guardian	52077741
Mystic Horseman	68516705	Ocubeam	86088138
Mystic Lamp	98049915	Offerings to the Doomed	19230407
Mystic Plasma Zone	18161786	Ojama Black	79335209
Mystic Swordsman LV 2	47507260	Ojama Delta Hurricane	08251996
Mystic Swordsman LV 4	74591968	Ojama Green	12482652
Mystic Swordsman LV 6	60482781	Ojama King	90140980
Mystic Tomato	83011277	Ojama Trio	29843091
Mystic Wok	80161395	Ojama Yellow	42941100
Mystical Beast Serket	89194033		
Mystical Elf	15025844		

CARD	PASSWORD	CARD	PASSWORD
Ojamagic	24643836	Pot of Greed	55144522
Ojamuscle	98259197	Power Bond	37630732
Old Vindictive Magician	45141844	Power Capsule	54289683
Ominous Fortunetelling	56995655	Precious Card from Beyond	68304813
Oni Tank T-34	66927994	Premature Burial	70828912
Opti-Camaflauge Armor	44762290	Prepare to Strike Back	04483989
Opticlops	14531242	Prevent Rat	00549481
Option Hunter	33248692	Prickle Fairy	91559748
Orca Mega-Fortress of Darkness	63120904	Primal Seed	23701465
Ordeal of a Traveler	39537362	Princess Curran	02316186
Order to Charge	78986941	Princess of Tsurugi	51371017
Order to Smash	39019325	Princess Pikeru	75917088
Otohime	39751093	Protective Soul Ailin	11678191
Outstanding Dog Marron	11548522	Protector of the Sanctuary	24221739
Overdrive	02311603	Protector of the Throne	10071456
Oxygeddon	58071123	Proto-Cyber Dragon	26439287
Painful Choice	74191942	Pumpking the King of Ghosts	29155212
Paladin of White Dragon	73398797	Punished Eagle	74703140
Pale Beast	21263083	Pyramid of Light	53569894
Pandemonium	94585852	Pyramid Turtle	77044671
Pandemonium Watchbear	75375465	Queen's Knight	25652259
Parasite Paracide	27911549	Rabid Horseman	94905343
Parasitic Ticky	87978805	Rafflesia Seduction	31440542
Patrician of Darkness	19153634	Raging Flame Sprite	90810762
Patroid	71930383	Raigeki	12580477
Penguin Knight	36039163	Raigeki Break	04178474
Penumbral Soldier Lady	64751286	Rain Of Mercy	66719324
People Running About	12143771	Rainbow Flower	21347810
Perfect Machine King	18891691	Rallis the Star Bird	41382147
Performance of Sword	04849037	Rancer Dragonute	11125718
Petit Angel	38142739	Rapid-Fire Magician	06337436
Petit Dragon	75356564	Rare Metalmorph	12503902
Petit Moth	58192742	Raregold Armor	07625614
Phantasmal Martyrs	93224848	Raviel, Lord of Phantasms	69890967
Phantom Beast Cross-Wing	71181155	Ray & Temperature	85309439
Phantom Beast Thunder-Pegasus	34961968	Ray of Hope	82529174
Phantom Beast Wild-Horn	07576264	Re-Fusion	74694807
Pharaoh's Servant	52550973	Ready For Intercepting	31785398
Pharonic Protector	89959682	Really Eternal Rest	28121403
Phoenix Wing Wind Blast	63356631	Reaper of the Cards	33066139
Photon Generator Unit	66607691	Reaper of the Nightmare	85684223
Pikeru's Circle of Enchantment	74270067	Reasoning	58577036
Pikeru's Second Sight	58015506	Reborn Zombie	23421244
Pinch Hopper	26185991	Reckless Greed	37576645
Pineapple Blast	90669991	Recycle	96316857
Piranha Army	50823978	Red Archery Girl	65570596
Pitch-Black Power Stone	34029630	Red Gadget	86445415
Pitch-Black Warwolf	88975532	Red Medicine	38199696
Pitch-Dark Dragon	47415292	Red Moon Baby	56387350
Poison Draw Frog	56840658	Red-Eyes B. Chick	36262024
Poison Fangs	76539047	Red-Eyes B. Dragon	74677422
Poison Mummy	43716289	Red-Eyes Black Metal Dragon	64335804
Poison of the Old Man	08842266	Red-Eyes Darkness Dragon	96561011
Polymerization	24094653	Reflect Bounder	02851070
Possessed Dark Soul	52860176	Regenerating Mummy	70821187
Pot of Avarice	67169062	Reinforcement of the Army	32807846
Pot of Generosity	70278545	Release Restraint	75417459

CARD	PASSWORD
Relinquished	64631466
Reload	22589918
Remove Trap	51482758
Rescue Cat	14878871
Rescueroid	24311595
Reshef the Dark Being	62420419
Respect Play	08951260
Return from the Different Dimension	27174286
Return of the Doomed	19827717
Reversal of Graves	17484499
Reversal Quiz	05990062
Revival Jam	31709826
Right Arm of the Forbidden One	70903634
Right Leg of the Forbidden One	08124921
Ring of Defense	58641905
Ring of Destruction	83555666
Ring of Magnetism	20436034
Riryoku Field	70344351
Rising Air Current	45778932
Rising Energy	78211862
Rite of Spirit	30450531
Ritual Weapon	54351224
Robbin' Goblin	88279736
Robbin' Zombie	83258273
Robolady	92421852
Robotic Knight	44203504
Roboyarou	38916461
Rock Bombardment	20781762
Rock Ogre Grotto	68846917
Rocket Jumper	53890795
Rocket Warrior	30860696
Rod of the Mind's Eye	94793422
Roll Out!	91597389
Root Water	39004808
Rope of Life	93382620
Rope of Spirit	37383714
Roulette Barrel	46303688
Royal Command	33950246
Royal Decree	51452091
Royal Keeper	16509093
Royal Knight	68280530
Royal Magical Library	70791313
Royal Surrender	56058888
Royal Tribute	72405967
Ruin, Queen of Oblivion	46427957
Rush Recklessly	70046172
Ryu Kokki	57281778
Ryu Senshi	49868263
Ryu-Kishin Clown	42647539
Ryu-Kishin Powered	24611934
Saber Beetle	49645921
Sacred Crane	30914564
Sacred Phoenix of Nephthys	61441708
Saggi the Dark Clown	66602787
Sakuretsu Armor	56120475
Salamandra	32268901
Salvage	96947648
Samsara	44182827
Sand Gambler	50593156
Sand Moth	73648243

CARD	PASSWORD
Sangan	26202165
Sanwitch	53539634
Sasuke Samurai	16222645
Sasuke Samurai #2	11760174
Sasuke Samurai #3	77379481
Sasuke Samurai #4	64538655
Satellite Cannon	50400231
Scapegoat	73915051
Scarr, Scout of Dark World	05498296
Science Soldier	67532912
Scroll of Bewitchment	10352095
Scyscraper	63035430
Sea Serpent Warrior of Darkness	42071342
Sealmaster Meisei	02468169
Second Coin Toss	36562627
Second Goblin	19086954
Secret Barrel	27053506
Self-Destruct Button	57585212
Senri Eye	60391791
Serial Spell	49398568
Serpent Night Dragon	66516792
Serpentine Princess	71829750
Servant of Catabolism	02792265
Seven Tools of the Bandit	03819470
Shadow Ghoul	30778711
Shadow Of Eyes	58621589
Shadow Tamer	37620434
Shadowknight Archfiend	09603356
Shadowslayer	20939559
Share the Pain	56830749
Shield & Sword	52097679
Shield Crash	30683373
Shien's Spy	07672244
Shift	59560625
Shifting Shadows	59237154
Shinato's Ark	60365591
Shinato, King of a Higher Plane	86327225
Shining Abyss	87303357
Shining Angel	95956346
Shooting Star Bow - Ceal	95638658
Silent Insect	40867519
Silent Magician Lv4	73665146
Silent Magician Lv8	72443568
Silent Swordsman LV3	01995985
Silent Swordsman LV5	74388798
Silent Swordsman LV7	37267041
Sillva, Warlord of Dark World	32619583
Silpheed	73001017
Silver Fang	90357090
Simorgh, Bird of Divinity	14989021
Simultaneous Loss	92219931
Sinister Serpent	08131171
Sixth Sense	03280747
Skill Drain	82732705
Skilled Dark Magician	73752131
Skilled White Magician	46363422
Skull Archfiend of Lightning	61370518
Skull Descovery Knight	78700060

CARD	PASSWORD	CARD	PASSWORD
Skull Dog Marron	86652646	Spirit Ryu	67957315
Skull Invitation	98139712	Spiritual Earth Art - Kurogane	70156997
Skull Lair	06733059	Spiritual Energy Settle Machine	99173029
Skull Mariner	05265750	Spiritual Fire Art - Kurenai	42945701
Skull Red Bird	10202894		
Skull Servant	32274490	Spiritual Water Art - Aoi	06540606
Skull Zoma	79852326	Spiritual Wind Art - Miyabi	79333300
Skull-Mark Ladybug	64306248		
Skyscraper	63035430	Spiritualism	15866454
Slate Warrior	78636495	St. Joan	21175632
Smashing Ground	97169186	Stamping Destruction	81385346
Smoke Grenade of the Thief	63789924	Star Boy	08201910
		Statue of the Wicked	65810489
Snatch Steal	45986603	Staunch Defender	92854392
Sogen	86318356	Stealth Bird	03510565
Soitsu	60246171	Steam Gyroid	05368615
Solar Flare Dragon	45985838	Steamroid	44729197
Solar Ray	44472639	Steel Ogre Grotto #1	29172562
Solemn Judgment	41420027	Steel Ogre Grotto #2	90908427
Solemn Wishes	35346968	Stim-Pack	83225447
Solomon's Lawbook	23471572	Stop Defense	63102017
Sonic Duck	84696266	Storming Wynn	29013526
Sonic Jammer	84550200	Stray Lambs	60764581
Sorcerer of Dark Magic	88619463	Strike Ninja	41006930
Soul Absorption	68073522	Stronghold	13955608
Soul Exchange	68005187	Stumbling	34646691
Soul of Purity and Light	77527210	Success Probability 0%	06859683
Soul Release	05758500	Summon Priest	00423585
Soul Resurrection	92924317	Summoned Skull	70781052
Soul Reversal	78864369	Summoner of Illusions	14644902
Soul Tiger	15734813	Super Conductor Tyranno	85520851
Soul-Absorbing Bone Tower	63012333		
		Super Rejuvenation	27770341
Souleater	31242786	Super Robolady	75923050
Souls Of The Forgotten	04920010	Super Roboyarou	01412158
Space Mambo	36119641	Supply	44072894
Spark Blaster	97362768	Susa Soldier	40473581
Sparks	76103675	Swarm of Locusts	41872150
Spatial Collapse	20644748	Swarm of Scarabs	15383415
Spear Cretin	58551308	Swift Gaia the Fierce Knight	16589042
Spear Dragon	31553716		
Spell Canceller	84636823	Sword Hunter	51345461
Spell Economics	04259068	Sword of Deep-Seated	98495314
Spell Purification	01669772	Sword of Dragon's Soul	61405855
Spell Reproduction	29228529	Sword of the Soul Eater	05371656
Spell Shield Type-8	38275183	Swords of Concealing Light	12923641
Spell Vanishing	29735721		
Spell-Stopping Statute	10069180	Swords of Revealing Light	72302403
Spellbinding Circle	18807108		
Spherous Lady	52121290	Swordsman of Landstar	03573512
Sphinx Teleia	51402177	Symbol of Heritage	45305419
Spiral Spear Strike	49328340	System Down	18895832
Spirit Barrier	53239672	T.A.D.P.O.L.E.	10456559
Spirit Caller	48659020	Tactical Espionage Expert	89698120
Spirit Message A	94772232		
Spirit Message I	31893528	Tailor of the Fickle	43641473
Spirit Message L	30170981	Taunt	90740329
Spirit Message N	67287533	Tenkabito Shien	41589166
Spirit of Flames	13522325	Terra the Terrible	63308047
Spirit of the Breeze	53530069	Terraforming	73628505
Spirit of the Harp	80770678	Terrorking Archfiend	35975813
Spirit of the Pharaoh	25343280	Terrorking Salmon	78060096
Spirit Reaper	23205979		

CARD	PASSWORD
Teva	16469012
The Agent of Creation - Venus	64734921
The Agent of Force - Mars	91123920
The Agent of Judgment - Saturn	91345518
The Agent of Wisdom - Mercury	38730226
The All-Seeing White Tiger	32269855
The Big March of Animals	01689516
The Bistro Butcher	71107816
The Cheerful Coffin	41142615
The Creator	61505339
The Creator Incarnate	97093037
The Dark - Hex Sealed Fusion	52101615
The Dark Door	30606547
The Dragon Dwelling in the Cave	93346024
The Dragon's Bead	92408984
The Earl of Demise	66989694
The Earth - Hex Sealed Fusion	88696724
The Emperor's Holiday	68400115
The End of Anubis	65403020
The Eye Of Truth	34694160
The Fiend Megacyber	66362965
The Flute of Summoning Dragon	43973174
The Flute of Summoning Kuriboh	20065322
The Forceful Sentry	42829885
The Forces of Darkness	29826127
The Forgiving Maiden	84080938
The Furious Sea King	18710707
The Graveyard in the Fourth Dimension	88089103
The Gross Ghost of Fled Dreams	68049471
The Hunter With 7 Weapons	01525329
The Illusionary Gentleman	83764996
The Immortal of Thunder	84926738
The Kick Man	90407382
The Last Warrior From Another Planet	86099788
The Law of the Normal	66926224
The League of Uniform Nomenclature	55008284
The Legendary Fisherman	03643300
The Light - Hex Sealed Fusion	15717011
The Little Swordsman of Aile	25109950
The Masked Beast	49064413
The Portrait's Secret	32541773
The Regulation of Tribe	00296499
The Reliable Guardian	16430187
The Rock Spirit	76305638
The Sanctuary in the Sky	56433456

CARD	PASSWORD
The Second Sarcophagus	04081094
The Secret of the Bandit	99351431
The Shallow Grave	43434803
The Spell Absorbing Life	99517131
The Thing in the Crater	78243409
The Third Sarcophagus	78697395
The Trojan Horse	38479725
The Unhappy Girl	27618634
The Unhappy Maiden	51275027
The Warrior Returning Alive	95281259
Theban Nightmare	51838385
Theinen the Great Sphinx	87997872
Thestalos the Firestorm Monarch	26205777
Thousand Dragon	41462083
Thousand Energy	05703682
Thousand Needles	33977496
Thousand-Eyes Idol	27125110
Thousand-Eyes Restrict	63519819
Threatening Roar	36361633
Three-Headed Geedo	78423643
Throwstone Unit	76075810
Thunder Crash	69196160
Thunder Dragon	31786629
Thunder Nyan Nyan	70797118
Thunder of Ruler	91781589
Time Seal	35316708
Time Wizard	71625222
Timeater	44913552
Timidity	40350910
Token Festevil	83675475
Token Thanksgiving	57182235
Tongyo	69572024
Toon Cannon Soldier	79875176
Toon Dark Magician Girl	90960358
Toon Defense	43509019
Toon Gemini Elf	42386471
Toon Goblin Attack Force	15270885
Toon Masked Sorcerer	16392422
Toon Mermaid	65458948
Toon Summoned Skull	91842653
Toon Table of Contents	89997728
Toon World	15259703
Tornado Bird	71283180
Tornado Wall	18605135
Torpedo Fish	90337190
Torrential Tribute	53582587
Total Defense Shogun	75372290
Tower of Babel	94256039
Tradgedy	35686187
Transcendent Wings	25573054
Trap Dustshoot	64697231
Trap Hole	04206964
Trap Jammer	19252988
Treeborn Frog	12538374
Tremendous Fire	46918794
Tri-Horned Dragon	39111158
Triage	30888983
Trial of Nightmare	77827521
Trial of the Princesses	72709014

CARD	PASSWORD
Triangle Ecstasy Spark	12181376
Triangle Power	32298781
Tribe-Infecting Virus	33184167
Tribute Doll	02903036
Tribute to The Doomed	79759861
Tripwire Beast	45042329
Troop Dragon	55013285
Tsukuyomi	34853266
Turtle Oath	76806714
Turtle Tiger	37313348
Twin Swords of Flashing Light	21900719
Twin-Headed Beast	82035781
Twin-Headed Behemoth	43586926
Twin-Headed Fire Dragon	78984772
Twin-Headed Thunder Dragon	54752875
Twin-Headed Wolf	88132637
Two Thousand Needles	83228073
Two-Man Cell Battle	25578802
Two-Mouth Darkruler	57305373
Two-Pronged Attack	83887306
Tyhone	72842870
Type Zero Magic Crusher	21237481
Tyranno Infinity	83235263
Tyrant Dragon	94568601
UFOroid	07602840
UFOroid Fighter	32752319
Ultimate Insect LV1	49441499
Ultimate Insect LV3	34088136
Ultimate Insect LV5	34830502
Ultimate Insect LV7	19877898
Ultimate Obedient Fiend	32240937
Ultimate Tyranno	15894048
Ultra Evolution Pill	22431243
Umi	22702055
Umiiruka	82999629
Union Attack	60399954
United Resistance	85936485
United We Stand	56747793
Unity	14731897
Unshaven Angler	92084010
Upstart Goblin	70368879
Uraby	01784619
Uria, Lord of Sealing Flames	06007213
V-Tiger Jet	51638941
Valkyrion the Magna Warrior	75347539
Vampire Genesis	22056710
Vampire Lord	53839837
Vampire Orchis	46571052
Vengeful Bog Spirit	95220856
Victory D	44910027
Vilepawn Archfiend	73219648
VW-Tiger Catapult	58859575
VWXYZ-Dragon Catapult Cannon	84243274
W-Wing Catapult	96300057

CARD	PASSWORD
Waboku	12607053
Wall of Revealing Light	17078030
Wandering Mummy	42994702
Warrior Dai Grepher	75953262
Warrior of Zera	66073051
Wasteland	23424603
Water Dragon	85066822
Water Omotics	02483611
Wave Motion Cannon	38992735
Weed Out	28604635
Whiptail Crow	91996584
Whirlwind Prodigy	15090429
White Dragon Ritual	09786492
White Horn Dragon	73891874
White Magical Hat	15150365
White Magician Pikeru	81383947
White Ninja	01571945
Wicked-Breaking Flameberge-Baou	68427465
Wild Nature's Release	61166988
Winged Dragon, Guardian of the Fortress #1	87796900
Winged Kuriboh	57116033
Winged Kuriboh LV10	98585345
Winged Minion	89258225
Winged Sage Falcos	87523462
Wingweaver	31447217
Witch Doctor of Chaos	75946257
Witch of the Black Forest	78010363
Witch's Apprentice	80741828
Witty Phantom	36304921
Wolf Axwielder	56369281
Woodborg Inpachi	35322812
Woodland Sprite	06979239
Worm Drake	73216412
Wroughtweiler	06480253
Wynn the Wind Charmer	37744402
X-Head Cannon	62651957
Xing Zhen Hu	76515293
XY-Dragon Cannon	02111707
XYZ-Dragon Cannon	91998119
XZ-Tank Cannon	99724761
Y-Dragon Head	65622692
Yamata Dragon	76862289
Yami	59197169
Yata-Garasu	03078576
Yellow Gadget	13839120
Yellow Luster Shield	04542651
Yomi Ship	51534754
YZ-Tank Dragon	25119460
Z-Metal Tank	64500000
Zaborg the Thunder Monarch	51945556
Zero Gravity	83133491
Zoa	24311372
Zolga	16268841
Zombie Tiger	47693640
Zombyra the Dark	88472456
Zure, Knight of Dark World	07459013

YU-GI-OH! DUEL MONSTERS GX: TAG FORCE 3

MIDDAY CONSTELLATION BOOSTER PACK
At the store, get to the booster pack menu and press Up, Up, Down, Down, Left, Right, Left, Right, ✗, ◉. The pack will now be available at the store.

YU-GI-OH! 5D'S TAG FORCE 4

HIGH NOON CONSTELLATION PACK
At the card shop, press Right (x5), ◉ (x7), SELECT (x3).

YU-GI-OH! 5D'S TAG FORCE 5

HIGH NOON CONSTELLATION PACK
At the card shop, press Up, Up, Down, Down, L, R, L, R, ◉, ▲.

CHEAT CODE OVERLOAD WINTER

DK/BradyGames, a division of Penguin Group (USA) Inc.
800 East 96th Street, 3rd Floor
Indianapolis, IN 46240

ISBN: 978-0-7440-1281-1

Printing Code: The rightmost double-digit number is the year of the book's printing; the rightmost single-digit number is the number of the book's printing. For example, 10-1 shows that the first printing of the book occurred in 2010.

13 12 11 10   4 3 2 1

Manufactured in the United States of America.

BRADYGAMES STAFF

Global Strategy Guide Publisher
Mike Degler

Editor-In-Chief
H. Leigh Davis

Digital and Trade Publisher
Brian Saliba

Operations Manager
Stacey Beheler

CREDITS

Sr. Development Editor
Chris Hausermann

Code Editor
Michael Owen

Book Designer
Keith Lowe
Doug Wilkins

Production Designer
Areva